How to

Get Into

the

TOP

COLLEGES

How to Get Into the TOP COLLEGES

Third Edition

RICHARD MONTAUK
AND
KRISTA KLEIN

PRENTICE HALL PRESS

PRENTICE HALL PRESS
Published by the Penguin Group
Penguin Group (USA) Inc.
375 Hudson Street, New York, New York 10014, USA
Penguin Group (Canada), 90 Eglinton Avenue East, Suite 700, Toronto, Ontario M4P 2Y3, Canada (a division of Pearson Penguin Canada Inc.) • Penguin Books Ltd., 80 Strand, London WC2R 0RL, England • Penguin Group Ireland, 25 St. Stephen's Green, Dublin 2, Ireland (a division of Penguin Books Ltd.) • Penguin Group (Australia), 250 Camberwell Road, Camberwell, Victoria 3124, Australia (a division of Pearson Australia Group Pty. Ltd.) • Penguin Books India Pvt. Ltd., 11 Community Centre, Panchsheel Park, New Delhi—110 017, India • Penguin Group (NZ), 67 Apollo Drive, Rosedale, North Shore 0632, New Zealand (a division of Pearson New Zealand Ltd.) • Penguin Books (South Africa) (Pty.) Ltd., 24 Sturdee Avenue, Rosebank, Johannesburg 2196, South Africa

Penguin Books Ltd., Registered Offices: 80 Strand, London WC2R 0RL, England

While the author has made every effort to provide accurate telephone numbers and Internet addresses at the time of publication, neither the publisher nor the author assumes any responsibility for errors, or for changes that occur after publication. Further, the publisher does not have any control over and does not assume any responsibility for author or third-party websites or their content.

PRINTING HISTORY
First Prentice Hall Press trade paperback edition / April 2000
Revised Prentice Hall Press trade paperback edition / September 2006
Third Prentice Hall Press trade paperback edition / August 2009

Third Prentice Hall Press trade paperback edition ISBN: 978-0-7352-0442-3

The Library of Congress has cataloged the first Prentice Hall Press edition as follows:

Montauk, Richard.
    How to get into the top colleges / Richard Montauk, Krista Klein.
        p. cm.
    Includes index.
    ISBN 0-7352-0100-5 (alk. paper)
        1. Universities and colleges—United States—Admission—Handbooks, manuals, etc.
        2. College applications—United States—Handbooks, manuals, etc. I. Klein, Krista.
        II. Title.
LB2351.2.M66 2000
378.1'61—dc21   99.-51497

PRINTED IN THE UNITED STATES OF AMERICA

10 9 8 7 6 5 4 3 2 1

Most Prentice Hall Press books are available at special quantity discounts for bulk purchases for sales promotions, premiums, fund-raising, or educational use. Special books, or book excerpts, can also be created to fit specific needs. For details, write: Special Markets, Penguin Group (USA) Inc., 375 Hudson Street, New York, New York 10014.

To my mother, who believed that education could change the world
—Richard Montauk

To Mom and Dad, who made sure
I received the best education possible and supported me
every step of the way
—Krista Klein

ACKNOWLEDGMENTS

We wish to thank those people who have been so helpful to the development and writing of *How to Get Into the Top Colleges*.

First, we thank the *admissions and financial aid directors* at top colleges in the United States and Great Britain, who have been so generous with their time and knowledge in discussing how admissions and financial aid decisions are made at their schools. In particular, we would like to thank those we interviewed for this book and who have allowed themselves to be quoted in the text:

Joe Paul Case, Katie Fretwell (Amherst); Leigh Campbell (Bates); Ken Himmelman, Meg Woolmington (Bennington); Bernard Pekala (Boston College); Walter Moulton, Richard Steele (Bowdoin); Michael Bartini, Michael Goldberger, James Miller (Brown); Nancy Monnich, Jennifer Rickard (Bryn Mawr); Rick Bischoff, David Levy (Cal Tech); Richard Black (UC Berkeley); Simon Goldhill (King's College, Cambridge); Ray Jobling (St. John's College, Cambridge); Paul Thiboutot, Leonard Wenc (Carleton); Alicia Reyes (University of Chicago); Parker Beverage, Steve Thomas, Lucia Whittelsey (Colby); Eric Furda (Columbia); Tim Cheney (Connecticut College); Tom Keane (Cornell); Karl Furstenberg, Virginia Hazen, Maria Laskaris (Dartmouth); Chris Gruber, Kathleen Stevenson-McNeely (Davidson); James Belvin, Christoph Guttentag (Duke); Julia Perreault, Dan Walls (Emory); Barbara Bergman, Charles Deacon, Patricia McWade (Georgetown); Ingrid Hayes (Georgia Tech); Marlyn McGrath Lewis (Harvard); Thyra Briggs, Youlanda Copeland-Morgan (Harvey Mudd); David Hoy, Jess Lord, Delsie Phillips (Haverford); Robert Massa (Johns Hopkins); Louse Burton (London School of Economics and Political Science); Marilee Jones, Stuart Schmill (MIT); Pam Fowler, Theodore Spencer (Michigan); Robert Clagett, John Hanson (Middlebury); Jane Brown (Mount Holyoke); Richard Avitabile (NYU); Stephen Farmer (University of North Carolina, Chapel Hill); Rebecca Dixon, Sheppard Shanley (Northwestern); Joseph Russo, Daniel Saracino (Notre Dame); Howard Thomas (Oberlin); Anne Daniel (Christ Church, Oxford); Michael Allingham (Magdalen College, Oxford); Eric Kaplan, Lee Stetson (Penn); Patricia Coye, Bruce Poch (Pomona); Don Betterton, Janet Lavin Rapelye (Princeton); Paul Marthers (Reed); Heather McDonnell, Stephen Schierloh (Sarah Lawrence); Debra Shaver, Myra Smith, Nancy Tessier (Smith); Catherine Thomas (USC); Cynthia Hartley, Richard Shaw (Stanford); James Bock (Swarthmore); Larry Burt, Kedra

Ishop (University of Texas, Austin); Lee Coffin (Tufts); Elaine Rivera (Tulane); Rollie Stoneman (U.S. Air Force Academy); Captain Susan Bibeau (U.S. Coast Guard Academy); Captain Robert Johnson (U.S. Merchant Marine Academy); Major William Smith (U.S. Military Academy); Captain Karen Frye (U.S. Naval Academy); Douglas Christiansen, David Mohning, William Shain (Vanderbilt); David Borus (Vassar); John Blackburn, Yvonne Hubbard (University of Virginia); Nanette Tarbouni (Washington University); Jennifer Desjarlais (Wellesley); Nancy Hargrave Meislahn, Barbara-Jan Wilson (Wesleyan); Kim Van Deusen (William & Mary); Dick Nesbitt, Phillip Smith, Philip Wick (Williams); Steve Van Ess (University of Wisconsin, Madison); Margit Dahl, and Donald Routh (Yale).

Second, we thank *counselors* at leading high schools across the country, who were similarly helpful: Antoinette Alonzo (Hirschi Math-Science IB Magnet High School, Wichita Falls, Texas); Sally Best Bailey (Fountain Valley School, Colorado Springs, Colorado); Peggy Blau (Brooklyn Technology High School, New York); John Boshoven (Community High School, Ann Arbor, and Jewish Academy of Metropolitan Detroit, Detroit, Michigan); Barbara Brown (Newton South High School, Massachusetts); Christine Brownfield (Rio Americano High School, Sacramento, California); Donna Cannon (Simsbury High School, Connecticut); Mark Davis (Upper Arlington High School, Ohio); Marlyne DeLima (Coral Reef Senior High School, Miami, Florida); Michael Denning (Noble and Greenough, Boston, Massachusetts); Claire Dickerson (Clayton High School, Missouri); Nick Faraco (Simsbury High School, Connecticut); Cheryl R. Feldsott (Bethesda–Chevy Chase High School, Maryland); Paula Garza (Simsbury High School, Connecticut); Michael Heeter (Hawken School, Gates Mills, Ohio); Kelly Herrington (University Prep, Seattle, Washington); Thomas Hughart (Wellesley High School, Massachusetts); Colette Johnson (South Texas High School for Health Professions, Mercedes, Texas); Gene Kadish (Hanover High School, New Hampshire); Robert Kostrzeski (Drew School, San Francisco, California); Laura Lamb (Shawnee Mission East High School, Kansas); Alan Loper (Chamblee Charter High School, Georgia); Marsha Lynch (Grosse Pointe South High School, Michigan); Andrew McNeill (The Taft School, Watertown, Connecticut); Marisa Ostroff (Tucson High School, Arizona); Maureen Penley (Denver School for the Arts, Colorado); Anne Perina (Whitefish Bay High School, Wisconsin); Nina Pitkin (Thomas Jefferson High School for Science and Technology, Alexandria, Virginia); Robert Pomer (Darien High School, Connecticut); Lynn Redmond (Shattuck–St. Mary's School, Faribault, Minnesota); Jonathan Reider (San Francisco University High School, California); Charlene Rencher (Cranbrook School, Detroit, Michigan); Jenny Rodriguez (Bronx Preparatory Charter School, New York); Barbara

Sams (St. Louis Priory School, Missouri); and Susan Thorngren (New Trier High School, Winnetka, Illinois).

Third, we thank our *clients*, from whom we have learned a great deal.

Fourth, we thank our *colleague*, Rebecca Hulse, for her indefatigable efforts.

—*Richard Montauk and Krista Klein*

ABOUT DEGREE
OF DIFFERENCE

Founded by Richard Montauk in 1991, Degree of Difference is an educational consulting firm that provides quality one-on-one service to individuals submitting applications for college and graduate study in a variety of fields. We help hundreds of individuals each year plan their college and graduate careers and complete successful applications to the top programs worldwide.

Our advice for you—a college-bound student set on attending one of the top schools—is informed not only by the years of service we have provided to successful college applicants, but also by our work with college graduates working on later steps in their educations and careers. Because our collective expertise extends beyond the realm of college, into the areas of graduate study and career advising, our perspective is like that of a wide-angle lens. (For more information on some of our advisory services to those preparing for post-graduate study, see *How to Get Into the Top MBA Programs* and *How to Get Into the Top Law Schools*, both by Richard Montauk and also published by Prentice Hall.)

We provide a full menu of services for college applicants and their families:

- **Matching students with colleges.** We begin the consulting process with each client by inquiring into past experiences and ambitions for the future. After learning more about you, your background, your education, and your goals, we help you research colleges and discover what programs and options are available to you. We help you select colleges that are most appropriate for your needs and desires, and also ensure that your final list of target colleges includes an adequate number of "stretches," "possibles," and "likelies."
- **Strategizing.** We help you develop a coherent strategy to follow during the college application process, as follows:
  —We advise you on whether you should consider applying Early Decision or Early Action to a particular college.
  —We help you develop a comprehensive positioning strategy. We teach you how to market your strengths, account for or overcome your weaknesses, and best position yourself to enhance your candidacy.

—We teach you how to tailor your applications to each particular school.

—We help you make decisions regarding applications to special programs for early entry into professional school or joint degrees.

- **Interviewing.** Interviews for undergraduate admissions are often daunting for high schoolers who have never experienced the interview process. We teach you how to approach your interviews with confidence and make a positive impression. This often involves one or more mock interview sessions.

    —We coach you on successful interviewing techniques, providing assistance not only regarding what to say but also regarding how to say it, what to wear, and how to act in a variety of formal and informal interview settings.

    —We provide mock interview sessions, either face-to-face in our offices or over the phone.

- **Soliciting recommendations.** Getting the most from recommenders is often one of the most difficult—and one of the most overlooked—tasks in the college application process.

    —We teach you how to look at your application in its entirety in order to determine what is most needed from your recommenders to fill in the gaps, enhance your strengths, and compensate for your weaknesses.

    —We provide advice on how to approach recommenders tactfully, and how to best provide them with the information you would like conveyed in your letters of recommendation.

    —We assist your recommenders (if desired) to develop high-impact letters of endorsement.

- **Completing applications.** A sloppy, unfocused application will do you no good. We are happy to review any and all of your written materials to ensure that all the necessary information is well communicated and correct.

    —We review all of the written product, including application data forms; listings of extracurricular activities, work experience, and community service; and responses to short answer and essay questions.

    —We will help you write a successful general or special talent résumé.

- **Essay writing.** For most of our clients, essay writing is an area of particular concern.

    —We help you craft themes in order to make your entire body of essays convey a set of consistent and solid messages.

—We provide advice on appropriate material for use in each essay. We help you fashion each set of essays so that it contains neither redundancies nor inconsistencies and makes the most out of your experiences and strengths.

—We edit essays and provide advice on essay structure and form, yet strive to do so in a way that retains a client's own voice, style, and personality.

Please note that we do not write essays for our clients under any circumstances.

HOW TO INITIATE A RELATIONSHIP WITH DEGREE OF DIFFERENCE

Some of our most successful clients sign up for our services one or more years in advance of actually applying to college in order to discuss long-term strategy and goals that need to be accomplished before applications are under way. This way, you will be best prepared to market yourself to schools when the time comes.

On the other hand, plenty of clients come to us at a later stage in the game—at the beginning of their senior year or even well into the college application process. We realize that many high school students have not given much thought to the college application process before it is suddenly upon them and they feel in over their heads. We are prepared to help you at any point in your college application work and encourage panicked students and parents who find themselves behind schedule to contact us for immediate assistance.

Please email us at **rmontauk@aol.com** or contact us at:

Degree of Difference Inc. (USA)
Tel. (415) 263-0567
www.degreeofdifference.com

Degree of Difference Inc. (UK)
126 Aldersgate Street
Barbican, London EC1A 4JQ
United Kingdom
Tel. (44) 171-608-1811

CONTENTS

Part II   APPLYING TO COLLEGE

Part III ON THE ROAD TO COLLEGE

Part IV OTHER OPTIONS

Part V FINANCING COLLEGE

Part VI APPLICATION ESSAY EXAMPLES

Part I

THE CONTEXT: WHAT YOU NEED TO KNOW BEFORE YOU APPLY

1

GETTING IN IS THE HARDEST PART

— KEY POINTS —

The college admissions process has become much more complex in recent years

Understanding admissions at leading schools is critical for getting good results

This book analyzes and explains every aspect of admissions at America's selective colleges

—What you need to know before you apply

—How to do bang-up applications

—How to respond to college decisions

—Alternative college options

—How to finance college

The role of parents is important—but should not supersede that of the applicant

INTRODUCTION

College admission has become immensely more complicated in recent years. The process has also grown more stressful, with students feeling increased pressure to get into a prestigious college. We have written this book to provide an in-depth guide to the admissions process at America's selective colleges to help readers sort through the complexity and thereby retain control of the process—as well as a measure of sanity.

Besides reducing readers' stress, we aim to help applicants discover and get into the best possible colleges for their individual needs. We stress: this does not mean we focus only on Harvard or the Ivy League, or even some notion of a "top 10" or "top 20." Instead, we look to help applicants (and their parents) find the schools at which they will grow and prosper. A higher ranked, perhaps more famous school may do little to develop the same person. In such a case, he or she would almost certainly be better off at a different school.

Although we emphasize fit over prestige in the pages that follow, we devote most of the book to analyzing admissions at the highly selective colleges, partly because this is where our readers and clients most want to go, and partly because this is where one can learn most about how best to approach the admissions process. The competition is stiffest at these colleges, in terms of both the number of qualified applicants trying to get in and the lengths to which they go to pitch themselves. Clearly, the strategies that work well at the most competitive colleges also work at less selective institutions.

THE EVOLUTION OF COLLEGE ADMISSIONS

College admission is more complicated than it once was for a host of reasons. First, vital information has been sucked out of the system:

- Fewer high schools calculate class rank
- High school grading is more lenient, with far more students graduating with high GPAs. Thus, it is harder to distinguish truly top students from good students
- SAT scores have been revalued upward, thereby crowding more students into the top score brackets

■ Fewer high school counselors reveal negative aspects of applicants' high school records (due in large part to litigious parents)

Second, the credentials applicants present are more complicated than they once were. Instead of just taking courses in high school, many take courses at local community colleges or regular colleges (during the summer), or get after-school tutoring in subjects not offered by their schools. It's not just in academic areas that matters have gotten more complicated. Whereas few students in the past participated in anything beyond a high school athletic team, some now participate in regional leagues, attend far-flung athletic camps, and so on. The same is true of the performing arts, volunteer activities, and employment.

Third, more high schools now offer candidates to the leading colleges. In prior generations, the leading private schools (especially the primary feeder school for a given university) and a limited number of wealthy public schools would pitch their graduates to the selective colleges. Now, hundreds upon hundreds of high schools do so. Recently, an increasing number of foreign high schools have entered the game. It is harder than ever for colleges to be able to compare applicants when they come from such diverse sources. How to compare someone with a 3.75 GPA from a suburban Detroit school with someone who is projected to get two A and one B grades on her A-levels in Birmingham (England, not Michigan)? How to compare someone taking the SAT in his second or third language with someone taking it in his native language? (This is also of concern regarding American immigrant applicants, who are more prevalent now than they were not long ago.)

Fourth, the colleges have made their task more complicated by moving away from selecting "well-rounded" students in favor of taking very angular (or, in the admissions vernacular, "hooked") students. In other words, rather than accept applicants who are pretty good at a bunch of classes and activities, colleges tend to favor those who are standouts at one or two things. This makes balancing a class—putting together a good mix of different sorts of people—a tricky proposition. In the old days, balance might have meant being sure that some applicants from farms and distant states were included. Now, in addition to geographic balance (which also includes foreign students), schools look for balance as to race and ethnicity, income, academic interest, extracurricular pursuits, and so on. In fact, this list does not do justice to the task facing admissions committees. In athletics, for example, the day of an athlete playing on three different college teams is long gone. Few athletes participate on more than one team. Also, the sports themselves are so specialized that one can no longer select a bunch of good basketball players and expect the basketball team to be competitive. Instead, one needs a point guard, a shooting guard, and so on. And this example is dwarfed by the need for specialists to fill a football team roster.

A fifth development complicating the job of admissions committees is that colleges now compete tooth and nail against one another. The impact of the college rankings, especially those produced by *U.S. News & World Report*, means that admissions decisions are weighed in light of their likely impact upon a school's ranking. Admissions committees constantly face questions about whether they should take a marvelous student who would, say, be a delight for the art history professors to teach, but whose SAT scores would drag down the school average (and thus sabotage the school's ranking).

The result of this complexity is that decisions at a given school are harder to predict. And because decisions are harder to predict, students apply to more schools—or apply Early Decision. Each of these phenomena contributes further to the system's complexity.

Don't worry. For one thing, this book explains the system—in greater depth than any other book manages. For another, there are plenty of very good colleges available. (One of the interesting aspects of researching this book is that, in talking at length with people in charge of admissions even at the country's most prestigious colleges, there is near unanimity among them that even the best students and their parents are wrong to target only the top 10 or top 20 or whatever.) And perhaps most importantly, the best study yet done of the incomes of graduates concludes that it is the person, not the college, that determines post-college career success.

HOW THIS BOOK CAN HELP

Most applicants to leading colleges are more than qualified to succeed academically and otherwise at the schools to which they apply. This puts colleges in the enviable position of having an excess of good applicants from which to choose, but it puts applicants in the unenviable position of having to stand out among a group of talented seniors. Given that most people who enroll at the leading colleges graduate successfully from them, the hardest part of college may be getting in.

The current college admissions process, which features an unfortunate combination of complexity and stress, rewards those who understand it. Those who don't understand it tend to put their efforts into applying to schools where they lack a realistic chance of admission, or undercut their chances by failing to understand what their target schools do and do not value. Those who do understand the process are best able to select schools that match their needs and offer a realistic chance of admission. They are also able to put together winning application efforts to these schools.

This book explains every aspect of admissions at selective colleges, so that you can maximize your own admissions results no matter where you apply.

WHAT IS INCLUDED IN THIS BOOK

This book analyzes and discusses each step of the college application process in a thorough, detailed fashion, with supporting comments from the admissions and financial aid directors at leading colleges.

The book contains six parts:

Part I, "The Context: What You Need to Know Before You Apply," provides the context for the decisions you will have to make during the college application process. It is important that you understand this context before starting your applications. The information in Part I will teach you how to decide where to apply. It will also give you a general introduction to the admissions process, showing you how it works at various schools.

Part II, "Applying to College," shows you how to plan and put together the various components of the application to achieve your best possible outcome. It introduces the idea of "positioning" and discusses in detail the three main vehicles for presenting yourself: essays, recommendations, and the interview.

Part III, "On the Road to College," contains information and advice to prepare you for the steps you should take after colleges notify you of their decision. This covers everything from what to do if you are waitlisted to how to prepare to get the most out of college.

Part IV, "Other Options," presents three different possibilities for applicants who may not follow the usual college path. One possibility is taking a year off before college. Another is going to a service academy (such as West Point or Navy). A third is going abroad for college, such as to Oxford or Cambridge. We explore what sort of person would be best served by pursuing each option as well as how to get the most out of it. And, of course, we offer advice on how to get into a West Point or an Oxford.

Part V, "Financing College," offers guidance to students and their families about college finances. It explores funding options, both short-term and long-term, from colleges and other sources. It examines the strategies that can be applied to get the best possible aid packages from colleges. It also considers other ways to make college more affordable.

Part VI, "Application Essay Examples," presents thirty-one recent essays from eighteen candidates to leading colleges. The essays are accompanied by our own critiques, explaining what worked and why. The essay writers come from a wide range of backgrounds; the essays themselves cover a host of different topics. What unites them is that they are uniformly well written and memorable.

OUR RESEARCH

This book is based on our own extensive experience counseling college applicants (Richard Montauk established our firm in 1991) and in-depth conversations with more than 100 admissions and financial aid directors at many of the country's leading colleges.

PRIVATE UNIVERSITIES	LIBERAL ARTS COLLEGES	OTHER SCHOOLS
IVY	Amherst	**STATE**
Brown	Bates	UC Berkeley
Columbia	Bennington	Michigan
Cornell	Bowdoin	UNC (Chapel Hill)
Dartmouth	Bryn Mawr	Texas (Austin)
Harvard	Carleton	Virginia
Univ. of Pennsylvania	Colby	William & Mary
Princeton	Connecticut College	Wisconsin
Yale	Davidson	
	Haverford	**TECHNOLOGY**
OTHER AMERICAN	Middlebury	Cal Tech
Boston College	Mount Holyoke	Georgia Tech
Chicago	Oberlin	Harvey Mudd
Duke	Pomona	MIT
Emory	Reed	
Georgetown	Sarah Lawrence	**SERVICE ACADEMY**
Johns Hopkins	Smith	U.S. Air Force
NYU	Swarthmore	U.S. Coast Guard
Northwestern	Vassar	U.S. Merchant Marine
Notre Dame	Wellesley	U.S. Military (Army)
Stanford	Wesleyan	U.S. Naval
USC	Williams	

Private Universities	Liberal Arts Colleges	Other Schools
Tufts		**BRITISH**
Tulane		Cambridge
Vanderbilt		London School of Economics
Washington U.		Oxford

The individuals we interviewed are cited by name and school in the Acknowledgments section of the book.

THE ROLE OF PARENTS

How to Get Into the Top Colleges is written for college applicants, but it is also written for parents of college applicants. Although the text is written as if to a college applicant, we realize that it may well be you, not your child, who first picks up this book. We indeed encourage parents to familiarize themselves with the college application process and, when appropriate, assist their children in preparing applications and making decisions.

You may in fact discover that you have to take a leading role in the college search and application process in order to get your son or daughter going. We urge you to trust your instincts as far as your involvement in your child's college applications is concerned. If your child genuinely needs your motivational encouragement (or motivational nagging), is used to your involvement in decisions and activities, or seems to encourage your input, by all means play a significant role. On the other hand, if your child is motivated to dive into the college research and application process on his or her own, is used to being independent and making his or her own decisions, or strongly discourages your input, try to let him or her have as much freedom as possible.

It will be difficult at times, as a loving and concerned parent, to balance the right amount of involvement with the right amount of distance. It may also be as tough for you as it is for your child to retain the proper perspective during the upcoming project. You will want to help and support your child through this difficult phase, but you should also think about giving him or her some independence. Your child is about to embark upon perhaps his or her first adult experience, to begin to live and work away from your embrace and in the company of other young adults. This is a good time to practice your new parenting role—one in which you care for your child from a distance, one in which you may become more friend and adviser than disciplinarian and protector.

Parents should also remember that their participation in the application effort can be unwelcome not only from their children but also from the perspective of admissions officers. When parents take over the process, it generally shows. Admissions officers recognize it and resent it: they would rather hear directly from the applicants.

SOME GUIDELINES FOR PARENTS IN THE COLLEGE ADMISSIONS PROCESS

- Do not start discussing college in serious terms when your child is in the eighth or ninth grade. Early discussions about college—even through sophomore year in high school—should be loose and exploratory, not serious or intimidating.

- Pay attention to what your child finds attractive about certain schools so that you can remain attuned to his or her desire and make helpful suggestions. Be on the alert, however, that there may be instances in which your child is merely mouthing the reigning attitudes of friends or others, rather than forming his or her own opinions. Try to help your child sort out his or her own needs when this is the case.

- Focus on finding the best colleges that will bring your child success and satisfaction rather than emphasizing getting into the school with the most famous name.

- View the college selection and application process as a matter of helping your child reach an outcome he or she will value, not an outcome about which you will be able to brag to your friends.

- Give help and guidance, but try to resist imposing your desires on your child.

- Do not let the college application process take over family life. Make sure you set aside time for activities in which college and applications are not discussed.

- Assist your child, but do not take complete control of the college application process. Help to keep your child on schedule, but do not do things for him or her. Do not, for example, ever write essays for your child.

- Remain realistic about your child's chances of getting into chosen schools. Help your child retain perspective, too.

- Interact with your child's college counselor on a regular basis. Make the application process a partnership.

A FINAL NOTE

Many applicants look upon the task of producing hundreds of details about their lives, writing dozens of essays about intimate or obscure topics, securing recommendations from teachers, and enduring interviews as a modern form of "death by a thousand cuts." They feel that it is trial enough simply to research the schools and figure out what they are looking for, let alone manage the intensive application process.

If that is your view, keep in mind that the application process, however imperfect it may be, forces applicants to think about where they want to go in their lives and careers—often for the first time. Too few people otherwise devote the time to take stock of their past, present, and future circumstances and opportunities. You are at a point where sensible decisions about these matters can yield a lifetime of benefits, and failure to consider your options carefully can result in missed opportunities. Confronting such important education and career decisions might open doors you never even realized exist. The application process may actually turn out to be more than just a painful experience—it may prove a helpful one.

2

WORKING WITH YOUR COLLEGE COUNSELOR

— KEY POINTS —

▪

Your high school counselor performs a host of important
functions from which you can benefit

▪

Understanding your counselor's role—as well as your
own responsibilities and those of your parents—will help
you get the most out of your working relationship with your counselor

▪

Establishing a good relationship with your counselor is valuable

▪

Hiring an independent college counselor is advisable
under some circumstances

An important aspect of the college application process is the working relationship you develop with your college counselor at school. Whether you are assigned to a counselor or are allowed to choose among a large staff, try to develop a strong working rapport with that person—he or she is a critical resource, and will play a significant role in your college selection and application process.

At some high schools, the college counselor plays a very public and active role in the lives of students, beginning perhaps as early as sophomore year. He or she teaches classes on the college process, meets individually with students, and makes him- or herself available for whatever assistance you require. At other schools, where counselors have a large caseload and perhaps other teaching or administrative duties as well, your counselor may not have as active a role in your life. If this is the case, you might have to take the initiative in getting to know your college counselor and seeking advice at the appropriate points.

The college application process is a team effort shared among you, your parents, and your college counselor. Understanding each party's responsibilities will help you get the most out of working with your counselor.

GENERAL RESPONSIBILITIES OF A COLLEGE COUNSELOR IN THE TEAM EFFORT

- Introduce students to the many resources available for learning about colleges.
- Conduct college research and planning sessions with students.
- Ensure that students and their families understand how college admissions works, how to evaluate their chances of acceptance at specific schools, and how to navigate the college application process.
- Track the admissions record of the individuals in each successive class of graduates (thereby providing a useful reference for understanding what it takes to get into different colleges).
- Help students devise a list of "likely," "possible," and "reach" schools that fit their needs.
- Arrange for representatives from colleges to visit the high school.
- Publicize opportunities, such as regional college fairs, for students and their parents to learn about colleges.
- Provide information about standardized tests, including the SAT, the SAT subject tests, and the ACT.
- Provide counseling about standardized testing options (which tests to take, when) and information about test preparation resources.

- Provide counseling on college essay writing. Help students choose appropriate and intriguing essay topics as well as develop their "voice" to create personal and self-reflective essays.

- Advise students and parents about college financial aid.

- Write a comprehensive counselor recommendation on behalf of each student for college applications.

- Create a "Profile" of the high school for college admissions committees, so that they fully understand the school's mission and philosophy, as well as academic offerings and standards.

- Attend national and regional admissions counseling conferences, visit college campuses, and read industry publications. Stay current on trends and controversies in the admissions field.

This list is by no means exhaustive. In particular, it does not include the ongoing efforts to ensure a student's intellectual and social development during the course of high school, without which the college application effort would be less successful.

Note: At some high schools, college counselors do not perform all of these duties because they are constrained by the size of their caseloads or by other responsibilities. Most authorities, including this book's authors, believe that a caseload of about 100 students per counselor is the maximum consistent with outstanding performance. The average at America's public high schools, however, is nearly 500 per counselor. Even education-focused Massachusetts, at the low end of the caseload spectrum, averages 415 students per counselor at public schools.

GENERAL RESPONSIBILITIES OF STUDENTS IN THE TEAM EFFORT

- Read all materials provided by the college counseling staff.

- Attend all mandatory college counseling meetings and complete all college counseling assignments on time and to the best of your ability.

- Check the college counseling center's website, notices, bulletin boards, or other materials on a regular basis to keep up-to-date on information and deadlines.

- Meet with college representatives when they visit your high school.

- Work with your college counselor to create a college application organization system to keep track of application materials.

- Give recommendation forms to teachers and the college counselor at least one month before the due date, or by school-imposed deadlines (if applicable).

- Talk with your college counselor to learn how college admissions works and how to evaluate your chances of acceptance at your target schools.

- Discuss your college preferences and ideas with your parents and your college counselor to keep them informed of your developing views and to solicit advice.

- Listen carefully when your counselor suggests colleges that you have not considered.

- Remember that you and your college counselor are on the same team.

GENERAL RESPONSIBILITIES OF PARENTS IN THE TEAM EFFORT

- Read all materials provided by the college counseling staff.
- Attend all college sessions for parents.
- Make an appointment for your family to meet with the college counselor together, if at all possible.
- Help your child complete the financial aid applications.

(See Chapter 1 for an in-depth discussion of the role of parents in the application process.)

WORKING WITH YOUR COLLEGE COUNSELOR

The better your college counselor knows you, the better able she (or he) will be to help you. For instance, her advice about which courses to take your junior or senior year will depend on her knowledge of such factors as how hard you are working, the extent to which you feel stressed and how you handle stress, your college and career goals, and so on. Note, too, that your college counselor will be called upon to write you a letter of recommendation (sometimes called a Secondary School Report) for college. This letter is meant to be a compendium of information gathered from your teachers, administrators, and formal report cards. However, it may also include your counselor's personal knowledge and observations of you, to the extent that she knows you.

Not all counselors have a reasonable enough workload to permit them to get to know their students as well as they might like. If your counselor does have the time (and inclination), however, you can certainly benefit by developing a relationship with her. Take advantage of the formal process she has established. Attend whatever college workshops and counseling sessions she has set up. If she is open to additional contact, by all means meet with her periodically to discuss your goals and progress. Keep in mind that this is an unusual relationship you are embarking on. She will want to understand your thoughts and will value honesty on your part. On the other hand, she may feel overly burdened if you routinely complain about all that annoys you, or if you try to see her every day. A few tips to keep in mind:

- Share your views about your academic and nonacademic interests and progress. She doesn't expect you to love every class, teacher, and assignment, but don't use her to vent at length about the Latin teacher from hell.

- Don't worry that she's seeing your views of what you want from high school, college, and life change over time. She is accustomed to this and will not find it odd.

- Be courteous and respectful. Don't be upset if you need to make an appointment several days in advance to see her. If you make an appointment, be sure to keep it. Understand also that she has busy periods during which you should minimize your demands on her.

Look to begin sharing your concerns and updating her on your progress before your junior year. Likewise, once the college application process is under way, it is important to continue communicating. Keep your counselor apprised of where you are applying (especially if your college list changes over time), of how your college interviews go, of decisions you have received from colleges, of changes in your interest level in the various colleges, and of waitlist offers you will pursue.

The more your counselor understands your personality and goals, the better he or she can help you choose appropriate colleges and make informed application decisions. Her perspective on the application process may differ from yours. Particularly in the early stages of your college search, you (and your parents) may be very excited about a famous college or two and therefore focused on maximizing your chances of getting in there. Your college counselor's main concern may be quite different. She may be more focused on finding colleges that best fit your needs rather than those that are most celebrated. In fact, nothing bothers most college counselors more than students (and parents) who obsess over prestige rather than identifying which colleges best match their learning styles, career goals, personal interests, and educational philosophies.

Remember that your college counselor has the best sense of your admissibility to various colleges, based on the performance of previous students from your particular high school. If he is encouraging you to widen your reach, it is probably for good reason. If you have trouble finding less competitive colleges (schools that would be considered "possibles" or "likelies" for you) that fit your needs, ask your counselor's advice, to see whether he or she can point you in the right direction.

Be sure to fully research and visit less competitive schools to follow your counselor's advice that you get serious about finding the right matches rather than concentrating exclusively on schools that may be extremely difficult to get into.

LITTLE THINGS MEAN A LOT

A few more tips for getting the most out of your relationship with your counselor:

- Stay on top of all standardized test registration deadlines.
- If you have a nickname or several names that you use, inform your college counselor which name you will use for all standardized test and college application purposes so that you can both adhere to the same format.
- Put your name on all materials that you give your counselor for review, and fill out the top portion of recommendation forms and Secondary School Report forms.
- Provide addressed envelopes and stamps for recommendation letters, if required by your counselor.
- Know where to find basic information, such as your school's College Board code or fax number, so that you don't have to pester your college counselor about trivial matters.
- Meet all application deadlines well in advance.

PET PEEVES OF COLLEGE COUNSELORS

Regarding Student Behavior

- Focusing on a school's "name brand" or prestige instead of how well it will fit you. If for no other reason, apply to several "likelies" ("safety schools") to help your college counselor sleep at night.
- Visiting (and even applying to) only your "reach" schools rather than a full range of colleges.
- "Trophy collecting": Applying to far too many colleges just to retain bragging rights in the spring regarding the number of schools that accepted you. (Most college counselors acknowledge that students who do their homework should be able to narrow their choices to a maximum of eight or ten schools.)

- Double depositing: Sending deposits to two schools in the spring, thus taking a space that could go to another deserving waitlisted student.

- Using less than knowledgeable independent counselors, especially those who interfere with the work of your high school counselor.

- Applying Early Decision to a school that is far out of reach or not a clear first choice.

- Screwing up senior year: Plenty of students with strong academic and behavior records take a dive senior year. This puts the counselor's reputation and the student's applications at risk.

Regarding Parent Behavior

- Maintaining unrealistic views of their child's chances of admission.

- Not respecting counselors' time (especially when deadlines approach).

- Ghostwriting their child's applications.

HIRING AN INDEPENDENT COUNSELOR

Most college applicants will find that their school's college counselor provides everything they need in terms of assistance and expertise in the college process. But if you find yourself in one of the following situations, you might consider hiring a private college counselor—someone outside your school who charges a fee for services—to help you with the college selection and application process:

- Your counselor at school cannot give you the attention you need, whether due to his or her own large caseload or for some other reason.

- Your counselor at school cannot determine a full range of schools (including "possibles" and "likelies") that fit your desires and needs, and you need professional help finding colleges that are good fits and where your chances of admission are strong.

- Your counselor pushes you to his or her pet schools, despite their being poor fits for you.

- Your counselor is unfamiliar with the schools, or types of schools, to which you plan to apply.

- You do not get along with your college counselor and prefer that another expert help you with the more personal aspects of the process, such as crafting strong essays. (Note that simply disliking your college counselor should not always lead to hiring an independent counselor. You may not like your counselor, but that hardly means he or she will fail to work well and hard on your behalf. If you can keep your feelings in check and do what is expected of you in this process, you will probably find that your counselor will do likewise.)

If you do decide to work with an independent counselor, be sure the person you hire is knowledgeable and right for your needs. A large percentage of independent counselors hang out their shingles with no more experience than helping one of their own children apply to college. See below for tips on hiring a good resource. (If you wish to hire us, see page *xiii* for contact details.)

BE CAUTIOUS WHEN HIRING AN INDEPENDENT COUNSELOR

- Investigate his or her credentials.
- If you are uncertain about a counselor's skills or reputation, ask for references and speak to several of them.
- Do not hire anyone who makes promises about your acceptance at certain colleges or tells you that he or she has connections to help get you admitted somewhere. (The system does not work that way. Someone who claims such connections or influence is probably lying or deluded.)
- Do not hire anyone who says he or she will do the application work for you. Private counselors should help you with the process in the same way that in-school college counselors do, but they should never perform the work for you. Not only is this unethical, but it is also likely to harm your chances when applying. Such help is obvious and very much disliked and distrusted by college admissions officers.
- Look for counselors who seek to retain your voice and personality in the application materials, with the aim of avoiding an "overprocessed" feel.

COLLEGE COUNSELORS GIVE ADVICE TO STUDENTS AND PARENTS

WHAT IS YOUR MOST IMPORTANT ADVICE FOR STUDENTS?

This process is about the match, not about what is most prestigious. Think about your hopes and dreams: What do you want to be doing ten years from now? What is the best way for you to achieve this goal? *Barbara Brown, Newton South High School, Newton, MA*

Be in charge of your process—you are the captain of your ship; your loving family and I are your crew. Start becoming opinionated about what you want and need, and work with me to find good matches. *Sally Best Bailey, Fountain Valley School, Colorado Springs, CO*

Do your homework. Don't take someone else's opinion about whether you would like a certain college. Don't be close-minded about variables like size, location, and distance from home—you can miss really good opportunities this way. *Jonathan Reider, San Francisco University High School, San Francisco, CA*

Spend time with your counselor. Get to know him or her personally. Colleges want personal anecdotes from us and we won't be able to provide them unless we know you. *Colette Johnson, South Texas High School for Health Professions, Mercedes, TX*

Don't slow down academically senior year. Many of our students apply to highly selective schools that require a mid-year report. Students must remember that schools have the right to refuse them for admission in the fall if they really let their grades slip significantly during their senior year. *Alan Loper, Chamblee Charter High School, Chamblee, GA*

How Do You Want Students to Work with You?

Don't wait until junior year to embark on working on your relationship with me. . . . My caseload gets larger every year, and I need all the time I can get to learn the uniqueness of *you* compared to the hundreds of other students I work with. If I am going to know you well enough by eleventh grade to make suggestions to you about college choices, then I need to know more about you than your GPA and test scores. *Marsha Lynch, Grosse Pointe South High School, Grosse Pointe, MI*

Be open-minded and inquisitive. Be a frequent visitor to my office. Help me get to know you by "dropping by" and updating me on your life. Be timely and responsive. *Barbara Sams, St. Louis Priory School, St. Louis, MO (and President, Missouri Association for College Admission Counseling)*

Please take the time to make an appointment with me during your junior year to talk about the college process. It is okay if you are "clueless." I can help you with the exploration and decision-making process. Check me out to be sure that you feel comfortable working with me on the college process. (We have five counselors in the office. You are not limited to just working with me.) This is your process, and you need to take responsibility for all aspects of the exploration and application process. I will help you, provide you with information, and answer your questions. It is, however, your choice and your application. *Gene Kadish, Hanover High School, Hanover, NH*

Come to me with questions, even if they seem silly. As a counselor, I would much rather provide correct information at the outset than deal with constantly patching the effects of bad information down the line. Students should meet with me starting in their junior year. Though many won't have college on their mind yet, working with a high school counselor is all about the relationship. If we have time to form one, and you grow to trust me, you will be able to trust that what I am telling you is accurate and benefit most from the services I have to offer. *Maureen Penley, Denver School for the Arts, Denver, CO*

Even if you think you are on the right track, run your ideas and plans by me. I may have helpful suggestions to get you where you are going. And, if I know where you are in the process and who you are as a person, I'll be able to plug your candidacy with the colleges I come in contact with. *Marlyne DeLima, Coral Reef Senior High School, Miami, FL*

It would be very helpful if students gave us all of their materials at the same time rather than a bit at a time. *Anne Perina, Whitefish Bay High School, Whitefish Bay, WI*

It is helpful when the student takes the time to make sure they are known on a personal level by the counselor. Students that want the most from their high school counselor should take the time to meet with him/her a couple times a year to let them know what is going on and how school is progressing. *Laura Lamb, Shawnee Mission East High School, Shawnee Mission, KS*

Junior students need to be committed to the college search and application process. For students, research and dialogue will help them clarify their personal goals and better understand which schools will help them thrive as individuals. The college counseling staff and the resources we provide are not effective unless the student commits to working with us throughout the entire process. *Charlene Rencher, Cranbrook School, Detroit, MI*

Not all counseling is alike. If you're not getting qualified help, seek it elsewhere. Counselors never take a graduate class in college counseling, so the experience is all over the map. *John Boshoven, Community High School, Ann Arbor, MI, and Jewish Academy of Metropolitan Detroit, Detroit, MI (and President, Michigan Association for College Admission Counseling)*

If students are working with an independent counselor, they should maintain a relationship with their school counselor. The independent counselor will be helpful with organization and structure, but may not always have the complete picture of a student that a school counselor will have from a student's cumulative file. In the end, it is the school counselor, and not the independent counselor, who will write the letter of recommendation. *Robert Pomer, Darien High School, Darien, CT*

The Best Way for Students to Gain Your Support

The best way for a student to gain my support in the college counseling process is to be just as interested in the outcome as I am. *Lynn Redmond, Shattuck–St. Mary's School, Faribault, MN*

I will help you put forth your best presentation to colleges when the time comes, but remember that my own reputation is on the line as well when I sign my name to your application. So be sure that our four-year relationship has been one built on honesty. *Marsha Lynch, Grosse Pointe South High School, Grosse Pointe, MI*

Counselors can work more effectively with students who invest in the counselor-student relationship. When students work consistently with their counselors, the counselor is able to provide opportunities for them, whether these are scholarships, internships, or recognizing a good fit at various colleges. *Susan Thorngren, New Trier High School, Winnetka, IL*

I certainly advocate for every student to the best of my ability, but those students who follow instructions and complete assigned tasks are easier to write for because they naturally leave the most positive impression on me. Those who avoid the process, and thereby me, give me less to work with, and subsequently and logically may not "read" as well to colleges. *Michael Heeter, Hawken School, Gates Mills, OH*

APPLICATION ADVICE FOR STUDENTS

I encourage my students to apply to no more than seven or eight schools. Some apply to fifteen or twenty, and that's too many. *Peggy Blau, Brooklyn Technology High School, Brooklyn, NY*

We encourage our students to apply to six colleges (they are required to apply to at least five). *Jenny Rodriguez, Bronx Preparatory Charter School, Bronx, NY*

Work with a teacher to produce the best possible college essays that you can! *Mark Davis, Upper Arlington High School, Upper Arlington, OH*

Get to know me by checking in with me a couple of times each year. I can write a better, more meaningful letter of recommendation for a student that I know well. It gives the college more confidence if I can demonstrate that I am well acquainted with the applicant. *Christine Brownfield, Rio Americano High School, Sacramento, CA*

CHOOSING COLLEGES

One of the most difficult challenges for students and parents during the college search and application process is to keep an open mind and set aside preconceived ideas of what constitutes a "good college." With the array of colleges from which students can choose these days, there is never just one college that will meet a student's needs. A successful college search process should help students discover the wide variety of opportunities available to them, opportunities that will suit their particular talents and aspirations. *Charlene Rencher, Cranbrook School, Detroit, MI*

Looking for colleges is similar to dating. Be wary of Early Decision unless you fall in love with one school. Some students do right away and some don't. The timing of a good fit is different for everyone. Nothing is wrong with you if one college doesn't jump out and a number of schools appeal to you.   *Donna Cannon, Simsbury High School, Simsbury, CT*

Visit a variety of different types of schools in the general area to get a feel for what appeals to you: large or small; secular or religious; urban, suburban or rural; civilian or military. Setting foot on a variety of campuses is the best way for students and their parents to start figuring out what type of school is the best fit, not which name appeals to them the most.   *Cheryl R. Feldsott, Bethesda–Chevy Chase High School, Bethesda, MD*

It is key to find at least one "safety" school that you would attend. It does no good to apply to one that you would refuse to go to.   *Barbara Brown, Newton South High School, Newton, MA*

It is not the name of the college you attend that will change your life. It is how you come out of that environment that can make a significant difference in your career choices and future development. Evaluate every college as to whether it is an "optimal growth environment." Look for not only academic experiences, but also social, personal, and athletic experiences.   *Nick Faraco, Simsbury High School, Simsbury, CT*

Trust data. High school guidance offices keep data on application results from year to year. It is easy to see what one student's chances are at an individual institution by comparing his/her profile to those of students who applied to that institution the previous year.   *Robert Pomer, Darien High School, Darien, CT*

Believe me when I tell you that all this hyped-up, who-got-in-where buzz is short-lived! Future employers are not going to care much about where you went to college, but they will care about what you learned. . . . Take time to really think about and identify the kind of environment that will help you learn and grow, and then find schools that have those characteristics at all levels of selectivity.   *Paula Garza, Simsbury High School, Simsbury, CT*

Parental Involvement in the Process

Parents, if you are working harder than your son or daughter at this process—stop!   *Thomas Hughart, Wellesley High School, Wellesley, MA*

Help support your children but realize that this is a rite of passage. Let your kids own the process and view them as they really are, not as you want them to be. Listen to them and think about schools that would support them and generate self-confidence, maturity, and growth.   *Robert Kostrzeski, Drew School, San Francisco, CA*

The most common mistake parents make in working with school counselors is that they do not allow their sons and daughters to "control" the application process. If a student is required to fill out all of the applications, submit all of the paperwork for the guidance office, and manage all aspects of the application process, he or she will feel a sense of control over the process. In a sense, so much of the admission decision is out of their hands—once the application is sent, it is up to the admissions office to make a determination. It is unfortunate for many students that the part of the process that they can control . . . is being usurped by parents. *Robert Pomer, Darien High School, Darien, CT*

Parents should not assume that the counselor knows their student as well as they do. They need to help the counselor know their student by keeping communication going both ways. *Nina Pitkin, Thomas Jefferson High School for Science and Technology, Alexandria, VA*

I advise parents to be involved. Make an appointment to meet with your child's counselor. Though we make an effort to reach out to parents, it would be nice to see more coming the other way. *Marisa Ostroff, Tucson High School, Tucson, AZ*

Parents should stay in close contact with their child's high school counselors. The college process has changed quite a bit since they went through it. They should rely on the counselor to describe these changes and usher them through. *Maureen Penley, Denver School for the Arts, Denver, CO*

COMMON MISTAKES STUDENTS MAKE

Three common mistakes I see: only visiting schools that will be very hard to get into, thinking that the process can be gamed and manipulated, and applying Early Decision to some school that is not a realistic option but that you hope will take you because you are applying Early. *Jonathan Reider, San Francisco University High School, San Francisco, CA*

Perhaps the most common mistake is not asking enough questions and not utilizing completely the assistance that a college counselor can provide. *Lynn Redmond, Shattuck–St. Mary's School, Faribault, MN*

One of the most common mistakes is being closed to new options—I have spent my professional career learning about colleges and universities throughout the country and world. It's my job to know about the wonderful but little known program at XYZ college that is exactly what you are looking for. Consider looking beyond the "known" lists. *Barbara Sams, St. Louis Priory School, St. Louis, MO (and President, Missouri Association for College Admission Counseling)*

I would like to see our students do more research on schools outside of New York. A lot of our students are first-generation-to-college students and they only know about NYU, Columbia, and Cornell. I advise them to look into other schools that may be equally good for them. *Peggy Blau, Brooklyn Technology High School, Brooklyn, NY*

There are lots of reasons students wait too long to come see me. Some feel overwhelmed and don't know where to begin, some are intimidated by the financial aid process, and for some it's just cold feet. Students should understand that the process is actually much easier—and more fruitful—if they come in to meet with me early. *Marlyne DeLima, Coral Reef Senior High School, Miami, FL*

Students should not assume that things can happen overnight. *Nina Pitkin, Thomas Jefferson High School for Science and Technology, Alexandria, VA*

COMMON MISTAKES PARENTS MAKE

One of the most common mistakes that parents make is having unrealistic college admissions expectations. *Claire Dickerson, Clayton High School, Clayton, MO*

They "do" for their students rather than "assist." They take charge and control over the college process. This does not foster the independence their children will need to be successful in college. *Kelly Herrington, University Prep, Seattle, WA*

Parents should not be afraid to call, stop by, or email a counselor. We are more than happy to talk. Some parents are intimidated or worried that they are bothering us. In fact, the more we are working together, the more beneficial it will be. *Colette Johnson, South Texas High School for Health Professions, Mercedes, TX*

If a family is going to invest money in a second opinion from an independent counselor, make sure the school counselor is in contact with the indy. The worst thing a family can do is force a kid to choose between two conflicting opinions. *Andrew McNeill, The Taft School, Watertown, CT*

Parents expect us to do all the work. We are (supposed) to . . . call the colleges for the parents, especially about any special concerns, set up campus visits, look into financial aid, email colleges for information for their child, etc. *Marsha Lynch, Grosse Pointe South High School, Grosse Pointe, MI*

3

Deciding Where to Apply

— KEY POINTS —

■

The process of choosing colleges is complex
—There are a lot of good schools and a lot of different criteria to consider
—Choosing colleges requires projecting yourself and your needs
five or six years into the future

■

Start early
—Expect the process to take a great deal of time and effort

■

Choosing the right colleges starts with analyzing yourself

■

Learn about colleges by reading college guidebooks and other literature,
looking at websites, meeting with college representatives, talking to
alums and students, and visiting campuses

■

Expect to apply to approximately eight schools
—Three or four "reaches," two or three "possibles," and two "likelies"

INTRODUCTION

Your selection of schools will be driven by two interrelated activities:

1. Analyzing yourself to determine your needs and desires, and
2. Investigating colleges thoroughly to find the best fits for you.

The more you analyze yourself and your needs, the more you will learn about what you require in a college; likewise, the more you investigate colleges, the more you will learn about yourself and your needs. Thus, you should conduct these two activities simultaneously in order to do the best job possible of choosing colleges that are ideal for you. You will find that with each successive round of investigation, you develop better and more precise ideas about the kind of institution you would like to attend.

To set in motion the iterative process just described, first analyze yourself, your needs and goals, and who you aim to become in college and beyond. Next, based on your desires and needs, determine what qualities are important to you in a college. Then use a variety of resources to research and investigate the colleges to decide where to apply.

AVOID THE COMMON PITFALLS ASSOCIATED WITH CHOOSING COLLEGES

There are two major errors that many students make when looking at colleges:

1. They focus on the "best" colleges rather than those that best fit their needs and goals.
2. They focus on one single "perfect" college.

Yes, you should aim high, but you should also realize that prestige and a name brand do not automatically make a college right for you. There are many excellent colleges to choose from. You should investigate carefully to be sure you are choosing schools that fit your needs, desires, and aims, rather than hoping to be accepted at a school just because of its rank in *U.S. News & World Report*. Students who apply to and ultimately accept an offer at one of "the best" schools without examining how that college fits their personal needs often end up unhappy.

To avoid the second mistake, resist going into the college selection process with the idea of "choosing *a* college." Even if you are the most talented and interesting person in America, there is never a guarantee that you will get into a particular college. For this reason, train yourself from the very beginning to think of the selection process not as one in which you deem one school "the favorite" and the rest completely unacceptable, but as one in which you determine general features of importance to you, and then match a set of schools to those features.

It is certainly all right to determine that one college fits your needs and desires a bit better than any other. As discussed in Chapter 5, some applicants indeed benefit from applying to a college Early Decision, a binding commitment that requires, among other things, that you have deemed that college your top choice. Even after applying to a college Early Decision, though, you must remember to spread your enthusiasm and energy sufficiently among all of the schools to which you will eventually make applications, in the event that this Early application is not successful. Be sure that no matter which college you deem your favorite, you continue to acknowledge the exciting possibilities that your other target schools pose. If you conduct the college selection process thoughtfully and carefully, you should not experience any serious disappointments in the end.

ANALYZE YOURSELF TO DETERMINE YOUR NEEDS AND DESIRES

You should analyze yourself in an attempt to make some decisions about what you are and are not looking for in a college before you begin visiting your target schools. Then, as you start visiting campuses and learning more about schools, you can refine and change your list of needs and desires as appropriate. There are several ways of going about the self-examination process. You might try one of the following exercises:

- Take half an hour or so to concentrate on your high school experience. Determine what was good and bad about your high school and make lists of each. This will help you decide what you should look for in a college and what you should avoid. For example, if the intimacy of your forty-five-person graduating class shows up in the "good" column, you can assume that you will probably be happiest at a small college. (See the sample self-evaluation on page 30.)

- Engage in a fantasy process, whereby you try to picture how you would be most satisfied and happy in college. After you have described your fantasy world, try to extract meaning from the outlandish portions of the description. Bringing your desires down to a level of reality can help you

---

**A SAMPLE SELF-EVALUATION:
AN EVALUATION OF MY HIGH SCHOOL CAREER**

WHAT WAS GOOD	WHAT WAS BAD
▪ I know every person in my 45-person class fairly well—feels intimate and cozy	▪ All-girls school—I want to attend a coed college
▪ Great art and drama departments	▪ Not enough diversity—too many students of my same background
▪ Beautiful campus—nineteenth-century architecture; pretty, rural surroundings	▪ Not enough focus on computing or technology
▪ Teachers are always there for us—I can ask for help at any time and receive plenty of individualized attention from them	▪ High pressure to succeed— students are too competitive with one another
▪ School's educational philosophy stresses importance of a balanced lifestyle	▪ Terrible food!

The student who wrote this self-evaluation might determine, for example, that she should attend a fairly small coed college, with an accessible faculty, in an appealing rural environment. It would ideally boast good performing and visual arts departments as well as state-of-the-art technology resources. The diverse and active student body would be concerned with more than just getting top grades. (In a perfect world, the on-campus dining facilities would also offer quality food, but this is likely to be one of the least important factors on the list.)

---

determine what you should be looking for in the place at which you will spend the next four years of your life. For example, perhaps in your dream world it snows 365 days of the year and you have enough time to hit the ski slopes every afternoon. You can assume that you might be happiest at a school in Colorado, where the ski season can last at least half the year and skiing is a way of life.

▪ Make a list of your values and needs. In the "values" column, cite what philosophies, principles, and lifestyle choices are important to you. "Close contact with my siblings" might show up in the values column; in this case, you might consider looking at schools fairly close to your home. In the "needs" column, list the circumstances, tangible objects, and other things that you require in your daily life.

A SAMPLE SELF-EVALUATION: MY VALUES AND NEEDS

Values	Needs
■ Quality time with family and friends	■ A lot of sleep
■ Honesty and personal integrity	■ Stimulation and intellectual challenges from peers and teachers
■ Independence and freedom—little constraint on personal desires	■ Community service options
■ Contributions to the community	■ Water sports

The student who wrote this self-evaluation should most likely attend a college with a strong residential system, best for maintaining close relationships and becoming a significant part of a tight-knit community. He might be especially attracted to schools with a serious honor code and significant community service programs. He would probably be happiest at a school with a very flexible curriculum rather than one with strict core curriculum or distribution requirements, so that he could have the freedom to design his curriculum. He would want to look at selective schools with bright and intellectual students, but maybe not somewhere so cutthroat that he might not be able to get a good night's sleep on a regular basis. He would want to look at schools located on either coast or near rivers and lakes so that he could be sure to continue participating in water sports while at college.

■ Start by visiting a few easily accessible or local colleges. It does not matter if they are the right caliber or style for you. The point is to visit a campus, talk to some students, and pick up admissions materials—doing so will trigger your thoughts about college. Visiting a school will likely encourage you to imagine what qualities you will be investigating when you look at the schools that *do* interest you. Before visiting a local university, for example, you might not even realize what it really feels like to be at a "suitcase school" on a Saturday afternoon. When you feel how dull and quiet the campus is with everyone away at home for the weekend, you will be sure to inquire about such circumstances at other schools you visit.

■ Use the following self-evaluation to begin thinking about your needs, goals, values, and educational philosophy, and where you want to be in the future. Thinking about the ideas presented in this evaluation will help you determine what you are looking for in a college.

**A SELF-EVALUATION TO HELP YOU IN
THE COLLEGE SELECTION PROCESS**

As you explore colleges to determine which are most suitable for you and your needs, you will realize that a thorough understanding of yourself will help you in the college selection process. Describing yourself, your habits, and your goals will help you begin to determine what is important in a college. The ideas presented in each of the eight sections of this self-evaluation will help you identify what is and is not important to you.

Respond to the statements as truthfully as possible—this is to be used only by yourself in your quest to make the smartest decisions regarding college. In each selection, you should either circle one of several alternative statements or finish the single given statement in your own words.

EDUCATIONAL PHILOSOPHY AND ACADEMIC ENVIRONMENT

■ I am more interested in learning and feeling intellectually engaged than I am in getting good grades.

I care more about my performance in class than I do about feeling intellectually stimulated.

■ I am independent and like to make decisions on my own, without help from parents or other adults.

I am not yet able to make decisions on my own and would rather have guidance from my parents, teachers, or other adults in doing so.

■ I would rather take a lot of different subjects than focus on one subject.

I would rather focus on my favorite subjects than take a lot of courses in areas that are not important to me.

■ I like to do extra projects and go beyond what is expected of me in the classroom.

Even when I am interested in the subject matter, I tend to do the bare minimum in a class rather than produce extra work.

■ I am ready to start thinking about my career and life after college.

I am not ready to start thinking about my career and life after college.

- I like to be challenged and work on my weaknesses.

  I would rather stick to improving my strengths than working on my weaknesses.

- I am good at making my own decisions.

  I am bad at making my own decisions.

- I do best when I feel confident that I am more capable than most of my peers.

  I do best when challenged by peers who are perhaps more capable than I am.

- I do best in an environment in which students are preoccupied with their studies and there is pressure to perform well.

  I do best in an environment in which students are relatively relaxed about their studies and there is no external pressure to perform well.

ACADEMIC PARTICULARS

- I participate heavily in class discussions and do not learn well if I am not an active contributor.

  I do not participate much in class and learn just as well (or better) when not required to contribute to discussions.

- It is very important to me to be able to seek attention and help from my teachers.

  It does not matter very much to me whether or not I am able to obtain personalized attention from my teachers.

- I enjoy and benefit from hearing other students' ideas and opinions in class.

  I do not especially enjoy or benefit from hearing other students' ideas and opinions in class.

- I am motivated on my own to do my schoolwork.

  I only do my schoolwork when reminded or badgered by my parents or teachers.

- I love to write and feel confident in my writing abilities.

  I do not love to write or do not feel confident in my writing abilities.

- I love to read.

  I do not like to read.

  I do not particularly like to read but am willing to do it for educational purposes.

- When I do not understand something or feel confused in class, I am not afraid to ask the teacher for help.

  When I do not understand something or feel confused in class, I am afraid or uncomfortable asking the teacher for help.

- I perform my best when motivated by "positive" reinforcement (i.e., praise for my strengths and accomplishments rather than criticisms of my weaknesses and failures).

  I perform best when motivated by "negative" reinforcement (i.e., criticisms of my weaknesses and failures rather than praise for my strengths and accomplishments).

- It is important for me to get to know my teachers and feel that they care about me and my progress.

  It does not matter to me whether or not my teachers play a role in my life or seem to take an interest in my progress.

- I like to speak in front of others in class.

  I do not like to speak in front of others in class.

- I am afraid to take a stand on something if I think that others disagree with me.

  I am unafraid to take a stand on something, even if I think that others disagree with me.

- My favorite subjects in school are . . .

- It is important that any school I attend have a strong department in . . .

OVERALL ENVIRONMENT AND ATMOSPHERE

- I enjoy community service and need to have a wide range of volunteer activities available to me.

  Community service is not very important to me.

- I read newspapers and news magazines regularly.

  I do not read newspapers or news magazines regularly.

- I like to play and watch sports.

  Sports are not a big part of my life.

- The "work hard/play hard" philosophy is appealing to me.

  I would rather work hard than play hard.

  I would rather play hard than work hard.

- I am attached to one or more special causes and feel my life would not be as full without my involvement in them.

  I am not particularly attached to any special causes.

- It is important for me to live within an international and globally oriented community.

  It is not important for me to live within an international or globally oriented community.

- My favorite extracurricular activities are . . .

- If I suddenly had an extra year in my life to do anything I wanted to do, I would spend it . . .

- The ways in which I spend my free time include . . .

SOCIAL ENVIRONMENT

- I am most comfortable and happy when surrounded by people more or less like myself.

  I thrive when surrounded by people who are different from me.

- I am happiest when surrounded by highly politicized people.

  I am uncomfortable with or indifferent to being surrounded by highly politicized people.

- I like socializing in small groups with just a few intimate friends.

  I like socializing in large groups with both friends and people I do not know.

- I prefer a calm social scene, where most socializing is done in small group gatherings and is confined to weekend nights only.

  I prefer a wild and crazy party scene, with social options every night of the week.

- The best social atmosphere for me is one in which I am a member of an exclusive club or organization.

  The best social atmosphere for me is one in which I am not a member of any special club or organization but free to socialize as I please, although I do not mind if others around me are members of such exclusive clubs.

  The best social atmosphere for me is one in which no one is a member of an exclusive club or organization.

- It is important for me to feel recognized and acknowledged by my peers and community, not an anonymous face or a number in a system.

  Recognition and acknowledgment from others are not important to me—I would rather be an anonymous face in a large crowd.

- I like being around others and do not enjoy being by myself.

  I like being alone and do not enjoy being around others.

  I value both time alone and time spent with others.

- I am religious and maintaining my devotion is important to me.

  I am not religious and do not like being around people who are.

  I am not religious but do not mind being around people who are.

- I adhere to an alternative lifestyle (in terms of sexual preference, a particular environmentalist stance, devotion to a certain cult or religion, etc.) and would do best in an environment that supports alternative practices.

  I do not adhere to an alternative lifestyle but would like to be part of a community that supports alternative practices.

  I do not adhere to an alternative lifestyle and would feel uncomfortable in a community that supports alternative practices.

- I want to be in an environment in which different racial and ethnic groups interact rather than merely live side by side.

  It does not matter to me whether or not different racial and ethnic groups interact in my environment.

LOCATION

- I like to be in an urban environment, surrounded by crowded city streets and plenty of cultural attractions.

  I like to be in a semiurban environment, not in a city itself but near enough to one to be able to enjoy it on occasion.

  I like to be in a peaceful, rural environment where there is plenty of natural beauty and perhaps limited access to cultural and entertainment venues.

- Attending cultural and entertainment events of national or international stature is important to me.

  Attending cultural events of national or international stature is not very important to me.

- Weather and climate are important to me—they affect my moods and productivity.

  Weather and climate are not important to me—they do not affect my moods or productivity.

- I am looking forward to being independent and have no reason to stay close to home when I leave for college.

  I am looking forward to being independent but need to stay fairly close to home when I attend college (for one reason or another).

  I am not looking forward to being away from my family and friends and want to stay fairly close to home when I attend college.

- My ideal home would be in . . .

Physical Features and Facilities

- The way my surroundings (architecture, landscape, etc.) look and feel is important to me.

  The way my surroundings look and feel is not important to me.
- It is important to me that the library I use is in top condition.

  It does not matter to me whether or not the library I use is in top condition.
- It is important to me that the computing facilities I use are in top condition.

  It does not matter to me whether or not the computing facilities I use are in top condition.
- It is important to me that the science labs I use are in top condition.

  It does not matter to me whether or not the science labs I use are in top condition.
- It is important to me that the athletic facilities I use are in top condition.

  It does not matter to me whether or not the athletic facilities I use are in top condition.
- It is important to me that the performing arts facilities I use are in top condition.

  It does not matter to me whether or not the performing arts facilities I use are in top condition.
- It is important to me that the dining halls where I eat my meals are in top condition.

  It does not matter to me whether or not the dining halls where I eat my meals are in top condition.
- It is important to me that my living quarters are in top condition.

  It does not matter to me whether or not my living quarters are in top condition.

Future Goals

- I view college primarily as an opportunity to prepare for my future career rather than as an opportunity to explore intellectual interests.

  I view college primarily as an opportunity to explore intellectual interests rather than as an opportunity to prepare for a specific future career.
- I know exactly what I want to do in my future career.

  I have no idea what I want to do in my future career.

  I have some ideas about what I want to do in my future career, but I am not certain about which ones I will pursue.

- My possible future careers include . . .
- My general short- and long-term goals are . . .

MISCELLANEOUS

- The reasons I want to go to college are to . . .
- I am most looking forward to . . . in the future.
- I am most afraid of . . . in the future.
- One bad decision I made in high school that I would like to avoid in college is . . .
- One good decision I made in high school that I would like to repeat in college is . . .

A PROCESS OF MATCHMAKING

Once you have some ideas about what you are looking for, the process of deciding where to apply is a little like matchmaking. You need to start investigating colleges, keeping in mind the key qualities discussed later in this chapter, and then identify which institutions fit your desires and needs best.

Start by giving every college a fair chance. If you do not assign a neutral position to all schools before examining them for yourself, you may prevent yourself from considering a school that could be ideal for you—just because your mother heard from her friend who heard from her daughter's piano teacher who heard from one of his students whose cousin went to the school that it is an awful place for anyone who does not passionately love football. Likewise, do not let Hollywood or the media shape your view of what colleges are like. Make informed decisions about schools based on your own research and observation rather than on hearsay or impressions you get from others.

RESEARCH THE SCHOOLS

First you should develop knowledge about colleges in general. You can do so by reading about the characteristics of colleges beginning on page 43; spending a few hours in your high school guidance counselor's office looking through college viewbooks and other materials; perusing college websites; or reading several publications devoted solely to the idea of how to choose colleges.

You should be able to generate a list of about twenty preliminary schools that interest you for one reason or another. This does not mean that you have to look seriously at each one—but if you cannot come up with a large number of schools that interest you based on your initial searches, you may be confining or limiting yourself unnecessarily. Now you need to begin to investigate the schools more closely:

1. Look at the information contained in guidebooks to colleges. You should have at least one of these at home for quick reference. For example, *The Fiske Guide to Colleges* is a good one to have on hand. These kinds of reference books should help you narrow down your most important criteria.

2. Get information from the schools themselves. Call, write, or e-mail each school to get its brochure, course catalog, and application materials. Here you can discover basic information about a college, such as the composition of its incoming class (by ethnicity, geographic origin, SAT scores, high school class rank, etc.), the majors and special programs it offers, and its graduation requirements.

3. Visit college websites. Instead of remaining sheltered within the admissions pages, jump around to find course offerings, look at the student newspaper, or become a participant in chat rooms for student groups. By perusing a school's Web pages, you can tune in to the pulse of the campus and all it has to offer. You can also subscribe to a college's newspaper, another good way of learning as much as possible about a school.

4. Learn when you can meet the school's traveling representatives. Most schools travel to college forums—gatherings held in cities around the country to introduce high schoolers to a variety of colleges. The colleges set up booths and give out information about their programs. You can meet representatives from the schools at these affairs, although they are often too crowded to get any decent conversation going. Colleges also send their representatives to individual schools around the country. These information sessions are often less hurried than are the larger forums, thereby providing the opportunity to question representatives and get more detailed feedback.

5. Talk with alumni of each school. Schools are generally glad to give you names of alumni in your area who have volunteered to discuss their colleges with prospective applicants. Recent alumni in particular can be good sources of information about the college's current atmosphere, strengths (and weaknesses, if they are willing to be honest), and the types of students who are happiest there.

6. Visit whatever schools you are able to. Visiting a school is an important part of your research. You should not visit only your top "reach" schools; becoming familiar with and excited about "possible" and "likely" schools is just as important. Visiting a school allows you to tap into its pulse in a way no other method of investigation can. See Appendix I for more detailed information on how to conduct campus visits.

CREATING YOUR FINAL LIST OF TARGET SCHOOLS

By this time, you should have a pretty good impression of what your original twenty or so colleges are all about. Now it is time to narrow down your list, so that you can come up with approximately eight final target colleges. Sometimes fewer is fine; sometimes more is fine, too—it all depends on how certain you are of what you want and how far you are reaching in terms of your chances for admission at each. You should spread your applications to schools representing a range of selectivity. Thus, your final list should probably include

- Three or four reaches,
- Two or three possibles, and
- Two or three likelies.

A reach is a school at which acceptance is possible but not at all certain. A possible is a school at which you have about a 50 percent chance of being accepted. A likely is a school at which you are almost certain to be admitted.

The best way to determine the likelihood of your gaining admittance to a particular college is to look at the statistics on its most recently admitted freshman class. Look at GPA figures, rank-in-class figures, and standardized test scores—looking at the average, median, or range of numbers for each—and then compare yourself with those in the freshman class. If your grades and scores place you below the average matriculated candidate, then the school is a reach for you. If your grades and scores place you around the middle of the freshman class, then the school is likely to rank as a possible. If your grades and scores place you in the top quarter or so of the most recently entered class, then this college is probably a likely. (Remember that the very best schools deny far more applicants possessing their average grades and scores than they admit. If your credentials place you among the college's averages for admitted students, you will probably have to position yourself exceptionally well or possess something valuable aside from academics—a special talent or athletic skill, for example—in order to get in.)

Adjust your determination up (or down) a notch if you have taken a particularly challenging (or particularly unchallenging) courseload. For example, if your grades and scores place you above the average student but they have been achieved in easy classes rather than Advanced Placement and honors classes, do not assume the school is a likely. Similarly, if you have very stellar (or very limited) extracurricular involvements or accomplishments, you will want to adjust the likelihood of your acceptance at a college up (or down) a notch.

The likelihood of your being accepted at a given school is generally improved if one or more of several factors are working for you:

- You are an athlete being recruited by a coach at the college.
- You are a legacy applicant (whose mother, father, or other direct relative attended the school).
- You are a "development" case, meaning that a prominent or wealthy relative of yours donated significant resources or funding to the college.
- You fall within the college's upper range of average admitted candidates *and* will apply Early Decision.

A spread in applications (among reaches, possibles, and likelies) will make it most likely that you will have choices about which college to attend. It will prevent you from missing a special opportunity, which might happen if you were to refrain from applying to any reach. Spreading out your applications will also prevent you from not going to college at all, which could happen if you do not apply to some likelies.

It is acceptable to have as few as one reach as long as you are not setting your sights on attending that one school. In other words, if your several top picks happen to be colleges at which you are more likely to be accepted, then do not worry about not having any reach on your list. You should worry, however, if you do not have at least two likelies. You need to apply to at least two likely schools that you would be happy to attend. They should not be schools you merely throw onto your list to satisfy your counselor at school. Your likely choices require at least as much (if not more) thought as your reaches and possibles require. There is a strong possibility that you might attend one of these colleges, so you should visit them and examine them with as much enthusiasm as you do your more competitive picks. You should also remember to continue to picture yourself at your likely schools, just as you might daydream about stepping into your top-choice school next fall.

**AVOID THE USUAL PITFALLS WHEN MAKING
YOUR LIST OF TARGET SCHOOLS**

1. Start the process early. You do not want to feel so rushed that you start eliminating schools because of time constraints or fail to investigate colleges thoroughly.

2. Do not take the rankings too seriously. They are no better than rough proxies for a school's quality and reputation. They also do not help you determine which colleges are the best fit for you based on an analysis of yourself and your needs.

3. Be aware that your interests may well change as you go through the search process.

4. Be aware that your academic interests may change during college. You should not pick a college based solely on its strong history department, for example. There should be other compelling reasons to choose the school.

5. Do not be swayed by spiffy college brochures or fancy websites. The quality of a school is not directly related to its admissions materials. After a while, you will begin to see that they all look more or less the same anyway.

6. Do not be swayed by one particularly warm or cold admissions officer, alum, or tour guide. Colleges are full of different personalities, and one person should not determine your ideas about an entire campus population.

APPLYING TO UNIVERSITIES WITH MULTIPLE SCHOOLS

Many universities have a whole set of undergraduate schools, some of which are easier to get into than are their sister schools. At Cornell, for instance, only a small minority of those entering the Hotel Administration School score 700s on each section of their SATs, unlike those entering the Engineering School. This does not mean, however, that you should try to get into the Hotel School if you intend to be an engineer! (Note, too, that universities usually permit you to apply to only one program in a given year.) It is generally not easy to transfer from one school to another, especially if the programs are as unrelated as are these two. It is also notoriously difficult to perform well in a program that does not interest you, and transfer evaluations are typically based largely on your college academic performance.

The strategy of trying to get into a top university via a back door needs to be considered in light of your other options. You should probably consider this route only if you intend to pursue a subject that is offered in more than one school at a given university. (The two most obvious areas are economics, which may be on offer in a liberal arts school and in a business school, and languages, which may be available in a liberal arts school and in a foreign service or diplomacy school.)

Consider the following factors before trying to get your foot in the door at a university by applying to one of its less selective programs:

- The ease of getting into each program (for you in particular, given your profile)
- The likelihood of truly enjoying each program
- The closeness of each program to your current interests
- The ease of taking a substantial number of courses in other schools or programs
- The number of required courses that you might otherwise prefer to avoid
- The extent to which a degree in this field will help or hinder your pursuit of your ultimate career goals
- The ease of transferring to your chosen program
- The likelihood of being able to get grades good enough to help you transfer

CHARACTERISTICS TO CONSIDER WHEN EVALUATING COLLEGES

There are whole books devoted solely to helping prospective college students identify the characteristics that make an educational institution a good fit for them. The main goal of this book is to help you prepare your application and get into those colleges once you identify them. We believe, however, that it is critical that students spend a significant amount of time and energy thinking about their college choices and selecting institutions that are best for them.

Hence, the rest of this chapter discusses the various characteristics to examine when choosing target colleges.

The following discussion offers general ideas about certain kinds of institutions, but these categories are not absolutes. You might find that a particular school does not act as you would expect it to according to a certain characteristic. A rural school nowhere near a big urban center might have a wonderfully diverse and international population, despite one's expectations of homogeneity and provincialism given the school's location. Use the material here as a guideline, but do your own detective work for each school you are interested in.

SIZE

One of the most basic decisions you should make concerns the size of the institution you want to attend. Colleges range in size from a few hundred students at the smallest schools to 50,000 or more at the largest universities. Generalities relating to an institution's size are often accurate, but be sure to examine each school yourself to gain a complete picture of how its size affects academic and social dynamics. Be warned against taking a simplistic view of large versus small.

You should not automatically assume, for example, that a large university will not give you any feelings of intimacy whereas a small school will provide a super-friendly environment. On the contrary, some large schools do everything they can to make their students feel more at ease—for example, grouping them in small living clusters so that students get to know a small segment of the population well and do not feel lost among the masses. Similarly, some small schools may not take special precautions to make their students feel at home, thus making social adjustments harder than they would be at a larger school.

Large Universities

Larger schools often project an abundance of perceived school spirit to the outside world because they tend to be well-known institutions with popular sports teams. But school spirit does not always equal a feeling of community within the campus itself. It is more difficult for a school with a large population to foster the same intimacy, common identity, and sense of community that a smaller school often does. The size of a larger university makes it possible to remain anonymous if that is what you desire. It also offers you the possibility of running into new people at every juncture in your four-year journey. If you find that you need a wealth of social opportunities to keep from becoming bored, a larger school is probably for you.

Large schools tend to be universities with a lot of graduate students. Thus, despite an impressive roster of senior faculty, a university may offer poor or suboptimal quality in terms of undergraduate level teaching because the graduate students do a large portion of it. At some universities, graduate students tend to teach the introductory courses, whereas at others they tend to teach the smaller discussion and seminar classes. For all your target schools, be sure to find out who does the teaching in all fields of interest to you.

Large schools tend to offer more courses and majors from which to choose. The breadth of options is usually better at a larger university than it is at a small liberal arts college. Larger universities also tend to have more "preprofessional" majors, such as business or nursing. But sometimes the size and structure of a university can prevent students from enjoying the breadth of options. Courses listed in the university's catalog may not be open to all students. At many large universities, access to certain classes is, for example, limited to those in the appropriate major. Access to certain classes, professors, and activities can also be constrained at larger institutions because students have to fight for limited space.

Similarly, bigger schools can offer you less and more all at the same time in terms of extracurricular activities. A larger student population generally requires more outlets and organizations than does a smaller student body; a larger number of students and their individual interests also encourage breadth in the kinds of activities offered. Because there are, however, so many students on a big university campus, it might be more difficult to earn a space on a sports team or to become the editor-in-chief of the newspaper there.

You have to be a self-starter to fare well at a large school. You have to be ready to fight for professors' attention, keep yourself on track in classes where you might not get much individualized help, and stick yourself out socially rather than waiting for opportunities to come to you. An active personality is key to survival at a large university; passive or lazy students tend to get lost academically and socially at a big school.

SMALL COLLEGES

Small schools usually foster intimacy and a solid sense of community. At a school of only several thousand students, you are likely to recognize most faces in your class by the time you graduate. If you thrive on intense relationships with a small number of people rather than on the breadth of your social sphere, you will do fine at a small school. On the flip side of the intimacy equation, the tight nature of a small school can mean that your business is everyone else's business. If you need to be able to hold a degree of privacy in your life, an especially intimate collegiate atmosphere might frustrate or discomfort you. Similarly, if you are constantly searching for new hands to shake, you might feel stunted or confined if you attend a smaller school.

The quality of teaching and caliber of faculty with whom undergraduate students have ongoing contact are often better at smaller schools. At a small college with no graduate facilities, you will generally have plenty of contact with professors and faculty because they teach their own classes rather than relying on graduate students. Most of the big cheeses at smaller colleges actually teach courses—even small discussion-style classes—and keep regular office hours so that you can seek their wisdom or advice on a regular basis. Similarly, at a small school you will usually have fewer large lecture classes and more intimate classroom settings. You will not often be able to get away with hiding when you have not completed your assignments. At the same time, you will not have to aggressively jockey for attention or time with a professor.

Smaller private colleges usually offer fewer courses and majors than public universities. Yet at the same time, small schools usually offer better access to classes for all students. Students at small schools rarely find themselves "stuck" in classes they do not want to take for lack of better options or because they are unable to secure a spot in a class of interest.

Smaller schools can also allow students to get more involved in activities—especially those in which they are novices or are not especially experienced—because competition for a place in an organization or group is not so fierce. Activities themselves, however, may be limited. A smaller campus population may not feature enough interested parties to put together a mime troupe or a classic Indian dance ensemble. A smaller campus may have two *a capella* singing groups rather than the ten at a bigger university.

PUBLIC VERSUS PRIVATE

Whether an institution is public and maintained by the state government or private and independently operated often shapes its character and the quality of its facilities.

PUBLIC INSTITUTIONS

Public universities were originally founded to educate state citizens and are subsidized by taxpayers' money. They are thus subject to state political currents and financial constraints. Dealing with the bureaucracy at a state institution can be difficult. It can take months (maybe even years) to get responses from state institutions, whereas the same problem at a private college might be handled by one person within a matter of days.

Public universities have far lower tuitions than do private schools, especially for state residents. But at some public institutions, you all too often get what you pay for. In other words, some of the facilities and resources at public universities do not always equal those at their private counterparts. Libraries may have fewer books (or not enough books to service the larger student population), technology and computing services may be of less than optimal quality, gyms and playing fields may not be kept up as well as expected, and clubs may not receive as much institutional support. This is, of course, not always true of re-sources at public institutions.

Public institutions tend to have more breadth in terms of course offerings, as well as pre-professional programs and honors programs for undergraduates. Because public schools service a wider and more academically diverse group of people, they have more to offer. Because of the large size of these schools, though, classes are more difficult to get into than they are at smaller private schools. At many public universities, certain classes are limited to students in the appropriate major.

Public universities also do not always attract the same caliber of students that top private schools do. Even the flagship state universities—which, of course, attract some stellar students—do not across the board boast the high-quality students that the very top private colleges do. As a result, most solid public institutions command respect within the state, but do not carry as much clout outside of the immediate area. Only the top flagship institutions, such as the University of Michigan or the University of California at Berkeley, command equal respect outside of the state.

Public schools also do not feature the same wealth of geographic diversity that private colleges do. After all, public institutions are constrained by the need to choose most applicants from within their own states.

PRIVATE INSTITUTIONS

Private schools are governed by their own internal politics, like any institution, and not by state political currents. Their trustees and administrators have free reign to make changes and institute their own rules. The bureaucracy at private schools is less cumbersome than it is at public universities, so that students and faculty have much more power to force change upon the school or move the college in a new direction.

Private schools charge high tuitions. (Note, however, that many private colleges have very healthy need-based aid programs.) Many private colleges maintain top-notch facilities: Their libraries are impressive, their computing centers are excellent and offer free laser printing, academic buildings and dormitories are well maintained, and organizations are subsidized so that their members can travel for special events and make necessary purchases.

Smaller private colleges usually offer fewer courses than public colleges. Students at private colleges generally have better access to all courses, though. Private institutions also do not generally offer honors programs or very many pre-professional undergraduate majors.

Private colleges can admit whomever they choose. Thus, student populations tend to be diverse in every way: ethnicity, socioeconomic background, geographical origins, personal and family backgrounds. You will not have to fear that you will end up sharing a room with two other people from your home state at most private schools. It is instead likely that you will come into contact with the widest range of students possible if you attend a private college.

EDUCATIONAL MISSION AND PHILOSOPHY

All educational institutions have their own mission and philosophy. Philosophical concerns dictate the manner in which each institution chooses to educate its students. Some schools believe strongly that every student should be educated in the classics, and thus require all students to take courses in the "Great Books" or ancient civilizations. Some schools think that every student should know something about the developing world, and thus require everyone to study a third-world culture. Many colleges have a foreign language requirement, so that every graduate has had at least minimal exposure to a language other than English. Many schools are heavily influenced by their religious roots, requiring everyone who receives a B.A. to have taken a few theology courses.

The most crucial and basic of all of the educational philosophies is an institution's stand on the relationship between education and future goals (i.e., whether higher education should direct a student toward one specific future career or merely provide a student with a strong foundation on which to build any future career he or she chooses). Some universities allow undergraduates to follow a pre-professional track, focusing nearly exclusively on business, architecture, communications, nursing, engineering, or another career-related field; other colleges require that every student, no matter what his or her major, follow a broad liberal arts curriculum.

Pre-professional Degrees

Public universities and some private universities offer pre-professional bachelor's degrees for undergraduates. At many of these universities, prospective students apply to a particular college within the university to follow a specialized degree, in business or engineering, for example. Students are not required to take the broad range of classes that students of liberal arts colleges must finish in order to graduate. Instead, they take a curriculum heavy in courses of direct relevance to their prospective careers. Applying to a particular non–liberal arts school means that as a high schooler, you must be certain about what you want to do in your career, because the classes you will take in college may well have real value for only one type of future.

LIBERAL ARTS CURRICULUMS

At liberal arts colleges, in contrast, there are very few pre-professional or specialized programs offered whatsoever (with the exception of classes that constitute premedical requirements, but these are taken as part of the liberal arts curriculum). The philosophy at these schools is that a liberal arts education teaches students how to think, read critically, analyze, reason, process complex ideas, and present opinions and facts through oral and written communication skills. These advanced skills, in turn, give students the strong intellectual foundation that will allow them to do anything they wish in the future, whether it be a job in finance or in journalism. The benefit of the liberal arts curriculum is that it is valuable no matter what the future holds. Students attending liberal arts colleges do not have to decide at the age of eighteen what they want to do in later life and can change careers many times, knowing that what they learned in college will be entirely relevant and valuable in all situations.

ACADEMIC STRENGTHS

Whether you want to follow a pre-professional or a liberal arts degree, if you have any inkling of what subjects are of interest to you, be sure to investigate the academic strengths of various colleges to be sure you will be getting the best quality possible in your given field.

DEPARTMENTAL STRENGTHS

Even the very best colleges have some departments that are weaker than others. You should know what the reputation of a department is before signing on to a college if you know what your major or fields of study will be. Balancing the quality of a department (assuming you know exactly what you will do in college) with the quality of a school overall is a tricky task. As an undergraduate, you do not want to sacrifice too much in terms of overall quality to have access to a better physics or English department—your future usually depends much more on the college you attend and your overall performance there than it does on the education you receive in one area.

It is difficult to measure the strength of an academic department in terms of the education it provides to undergraduates—there is no surefire or accurate way to grade each department in a college. Considering several factors in tandem, however, can serve as the best possible proxy for such quality. First, if the college has a graduate program in the field, do some research to find out how strong it is. Generally speaking, the stronger the graduate program in a field, the stronger the undergraduate program is as well. Then find out about the undergraduate classes offered in the field. Examine what teaching structures are used as well as how big the classes are. How many classes with over one hundred students are there? What about classes with fewer than ten or twenty students? The greater the number of small classes, the better the education is likely to be. Are there opportunities to take small seminars and do independent studies? Look at the student-faculty ratios for all classes taught in the department. Look at the breadth of classes offered, as well as the depth that upper-level seminars reach. Get your hands on an "unofficial" student-published guide to the school. Such guides, often published by the student assembly or student union on campus, usually feature a section on academics in which polled students give candid opinions about classes and faculty members. The books usually give a good clue to the strongest departments and teachers on campus.

Major and Graduation Requirements

You should also research the academic requirements at each school so that you are clear about what is necessary to graduate. At some schools, for instance, it is very difficult to double major because each major requires that nearly half of one's classes be devoted to it. For someone who is certain she wants to double major in economics and mathematics, such strict major requirements at one school might be a reason to consider different schools, where doing the same double major would be feasible. Some schools offer no minors. At some colleges, some fields require that all candidates majoring in those areas write a thesis in order to graduate. Other schools require that all seniors in all fields write a thesis in order to graduate. Be aware what core curriculum, general distribution, and other graduation requirements exist at each of your target schools so that you can choose a college that best matches your own academic desires and needs.

Special Programs

Some colleges have special programs or academic features that are of great advantage to the right applicants. Some schools, for example, offer prestigious and competitive medical programs in which students applying for freshman admission are also admitted (conditionally) to the medical school. This is a great boon for strong high school students who know with certainty that they want to attend medical school and are interested in getting a jump start on their careers. Similarly, many of the public universities offer honors programs in which admitted students get special and exclusive educational benefits to help them get ahead in their careers even before graduating from college. Honors program benefits often include independent study opportunities, research opportunities, internship opportunities, contact with top tenured professors, attendance at guest lecture series, and financial rewards.

NONACADEMIC STRENGTHS

Just as each college boasts particular strengths in academic fields, each school also possesses certain nonacademic strengths. Some schools are known for the power of their women's ice hockey teams, others for their wonderful theater productions, others for their provocative newspapers or literary magazines, still others for their talented stand-up comedy acts. If you have a special hobby or activity you want to pursue further during college, be sure to find out about the existence of such an organization on target college campuses.

LOCATION

CLIMATE AND WEATHER

Do not underestimate the influence of geography on a campus's desirability or fit with your needs. The location of a college obviously dictates the climate and weather patterns that prevail there. If you are someone who is affected mildly or seriously by weather and climate, you should definitely make location a primary consideration when choosing colleges. Consider whether you want to live in a place—most likely in the Northeast or Midwest—with four distinct (and perhaps severe) seasons. If you love winter weather, you might want to be far north so that you can enjoy the cold and snow for longer periods of time each year. Or perhaps a mild climate with little seasonal change is what you most desire, making colleges on the West Coast particularly attractive to you. If you are strongly partial to warmth and sunshine, consider the weather patterns in the locations of your target colleges before setting your heart on any of them. Four years is a long time to spend in long johns if you hate the cold.

LOCAL CULTURE

Location also affects an institution's cultural value, which you should take into account in your investigations. Be well aware before making your college visits that there are distinct regional differences in the United States. Plan to look into these differences and how they affect campus life during your travels.

The prevailing stereotypes of people in each region are not entirely accurate, although a visit to each area of the country will most likely assure you that there is some truth to them. You should be sure that you can handle the cultural differences between North and South if you plan to go from your Boston high school to college in the South. It is likely that the academic atmosphere will be more relaxed, the people will be more homogeneous and conservative in their views, and students might dress up on Saturdays to attend football games. If you are not anxious to experience a culture of this sort, you will want to rethink your college choices. (Note, too, that there are exceptions to this description—several of the most interesting liberal arts colleges happen to be in the South.)

Remember, as always, to keep an open mind when starting the process of looking at schools in different areas of the country. Do not automatically resort to a "nothing west of the Mississippi" stance if you have never even been west of the Mississippi to judge for yourself what it is like! Begin your college search with an adventurous spirit until you examine issues on your own to determine what is right and wrong for you.

PROXIMITY TO URBAN OR RURAL RESOURCES

Along with thinking about a school's general geographic location, you must also consider how a college is shaped by its immediate surroundings. A college located in an inner city will feel a lot different from one located in the mountains, two hours away from the nearest urban center. Apart from how an urban or rural location shapes a school's personality and determines the kinds of students it attracts, location also influences the realities of daily life on a campus.

URBAN AND SEMIURBAN LOCATIONS

A college in an urban center is likely to be throbbing with vitality. Urban areas—and usually semiurban areas as well—offer students a wealth of social and cultural opportunities and the chance to escape the confines of the campus environment. Urban areas also offer a range of internship and work opportunities for students embarking on career discovery. Similarly, a host of urban problems can inspire the growth of a diverse range of community service outlets.

It is difficult to feel stifled in a large city, where the social sphere may start within the campus walls but inevitably extends far into the larger urban outpost. Students at city universities and semiurban schools have more and better cultural venues—such as theater, performing arts, or museums—to enjoy, more restaurants to choose from, and more opportunities to meet people outside the school environment. But often the energy on a city campus feels a bit diffused, because the attention is focused not only on campus life but also on what goes on outside.

SUBURBAN LOCATIONS

A suburban campus may have the best of both worlds—urban and rural—because it is located somewhere in between. A suburban campus can be a perfect answer to finding proximity to diverse cultural outlets along with adequate access to the beauty of the outdoors.

RURAL LOCATIONS

Rural schools often evoke a strong sense of community among their students and faculty because of their positions as oases of intellectual and cultural vibrations. The beauty of rural campuses is what first attracts many students. Access to the great outdoors and all that one can do in it—hiking, canoeing, skiing, camping, even simply running in a peaceful setting—is often what makes the final case for attending a school far away from an urban center. Taking advantage of all that a rural setting offers can be what makes a student's collegiate life so special—especially for those who end up spending the rest of their lives sweating it out in a skyscraper on Wall Street.

But there are also limits to life in a country setting. College towns often have only a handful of restaurants, one pharmacy, one grocery store, and one movie theater. Access to serious shopping is often limited, and cultural opportunities may be few and far between as well. This is not true in all rural towns, of course, since many of them have changed to cater to their young collegiate populations.

SAFETY ISSUES

In Urban and Semiurban Locations

Safety is a concern that is closely related to location. At urban universities, safety tends to be more of a concern than it is at schools that are not located in the midst of a metropolitan area. These days, urban campuses (and many nonurban campuses as well) are patrolled well, operate safety escort services for students who need to get across campus at night, and maintain secure dormitories for living. Still, if you have never lived near an inner city, you should spend a few days learning what life is like on an urban campus (you will have to learn to lock your doors, keep your purse zipped and gripped tightly, and take taxis rather than walking alone at night) before deciding to attend a city school.

In Suburban and Rural Locations

Rural and suburban schools are often safer than city schools because of their sheer distance from most security risks. However, less attention to and awareness of security issues (from both students and campus administrators) can result in mishaps. Students should not be fooled into thinking that rural and suburban campuses are 100 percent safe and risk-free, although these kinds of schools tend to be safer than urban universities. Be sure to ask about safety concerns at all the schools you visit.

For further information about the safety of various colleges, visit the website www.securityoncampus.org/crimestats/index.html or plug in the school's name at www.ope.gov/security/main.asp.

COST OF LIVING

Cost of living is also closely related to location. Do not underestimate the degree to which the cost of living varies from one location to another across the United States. Visit grocery stores, look at rental and real estate sections in newspapers, and pass by some gas stations near the colleges you visit—a little of your own detective work will go a long way in giving you a sense of how prices differ from place to place.

In Urban, Semiurban, and Suburban Locations (Especially on Either Coast)

Cities, semiurban, and many suburban areas—especially those located on the East and West Coasts—tend to be more expensive than small towns or rural areas. Rents are more expensive, gas is more expensive, groceries are more expensive—even movies are more expensive in large and cosmopolitan areas near big cities.

In Rural Locations (and Some Noncoastal Areas)

In rural areas, as well as many noncoastal areas, the cost of living is generally lower. You can save hundreds of dollars a month on rent if you attend college in Maine rather than in the greater San Francisco area, for example.

SOCIAL LIFE CONDUCTED ON OR OFF CAMPUS

In Urban or Semiurban Locations

A campus's location also has an impact on how social activities are conducted. At some schools, a lot of socializing takes place off the college property, and often in an environment far removed from the feel of the college setting. At urban and semiurban colleges, this is usually the case. Colleges located in urban or metropolitan areas are surrounded by restaurants, bars, night clubs, civic centers, concert halls, museums, sporting arenas, and other facilities common to large population centers. Students thus have a wealth of options available to them when planning weekend or evening entertainment. When not constrained to a campus's limited social venues, students tend to seek after-hours livelihood elsewhere, partially because it helps them forget the stress associated with the campus, and partially because off-campus settings are simply more abundant and more glamorous. Some prospective college students relish such opportunities to socialize in a variety of locations, thus making urban or semiurban colleges more attractive options for them. Other students, however, find the lack of campus identity and spirit unnerving and would rather attend a college where few off-campus activities interfere with the pulse of campus life.

In Suburban or Rural Locations

At other schools, nearly all social activities take place on or near campus. At rural and suburban schools, students tend always to congregate and party on campus because there are not many off-campus facilities for holding social events. Some prospective college students find that they prefer to attend such a college, where there is an intimacy and a sense of community fostered through students' remaining on campus as much as possible. Other students feel bored or restrained when not presented with plenty of options and opportunities to get away from the tiny hub of campus life.

OPPORTUNITIES FOR EMPLOYMENT

Many students setting off for college—especially those who are not on financial aid or who do not need to work for wages during college—forget that higher education often becomes most valuable when accompanied by work experience. In order to best prepare for a successful life after college, many students find that they want or need to acquire serious work experience of a career-related nature while in school. Some students are satisfied doing so during summer vacations, when they are mobile and can go elsewhere to work; other students like or need the option of working when class is in session as well. Visiting the career services centers on college campuses can help you learn what kinds of opportunities are available locally for students on the campus.

IN URBAN AND SEMIURBAN AREAS

In general, students attending colleges in cities and semiurban areas have much better access to career-related jobs during their college years. Students at schools in urban or metropolitan areas can find a wealth of paying jobs and internships at law offices, consulting firms, banks, technology firms, museums, major nonprofit institutions, and other such employers. If you know that you intend to seek a professional career (especially in law or business) and want to work during college, this is something to consider.

IN SUBURBAN AND RURAL AREAS

On the other hand, all areas—whether urban, suburban, or rural—offer limited opportunities to work at hospitals, schools, small businesses, local community service centers, and other such employers that are found everywhere, no matter the location. If you do not plan to attain significant work experience when class is in session, it may not matter if the area surrounding your college does not offer the same wealth of job options as would a different location.

RESIDENTIAL SYSTEM

Campus residential systems can affect how students interact with one another and the sense of community fostered on campus as well. Most colleges realize that the quality and type of housing arrangements on campus are important priorities for prospective students, so they are eager to share their housing options with you. If a school does not offer much information about housing and residential systems, definitely ask about it.

RESIDENTIAL HOUSE OR CLUSTER SYSTEMS

Some colleges place students in residential "houses" (generally clusters of buildings that together form one residential unit), where they remain for the duration of their time in college. Students live, eat their meals, and socialize within the house, and much of campus life is focused on these small residential quarters.

These kinds of residential systems foster a unique social living experience in which students have the opportunity to get to know very well a small portion of their classmates (as well as students in other classes, too). Students at these schools tend to develop a strong identity rooted in their living cluster. Living in the same cluster with the same students year after year instills a sense of "home" and "family." At the same time, though, some students may feel bogged down by these types of residential situations because they do not encourage students to make new friends during their later years of college or search out alternative social outlets. Some students may feel that the residential house system feels too cliquey, almost fraternity-like in nature, because it fosters an inward orientation rather than an outward or all-embracing orientation.

HIGHLY RESIDENTIAL CAMPUSES

At other highly residential colleges, students may not necessarily live in the same house or living cluster during all four years of college, but they are required or strongly encouraged to stay on campus throughout their education. Colleges that are highly residential in this manner often instill a real sense of community among their students, in the same way that colleges located far from urban or noncampus social resources do.

CAMPUSES WITH SIGNIFICANT OFF-CAMPUS RESIDENCY

Some colleges do not have strict campus residency policies, often because they do not possess sufficient housing for all students in the first place. A residency policy that is flexible regarding students' wishes to live where and how they desire can foster a valuable sense of independence in students who choose to live off-campus. Students who have an opportunity while in college to deal with landlords and real estate companies, pay rent and utility bills, buy groceries, and cook their own meals often find themselves better prepared for "real life" than those who have never taken on such responsibility. In addition, students at colleges with lax residential systems may (if rents in the area are reasonable and the student knows how to cook for himself or herself) have more of an opportunity to save money on living expenses than those who are forced to remain in college dorms and on college meal plans. But colleges that allow a large percentage of students to live off-campus also may feel lacking in school spirit. When students are diffused over a wide geographical area rather than concentrated within a small campus environment, they often become less connected to the school and more dependent on outside resources.

QUALITY OF LIFE ISSUES

Gather facts about important aspects of living on each campus you visit. Find out about dorm living—living in a high-rise built in 1962 offers quite a different experience from living in a nineteenth-century brick building, your room adorned by a fireplace and a window seat. Find out how many roommates you will have and whether or not there are special living options, such as smoking rooms, foreign language halls, or substance-free dorms. Ask about dining options. What kinds of cafeterias are there? What are their hours of operation? Are there healthy alternatives to the usual college fare? Find out about the athletic facilities or exercise-class options if those are important to you.

SOCIAL ATMOSPHERE

Find out as much as you can about the nonacademic side of things at every school you visit. The social experience you receive at college will be every bit as important as the academic experience. Spend a weekend at some of your target campuses to test out the goods. Find out if students go to fraternity parties or to off-campus events. Are there enough activities that are predominantly nonalcoholic? Do students go to cultural events together or do they head off to the bar as soon as dinner is over?

DOMINANT GREEK SYSTEMS

Colleges with strong Greek systems feel very different from those without fraternities and sororities. Schools with Greek life tend to be cliquey, especially if the majority of students on campus belong to a house. The social life of such colleges is frequently dominated by Greek-sponsored parties, all too often meaning large, loud, drunken bashes held in unglamorous spots, such as the fraternity's basement. Fraternity and sorority life is attractive to some people and not attractive to others; you need to decide for yourself how much it appeals to you, or at the very least if you would mind attending a school that offers such options. Going to a school with a Greek system does not mean that you have to participate in it, but you should be aware that these are the kinds of events that many of your peers at such a college will be attending.

DOMINANT CLUB SYSTEMS

Some colleges feature exclusive clubs (called "eating clubs," "finals clubs," etc.) instead of Greek fraternities. The effect on the social life of a campus is largely the same, either way. Clubs sponsor the major parties on campus and breed the dominance of cliques and small exclusive groups on campus. Again, some students desire to be part of such a formalized intimate group; others do not wish to be part of such a system but do not mind its existence; and still others do not want to attend a campus that even offers exclusive clubs as a social option.

STRONG CULTURAL VENUES

At some schools, cultural entertainment is an important part of the social scene. If you would like to attend a school where most students check out a modern dance performance or attend a sculpture opening before letting loose for the evening party scene, try to catch a glimpse of the cultural events and get a sense of their dominance in the social life at each campus you visit.

ACADEMIC ENVIRONMENT

Find out about the academic environment at colleges you visit if that aspect of a school's personality is apt to influence you positively or negatively. Some students like to be in a pressure-cooker environment because it inspires them to perform well. Other students, on the contrary, dislike such an intense atmosphere because it makes them nervous and unable to relax or perform their best. Determine whether the competition at the school is cutthroat or whether students seem relatively easygoing about academics. Do premeds ruin other students' lab experiments in order to get ahead? Or do students seem cooperative and more interested in learning for learning's sake? What is the campus like during exam period? Are people bursting into tears at every desk or is there a positive energy generated by all those minds pushing forward through the last battle?

STUDENT BODY COMPOSITION

The composition of the student body is likely to influence your thoughts about a college. At each college you consider, you will want to investigate the gender balance; the number of minority, international, and out-of-state (at public institutions) students; the diversity of the population in other regards; and the degree to which the various groups on campus mix with one another.

A single-sex environment is, of course, going to feel very different from a coeducational one. If you are considering an all-women's college and have never before attended a girls' school, you should definitely visit the campus, ideally spending a weekend there. An all-women's environment is highly appropriate for some students, but not the right atmosphere for all women. You might find that the absence of a male viewpoint in some classes is a problem. Similarly, on the social scene, you may be disappointed if you sense that the focus of student life shifts to other campuses on the weekends. There are a few coeducational schools where gender balance is a problem as well, since even most coeducational colleges have more women than men.

If you are a minority or international student, you will want to confirm that you will feel welcome and comfortable at the school you attend. Although your status might serve you well in being admitted to the college if it attracts few students of your race, ethnicity, or citizenship, you may not feel comfortable being part of a particularly small group of students on a campus. You will want to get a good sense of how students like yourself live and learn on the campus, and whether or not they are happy and satisfied with their experience there.

No matter who you are, you likely have a good idea of how much diversity you want or need on campus. Some campuses are particularly diverse, featuring large percentages of certain American minorities or international students, whereas other campuses are much more homogeneous.

Aside from looking at the numbers of various kinds of students featured in a student body, you should also closely examine relations among the various groups on a campus. At some campuses, even some that are not especially diverse in terms of numbers of minorities or international students, there is regular and frequent mixing among the various races and ethnicities. Students mix socially with those unlike themselves, interracial dating is common and accepted, and minority groups do not feel isolated. Some campuses, on the contrary, are very racially or ethnically segregated. Students nearly exclusively socialize with those of their own kind, interracial dating is uncommon or not widely accepted, and minority groups keep to themselves. This can be a problem, even at schools where the numbers paint a picture of diversity. Diversity does not benefit a student if he or she has no access to or interaction with those who are different.

POLITICAL PERSONALITY

Although most college campuses are predominantly moderate to liberal, you should decide for yourself if you like the feel and tempo of a university's political atmosphere. Even if you are not politically active yourself, you might find that you value an open political atmosphere in which all groups are welcome, regardless of the dominant ideology on campus.

Some campuses are particularly liberal or feature vocal radical groups that give a certain flavor to college life. At a few schools, an excessive liberal edge might mean that conservative groups are marginalized, unwelcome to address issues in their own manner. For some prospective students, this is not a problem; for others, even those who consider themselves liberals, the squeezing out of minority ideologies might be bothersome. Other schools lean farther into the conservative realm because of particularly vocal Republican or conservative groups. This flavor, similarly, might not feel right to some students.

Check out the number of liberal and conservative political clubs and publications. What is the reaction of most students on campus to those groups or publications? Are any groups marginalized? Is there enough political debate on campus for your needs? Are there weekly rallies for local, national, or international causes at the campus center? Do students seem to care about what goes on in the outside world? What are their positions on certain issues?

RELIGIOUS OVERTONES

The student body at most schools represents a broad spectrum of religions. At most colleges, there is no one dominant religious group, nor are there any particularly religious overtones to campus life. If you are devoutly religious, you will want to ensure that you will feel comfortable and have access to appropriate channels of worship at any of the schools to which you apply. A Mormon, for example, might feel especially uncomfortable at particularly liberal East Coast institutions and may discover that he or she has little access to religious connections at some of these schools. If religion is a concern in your life, be sure to inquire about the existence of fellow believers and talk to others like you about their experiences at the school.

Similarly, those applying to schools with religious roots should be aware that many of these schools are still somewhat dominated by their founding philosophies. If you are not part of the majority religious group, you will want to talk to others like yourself on campus to get a glimpse of what it is like to be a religious minority there. (Remember, though, that there may well be positive implications for applicants to these schools who are not of the majority religion. For instance, non-Jewish applicants to Brandeis may be particularly attractive to its admissions board, whereas Jewish or Hindu applicants to Notre Dame stand out in comparison to the rest of the pool.)

Some schools that are not religious by nature attract large or particularly active groups of people with certain religious ties. Schools with especially dominant or cohesive religious groups may be particularly attractive to some applicants and unattractive to others. Thus, the Jewish populations at the Midwestern Universities of Michigan and Wisconsin have long-standing connections with the East Coast Jewish establishment, making those schools especially attractive for Jews who want to stake their careers on the East Coast. On the other hand, Jews and Catholics (and others) applying to southern schools, for example, should inquire about the existence of fellow religious minorities before committing themselves to attending. The South still cultivates a predominantly Christian Protestant ethos, often a surprise to Jews and Catholics from the northern or western parts of the country.

GENDER RELATIONS

Apart from the issue of gender balance on a campus is the issue of relations between the sexes. At some campuses, gender relations are peaceful and students seem generally satisfied with the prevailing dating and relationship networks. At other colleges, especially those featuring radical feminist organizations or a male-dominated Greek system (or both), a campus can feel like a war zone rather than like a solid community.

Find out what the dating scene at each college is all about, too. At many colleges, students complain that there is not a lively dating scene; instead, students get to know one another in groups rather than going out one-on-one in order to form intimate relationships. Do students seem to have meaningful relationships or just casual sexual encounters? How do they meet one another, and how are dates arranged? Do the men on campus flock to a nearby women's college for fun? Find out about the dating scene for gay students if that is a concern for you. Are there enough openly gay students to ensure the chances of forming positive relationships? Is gay social life integrated into the larger social life of the community or are gays marginalized, forced to socialize within their own clusters?

Women should also inquire about the legal and safety implications of gender problems. Ask about sexual harassment, for example, if this concerns you. Safety officers might have official information, but talking to students on campus might be just as informative when it comes to finding out about women's safety issues.

RESOURCES

There are innumerable guides to American colleges. Two sensible choices, each of which discusses about 300 schools and is revised annually, are:

- Edward B. Fiske and Robert Logue, *The Fiske Guide to Colleges*
- Yale Daily News, *The Insider's Guide to the Colleges*

Loren Pope provides a different look at colleges, making a strong (if overstated) argument on behalf of smaller, liberal arts schools:

- Loren Pope, *Looking Beyond the Ivy League: Finding the College That's Right for You*
- Loren Pope, *Colleges That Change Lives*

WHAT THE ADMISSIONS DIRECTORS HAVE TO SAY ABOUT CHOOSING COLLEGES*

Think about the kind of person you are and what kind of environment will be best for you. Choose as if nothing will come after college—no job, no graduate school. Choose on the basis of where you'll have your best four years. If you do, you'll be happy, you'll do well, and you will have the best possible range of opportunities after graduation. *Rick Bischoff, Cal Tech*

It's very important that prospective students investigate the colleges carefully and make wise choices. We are different from one another. Stanford, for example, has significant focus on interdisciplinary study and undergraduate research and commitment to the quality of the undergraduate experience while being a major research university. A student might get a very different feel or focus at other campuses. Candidates need to know what they're looking for and in what environment they will be happy. *Rick Shaw, Stanford*

Students should be careful about college application information they come across on the Web. It often presents itself as bias-free, which it seldom is, and can often consist of terrible advice. *Bruce Poch, Pomona*

I think students should broaden their searches and keep an open mind. That is, investigate colleges they've never heard of. Many times students will only apply to "name" colleges. They miss a lot of gems that way. *Debra Shaver, Smith*

Students should not assume that all schools of the same type are the same. As similar as Connecticut College is to many of its peer schools, there are significant differences that might either put you off or make it especially appealing. *Tim Cheney, Connecticut College*

Students should not hinge their choice of college on name recognition. It's not about having a certain bumper sticker on your car. It's about finding an institution that meets your needs. *Chris Gruber, Davidson*

We see kids visiting earlier and earlier each year. We joke that soon we'll have seventh graders asking us for viewbooks. It's part of the trend toward Early Decision and a general acceleration of the college search process. *David Borus, Vassar*

I went to college without even visiting the school! Today students are much more serious about choosing schools and doing their applications. People come to visit the campus a few times rather than just once, for example. Applicants are really doing their research on Brown so they know what we're all about before applying, which is to their advantage. *Michael Goldberger, Brown*

Don't get stressed-out! Try and match what you really care about with what the school has to offer. Sometimes students will choose colleges for random, impressionistic reasons—like whether it was rainy or sunny on the day they took a campus tour. Make sure you are making decisions based on what is really important. *Stuart Schmill, MIT*

How Has Technology Changed the Way Prospective Students Learn about and Choose Schools?

The Internet has really helped students look at colleges. There are virtual tours, and prospective students can look at our student newspaper and class information over the Web. This is a wonderful source of information. *John Blackburn, University of Virginia*

What Are the Most Common Mistakes Students Make When Choosing Colleges?

The most common is pulling out a book, or rankings, and saying "these are the schools I want to apply to." That leaves out a lot of great places—we're fortunate to live in a country that affords us so many opportunities and choices. Students have lots of time to explore types of schools—size, location, etc., and to see what fits best for them. They also need to think about what colleges will still "fit" after they've grown and changed—academically and socially. *Nanette Tarbouni, Washington University (St. Louis)*

Students listen too much to others and not enough to their own hearts. If they've done a good search and chosen to apply to colleges that are good matches, in the end they need to think about what "feels" right to them . . . not what feels right to their parents, friends, or neighbors. *Debra Shaver, Smith*

The most common mistake students and parents make when choosing colleges is relying too heavily on rankings. One year, *U.S. News & World Report* ranked a certain college at number 9. All of a sudden, droves of students had that college on their lists when the year before very few would even have considered it. Students and parents need to understand that these ranking systems are highly variable and arbitrary. Far better to make choices on personal needs and preferences than to rely on rankings. *Paul Marthers, Reed*

Students and parents initially, and often throughout the process, focus too much on schools' prestige and not enough on finding the right fit. Instead, you should search out the institution—or type of institution—that will be a good match for your son or daughter. Perhaps they'll end up at a well-known school. But if you do the process well, perhaps they'll end up at a college you know little about right now. If this is the right place for them, they'll be able to develop and grow there—and that's the goal of this process. *Janet Lavin Rapelye, Princeton*

The biggest mistake students make is to base their decision of where to apply on what other people say—be it rankings, parents, friends, or any outside source. Students should develop their own ranking system that is not based just on quantitative information, but on qualitative information subjective to their own interests and needs. *Jennifer Rickard, Bryn Mawr*

A common mistake parents and students make in selecting colleges is ruling out options too quickly. Students aren't buying a product, they are choosing what kind of education they want. The difficult question is how to think about that. What is it that you *really* want from college? *Ken Himmelman, Bennington*

A big mistake students make is applying to too many schools. If you're applying to 16 schools, that should signal a problem. *Stephen Farmer, UNC Chapel Hill*

The most common mistake students make in choosing colleges is relying only on the name. What's in a name? Too often it's athletic prestige or place on a rankings list. No one is looking at who has the best French department or what the best school is for someone interested in becoming a vet. The resources are out there—find out what makes a school attractive to your personal needs and goals. *Lee Coffin, Tufts*

WHAT ARE THE MOST COMMON MISTAKES PARENTS MAKE IN THE COLLEGE CHOICE PROCESS?

This process is about the student. It's not a report card on the parents' parenting. It is about finding the right match for the student. *Janet Lavin Rapelye, Princeton*

The greatest mistake that parents make is thinking it's their search. It's not about them . . . it's about their child. Parents often put too much pressure on their children. Frankly, students "get it." Everyone is always talking about college and tests and essays and interviews. Parents don't need to add to the stress. Parental concern is coming from the right place—parents want their kids to have the best opportunities. But it morphs into enormous pressure being put on kids today. I worry that parents aren't allowing their kids to have some fun in high school! *Debra Shaver, Smith*

Parents should not assume that because they loved their alma mater their child therefore will. Selecting schools is about finding a good match; what was good for you may well not be the best fit for your child. *Daniel J. Saracino, Notre Dame*

Parents should not be looking for a school to impress their colleagues at work. They should be helping their child find the best environment for their son or daughter to learn and grow as a person. *Paul Marthers, Reed*

Parents need to be realistic about how their kids look on paper (i.e., the transcript). *Janet Lavin Rapelye, Princeton*

---

*The term "admissions director" is used generically, as a catchall title, to denote those in charge of the admissions process at their respective schools, as most people quoted in this book are—whatever the vagaries of the specific title accorded them.

Appendix I

THE COLLEGE VISIT

INTRODUCTION

Visiting a college is an important part of your research. The visit brings to life a campus that has heretofore been only an imaginary place fashioned by rumors, hearsay, website information, guidebook blurbs, and statistics. Visiting colleges impresses on a student that the college experience is minimally about grades and scores and far more about interactions with people, involvement in a multitude of activities, and the pursuit of intellectual endeavors.

In addition to partaking in the usual introductions to campus (a tour, an information session, an interview), a prospective student should attempt to experience the life of students at the campus. This can be done by sitting in on a class, meeting with a professor, reading the school newspaper, hanging out where students tend to congregate (the student union, library, cafeteria, or dorms), attending an extracurricular event, or spending the night in a dorm. Although you will probably not have time to do these things at every college you visit, you should attempt to do many of them at the colleges in which you are most seriously interested.

WHY VISIT A CAMPUS?

- A visit can jump start the college application process and provide you with the energy necessary for getting through its anxieties. It makes the college admissions process a reality (if it was previously not at the forefront of your mind) and makes you excited rather than bored about diving into the task.

- A visit puts a face on something that was previously only about average SAT scores and GPAs. It can make a competitive college seem more human, thus reducing your fear of the admissions process.

- A visit gives you your first taste of college life. By spending some time on a college campus, you can learn what it will be like to be far away from home, live in a dormitory with roommates, interact with a diverse group of people, and eat your meals at a dining hall.

- A visit helps you in the application process because it gives you a better sense of what the school is about and what it is looking for from its candidates.

- A visit signals your interest in the college to the admissions officers. Most admissions offices record the visits of prospective students and look favorably on their "demonstrated interest." Unless you have a good reason for not visiting (because you lack the financial resources or you live particularly far away), admissions officers will doubt your true interest in a school if you do not investigate it thoroughly.

- A visit gives you an opportunity to make a positive impression on admissions officers (if you interview while on campus) as well as professors or coaches, which could positively influence your chances of being admitted.

- A visit to a school you particularly like inspires you to continue performing well (or to buckle down).

- A visit to a school that you were not very attracted to based on its publications or description in guidebooks can prove beneficial by demonstrating it to be a much better place in reality.

WHEN TO VISIT

Ideally, you should visit colleges during your junior year or early in the fall of your senior year. Visiting as close as possible to the beginning of the admissions process in the fall of your senior year will best help you determine to which schools you should apply. However, there is no reason you cannot begin looking at colleges a lot earlier if you want to—even as early as your freshman year. For example, if you are vacationing in close proximity to a college that might interest you, take advantage of the opportunity to see it.

Although often difficult for high schoolers to manage, it is best to visit a college when school is in session so that you can get the right feel for campus and student life. If at all possible, try to visit schools when classes are in session, but not during exam period. Attending campus when school is in session will give you an opportunity to interact with students, who are the best reflection of a school and what it is all about. At exam times, however, you may get a poor impression of the school because students may be stressed out; they may not have an interest in (or time for) talking to prospective students. Furthermore, if you visit during exam time, you will see students holed up in the library but will not get to see the usual dynamics of the campus—there will be few student soccer games taking place on the playing fields, students lounging around and laughing together in the common areas, or students participating in rallies or public activities.

You should also try to visit a campus on a weekday in order to get the best sense of the school. Weekday visits will allow you to see students interacting and to attend a class. Staying for a weekend night is a good idea if you have the time to spare but should be secondary to seeing the school when regular classes and activities are going on. Remember that at college, social activities take place all nights of the week—not just on Fridays and Saturdays. So there is a good chance you will get to attend a social activity or two if you are staying overnight during the week rather than during the weekend.

Spring or summer break might well be the only time when you can get away to visit schools. If this is the case, bear in mind that you are unlikely to get an accurate impression of a school when the campus is void of activity. During spring and summer vacations, the campus is likely to contain only the limited energy of a handful of students. It is better to visit a school during a break than not at all—you will at least be able to talk to admissions officers, see the facilities, and picture yourself living and studying there.

It is not a bad idea to revisit schools you are seriously considering after you have been accepted in order to arrive at a final decision. This is especially true if your original visit was early on in your research. You will want to be sure as a high school senior that the college fits your current needs.

ADMISSIONS DIRECTORS DISCUSS THE VALUE OF VISITING CAMPUSES

Not visiting the campus for a school you are considering enrolling in is a critical mistake. The campus visit is probably the most important component in the decision process for a student.   *Theodore Spencer, Michigan*

The main benefit of visiting a school is to home in on whether or not you would be comfortable there. The best kind of visit is one in which you can experience the school as a current student would, for example, sitting in on a class, eating in the dining hall, talking to students and faculty, and so forth. . . . Visiting schools can be difficult to fit into your schedule during the school year. Often students will embark on college tours during the summer—which is a fine way to get first impressions. If possible, however, I strongly recommend visiting your top choices when school is in session so that you can get as authentic an experience as possible before making a final decision.   *Stuart Schmill, MIT*

If at all possible, students should visit schools they are considering. They may find that the decision they made with their head (that they like a school or not) conflicts with the sensation they have in their gut when they get there. That's an important tension to resolve.   *Steve Thomas, Colby*

When choosing a school, students should spend a few days on campus "kicking the tires." During the admissions process we evaluate applicants, but equally important is applicants taking time to evaluate us.   *Daniel J. Saracino, Notre Dame*

BEFORE THE VISIT

Follow the guidelines recommended in Chapter 3 regarding the kind of research you should do before visiting colleges. By the time you start out on your college trips, you should have completed the following tasks in order to get the most out of your visits.

- Plan to visit a range of colleges. If you are not certain what you are looking for, this is extremely important. Visiting different kinds of schools is a smart move even for those who think they know what they want. You might be certain, for example, that you want to attend a large university because your high school felt too small and limiting—but actually visiting a range of schools might help you see that you would feel lost at a really big place. Visit small and large schools; public and private colleges; urban and rural schools. Also, be sure to visit a range of colleges in terms of selectivity. You need to visit not just your reaches, but also your possibles and your likelies.

- Familiarize yourself thoroughly with the colleges you will be visiting—use college guidebooks, check out the school's website, contact students you know on campus, browse the school's brochures and viewbook. You should be familiar with all the basic facts about a school before getting to the campus, where your job is to refine your impressions and conduct a more detailed investigation. Start a college notebook, allotting a few pages to each school you will visit. Record all the basic data as well as any questions you have about the school so that you will have it on hand when you are on campus. Leave blank pages for each college so that you can record your impressions and answers to questions after the visit.

■ Plan your trips thoroughly. Make sure that you take care of all the logistical details before getting into the car or onto the airplane. Reserve rental cars and airplane seats ahead of time. Map out car trips before hitting the road: Be sure to have both general highway maps and detailed ones of each college town. Get specific directions to each campus from the college admissions office—most websites and viewbooks give detailed information about how to get there from any direction. Make all hotel reservations or arrangements to stay with friends before setting out. Ask admissions office staff for their recommendations on inexpensive overnight options.

　　When making your arrangements, be realistic about the number of activities and travel you can cram into one day. You should ideally visit only one school per day if you want to explore thoroughly and get the best sense of the college's environment.

　　Allow at least three to four hours per campus if you are attending an information session, going on a campus tour, and being interviewed. Allot even more time if you have arranged an additional meeting with a professor or a student. Contact the admissions office to determine times of tours and information sessions. Do not hesitate to talk to the staff at one school about how to get to other nearby campuses. They realize that students visit a number of colleges on one trip and will not be offended to know that you are interested in more than just their own school!

■ Arrange for formal or informal (depending on the school) interviews with admissions officers. Call to schedule an appointment as far as possible in advance, especially for formal admissions interviews.

■ Arrange meetings with individuals in areas of interest to you—coaches, instructors in the performing arts, and professors. Professors are especially good contacts if you have an interest in a major that is less popular on a particular campus—faculty in these fields are always looking for interested applicants to bolster their programs and might even become your advocate in the admissions process if you convey genuine enthusiasm for their discipline. The admissions office is usually helpful in tracking down email addresses or phone numbers of such people.

■ Arrange to speak with a financial aid officer. Again, the admissions office can help you in contacting someone with whom you can speak about financial aid and overall college financing concerns.

■ Create a list of questions to ask in order to get a comprehensive and honest view of the school. See page 76 for suggestions.

■ If possible, arrange to stay overnight with a friend on campus or contact the admissions office to inquire if they have an overnight program in which you can arrange to room with a student.

WHILE ON CAMPUS

While you are on a college campus, you have a lot of options in terms of what to do to get the best feel for the place. The basics include taking the campus tour, attending an information session, and going on an interview or meeting with an admissions officer. Here is a full range of activities you might consider doing on any given campus.

TAKE THE CAMPUS TOUR

The campus tour gives you a feel for the college landscape and facilities. The better ones also introduce you to the college's history, philosophy, academic offerings, and other special features. The tour gives you a chance to walk around and see some typical scenes from "a day in the life" at the college. You can check out the kinds of students the campus attracts and notice if they appear to be happy or dissatisfied, stressed-out or generally at ease. Tours typically last between forty-five minutes and an hour. Tours are almost always led by students who are trained by the admissions office. Take advantage of this opportunity to ask them questions, but bear in mind that these students are salespersons for the school and might not always be completely forthright in their responses.

ATTEND AN INFORMATION SESSION

A group information session is a useful tool for gaining basic information about a school and its admissions process. Usually led by admissions officers or students who work in the admissions office, these sessions give a student an overview of the school's tradition and philosophy as well as the multitude of academic, extracurricular, residential, and other opportunities available on the campus.

Although admissions officers often lead these sessions, this is usually not a time to try to stand out from the crowd by impressing them. Most admissions officers report that they very rarely have an opportunity to take note of prospective students at these meetings, which often include a few hundred high schoolers and their parents at one time. Applicants who try to dominate sessions or gain attention with too many questions that are not of interest to everyone are frowned upon by admissions officers.

VISIT THE ADMISSIONS OFFICE

At many campuses, you can visit the admissions office and ask to speak with an admissions officer, even if you have not prearranged an interview. An officer might be willing to give you a few minutes of his or her time to answer questions and address concerns. Express your interest in the school and ask questions that show you are serious. If you have a special interest in a particular area (and you have not already prearranged a meeting with an individual in that area), ask the admissions officer whom you might contact to discuss pursuit of this interest.

Here you have the chance to impress the admissions officer in a way that might benefit you, so be on your best behavior and be sure that your questions and comments show your overall knowledge of the school and your general intelligence. Stanford's admissions officers, for example, say that they often take note of students with whom they talk in brief informal meetings that occur when they are on the road giving presentations or when a student pops into the office while visiting the campus. If a prospective student really impresses one of them or seems particularly intelligent, they might slip a note into the student's file so that their impressions become part of the admissions record. This can be especially helpful in admission at places such as Stanford, where there are no interviews.

VISIT THE FINANCIAL AID OFFICE

In speaking to a financial aid officer, you will get a better sense of how financial aid works at a school, if there are any packaging policies that might benefit you, and if there are any special opportunities or awards you should apply for. Students should not let their parents attend the financial aid office appointment on their own. You should show a college that you are serious about your future and concerned about your own financial affairs (as well as those of your family) by sitting in on the meeting. There may, of course, be details that are best left up to your parents. If this is the case, you might try to take advantage of this opportunity to separate from them for a while to explore the campus on your own.

ATTEND A CLASS

Upon contacting the admissions office to arrange your visit, ask about the possibility of sitting in on classes. This is a great opportunity to get a feel for professors, students, and the quality of teaching at the school. If you have time, you might want to try to sit in on a variety of classes: different subjects, different teaching contexts (e.g., a lecture course, a small group discussion), and different faculty members.

SPEND THE NIGHT WITH A FRIEND OR STUDENT

It is always a good idea to spend the night at a school. Some schools arrange for overnight stays with students on campus, or you might already know a student with whom you could stay. Your host should ideally be someone who lives on campus in a regular dormitory, rather than off-campus in an apartment with just a few other people. This is a great opportunity to sample college life, particularly the social aspects, as well as to get an honest assessment of the school from students. Try to go to a campus party if you can, or at least have a meal with a group of students. Attend a guest speaker event, participate in an evening dorm activity, or go out to the late-night pizzeria—anything you can imagine yourself doing as a student once you get to campus and at which you will have the opportunity to talk with a variety of students.

EAT IN A CAMPUS DINING HALL OR CAFETERIA

You will almost certainly have a chance to see the campus eating facilities and sample the food if you stay overnight. But even if your visit is just a day trip, you should consider taking a meal in one of the college's student dining halls. This will allow you to sample some of the food (remember that campuses often have a variety of dining options so one place is not necessarily representative of all the facilities on campus) and observe students in an informal setting.

VISIT THE GYM OR ATHLETIC FACILITIES

If sports and physical exercise are important parts of your lifestyle, you will want to check out the athletic facilities at your target campuses. Many colleges will allow you to use the equipment or facilities if you tell them you are a prospective student. Look at the athletic fields and fitness rooms, observe or participate in an exercise class, take a look into the locker room.

PICK UP A COLLEGE NEWSPAPER AND CHECK OUT CAMPUS BULLETIN BOARDS

To discover the real pulse of a campus, read the college newspaper and look at various bulletin and message boards, usually located in the student center, near the student mailboxes, in dining facilities, and in the library. The newspaper will alert you to current campus issues, including those that administrators and students might be hesitant to voice. Bulletin boards are full of announcements about campus activities—they let you know what kinds of things take place at the school as well as giving you an opportunity to actually attend an activity if you so desire.

GO TO THE LIBRARY

Visit the main library on campus. Visit the various study halls; check out the online library catalog; inquire about whether the library maintains "open" or "closed" stacks. If the stacks are open to student perusal, duck into them to see what a huge college library is all about.

VISIT THE BOOKSTORE

Most prospective students make a trip to the bookstore to pick up college gear before heading home. But you should also take the opportunity to look at the textbook section of the campus store. Most campus bookstores post listings of required reading for all courses in session in the textbook section—you can check out some of the materials you might be using once you get to college.

THE ROLE OF PARENTS ON THE CAMPUS VISIT

The practical realities of traveling to colleges usually require that students go with a parent—and there is no reason your parents should not want to sample schools with you and give you their input. Parents are preparing to go through as much of a transition as you are, and college visits often help them ease into the idea of your leaving home. It is important that you remain as sensitive to *their* emotions during the college application and preparation process as they are trying to be of yours. Furthermore, you should be appreciative of all the help they are giving you in this difficult and logistically complex process. Ideally, though, you will have ample time to explore college campuses by yourself or with a friend in order to get a true feel for being on your own in the college environment. Spending time on your own also lets you avoid being too influenced by your parents' opinions about a school.

It can be a little tricky balancing your own needs with those of your parents during college visits. You both want to see the campus and determine how appropriate it is for you, but your parents are likely to have different concerns than you do. You will probably want to have some time on your own at a campus, whereas your parents might not want you to stray too far, fearing that you will get lost, be late for your next appointment, or develop ideas about the school to which they cannot relate because they missed out on a certain experience. All parties need to try their best to understand and respect one another's needs on these visits.

Instead of planning to ditch your family as soon as you arrive on campus, you should discuss beforehand your mutual expectations of how your parents will act and what role they will play. Try to draw a compromise between spending time on your own and tackling the visit with your parents. In other words, you might decide to take the campus tour with your parents, and maybe even take them with you to a class. But also try to spend some time apart from your parents if possible, exploring the campus and interacting with students and professors on your own. Staying overnight on campus—while Mom or Dad stays in the motel down the highway—is often the most convenient way to do so.

Admissions officers are used to parents accompanying their children on campus visits. But parents should be careful not to dominate conversations with admissions officers or faculty. And a parent should never try to enter the meeting room with his or her child when the student goes into an interview. College officers want to know that students themselves are serious enough about the school to prepare their own questions—and they are interested in knowing more about a prospective student from herself, not from her parents' point of view.

BE AWARE OF YOUR PREJUDICES

Many things can skew your impressions of a campus for better or for worse, thereby affecting your ability to evaluate it. Therefore, pay attention to these points:

- Do not let your like or dislike of a single person (tour guide, admissions officer, student, professor) influence your overall impression of a school.
- Bear in mind that weather is a transitory thing and you might be visiting a school on the rare sunny day or the rare rainy day.
- Remember that depending on when in the term you visit (i.e., at the beginning of the term or during midterm exams), students might be more or less engaging.
- If you sit in on a class, recognize that the material is likely to be far more advanced than in high school. Hence, do not be discouraged if you are unable to follow along.
- Remember that part of a school's goal is to attract students. Thus, official school representatives might try to sell you. The more people you talk to (particularly students, because they are not as concerned about attracting more students to the school), the better able you will be to sift through the embellishments.
- Even though a school might have a prestigious name, it is not necessarily the best school nor the best school for you. Remember to determine what is important to you in a school before visiting most campuses (and certainly before making final decisions about where to apply). During the visit, you will then be better able to analyze how well the colleges you visit match up to your needs and desires. Remember that college decision making is an iterative process—as you visit and examine schools, you will learn more about your own needs; and as you learn more about your own needs, you will make further decisions regarding which colleges are best for you.
- Appreciate and observe the school for what it is rather than obsessing about your chances of admission there. If you focus too much on the latter, you will limit your ability to accurately assess the school.

THINGS TO NOTE ON YOUR CAMPUS VISIT

- The school's appearance: Is it clean and well kept? Are the facilities functionally modern? What kind of architecture predominates?

- The diversity of the student population: Is the student population homogeneous, or does there appear to be a good mix of people? Do different ethnic and racial groups interact?

- The students: Do they appear happy or glum? Stressed-out or at ease? Engaged or apathetic? (Remember that the timing of your visit can affect the way students are acting.)

- The professors: Do students and professors interact outside of class? Do professors seem weary and bored with their material, or are they energetic and uplifting?

- The pulse of the campus: What sorts of activities and events are advertised on bulletin boards? What issues are important to students? (You can discover the latter by talking to students, listening to conversations in eating facilities or dorms, and reading the school newspaper.) What is the overall "feel" of the campus?

- The computer labs: Are there enough computers to support the student body, or is a personal computer a better bet? Is free laser printing available? Is the equipment state-of-the-art?

- The library: Are students utilizing it? Is it attractive? Does it offer both private study carrels and areas for group meetings? Is there an area with comfortable chairs for light or less intense work? Is the atmosphere conducive to studying?

- The dining facilities: Are they clean and attractive? Do the menus offer enough variety? Are there healthy options at all meals? Are the dining halls open at convenient hours?

- The dormitories: Is there variety in living arrangements? Do dorms have common areas and common kitchens? Are bathrooms single-sex or coed? Are bathing facilities clean and modern? Are there singles? What is the greatest number of students living in one room? Are the rooms spacious? Is the furniture comfortable? Is there room for privacy within shared living quarters? Is it possible to ask for a room in a quiet area?

- Student life after 10:00 p.m.: On weeknights, between 10:00 p.m. and midnight (or even later), what do students do? Do they continue studying? Argue about politics or social issues? Drink beer? How does this fit with your tastes?

UPON LEAVING CAMPUS

RECORD YOUR IMPRESSIONS

Keep detailed notes of the colleges you visit. Buy a notebook for your campus visits and allot a few pages to each school. After each visit, record your impressions of campuses and responses to questions you asked. It is best to make these notes soon after the end of the visit (this can be a great opportunity to sit at a campus cafe or in an easy chair in the library for a few minutes). Do not wait until the end of a trip—or even the end of a multicampus day—to record your impressions. By the time you have gone to even one other campus, some of your memories from a previous site are bound to have faded.

SEND THANK-YOU NOTES

Send thank-you notes to key people with whom you interacted. This can include interviewers, financial aid officers, professors or other faculty who took time to chat with you, and students who hosted you. E-mail notes are perfectly acceptable, but traditional, handwritten notes are especially appreciated. It is not necessary to send notes to people who conducted large information sessions or tours. It is the individualized treatments that should be addressed with letters of appreciation.

QUESTIONS TO ASK WHILE ON CAMPUS

You should use your campus visit to ask as many questions of admissions officers, administrators, students, and faculty as possible. Asking the same question of a variety of people will often give you different perspectives on an issue. For more ideas about questions to ask (especially of admissions officers and faculty who might influence your chances of admission), see "Intelligent Questions to Ask Your Interviewer" on page 416.

- Who does the teaching here? (Many large or research universities use teaching assistants or graduate students to teach undergraduate courses while professors are off doing research or teaching graduate or upper division courses. Find out who teaches the core or distribution courses typically taken by freshmen and sophomores.)
- What do you particularly like and dislike about the university? What do you see as its benefits and shortcomings?

- If you could change one thing about your school, what would it be? (Even a student who adores his school should be able to come up with something.)

- Is it common for students to have close relationships with their professors? What opportunities exist for students to foster relationships with professors?

- What do students do for fun? What is a typical weekend like? Is the social life primarily about on-campus activities? How prevalent is the Greek system? Will you have a social life if you're not involved in the Greek system?

- How big do freshman classes tend to be? (Many freshman introductory courses are very large. If this is a concern for you, ask questions to determine the amount of one-on-one attention that will be available to you through the professor's office hours or the use of teaching assistants and tutors.)

- What campus and world issues are most important to students?

- What do you feel are the strengths of this school relative to its competitors? (To students only:) Why did you choose this school over other schools?

- What are the most popular majors?

- What are the most popular extracurricular activities?

- What sort of advising services—overall, academic, career, health, mental health—are available to students?

- What special academic programs—overseas study, research opportunities, seminars, independent study—are available to students?

- What are the strongest and weakest departments?

- I'm interested in X as a major—how strong is the program here? Are there any special opportunities available to students in this major?

- What if I'm undecided about my major—will I get an opportunity to explore various disciplines before choosing one?

Do Not Ask . . .

- Avoid asking questions about admissions requirements for GPA and SAT scores or any other questions to which you can find the answers by simply reading admissions brochures and publications.

- Avoid grilling an admissions officer only about the school's weaknesses. Remember to be positive and ask about strengths as well.

4

How to Use the Rankings

— KEY POINTS —

Schools are routinely ranked by various organizations

The rankings provide no more than rough-and-ready guides
to schools' reputations
—Recognize their limitations as well as their strengths

Consult them at the beginning of your search, but do not rely on them
—To get the most out of them, consider the consensus
view of individual schools

You can devise your own rankings to suit your needs

INTRODUCTION

The purpose of *How to Get Into the Top Colleges* is not to rank schools nor to place one particular school on a list of "top" colleges and relegate another school to a list of second-tier institutions. Other publications devote substantial effort to evaluating and ranking colleges, and the field will be left to them. This chapter examines some of the rankings available, discusses the methodologies they employ to reach their conclusions, and suggests how you can use the rankings without being misled by them.

USING THE RANKINGS

The ranking and rating of colleges is a very uncertain science. Organizations that undertake such evaluations are confronted by daunting methodological problems. For example, how important is it to have a library of 20 million volumes rather than 5 million volumes? How about median SAT scores of 730 per section rather than 710? Is the school with 20 million volumes and SAT averages of 710 better than, equal to, or worse than the school with 5 million volumes and SAT averages of 730? It is not obvious how the two schools should be compared, even when two relatively simple quantitative measures are employed. The problem is made infinitely more complicated when numerous other factors are considered, especially because many of these are inherently subjective rather than accurately and objectively quantifiable.

SOME WARNINGS

Rankings are useful as a rough guide to the reputation and quality of different schools. Most people take them far too seriously, however, when considering where to apply. It is inappropriate to take the latest *U.S. News* rankings and limit yourself to the top five schools in one of its lists. The various schools differ enough in their goals, philosophies, academic strengths, and atmospheres that a person who will be well served by one may be very poorly served by another. To take an obvious example, an applicant interested in becoming an actor rather than a nuclear physicist should probably put Yale, Northwestern, and

Carnegie Mellon before Princeton, Cal Tech, or Chicago because the first three also have top-flight theater training available. The latter threesome is an exceptionally good set of schools—but for quite different purposes and thus quite different students.

Chapter 3 lists many criteria that are relevant to choosing the right program. Not all are equally significant. But it would be silly to opt for a school ranked fourth by *U.S. News* over one ranked eighth solely because of these rankings. If the college ranked fourth had an unsuitable atmosphere, had weak departments in your areas of interest, or suffered from one of many other critical weaknesses relevant to your educational and personal goals, then it would not make much sense to choose it over one that was listed below it. There is no precision to the rankings; the same publication might even reverse the rankings of the same two schools next year! (In fact, the volatility of its rankings helps *U.S. News* sell magazines, which is evidently its underlying motivation.)

RULES TO REMEMBER WHEN CONSULTING COLLEGE RANKINGS

1. Use rankings primarily to determine the approximate level of a school's reputation.

2. Note that a ranking of a school is not the same thing as a ranking of each department and program within the school, and some departments and programs within a school will be substantially better than others.

3. Consult multiple rankings, rather than just one, because the consensus view tends to be more valuable than any one ranking.

4. When rankings are suitably detailed, as is true of the *U.S. News* rankings, examine them to see what questions are raised in addition to what answers might be provided. For example, if a school has a substantially lower graduation rate than its peers, you should investigate what underlies the disparity.

5. Since you should be looking for the best college to meet your specific academic and extracurricular needs, with an atmosphere in which you will thrive, the rankings should play only a modest part in helping you determine the best schools for you. They have little to say, after all, regarding which school will provide the courses that you will find most useful or the social environment that will most stimulate you.

6. More important than the rankings is the research you conduct to evaluate particular colleges and their offerings, as discussed in detail in Chapter 3.

THE RANKINGS*: UNIVERSITIES

	U.S. News & World Report	Top Colleges' Selectivity	Professional Schools' Feeders	Doctoral Programs' Feeders	London Times	Shanghai Jiao Tong
Princeton	1	3	3		3	7
Harvard	2	1	1		1	1
Yale	3	2	2		2	9
Stanford	4	6	4		11	2
Cal Tech	5	4	28	1	4	5
Univ. of Pennsylvania	5	12	16	10	9	13
MIT	7	5	8	5	6	4
Duke	8	11	6		8	24
Columbia	9	8	11		7	6
Chicago	9	23	14	9	4	8
Dartmouth	11	7	7		25	55–70
Cornell	12	17	25		12	10
Washington U. (St. Louis)	12	10	47		54	20
Brown	14	8	12		16	43
Johns Hopkins	14	19	24		10	17
Northwestern	14	17	21		15	21
Emory	17	23	36		27	55–70
Rice	17	13	20		34	49
Notre Dame	19	16	35		51	
Vanderbilt	19	25			31	31
UC Berkeley	21	20	41		14	3
Carnegie Mellon	22	22			12	40
Georgetown	23	14	17		38	
Univ. of Virginia	23	27	33		40	55–70
UCLA	25	26			18	11
Michigan	25	30	30		17	18
USC	27	20			42	37
Tufts	28	15	45		52	55–70
UNC Chapel Hill	28	28			50	39
Wake Forest	30	29				

Other universities ranked in the American top 25 by:
London Times: Boston University, NYU, Texas (Austin), University of Washington, Wisconsin (Madison), UC San Diego
Shanghai Jiao Tong: UC San Diego, University of Washington, Wisconsin (Madison), UC San Francisco, Illinois (Urbana Champaign), NYU, Rockefeller

*The Professional Schools' Feeders survey ranked 50 schools; the Doctoral Programs' Feeders survey, 10; the London Times, 56 (American); and the Shanghai Jiao Tong, 88 (American). Data for the latter two in the chart above exclude non-American schools. The Professional Schools' Feeders and Doctoral Programs' Feeders surveys included both universities and liberal arts colleges.

THE RANKINGS*: LIBERAL ARTS COLLEGES

	U.S. NEWS & WORLD REPORT	TOP COLLEGES' SELECTIVITY	PROFESSIONAL SCHOOLS' FEEDERS	DOCTORAL PROGRAMS' FEEDERS
Williams	1	4	5	
Amherst	2	2	9	
Swarthmore	3	3	10	4
Wellesley	4	16	15	
Carleton	5	11		6
Middlebury	5	9	23	
Bowdoin	7	7	19	
Pomona	7	1	13	
Davidson	9	16		
Haverford	10	8	18	
Claremont McKenna	11	5	22	
Grinnell	11	22	44	
Vassar	11	15	32	
Wesleyan	11	11	27	
Harvey Mudd	15	6		2
Washington and Lee	15	10	48	
Colgate	17	16		
Hamilton	17	19		
Smith	17	25		
Oberlin	20	23		7
United States Naval Academy	20	13	37	
Colby	22	20	46	
United States Military Academy	22	13	34	
Bates	24	21	40	
Bryn Mawr	24	24	26	8

*The Professional Schools' Feeders survey ranked 50 schools; the Doctoral Programs' Feeders survey, 10. These two surveys included both universities and liberal arts colleges.

U.S. NEWS & WORLD REPORT

In this section, we analyze the *U.S. News* rankings in greater depth than we do the other rankings provided here because its methodology is the most detailed and includes both subjective and objective elements, and it is the most influential of the various rankings. As such, it provides the right vehicle for understanding issues critical to any college rankings.

METHODOLOGY

OVERVIEW

U.S. News & World Report's rankings involve a three-step process. The colleges are separated into their different categories based on groupings determined by the Carnegie Foundation for the Advancement of Teaching. The two groups of schools whose rankings we list here are the National Universities, which offer a full range of undergraduate majors plus master's and doctoral degrees, and the National Liberal Arts Colleges, which offer almost exclusively undergraduate education.

Second, *U.S. News* gathers data on fifteen indicators from these institutions. It uses seven main categories, all given different weights in the final rating, in evaluating each school: academic reputation, now called peer assessment (25 percent weighting); retention of students (20 percent); faculty resources (20 percent); student selectivity (15 percent); financial resources (10 percent); graduation rate performance (5 percent); and alumni giving (5 percent).

Third, *U.S. News* inserts the data into a series of formulas to rank each college against others in its category.

THE SEVEN RANKING CATEGORIES

U.S. News computes each institution's *peer assessment* score by surveying the administrations at other colleges and universities in the same college category. Responders to questionnaires are required to rate each of these other schools in various programs, on a one- to five-point scale. The responses for each school are then averaged.

The *retention of students* figure refers to a combination of two separate indicators: the percentage of students graduating within six years of entry (80 percent of the retention score) and its freshman retention rate (i.e., the percentage of freshman returning to the school; 20 percent of the score). Retention is used here as a proxy for several hard-to-measure underlying factors, including student happiness with academic and nonacademic situations.

The *faculty resources* score takes several indicators into consideration: class size, comprising the proportion of classes with fewer than twenty students (30%) and classes with more than fifty students (10%); faculty salary, which is average faculty pay plus benefits, adjusted for regional cost of living differences (35%); proportion of professors with the highest degree in their field (15%); student-faculty ratio (5%); and proportion of faculty who are full-time (5%). The basic rationale for this score is that having relatively many professors, paid a lot of money, is a proxy for good teaching.

Student selectivity is calculated using several factors meant to measure the caliber of the student populations at the colleges: the SAT or ACT scores of accepted students (50%); the proportion of freshmen who graduated in the top decile of their high school classes (40%); and the acceptance rate, or ratio of accepted students to total applicants (10%). (For the 2009 rankings, these figures were taken from the class entering college in 2008.)

The *financial resources* measure looks at the total spent on student services, libraries, research, and various other educational items. (For the 2009 rankings, these figures were taken from the 2007 and 2008 fiscal years.) The underlying belief is that the more that is spent on students, the better the educational experience they must be having.

The *graduation rate performance* score measures the difference between the percentage of students who actually manage to graduate within six years and the predicted six-year graduation rate, using a recent class at the college. (For the 2009 rankings, for example, figures were computed for the class that entered college in 2002.) The predicted six-year graduation rate is calculated using a formula that rests on two variables: the "quality" of the incoming class, as based on the class's average standardized test scores, and the amount of financial resources expended per student. If the actual graduation rate exceeds the predicted rate, *U.S. News* credits the school with "enhancing the students' achievement."

The *alumni giving* rate is the percentage of alumni who contributed money to their school in a recent two-year period, which is meant to reflect alumni satisfaction with the school.

PUTTING THE DATA TOGETHER

A score is calculated for each indicator within each of the seven categories. The schools with the highest value for each indicator are assigned a "grade" of 100. Then every other school's score for that indicator is calculated as a percentage of that highest value. The resulting scores are then weighted, as set forth previously, and totaled to determine the scores for each category. Those scores, in turn, are then weighted and totaled to determine a final score, rounded to the nearest whole number, for each school. Schools are then ranked according to those scores. When two or more schools receive the same overall (rounded) score, they are assigned the same ranking.

ADVANTAGES OF THE *U.S. NEWS* APPROACH

There are definite advantages to this approach. First, it looks at a host of factors to arrive at a ranking, rather than depending on any single factor. Given the complexity of the education experience that *U.S. News* is trying to measure, no one factor is likely to suffice in arriving at a sensible ranking. Second, the statistics that the magazine uses are presented for scrutiny and possible manipulation by applicants and their advisers. Thus, a reader can use this same statistical information for his or her own purposes, such as by reweighting factors to more accurately reflect his or her own needs. Third, the data is gathered each year, providing a useful time series for viewing schools' results. Fourth, the data-driven methodology restricts the ability of the magazines' editors to help or harm a school's ranking due to their subjective preferences.

SOME LIMITATIONS OF THE *U.S. NEWS* APPROACH

Factors Not Included

Innumerable factors that might be relevant to you are not included in this (or any other) ranking. For example, there is no direct measure of the actual quality of teaching or of faculty accessibility, no department-by-department analysis of each school, and so on.

No One Weighting of Factors Will Appropriately Reflect All Readers' Needs

One of the major problems in producing a ranking of colleges is that different students want different things in a college. For example, George may prefer a school with a huge library but limited computer facilities to one with a small library but wonderful computer facilities, whereas Lisa may prefer the opposite. Producing one ranking, based on whatever weighting of these two factors is chosen, cannot do justice to the needs of both George and Lisa. (To its credit, *U.S. News* now recognizes this problem. It suggests that students consider doing their own ranking of schools by determining what weight to give to each factor *U.S. News* has calculated. This can be done on its website.)

This problem of determining what weight should be given to each factor is potentially very important. For example, consider Cornell and Brown. The following chart summarizes the recent *U.S. News* rankings of the schools, with a + indicating that a school received a better ranking on the given factor.

FACTOR	CORNELL	BROWN
Peer assessment	+	
Freshman retention		+
Graduation rate		+
Faculty resources	+	
Percent of classes <20		+
Percent of classes >20		+
Student-faculty ratio		+
Full-time faculty	+	
Selectivity: SAT scores		+
Selectivity: Top 10% of high school class		+
Selectivity: acceptance rate		+
Financial resources	+	
Alumni giving		+

Insofar as Brown scored better than Cornell on nine of thirteen criteria, you will be forgiven for assuming that it was ranked higher than Cornell. Not true. Cornell's higher ranking was due to the fact that the criteria on which it outscored Brown were given greater weights in *U.S. New & World Report*'s ranking methodology. Thus, a slightly different weighting of the various factors might have reversed the rankings. Even if you decided that *U.S. News* was considering all the relevant factors and assessing them perfectly—matters about which the rest of this section should raise very serious doubt—it is clear that two students could weight the various factors differently, resulting in one favoring Brown; the other, Cornell.

POTENTIAL IRRELEVANCE OF DATA

Some of what *U.S. News* evaluates may be quite accurate, but that does not mean that it will pertain to you. For example, even though small classes are generally preferable to large ones, seeing that College X has 20 percent of its classes with fifty or more students whereas College Y has only 10 percent with fifty or more students does not necessarily mean that even on this dimension College Y is the better choice for you. If you are going to major in history and not take any biology courses, for instance, the question becomes whether the history courses you would wish to take are large or small, not whether the biology courses are invariably large.

ACADEMIC REPUTATION

Two obvious markets exist for the graduates of top colleges: employers and graduate or professional schools. Unfortunately, *U.S. News* does not attempt to assess directly the market value of graduates of different schools, preferring instead to get the views of relatively uninformed, distant observers—undergraduate deans and presidents. These college administrators are not in a position to render sophisticated, up-to-date judgments about the value of other schools' outputs, but they *are* an inexpensive way for *U.S. News* to get some measure of school reputation. Thus, the magazine does not examine the hiring practices of the top management consulting firms and investment banks, publishing houses and newspapers, scientific research institutes and biotechnology firms, and so on. Neither does it survey those in charge of hiring at such companies. *U.S. News* similarly fails to examine the success of schools' graduates in getting into leading graduate and professional schools; neither does it survey those schools' admissions directors to understand their perspective on the quality of undergraduate institutions.

RETENTION

Graduation Rates.   Having a high graduation rate is probably a good thing overall. Having few students graduate within five or six years would suggest that many who had been admitted found the work too difficult or the atmosphere too unpleasant to complete the required coursework. There is surely another possibility, however: Schools might be tempted to make it too easy to graduate by making sure that few failing grades are handed out. Therefore, having some students fail to graduate within six years may actually be a good thing, indicating that a school is keeping up standards, which helps guarantee the quality of the degree conferred.

There is a second problem in regarding very high graduation rates as a good thing. Should a school be penalized for students who leave after a couple of years of study to take advantage of great opportunities that were offered to them because the school prepared them so well in their fields? For example, consider an actress who is able to get a start on Broadway at twenty. If she does not graduate until she takes a break from acting at age thirty-five, it is certainly arguable that her college had actually done very well by her rather than failing her.

FACULTY RESOURCES

The amount spent on the faculty may or may not correlate with faculty quality. There are a number of problems with this notion, however, some of which are dealt with under the "Financial Resources" section, later in this chapter. One problem concerns the fact that engineering and science faculty are more expensive to employ than are classics professors. Should a school such as Cal Tech be ranked above a school like Columbia simply because it has more science faculty than classics faculty—due, of course, to its having a preponderance of science students? Another problem is that this measure inherently rewards slothful management: Schools that fail to minimize the amount they pay for a given quality of faculty are rewarded. For example, a school would be much better ranked this year than it was last year due simply to doubling its faculty pay, even if it still had the same faculty, teaching the same courses in the same way.

Part-Time Instructors Are Not Necessarily Evil.   These rankings reward schools for having full-time rather than part-time instructors. This may be an appropriate standard when distinguishing between one lesser college and another, but it is highly inappropriate for distinguishing among the leading schools.

Lesser colleges often try to hold down their expenses by using a large percentage of part-time instructors. A faculty filled with part-timers is likely to interact less frequently with students outside of class than a faculty brimming with full-time instructors. Similarly, such a faculty may face continuity problems, with a great deal of annual turnover among instructors, impeding students' planning for classes in future years. Therefore, a faculty with 80 percent full-time faculty will ordinarily be preferable to one with 10 percent full-time faculty.

The problem comes when looking at the top colleges. It is not at all clear that a faculty with 100 percent full-time instructors is better than one with 95 percent full-timers. Having no part-time faculty means that a school forgoes bringing in practitioners on the cutting edge of new developments in their fields, people who would never give up their practices in order to be full-time professors but would enjoy teaching now and again. This is more important in some fields than others, of course. Computer science or biotechnology professionals, rather than historians, are likely to be missed due to this policy.

Penalizing a school for having Bill Gates give a class on expected developments in information systems, or having Richard Holbrooke lecture on diplomacy, or having Trevor Nunn discuss how to direct Shakespeare for modern audiences seems perverse. The optimal percentage of full-time instructors is unclear, but it is clear that the appropriate figure is less than 100 percent.

STUDENT SELECTIVITY

Freshmen in Top Ten Percent of Class.   There are numerous problems with this measure. First, it pays no attention to the quality of competition at different high schools. Graduating number 95 in a class of 1,000 at a poor-quality school where few are serious about grades may be less of an academic accomplishment than graduating number 11 in a class of 100 at an intensely competitive, seriously academic school, but this measure takes no account of such distinctions. Second, this measure ignores how different high schools calculate class rank. Some give extra value to grades earned in difficult classes whereas other schools do not. (In the latter case, a student who takes only the easiest classes and avoids all advanced ones will not be penalized.) The result is another apples and oranges problem: It is hard to compare results when they are arrived at in such different manners. Third, it can be hard to determine whether some students are or are not in the top 10 percent of their classes, given that a very substantial number of high schools no longer calculate class rank.

Acceptance Rates.   Acceptance rates can be managed in a variety of ways. The key way to "game" the numbers these days is to try to determine which applicants are most likely to attend the school and then admit only them. This results in higher "yields"—the percentage of those accepted who actually matriculate—which allows schools to accept fewer applicants to fill the class. The result is that many strong applicants, including many who are better candidates than those actually accepted, may be rejected because the school did not believe that they would actually attend.

Schools can determine which applicants are most likely to attend by considering whether they visited the school (and how many times they visited!), interviewed, filled out the school's own application form rather than the Common Application, communicated by email with school admissions officers, and so on. In the case of applicants from high schools with active college counselors, especially those who are well known to the college, admissions officers can have informal chats with the college counselor to learn whether their school is the applicant's first choice.

Schools often use the waitlist to placate those with strong credentials suspected of intending to go to another college. Schools also use the waitlist to figure out an applicant's intentions: If the person stays on the waitlist and campaigns hard to get into the school over the summer, she is admitted on the assumption that she really does intend to attend.

Another unfortunate aspect of the emphasis placed on acceptance rates is that admissions offices are under pressure to push up the number of applicants to their schools, so as to push down the acceptance rate. This all too often results in encouraging people to apply even when they have absolutely no chance of being accepted, because this helps the schools' numbers. Basing any ranking on the number of unqualified and unrealistic applicants to schools is essentially meaningless.

There is one other obvious difficulty with acceptance data. Some universities, such as Cornell and NYU, are made up of a set of "schools," such as Industrial Relations, Arts and Sciences, Hotel Administration, and so on. Some of these schools are much harder to get into than are others. Using admissions data applicable to the whole university (i.e., aggregating the data for each constituent school) risks distorting more than it reveals about the different schools clustered together under the umbrella of this university.

FINANCIAL RESOURCES

The financial resources measure used by *U.S. News* is inherently subject to problems. First, schools that prepare a large number of science and engineering students tend to need more expensive facilities, such as laboratories, to provide a suitable education than a school educating a greater proportion of classics majors. Thus Cal Tech, MIT, Stanford, and Johns Hopkins, all of which are famous for their focus on science and engineering education, are atop the financial resources lists. If, hypothetically speaking, Cal Tech provides $250,000 worth of laboratory facilities per science and engineering student and Cornell does the same, should Cal Tech receive a higher ranking simply because a higher percentage of its students are indeed science and engineering students?

Second, consider the following case. Imagine that College X built a marvelous library in 1948, with many plush reading rooms and other useful extras, whereas College Y is currently building a trashy library without sufficient space to house its book collection, let alone such extras as marvelous reading rooms. Because College X has long ago ceased paying for its plush building (or even depreciating it on its financial statements), and College Y is currently spending money for its trashy building, the latter will be ranked higher on this measure.

Thus, a school's accounting policies, such as the means of depreciating different capital assets (e.g., buildings and laboratory equipment), is but one example of the arcane matters that can affect these rankings, potentially adding substantial volatility to a school's ranking. (Further discussion of the fine points of financial accounting is beyond the scope of this discussion.)

Third, where buildings and other matters are concerned, a school might have to pay more for any given product if it is in a high-wage, highly unionized area than another school would in a different labor environment. The same is true regarding *when* it has work done. Building during a boom period may necessitate spending more for hard-to-obtain resources than would be necessary during a recession, but the resulting buildings would not necessarily be any better for students.

The major problem with input measures, especially financial measures, is that one can spend money well or poorly. As many a major league baseball, basketball, or football team could attest, it is not difficult to spend a fortune and fail to win a championship. The academic market is a much more opaque one than the sports market, so it is likely to produce even weaker correlations between spending and actual results. In general, these input figures say nothing about the quality of spending (i.e., whether much or little has been wasted).

GRADUATION RATE PERFORMANCE

The difference between predicted and actual graduation rates is arguably the single weakest element of the *U.S. News* rankings. The predicted rate is based on only two factors: the standardized test scores of incoming students and the amount of money that the school spends on them. That rate is then compared with the actual graduation rate. The difference between the two is assumed to be due solely to the quality of the school's education. This assumption is heroic, indeed.

Other possible causes of students graduating or failing to graduate in six years are legion. A few of the innumerable other possible causes are:

- Taking chances on applicants from weak high schools. These candidates are more likely to drop out than are those from tried-and-true feeder schools, even though taking such chances can produce a more interesting, diverse class.

- Recruiting a disproportionate number of students from far away. These students may drop out more often because they cannot readily go home when struck by homesickness. A geographically diverse class is ordinarily considered beneficial but could work against a school's ranking.

Numerous other factors affecting graduation rates could, of course, be offered. Suffice it to say that using only two factors to predict graduation rates—and considering any variances from the predicted graduation levels to be something to be held for or against the school—borders on the absurd.

ALUMNI GIVING RATE

Using the alumni giving rate as a proxy for alumni satisfaction with their alma maters is by no means absurd, but it suffers from some serious drawbacks. First, it looks at whether someone donates at all rather than the amount donated. If College X has 50 percent of alumni donate $10 apiece, it fares better in the rankings than College Y, which has 40 percent of its alumni donate $1,000 each. In other words, the strength of alumni feelings is not incorporated in this measure. Second, it ignores the fact that some people donate substantial amounts in major "pledge years" and nothing in between. This causes a degree of volatility in this measure from year to year that does not reflect shifts in alumni feelings. Third, it is substantially biased against public universities, the alumni of which tend not to donate money in the belief that these schools are meant to be funded by taxpayers' dollars.

TOP COLLEGES' SELECTIVITY

The authors of this book have put together a very simple, rough-and-ready ranking of colleges based on two measures of selectivity: the average SAT score and percentage of applicants accepted for each college. We calculated the average SAT by taking the midpoint of the 25th and 75th percentiles reported by the schools. We then ranked the top thirty universities in the *U.S. News* survey (against one another, only). Next, we ranked the same universities on the basis of the percentage of applicants they accepted, with the highest ranking given to those schools accepting the fewest applicants. We combined the two rankings—for SAT score and acceptance percentage—to produce an overall ranking, which is what we have reproduced in the chart on page 82. We repeated the process for the liberal arts colleges.

There are, to say the least, some methodological issues with our approach. We consider only two factors, despite the fact that the worth of a school is hard to summarize in as few as a dozen factors. We give equal weight to the two factors for no particular reason. And so on.

So, you might ask, why bother? For a number of reasons. First, the inputs are easy to understand. Second, the two factors chosen do reflect important factors for judging a school. The average SAT score is a reasonable proxy for the academic strength of the incoming class (and it does not suffer from the terminal problems of GPAs and rank in class, as discussed regarding the *U.S. News* rankings). The percentage of applicants accepted is, likewise, a reasonable proxy for how selective the school can be in choosing students. The quality of one's classmates is arguably as important as anything else (or everything else) in determining the amount and nature of learning likely to take place in college. The percentage accepted is also a measure of how desirable applicants find the school. In other words, it is akin to a vote by applicants, thereby taking into account whatever factors they consider important. Third, and perhaps most important, we think that our ranking is every bit as reasonable as any of the others discussed here (or elsewhere). Take a look at the schools that we value more highly than does *U.S. News*, for instance. Are we clearly wrong? Do the same for the schools we value less highly. Again, is it obvious that we are mistaken?

Our fundamental points are that:

- For all the apparent sophistication of *U.S. News* and other surveys, there is no hard and fast means of saying which school should be number nine and which number thirteen.

- It is easy to put together your own ranking, regarding whatever factors matter most to you. (See "Create Your Own Rankings" on page 97 for more about this.)

PROFESSIONAL SCHOOLS' FEEDER COLLEGES

The *Wall Street Journal* recently ranked America's colleges according to the extent to which their graduates enrolled in various elite professional schools. The *Journal* selected five MBA programs (University of Chicago, Dartmouth's Tuck School, Harvard, MIT's Sloan School, and the University of Pennsylvania's Wharton School); five law schools (University of Chicago, Columbia, Harvard, Michigan, and Yale); and five medical schools (Columbia, Harvard, Johns Hopkins, UC San Francisco, and Yale). Its reporters counted the number of graduates of the various undergraduate colleges attending these fifteen professional schools and then discounted the numbers according to the size of the graduating class at each college.

There are some obvious potential problems with the data used here. For one example, the schools chosen are by no means the only ones that could have been used. Thus, in law, the top five schools would undoubtedly have included Stanford rather than Michigan. The choice of schools matters because of the potential bias that it introduces. To the extent a graduate school favors its own undergraduates in admissions, or those same undergraduates prefer to remain at the same university at which they have done their undergraduate work, the survey will be biased in favor of the chosen five schools in each subject. Harvard is likely to be the greatest beneficiary of this, given that it is on each of the three lists. Cal Tech, MIT, and Princeton—which have no business, law, or medical schools—are clearly not advantaged by the nature of this survey. The greatest oddity, however, may be that Stanford, which arguably has a top-five program (if not better) in each of the three professional fields included here, is not on any of the lists.

Another potential problem is that the ranking is very limited in scope. Although it considers professional schools, it does not include architecture, dentistry, engineering, or veterinary medicine. It is incomplete in another way, too. It does not include graduate programs outside the professional realms. In other words, master's and doctoral programs in economics, history, physics, and so on are ignored.

Despite these clear limitations, this survey is intriguing and valuable insofar as it considers the outputs of colleges (what its graduates do and how they are evaluated) rather than just inputs (such as how much colleges spend).

DOCTORAL PROGRAMS' FEEDER COLLEGES

The Higher Education Data Sharing Consortium has gathered data for its constituent colleges concerning the percentage of graduates who go on to do doctorates in a host of fields. It then ranks colleges according to the percentage of their graduates who eventually pursue doctorates. This can be read as a complement to the Professional Programs' Feeder College study produced by the *Wall Street Journal*, which looked at professional schools rather than academic graduate programs.

This study is relatively narrow in focus, considering only doctoral programs, and only those doctoral programs in academic fields (not including accounting, for instance). The bigger problems, however, are that the survey only ranks ten schools and that the consortium is not currently publishing its results, preferring to hoard them for its member colleges.

INTERNATIONAL RANKINGS

The next two rankings to be discussed here are international in scope. We include them because, in a global marketplace, the opinions of non-Americans are of value. After all, you may end up working abroad—or in the United States for a foreign employer, or you may look to do a graduate degree abroad. In addition, the approaches taken by the two surveys are interestingly different from those discussed above. (Note, by the way, that the two international rankings do not limit themselves to just the undergraduate component of universities. Thus, they tend to rate highly those schools with strong graduate departments and all but ignore purely undergraduate institutions, such as the liberal arts colleges.)

LONDON TIMES

The *London Times Higher Education Supplement* has recently started ranking universities on a worldwide basis. It currently ranks the "top 200" globally, of which fifty-six are American. Although its methodology is likely to evolve with experience, at the moment its rankings are based on:

- Peer assessment (measured by a survey of academics): 50 percent of total score
- Research impact (measured by the number of citations per faculty member): 20 percent
- Faculty-student ratio: 20 percent
- Percentage of overseas students: 5 percent
- Percentage of overseas faculty: 5 percent

Although this is a relatively new ranking, it is likely to become quite significant, especially because it takes a somewhat different approach from the other internationally noteworthy survey (discussed below). Rather than take a purely quantitative approach—counting the number of Nobel Prizes in Physics won by the faculty, for instance—it places greatest weight on scholarly opinion. This is by no means unreasonable, but it is certainly subjective and hard to measure accurately. How many physicists rather than creative writing professors should be included in the survey? How many of each from a given country or region? And so on. Another methodological issue: The percentage of students from overseas is a measure ill-suited to the American market. The ability to attract students from abroad may distinguish one school from another in some countries, but at the top end of the American market, the percentage of foreigners attending a school is almost totally dependent upon that school's admissions (and perhaps financial aid) policies rather than demand. The number of foreigners attending Yale doesn't tell us how popular Yale is abroad; it merely tells us what balance between Americans and foreigners Yale prefers.

The rankings are probably best interpreted as a measure of the international fame and reputation of a university, with graduate programs inevitably accounting for the bulk of the results. As a result, American universities without large graduate schools (such as Brown and Dartmouth in the Ivy League) will tend to fare poorly. Universities with large graduate schools (such as Berkeley and Michigan) will tend to make out well. Unlike the Shanghai Jiao Tong rankings, its results are not heavily math and science oriented, so it may provide a better measure of reputation across disciplines.

SHANGHAI JIAO TONG

The Chinese interest in getting their universities up to the mark as quickly as possible inspired one Chinese university to start ranking its competitors—or, to put it more genteelly, the universities against which it would benchmark itself. This ranking awards credit for:

- Articles published in *Nature* and *Science*: 20 percent of total score
- Articles in science, social science, and arts and humanities citation indices: 20 percent
- Staff of university winning Nobel Prizes (in chemistry, economics, medicine, or physics) or Fields Medals in Mathematics: 20 percent
- Highly cited researchers: 20 percent
- Alumni of university winning Nobel Prizes or Fields Medals: 10 percent
- A further calculation discounts (or increases) the above results on the basis of the university's size: 10 percent

This was the first such ranking to be used broadly in international education. It is well regarded in large part because it is based on hard, quantitative inputs—number of Nobel Prizes won, for instance. The problems with this ranking, however, are as clear as its virtues. Its methodology is muddled: It relies on two overlapping citation indices without the overlap being taken into account. Partly as a result, it values math and science much more than other fields, even though it has evolved and broadened the items for which it gives credit (and thus gives at least some credit for the arts, humanities, and social sciences). And, on a more mundane note, it is not clear how much credit should be given to a university for having produced a 1933 graduate who managed to win a Nobel Prize in 1977.

DEPARTMENTAL RANKINGS

It is not just colleges that are ranked; numerous rankings of specific departments or programs are also constructed. Both *U.S. News* and the National Research Council (an arm of the U.S. National Academies of Science and Engineering) rank a large number of graduate departments. Although your primary focus is likely to be on undergraduate departments, these graduate rankings are nonetheless useful proxies for the overall strength of the respective departments.

Note, too, that various magazines rank departments in specific fields. For instance, *Business Week* magazine ranks undergraduate business programs and *Foreign Policy* magazine ranks undergraduate foreign relations programs. If your fields of interest are the subjects of such magazines, by all means check to see whether they have produced a ranking of relevant departments or programs. (But be sure to check the methodology they used, too.)

CREATE YOUR OWN RANKINGS

Obviously, the rankings cited in this chapter may not cover all of the issues and concerns you might have about colleges. This leaves you with the opportunity to craft your own rankings, tailored to whichever criteria you deem to be most important. Following are the bases for a few of the many rankings you might consider helpful:

- Number (or percentage) of graduates winning specific scholarships (Rhodes, Marshall, Fulbright, et al.) or grants (National Institutes of Health, National Science Foundation, et al.)
- Number of graduates hired by your target employer(s)
- Number of courses or professors in your chosen field
- Number or nature of foreign exchange opportunities
- Percentage of incoming freshmen over the age of twenty-five
- Percentage of foreign students

- Percentage of students in fraternities or sororities
- Percentage of men (or women)

A three-step process should get you started:

1. Select an initial group of schools likely to be of interest to you.
2. Ask your parents, high school counselor, or other trusted advisers for possible additions to your list.
3. Pull together data relevant to your chosen method of ranking, whether from school websites; general college guidebooks; or specialist websites, such as that of *U.S. News* (which includes substantial information about schools not included in its own rankings).

And then, let the ranking begin!

PUTTING IT ALL TOGETHER

Looking at any one survey's results is less helpful than considering those of multiple surveys. For instance, if you look at Cal Tech's rankings, you may see that it ranks high in producing students who go on to doctoral programs, but that it ranks less high in producing students who go on to business, law, or medical schools. The two phenomena are, of course, related: Cal Tech's students are hardly considered unfit for professional schools. Instead, a disproportionate number of its graduates choose to do doctoral rather than professional studies. So, too, for Bryn Mawr. Looking at only one ranking would have revealed less about each school.

And, of course, creating your own ranking based on whatever factors matter most to you may provide the most useful measure of all.

SOURCES

U.S. News & World Report, America's Best Colleges

The *Wall Street Journal*'s Professional Programs' Feeder Colleges rankings www.wsjclassroomedition.com/college/feederschools.htm

Higher Education Data Sharing Consortium's rankings
http://hseagle.sas.edu.sg:8068/hscounseling/College/phds.htm

London Times Higher Education Supplement rankings
www.thes.co.uk/downloads/ranking

Shanghai Jiao Tong rankings
http://ed.sjtu.edu.con/ranking.htm

National Research Council rankings
www.nationalacademies.org/nrc

BusinessWeek rankings
www.businessweek.com/bschools/undergraduate

Foreign Policy rankings
www.foreignpolicy.com

ADMISSIONS DIRECTORS DISCUSS COLLEGE RANKINGS

WHAT IS THE APPROPRIATE USE OF THE *U.S. NEWS* AND OTHER RANKINGS?

Some people seem to start with the *U.S. News* list in hand and won't go below a certain number on the list. As a result, they miss numerous truly outstanding institutions—this is especially true amongst the liberal arts colleges. Even in the sciences, many of these liberal arts colleges offer outstanding educations.   *Rick Bischoff, Cal Tech*

Rankings may be useful to identify which are the best, say, 100 or 200 schools in the country. It's the ranking part that goes overboard. The difference between number 15 and number 30 simply isn't that significant. As between the two, the school ranked 30 might be far more preferable to a certain student for a variety of important and personal reasons.   *Paul Marthers, Reed*

The whole point of going off to college is increased autonomy—thinking for yourself. If the college search process is approached appropriately, it ends up being a pretty good primer for the college experience. When students start to depend too much on one source, be it parents, a counselor, or a ranking, the irony is that it's defeating the purpose of being the self-sustaining person you hope to be once you're in college.   *Stephen Schierloh, Sarah Lawrence*

I am not a huge fan or a huge critic of rankings systems. Some are very forthright about what factors they are weighing. Students should just be clear that there are a lot of value judgments embedded in rankings that may not match their own values.   *Stephen Farmer, UNC Chapel Hill*

The Internet is far more useful than any rankings system. You get better search results. If you are interested in a particular academic field, I recommend

Google over *U.S. News & World Report* any day in terms of identifying schools with strengths in areas you care about.   *Lee Coffin, Tufts*

WHAT ARE THE LIMITATIONS OF THE RANKINGS?

It's a very imperfect attempt to quantify the characteristics that would allow you to do any kind of true ranking of colleges.   *Charles Deacon, Georgetown*

Oberlin has a music conservatory, Wesleyan doesn't. The *U.S. News* ranking doesn't factor this difference in. Yet this distinction is certainly critical to many applicants, particularly those with a music interest, and would be missed if they relied only on the rankings. Rankings such as *U.S. News* are terribly blunt instruments being used for what people believe are precise measurements. The results are developed into instruments that feature what I call "artificial precision."   *Bruce Poch, Pomona*

For each individual there are schools that are good fits and schools that aren't. There is no absolute scale that applies to everyone. Rankings are not tailored to any one person. The only solution is to make your own individualized ranking based on criteria that are important to you.   *Stuart Schmill, MIT*

Colleges don't want to be reduced to a numeric ranking any more than high school students want to be reduced to their SAT score. We appreciate the data that accompanies the rankings; it's only the ranking part we take issue with. Students and families should take stock of the data and make their own assessments. They should not depend on a third-party formula to make decisions for them.   *Stephen Schierloh, Sarah Lawrence*

Rankings are too often taken as gospel. In truth, they are a poor substitute for doing the research yourself.   *Ingrid Hayes, Georgia Tech*

It's important for students to get beyond the superficiality of the rankings. They present very general information, but there is little about the quality of instruction, the nature of the student body, the faculty, or the institution itself. *Jennifer Desjarlais, Wellesley*

5

UNDERSTANDING ADMISSIONS AT THE TOP COLLEGES

— KEY POINTS —

▪

A thorough understanding of how admissions works—
including the terminology used, the priorities of the admissions
department, and the way in which decisions are made—will help you
fare your best in the application process

▪

Understanding the various cycles of admission will allow you to make the
critical decision of whether to apply Early Decision or Early Action

▪

Admissions committees examine your academic potential, nonacademic
pursuits, and personal attributes to evaluate your candidacy

▪

Colleges seek diversity and want to craft a "well-rounded" class, which is
not necessarily composed of "well-rounded" individuals

▪

Colleges have different educational philosophies and values, which play
a role in admissions, as well as different methods of evaluating
candidates for admission

INTRODUCTION

A thorough understanding of how colleges make their admissions decisions is essential for you to do the best job possible in completing and submitting your applications. This chapter will help you understand the basics of college admissions. You will learn about the various application timing options (Early Action, Early Decision, Regular, and Rolling), which will help you determine whether or not you should apply early to a college. The chapter will also show you what criteria the college admissions committees evaluate, who is involved in the evaluations, and how these evaluations are performed.

THE ROLE OF ADMISSIONS

Admissions departments play a dual role. They are responsible for selling the college to prospective students and evaluating applicants for admission. Admissions officers are meant to be ambassadors of the school, bestowing prospective applicants with positive information about the college and its offerings. Most travel the country and the world in order to publicize their schools and stir up interest in attending them among future college entrants. These same officers work together, beginning in November each year and continuing through the winter months until April, to read applications and make decisions about which candidates to admit.

ADMISSIONS PRIORITIES

Before reading further in this chapter, it is important that you command an overview of the various priorities that admissions committees must juggle when evaluating students. Obviously, colleges want students who will be successful in college and beyond. As discussed later in this chapter, the three fundamental criteria on which you will be evaluated for admission to a college are your academic potential, your nonacademic pursuits and talents, and your personal attributes.

Admissions committees must also, however, fulfill specific needs of the college. They must first of all ensure that the college maintain or enhance its "profile," which is the information submitted to the public about the college.

Colleges know that the public judges their quality based on information such as the college's rate of acceptance in admissions, the SAT scores of the most recent incoming class, and the college's yield on accepted applicants (the percentage of accepted applicants who decide to attend the college). For this reason, colleges want as many applications as possible (so that they can push down their rate of acceptance), look for students with high SAT scores, and want to accept students whom they believe are most likely to attend their institution.

Colleges have other priorities as well. Most look to diversify their classes as much as possible, which means that they are concerned not only with each applicant as an individual but also with how each applicant will add to the college's composition, often referred to as the "composite." Most colleges set loose targets for the numbers of minority or international candidates they want to accept, for example. See pages 124 through 126 for an in-depth discussion of diversity's role in college admissions.

Colleges also must abide by certain policies set by the college's administration, in conjunction with a board of directors or other decision-making bodies. The most important of these policies might concern, for example, the need to compose a high-performance hockey or basketball team or to satisfy wealthy contributing alumni by admitting their offspring at higher rates than other applicants. One of the most important policies that govern college admissions concerns the college's ability to admit students who cannot afford its tuition. This refers to a college's stand on need consciousness in its admissions process.

NEED CONSCIOUSNESS IN COLLEGE ADMISSIONS

Perhaps the most important policy governing admissions is a college's approach to evaluating candidates with financial need. Many of the very elite colleges have financial aid budgets strong enough to allow them to evaluate applicants without concern for their financial situation at all. Such a system, called a "need-blind" admissions policy, means that a college's admissions officers evaluate a candidate without having any information about his or her financial situation available to them. If the candidate is admitted, the financial aid office then puts together an aid package and presents it to him or her upon receipt of the acceptance letter from the college. (Note that not all colleges that are need-blind also agree to meet the full need of all students admitted. A college can admit a student need-blind, but then offer him or her an aid package that is not sufficient to cover the costs of attending the school.)

At colleges that are *not* need-blind, some or all applicants are evaluated with some consideration of their ability to pay for college. Especially when admitting the last students in a class, the admissions committees at schools that are not need-blind (often referred to as having "need-aware" or "need-conscious" admissions policies) will admit students with little financial need over those with great financial need. Thus, if you are an extremely well-qualified applicant, likely to be highly desirable to the college, then it likely will not matter—even at need-conscious schools—if you have great financial need. If you have great financial need and are at the bottom of the college's list of possible admits, though, it will be more difficult to gain admission to the college.

THE FOUR POSSIBLE OUTCOMES OF AN ADMISSIONS DECISION

The decision that an admissions committee makes regarding your application will be one of four possibilities: admit, deny, waitlist, or defer.

To **admit** an applicant is to offer the student a place in the incoming class. To **deny** a candidate admission is to notify the candidate that, although he or she may be qualified to attend the school, he or she is not being offered a place in the class. To **waitlist** an applicant is to notify the candidate that he or she is not being offered a place at the school at the present time, but there is still a possibility of being admitted in the future if there is space in the class after all admitted applicants notify the school of their decisions. To **defer** a student is essentially to put the applicant "on hold." Deferring an applicant delays a final decision until more information about the student can be evaluated or until the admissions committee can better compare the student against other applicants. Deferring a student does not occur in Regular Admissions cycles, but only during Rolling Admissions, Early Decision, or Early Action cycles.

THE FOUR TYPES OF ADMISSIONS CYCLES

There are four different types of college admissions cycles: Regular Admissions, Rolling Admissions, Early Decision, and Early Action.

REGULAR ADMISSIONS

Regular Admissions is the standard admissions evaluation cycle, which requires an applicant to submit the application by a particular deadline (usually in January or February of the year in which he or she wants to attend college). After the deadline, the admissions team begins to evaluate all applications at the same time. All students are notified of the college's decision several months later (usually in late March). Because of concern for the composition of the class as a whole, most decisions are not finalized until all applications have been reviewed. Most schools notify students who applied for Regular Admission in late March to early April and stand by the Candidates' Common Reply Date of May 1. This means that students applying to most colleges are not required to notify schools of their decision to attend or not attend until May 1, allowing them to receive notification from all colleges before making a decision.

ROLLING ADMISSIONS

Rolling Admissions is an admissions evaluation cycle that allows applications to be reviewed and decided on as they arrive in the admissions office. A Rolling Admissions policy might, for example, open its season on October 1, requiring only that all applicants get their applications in by a certain deadline in the winter or spring. (For Rolling Admissions, it is generally beneficial for the applicant to get his or her application in as soon as possible.) Under most Rolling Admissions policies, a candidate is notified of the college's decision four to eight weeks after receipt of the application. Rolling Admissions cycles are used mostly by large public universities.

EARLY DECISION

Early Decision (ED) is a policy offered by many private and some public colleges for students who know what their first-choice college is by the beginning of the senior year. In Early Decision, a student applies to the college under a *binding contract* early in the fall (the deadline is usually November 1 or 15), is notified several months later of the college's decision, and is *obligated* to attend the school if admitted. A student applying Early Decision to one school cannot apply Early Decision to any other school.

EARLY DECISION II

A few schools, such as Bowdoin, Colby, Middlebury, Tufts, and Wesleyan, now conduct two rounds of Early Decision, one with applications due by the early November deadline and another with applications due by a January deadline. Early Decision II, as it is often called, referring to the January deadline, is still a binding contract in which candidates are obligated to attend the school if accepted. They are notified within a month or two, before regular January applicants are notified.

The benefit of the ED II policy is that students have more time to investigate colleges and think about where they want to go before committing themselves, yet still get the benefit of proclaiming that a school is their definite first choice (a plus for your candidacy in the eyes of admissions officers). The drawback to ED II is that students cannot wait until they hear the decision to complete applications to other colleges, so the option does not save candidates any work or energy.

EARLY ACTION

Some colleges have Early Action rather than Early Decision policies. Early Action also allows a student to apply to a college early and be notified by the school a few months later. It differs from Early Decision in that it is not a binding contract. Those who apply Early Action are not obligated to attend the school if they are accepted but can wait until hearing from other schools (during the Regular Admissions round) to make a final decision about where to attend. Colleges with Early Action formats do not have uniform policies regarding applying Early Action or Early Decision to other colleges. Some openly allow candidates to apply elsewhere Early, whereas others prohibit the practice. The latter often call their format single-choice Early Action.

THE BENEFITS OF THE EARLY OPTIONS FOR COLLEGES

Because one is a binding policy and the other is not, Early Decision and Early Action confer quite different benefits on the colleges' admissions committees. Early Decision is beneficial for colleges because it helps them choose good candidates to form a foundation for the upcoming class, knowing for certain that those students will attend the school. This helps them improve their "yields" (the percentage of accepted students who decide to matriculate at the college) because they know that the students admitted Early will attend. Early Decision also benefits the college by ensuring that a portion of the class is extremely enthusiastic about attending the school, declaring it their first choice early on. Every college wants to be sure that its students are happy, motivated, and productive. When a large portion of the entering class strongly supports the college, the feeling can be contagious, thus boosting the morale of everyone on campus. An Early Decision policy gives colleges a great deal of control over class composition, knowing for certain that students admitted Early will matriculate at the college.

Early Action, on the other hand, is not as beneficial for colleges because it does not allow them to admit a student knowing for sure that he or she will attend. Early Action does not give colleges as much control over their future classes. (It is important to note, however, that colleges usually get a better yield from their Early Action applicants than they do from their regularly admitted applicants.)

THE BENEFITS OF THE EARLY OPTIONS FOR APPLICANTS

The real question is how beneficial Early policies are for applicants. Most of this discussion focuses on Early Decision, since an application under this binding policy involves much more thought and commitment, and potentially confers more benefits—albeit at a high risk of making a grievous, hard-to-reverse error—on an applicant who chooses an ED target wisely than does an Early Action application.

Over the past decade, many colleges have continued to fill greater and greater portions of their freshman classes with Early Decision (and Early Action) applicants. Most of the very competitive colleges fill between 30 and 50 percent of their freshman classes with Early applicants.

The acceptance rate (the percentage of applicants who are admitted to the college) at most schools is higher among Early Decision (and Action) applicants than it is among Regular Admissions applicants. It is indeed easier at most private (and some public) colleges for students to gain admission Early Decision (and often Early Action as well). As an added benefit, if you are accepted under a college's Early Decision or Action policy, you will not have to commit as much time to the application process as you would if you were to apply to a large number of schools. You can breathe easily for the rest of the year in a way that other seniors do not have the luxury of doing.

Inevitably, high school students are now concerned that they need to apply somewhere under an Early Decision or Action policy in order to boost their chances of acceptance. The result has been a huge surge in the number of Early applications—a kind of mad frenzy among high school seniors, especially those at independent high schools, to decide on a favorite college and apply Early in the fall.

College admissions officers and high school counselors alike are worried about the repercussions of this trend toward applying Early, especially under Early Decision policies. It means that many students are applying under binding contracts to colleges that may or may not end up as their first choices. Many students are simply not ready by the very beginning of their senior year to make a final decision about their top-choice school, and yet they are applying Early Decision to colleges despite this uncertainty, for fear of not being accepted in the Regular Admissions round.

WHO SHOULD APPLY EARLY

Applying Early is likely to make sense to the extent that most or all of the following factors are true of your situation:

- You know the college you most want to attend, and your decision is unlikely to change
- Your chosen college favors Early applicants
- Your chance of acceptance Regular Decision would be moderate
- Your credentials will not improve substantially during your senior year
- You do not need substantial financial aid—*Or*, you need substantial financial aid, but your target school fully meets financial need
- You are organized early enough in your senior year to do a good application
- You are a legacy (see Chapter 7)

You Know the College You Most Want to Attend, and Your Decision is Unlikely to Change

If you have done substantial homework about colleges before senior year, you may have determined which one would be right for you. If so, applying Early to that school may be a good idea. The better you know yourself, and the more investigation of colleges you have done (including substantial visits to likely choices), the more probable it is that your choice will indeed be a good one for you. Those who have not done much thinking about both their own needs and the relevant differences among colleges are more likely to find their number one choice changing through the course of their senior year.

**ADVICE FOR THOSE WHO LIKE
SEVERAL SCHOOLS EQUALLY WELL**

Some counselors believe you need not have targeted one and only one school for Early application. If several schools are of roughly equal appeal to you, they think you might well apply Early to one of them in recognition that you would not be much better off going to any of the others.

This advice—apply Early somewhere if you have several equally attractive schools in mind—is strategically correct. If may also lead to trouble. In our experience, too many applicants who find themselves in the situation of liking a bunch of schools equally have not in fact done their homework. They generally don't yet fully understand their own needs; neither do they have a clear picture of the schools on their list. Despite this, they succumb to the pressure to apply somewhere Early Decision. The result is often one of buyer's remorse: they are sorry they chose a school they have come to recognize is not a good fit for them.

Your Chosen College Favors Early Applicants

Most selective private colleges favor Early applicants. As the quotations from admissions officers at the end of this section suggest, however, by no means do all selective colleges favor Early applicants. (You can assume that those schools admitting students with lesser SAT or ACT scores and class ranks than they do during the Regular Admissions cycle favor Early applicants. Where this is not the case, and the credentials of those admitted Early are indistinguishable from—or better than—those admitted Regular Decision, you will know that applying Early confers no advantage.) If there is no admissions advantage to applying Early at your chosen school, then it is likely to be a bad idea to apply Early.

YOUR CHANCE OF ACCEPTANCE REGULAR DECISION WOULD BE MODERATE

Those whose chances of admission are increased most by applying Early are those whose chances of applying Regular Decision would be moderate. The applicant who would almost certainly be admitted Regular Decision clearly has little to gain. Perhaps surprisingly, the same is true of someone with essentially no hope of being admitted Regular Decision. Instead, it is those whose chances of applying Regular Decision would be one-in-five or three-in-five who are most advantaged by applying Early.

The trick, then, is being able to estimate your chances. Consult Chapter 3, "Deciding Where to Apply," and Chapter 4, "How to Use the Rankings," for a discussion of the relevant factors. Then discuss the specifics of your case with a knowledgeable college counselor, preferably your high school counselor. A good high school counselor is likely to have detailed information about the admission success of recent graduates of your school, which should allow the two of you to estimate your chances via a bit of extrapolation. For instance, you may see that in the last two years, twelve seniors from your school have applied Regular Decision to a handful of schools approximately as selective as your target school. You can see the results each senior had and, with your counselor's help, determine how strong a candidate you are relative to each of the dozen.

EARLY APPLICATION BENEFITS FOR *BWRKs*

Students who are considered good academic performers with nothing extra special to offer are often termed "bright, well-rounded kids"—or BWRKs, in admissions jargon. If your high school record is strong, your test scores fall around the median of those submitted by a college's most recent incoming class, and your extracurricular involvement and leadership are healthy, but you do not possess any hook (by virtue of your race, ethnicity, geographic origins, legacy, or athletic recruit status, etc.) that will set you apart from other similarly solid candidates, you are likely to be considered a BWRK.

In a prior age, being considered a bright, well-rounded kid was an advantage in the college admissions game. That has not been the case, however, for more than a generation. Colleges now seek "hooked" candidates (discussed in detail in Chapter 7). In fact, a substantial majority of a leading school's incoming class will consist of legacies, development cases, recruited athletes, and the like—people with hooks, in other words. Those who are not legacies, development cases, or recruited athletes or musicians therefore face an uphill battle.

Most colleges, however, will end up taking some BWRK applicants. Given the large number of BWRKs they have to choose from, they prefer to do so as painlessly as possible. (Limiting the number of offers they make to fill their class not only cuts down on their workload but also helps their *U.S. News* ranking.) This means that they would prefer to accept only those who (appear to) adore their college and are guaranteed to matriculate if accepted. Thus, they favor BWRKs who apply Early Decision (and, to a lesser extent, Early Action).

Note, however, that this admissions benefit will be more than outweighed if you end up admitted to a school that turns out to be a poor fit for you.

YOUR CREDENTIALS WILL NOT IMPROVE SUBSTANTIALLY DURING YOUR SENIOR YEAR

If you are not going to improve your profile substantially early in your senior year, you may benefit from applying Early Decision. On the other hand, if you will be a much stronger applicant in a few months, this additional strength may outweigh the Early application advantage. An applicant whose academic performance has improved of late, particularly in the second half of junior year, may wish to consider his likely performance in the first half of senior year. If he is headed for very strong first-semester grades, he is probably better off waiting for Regular Admissions. The same is true for other types of performance as well: standardized tests, athletics, performing arts, and so on.

YOU DO NOT NEED SUBSTANTIAL FINANCIAL AID

Some schools give lesser aid packages to those who apply Early because these applicants are committed to attending. If you do not need or will not qualify for financial aid, the chance of missing out on some financial aid dollars is obviously irrelevant to your decision making. On the other hand, if maximizing financial aid is important to you, having an opportunity to consider various schools' aid offers—and perhaps to bargain with some of them—will push you toward applying Regular Decision. (The strategic implications of your financial situation are discussed in Chapter 20.)

OR, YOU NEED SUBSTANTIAL FINANCIAL AID, BUT
YOUR TARGET SCHOOL FULLY MEETS FINANCIAL NEED

Even if you need financial aid, you need not apply to multiple schools—with the intention of comparing (and perhaps bargaining over) aid offers—if your target school gives financial aid only on the basis of need (rather than merit) and clearly meets the full financial need of its admitted students. A school such as Princeton, for instance, has long since determined that it would expect little self-help (loans and work) from its admitted students. Also, its aid offers are not dependent upon whether a student was admitted Early or Regular. Thus, applying Early to a school such as this does not involve a financial aid penalty.

The tricky part may be ascertaining whether your target school is one of these generous schools. Recognize first that the schools with generous financial aid policies tend to be among the country's most selective and to have the largest endowments. With this in mind, examine the stated financial aid policies of your target school. A school that describes itself as meeting full financial need is what you want. Consult the various personal finance magazines, such as *Consumer Digest*, *Kiplinger's*, and *Money*, which run articles showing the extent to which different colleges meet applicants' financial need. Finally, check with your college counselor, who may well have additional sources of information about the school's aid policies.

You Are Organized Early Enough in Your Senior Year to Do a Good Application

Applying Early confers a potential admissions advantage, but only if your application is well done. A hasty application that does not reflect suitable thoughtfulness on your part is likely to dissipate that advantage, thereby wasting an opportunity. If you decide to apply Early only days before the Early deadline, it is likely a bad idea. Not only will you probably put together a less than optimal application, but the timing of your decision also suggests that you have not done sufficient homework about yourself and colleges to be reasonably sure of having found the right college for you.

IMPLICATIONS OF EARLY APPLICATION

The potential admissions impact of applying Early is sufficiently great to warrant seriously considering it. This does not mean that you should necessarily apply Early, but you should certainly start the process junior year so that applying Early will remain a viable option for you. Take the following steps:

■ Assess your own needs and potential college choices early on. You cannot leave these matters to the summer before senior year. Making hasty decisions about colleges invites disaster. You need to know what matters most to you and what schools best fit your criteria long before an Early application deadline.

■ Take the standardized tests early enough to reach your potential for Early application. This means taking at least some of them junior year.

■ Determine your chances of admission at the schools of interest to you, so that you can start making the strategic trade-offs between first and lesser choices discussed in the previous section.

- Assess your financial aid needs with your parents in a realistic fashion. Then examine the financial aid profile of your target schools to determine which of them are viable Early application targets for you.

- Start putting together your application during the summer before senior year. Writing suitable essays, sourcing recommendations (with enough time given to your recommenders to write on your behalf), and completing the various application elements soaks up more time than you will have available during the first half of senior fall term. We recommend that you at least have good drafts of your essays before school starts.

BACKING OUT OF AN EARLY DECISION ACCEPTANCE

Some applicants, no longer wishing to attend their Early Decision choice, try to back out of their acceptance. Colleges will generally permit a student to back out if the family considers the financial aid package insufficient. Some colleges will permit a student to back out for other reasons, such as not wanting to attend a college her parents pushed her toward or failing to get into an academic program they wanted.

On the other hand, colleges do everything they can to prevent students from trying simply to trade up to a more prestigious college. Consider, for instance, a student who applies Early Decision to Tufts and is accepted. If she applies regular decision to Harvard and is accepted, Tufts is not likely to permit her to ignore her agreement to attend it because she now has a better offer. Instead, Tufts will contact Harvard to see that it rescinds its admissions offer (which it will do). In fact, many colleges exchange Early admission lists to prevent this from happening in the first place. High schools, fearful that this sort of behavior will damage the chances of their future applicants, also tend to police this.

ADMISSIONS DIRECTORS TALK ABOUT EARLY DECISION

WHAT EARLY APPLICATION SYSTEM DO YOU HAVE? WHY?

We know that there are a number of students every year who have figured out by the fall of their senior year that MIT is the place they most want to come. We let them apply Early, and if they are admitted it can be a real stress reliever for the rest of their senior year. But our Early Action program is very student-centric. Students are free to apply Early to MIT and apply Early elsewhere (provided those other schools allow it). Our Early Action program is not binding, which means that if you are admitted Early, you do not have to attend. *Stuart Schmill, MIT*

Middlebury uses binding Early Decision. What we like about it is that it encourages students to go through the full process of truly deciding whether Middlebury is their first choice. *Robert Clagett, Middlebury*

We use the Early Decision option. We feel it gives students an opportunity to indicate their desire if they truly would like to matriculate at Vanderbilt as their first choice. We only believe in Early Decision if it is run in a holistic manner as part of the full process. When schools give too many spots away in Early Decision, they risk the less sophisticated students in the college application process being disadvantaged. Early Decision has to be run in an ethical manner. *Douglas Christiansen, Vanderbilt*

The original intent of Early Decision programs was to give students an opportunity to indicate that a particular school appeals more than any other. Now Early Decision programs have become a way for applicants (and institutions) to try and game the system. We have tried to restore the original intent of Early Decision by offering a binding Early Decision option only. *Lee Coffin, Tufts*

Our Early Decision process enables us to be more focused in the crafting of our class. We can be assured that we are getting that cellist, or that student from Bulgaria. It gives us a little more control, and it gives students a little more control in knowing where they are headed early on. *Chris Gruber, Davidson*

We do Early Action with the limitation that people applying Early Action cannot at the same time apply Early Decision somewhere where they're bound. Otherwise, they can apply anywhere else they want at any time. The advantage of this system is that we have an applicant pool of very strong applicants who are not yet necessarily ready to commit and it allows us to select the best candidates we possibly can. We don't care so much how much the candidate wants to come here as how much we want them. *Charles Deacon, Georgetown*

We have a nonbinding Early Action program at Notre Dame. Students accepted Early are invited to come back and spend time to see if it really is a good match. *Daniel J. Saracino, Notre Dame*

We used to have a binding Early Decision alternative, but we got tired of students asking questions about admissions rather than questions about the character of our school. *Stephen Farmer, UNC Chapel Hill*

We are a unique enough place that you don't apply to Bryn Mawr on a whim. We have the luxury of Early Decision applicants who tend to know us well and know what they are getting. *Jennifer Rickard, Bryn Mawr*

The reason we have a second round of Early Decision is to provide that option for students who haven't known about Wesleyan all along, who discover us during the fall of senior year, or for whom their fall semester senior grades are going to be an important factor in the admission decision. The November Early Decision pool is very homogeneous—mostly white, affluent, East Coast kids who have known about Wesleyan for a long time, usually visited once or twice before senior year, and known others who have attended. ED II draws more students from outside the northeast and from a broader range of backgrounds. *Nancy Hargrave Meislahn, Wesleyan*

We have a second round of Early Decision at Pomona because there are students who come to their decision a bit later than the first round allows. Many are involved in sports or other activities that make it difficult to focus on the college choice earlier. Others have just come later to the information. *Bruce Poch, Pomona*

Georgia Tech does not offer an Early Admissions option. We do not want to add an additional layer of pressure for students to commit to our school without fully exploring their options. That's not to say that this is the intent of schools that do use this method; it's simply that we choose not to. *Ingrid Hayes, Georgia Tech*

WHO SHOULD/SHOULD NOT APPLY EARLY? FOR WHOM DOES IT NOT MUCH MATTER?

A student should apply Early if they have gone through the full process of learning about different schools and found the best fit for their needs. I like the Early Decision option because it allows students to know where they are going earlier in the process, which can alleviate a lot of stress. However, Early Decision doesn't work if the student is simply trying to game the process to get into a selective school. The most critical component of the application process is trying to match specific students to specific schools where they will have the most success in and outside of the classroom. Gaming an Early Decision process doesn't serve this goal. *Douglas Christiansen, Vanderbilt*

Students should be careful not to apply Early to a school as part of an admissions strategy. Applying Early to a school is a way of demonstrating intent to come. If you do not intend to come, or are not sure about your choice yet, you do yourself a disservice by applying Early. *Paul Marthers, Reed*

Early Decision is good for very, very few students. Students change between October and April of their senior years, often tremendously. Committing yourself in October means you need to be very sure of where you want to go. Nonbinding Early Action, on the other hand, is not so constraining. It requires that you be organized, nearing the end of your college search, and able to get your application in by November 1. You don't need to commit until May 1. *Rick Bischoff, Cal Tech*

Don't apply Early if you are simply looking for admissions leverage. Early Decision works best when it is approached in its purest form: when a clear first choice emerges after thorough research, a campus visit, and careful consideration. *Tim Cheney, Connecticut College*

Anyone can apply Early, but we're going to restrict admission to those who are high in everything. Not only must they have strong personal characteristics but in this case they also need to have a strong academic record in every respect: grades, test scores, etc. In the regular pool, we're much more willing to let strong personal characteristics overcome a less than very top academic record, but Early must be top across the board. *Charles Deacon, Georgetown*

If a student wishes to include first semester or trimester senior year grades or specific standardized tests, Early Decision Round II rather than Early Decision Round I may be the best option for them. *Tim Cheney, Connecticut College*

How Much Impact Does Applying Early Have?

Without getting into the complexities of managing enrollment using rolling admissions at a very selective school, suffice it to say we strongly encourage students to apply Early to maximize our consideration of the application for admission. *Theodore Spencer, Michigan*

Applying Early has little or no impact on admissions decisions. If anything, the bar for the Early Admissions pool is raised a bit. If there is any doubt about a file, we will defer. It's important for students to understand that there is no strategic advantage to applying Early. They should only do so if they have decided through careful thinking that Middlebury is their first choice. *Robert Clagett, Middlebury*

There is no disadvantage to applying Early at MIT, so I would never discourage anyone from applying Early here. However, it will not help your admissions chances to apply early to MIT, so doing so should just be a reflection of where you are in the search process. If you are far along, applying Early can make sense. If not, it's not going to hurt your admissions chances to wait and apply regular action. *Stuart Schmill, MIT*

Applying Early gives applicants a slight advantage at Reed—it can be the tiebreaker because, all other things being equal, it shows us that the student is committed to coming here. *Paul Marthers, Reed*

At Notre Dame, we do not give preference to Early applicants. In fact, the quality of the Early applicant pool tends to be better, making it more competitive. Students with a modest academic record will not gain any advantage by applying Early here. *Daniel J. Saracino, Notre Dame*

Applying Early does make a difference in terms of signaling to admissions that you've made a commitment to our school. During Regular Decision, the admission committee reads and reviews nearly 4,000 applications for approximately 300 remaining places in the freshman class, but the committee has no way of knowing if Connecticut College is your first choice or your safety school.   *Tim Cheney, Connecticut College*

We apply the same admissions standards to Early applicants as to those in the regular pool. Students should not expect to be getting a leg up in admissions by applying Early to Tufts.   *Lee Coffin, Tufts*

If you look at it statistically, which cagey parents do, we accept a higher percent of the Early applicant pool than we do in the regular round. Does it make a difference? Yes, but only for a handful of kids.   *Steve Thomas, Colby*

We're probably the only college in the country that will admit only the same percentage—or at a lower percentage rate—we use for Regular Admission, which is about 20 percent.   *Charles Deacon, Georgetown*

There is no advantage in terms of admissions rates to applying Early Decision to the College of William and Mary. The advantage for the student is knowing as early as December of the senior year where he or she will be next fall.   *Kimberly Van Deusen, William & Mary*

What Are the Most Common Mistakes Students Make Regarding Early Application/Decision?

I have come across students who have explained, "I am applying Early, I just don't know where." That is the wrong approach. You should think about an Early Decision application after your college search has concluded and you realize there is a clear front-runner. If you don't have that sense, don't limit yourself by applying Early to a school you are not 100 percent sure about.   *Lee Coffin, Tufts*

I often advise high school students not to settle on a school too early in their high school careers. Remember that interests and learning styles change. Give yourself room to grow.   *Stuart Schmill, MIT*

When students are thinking about a binding Early Decision commitment, they should be doing so for the right reasons: because they have already visited and done their research and know that a college is RIGHT for them. Most don't know this so early—again, because of all the choices. Early Decision is not about "hurrying up and getting it over with"—tempting though that may be.   *Nanette Tarbouni, Washington University (St. Louis)*

Do Your Offers of Aid Differ for Those Applying Early?

Applying Early does not affect offers of need-based aid, but it does affect offers of merit-based aid. We don't require a separate scholarship application. The university's Office of Financial Aid, and the specific schools and colleges, use the admissions application as scholarship application. They immediately start reviewing files of admitted students for consideration for merit aid. To be competitive for merit-based aid we recommend students apply as early as possible, but certainly before December 1. *Theodore Spencer, Michigan*

Some schools give less money to Early admits on the theory that they will come no matter what aid they are provided. We consider this unethical. All our financial aid is based upon "need," not on perceived desires of students. *Daniel J. Saracino, Notre Dame*

We don't offer students who apply Early Decision any less grant money because they applied Early. Whether or not you apply Early has no impact on the amount of financial aid you will get. *Thyra Briggs, Harvey Mudd*

Aid offers do not differ for those who apply Early. We do nothing differently in calculating Early applicant and Regular applicant aid. *Steve Thomas, Colby*

Our offers of financial aid are exactly the same for those applying Early and those not. *Rick Bischoff, Cal Tech*

What Happens to Applicants Who Are Not Accepted?

No one is denied early. We simply accept or defer [until Regular Admission]. *Charles Deacon, Georgetown*

Students that apply Early to Bennington and are not admitted by December are automatically deferred to the Regular Decision pool of applicants. Not being admitted Early Decision in no way affects your ability to get in during Regular Decision. *Ken Himmelman, Bennington*

Early Decision candidates are telling us that their interest in Northwestern is very high. In light of this strong and well-informed interest, we offer admission to all those we can. If we cannot offer admission to a candidate, we say so rather than offer to defer for later consideration. This is different from what other schools with Early Decision do. *Sheppard Shanley, Northwestern*

WHAT AN APPLICATION REQUIRES

THE ELEMENTS OF THE APPLICATION

Applications to college generally require the following elements, which together provide the set of criteria on which you will be evaluated for admission. (Note that larger universities and less selective colleges might not require all of the following.)

■ High school transcript

■ High school profile

■ Standardized test scores

■ Written application (including basic data sheets, activity lists, short answers, and essays)

■ Financial aid application (if you are applying for financial aid)

■ Interview

■ Counselor recommendation/Secondary School Report

■ Teacher recommendations (one or more)

The **high school transcript** is the official record of all your classes and grades over three years; grades from the senior fall are also evaluated (except in the case of Early Action and Early Decision applicants, who are sometimes required to file unofficial quarter grades). Senior fall grades are often called "seventh semester" grades.

A **high school profile** is provided by the counselor at your school. The profile contains a description of your high school and its students. It often also offers information about your school's mission and philosophy, course offerings, grading scale, and which colleges (or types of colleges) recent graduates have chosen to attend.

Standardized test scores are the results from your SAT and ACT tests. Most colleges will also evaluate Advanced Placement (AP) scores if included.

The **written application** consists of several pieces. At a minimum, the basic application requires forms with identification and background information. Most applications, including the Common Application, ask for lists of your activities, including your specific roles, the amount of time you dedicated, and the length of your participation. Some applications also require short-answer responses, and one or more longer essays.

The **financial aid application** contains basic information about your family's income, assets, and financial situation, and generally requires detailed information from the most recent year's tax form. Some colleges require that you file only the Free Application for Federal Student Aid (FAFSA) or the College Board's Profile; other colleges require their own forms in addition to one or both of the above. (See Chapter 20 for more information.)

Some colleges offer or require an **interview**, either on-campus or in your local area. These may be conducted by college admissions officers, alumni of the college, or, in some cases, current students of the college.

Most private colleges and some public universities require an applicant to submit a **counselor recommendation** and/or a **Secondary School Report**. Such a report is generally based on information the counselor gathers from the student's teachers and administrators. It is meant to be a comprehensive recommendation that both highlights an applicant's strengths and weaknesses and provides the necessary context for this candidacy to be evaluated.

Most colleges ask for one or two **teacher recommendations**, although some will permit more to be filed.

Each of these important parts of the application is discussed in detail in Part II of this book, except for financial aid, which is discussed in Part V.

OBJECTIVE CREDENTIALS VERSUS SUBJECTIVE PRESENTATION

The high school transcript, high school profile, and standardized test scores together make up your academic credentials. Academic credentials are bits of hard, objective information that, for the most part, you can do little about changing after the fact of your performance. There are ways in which you can overcome the impact of a negative grade or negative test score, or compensate for a weakness in your record, but there is nothing you can do to change the original record itself. (See Chapter 8 for further details on how to make up for academic weaknesses after the fact.)

The credentials you bring to the application are one thing, but your presentation of them is another. Your presentation, which is conveyed through the written application, the interview, and the recommendations, matters a great deal for several reasons. Most important, you have the opportunity to color the interpretation of all the objective data—your academic credentials—by providing a context and explaining how all of the different pieces fit together. The objective data can look quite a bit different when viewed through a subjective lens. Strong credentials lose their ability to impress when the supporting presentation is not compelling. Weak credentials are boosted when the supporting presentation is particularly powerful.

In addition, sharp admissions officers will cross-check the information provided in the various parts of your application for consistency. They will compare your essay assertions, for example, with what you say (and how you say it) in your interviews, to get as honest a picture of you as possible. This means that your presentation must be meaningful and fine-tuned.

Your total presentation (delivered through the written application, interview, and recommendations) also provides information that is important to admissions decisions yet not evidenced by the objective credentials. This subjective information is crucial to the overall picture that is created. The essays, for example, reveal your writing ability and your ability to sustain a closely reasoned argument. The recommendations reveal the extent to which you have impressed your teachers and also qualities such as intellectual passion. The interviews reveal your personality, oral communication skills, and maturity, among other traits.

Although it is always easier to make an impressive presentation when your substantive credentials are strong, the extent to which you take full advantage of the opportunity to present your case as effectively as possible can change how the admissions officers think about you. Because of their role in your presentation, we regard the written application (particularly the essays, but also the nonacademic activity presentation and short-answer responses), the interview, and the recommendations as your three main presentation vehicles. Each of these is discussed in further detail in Part II.

MIT EXPLAINS THE GOALS OF ADMISSIONS COMMITTEES

The goal of the admissions process is to create a community that bubbles with motivated, passionate students. We start with people we know can handle the work, then mix in an unpredictable blend of interests, talents, and activities.

There's room for all types, from the kid whose main hobby is cloning dinosaurs to the jazz pianist to the captain of the All-State soccer team. That means we don't have a magic formula for the perfect applicant. We look for intellectual commitment and potential, creativity, and character. Those are not exactly quantifiable but we can tease them out of the information you supply.

Most of our applicants have top-notch academic credentials, so we look beyond the numbers. We base our more subjective evaluation of your personal characteristics on the application itself and the letters of recommendation, secondary school report, and interview. The application forms are designed to allow you to describe what makes you tick: use them to describe your activities, personality, interests, and dreams. Your activities list gives us a sense of how you spend your time outside the classroom, while teacher references offer insight into how you do in the classroom and school community. *Application for Freshman Admission and Financial Aid*

THE EVALUATION CRITERIA

Through these many materials—from the high school transcript down through the letters of recommendation—a college's admissions committee can gather all the information on which they examine their candidates. The colleges are most concerned about your academic record, but it is important to recognize that this is only one piece of the complete picture they will take from your application. The most fundamental criteria on which admissions officers evaluate prospective students are:

- Academic and intellectual potential,
- Nonacademic pursuits and talents, and
- Personal attributes.

These main elements that they seek are evidenced in different ways and to different degrees by the elements of your application discussed previously. The following chart explains where the admissions committees look to find out whether you have the academic potential, nonacademic pursuits, and personal attributes they desire.

CRITERIA	PRIMARY SOURCES	SECONDARY SOURCES
Academic/intellectual potential:	High school transcript High school profile Standardized test scores Recommendations	Written application Interview
Nonacademic pursuits/talents:	Written application	Interview Recommendations
Personal attributes:	Written application Interview Recommendations	

ACADEMIC AND INTELLECTUAL POTENTIAL

In terms of academics, the most selective colleges of course want to see top grades and scores. They also look for students who have consistently performed well or improved academically over time; the selective schools are not inclined to admit students who provide evidence of strong academic performance in the past but have regressed over time. Just as importantly, though, the more selective the college, the more it will require that you challenge yourself by taking the most rigorous courseload available to you. Admissions committees also learn about certain aspects of your personality through academics. All colleges are looking for students who like to challenge themselves intellectually, test their limits, expand their knowledge, and investigate their curiosities. They like students who express enthusiasm for the learning process and passion for particular subject areas. See Chapter 8 for further information about the academic credentials colleges value most.

NONACADEMIC PURSUITS AND TALENTS

In terms of nonacademics, the colleges are most interested in seeing how you spend your time outside of the classroom and what kind of person you are, as demonstrated by what you do. If you have a special nonacademic talent, then the level of your accomplishment in that activity can substantially help you gain the attention of admissions officers. For others without particularly advanced or specialized nonacademic talents, it does not matter what worthwhile activities you enjoy as long as you demonstrate commitment to certain ones among them (through the length of time you have participated in them and the number of hours you devote to them) and can discuss *why* these endeavors matter to you above others. Colleges also generally want to see that applicants have taken full advantage of the opportunities given to them.

Excellence in and special commitment to certain activities is important, while trying to demonstrate that you do a little bit of everything is not ideal. Still, some versatility is advisable. The colleges are looking for students who possess particular strengths but are also complex, multidimensional human beings. One-dimensional candidates—even talented one-dimensional candidates—appear dull and unimpressive when matched against candidates with a multitude of orientations, values, and pursuits. A brilliant computer whiz kid who devotes every spare moment to working in computer labs and designing software does not match up to a brilliant computer whiz kid who also publishes poetry or raises seeing-eye dogs for the blind. See Chapter 9 for more information on how to build an impressive profile of nonacademic pursuits.

PERSONAL ATTRIBUTES

Just as with academics, college admissions committees can learn about your personality traits by the way you describe and discuss your extracurricular activities and other life experiences. Some of the personal traits colleges tend to look for in prospective students include the following:

Passion	Devotion	**Interpersonal**	Leadership
	Commitment	**Skills**	Teamwork
	Enthusiasm		Cooperation
	Energy		Sense of humor
	Dedication to	**Creativity**	Entrepreneurism
	learning		Originality
Perseverance	Follow-through		Innovation
	Ability to		Imagination
	overcome	**Maturity**	Independence
	obstacles		Judgment
	Fortitude		Thoughtfulness
Compassion	Kindness	**Honesty**	Integrity
	Humanity		Honor
	Generosity		Morality
	Selflessness	**Curiosity**	Adventurousness
	Community		Willingness to take
	awareness		calculated risks
	Tolerance		Inquisitiveness

Before applying to colleges, you will need to think about which of the preceding characteristics you possess (and which are most clearly emphasized through the evidence you can make available to admissions officers). It is important to make your most desirable personal attributes well known through the academics, extracurricular activities, and life experiences you present in your applications. There is no one prescription or formula that you can follow to give the admissions committees what they are looking for. The reason for this is quite simple: The top colleges are not looking for one particular type of applicant.

The most selective colleges want to include in their classes as many different kinds of people as possible—people who, despite being different in their backgrounds and strengths, are nonetheless similar in that they are all talented and special in some way. All colleges desire well-rounded *classes,* meaning classes composed of a wide range of individuals. They do not, however, necessarily want to populate those classes with well-rounded *people,* contrary to popular myth. Successful applicants are not those who show evidence of doing or being a little bit of everything. Successful applicants are instead those who show that they excel and surpass others, whether it be with their academic pursuits, nonacademic talents, personal attributes, or some combination of the three. Attaining such excellence nearly always requires the kind of focus that prevents one from doing or being many other things. The most successful applicants are those who can prove to the admissions committees that their excellence—attained in as few as one, two, or three areas—will allow them to better contribute to and benefit from an education at a top college than other applicants would.

THE ROLE OF DIVERSITY IN ADMISSIONS

Admissions decisions are more complicated than the three basic admissions criteria suggest because the desire for diversity is thrown into the mix. Nearly all colleges are committed to the virtues of diversity. The kind of diversity they desire goes beyond creating a community that is merely well-rounded in terms of the academic talents, nonacademic pursuits, and personal characteristics contained therein.

The leading institutions of higher education strongly uphold the value of incorporating a wide variety of people in their communities in order to spread the value of higher education; create learning environments that are representative of a wealth of ideas; improve the number and strength of academic and nonacademic pursuits on their campuses; and increase communitywide tolerance for differences in thought, belief, or culture. In diversifying their classes, the colleges want to include not only students who represent a wide variety of academic talents, nonacademic pursuits, and personalities, but also students who represent a wide variety of races, ethnicities, nationalities, geographical locations, family backgrounds, and personal histories.

In creating an environment that supports a diversity of ideas, the college admissions officers are looking for students of all shapes and sizes—this includes a variety of minority students and international applicants, those from single-parent households as well as from large united families, those from the inner city as well as from remote rural areas, and those with unique religious or philosophical outlooks. Some admissions officers focus on looking beyond superficial labels (such as "Latino" or "resident of California") to find *real* diversity. In other words, if you claim a certain background or label but do not evidence any sort of connection to it, you may not be considered as valuable to the college as someone who clearly identifies with that background or label. You cannot rely only on brief tags and labels to convince an admissions committee that you will add to its desired mix of students.

The desire for diversity means that each candidate is judged not only as an individual but also as one of many individuals who make up a class and a community. Each candidate is evaluated on the basis of how he or she can contribute to campus life and complement the virtues of the others admitted alongside him or her. A candidate whose academic potential is not deemed as strong as others in the applicant pool might be admitted over others because he hails from a small town in Arkansas, a state with little representation in the applicant pool, and is a fine trombone player, desperately sought by the college's marching band. Another candidate might be regarded especially highly by the admissions committee because, alongside her strong academic record, she represents the first generation in her Ukrainian immigrant family to attend college. Another candidate might rise above other upper-middle-class white males from the Northeast because of his particular draw as an All-State hockey champion and his leadership as the head of a community society for the prevention of cruelty to animals.

Thus, the admissions committees weigh criteria differently depending upon the applicant. They do so in order to admit a wide variety of individuals into their classes, with the goal of improving and enhancing the education and experience that each member of the collegiate community receives.

ADMISSIONS DIRECTORS DISCUSS DIVERSITY

A diversity of ideas is what we're after. We're looking for students who will add something to the class: kids from single-parent households, students from small rural schools, others from big inner-city schools, students who have overcome serious challenges, original thinkers. *John Blackburn, University of Virginia*

We look to bring all perspectives, interests, opinions—especially those that are not well-represented in mainstream communities—to our campus. We are interested in all facets of diversity, including diversity of political views or sexual orientation. Often, however, certain unusual or rare aspects of a person's experience or way of looking at the world are not brought to our attention, so we are not in a position to take them into account in evaluating a candidate. *Katie Fretwell, Amherst*

I find it's important to look beyond the superficial labels to find real diversity. Someone whose family has for generations lived in southern Florida is very different from a candidate who now happens to live in Florida but just moved there a year and a half ago from Long Island. *Nancy Hargrave Meislahn, Wesleyan*

This institution is mission-driven and committed to serve the state and we want to represent the whole of the state. We seek ethnic, cultural, international, high school background, and geographic diversity, and to expose our top-ranked programs to a national and international group of prospective undergraduates. *Kedra Ishop, Texas (Austin)*

As a state school, we look for diversity throughout the state. Applicants from different parts of Virginia offer different strengths, and we want our student body to reflect that diversity. *Kimberly Van Deusen, William & Mary*

We don't move into the admissions process with some overall game plan, but we *do* want to make sure we get a balanced class. We think part of a student's growth at Stanford comes from being exposed to different kids with different backgrounds and experiences. The student who grows up on a sheep ranch in Wyoming provides a nice contrast with an urban student from Los Angeles. *Rick Shaw, Stanford*

We're very conscious of building pools, so that we are never in the position of accepting a candidate just because she's the only one of her kind—let's say the only student from South Dakota—in the pool. We want diversity but we also want to keep our options open. *Katie Fretwell, Amherst*

We don't have to engineer our incoming class to include students of different backgrounds. That takes care of itself through the range of applications we receive. *Sheppard Shanley, Northwestern*

We want a class that represents a good cross-section of America. *Dan Walls, Emory*

STANFORD WARNS APPLICANTS
THAT THE SCHOOL'S AIM OF SHAPING AN ENTIRE CLASS
MEANS THAT SOME FACTORS IN ADMISSIONS ARE
BEYOND YOUR CONTROL

Bear in mind that while we are focusing on each individual applicant, we are also putting together a class that cuts across a number of dimensions. Consequently, many factors may enter into the process over which individual candidates have no control. A high proportion of those applying are capable of succeeding scholastically at Stanford, and many more academically qualified students apply each year than we have places for in the class. *Stanford Today*

THE ROLE OF "FIT" IN ADMISSIONS

Each college also possesses its own distinct personality and educational philosophy, which in turn governs the way in which its admissions committee evaluates applicants. Many applicants overlook the fact that schools of a similarly high quality are in fact very different places, and thus may have different emphases in terms of what they are looking for in their future students. These emphases play an even greater role in admissions as applicant pools grow and, more significantly, as the number of equally qualified students in those applicant pools increases. When forced to choose between several candidates of equal talent, a college's admissions team often looks for the best "fit" between a candidate and the school in order to make the best decision.

A fit or match between a student and a school can exist as a result of many different factors. Chapter 3 discusses many of the academic and nonacademic qualities you should examine before deciding which schools best fit your needs and where to apply. Fully examining these many characteristics when looking at colleges will help you not only determine which schools represent the best fit for you but also communicate this fit to the admissions committees. Admissions officers are pleased and impressed by an applicant who can provide evidence that their particular college offers the most ideal circumstances for the applicant's goals. An inner-city candidate wanting to attend Bowdoin or Dartmouth, for example, might write an essay about working as a Fresh Air Fund counselor in a small rural town. In showing how this experience helped him discover new skills and personal attributes, he can also incorporate a discussion of how he aims to build on these attributes by spending the next four years in a similar type of setting, thus providing evidence of a match between the school and himself.

THE ROLE OF EDUCATIONAL PHILOSOPHY IN DETERMINING "FIT"

A college's educational goals and philosophy represent the primary qualities with which admissions committees yearn to match applicants. MIT is a prime example of a college with a very distinct value system, which comes across clearly in its admissions procedures. MIT's culture is initiative-oriented. In order to succeed there, students have to be willing to take risks and even occasionally to fail at their endeavors. The admissions officers thus look for applicants who have demonstrated not only leadership and self-initiative but also resilience. The admissions committee wants students who are independent and who can claim responsibility for their own development and actions.

MIT's emphasis on initiative in admissions came about as a way in which to distinguish the most appropriate applicants from the rest of the talented pool. Some of the students who apply to MIT tend to have been pushed by their parents to succeed rather than creating goals and dreams of their own, which is something the school frowns upon. Applicants to MIT, keeping the school's values and educational philosophy in mind, will do themselves a great service by showing that they are capable of self-starting and risk taking.

The phrase Stanford's admissions officers use to describe the special quality that matters most to them is "intellectual vitality." Stanford relies on this value so much that it long ago adopted "Intellectual Vitality" as one of the areas in which all applicants are rated (on a scale from one to six) in the admissions evaluation process. A successful application to Stanford nearly requires that you be able to provide clear evidence of passion for intellectual endeavors, whether it be through discussing intellectual pursuits outside of the classroom, soliciting recommendations from teachers who can attest to your stimulation and initiative in pursuing academic subject matter, or writing an essay about a special academic commitment.

As another example, Amherst's admissions officers describe the college as a "very verbal place." Amherst's educational philosophy relies heavily on the importance of the written word, and this is emphasized in its admissions process. Amherst leans very heavily on the essays when evaluating applicants and does not interview candidates for admission at all. Candidates for admission to Amherst should take the school's particular emphasis on the written word to heart when completing its application.

Brown's method of education places a great deal of responsibility on the student through the lack of core curriculum and distribution requirements. Brown's admissions officers thus look closely at applicants to ascertain whether or not they can handle the academic independence and benefit rather than fall to pieces in a flexible academic environment. Any student applying to Brown should try as best as possible to give positive proof of intellectual independence (discuss independent projects, outline classes taken outside of school, or demonstrate your intellectual creativity) as well as demonstrate maturity and sound decision-making skills. Show the admissions officers that you are capable of succeeding without an academic road map.

Columbia's educational philosophy, on the other hand, is nearly the opposite of Brown's. Everyone at Columbia takes the Core Curriculum, a structured set of small seminar classes. The admissions officers thus look for candidates who demonstrate that they are well-suited to both the relative structure in the undergraduate curriculum and the educational philosophy that governs that structure. Applicants should be able to demonstrate that they seek an education that is, in part, somewhat inflexible and emphasizes traditional learning—i.e., studying the classics of Western literature and world civilizations.

It is important to realize that although the top schools are looking for many of the same general traits in their candidates, some are also looking for prospective students who possess particular characteristics deemed necessary to fulfilling the school's educational mission and goals. By doing your homework and knowing a school well, you can determine on your own what a particular college claims as its educational philosophy and communitywide values. Understanding what is fundamental to the life of a school will help you decide if that college is right for you as well as help you fashion your application with the proper foundation and ideals in mind. A college's educational mission, philosophy, and personality usually come across in admissions materials and brochures, campus websites, and conversations with admissions officers.

DEMONSTRATED INTEREST

Closely related to the idea of "fit" in college admissions is what colleges often call demonstrated interest or demonstrated intent (to attend). In an effort to gauge both which students are truly excited about their college and which students are most likely to attend their college, many admissions offices at private schools now track demonstrated interest. In other words, they record information about how much contact you have had with the college in performing your application research and in applying.

At some colleges, the amount of interest you have demonstrated counts very much in the admissions process, so it is generally best to follow the rule of making maximum contact with each private college to which you will apply. (At least insofar as in-state applicants are concerned, public universities are not concerned about "interest," given that they are meant to provide a service to local citizens. In addition, they face such large application volumes that tracking such interest would be burdensome. If you are applying to a public university out of state, however, it might help to demonstrate such interest.) It is just as important to demonstrate interest in colleges to which you figure you are likely to be admitted because safety schools are often the ones that look most closely at highly desirable candidates to determine whether they will actually attend if admitted. You have probably heard stories of the honors student with high SAT scores and extracurricular talents who did not get in anywhere, even though she applied to several "safety schools." It is likely that she did not show these schools that she was truly interested, resulting in the schools assuming that she would reject them (once she was admitted to a more competitive school). In order to keep their acceptance percentage as low as possible, these schools might have opted simply to reject her outright.

Many candidates believe that it takes a lot of money to demonstrate interest in a college, but this is not the case. Of course one of the ways to demonstrate your enthusiasm is to visit the campus, but you may not be able to visit all the schools that interest you. There are, however, other ways to show your interest. You can request to be put on the school's mailing list; attend the college representative's visit at your school; attend a college fair or consortium in your area where the college will be represented; ask to interview with the school, whether or not an interview is mandatory; strike up an email or telephone correspondence with an admissions officer; or become friendly with one or more students, professors, or coaches through email or telephone inquiries. Similarly, you can develop a relationship with your chosen college's regional representative (the person assigned to your state or region), who is tasked with visiting your school and attending local college fairs. It is also important to keep your college counselor apprised of which school or schools remain favorites, so he can notify the relevant admissions officers when given the opportunity.

ADMISSIONS DIRECTORS DISCUSS WHAT IMPORTANT ISSUES CANDIDATES SHOULD CONSIDER WHEN COMPLETING COLLEGE APPLICATIONS

How Important Is It That a Student Demonstrate Fit with a Particular College?

If we feel that an applicant does not know Brown, or states a determination to do something we don't offer here, chances are we might not take him. *Michael Goldberger, Brown*

"Fit" is critical. It is important that a candidate fits with Wesleyan's values and expectations. For example, ours is an open, flexible curriculum; there is no core. A student coming to Wesleyan needs to be prepared to take responsibility for his or her own education, be the driving force, and be ready to work closely with faculty advisers. *Nancy Hargrave Meislahn, Wesleyan*

"Fit" is a complex issue. We want to know, if a candidate attends Stanford, how will he or she play a role in who we are. The 8,000-acre, self-contained campus makes this a place oriented toward community; there are 640 plus organizations to be a part of. We want to measure how well candidates match to our focus and atmosphere. *Rick Shaw, Stanford*

"Fit" is crucial. We go beyond the assessment of whether a student can succeed here academically. This isn't the kind of institution where you can muddle through for four years and everything will be okay. You need to want to think about and talk about science all the time—like everyone here does. *Rick Bischoff, Cal Tech*

We have some fundamental expectations for how a student will take advantage of their Haverford experience and, as such, demonstrate their fit: that they will invest in the residential experience, for instance, and that they will invest in the liberal arts approach to academics—valuing a broad range of courses. We pay attention to these matters and define "fit" along these lines. But when we talk about fit, we are not talking about all of our students being the same, and we certainly do not mean things like whether an applicant will be close to the average socioeconomic background or the political views of other students here. *Jess Lord, Haverford*

For us, demonstrating "fit" is extremely important. Use the personal essays and interviews to show us why you believe you are a great fit for our community. *Tim Cheney, Connecticut College*

Amherst is a very verbal place—we're very committed to the written word. And this is emphasized in our admissions process. We look for students who we think appreciate and can contribute to our ideals. *Katie Fretwell, Amherst*

How Does Your School's Institutional and Educational Philosophy Play a Role in Admissions?

Our curriculum puts more responsibility on the student. There is no core curriculum, there are no distribution requirements. So we need to look closely at applicants to be sure that we think they are prepared to take on this kind of independence and responsibility. *Michael Goldberger, Brown*

From our perspective, we offer a unique education. Everyone at Columbia takes the Core Curriculum, which is a structured set of small seminar classes. Our intellectual atmosphere and our location in the city of New York also create a very unique learning experience. It's very important to us that students be able to articulate that there is a match between themselves and Columbia. *Eric J. Furda, Columbia*

In our admissions statement, we talk about the importance of social justice. So to the extent we can, we hope people have exhibited some kind of concern for others through volunteering or in other ways. The desire to make the world a better place, rather than simply being involved in religious activities, is more likely to affect us. *Charles Deacon, Georgetown*

At MIT it's *what you do*, not where you come from. This sentiment is at the center of our educational and institutional philosophy, and it's at the center of our admissions philosophy, too. There are, for example, no legacy admits here. All groups are evaluated the same way; all admissions are based solely on merit. We don't lower the bar for any group. That philosophy infuses every aspect of this campus. *Stuart Schmill, MIT*

Our educational philosophy has a strong global orientation. This has always been one of Middlebury's strengths and unusual characteristics. There is a real overlap between this philosophy and admissions—we have a strong commitment to international admissions that carries through to the curriculum. *Robert Clagett, Middlebury*

Wellesley's mission is to educate women who will make a difference in the world. Everything we do in admissions is framed within that mission. Our priority is to extend Wellesley's reach to find students—who may come from many different experiences and backgrounds—who will fulfill that mission. *Jennifer Desjarlais, Wellesley*

How Important Is It That an Applicant Show Enthusiasm for Your College in the Application?

Early Decision is for those with a really compelling interest in Duke. Otherwise, the desire to attend Duke is not really a factor in admissions. We're interested in attracting the best possible students. We don't want to sacrifice the quality of the students for the sake of yield. *Christoph Guttentag, Duke*

We treat everyone who has applied as if they want to come to Brown. There are, however, things that can turn us off on a candidate because they signal a *lack* of care for our application—a poorly thought out presentation or misspellings, for example. *Michael Goldberger, Brown*

The only thing that really matters is whether or not we think you will be a good match to MIT—if we think the things you've done in (and out) of high school match the culture here, and if we think that you would thrive academically here. Telling us you love MIT or that it's your first choice doesn't help us make this determination. *Stuart Schmill, MIT*

It's always important that an applicant knows who we are. What is critical is that you use discretion and balance. Over-the-top "rah-rah Vanderbilt" is not good at all. We want to see that students know what Vanderbilt is about. But we don't want our egos stroked. Rather, we want to see that what the student likes about Vanderbilt matches that student's needs and interests. If a student can articulate why Vanderbilt specifically is a good match, that can go a long way. Empty praise of the school that does not demonstrate a good fit gets no traction. *Douglas Christiansen, Vanderbilt*

We don't ask specific questions about the applicant's level of interest in Middlebury in the application. That is not an admissions factor for us. We don't expect students to extol the virtues of Middlebury in their essays. It won't necessarily hurt you to do so, but we're far more interested in getting to know the applicant better. *Robert Clagett, Middlebury*

Desire to attend Penn doesn't *drive* our decisions but it can certainly *inform* our decisions. *Eric Kaplan, Penn*

We have a question on our application asking applicants how they became interested in Northwestern. The details, language, and slant of the answer can be important, but we do not use enthusiasm for Northwestern as an admissions criterion. If a student lives nearby we find it strange if she doesn't visit the campus. Obviously, if a candidate lives in Bangladesh, we won't necessarily expect a visit. *Sheppard Shanley, Northwestern*

A candidate's enthusiasm for the school is irrelevant in our decision-making process. *Maria Laskaris, Dartmouth*

It's not a factor. *John Blackburn, University of Virginia*

It's less gushing enthusiasm that we're looking for and more demonstration that a student understands what kind of institution we are. *Eric J. Furda, Columbia*

Is the applicant's desire to attend important? I don't let my staff ask this question. We're up against a lot of different great colleges. I don't want to get into playing the game of guessing who's going to come here. *Richard Steele, Bowdoin*

How Important Is It to Discuss What You Intend to Study?

We do ask for their top three choices of potential majors. We also recognize that 70 percent of those who come to Princeton change their minds, so we're not overly concerned about it. We do get interested in what they say if they have a clearly defined academic interest, but it's not a requirement for us. We admit students to Princeton, not to a department. *Janet Lavin Rapelye, Princeton*

Thinking about what you're interested in studying matters, but it doesn't matter which subject you intend to study. In other words, it isn't essential that you have figured out which subject you'll study; but it does matter that you devote serious thought to the issue rather than being undecided as a default. When you do indicate an area of interest on your application, though, we can use this to contextualize some of the choices you've made, such as courses you've chosen and extracurricular activities you've engaged in. *Jess Lord, Haverford*

What Is the Importance of Demonstrated Interest (Intent)?

With 16,000 applicants, seeing an applicant's enthusiasm for Princeton is not our overriding concern. For us it doesn't matter as much as their performance in the classroom, in their other activities, and in the development of their intellectual curiosity. We care most about whether they're ready to excel at Princeton, at a very high level. *Janet Lavin Rapelye, Princeton*

Interest in Emory can be a "tip" factor. It doesn't come into play all the time, but there certainly are cases where intense interest in Emory helps a student get in. This is particularly true for waitlisted students. Indifference, however, may result in a student failing to get in. A lack of research, lack of knowledge of the institution, or lack of taking the opportunity to interact with the admissions office can be detrimental. *Dan Walls, Emory*

"Demonstrated interest" is not a factor in admission to Smith. Students often change their minds in the senior year. In fact, in the weeks leading up to the May 1 deadline, many students are still changing their minds! That's part of what it means to be seventeen. I know that the better students get to know Smith, the more interested they become. How they feel about the college at the time of application may be different from how they feel in April. I want to give them the freedom to change during their senior year and not to pressure them into letting me know where Smith falls on their list. I assume they're really interested just by the fact that they applied. *Debra Shaver, Smith*

Showing enthusiasm for Haverford is a plus; this is, for example, one of the reasons we value Early Decision. It is not, however, a prerequisite for being a compelling candidate. What can hurt, however, is when we see a candidate who shows "active disinterest" in the school—not filling out the required supplement to the Common Application, for instance, or not showing up for scheduled interview appointments. *Jess Lord, Haverford*

We tend not to focus on demonstrated intent on the theory that we are trying to create a level playing field. Not everyone can come visit, and not everyone is knowledgeable that showing your desire to attend can be an important factor in college admissions. *Jennifer Rickard, Bryn Mawr*

The heightened interest in students' demonstrated intent to go to a particular school is a direct result of college applications becoming easier to submit. With the Common Application, and advent of online applications, students can apply to colleges with a simple "point and click." This trend has left colleges trying to figure out who's clicking to apply arbitrarily and who is genuinely interested in their school. *Lee Coffin, Tufts*

Interest is a part of the admissions decision, but we do not quantify it. If you want to play the "demonstrated intent" card, apply Early. That's what it's intended to tell us. *Steve Thomas, Colby*

Demonstrated intent is not part of our process. We keep track of campus visits for our own statistical analysis, but we do not rate students based on the number of contacts as some other schools do. *Kimberly Van Deusen, William & Mary*

DEMONSTRATING INTEREST

We keep a record of a student's contacts with Wesleyan, so we know in the admissions process how the student became interested in the school and whether he or she has visited campus, etc. This is not something that is factored into the admission decision formally, but it does help us to know how a student came to know and have interest in the university. *Nancy Hargrave Meislahn, Wesleyan*

There is no magic formula for measuring how interested someone is. On the other hand, it makes sense to check in with the admissions office and perhaps go through the formal welcome if you visit the campus, to make sure that your visit is registered. *Dan Walls, Emory*

As part of our effort to discern who is serious about Tufts, we ask students to tell us what it is about Tufts that appeals to them. When applicants tell us they want to come because Tufts is such a great school, we are far less impressed than we are by those who provide specific reasons—for example, their desire to study with a certain professor or take certain classes. *Lee Coffin, Tufts*

THE CANDIDATE EVALUATION PROCESS

WHO EVALUATES APPLICATIONS FOR ADMISSION

ADMISSIONS OFFICERS

The employees in a college admissions department include the senior admissions officers (directors, deans, and their associate or assistant counterparts); junior admissions officers; and the administrative staff. Senior admissions staff generally oversee the activities of others in the office and make final decisions about candidates when there is no consensus. They also usually take part in some or all of the duties of junior officers, which include talking to prospective students on campus; visiting high schools and attending college events in particular geographical areas; and evaluating candidates' files. Most admissions offices divide up the United States (by state or region) and the world (by country or region), assigning particular areas to each active admissions officer. An officer might be responsible, for example, for the following five geographical regions: Oregon-Washington; Florida; Illinois-Indiana-Ohio; the greater Los Angeles metropolitan region; and all the African nations. Responsibility for a geographical region requires that an admissions officer visit its high schools, getting to know the various guidance counselors and talking to students; attend college consortiums, fairs, and other regional events as a representative of the school; become the in-house authority on the area's high schools, communities, and culture; and oversee the applications from the region, making sure that they are evaluated properly during the admissions decisions.

The admissions officers at most colleges tend to be intelligent, perceptive, impressive people who, for the most part, attended leading colleges themselves. Many of them teach on their college campuses in addition to serving as admissions officers, have graduate degrees, and publish articles in industry journals and magazines. They are interested in both general educational issues and the educational priorities of young people. Most college admissions committees also include some junior staff members who are recent graduates of the college (or one of its peers). At many schools, acquiring one of these limited postgraduate positions in the admissions department is considered a very prestigious honor, one for which many seniors and other recent graduates compete. Thus, you can be sure that those reading your applications will be highly capable and well aware of what qualities make a successful student at a demanding college.

The officers at the top colleges are experienced in admissions and talented at evaluating all kinds of candidates, no matter what their particular strengths or selling points. They may or may not have advanced knowledge of a given subject—whether it be Swahili, gene therapy, or tap dancing—but that does not mean that they are incapable of evaluating a student with an interest or talent in it. After all, many food critics cannot cook.

You must therefore fashion your application so that it is impressive to an intelligent reader but comprehensible to someone unschooled in your particular areas of discussion. You need to explain anything that is not common knowledge, but should not make the mistake of "talking down" to your readers. Do not turn a serious subject into the "lite" fluff version in fear that a sophisticated discussion will befuddle your readers. These people are not dummies and they desperately want to be impressed by you. Furthermore, admissions officers defer to the opinions of faculty experts, when necessary, in evaluating candidates whose special talents they cannot measure themselves.

Faculty and Students

Some schools also include faculty or students on their selection committees. At Cornell, for example, there is faculty involvement in each of the committees responsible for admitting freshmen to the seven undergraduate schools. At some schools, faculty input is sought when evaluating students interested in studying particular academic fields. At Duke, for instance, engineering faculty help in the selection of engineering candidates but are otherwise not involved in admission. At some schools, such as Cal Tech, students are even involved in the admissions selections.

THE EVALUATION PROCESS: A GENERALIZED DESCRIPTION

Each college has a slightly different procedure for evaluating admissions files. At many schools, the process approximates the following scenario, with minor differences from school to school:

The evaluation process begins soon after the application deadline (or after Rolling Admissions begin) with a "first read," which is a thorough reading of everything in a candidate's file, for every application submitted. At some schools, the first reader of a given application is the admissions officer responsible for the geographical area in which the student lives; at other schools, files are divided alphabetically or sorted randomly between all the first readers. First reads are the longest and most careful evaluations of candidates; most schools ask their officers to spend between fifteen and thirty-five minutes when acting as the first reader of an applicant's folder.

First readers are usually responsible for filling out a form with hard data and basic information about the candidate. The data sheet provides information at a glance to readers who visit the file after the initial evaluation. They often include information such as class rank, standardized test scores, an applicant's race or ethnicity (if provided on the application), and any special status information (if the candidate, for example, is a legacy applicant or a recruited athlete, or possesses a special talent). The data sheet usually also includes ratings determined by the first and subsequent readers in a number of different areas, such as academics or extracurricular involvement. Most colleges use numerical ratings so that readers of an application can make judgments of candidates in a variety of areas, which become useful for purposes of comparison against other applicants.

At the end of a first read, the initial reader has the opportunity to indicate whether he or she thinks the candidate should be admitted, denied, or discussed further. Files generally then go to a second reader. The second reader also looks over all material in the file thoroughly and provides his or her own opinion as to whether the candidate should be admitted or denied, or falls somewhere between the two extremes. At many schools, if the first and second reader agree wholeheartedly that a candidate should be either admitted or denied, the folder does not generally go to a committee for further discussion but usually gets passed to a dean or director of admissions, who authorizes the decision to admit or deny the candidate. At most colleges, only the borderline applicants (usually a large majority of the applicant pool) are discussed in a committee setting.

The files of applicants who fall somewhere between the "certain admit" and "certain deny" categories, as well as those who received inconsistent evaluations from the first two readers, often go to a committee for further evaluation. Committees are made up of several people who present candidates to one another; talk about the applicants together; and then vote on whether to admit, deny, or waitlist each. As the admissions process moves ahead, the department usually keeps track of the entire pool of admitted candidates to determine what it looks like as a whole. At the end of the committee's decision-making process, the admissions department ensures that the class composition is ideal for its own diversity needs and goals before letters of acceptance are sent out. Sometimes last-minute adjustments or changes are made, for example, if there is a great gender imbalance or if the class is not deemed adequately diverse.

THE EVALUATION PROCESS: FEATURES UNIQUE TO PARTICULAR COLLEGES

The extent to which each school follows the basic pattern just described in its admissions evaluations differs.

READERS AND COMMITTEES

At some schools, more than two reads occur before a file is either decided on or sent to committee for further evaluation. At Middlebury, for instance, all candidates who are probable or possible admits, in the eyes of the first two readers, go to committee for evaluation. No one is admitted to Middlebury without a committee's agreement, although candidates can be denied without being discussed by the committee. Even so, all denied applicants are seen by at least four admissions staff members before the decision is made. Middlebury encourages disagreement among members as a way in which to ensure that each applicant is evaluated fairly, from a variety of perspectives.

Taking the group-decision philosophy to its extreme, some schools send *all* files to committee so that all candidates are discussed among many individuals before being admitted or denied admission. At Wellesley, for example, after the first two or three reads are completed, every candidate is discussed in committee and voted on. Harvard similarly makes no admissions decisions before sending a candidate's file to a committee discussion for final vote. No applicant to Wellesley or Harvard is accepted or rejected before being discussed and evaluated by a group of officers.

Some schools, on the opposite end of the spectrum, do not use formal committees or group decision-making structures at all. At Northwestern, for example, all officers read files individually. First or second readers hand all files—whether deemed probable acceptances or denials—to senior officers for final decisions. Four of the senior officers do nothing but make final decisions on candidates.

Stanford's evaluation process is unusual in that the first read is not a careful, in-depth evaluation but a quick skim intended to cut the applicant pool down to a more manageable size. This first step in Stanford's evaluation process is called "sorting." Only very experienced readers take care of the sorting round, in which brief reads result in denials for a large percentage of the applicants.

RATING SYSTEMS

The way in which each school rates its candidates also differs tremendously from school to school. Many colleges, for example, assign two codes to every applicant, one based on academics and the other based on personal criteria, which takes into consideration extracurricular involvement, special talents, and personal attributes.

At MIT, all applicants are evaluated in two ways in order to be placed on a graph or table that determines their desirability as candidates for admission. First, the admissions staff calculates a numeric index, or NI, for each candidate, using an algorithm that takes a student's grades, class rank, and standardized test scores (SAT and subject tests) into account. The NI is a number between one and five, with five being the best rating possible. Each candidate also gets a subjective rating—also on a one through five scale, with five being the best score—that is based on his or her cocurricular activities (learning-oriented activities outside of the classroom), interpersonal skills, and extracurricular activities. The objective rating is mapped backward on an *x*-axis and the subjective rating is mapped backward on a *y*-axis, so that every candidate ends up being placed in a "cell" on this table, with those located in the lower left-hand corner representing the admissions committee's top candidates.

RESOURCES

Bill Paul, *Getting In: Inside the College Admissions Process*. Somewhat dated look at the admissions process at Princeton, largely from the perspective of five applicants.

Jacques Steinberg, *The Gatekeepers: Inside the Admissions Process of a Premier College*. A look at the admissions process at Wesleyan from the perspective of one admissions officer.

Although both of these books are a bit dated, together they give a good feel for the two sides of the admissions process at selective colleges.

ADMISSIONS DIRECTORS EXPLAIN HOW THEIR CANDIDATE EVALUATION PROCESSES WORK

An outsider would consider our admissions process a very inefficient system; we are painstakingly thorough. *Marlyn McGrath Lewis, Harvard*

We look at the entire application and have a very holistic reading philosophy. We look at the whole person, not how they stack up against ten other applicants. Each file gets two reads. A third read is done by a more senior member of the admissions staff who signs off on the decision. Applications that fall in the middle ground go to a committee where they are vetted and discussed. *Douglas Christiansen, Vanderbilt*

Every student who is admitted, with no exceptions, has gone through at least five different stages. Every file is reviewed by most of the staff multiple times, and by senior staff at least twice. We have two different scales. One is objective (using a weighted average of grades and standardized test scores). Then we have a subjective scale, which includes level of engagement and talent on the academic side and level of engagement and talent on the non-academic side. Both scales are numerical and we use these numbers to come up with a grid. Where you fall on the grid informs the admissions committee, but we don't make cut offs or decisions based upon it. Every admissions decision is a very human decision. *Stuart Schmill, MIT*

Everybody from one area, from each high school, is presented together. This is not to compare kids against others from the same school. The purpose is so that we can get to know the high schools—their courses, teachers, grading systems— really well. Applicants are not competing against others from their high school, though. *Michael Goldberger, Brown*

Our evaluation process is rather complex because we need to adjust our thoughts for four different undergraduate schools, as well as for in-state and out-of-state applicants. *John Blackburn, University of Virginia*

Our process is cumbersome, but we feel we really know the candidates by the end. *Richard Steele, Bowdoin*

There's still an art to admissions. You can't capture the process through a formula. *Dan Walls, Emory*

We first make tentative decisions about our class. Then in mid-March we do a number of reviews to see what various subgroups of the class look like. We try to do some shifting at that time to make the overall class look the way we want it to. *David Borus, Vassar*

An application will receive two thorough reads by admissions officers. The first reader of a file will be an admissions officer at-large; and the second reader will be the admissions person in charge of the candidate's area, who also brings specific context (regarding the area and the school) to bear. Both readers evaluate the application and make suggestions as to whether the candidate should be admitted, denied, or discussed. Then, I look over the file. If both readers have suggested that we deny the candidate and I agree, we do deny him. This happens to about 25 percent of candidates; the other 75 percent go to the full admissions committee for discussion. *Jess Lord, Haverford*

Texas high school students who are in the top 10 percent of their class when they apply are admitted on the basis of their rank, per [Texas statute] HB 588, but must complete the application. These automatically admitted students make up 69 percent of the class of 2005. *Kedra Ishop, Texas*

The files of the candidates who are not automatically admitted [by virtue of being in the top 10 percent of their Texas high school class] are randomly assigned to a reviewer who holistically evaluates their file. First, they evaluate and score each of the two essays. Second, they read and score the rest of the file, looking especially for leadership experience, innovation, persistence, creativity, and overall "well-roundedness." These scores, combined with the academic credentials [class rank, course selection, and test scores], form the basis for final decisions. . . . Our process aims to balance academics, writing ability, and leadership potential. *Kedra Ishop, Texas*

The first reader is an admissions officer. About half of the files are forwarded to me as uncompetitive for admission. I generally agree, but if there is an argument to be made for anyone, I'll send the file on for further evaluation. One faculty and one student will read these and the other half [the most competitive] of the files. If all three evaluators agree—that the candidate should be admitted [or rejected]—then we generally follow their suggestion. If there is disagreement, the file then goes to the admissions committee, which includes an equal number of faculty, students, and admissions officers—all with equal power. About 10 to 15 percent of files end up in committee. *Rick Bischoff, Cal Tech*

We look at the candidate evaluation process from a positive perspective. We look for reasons to admit students, not for reasons to reject them. *Maria Laskaris, Dartmouth*

How Do Your Evaluation Committees Work?

We pride ourselves on the fact that every file comes to committee. Before it comes to committee, it's read carefully by at least two people—three if you are an athletic recruit, an eight-year medical program finalist, an engineering applicant, or someone who has received very different reads from the two original readers. *Michael Goldberger, Brown*

Each of the readers of a case writes notes all over the applicant's file, then we discuss every case in committee and make a decision by majority vote after a series of excruciating comparisons. I think you could call this "the lunatic fringe of democracy." *Marlyn McGrath Lewis, Harvard*

Our process is fairly straightforward. We review all candidates randomly, one candidate after another. Each applicant is usually evaluated by two readers before coming to me for a final read. I see all applicants except for obvious denies—and even those are seen by the Director of Admissions before a final decision is made. We use a committee at the end of the process for candidates who receive different evaluations from the various readers. *Maria Laskaris, Dartmouth*

The territory manager is the first reader of a file and is responsible for presenting the best candidates from the region to the committee for further evaluation. This admissions officer is a kind of advocate for applicants in his or her area. Our admissions officers have a lot of responsibility in that they provide quality control before bringing up files for discussion in committee, so that we don't have to discuss every case there. *Rick Shaw, Stanford*

We pass files among ourselves to arrive at a consensus—rather than by group discussion and vote. There are no committee meetings here. *Sheppard Shanley, Northwestern*

We have a three-reader system. The first reader probably does about thirty-five first reads per day. He or she rates each file: offer, waitlist, or deny. It gets passed on to a second reader and then to myself or an associate dean for the final read. If there's no consensus, the file goes to committee. *John Blackburn, University of Virginia*

Are Students or Faculty Involved in the Selection of Candidates?

Faculty are involved in the selection of our engineering candidates, but otherwise they are not involved in admissions. *Christoph Guttentag, Duke*

Faculty are involved in our admissions decisions. About one-fifth of the applicants are evaluated by faculty members—these are generally applicants with interests or strengths in math and science. Faculty in the arts also review portfolios and evaluate recordings of musical talent. *Eric J. Furda, Columbia*

Reed is a faculty-governed school, so we feel it is important to let faculty in on the admissions process to a degree. We try to deliver to the faculty students they are interested in teaching. We therefore like to have faculty input, especially on the borderline cases. *Paul Marthers, Reed*

Students are not involved in the selection process, but we do have faculty members who read applications on occasion, particularly for applicants with very obvious academic niches. In such cases, we'll get faculty involved to help us interpret essays or submitted material. *Robert Clagett, Middlebury*

WHAT KINDS OF RATING SYSTEMS DO YOU USE TO EVALUATE AND COMPARE CANDIDATES?

We use codes to rate applicants in several different areas—academics, extracurricular contributions, and personal qualities—but we don't combine them together afterward to come up with any kind of definite ranking or ordering system. *Marlyn McGrath Lewis, Harvard*

There are six types of numerical ratings here. We give ratings on strength of curriculum, performance in class, standardized tests, extracurricular activities, the essay responses, and the letters of recommendation and the interview combined. *Christoph Guttentag, Duke*

We rate students on many different aspects: academic outcomes, intellectual vitality, success outside the classroom, teacher and guidance counselor recommendations. Ratings are not used in any formulaic way to help us decide definitively who gets in and who does not. *Rick Shaw, Stanford*

We don't use an algorithm or quantitative formula for any of our ratings, but all applicants get rated in five different categories: academic achievement, intellectual curiosity, commitment, personal qualities, and extracurricular performance. *Nancy Hargrave Meislahn, Wesleyan*

We give one to six points (six being highest) for each of eight categories: academic achievement, intellectual curiosity, potential, commitment, extracurricular achievement, communication, initiative, and personal. We then give an overall ranking for the academic and personal, but these are somewhat impressionistic summaries rather than a simple averaging of the scores in each subcategory. *Jess Lord, Haverford*

We don't use numbers to rate students anymore. *John Blackburn, University of Virginia*

We have three ratings. One is for academics; one is for involvement and recognition in extracurricular activities; and one is for what we call "Self-Presentation"—which evaluates the applicant's skill at completing the application. *Sheppard Shanley, Northwestern*

All applicants are given two separate numerical ratings: one reflects a student's academic achievements, the other a student's nonacademic achievements. Each of the two readers assigned to a candidate rates the applicant and prepares a narrative assessment. The ratings themselves are descriptive, not prescriptive. *Katie Fretwell, Amherst*

We don't use ratings here—mostly because of how small we are. We do a narrative evaluation of every candidate. *James Bock, Swarthmore*

The Academic Index is a measure that was devised by the Ivy League to rate or compare academic credentials of recruited athletes. It has no decisive role in our decision-making process. *Marlyn McGrath Lewis, Harvard*

ONE TOP COLLEGE'S DATA SHEET

The following is the data sheet that one of the top colleges uses in its admissions process. Such a sheet is filled out by the first and subsequent readers of an applicant's file and then attached to the front of the file. It becomes a running record of each reader's opinion on the candidate. The terms used on the sheet are described below. Similar types of sheets are used by all the colleges in order to place certain crucial information and ratings of a candidate in one location so that they can be easily accessed by other admissions officers.

Explanation of Terms

Explanations of words used on the following data sheet are given for the nonobvious terms, starting with those in the upper left corner of the sheet, continuing down the left column, and then moving to those in the upper right corner of the sheet and continuing down the right column.

Affiliation = Affiliation. Comments on an applicant's relation to a current student, alum, or employee of the university.

12th & 1st = Twelfth Grade and First Semester PG Year. Refers to a candidate's academic performance during senior year as well as the first semester of any additional postgraduate study the candidate has performed.

Rank in Class U W = Rank in Class Unweighted or Weighted. One of the two terms after Rank in Class is circled to indicate how the rank is calculated.

7 = Seventh Semester. Refers to the fall semester of senior year (the seventh of eight semesters of high school).

GPA-SSR/Transcript = GPA-Secondary School Report/Transcript. The candidate's GPA (found either on the Secondary School Report or on the candidate's own transcript—the reader circles the source).

% to 4 yr = The percentage of seniors at the candidate's high school who attend four-year colleges.

C COMPETITIVE = Readers are asked to write a "C" in all the spaces in which the candidate would be considered especially noteworthy or competitive.

NC NONCOMPETITIVE = Readers are asked to write "NC" in all the spaces in which the candidate would be considered especially deficient or noncompetitive.

Program = The quality of the high school and academic curriculum that the candidate has followed.

PQ's = Personal Qualities. A candidate's personality and other characteristics.

Support = Teacher or guidance counselor recommendations.

Self-Presentation = Essays.

Solid All Around = Refers to a candidate's stance as a "solid" or "well-rounded" person.

Use of Resources = Refers to whether or not a candidate has taken advantage of available opportunities.

Glue = Refers to candidates who are especially spirited or well-liked (i.e., those loved by everyone, with great interpersonal skills, to whom others turn for support and help).

Yrs. in U.S. = Years in the U.S. Refers to how long the candidate has lived in this country, if he or she immigrated from somewhere else.

Home Lang. = Home Language. Refers to the language a candidate speaks at home with his or her family.

Academic Program: Avg AA Rg MRA = Academics: Average or Above Average Regular or Most Rigorous Available. Readers must circle one of the choices to indicate the candidate's academic curriculum.

HSR = High School Record.

AC: = Academic Rating. Readers must rate the candidate on overall academics.

JIL = Joy in Learning. Readers must rate the candidate on his or her demonstration of "joy in learning," also sometimes called intellectual curiosity.

Athletics: B R _____ = Athletics: Blue-Chip or Red-Chip _____. Readers are asked to circle whether or not a recruited athlete candidate is a "blue-chip" recruit, meaning a high-priority athletic recruit, or a "red-chip" recruit, meaning a low-priority athletic recruit. The space is for noting the sport.

Work: HPW = Work: Hours Per Week. Indicates how many hours of paid work the candidate performs per week.

NONAC: Nonacademic rating. Readers must rate the candidate on overall nonacademics.

EL = Enthusiasm Level. Indicates an admissions reader's enthusiasm for the candidate.

RECOMMENDATION _____ A H D = Recommendation _____ Admit or Hold or Deny. Refers to a reader's opinion on what the decision on the candidate should be. "Hold" means to defer the decision and send the candidate's file to another evaluator.

Unusual circs./Q's = Unusual Circumstances or Questions. Readers make any notes or ask questions they would like answered about the applicant's candidacy.

RAD = Regional Admissions Director. A space for the officer responsible for the student's region of the country or world to make comments.

A H D WL 7 DEF = Admit or Hold or Deny or Waitlist or Seventh Semester or Defer. Refer to the decision made on a candidate.

FRESHMAN

Round 2 Reader _____ Date _____ ED: _____

Academic: Avg AA

Program: Rg MRA 7th:

AP's/Awards:

Tests 1 2 3 4 5 6 _____

HSR + N M — _____

AC: 1 2 3 4 5 6

JIL 1 2 3 4 5 6 _____

Ethnicity: ___ ___ Decline to State☐ Citizenship _____

Permanent Resident: Financial Aid:

Gender:

Affiliation:

	A's	B's	C's	D's	F's	P's	GPA	Rank in Class U W
Transcript 10th								(of ___)
11th								7 (of ___)
10th & 11th								GPA-SSR/Transcript
12th & 1st								U W

Test Scores   % to 4 yr ___

Nonacademic: Work: HPW _____

Athletics: B R _____

Art: _____

Dance: _____

Drama: _____

Music: _____

NONAC: 1 2 3 4 5 6 _____

Self-Pres. + N — _____

Support + N — _____

PQ: + N — _____

EL + N — _____

RECOMMENDATION _____ A H D

Unusual Circs./Q's

Round 2 Comments

_____ Date: _____

_____ Date: _____

Round 1 Reader _____ Date _____

C COMPETITIVE		NC NONCOMPETITIVE
___ Academic Record	___ Use of Resources	___ H.S. Record
___ Rank in Class	___ Background	___ Rank in Class
___ Program	___ Area/Geography	___ Program
___ Scores	___ Diversity/Mix	___ Scores
___ Intellectual Vitality		___ Nonacademics
___ Nonac.Achieve	___ Special Circumstances	___ PQ's
___ Special Talent	___ Glue	___ Support
___ PQ's		___ Self-Presentation
___ Support	___ Other ___	___ Not Outstanding
___ Self-Presentation		___ Other ___
___ Solid All Around		

RAD

Search: Clear Admit _____ Estimated GPA _____

Round 1 Comments

Hold Round Comments _____   Date _____

XYZ

Dean Comments

Yrs. in U.S. _____ Home Lang. _____

Major/Career: _____ ☐M

☐O ☐V ☐S ☐U ☐F

☐L ☐D _____

AC JIL Non-Ac	A	H	D	WL	7	DEF

Figure 5-1. Data Sheet.

Appendix II

COLLEGE PREPARATION AND APPLICATION TIMETABLE

FRESHMAN YEAR

THROUGHOUT THE YEAR

- With the help of an adviser or counselor, tentatively plan out your curriculum for the next four years, making sure to take challenging (albeit manageable) classes. In general, selective colleges like to see four years of English; four years of a foreign language (preferably the same language throughout); four years of math (algebra I, geometry, algebra II, and an advanced math course such as calculus); four years of natural sciences (physical science, biology, chemistry, and physics); and four years of social science classes (history, government and politics, ethics, etc.). Furthermore, colleges like to see that you've taken advantage of available AP, IB, or other honors programs. See Chapter 8 for more details on high school curriculum planning.

- Get seriously involved in a few extracurricular activities, planning to maintain your commitment to one or two of them throughout the next four years. It is best if these activities also allow for growth or change in your role over time. Remember that sustained commitment to at least one or two extracurricular activities is critical for admission to a top college. Feel free to sample a number of endeavors at this time so that you can find two or three you really like. Also note that at some point during your high school career you should partake in some sort of community service work. It does not have to start during your freshman year, but do not let it slip through the cracks over the next three years.

- Plan for a meaningful summer experience—employment, volunteer work, extracurricular programs (such as athletic and/or other recreational theme camps or art programs), summer school, or academic enrichment programs (to get a jump start on the following year or to explore new areas of academic interest).

- Take advantage of opportunities that may arise to visit colleges—just to start getting a feel for them. Check out local colleges or visit campuses convenient to family vacation spots. It is not yet necessary to be overly evaluative on these visits; it is merely helpful for a student to have a feeling for what college campuses are like before starting the self-assessment and research process during junior year.

SOPHOMORE YEAR

THROUGHOUT THE YEAR

- Continue to follow a challenging curriculum.

- If you have not already committed to one or two extracurricular activities, do so now.

- Continue to visit colleges when the opportunity arises. You may want to attend a college fair or a multicollege consortium to look at a few campus publications, listen to current applicants' questions, and get a feel for what kinds of things will be important to you when you start to look more seriously at colleges.

OCTOBER–DECEMBER

- Take the October PSAT in preparation for the junior year PSAT/NMSQT. The results you receive on your first set of practice PSATs will let you know what your weak spots are so that you can start to better prepare for future standardized tests.

- Students who plan to take the ACT should take PLAN as a practice run.

- Start to plan for a meaningful summer experience. Continue in an activity in which you were involved the previous summer if there is a way to advance within it; otherwise, do something new.

JANUARY–MARCH

- Students and parents should at this time familiarize themselves with the nuts and bolts of college financial aid. You should also take a preliminary look at FAFSA and PROFILE forms to prepare for the kinds of information you will be required to offer. (Parents: You must begin to prepare this early for financial aid applications because you have to allow time to make any and all legal adjustments to your financial situation before January of your child's junior year of high school. The year that runs from January of the junior academic calendar year to December of the senior academic calendar year is the one on which all college financial aid considerations are made.)

MARCH–JUNE

- Assess your needs and interests against the curriculum at your high school. This is the time to start thinking about whether or not you would benefit from taking a course at a local community college during your junior or senior year. Talk to your guidance counselor and teachers about the possibilities open to you.
- Take the SAT subject tests in subjects you complete sophomore year.
- Take AP exams in AP courses you complete sophomore year.

JUNIOR YEAR

Junior year is generally considered the most critical year in terms of your admission to colleges. Therefore, you need to start the year prepared to give your best performance in challenging classes as well as assert yourself in extracurricular activities. You also need to make any final moves toward preparing for the college application process, such as arranging for testing improvement courses or hiring a private college consultant.

THROUGHOUT THE YEAR

- Continue to follow a challenging curriculum.
- Continue to commit yourself to extracurricular activities. If you have not yet participated in substantial community service activities, you should plan to do so now.
- Buy a basic guidebook to the colleges if you have not already done so.
- Do some preliminary self-assessments in order to formulate ideas about what you are looking for in a college as well as what your positioning efforts might be. Use the guidelines provided in Chapter 3 in doing these self-assessments.

- Continue to inform yourself about colleges. Speak with friends in college and alumni of colleges in which you are interested. Take advantage of gatherings with adults and college-age students to learn what you can about various schools—holiday parties, church or temple events, and neighborhood happenings are good opportunities for doing this. Also learn about colleges by attending college fairs or information sessions with college representatives, surfing the Web, and reading guidebooks.

- Develop a preliminary list of appropriate colleges for you based on your self-assessment and college research.

- Examine any application forms you can get your hands on to get an initial feel for what the application process will involve.

- Create a résumé of accomplishments and experiences. It will be useful when it comes time to solicit recommendations, go on interviews, and write your applications.

- Reassess your needs and interests against the curriculum at your high school. Decide (with the help of guidance counselors and teachers) whether or not you would benefit from taking a course at a local community college.

- Take advantage of any opportunities to interview (for jobs or volunteer positions) in order to develop interviewing skills.

SEPTEMBER–OCTOBER

- Register for and take the PSAT/NMSQT. The PSAT qualifies you for National Merit Scholarships and prepares you for the SATs.

- Register for and take the fall ACT if that test is right for you (see Chapter 8). As you compare your ACT and PSAT/SAT performance, you will be able to determine which testing option is going to be best for you.

- Determine whether or not you would benefit from a class (or tutor) to improve your standardized test scores and arrange for one of these before the spring tests.

- Start to plan for and arrange college visits for the spring of this academic year.

- Students and parents should take care of any adjustments or changes to the family financial situation that will need to be made for financial aid consideration purposes before the beginning of the next calendar year.

NOVEMBER–DECEMBER

- Start to plan for an especially meaningful summer experience. Many college applications ask you to write about your past summer, so you will want what you do between your junior and senior years to be something from which you can extract a lot of meaning. Many interviewers also ask college candidates about their past summer experience.

- Start to consider who should write recommendations for you. If there are junior year teachers whom you will want to write your recommendations, then you should continue to foster your relationships with them, especially if they will not be teaching you at all senior year.

JANUARY–JUNE

- Take the SAT (and the ACT, if you choose to do so).
- Take the SAT subject tests in subjects you complete junior year.
- Take AP exams in AP courses you complete junior year.
- Complete arrangements for spring and summer college visits.
- Complete arrangements for a meaningful summer experience.
- Meet with your high school guidance counselor for preliminary talks and planning, even if your school does not require you to do so at this time.
- Start to think about any supplemental application submissions you will need for special talents in the performing or fine arts. Consult with a teacher or instructor about your best work and how to go about preparing it for college submission purposes. Continue to work on the planning and execution of these materials throughout the summer and senior fall.
- Register with the National Collegiate Athletics Association (NCAA) Clearinghouse once the junior academic year is complete if you are an athlete who intends to be recruited by Division I and II schools. (The NCAA needs an academic record containing six semesters or three full years of high school study in order to register a student for Division I or II recruiting, so you must wait until after your junior year grades are processed to do so.)
- Reassess the need for a course (or tutor) to improve your standardized test scores and arrange for one of these over the summer, before your final testing opportunities in the fall of your senior year.

SENIOR YEAR

Students need to remember that despite the primary importance of the junior year, senior year is no time to slack off! Colleges look closely at academic records from the fall of the senior year and often contact high schools during the spring decision-making process to inquire about continued performance.

THROUGHOUT THE YEAR

- Continue to take a challenging courseload.
- Continue to commit yourself to extracurricular activities.
- Continue to inform yourself about colleges by speaking to alumni, attending college fairs and information sessions, and surfing the Web.

SEPTEMBER–OCTOBER

- Formalize your list of target schools.
- Request or download applications from schools to which you are considering applying.
- Acquire the Common Application in the event that you will be applying to any schools that accept it.
- Request your high school transcript and review it to verify that all information is correct.
- Start a college application organizational system. Allocate a corner of your bedroom or the den for all the college publications and flyers you receive. Keep a folder for travel and logistics information about college visits you are planning. Keep another folder for all the applications you will file, with notes about each particular college's application details. Start a filing system in which you maintain separate folders for each college in which you are particularly interested. Each file should contain your notes on that school as well as the college's brochures, publications, and application.
- Decide whether or not you will be applying Early Decision or Early Action to any school.
- *Early Decision and Early Action candidates:* Applications for ED and EA are usually due on November 1 or 15. (A few colleges now have a second round of Early Decision called ED II, for which binding-commitment applications are due in January.) All Early Decision and Early Action applicants must both initiate and finalize all aspects of the application process for their ED or EA application college during these two short months. Note that you should continue to follow the timeline regarding applications to other colleges. Do not wait until late December, when you will hear from the Early application school, to move forward with other applications; if you are deferred or rejected from the college to which you applied early,

you will have a lot of work to do while also suffering from a waning confidence level.

- Register for and take the SAT, ACT, and SAT subject tests.
- Start rough drafts of essays and personal statements. The sooner you complete a rough draft of an essay, the more time you will have to rework it to get it into its best shape.
- Continue to visit schools.
- Arrange for interviews at schools that require or recommend them.

OCTOBER–NOVEMBER

- *Rolling Admissions candidates:* If you are applying to a school with Rolling Admissions, submit your application as soon as the school will start accepting them. The sooner you get it in, the better chance you have of being admitted. Rolling admissions candidates generally receive a reply from the school four to eight weeks after the submission of the application. Note that you should continue to follow the timeline regarding applications to other colleges.
- Approach recommenders and request recommendations. Give them at least a month in order to write you the best recommendation possible. The more time you give a recommender, the more willing he or she will be to support you—you do not want to get off on the wrong foot here!
- Continue to revise and complete final drafts of application essays.
- Complete final drafts of application forms.

DECEMBER–FEBRUARY

- Most Regular Admissions applications are due to college admissions offices in December, January, or February.
- *Early Decision and Early Action candidates:* Early Decision and Early Action candidates generally receive their notices of admission, rejection, or deferral in December. If admitted, send in your reply along with your deposit. (Early Action candidates should reply positively and send in their deposits only if they are certain they will attend the school.)
- Check with teachers and your guidance counselor to confirm that recommendations and transcripts have been sent to target schools.
- Request FAFSA and PROFILE financial aid forms. Complete the forms and return them as soon as possible.
- Contact schools that have not yet acknowledged that your file is complete.

MARCH–JUNE

- Notify schools of any new information, such as awards, honors, and scores, that might benefit you in the admissions process.

- Continue to perform well academically! Do not slack off, especially if there are schools from which you have not yet heard. Admissions committees often call schools for updates when they are forced to make tough decisions or to choose among two candidates.

- Most schools notify candidates of admissions decisions by April 1.

- Visit schools you have been admitted to in order to make your final decision. Take advantage of yield enhancement events and prospective student weekends offered at schools to which you have been admitted. These give you a comprehensive view of the school's academics, extracurricular offerings, and social atmosphere, as well as an opportunity to room with current students and meet prospective future classmates.

- Notify your recommenders of schools' admissions decisions and tell them what college you plan to attend. Thank them again for their assistance.

- Notify the schools of your acceptance or rejection of their admissions offers. Most schools require replies from their admitted candidates by May 1. Send in your deposit to your school of choice.

- If you have been put on the waitlist at a school, notify it that you would like to remain active on the waitlist if you still want to be considered for admission. Write a letter reiterating your interest in the school, send in any additional information that will help your case, and request recommendations from those who can support your interest in the school.

Part II

APPLYING TO COLLEGE

6

POSITIONING YOURSELF: GENERAL PRINCIPLES

— KEY POINTS —

▪

Understand how you compare with the competition

▪

Learn how admissions officers will view your candidacy based on their expectations of people from your educational and personal background

▪

Capitalize on your strengths, while minimizing your weaknesses

▪

Show how you bring unique value to the school
—Learn how to position yourself so that you stand out relative to others
—Maximize your reward/risk ratio

▪

Use themes to focus your positioning effort

INTRODUCTION

Schools want candidates who will be successful college students and, by extension, prominent scholars, civic leaders, entrepreneurs, artists, scientists, inventors, athletes, doctors, business executives, teachers, politicians, and humanitarians. To find these future success stories, colleges assess a great deal of information. Some of this is objective and quantifiable, such as your standardized test scores and high school grade point average (GPA). Some of it is not readily quantifiable, whether it is your family background or display of leadership, or simply the reasons for what you have done.

The objective elements of a candidate's application, such as basic academic credentials, are extremely important to good colleges. They are, in fact, generally responsible for putting you in the running at leading schools. (Note, however, that this need not be the case with recruited athletes or other applicants who are particularly compelling for another, nonacademic reason.) The subjective elements, however, are ultimately every bit as important as the objective ones in determining admissions results. This means you have an opportunity to become more than just a set of numbers—or a pawn in a game of numbers. You in fact have a real chance to help yourself in the college admissions process by presenting your materials, and thus yourself, in the most effective way possible.

You therefore have many choices for what to focus on in your application. The first part of this chapter shows you how to determine what you should emphasize. Your areas of emphasis depend on several factors: what leading schools want, what your competition offers, and how your relevant strengths and weaknesses compare to the competition. The rest of the chapter begins the discussion of how to capitalize on your strengths and make the strongest possible argument for your acceptance. This discussion continues throughout the following chapters, which explore the communication vehicles you need to master: the essays, recommendations, and interviews.

CREATING A POSITIONING STRATEGY

To begin the process of putting together a successful positioning strategy, you must first closely examine all the schools to which you will apply. You already know from Chapter 5 what schools are generally looking for in candidates. They want brains. They want special artistic, athletic, and other kinds of talent.

They want leadership potential. They want independent thinkers who can also perform well within a community or group. They want students who take initiative, make things happen, and follow through.

But you must also gather relevant data about each school to which you will send an application so that you can be sure to effectively tailor your message to each one. School and entering-class profiles can usually be found in the information packages schools send out about themselves; they can also be found on college websites, in college guidebooks, or in your high school's college counseling office.

You will want to examine the following data on the most recent incoming freshman class of each school:

- Average SAT and ACT scores
- Average high school GPA/rank in class
- Distribution of geographic origins
- Percentage from public versus private schools
- Percentages of various ethnic groups

You also need to know about the school's strengths and requirements, and facts about the student body at large:

- What are the school's strong departments or fields of study?
- What departments or fields of study are undersubscribed?
- What kinds of foreign language and/or foreign culture requirements are there?
- What kinds of study abroad programs does the school offer?
- What varsity and club sports teams does it field?
- What kinds of newspapers and special publications does it offer?
- What kinds of art, music, dance, or drama programs does it feature?

You need to get a real sense of what a school is looking for as well as what it already has enough of. This will allow you to refine your message to meet the school's specific needs and interests.

MAXIMIZING STRENGTHS, MINIMIZING WEAKNESSES

With this information in hand, it will be easier to see how you stack up against your competition for each school. You need to determine what an admissions officer is likely to see as your strengths and weaknesses. Then you need to capitalize on your new understanding of yourself as one college applicant amid a huge pool of competition.

Admissions officers would like to get to know their applicants as well as possible when making judgments about them; they will certainly view your entire application with as much care as they can (given time and energy limitations) to make decisions about who you are and how you compare with other applicants. If you follow our guidelines in this and the following chapters, your message will be sophisticated and multifaceted, yet crystal clear. You will thus not be merely a "category" to the admissions people you are trying to impress; you will become an individual. In other words, you will not be just "a jock" but "the fantastic field hockey player and shot-putter who also volunteers at an animal shelter and wants to become a veterinarian."

TRANSCENDING CATEGORIES

In order to transcend the boundaries of any categories in which you might fit, though, you should understand how admissions departments might view you given some basic information about you. There is no denying that people can, consciously or unconsciously, make judgments based on little information, and admissions officers are no exception to this rule. Although admissions officers certainly realize that not all "children of immigrants" are the same, they probably have some basic presumptions about what a child of immigrant parents is like, and what strengths and weaknesses he or she might bring to the college. Keep in mind that your strengths and weaknesses when compared to those of the rest of the applicant pool might be valued differently from school to school. Columbia, located in Manhattan and attracting a generally sophisticated and ethnically diverse crowd, might not place as high a value on your cosmopolitanism or your Hispanic roots as does Colby, a small school in rural Maine where minorities make up a smaller percentage of the student population.

The chart presented here is intended to make this process of identifying where to focus your efforts a bit easier by showing likely presumed strengths and weaknesses of different categories of applicants. These may give you some ideas for things you can emphasize as strengths, while also showing you what weaknesses you might want to think about disproving. Remember that a single applicant can certainly embody more than one category or type.

CATEGORY	STRENGTHS	WEAKNESSES
Academic Superstar	Intelligent, focused on academics, career-oriented	Dull, no sense of humor, poor interpersonal skills, not necessarily a leader, quiet loner type
Jock	Dynamic and energetic, strong team player, strong interpersonal skills, strong leadership skills	Less intelligent, not focused on academics

CATEGORY	STRENGTHS	WEAKNESSES
Student from a Disadvantaged Background	Strong work ethic, determination, unique or underrepresented perspective	Culturally unsophisticated and unsavvy, unprepared for rigors of college, difficulty fitting in
Student from a Wealthy and/or Advantaged Background	Rich experiential knowledge, culturally sophisticated and savvy, prepared for rigors of college, future success nearly inevitable	Arrogant, weak work ethic, spoiled
Artsy Type	Creative, culturally sophisticated and savvy	Poor analytical and quantitative skills, romantic dreamer rather than pragmatist, postcollegiate employability and potential for success uncertain
Verbal/Language Type	Strong communication and writing skills, dynamic, creative	Poor analytical and quantitative skills
Math/Science Type	Strong analytical and quantitative skills	Poor communication and writing skills, uncreative, dull and undynamic, nerdy
City Kid	Culturally sophisticated and savvy, ability to relate to diverse classmates	Arrogant, tendency toward boredom in collegiate environment if in small town
Suburban Kid	Solid and grounded	Ordinary or lacking in uniqueness, spoiled
Rural Kid	Unique and underrepresented perspective, solid and grounded, strength of character	Culturally unsophisticated and unsavvy, unprepared for rigors of college, difficulty fitting in
Immigrant/Child of Immigrant Parents	Unique or underrepresented perspective, strength of character, strong work ethic, determination	Weak English language skills, too focused on academics (lack of interest in extracurricular aspects of college), difficulty fitting in
Elite Private or Boarding School Student	Prepared for rigors of college, focused on academics, career-oriented, future success nearly inevitable	Arrogant, spoiled
Physically Handicapped Student	Strength of character, strong work ethic, determination	Difficulty fitting in
Learning-Disabled Student	Strength of character, strong work ethic, determination	Unprepared for rigors of college
Older, Nontraditional Student	Rich experiential knowledge, career-oriented, focused on academics	Difficulty fitting in, inability to work and associate with fellow students, lack of interest in extracurricular aspects of college

HOW TO PREPARE YOUR POSITIONING STRATEGY

After examining how you stack up against a school's competition and how the admissions officers might view you, given your profile, you must figure out how to pitch yourself. Start by making a list of general ideas or facts about yourself. You can make the list yourself, or you can fill in our Personal Profile Worksheets, provided in Appendix III. If you are making your own list, divide it into five categories: academics, extracurricular activities, work experience, summer activities, and personal background. First write down everything you can think of to say about yourself in the area of academics: your academic interests, what kind of grades you receive in various areas, how your grades have changed over time in various areas, special projects you have done, any awards you have won, etc. Do the same for each category, basically attempting to make a list of data that would cover nearly every aspect of your life, whether or not you deem it important.

When you are through, you need to take each piece of information and regard it objectively, to determine whether you should characterize it as a strength or a weakness. You must look at each piece of data the way an admissions officer would, rather than simply judging whether the experience has *felt* positive or negative to you. In other words, you may think that the experience of growing up in a poor, rural area has been nothing but negative; you would rather have grown up advantaged, with a lawyer rather than a dairy farmer as a father. But remember that from an admissions standpoint, your background gives you no negative points. It is a strength, or can easily be pitched as a strength; for example, performing farming chores to help support the family has given you a strong work ethic and taught you the meaning of responsibility. Similarly, taking the cinch English class instead of the challenging (but doable) AP variety might have affected you positively in the short term, giving you an easy A grade and fewer papers to write each semester and thus more time to spend with your girlfriend. But to an admissions officer, this piece of data would be a weakness: You took the easy way out rather than challenging yourself.

You need to turn each piece of information around in your head to envision what it will look like to the admissions committee. You might well need a college counselor, a friend, or a teacher to help you in this exercise. First, you must be sure that you have included every piece of information possible on your five-category list. This is often difficult to ascertain on your own. After all, from your own internal perspective, certain parts of your life might escape your attention or be deemed unworthy of mention because they have become so commonplace to you. For example, if you have cared for your now 3-year-old sister for several hours every day after school since she was born, that is a significant piece of information. But because this aspect of your life has become so ordinary, perhaps even tedious, you may neglect to realize its value as material in a college application.

After making your lists of strengths and weaknesses, you need to mold them into a strategy. First, you will want to support any obvious strengths. You can relate stories in your essays, for example, that demonstrate these strengths. You will choose recommenders who are likely to provide supporting examples of your best assets as well. The interviews give you a further opportunity to amplify your strengths. The following chapters show you how to use these three communication vehicles most effectively. Next, you must do whatever you can to minimize your weaknesses or, better yet, show that you do not suffer from them. Once again, it is a matter of addressing them through each of the vehicles at your disposal: the essays, recommendations, and interviews.

If you would like individualized help in formulating and executing a positioning strategy, contact us. See page *xiii* for how to initiate a relationship.

MAXIMIZING YOUR REWARD–RISK RATIO

To maximize your reward-risk ratio, place all of your strengths (the rewards a college will reap if it gains you as part of its student body) on the top of the ratio equation, or as the numerator of a fraction; then place all of your weaknesses (the risks a college assumes if it decides to accept you) on the bottom of the equation, as the denominator. Rewards include academic strengths, athletic talent, leadership potential, social skills, a unique geographical background, and the like. Risks include the possibility of your failing academically, dropping out of school, having disciplinary or substance abuse problems, or simply being unhappy and "needy" as a student. You want the rewards to far outweigh the risks, thus making the ratio or number as large as possible. This is what we refer to as maximizing your reward-risk ratio.

A popular and well-rounded student with an A– GPA but nothing particularly unique to offer has a far different task in maximizing the reward-risk ratio than does a right-wing political aficionado whose grades are mediocre but who has founded a thriving forum for archconservative speakers in his community as well as run local election campaigns. The well-rounded good student is likely to be regarded as someone who would do fine and fit in with her classmates, without being much of a risk. She brings solid academic skills and experience to the school. It might look as if it would be an absolute cinch for her to gain admission because of her steady and solid record. But her problem is that she is but one among thousands of solid, well-rounded students applying to the school, all of whom bring similar qualities. In other words, she poses no risk to the school, but she also brings no readily identifiable rewards.

To improve her chances of admission, she must show that she is quite different from other adequate but not unique students. She can do so by showing the extreme consistency of her work over time and across disciplines, a dedication to a certain area of academics, the breadth of her capabilities, or perhaps even a sophisticated portrayal of her future career ambitions.

The right-winger is in a nearly opposite situation. In his case, the problem is not what he brings to the program or how he is unique. His unpopular politics (and self-confidence in expressing them) are rather unusual within most college environments today, which are populated for the most part with moderate to liberal-minded students. His initiative in creating a speaker's forum for his community is impressive, as is his successful record in coordinating election campaigns at such a young age. He has considerable uniqueness value to start with. His problem involves the risk side of the ratio. An admissions director is likely to worry that he spends too much time on his political passions and not enough effort on academics, or perhaps that his mind for academic matters is simply not that sharp. As someone who has not proven himself academically, what if he were not able to handle the demands of the college? An admissions officer may also worry that his politics will be distasteful to most of his peers and perhaps alienate him in some way. In other words, this candidate brings high rewards *and* high risks.

To improve his chance of admission, he must strive to use the three main admissions vehicles (the essays, the recommendations, and the interview) to his best advantage to show maturity, sensibility, and academic capability. He must discuss his views in ways that do not offend others and are easily and logically supportable. He should demonstrate that he understands that the general atmosphere of the campus may not be conducive to his particular views and activities. He must be able to "prove," perhaps through a discussion of one of his extensive extracurricular activities, his brainpower in order to make up for the brilliance not demonstrated in his academic record. He might want to show a sense of humor to take the edge off his profile and provide some comic relief to an otherwise serious set of application considerations.

The well-rounded student would make a mistake if she were to concentrate on the risk side of the ratio; she should focus on the reward side by showing her unique value. The right-winger would make a mistake if he were to concentrate on the reward side of the ratio; he should reduce the risk he poses.

FIT IN–STAND OUT

No matter who you are or where you are applying, tailoring your message depends first and foremost on the "fit in–stand out" issue. Fitting in means that you will be able to handle the coursework, you will subscribe to the school's mission and overall philosophy of education, and you will be accepted by your peers and get along well with them. In other words, you will be happy and thrive at the school, and will best benefit from the resources it offers. Standing out means that you bring something unique and special to the college, something that distinguishes you from other students. In other words, you will offer your resources to classmates and the greater community so that others may benefit from your talents.

Admissions officers view the relationship between an individual student and a college campus as a synergistic one. Admissions officers want to be sure that you will benefit from their school (thus, you want to show that you fit in), but they also want to know that the school community will be richer because of your presence (so you also need to prove that you stand out). Instead of merely throwing a bunch of your foremost accomplishments and qualities at the admissions officers, forcing them to imagine on their own how you might give back to the school if you matriculate there, it is better to be explicit about how you plan to contribute to the campus community. Many applicants, though they know they must impress admissions officers, concentrate more on showing a school how they will personally benefit from going there. This helps show how you will fit in, but does not necessarily help you stand out. Rather than discussing only that you want to attend a certain college because you would like to work on its award-winning daily newspaper, which will give you competitive skills for your future career in journalism, you also want to emphasize that the newspaper (or some other outlet) will be better off with your input. Showing how your future contributions to the campus will be distinct will help separate you from the crowd.

The trick is to fit in *and* stand out at the same time. It is not sufficient to do only one or the other. Arguing that you really fit in, that you look like a composite of all the other students, gives the school no reason to want you there because you bring nothing different or new. Saying that you really stand out, that you do not resemble the student body in any way, is similarly useless because you will be seen as too risky to invite into the community. Colleges do not want to matriculate unhappy or unsatisfied students; they want to keep their graduation rates up, their transfer rates down, their mental health clinics empty—and they want to produce successful alums whose positive memories of their college years will encourage them to donate money to the school in the future.

A good way to straddle the fit in–stand out divide is to fit in with regard to certain key dimensions and stand out with regard to other aspects. More people will fall on the "fit in" side than on the "stand out" side. Unlike specialized technical schools or graduate programs, most four-year undergraduate institutions offer a vast variety of programs, which also ensures that their student bodies are quite diverse. The majority of high schoolers—even those with fairly unique qualities—will not have to worry about showing that they fit in. You probably do not need to worry about fitting in unless you can identify yourself as belonging in one of these risky "categories":

- The quiet and shy loner
- The proverbial troublemaker
- The spoiled rich kid
- The fanatic with a singular passion

THE QUIET AND SHY LONER

The quiet and shy loner is easily identifiable from his list of extracurricular interests and hobbies. He engages in individual rather than group activities. He plays chess or collects butterflies rather than engaging in interactive activities. If he's athletic at all, he probably runs cross-country or swims rather than participating in a team-oriented sport such as soccer or water polo. He might perform solo guitar at a local coffeehouse, but probably does not play an instrument in the school orchestra. He refrains from working on school committees or in group projects. If he writes, it is on his own and not as part of the editorial board of a school literary journal. You will give yourself away as a shy loner type if you claim yourself to be wildly passionate about your activities or hobbies without ever being involved in any group outlets devoted to them. The quiet loner can also usually be identified during an interview. Traits giving away this personality are often divulged (consciously or unconsciously) in teacher recommendations, and sometimes even in one's own essays.

This is not to say that you must change your personality if you are a shy, quiet person and enjoy being on your own rather than interacting in groups. You should simply be aware that some admissions officers might stereotype you as antisocial or unfriendly in some way; they would be more confident about admitting you if you can show that you have the positives of the quiet, shy personality without the negatives. In fact, you can play up this aspect of your personality for all of its strengths (introspection, strong sense of identity, peaceful by nature, etc.). But it is probably best if in at least one way you can prove yourself to be capable of interacting with others and performing well in a group setting.

You can inspire confidence in your sociability in one of several ways. You can write an essay that shows you in a communicative and social role, even if it is with only one other person. For example, in writing about an event that significantly changed your life, you could write about tutoring younger children from your community in reading; caring for a sick grandparent; or befriending your newly immigrated neighbors and helping them adjust to life in the United States. You can similarly ask teachers who are writing recommendations to be aware of issues concerning your personality type, perhaps documenting your involvement in team or group activities and otherwise assuring your friendliness or ability to interact with your peers.

It would also be wise to go against your natural instincts and become involved in one serious and committed activity in which you interact with others. Sometimes such an activity can be a group or team effort, when your role or contribution is still fairly independent. In other words, it might serve to erase any worries regarding your sociability on the part of admissions officers yet not prove too painful or uncomfortable for you. For example, you could become part of the Golden Key society that promotes your school to outsiders, something that is widely assumed to require interactive skills, if not a bubbly cheerleader personality. But you could join specifically to edit the group's newsletter or to develop its website. In joining a group activity, you might even find you like the team spirit involved. Anybody can demonstrate sociability or ease in communication by merely showing a link between himself or herself and a group of people.

If you are painfully shy, become nervous easily, or are worried about how you will come across in a college interview, you should make efforts to improve your interviewing and discussion skills. Your college counselor or a mentor can coach you and help prep you for interviews of many kinds; sitting through several mock interviews and receiving feedback from a school adviser can help you improve your ease and grace in communicating with others. You can also have a friend, parent, or adviser videotape you, so that you can watch yourself in action to determine what features of interviewing you need to improve. Again, do not think you must change your personality to get into college. Colleges are happy to take quiet types, too—you just need to minimize any weaknesses associated with your personality type. (For more on interviewing, see Chapter 14.)

THE PROVERBIAL TROUBLEMAKER

The proverbial troublemaker is spotted by his school (or civil) record of disturbance and misbehavior. Any formal citations against your behavior (probations or suspensions from school, serious arrests) will be evident from your official record. But even informal infractions and questionable behavior are often conveyed to college admissions officers through a school guidance counselor or teacher recommendation. A high school counselor is ethically obligated to pass on behavioral information about you so even if you were only reprimanded by the principal rather than formally suspended for playing hooky or getting caught tying underwear to the flagpole, it might be transmitted to colleges.

It is difficult for troublemakers to convince college admissions officers of their worth if their record is particularly heavy with blemishes and those blemishes have continued on through junior and senior years. But if you have only one infraction of the rules counting against you, or have demonstrated that your pattern of disturbing behavior improved or stopped by junior year, you may be able to save yourself. First, you need to come across as maturely and properly as possible during your interview. Dress particularly well, be clean, arrive early, be particularly polite. If you have a logical, mature, and sincere way of addressing your behavior in the interview or in an essay, certainly do so—but do not whine, blame others for your mistakes, or carry on too long about your past. And certainly do not offer additional details that will not be revealed elsewhere! Second, and better yet, you can have a teacher that you know and trust write you a recommendation, specifically addressing the bad behavior. You will want someone who likes you and seems to have understood and forgiven your transgressions to do this job.

The Spoiled Rich Kid

Spoiled rich kids are not necessarily risky in that they will "stick out" at college (after all, all colleges have their fair share of the well-to-do). But many admissions officers will want to see that you have truly taken advantage of your opportunities if you are well off. Your family's wealth and opportunity is readily evident through your application (as is discussed elsewhere in this book)—even if you are not applying for financial aid—and you cannot change that. But you can make sure that if you come from privilege you do not come off as ungrateful for your opportunities, spoiled rotten, or unaware of the circumstances of those who are less fortunate. You would appear to be spoiled and unlikeable if you wrote an essay about your family's trip to Greece and concluded with a caustic remark mourning the plight of fellow classmates who had to stay home in Indianapolis to work for wages over the summer.

The simplest and easiest way to combat your "disadvantageously advantaged" profile is to make sure you are involved in serious community service throughout your entire high school career. This means volunteering in a capacity that truly helps those less fortunate. You can also readily acknowledge the advantages with which you've been blessed in an essay or the interview. When asked in an essay about her favorite childhood story, one young woman we know used Dr. Seuss's "How Lucky You Are" as her response, incorporating a discussion of how her parents taught her to be grateful for all the special opportunities she had enjoyed.

COMBATING A PRIVILEGED IMAGE

Do:

- Conduct community service.
- Show that you have taken advantage of all opportunities.
- Demonstrate that you have crossed social and other divides or experienced the plight of (and sympathize with) others who are less fortunate.

Don't:

- Discuss shopping, expensive trips, or glamorous events you have attended.
- Describe your parent as managing partner of Chicago's largest law firm— "lawyer" will suffice as a description.
- Sound arrogant, spoiled, or unappreciative of your opportunities.

THE FANATIC WITH A SINGULAR PASSION

It is, generally speaking, always a good idea to show admissions officers that you are passionate about and devoted to your activities and studies. But you must be careful not to overdo it here, especially if you have a singular activity to which you commit most of your time, and that activity's value could be considered questionable or ordinary by others. If you are obsessed with computers and spend virtually all of your free time surfing the Web, learning programming languages, and playing games, do not expect admissions officers to be impressed. There are far too many other applicants with this profile for you to readily stand out. You are likely to need to involve yourself in other activities and passions to impress them. Activities such as computing or playing poker do not on their own instill the full range of qualities that an admissions officer wants to see in an applicant. You do not want to come across as a true fanatic with a singular passion that prevents you from devoting energy and time to other valuable activities if that passion is of questionable or minimal worth.

Note that if your single extracurricular activity is playing tennis and you are ranked as the number three singles player in the United States in your age group, this is a different story. Here, devotion to your sport, for which you have superior proven talent, would quite naturally prevent you from doing a lot of other things with your free time. In this case, your tennis career requires not only passion but also a willingness to forgo other activities. Furthermore, there is no question about the value of this talent. Your athletic skill will likely be one of your most attractive qualities to colleges; commitment to a sport and a team, as well as the social and life skills tennis can teach, will also become valuable parts of your profile. In this case, a near fanatical devotion to the activity would not detract from your overall application.

ADMISSIONS DIRECTORS TALK ABOUT THE KINDS OF STUDENTS THEY ARE RELUCTANT TO ACCEPT

Our process gives everyone a fair chance to compete; however an obvious, serious lack of any of the desired attributes will be a problem—for example, someone with a near perfect SAT score who's in the bottom tenth of his or her class or someone who does a notably poor job of writing the required essays. *Kedra Ishop, Texas*

Students who are overly committed and zealous about only one thing—to the detriment of other areas of development—always worry me. I'm talking about the kid who may be really bright and started his own computer business, but he hasn't done much outside of computers. Passion is a very good thing, but one-dimensionality is not. *Nancy Hargrave Meislahn, Wesleyan*

We are very reluctant to accept kids who market themselves—we can smell that. We are looking for an authentic voice in an application, not one that is manufactured to please. Think about what your authentic narrative is—what do you care about? This is what you should communicate in your application. *Lee Coffin, Tufts*

I am reluctant to accept applicants I can't get a handle on—applicants for whom we don't have a clear picture after we've reviewed their file. Sometimes it feels like we have three applicants instead of one. When the disparity within a file is big enough, we often call a high school counselor or a recommender to try and sort out who the applicant is. *Steve Thomas, Colby*

There are applications we read and aren't convinced the kid loves math and science enough. Just being good at it or having a passing interest isn't enough. Kids here eat and breathe math and science. *Rick Bischoff, Cal Tech*

At Reed, we are reluctant to accept the student who misjudges us. Students often underestimate how traditional our academic values are—contrary to popular perception, we have grades, we have structure. *Paul Marthers, Reed*

UNDERACHIEVING STUDENTS

We are most reluctant to admit students who clearly have ability but who have not achieved to their potential in high school. *Dick Nesbitt, Williams*

We are reluctant to accept students who ask us to take a leap of faith based on a record of underachievement. To take you on this basis, we need to see more evidence of your ability and drive to succeed than a blank statement that you'll try harder when you're here. *Paul Marthers, Reed*

We are very reluctant when we see an applicant with high scores but low grades. An applicant with great grades but modest scores is far more appealing. *Jennifer Rickard, Bryn Mawr*

Personality Issues

Students who are not resilient. That is, students who are reluctant to take a chance or to make a mistake. That's part of what college is about, and students can't be paralyzed by that experience. College may be the first time a student gets a bad grade or doesn't achieve something they've worked for. Well, that's life. You need to get right back up and try again. College is the perfect time for this . . . it's a time when there's enormous support to try new things and have new experiences. Students need to be open to it. *Debra Shaver, Smith*

Students who are arrogant will have a difficult time here. This place is too demanding and too humbling for arrogance. The undergrads on the admissions committee are incredibly hard when they see arrogance in applicants. *Rick Bischoff, Cal Tech*

I am reluctant to accept students who are bad citizens—students who are arrogant, uncharitable, unkind; students who look to get ahead on the backs of others or who think that being smart or successful is the most important thing in the world. *Stephen Farmer, UNC Chapel Hill*

MAXIMIZING THE IMPACT OF YOUR APPLICATION

An admissions officer is confronted with thousands of applications for each class. She is meant to read far too many lengthy folders on these candidates, containing data sheets, lists of schools and extracurricular activities, transcripts, essays, recommendations, interview write-ups, and so forth. As if this onslaught were not enough, every time an admissions officer ventures into a public forum, there are applicants trying to grab her attention. Most of these applicants are qualified, meaning that they could successfully complete the work at the college. If you are not careful, you will remain part of this undifferentiated mass of applicants. The key to standing out from the crowd is positioning yourself well.

POSITIONING

Positioning is a concept that is meant to deal with the problem of too many applicants trying to capture the attention of admissions officers at popular colleges. To cut through the haze, you must have a sharp and clear image that is readily noticed, valued, and remembered.

Let's look at an example of how this works. There are many different manufacturers of ice cream, even premium ice cream. But a number of ice cream products are distinctively positioned to stand out and attract the attention of consumers. For example, Ben and Jerry's offers premium ice cream made from "all natural" ingredients and "the milk of Vermont cows." The company heavily publicizes its commitment to various social causes and world peace through the Ben and Jerry's Foundation, into which 7.5 percent of the company's pretax profits are funneled; Ben and Jerry's Peace Pops even carry a "1% for Peace" slogan on their labels. The various flavors are given wild and crazy names, some even commemorating famous icons of liberalism: Cherry Garcia, for example, is named after the leader of the Grateful Dead. The colorful cartons promote the notion that the company is "fun" and "zany." Its community-oriented and hippie-ish founders have positioned it uniquely to attract civic-minded, humanitarian, and socially liberal consumers.

Häagen-Dazs, on the other hand, markets itself as a food product for the socially refined and sophisticated. The company has given itself a Dutch name and advertises its product essentially as a dessert for snobs with high standards. Flavor names are sophisticated in their austere simplicity: Coffee, Vanilla, Chocolate.

These two products—Ben and Jerry's and Häagen-Dazs—compete in the very high end of the ice cream market, yet each is positioned to be completely unique. Their marketing efforts aim to make it very clear what key attributes they possess, and they are very successful. The result is that each may claim a premium price for its distinctiveness that would be impossible were they positioned head-to-head. In other words, both may exist and succeed in the market at the same time because both are positioned so favorably.

How does this apply to you and your college applications? You must distinguish yourself from others in the applicant pool. Even if you are of "undisputed" high quality as far as college applicants go, there are many other applicants out there just as qualified as you are. You need to position yourself so that you can compete head-to-head with others applying to college.

College applicants are not all the same. Your job is to show your uniqueness. By appearing unique, you increase your value. After all, if you are the same as the 15,000 other applicants, what school will really care if it gets you or someone else just like you? By making yourself unique, you also make yourself more memorable.

DIFFERENT POSITIONING TACTICS FOR DIFFERENT SCHOOLS

To what extent should your positioning differ from school to school? Most serious four-year colleges are fairly similar, but you might want to position yourself slightly differently for different schools. For example, let's suppose you are a stellar mathematician *and* an accomplished actor, and you are applying to both MIT and Yale. You would want to rely strongly on the math skills to distinguish yourself from the crowd of applicants at Yale, where the world-renowned drama department sees its fair share of serious thespians; but you would want to emphasize your theatrical skills more in your application to MIT, since math whizzes are a dime a dozen there. Acting and math would be important pieces of both applications, but the emphasis would change according to the school. The difference is merely in focus. Have a general positioning strategy that you can fine-tune to fit the needs of specific schools without making major changes in your application. Emphasize different aspects of your experience for a given school rather than trying to re-create yourself for it.

ADMISSIONS DIRECTORS REVEAL WHAT TYPES OF APPLICANTS THEY ARE ESPECIALLY INTERESTED IN ATTRACTING

We are looking for students who will embrace the culture here. It's open, transparent, and merit based. It's a place where we have great optimism for the power of science and technology. We're looking to solve the problems of the world. We want students who are aiming that high. *Stuart Schmill, MIT*

The states of South Dakota and Wyoming are often underrepresented in our pool. We're always looking for students interested in anthropology and linguistics—we have a great linguistics department, but most 17-year-olds have no experience with this yet. There are lots of ebbs and flows in what we're after, though. *Lee Stetson, Penn*

We're committed to ensuring we have a good representation of kids from the Carolinas—we generally want 15 percent of the class from the states of North and South Carolina. *Christoph Guttentag, Duke*

We're always looking for more Hispanic and Latino students, as well as black students—there aren't as many of these minorities in Virginia as there are in other areas of the country. I am personally interested in finding students who have overcome challenges or are original thinkers. *John Blackburn, University of Virginia*

We're always looking for more musicians and artists—when I came here, I determined to make that a priority for us. We're also always looking for kids who represent the first-generation-to-college and students from small rural high schools—I call them the "tiny towners." *Richard Steele, Bowdoin*

There is a misperception out there that we are looking for a well-rounded student. In fact, we are trying to create a well-rounded student body. We are looking for academically outstanding students who also have unique traits or talents to share with our community. *Daniel J. Saracino, Notre Dame*

I'm interested in smart, creative risk-takers. I'm looking for students who want to learn to make a difference. I want students who aren't afraid to be made intellectually uncomfortable because that's where learning really takes place. I want students who are curious and not afraid to question. *Debra Shaver, Smith*

We are looking for students who will thrive in and contribute to a diverse community of active learners. *Dick Nesbitt, Williams*

We are especially interested in attracting students who want to learn for learning's sake. *Thyra Briggs, Harvey Mudd*

We are looking for students interested in participating in the broader life of the college. We are a small school, and yet we have over seventy clubs, nearly thirty sports teams, and a commitment to volunteerism that had students contributing nearly 30,000 hours in community service last year. We need people with a history of engagement to help fuel this energy on campus. *Tim Cheney, Connecticut College*

We are especially interested in attracting high ability, low income students, a group that has been underrepresented at the nation's most selective colleges. *Dick Nesbitt, Williams*

We are looking for students who are self-reliant in and out of the classroom. That is a commodity that is becoming harder to find, especially as parents are becoming more involved in the application process. *Thyra Briggs, Harvey Mudd*

The Mechanics of Positioning: Using Themes

Positioning is a method for presenting a very clear picture of yourself. A simple way to achieve this is to use several themes to organize your material. When writing the essays, for example, relate all or most of your material to your chosen themes. If your material is organized around three or four themes, your positioning will be very clear and easy to grasp. In other words, with strong themes you can better guide the way in which admissions officers will think about you. You will have more control over the application process and reach better outcomes.

The themes you use will be different from those that your next-door neighbor will use. Nevertheless, as noted before, colleges are looking for a few of the same general features in their candidates. They want students who will accomplish things, despite any obstacles in their way. They want students who are relatively mature and have begun to explore their identities and their futures with seriousness. They want people who are determined and willing to work hard and persevere in order to attain goals. Remember these generalities when fashioning your themes, but do not focus only on such broad ideas.

Instead, keep those general positive qualities in the back of your head while coming up with ways to modify them to fit you more particularly or to become especially memorable to administrators. For example, rather than using the theme of "leader," you can go a few steps further. Instead of merely showing yourself to be an all-around leader, you can show that you are actually an initiator of new ideas and events. You create new ideas, are successful at persuading others to rally around them, and can guide a group to accomplish the task that you originally set out to attempt. Or you can show that you are someone who has taken advantage of skills learned through formal leadership roles to apply them even in situations involving informal leadership. In other words, your leadership is such that you can take the bull by the horns in any situation you encounter, even when no one has specifically designated that you be in charge.

Here are some examples of the kinds of themes successful college applicants have used:

- Warm, loving, good citizen type: Started a neighborhood baby-sitting service, volunteers in a senior citizens' home, and comes from a strong, close-knit family of eight.

- Polyglot: Speaks three languages fluently and has been a part of many different cultural influences as the daughter of a French mother and an Egyptian father.

- From an unusual background: Grew up on a ranch on the Texas–New Mexico border, living 21 miles away from the nearest neighbor.

- Risk taker or adventurer: Studying for a pilot's license, went on an animal safari to Africa last summer, and participated in an exchange program with a troubled inner-city school during junior year.

- Determined youth from a disadvantaged background: Grew up in a housing project with a single mother and works after school at a grocery store to help care for three siblings.

- Change-the-world type: The community's junior United Way chairperson, spearheaded the school's recycling efforts, and plans to become a social worker.

- Quiet, introspective type: A knowledgeable bird-watcher who goes out alone at dawn on Saturdays to do fieldwork, has kept a journal since first grade, and plans to get a PhD and go into academia.

There are practical limitations to the number of themes that will help you. If you use too few, you have very little maneuvering room in writing your essays because everything has to fit into just one or two organizing themes. If you use too many, you end up doing no organizing whatsoever and your positioning will no longer be clear. (Using too many themes is the equivalent of not devising themes at all.) The trick is to provide a balance. Using about three themes is generally appropriate because with that number, you do not constrain your efforts so much that you appear boring, but you are focused enough that admissions committees reading your application will know what you are about and remember you.

As discussed before, you have three primary vehicles for getting your message across to colleges: essays, the recommendations, and interviews. You will need to be consistent within and across all three vehicles to gain the maximum positive impact. The following chapters show how to make the most of each.

A SIMPLE POSITIONING EFFORT

"My love for science began when I developed a bug collection for a first-grade science project. I somehow persuaded my parents and my three older siblings (one of whom is now studying for his doctorate in organic chemistry) to help me dig around in our backyard for beetles and crickets. My passion for the biological sciences grew over time, as did the number of antfarms, aquariums, and hamster cages cluttering our garage. As a sophomore in high school, I led a team of five to the state Science Fair finals with our study and report on the Human Genome Project; in my junior year I began to volunteer in the emergency room of a local hospital to receive more exposure to science in the form of medicine. Over the last several years, my focus on human biology has deepened (though I do still maintain a 300-gallon fish tank at home!) and I have begun to shape plans to follow a premedicine curriculum in college. My plans to become a doctor took on more meaning last year when my mom was diagnosed with breast cancer. In an effort to find the best treatment possible and help her cope with her condition, my entire family has engaged in extensive cancer research. Despite my lifelong love of science, I never would have guessed that I would be opening a medical textbook at the early age of sixteen."

That paragraph represents a no-frills positioning effort. It is not meant to be a realistic college essay. Instead, it is meant to illustrate that it is possible in a short space to develop some important organizing themes. We know, in just a few short lines, that this candidate has a passion for science, especially biology. We know that she is serious about academics as well as accomplished in her field. We know her family is important to her and seems to have encouraged her to develop strong values; she cares not only for her own family but also for the well-being of others. This mini-portrait shows several clear themes: a deep-rooted passion and aptitude for biological sciences; a conviction about developing a future in medicine; and strong family ties. It is a fundamental but powerful positioning effort.

ADMISSIONS DIRECTORS STRESS THE IMPORTANCE OF PROVIDING AS MUCH CONTEXTUAL INFORMATION AS POSSIBLE WHEN MARKETING YOURSELF

Build a three-dimensional case for yourself—a richer picture comes through if you make connections between the various pieces of your life. *Eric J. Furda, Columbia*

Context is absolutely important. Understanding the context of a student's family situation and community is critical, so applicants must paint a complete picture for us. *Nancy Hargrave Meislahn, Wesleyan*

Contextual information is critical to our ability to rate your candidacy. We are looking for students who not only succeed but also enjoy learning. We look for context to show us your motivations and what matters to you. *Paul Marthers, Reed*

Everything needs to be explained and placed in a context. As an example, it can look like you're not involved if you have to commute long distances to school, which often prevents students from participating as much in extracurriculars. This kind of thing should be noted in the application so we can understand. *Dan Walls, Emory*

If I have one piece of advice for applicants it's that they must point us in the right direction at all times. For example, if they're working, why? Is it to support family? Is it because of a drive to create a career in computers? They need to explain everything so that we can determine where they are coming from. *Richard Avitabile, NYU*

Appendix III

PERSONAL PROFILE
WORKSHEETS

The following prompts and questions are designed to help you determine how to position yourself for college. Complete the work on a separate piece of paper to give yourself enough space to answer the questions thoroughly.

ACADEMIC PROFILE

High school curriculum and grades (List all courses taken and grades received or use a current transcript as the first "page" of your profile.)

	COURSE	GRADE 9	GRADE 10	GRADE 11	GRADE 12
English					
Math					
Science					
Social science					
Foreign language					
Performing/Fine arts					
Other					
Other					

Overall GPA   **Class rank** (if applicable):

Other academic work (List all institutions, courses, dates of attendance, and grades received.)

	COURSE	INSTITUTION	DATES OF ATTENDANCE	GRADE
Course I:				
Course II:				
Course III:				
Course IV:				

Standardized test scores (List best scores or use a current score report for this "page" of your profile.)

SAT

ACT

SAT Subject

SAT Subject

SAT Subject

SAT Subject

AP

AP

AP

AP

Awards and honors (List awards, institution granting award, date of receipt, and basis of award receipt.)

	AWARD	INSTITUTION	DATE OF RECEIPT	BASIS OF AWARD RECEIPT
Award 1:				
Award 2:				
Award 3:				
Award 4:				

EXTRACURRICULAR ACTIVITY PROFILE

List extracurricular activities performed in high school; your role; the number of hours per week you spent (spend) on the activity; years of participation. You may choose to include volunteer work and community service here or in the Work Experience section.

	ACTIVITY	YOUR ROLE	HOURS/WEEK	GRADE 9	GRADE 10	GRADE 11	GRADE 12
Activity 1:							
Activity 2:							
Activity 3:							
Activity 4:							
Activity 5:							
Activity 6:							

Choose up to four activities to describe in detail. These activities should be those in which you have demonstrated the most commitment (in terms of years of involvement and/or importance of your role) or those that are most important to you.

Detailed description of the activity:

How has your role changed over time?

What has your involvement taught you?

Have you shown leadership in this activity? If so, explain.

Why is this activity special or important to you?

Do you plan to participate in a similar activity in college and/or beyond? If so, explain.

WORK EXPERIENCE PROFILE

List all work performed in high school; your role; the number of hours per week you worked; years of participation or specific dates. You may choose to include volunteer work and community service here or in the Extracurricular Activity section.

	JOB	YOUR ROLE	HOURS/WEEK	GRADE 9	GRADE 10	GRADE 11	GRADE 12
Job 1:							
Job 2:							
Job 3:							
Job 4:							

Choose any (one or more) of your jobs to describe in detail. These jobs should be those in which you have demonstrated the most commitment (in terms of years of involvement and/or importance of your role) or those that are most important to you.

Detailed description of the job:

Why did you take this job?

How has your role changed over time?

What has this job taught you?

Have you shown leadership in this job? If so, explain.

How have you contributed to the organization's overall success?

Do you plan to continue in this line of work in college and/or beyond? If so, explain.

SUMMER EXPERIENCE PROFILE

Discuss your summer activities and experiences. You do not need to repeat information included elsewhere in the worksheets, such as material on jobs or extracurricular activities.

Summer between freshman and sophomore year:

Summer between sophomore and junior year:

Summer between junior and senior year:

PERSONAL LIFE PROFILE
Childhood and Family Life

Write about a favorite childhood memory.

Where were you born, where have you lived during your life so far, and how have these places shaped who you are today?

Write about your family here. Include details about how your family composition has changed over time, the people who make up your immediate family, and other relatives.

Write about a favorite recent occurrence that involves you and one of your family members.

Describe your upbringing: what your parents do, what kinds of activities you enjoyed as a child, what kinds of activities your family performs together, what values have shaped you, etc.

EDUCATIONAL PROFILE

Elementary schools attended:

Middle schools attended:

High schools attended:

How has your particular education—including schools, teachers, educational philosophies, and other school-related influences—shaped who you are today?

Under what circumstances do you perform your best academically?

TRAVEL PROFILE

Talk about your favorite travel experience. The experience need not be exotic—many people have not had the opportunity to travel very far from home. You can discuss visiting your grandmother's town, for example.

PERSONAL INTERESTS

Besides your formal extracurricular activities, what do you like to do in your leisure time?

What is your favorite book and why?

What is your favorite movie and why?

Describe how you would spend an ideal Saturday.

OVERALL PROFILE

Based on everything you have written about so far on these Personal Profile Worksheets (as well as anything you have not yet included), think about the following questions and answer them accordingly.

Who are the three or four people who have most influenced you?

What has been your greatest accomplishment? Why do you consider it an accomplishment?

What has been your greatest failure? What did you learn from it?

What is your greatest leadership experience?

What is your greatest fear?

What fear or hardship have you overcome?

What are the four or five key words that best describe you?

What do you think your friends and family most like and dislike about you? (In other words, what are your strengths and weaknesses?)

What is your most important value? Can you give an example of how you uphold this value?

What events or time periods in your life represent turning points or inflection points (i.e., points at which you experienced significant change or new beginnings)?

In what way are you different from five years ago?

What are your future goals, including both personal life goals and career goals?

OTHER COMMENTS OR NOTES:

POSITIONING YOURSELF: SPECIAL CASES

— KEY POINTS —

■

The following types of applicants are sufficiently unique to warrant special attention:

—International Applicants

—Older Applicants

—Minority Applicants

—First-Generation-to-College Applicants

—Home-Schooled Applicants

—Learning Disabled Applicants

—Physically Disabled Applicants

—Legacy Applicants

—University Professors' and Employees' Children

—Recruited Athlete Applicants

—Transfer Applicants

INTRODUCTION

Most colleges are like athletic teams that seek to fill specific positions (left-handed relief pitcher, point guard) rather than just recruit the "best athlete" available. Thus, these colleges want an incoming class with kids from the inner city as well as those from France, kids who throw great screwballs as well as those who can translate hieroglyphics, and so on, rather than just admitting candidates with the highest SAT or ACT scores. (There are exceptions to this. Foreign universities, as discussed in Chapter 19, tend to value pure academic performance and promise more highly than do typical American universities. The same is true for technology schools in the United States, such as Cal Tech and MIT.)

The attributes colleges value are known in admissions jargon as "hooks." "Hooked" applicants now comprise 60 to 70 percent of a typical incoming class. This has two important implications for applicants. First, competing for the remaining 30 or 40 percent of seats is to take the difficult route into college. Second, those who have a "hook" available to them should do their best to identify it—and then figure out how best to take advantage of it.

This chapter considers special cases (or "hooks") that warrant extra attention, particularly because they raise critical application issues. Our purpose here is to help you understand both the benefits you stand to reap by qualifying as one of these special cases and the strategies you should employ to get the fullest value out of your status. However, all applicants—regardless of their special-case status—should first read Chapter 6 to understand how to position themselves in general before reading the section in this chapter specific to their individual circumstances.

INTERNATIONAL APPLICANTS

SPECIAL CASE STATUS

Overseas student admission is an important priority for all of the top colleges. Because colleges generally want to create student bodies that are as diverse as possible, international students are valued. You bring a unique perspective, background, and cultural heritage to the campus. You are also a special case because of how you are treated in admissions.

You will become part of a separate overseas applicant pool and will be evaluated largely against other international students rather than against U.S.

citizens or residents. Most colleges have notional targets dictating how many overseas applicants they will admit in any given year (generally a certain percentage of the freshman class). International students need to realize they are generally competing not only against all other applicants in the overseas pool, but especially against those from the same country or region of the world. The main objective in the admission of international students is to create a diversity of backgrounds, cultures, and perspectives on campus, so each college wants to avoid stuffing the international group with too many students from the same background. If you are applying from India or China, countries from which the top colleges generally receive many applications each year, you might face stiffer competition than if you were applying from Sierra Leone or Finland, countries that are not well-represented on American college campuses. (Note that colleges have their own particular recruiting priorities and international connections, so each college will differ in its number of applicants from various countries or areas of the world.)

You will be evaluated in a context particular to your background, educational history, and nationality, based on what the admissions officers know about the life, educational systems, and cultural norms of your area of the world. Most other cultures do not provide the same extracurricular and leadership opportunities to high-school-aged students as do the schools and communities in the United States, for example. Admissions officers know this and do not expect international applicants to have achieved the same recognition or success in nonacademic activities as have their American counterparts. Like regular American applicants, you will be evaluated for how you have utilized the opportunities open to you.

PERCEIVED STRENGTHS OF YOUR POSITION

As an international student, you enjoy a coveted position as a candidate with an easy and clear way to position yourself in the applicant pool. The problem that most American students have in applying to the top schools is finding a way to make themselves stand out in the admissions pool so they can claim they bring something special to the campus. You may not need to dig for any distinguishing features because they may be inherent in your international status.

It is likely that a particular aspect of your background gives you a desirable skill or characteristic. For example, if you have been educated in England, thus having focused on a few subjects for the past few years before taking your A-level exams, your extensive knowledge in those areas is of value to American colleges. Or, if you have been raised in a large agricultural family on Sumatra as one of nine siblings who helps your father with the rice harvest each year, you probably possess personal qualities that many others in the admissions pool could not claim. Such a lifestyle could be positioned as having cultivated traits of responsibility, family values, and selflessness.

PERCEIVED WEAKNESSES OF YOUR POSITION

The weaknesses of your position depend on your individual case as an international student. Your weakness may result from your educational background, which may not have been as rigorous as the preparation that most applicants to the college have had. Your cultural background may be so different—if you are a female who has lived a sheltered existence in a very conservative Islamic society, for example—that admissions officers may be unconvinced that you would be happy and fit in on the campus. Or your weakness may lie in your English language proficiency.

Sometimes the weakness in an international applicant's profile can be a result of belonging to a large group of applicants from one particular region, thus preventing him or her from seeming as unique as possible. If you are a Chinese student competing against many other Chinese applicants in the pool, for example, it is more difficult to win a place in the class over others like you.

There may also be problems inherent in your financial situation. Most colleges do not give full financial aid to all overseas applicants, thus forcing them to pick international applicants who can afford the college on their own rather than more qualified applicants who cannot pay their own way.

APPLICATION TIPS

Develop a profile that suggests you will be able to fit in and stand out at the same time. In other words, you should show that you can be comfortable in the college's environment and be successful there, but you also need to play up your uniqueness in order to sell yourself.

To show that you will fit in to a certain degree, you need to demonstrate that you are academically talented, proficient in the English language, and able to live your life in an American environment. You can instill confidence in your ability to live and learn on an American college campus by discussing any experiences abroad (especially if they were in the United States) or showing what you have learned from interacting with Americans or other foreigners. As part of your research, talk to each college's international admissions officer to find out more about the school's environment and what qualities are generally considered crucial for obtaining a place there.

More important than showing how you will fit in, you should use the inherent way in which you will stand out to your utmost benefit. Rather than play down your differences, you need to do just the opposite. Whereas in some other cultures conforming to a certain norm and showing that you fit a certain mold are the best ways of demonstrating your fitness for an educational opportunity, it is just as important to show what differences you can bring to the mix at one of America's top colleges. For instance, show how your experiences (country x, city y, educational system z) shaped who you are, the values you hold, your educational goals, and so on. Then discuss how this has led you to want to study in the United States—and at this school in particular. Given that the American educational system is different from most other (especially non-Anglophone) systems, you have a made-to-order rationale for why you want to experience it.

A few words of warning:

- International applicants qualify for financial aid at relatively few schools (including Harvard, Yale, MIT, Princeton, and Middlebury), so if you will need substantial help consider applying to the generally cheaper Canadian schools.

- If your English is not up to snuff, consider taking a postgraduate year in an American (or other English-speaking) high school before trying to survive in an American college. At a minimum, spend the summer before college taking courses at an American university, to become accustomed to both the language and the nature of American education.

**WHAT ADMISSIONS DIRECTORS SAY ABOUT
INTERNATIONAL STUDENTS**

Most important is their academic achievement in their home system. They have to be eligible for admission at their home universities. Based on the country, that might itself be a very high standard. Generally, it's the academic performance. Standardized testing is not as important because of the English language difference. Also, most of these systems don't have the same kind of extracurricular activities that we have here. So the academic record becomes the most important item. *Charles Deacon, Georgetown*

The biggest admissions challenge for non-English-speaking international applicants is to demonstrate the ability to successfully complete the curriculum in English. Their oral, written, and reading comprehension must be excellent. For those international applicants who have mastered English, we look at the same set of factors as for domestic candidates. *Lee Coffin, Tufts*

We're very proud of out involvement with international applications. We are now visiting students in other countries, and we are preparing to add more international outreach in the near future. The inclusion of international students in our incoming class greatly adds to the total learning experience. They bring a very important perspective to the academic and social experience. *Rick Shaw, Stanford*

We get clusters of international applicants from certain geographic areas such as China, Bulgaria, and India. As a result, applicants from these countries may have a more difficult time compared to an international applicant from a less represented country or region. *Jennifer Rickard, Bryn Mawr*

WHAT CRITERIA ARE EVALUATED IN THE ADMISSION OF OVERSEAS STUDENTS?

We look for the same qualities in international students that we look for in the rest of the applicant pool: a deep interest in science and technology, potential to make a lasting impact on the world, and potential to enhance our community. . . . With all applicants, including international applicants, we look at the applicant in context. How and what is the applicant doing in his or her environment? This can be particularly important for international applicants. For example, in some cultures extracurricular activities are unheard of. Our admissions process takes this into account. *Stuart Schmill, MIT*

We use the same criteria when evaluating international students as we do for domestic students. We are looking for academic ability, rigorous studies, and contributions to their communities. *Douglas Christiansen, Vanderbilt*

Fluency in English—oral and written—is especially important at Sarah Lawrence because we are a writing-intensive college. Clear writing ability is a prerequisite. When we review applications from international students, we very much hope we are getting a true picture of their English ability so they are able to hit the ground running when they arrive, as opposed to being set up for a struggle at the outset. *Stephen Schierloh, Sarah Lawrence*

Usually international students don't present much in the way of extracurriculars, so they don't come across with great leadership or community service experience. We tend to rely more heavily on academics for international admission. *John Blackburn, University of Virginia*

The way we view standardized test scores from international applicants varies according to their language ability. *Sheppard Shanley, Northwestern*

We understand that in some cultures, community service is not available or encouraged as an extracurricular option in the same way it is in most places in the United States. We look for international applicants who have demonstrated some level of excellence in the classroom and in activities in which they have participated. *Ingrid Hayes, Georgia Tech*

We really try to calibrate the use of recommendations for overseas students relative to what we know about the culture and educational system there. For example, in England, teachers are very honest—to the point of being harsh. They often discuss shortcomings as much as they do positive attributes. In many countries there is absolutely no grade inflation, and it is actually much tougher to get top grades than it is in our schools. We take all these things into account when reading recommendations for international applicants. *Maria Laskaris, Dartmouth*

FINANCIAL AID

International students with financial need should be aware that there may be a different review system applied to their candidacy. A college cannot tap federal and state aid, which foreign applicants are ineligible to receive. Dollars, therefore, go farther for U.S. citizens and permanent residents ("green card" holders). Foreign applicants with financial need may therefore have a tougher time than domestic applicants, unless the school has an endowment or other monies set aside for foreign student aid. *Bruce Poch, Pomona*

There are very few U.S. colleges that are need-blind for international students. Many of us worry that international applicants are not being honest when they check the box indicating they do not need financial aid. Are they doing it to try to gain admission? This is a tricky strategy: if you are accepted without financial aid, the money to come won't just appear. *Anonymous Admissions Director*

OLDER APPLICANTS

SPECIAL CASE STATUS

Older (sometimes referred to as "nontraditional") students are a fast-growing segment of the college population. Although the majority of the colleges in the United States report surges in the numbers of applications they receive from candidates who have been out of high school for several or many years, the most competitive colleges have not felt the trend as strongly. This is potentially to your advantage if you are planning to apply to some of the nation's leading schools, because it means that you can stand out more clearly in the admissions pool.

Each college treats older applicants differently. Whereas some colleges have special programs for applicants who are twenty-five and older or have been out of the educational system for a given length of time (such as Wellesley's Davis Scholars program), other schools treat them as part of the regular admissions pool. Some colleges take older students only through their transfer programs, requesting that anyone who has been out of the educational loop for five or more years start at a community or other college first, and then apply for admission to the sophomore or junior class. Colleges differ as to the criteria upon which they base the admission of older students as well. Although some schools require standardized test scores and high school transcripts from older applicants, other colleges base their admission of older applicants on an entirely different set of criteria from that upon which regular freshman admits are judged.

PERCEIVED STRENGTHS OF YOUR POSITION

As an older applicant, you are in a position of strength in that it is easy for you to show how you stand out among other applicants. You are quite naturally different from most applicants and bring something interesting to add to a college's mix of perspectives and personalities.

Older students are seen as being more mature and more directed than younger applicants. Because they have generally spent time in the working world and have grown into adulthood, they generally know what their life goals are and what kind of a career or focus they would like to follow. They know themselves better than do seventeen-year-olds and can often speak from a strong position of self-awareness.

Applying to college after a long time out of the educational system requires the kind of initiative that admissions officers like. Older applicants intent on going to college at an untraditional age tend to have an appreciation for learning and education that younger applicants do not. Whereas many high schoolers apply to college merely because they are following what is assumed and expected of them, older applicants who either lacked or missed the opportunity to go to college directly out of high school know exactly why they want to go to college. The kinds of people who apply to college at an older age tend to have a strong work ethic and demonstrate great motivation.

Most important, older applicants possess a wealth of life experience—whether it be from working, raising a family, traveling, or a host of other activities—that younger applicants cannot possibly have. They provide a perspective in academic and nonacademic situations that is particularly valuable on campuses where student bodies tend to be diverse in every way except for age.

PERCEIVED WEAKNESSES OF YOUR POSITION

Your difficulty in the admissions process is not in demonstrating how you stand out but in showing how you fit in. First and foremost, admissions officers worry that people who have not been in an academic environment for a long time will have a hard, perhaps ultimately unsuccessful, time settling in at a rigorous educational institution. After all, the requirements for doing well in tough classes are often very different from the requirements for doing well in many careers and occupations. This can be an especially daunting obstacle for those who did not perform well in high school but are applying to demanding colleges after years of developing as a successful person in other realms of life. Colleges also worry that adults—who often have children to care for, spouses to support, and adult-level problems to contend with—will not have time or energy to contribute to campus life. The schools want to know that you will be able to live, learn, associate, and communicate with your peers, who will be much younger and generally different from yourself. Many adults do not have enough patience to deal with the naiveté and inexperience of college-aged students; other adults cannot add to the campus environment because they are prevented from doing so by their personal responsibilities.

APPLICATION TIPS

You need to do your best, like all applicants, to maximize the rewards and minimize the risks inherent in your profile. To maximize the benefits of your special status, concentrate on the perspective and knowledge you bring because of your age and experience. Show through your essays, recommendations, and the interview that you are mature, self-aware, focused, and goal driven. Discuss in detail how you have gotten where you are today, tracing the major developments that have affected you since you left high school. Make sure that admissions officers can evaluate your application in the proper context by explaining why you have taken the route that you have, how you have grown through your various jobs or endeavors, and what motivates you to seek a college degree at this point in your life. Demonstrate what unique perspectives, ideas, and life experiences you will bring—try to describe them in ways that make it clear that no other applicant can add what you will to the class.

To minimize the risks inherent in your profile, you should first attempt to make the admissions committee as confident as possible of your academic ability. This is especially true if you had a less than stellar high school record. To ensure the best possible success in college admissions, it is a good idea (even if your high school record is unblemished) to take classes at a nearby college. If you have done well in recent college-level classes, you are providing the college with further evidence that you have what it takes to succeed there.

You also need to show your target schools you can fit in and become an active and valuable member of the college community. Try to provide evidence that you are tolerant of others' perspectives and that you are capable of occupying a unique position of difference in a largely conformist community. Demonstrate that your family or other burdens will not prevent you from spending significant time and energy studying for your classes as well as participating in campus organizations and events.

WHAT ADMISSIONS DIRECTORS SAY ABOUT
ADMITTING OLDER STUDENTS

We have a special program for students twenty-five or older, who have been out of the educational system for five years or more—the Resumed Undergraduate Education (RUE) program. Some of the applicants have really abysmal high school records—we ask to see them, but mostly because it's helpful to see how far they've come since that period in their lives. Poor high school records don't really hurt these applicants. We don't require standardized test scores from these candidates, either. *Michael Goldberger, Brown*

We certainly welcome older students, but it is important that they are interested in embracing the whole Haverford experience. We're not looking for someone who just wants to take courses without being involved in the extracurricular life of the college. If they're married with kids, we wouldn't expect them to live in the dorms—but otherwise we would. . . . You need to show that you know what you're getting yourself into and that this is what you want. *Jess Lord, Haverford*

It is important for older applicants to present recent academic work. It is hard to admit a student you believe to be capable based on a 15-year-old transcript. You will really improve your chances if you have done a few semesters at a community college. *Stephen Farmer, UNC Chapel Hill*

WHAT CRITERIA DO YOU EVALUATE WHEN STUDENTS HAVE BEEN OUT OF THE EDUCATIONAL LOOP FOR A LONG PERIOD OF TIME?

We don't look at the high school record of older applicants. Instead, life experience becomes a very important factor in admission for these people. *Maria Laskaris, Dartmouth*
When we evaluate older applicants, we are looking for a strong commitment to the ideals of a liberal arts education. Often older applicants are more pragmatic about school, and that's not necessarily a bad thing. But we are looking for a desire to stretch themselves intellectually. Also, we are looking for evidence that the older candidate has remained intellectually engaged since last in school. Otherwise, the transition can be very difficult. *Robert Clagett, Middlebury*

For older applicants, we are looking for academic seriousness. We want to know why you want an environment like Bryn Mawr as opposed to, say, night school or one of the other more traditional venues for older students. *Jennifer Rickard, Bryn Mawr*

If we do have concerns about older applications, they are lower order concerns having to do with logistics of presenting and processing an application. We are the kind of place that can be flexible with these applicants. For example, we'll commonly accept recommendations from current employers or supervisors if high school teachers or guidance counselors are less in touch with the applicants' current circumstances. In these instances we're happy to work with the applicant to tailor the application.　*Stephen Schierloh, Sarah Lawrence*

WHAT LIABILITIES MIGHT OLDER APPLICANTS BRING WITH THEM TO CAMPUS?

Our older, nontraditional applicants tend to be really interesting, accomplished people. But occasionally there is the problem of an older applicant not being able to handle the particular rigors of the collegiate environment, a problem shared by many traditional applicants, too, of course.　*Marlyn McGrath Lewis, Harvard*

WHAT SPECIAL POSITIVE QUALITIES DO OLDER APPLICANTS GENERALLY EXHIBIT?

They really add to the mix. They're some of the most interesting applicants. We have a very strong and valued transfer program from where we draw the majority of these students.　*Rick Shaw, Stanford*

We don't see a lot of negatives associated with older, nontraditional students. To some extent they parallel transfer students in having, for example, heightened maturity, sense of purpose, and appreciation for what they will get out of their educational environment. Plus, they have increased breadth and depth in academic and real-world experience.　*Stephen Schierloh, Sarah Lawrence*

The faculty like older students—those who have taken years off. They have a different perspective, which makes them interesting to have in class.　*Dan Walls, Emory*

MINORITY APPLICANTS

SPECIAL CASE STATUS

The recruitment of minorities—especially African Americans, Hispanics, and Native Americans—is a top priority at virtually all of the leading colleges. If you have performed well in academics as one of these kinds of minority candidates, you stand a good chance of doing very well in the college admissions process. Asian Americans, on the other hand, are at a disadvantage in relation to other minorities in the applicant pools at most of these colleges because the number of strong Asian American students has grown tremendously over the past few decades. Whereas being an Asian American once gave an applicant a distinct edge in admissions, at some colleges (those where Asian American pools are huge), such a status can be a substantial disadvantage. The colleges may not maintain quotas for the numbers of minority applicants they take, but no leading college wants overrepresentation of any group, be it students from Connecticut or Korean Americans.

PERCEIVED STRENGTHS OF YOUR POSITION

Minority applicants benefit from being in a position of great value to the colleges. In their efforts to bring the greatest amount of diversity possible to their communities, colleges seek American minority students in significant numbers. Your status as part of a minority is valuable in and of itself, and it can become more beneficial if you show that you possess certain perspectives, ideas, or strengths because of it. Minorities are generally perceived as having fortitude and strength of character for having to endure systematic discrimination, especially if they have not grown up in luxury. Those minority applicants who live in situations of poverty and in communities where educational and other resources are inadequate are seen as having great perseverance for having to overcome obstacles in order to find success.

PERCEIVED WEAKNESSES OF YOUR POSITION

There are no inherent weaknesses in your position if you are an African American, Latino American, Pacific Islander, or Native American applicant. (If you are an Asian American applicant, you may face a challenge stemming from the fact that you are competing against many other very talented and bright students of similar background in the admissions pools at the top schools.) A weakness that can arise as an *indirect* result of minority status is a lack of academic preparation stemming from the type of school you have attended. Those minorities attending school in poorer public systems that do not offer AP classes, test preparation, and other similar opportunities may do well in school yet still be regarded as less prepared for college than are applicants who have done well in much more rigorous curriculums. (This would also be true of Caucasian (nonminority) applicants coming from the same poorer school systems.)

APPLICATION TIPS

First, it is important that you note your minority status in order to benefit from it. Make sure when taking standardized tests and filling out college applications that you check the right box to notify the colleges of your particular background.

You can also use your background as a profiling point, making it one of the ways in which you position yourself in the application. Make sure when doing so to avoid clichés or sounding as if you are trying to manipulate the colleges with your status. Do not resort to trite statements such as "By persevering through extraordinary prejudice, I have become a stronger person." This is a fine theme to use, but you need to tell detailed stories full of self-analysis and meaning in order to make the theme come through without actually stating it.

Do not make your minority status into something it is not, either, because the admissions officers will probably be able to sense when you are stretching the truth. If you live at a fancy address in Brentwood and your parents are professionals (both pieces of information are readily available to admissions officers from your application data sheets), do not write an essay about the poverty and difficulty you have endured as a black male growing up in Los Angeles. Last, be sure to show that you have taken advantage of every opportunity available to you and done as best as you can given the resources available to you if you have gone to school in a less than ideal environment.

A note for African American students applying to the Historically Black Colleges and Universities (HBCUs): You might assume that because you are applying to colleges where nearly all the applicants are minorities like yourself, you should not bother to discuss in your application your minority status and its impact on you. On the contrary, even though your minority status does not set you apart from others in the HBCU applicant pool, these colleges embrace students who have strong African American identities and have reflected on what their heritage means to them.

ADMISSIONS DIRECTORS SPEAK ABOUT MINORITY APPLICANTS

We are always looking for more African American and Latino students. *Christoph Guttentag, Duke*

Among underrepresented applicants including minority and first-generation-to-college applicants, we often see a lack of knowledge about the importance of meeting financial aid deadlines. They may submit a beautiful application, and do so on time, but there's oddly a perception out there among some that financial aid deadlines can slide until results are in from admissions. Unfortunately this is not the case. Applicants need to be vigilant about deadlines both for applying and for financial aid. *Stephen Schierloh, Sarah Lawrence*

Underrepresented students should use their authentic voice. Tell us what matters to you. Communicate how you would add to the richness of campus. If you have experiences related to your background that are germane, tell us how these experiences can shape life on campus and add to this community. *Douglas Christiansen, Vanderbilt*

My advice to minority candidates is not to be daunted by schools' profiles. Schools like Colby prize diversity of all kinds. Minority students interested in a school should investigate any school that piques their interest, and they should talk to someone at that school. At Colby, we work closely with applicants of color to respond to any concerns or questions. *Steve Thomas, Colby*

FIRST-GENERATION-TO-COLLEGE APPLICANTS

SPECIAL CASE STATUS

Many colleges have recently prioritized the recruitment and admission of students who represent the first generation in their families to attend college. In other words, if neither of your parents (or their ancestors) attended four-year college—even if you have an older sibling who has gone on to college before you—you are considered a valuable commodity at many schools. Although most colleges do not have quotas for "first-generation" students, they want to do their part to spread educational equality in our society.

PERCEIVED STRENGTHS OF YOUR POSITION

First-generation applicants benefit from being in a position of substantial value to the colleges. Accepting you helps a college play a role in spreading education to deserving but not advantaged applicants. Colleges generally assume that if you come from a family where college education is not the norm, you likely have not had the same expectations placed on you as have students whose parents always assumed their children would attend college. In other words, you have likely had to work a little harder and perhaps even create your own educational map rather than relying on one established for you by your family. If your family is working-class or poor as well, then you are at a double advantage in the application game: you are assumed to have had to overcome substantial obstacles to succeed in your education to this point.

PERCEIVED WEAKNESSES OF YOUR POSITION

There are no true weaknesses associated with your candidacy, unless your preparation for college has been hampered by your family's lack of education. If you have attended weak schools or been required to spend an inordinate amount of time dedicated to earning money, your preparedness for college may be lacking. Still, most applicants can turn these apparent liabilities to their advantage in the application process.

APPLICATION TIPS

On some applications, there is a question asking you specifically whether your parents or relatives have attended college. Do not, by any means, be embarrassed if the answer is no, and make it known that you are indeed the first generation in your family to seek higher education. If there is no direct question like this, never fear: colleges will easily determine your family's background in the data section where it asks for information about your parents' educational backgrounds and alma maters.

Being part of the first generation of your family to attend college will probably not merit an entire essay on its own. There are, however, many handy ways of slipping this information into other essays if this has been a critical aspect of your development or goal setting. On the other hand, if your family has opposed your educational goals or clearly does not support your attending college, you may want to make this a substantial part (or all) of an essay. In such a case, it is important for colleges to understand how much determination to succeed your situation requires of you.

Whenever you write about a need to overcome an obstacle, be careful not to overplay your hand. Do not appear to be appealing for an admissions officer's sympathy. Instead, let the facts speak for themselves.

ADMISSIONS DIRECTORS DISCUSS FIRST-GENERATION-TO-COLLEGE APPLICANTS

WHAT CRITERIA ARE MOST IMPORTANT?

We're not trying to evaluate students on the basis of what they've accomplished up to this point; we're not even trying to measure how well they'll do in their first year here. We're looking at who the student will become given the resources of Cal Tech. Who will they be upon graduation, in grad school, or as a professional? Many first-generation students haven't had a supportive environment, so it would be wrong just to line up applicants on the basis of who has the best credentials today.   *Rick Bischoff, Cal Tech*

It is common for applicants who come from underserved areas to be intimidated by the idea of applying to a place like MIT. They may not have access to the counseling resources that motivate them to reach. What they don't understand is that you don't have to be perfect to be accepted to MIT. Students are evaluated based on the context from which they come. We don't expect all students to have had the opportunity to participate in science fairs or on math teams. We are looking for talented students from all backgrounds.   *Stuart Schmill, MIT*

MOST COMMON MISTAKES

There is a tendency for applicants whose families don't have experience with college to be more tentative and less aggressive in the admissions process. Sometimes it is charming, but sometimes it means we don't get the information that would make a student's application as strong as it could be.   *William M. Shain, Vanderbilt*

They should use the essays and résumé as an opportunity to represent to us what makes them different and unique. First-generation college students, in particular, may be less savvy about the college application process and often shortchange their experiences and fail to give full credit to what they will bring to our school. *Kedra Ishop, Texas*

Students and parents may overlook highly selective schools, where the "sticker price" is high, but generous financial aid packages may make those colleges even more affordable than a local state university.   *Dick Nesbitt, Williams*

First-generation-to-college students commonly make the mistake of interpreting "extracurricular" too narrowly. "Extracurricular" should include anything you do when you are not in school. If you work, tend to siblings, or are active in your church, these are all the types of activities we also want to hear about. *Daniel J. Saracino, Notre Dame*

First-generation-to-college kids generally don't talk to us enough—whether that means picking up the phone, emailing us, or visiting the school. These are the ways you learn about the institution, and that knowledge shapes the application.   *Rick Bischoff, Cal Tech*

First-generation-to-college applicants should not make the mistake of thinking doors are closed to them. We want first-generation-to-college applicants to know that they will be welcome at places like Bryn Mawr.   *Jennifer Rickard, Bryn Mawr*

Unlike some students whose parents practically write their application for them, we often find that first-generation-to-college students truly have the onus of running the entire process, often without any resources or assistance whatsoever. Not only that, many must interpret the process back to their parents. It's in those situations when, not surprisingly, some important details (like financial aid deadlines) fall through the cracks.   *Stephen Schierloh, Sarah Lawrence*

People who are the first in their family to go to college—like I was—should resist the temptation to exclude schools because of cost. Talented first-generation-to-college students should apply to the same schools a talented wealthier student might consider. Schools are very interested in recruiting first-generation-to-college students. . . . First-generation-to-college applicants need not feel that they are beggars at the table of higher education. They belong here, too. *Stephen Farmer, UNC Chapel Hill*

WHAT SPECIAL POSITIVE QUALITIES DO THEY EXHIBIT?

Since many of these first-generation students have had to overcome obstacles that their more affluent counterparts have not faced, they often exhibit a resiliency and determination to succeed that translates to overachievement in the classroom. *Dick Nesbitt, Williams*

HOME-SCHOOLED APPLICANTS

SPECIAL CASE STATUS

The trend toward home-schooling is one that has been felt in certain pockets of American society but has not yet had an overwhelming effect on admissions at the nation's most selective colleges. Most of the leading schools receive a substantial number of applications from home-schooled applicants each year and have developed guidelines (whether formal or informal) for these applicants but have not yet made home-schooled admissions a real priority for their staffs.

Home-schooled applicants are special cases in that they must be careful to do all the right things when preparing and applying to colleges, or they risk faring poorly in the process. Most colleges want home-schooled applicants to approach their applications a bit differently than do regular applicants. Home-schooled applicants are warned by most colleges that their standardized test scores will count very heavily in their evaluation. They are encouraged to submit more than three SAT subject test scores and to take AP exams to prove their academic preparation for college. Many colleges want them to submit detailed information about the curriculum used in their classes. Home-schooled candidates are almost always advised to sit for an interview, with an admissions officer rather than an alum if that is available at the school, even at colleges that do not necessarily put a large emphasis on the interview for other applicants. The colleges also generally hope that a home-schooled applicant has taken some classes at a nearby school or community college, so that there can be the benefit of an academic recommendation other than one written by the parent.

PERCEIVED STRENGTHS OF YOUR POSITION

Some of the differences inherent in your position are generally viewed as strengths from an admissions officer's point of view. Home-schooled applicants are generally thought to be independent, capable of learning and pursuing topics on their own. They demonstrate the kind of entrepreneurism and intellectual curiosity that schools love. They are seen as being academically mature, motivated, diligent, and self-aware. Many home-schooled students have benefited from being able to pursue particular interests (often academic ones that are not available at most high schools—a particular language or the study of architecture, for example) to a depth far beyond what the average applicant has accomplished. They have often begun to focus on a particular field or subject matter at a young age and have even benefited from jobs or internships in those fields, giving them a bit of life experience that other high schoolers do not possess.

PERCEIVED WEAKNESSES OF YOUR POSITION

Some of the differences inherent in a home-schooled applicant's profile are considered weaknesses rather than strengths. Many schools worry that students who have learned at home, through their parents' teaching methods, are ill-prepared for a rigorous college curriculum. Because they cannot be certain that a home-schooled applicant has covered all the material that is studied by a student in public or private school, admissions officers often feel less than confident about a home-schooled applicant's academic readiness for college. They also wonder if the student can follow a curriculum with rigorous and inflexible requirements after getting used to learning what and when he wants to study.

Colleges are enormously concerned about home-schooled applicants' social and communication skills. Leading colleges employ curriculums that require a lot of interaction between students inside the classroom. They are also for the most part residential communities where students must cooperate and live peaceably with one another. Many admissions officers are wary that home-schooled applicants will have a hard time adjusting to living and learning with other students after spending so much time on their own. Many admissions officers view home-schooled applicants as academically mature but socially immature. This becomes a more obvious pitfall for those home-schooled applicants applying to college at very young ages.

APPLICATION TIPS

First, all home-schooled applicants must contact the admissions committee of each of their target schools to discuss their candidacy and what they can do to ensure the best treatment in the admissions process. This is crucial for all candidates applying to colleges from a current home-school status as well as those applying to colleges as regular high school seniors who have been home-schooled at some point in their high school careers. Each school has different recommendations for home-schooled applicants, so you need to talk with someone at each college—this will help to put you on their radar screen as well as clue you in as to what you need to do when applying. Many colleges now assign one particular admissions officer the responsibility of overseeing home-schooled applicants. You can benefit from getting to know this individual.

Be sure to follow all of the colleges' guidelines. If a college tells you and your parents that it wants a curriculum list, take the request seriously. Do not send some Post-It notes with the names of books scribbled down on them. Call your local school system to see what a curriculum guide contains and how it is put together. Send the colleges a formal printed list containing substantial and detailed information. It is a good idea for all home-schooled applicants to offer curriculum lists, even when they are not requested. Be sure to follow each school's testing requirements. It is best if you can take (and do well on) as many SAT subject and AP exams as possible.

It is also in every home-schooled candidate's best interest to take classes at a school or community college, not only for the objective grades you can then show for yourself but also for the teacher recommendations you will be able to solicit. Joining activities and organizations in the community or at a school is a smart way to ensure that you receive recognition for your pursuits and to extinguish any thoughts on the part of admissions officers that you are antisocial or unable to work well with others. You should always sit for an interview, on campus with an admissions officer if the school offers such interviews. Because one of the concerns that admissions officers have about you is regarding your social, interaction, and communication skills, the interview is an ideal way in which to put their fears to rest. It also gives you an extra opportunity to elaborate on your experiences and provide the proper context for an evaluation of your candidacy.

Capitalize on your strengths as much as possible. Your independence, self-motivation, intellectual maturity, and passion for learning should become critical aspects of your profile. If you have a particular interest that you have been able to pursue in depth through your unique education, use that material in your essays. By doing your best to prove that you have none of the weaknesses inherent in your profile and playing up the unique benefits of a home-school education, you can win over the admissions committees and find a place in their hearts.

**WHAT ADMISSIONS DIRECTORS SAY ABOUT
HOME-SCHOOLED APPLICANTS**

Home-schooling is certainly a growth industry. Every year we see and take a few more home-schooled students than the year before. *Marlyn McGrath Lewis, Harvard*

It always involves a bit of a leap of faith to take them, but some of them are superb. *David Borus, Vassar*

We try to be very user friendly to home-schooled applicants at Colby. We don't look down on the home-school experience, and we don't diminish the customization of your education. But we do want to know the motivation behind your home-school decision, and to be more aware of the context. *Steve Thomas, Colby*

The thing that home-schooled students can't automatically give us is context. They are studying in a "group of one" instead of a group of 100 or 1,000. As home-schooled applicants are assembling their application, they should err on the side of giving us more than we asked for to help provide the missing context. *Stephen Farmer, UNC Chapel Hill*

Home-schooled students may not have made the same kinds of contributions to their community as more traditional students (student clubs, student government, etc.). However, we recognize that there are other ways to demonstrate leadership and service. We are looking to see how this person is going to move our campus forward, and to see whether our school is a good fit that will move them forward, too. *Douglas Christiansen, Vanderbilt*

Most important is understanding what opportunities they did and did not have. Many will be in educational environments without an AP curriculum, for example. We don't expect them to take advantage of opportunities that don't exist for them. Instead, we look at how they have achieved in the context of what's available to them. *Rick Bischoff, Cal Tech*

What Advice Do You Have for Home-Schooled Applicants?

We prefer that home-schooled applicants take five SAT subject tests instead of the usual three. *Eric J. Furda, Columbia*

I would suggest that all home-schooled students interview as well—we try to be sure they do if they are nearby. *Christoph Guttentag, Duke*

The more SAT subject tests home-schooled applicants can take, the better—take a dozen if you can. *Rick Shaw, Stanford*

It's much easier for us to evaluate a home-schooled student if he or she has gone to community college or taken some classes at local schools—especially when recommendations come from these outside sources. *Michael Goldberger, Brown*

Because of the nature of their grades, we like to see as many SAT [subject] scores as possible from home-schooled applicants. We also hope that they've taken a few courses at a local school or college. We urge them to come for an interview. Here's where an interview at UVA might matter. *John Blackburn, University of Virginia*

Home-schooled kids have a great responsibility to summarize their educations in a way that makes sense, while keeping to the confines of our application. This requires dedication to the application process. They have to show what they've studied and how they've studied. We need to see how their education has evolved and what they've learned along the way. *Janet Lavin Rapelye, Princeton*

Home-schooled students should be careful about their curricular choices. If their parent [or home-based program] is uncomfortable with a subject or lacks the resources for proper instruction, students should pursue that subject outside the home or program. For example, if the parent is not strong in a foreign language, this is a perfect opportunity to look for foreign language courses in other settings such as the local community college. This has the added benefit of supplying a nonparent letter of recommendation and allows the student to compete with many applicants who have four years of a foreign language on their transcript. *Kimberly Van Deusen, William & Mary*

There is more pressure on home-schooled students to explain and define their curricular experience. This can best be accomplished by amassing as much objective data as possible—SAT subject test scores, grades from community college or high school courses, recommendations from others besides their parent-teachers, etc. *Lee Coffin, Tufts*

Recommendations are the biggest challenge. Candidates need to start thinking several years in advance about the kinds of people they will be asking for recommendations. These recommenders will need to talk about their ability to do demanding coursework. It can be tough to persuade us when the only recommendations are from Mom and Dad. *Rick Bischoff, Cal Tech*

Home-schoolers have to work harder to make themselves "fit" into the traditional nature of college applications. They may not have the more traditional organizations and academic backgrounds; thus, they have to think "outside of the box" and make sure that their application represents the uniqueness of their experience but also allows them to compete in the applicant pool. *Kedra Ishop, Texas*

A rule of thumb for home-schooled applicants is that the more they can tell us the better. A liability home-schooled applicants can face is not enough documentation in their application. Give us reading lists of the books you've read. Tell us about the mentors who have been involved in your instruction. Taking time to document each aspect of your education is very helpful. *Stephen Schierloh, Sarah Lawrence*

We look to see that home-schooled applicants have also engaged in the world beyond their home. It's beneficial to provide recommendations from someone other than a parent for added perspective. As a parent, I can tell you from experience that parents can often be biased. [Also] we find that the interview becomes important to try to tease out an applicant's level of involvement with the world. *Stuart Schmill, MIT*

Those who have never had outside evaluation—no high school or community college courses, for instance—have to take a step back and explain carefully what they have done. They should never assume that we understand what they've done, absent their own full explanation. *Janet Lavin Rapelye, Princeton*

We need details of the work they've done and how it has been pursued, whether they've done it independently or by one-on-one tutoring, online classes, or community college courses. They should err on the side of giving us too much information. In fact, if a question is not answered thoroughly—such as not describing in detail the math and science curriculum they've covered—we won't assume that a home-schooled candidate has managed the same curriculum as an average applicant. *Jess Lord, Haverford*

ARE STANDARDIZED TEST SCORES MORE IMPORTANT FOR HOME-SCHOOLED APPLICANTS?

Here is where we suspend our admissions philosophy of subordinating quantifiable criteria. We have to look at test scores carefully with home-schooled applicants. We can't avoid it—we don't know what their grades mean. *John Hanson, Middlebury*

Standardized tests take on a greater weight for home-schooled students. *Christoph Guttentag, Duke*

I tell students who are schooled at home to get as much external validation of their abilities as possible—especially in math and science. Taking AP exams and SAT subject tests are good ways to do so. *Nancy Hargrave Meislahn, Wesleyan*

We just changed our policy in regard to testing for home-schooled applicants. We still don't *require* that they submit test scores, but we highly recommend that they submit as many scores as possible. We end up not taking students if we can't see test scores and the only grades and recommendations are from parents. *Richard Steele, Bowdoin*

WHAT ARE YOUR BIGGEST AREAS OF CONCERN WITH APPLICANTS WHO HAVE BEEN HOME-SCHOOLED?

Our greatest concern with home-schooled applicants is regarding their social maturity. They often apply to college at a very young age and don't have the experience of interaction in the classroom that others have. *Rick Shaw, Stanford*

My biggest concerns with home-schooled kids are regarding social interaction and maturity. Engagement with fellow learners is critical to higher education, and we need to know that our students can hold up their end of the responsibility here. *Nancy Hargrave Meislahn, Wesleyan*

In the case of home-schooled applicants, we are often unconcerned about self-direction (which we value highly here) and intellectual capacity. In some cases we do worry about maturity and social IQ. Anything home-schooled applicants can do to allay these concerns in their application is helpful. *Stephen Schierloh, Sarah Lawrence*

Parents of home-schooled kids shouldn't expect their child to be the lone exception to the rules regarding admission here. They should understand the requirements for admission as well as for participation once they're here. *Janet Lavin Rapelye, Princeton*

The home-schooled applicants we see don't present unusual challenges. They have usually documented their progress, oftentimes by taking courses at local colleges or through reputable online programs. This is particularly true of math and science courses. Problems do arise if we can't tell what they've studied. We need to be certain they've taken sufficient math to be able to step into our courses. *Rick Bischoff, Cal Tech*

WHAT SPECIAL POSITIVE ATTRIBUTES DO HOME-SCHOOLED STUDENTS TEND TO EXHIBIT?

They tend to be very mature and independent. *Maria Laskaris, Dartmouth*

Home-schooled applicants have the ability to show really extended development in one area—that's the draw. They can often go farther in music or science—whatever they're into—than other students can. But they also need to have some balance. *Sheppard Shanley, Northwestern*

LEARNING DISABLED APPLICANTS

SPECIAL CASE STATUS

If you have been diagnosed with a learning difference, you should treat your college admissions situation as a special one. Colleges cannot legally require you to disclose information about a disability. If you have a disability that has affected your academic performance, though, you would be wise to discuss it appropriately. Providing the colleges with as much contextual information as possible enables them to have more confidence in your ability to perform there. For example, if a learning disability helps them understand why your grades in math have fluctuated dramatically despite your having done consistently well in all other subjects, then you need to explain the situation.

PERCEIVED STRENGTHS OF YOUR POSITION

The likely strength of your status is what you can claim from having battled a problem, come to terms with it, overcome it, and found ways to live your life around it. Showing that you sought help for a learning issue and worked to overcome it indicates initiative and the ability to persevere.

PERCEIVED WEAKNESSES OF YOUR POSITION

The weaknesses of your position stem from the limits imposed by your disability on your academic capabilities. Learning disabled students who have performed well after the diagnosis was made and solutions found largely escape any problems associated with their position. If you have already proven that you are capable of doing well by using certain learning and study strategies, then you will not suffer in the admissions process. Learning disabled students who have not yet performed well in spite of diagnosing the problem and applying particular study tactics may have a hard time convincing admissions officers that they have what it takes to succeed at a demanding college.

CHOOSING COLLEGES

All colleges—even the most elite ones—now offer services for students with learning differences. Such services include writing centers, one-on-one tutors, note-taking services, study-skills classes, and the offering of accommodations such as extended time on major exams for those with diagnosed disabilities. If you have a learning difference, you will want to investigate how extensive such services are at your prospective colleges, and to speak to someone at each learning center to make sure your needs can be met. If your needs are great, you may want to look into special programs with comprehensive four-year services, such as the University of Arizona's SALT program or the University of Denver's LEP program. Programs of this nature require an extra application in which you discuss your learning issues and requirements in-depth.

Whether or not you apply to one of these programs, by all means seek evaluation of your issues while in high school. A sophisticated evaluation will help you develop appropriate coping strategies and skills. It will also help you target appropriate colleges—and discuss your abilities and needs with these colleges when the time comes.

APPLICATION TIPS

As mentioned previously, you should definitely offer the admissions committee as much information as possible about your issue and, if possible, provide evidence that when applying the right strategies, you can and do perform well. Colleges are not concerned with what particular strategies you use to achieve success, they merely want to see that you can achieve your goals with proper accommodations.

The question is not *whether* to disclose information about the disability but *how* to disclose that information. Colleges have slightly different opinions about this. Most schools agree that a guidance counselor is often best able to provide appropriate information in a way that does not sound like an excuse for poor performance and is accompanied by some amount of perspective on the problem. Some schools also want candidates or teachers to address the issue, whereas others prefer that the problem not take up too much of the application's focus. You should contact each target school to ask an admissions representative's advice on how to approach the application.

The personal strength you have gained from battling a learning difference is not one you should dwell on too much, though. Being as succinct as possible in discussing this kind of disability is usually more effective than making it the only message that comes through. You do not want to be known as the girl with the learning disability; you want to be known as the great candidate who has the best record in her league for the 400-meter run—oh, yes, and also happens to have a learning disability that she has fought and overcome. Find other positive qualities and strengths with which to position yourself.

Note that the College Board and ACT transcripts do not indicate whether you have had accommodations for their tests. However, it can be advantageous to mention your receipt of accommodations on your college applications because both the College Board and the ACT organization have become quite strict about their services for students with disabilities (SSD) offerings. Evidence of accommodations on standardized tests generally shows that your learning issue is legitimate.

ADMISSIONS DIRECTORS TALK ABOUT APPLICANTS WITH LEARNING DISABILITIES

We often don't know about learning disabilities during the admissions process. But if a student has taken the SAT untimed, or there is evidence of a disability, the student should tell us more so that we understand something about the conditions under which the candidate has succeeded. *Katie Fretwell, Amherst*

We are interested in *performance*—how a student has performed over time. We're not so interested in the strategies a student has used to achieve that performance as we are in the end result itself. Learning disabilities in and of themselves do not discourage us from admitting an applicant. *Marlyn McGrath Lewis, Harvard*

There is perhaps more of a burden in the college choice process on students with learning differences than those without to find a good match. Different colleges offer different degrees of support. If you are in this situation, contact the people or offices providing those services directly. Find out which school will make it most possible for you to flourish.   *William M. Shain, Vanderbilt*

It is 100 percent the student's decision whether or not to disclose a learning disability. For those that choose to, it can be a good vehicle for providing context about performance and lead to a better understanding by admissions officers about how the applicant has developed compensation mechanisms. The focus of admissions officers will be on performance. Good performance for a student with a learning disability will be a good demonstration of the student's ability to have compensated. Poor performance, however, is poor performance, and won't be a good predictor of future performance in some environments.   *Bruce Poch, Pomona*

We tell applicants with concerns about a disability to be in touch with the campus coordinator for students with disabilities while applying. All conversations with that office remain confidential—records of the contact do not go to the admissions committee. I recommend full disclosure of disabilities, though—students who do the best job of presenting themselves give us a full context in which to make our decisions.   *Nancy Hargrave Meislahn, Wesleyan*

We don't factor a learning disability into the admissions process. It may give us perspective to know about it, but our policy is that those students still need to meet our regular admissions standards. Once they are here, they will have a wealth of services to help them continue to succeed academically.   *Ingrid Hayes, Georgia Tech*

We think it's to a student's advantage to tell us about a learning disability. It allows us to understand them better.   *John Blackburn, University of Virginia*

Is It Best for an Applicant, a Teacher, or a Guidance Counselor to Disclose the Disability?

I don't suggest that the disability come through in every part of the application. If everyone—the student, the counselor, a teacher—discusses it, it starts to become the only thing we see.   *Sheppard Shanley, Northwestern*

If a student decides he'd like to disclose a disability during the admissions process we feel it is a plus for the student to tell us about it in his own words. This conveys a sense of awareness, ownership, and control over the disability. That said, there is of course no harm done if someone else discloses this information for him. *Stephen Schierloh, Sarah Lawrence*

It can be helpful if the student addresses the disability and a teacher or guidance counselor does the same in a recommendation—so we get a few perspectives on the issue.   *Nancy Hargrave Meislahn, Wesleyan*

PHYSICALLY DISABLED APPLICANTS

SPECIAL CASE STATUS

If you have a physical disability, you should treat your college admissions situation as a special one, even though it will not be deemed so by the schools themselves. Colleges cannot legally require you to disclose information about a disability. Nowhere on the college application forms will you be asked about such situations. All of the schools have offices for students with disabilities and provide assistance for those in need of help in performing academically, living comfortably on the campus, and contributing to the campus community. You will find students possessing every kind of physical disability—from blindness to multiple sclerosis—on the campuses of the leading colleges.

If you have a disability, even if it has not affected your academic performance whatsoever, you should by all means let the colleges know. By providing the colleges with as much contextual information as possible, you enable them to understand and appreciate your situation all the more.

PERCEIVED STRENGTHS OF YOUR POSITION

You derive enormous strengths that can benefit you in the college admissions process from coping and living with a physical disability, which, at a minimum, shows that you possess inner fortitude. If you have a serious disability and have still managed to perform well academically and reach your goals, you demonstrate an ability to bound over obstacles and deal with an affliction likely to be unique among the college applicant pool. You are also seen as possessing strength of character through facing discrimination and marginalization.

PERCEIVED WEAKNESSES OF YOUR POSITION

There are no weaknesses inherent in your position, unless your academic performance suggests that you might not be able to live and learn on the college campus because of the limitations of your physical disability.

APPLICATION TIPS

Discuss your disability situation as part of your profile, but do so with great care. You do not wish to appear as if you are "using" your position to gain sympathy from the admissions staff, nor should you risk sounding crass, angry, or resentful of others. Discuss your disability in a meaningful way, do not whine, and avoid using clichés to show how you have been formed by your life experiences. It is also a good idea to contact each target school's office for disabled students. You will need to start preparing to live in a new environment, but contact will also be helpful for your own fact-finding purposes. Discussions with the office for disabilities can teach you more about the school and how it meets your needs and desires as a special student. This information can in turn be used in your admissions materials to demonstrate your fit with the college. In addition, a counselor in the disabilities office may even become a supporter of your case in the admissions process.

**ADMISSIONS DIRECTORS DISCUSS APPLICANTS
WITH PHYSICAL DISABILITIES**

Physical disabilities are very important to discuss—students shouldn't hide them! A discussion of a disability often gives us a very good picture—a positive impression—of the candidate. We want to know what obstacles an applicant has overcome, what makes that applicant unique, what affects the day-to-day life. *Maria Laskaris, Dartmouth*

It is completely up to the student to decide whether or not to disclose a disability. Some students have powerful reasons not to. It will never hurt to disclose [it]. . . . If a student wants to disclose a disability, passing mention in an essay or recommendation is not enough. Our admissions materials explain how to go about it properly. *Stephen Farmer, UNC Chapel Hill*

Unless the student thinks it's a story worth telling, there is no reason we need to know about a disability. It might be good to bring it up in an essay as a challenge faced, but we leave it to students to decide. Only after a disabled applicant is admitted do we ask for this information so we can accommodate their needs. *Daniel J. Saracino, Notre Dame*

LEGACY APPLICANTS

SPECIAL CASE STATUS

Being a "legacy"—that is, related to someone who attended a given college—can greatly improve your chances of admission. Note, however, that many universities will only consider those whose relative attended the undergraduate college to be a true legacy, entitled to potential admissions favor.

Schools vary in how much favor they extend legacies. Three factors tend to be influential in determining the admissions advantage to be gained:

■ The closer the relationship to your relative, the better. If one of your parents attended a school, the impact will tend to be greater than if an uncle were the alum.

■ The more active in alumni and school affairs, and the more the relative has donated to the school, the better.

■ Private schools tend to put more weight on legacy status than do state schools, due to the latter traditionally relying on public rather than private funding and having their admissions decisions subjected to more scrutiny.

The impact of being a legacy can be substantial:

■ It makes it easier to get into a school (i.e., the "bar" may be set lower).

■ Special admissions procedures may be put into effect. Thus, counseling about how best to fashion an application may be offered. Legacies may be given the chance to interview, even when other applicants are not. And legacies are often given the chance to respond to an admissions office's concerns about his or her candidacy.

■ At state schools, the candidate is likely to be considered as an in-state applicant, thereby making it easier to get in and also lowering the amount of tuition to be paid.

Not all schools, even private ones, give preference to legacies, but most do. At the most selective schools, legacies comprise 10 to 15 percent of the student body. They are more than twice as likely as nonlegacy applicants to be admitted. Part of this advantage may derive from the fact that alumni do much of the interviewing for schools and tend to favor their old classmates' children.

PERCEIVED STRENGTHS OF YOUR POSITION

There are three strengths that you are thought to exhibit by way of your legacy status. The first is that you are more likely to attend the school than others in the applicant pool who do not have family ties. The second strength of your profile is that of your connection with alums of the school. By admitting you, the school keeps a contributing and supportive alum happy. The third is that you are likely to be a very engaged student, and then a dedicated alum of the school.

PERCEIVED WEAKNESSES OF YOUR POSITION

There is no inherent weakness in your position as a legacy unless you show insufficient "demonstrated interest" during the application process. Colleges want to know that legacies have fully evaluated their programs rather than deciding to apply simply because of a family connection.

APPLICATION TIPS

As a legacy applicant, you should do everything in your power to make the admissions committee confident that your interest in the school stems not only from your family connection but also from your own research and investigation. Although admitted legacies generally attend their target colleges in higher numbers than do nonlegacies, admissions officers are also aware that there are plenty of legacies who have applied to their colleges to use them as safety schools. Many students end up applying to Mom's and Dad's alma maters not because they really want to attend but because they think that they might have an easier chance at getting in. You should thus show to the admissions officers that you have substantial and mature reasons (i.e., reasons other than the fact of your perfect football game attendance record since the age of five) for wanting to attend the school and that you would choose it even without the family push.

Make sure to solicit materials from the school, visit its website, and make a formal prospective applicant visit, even if you think you already know all there is to know about the school. You are bound to discover something new, which you can use to show your fit with the school in your admissions materials. You also need to show "demonstrated interest" in the school to admissions officers, who have no way of knowing that you have been reading Dad's alumni magazines and staying in the dorms during alumni reunion weekends all your life.

The admissions committees will look with special care at your case if your parent or relative is a long-standing or generous donor to the campus or occupies a position of leadership in an alumni organization. If your alumni relative is not an important priority to the college, your application will still be treated with great care by the admissions committees, but you may not get much of an edge over other applicants in the process. This is particularly true, at the most selective schools, if you apply for financial aid.

WHAT ADMISSIONS DIRECTORS SAY ABOUT LEGACIES

Our alumni are our taxpayers, so we can't ignore them. There is some level of preference for alumni children who come to us in Early Decision. Those in the regular admissions pool get little preference, though.   *Lee Stetson, Penn*

We read the files of children of our graduates as we read everyone else's. We do admit legacies at three times the rate of others, but the qualifications of legacies admitted here are exactly the same as those of the rest of the class. They tend to have gone to good schools—their parents have valued good schools, as they did their own education at Princeton, and they've sought out good programs in and out of school for their children. So these are students we'd want anyway, regardless of whether they were legacies. *Janet Lavin Rapelye, Princeton*

Legacies are an important demographic—they are part of the college family. As long as our standards are met, those candidates can be the beneficiaries of a "legacy bump." *Tim Cheney, Connecticut College*

Our criteria for legacy candidates are the same as for nonlegacy candidates. The difference is that they get a fourth read while most applications get three. We are looking for reasons to take legacies, but will not do so if the academic foundation of the application is not sufficient. *Steve Thomas, Colby*

Legacy candidates are given special consideration, but legacy status is not a guarantee of admission. If all other things are essentially equal, preference is given to children of alumni. But all other things must be equal. *Kimberly Van Deusen, William & Mary*

It is very interesting: we are at the point in Wesleyan's history where we are beginning to see "double-legacies"—students whose parents are both Wes alums. Sometimes they ask if they can get twice the push! Just kidding, of course. In all seriousness, we try to make the best decision we can for students with a family history and connection to Wesleyan. That means they get another "extra look" before a decision is final. And, if the answer is not going to be positive, we work with colleagues on campus to determine if any special notification or special follow-up is needed. *Nancy Hargrave Meislahn, Wesleyan*

Being the son or daughter of a Yale graduate does not by itself make one a competitive candidate. Legacies have to survive initial comparison with everyone else in our applicant pool and appear to be competitive in their own right, and at that point there is additional weight given to their application in the review process. We look for the same qualities in legacies as we do in other applicants—strong academic performance and the ability to bring other qualities to Yale such as energy, motivation, curiosity, and the capacity to be committed to extracurricular pursuits and to the Yale community. *Margit Dahl, Yale*

Legacy candidates are evaluated along with everyone else—they are not placed into a separate pool or anything like that. And, as at other schools, being a legacy can become a plus when a student is right on the border. *Maria Laskaris, Dartmouth*

I've had alumni tell me that they appreciate our system of no favors for legacies even when this policy works against their child. They appreciate that MIT is truly about merit and are proud of that. *Stuart Schmill, MIT*

We of course accept a greater percentage of legacies than of nonlegacies. But that's really not so terrible as some people make it out to be. If an applicant has a parent who went to Amherst, we would expect that he or she grew up in a home where reading is valued, good books are always around, and intellectual pursuits are common. So there is probably more likelihood of that student being a good fit with Amherst anyway.   *Katie Fretwell, Amherst*

Our Quaker roots obligate us not to give preferential treatment to legacies—our alumni all respect this policy.   *James Bock, Swarthmore*

Tradition and connections are especially important at small schools, so extra weight is given to legacies. We give a legacy folder an especially careful read. *David Borus, Vassar*

The Most Common Mistakes Legacies Make

I don't feel that legacies make any more mistakes than anyone else. Some may feel that their legacy connection will "get them in," when it is only a part of a much larger consideration; but then again, some nonlegacies may feel there is something in particular that will "get them in" as well. My advice would be to try to separate family affiliation with a college from the question of whether that school is a good fit for you, and not to feel pressured to attend that school just because all of your siblings and your parents have gone there. It may be a great choice for you—but if you don't feel that it is, have the courage to look elsewhere.   *Margit Dahl, Yale*

Legacy students should be sure to familiarize themselves with the school—it's not the same place as when Mom or Dad went there. Make sure that you are basing your decision to come on more than yarns from yesteryear.   *Tim Cheney, Connecticut College*

What Special Positive Qualities Do Legacies Exhibit?

It depends on the student. Many legacies bring with them a deeper knowledge of Yale and an inherent loyalty to this institution based on their family's involvement with Yale over the years—but others do not. I have no concerns about legacies that I wouldn't have for any other students adjusting to a school as challenging as Yale.   *Margit Dahl, Yale*

UNIVERSITY PROFESSORS' AND EMPLOYEES' CHILDREN

SPECIAL CASE STATUS

The children of a university's faculty, administrators, and other employees face a situation very similar to that of legacy applicants. Not all such children will receive a substantial admissions boost, of course. Some colleges limit the admissions benefit to those whose parent:

- Is a faculty member (perhaps further limited to those who are tenured) or senior administrator

- Works full-time for the school—and has done so for a specified number of years

- Works for the college (rather than the medical school, for instance)

Those who do qualify receive a very substantial admissions boost at almost every school.

Note, however, that even those who fail to meet the official guidelines may be advantaged in the admission process. After all, the school (presumably) wants to keep its employees happy.

PERCEIVED STRENGTHS OF YOUR POSITION

There are several strengths to your position. First, you are probably knowledgeable about and interested in the school and thus likely to be an engaged student. Second, you are likely to attend the school, thereby increasing the school's yield statistics. Third, and most important, the school attracts faculty and administrators on the basis of promising to educate their children free of charge (or for a greatly reduced amount), a tax-free benefit greatly valued by recipients. Keeping its side of the bargain is critical to keeping these employees happy. Failing to do so would not just poison relations with these people, it would also make recruiting others in the future much more difficult.

PERCEIVED WEAKNESSES OF YOUR POSITION

The only likely weakness—apart from academic underperformance, of course— is that you may seem blasé about attending your parent's school. In the grand scheme of things, this is a minor consideration.

APPLICATION TIPS

Apart from making sure you do not appear unexcited about attending this school, there is nothing specific to your situation as a professor's or administrator's child that warrants attention. That said, you maximize your chances by following the general marketing approach suggested in this book, with particular attention to maximizing your academic profile. In considering professors' and administrators' children, schools are least likely to admit those who appear to be academic risks. The lack of sparkling extracurricular credentials is less likely to be cause for concern.

RECRUITED ATHLETE APPLICANTS

SPECIAL CASE STATUS

Athletics is a big part of collegiate life, and virtually all schools pay a great deal of attention to athletics in the admissions process. If you are a high school athlete looking to attend a world-class institution, it would be a mistake—and a potential opportunity lost—to assume that this emphasis on athletics is found just at "jock schools." Few colleges have de-emphasized athletics; the Ivy League schools, for example, are heavily invested in winning at each of the many varsity sports they play.

Many of the most competitive colleges, including the Ivy League schools and the small, competitive liberal arts colleges, do not grant athletic scholarships. They do, however, seek talented athletes and are willing to stretch to admit less able students who are gifted athletes.

The impact upon admissions tends to be substantial. A typical small school participating in twenty-five sports (men's and women's) will tend to set aside between 150 and 200 seats for recruited athletes. At the medium-sized Ivy League schools, approximately 8 to 15 percent of an incoming class will consist of recruited athletes. Few of these recruits would get in without the admissions boost they receive.

Coaches of minor sports (fencing, gymnastics) can expect to get their top few recruits admitted at about an 80 to 90 percent rate, with the next set of (lesser) recruits admitted at a 60 to 75 percent rate. (Thus, knowing where you stand on a coach's list can be very important.) Coaches of major revenue sports (football, basketball) can expect to succeed with far more of their recruits. Coaches with long records of success tend to have more influence over the admission process than do new or less successful coaches.

THE DEMAND FOR ATHLETES

Numerous changes in the nature of collegiate athletics have increased the recruiting of athletes:

■ Title IX has indeed leveled the playing field for women, which has meant that the number of athletes participating on varsity teams has all but doubled in recent years.

■ The increased competitiveness of college teams—with few administrations accepting mediocre, let alone poor, results in any sport for long—has meant that coaches no longer rely on "walk-ons" (unrecruited athletes who simply try out for a team at the beginning of a season) and instead recruit heavily.

■ The increased professionalism of college—and indeed of high school and grade school—sports means that there are no longer many multisport participants. The result is a need for more athletes.

■ At schools that are forbidden to give out athletic scholarships, the increased demands on athletes means that many simply quit their sports partway through college (since they are financially free to do so). To take account of the likely dropout rate, coaches recruit more athletes.

PERCEIVED STRENGTHS OF YOUR POSITION

Virtually all colleges are looking for accomplished student athletes. Even if you are not near the top of your high school class, the combination of a solid academic record and your athletic prowess may prove to be a combination that you can leverage into an acceptance at a very selective college. The opportunity for self-promotion is stronger for the ambitious, accomplished student athlete than it is for almost anyone else in the admissions pool.

Part of this is due to the impact you may have on a college team's prospects. Part of your value also resides in the personal qualities you are assumed to possess. Being the successful captain of your outstanding soccer team, for example, indicates personal attributes such as perseverance, leadership, teamwork, and the ability to juggle many different responsibilities at once.

PERCEIVED WEAKNESSES OF YOUR POSITION

There are two potential weaknesses that you may need to overcome, depending on the sport you play as well as your own profile. If you are a male, playing one of the "macho" sports—football, ice hockey, basketball, wrestling, and perhaps track and field (albeit not distance running) or baseball—you risk being stereotyped as an inconsiderate, even potentially violent fellow, if other aspects of your candidacy also point in the same direction. For example, a wrestler who has been suspended from school for drinking will need to counteract this poor impression. (This is particularly true if there is even a hint of trouble in his file regarding the treatment of young women.) The other potential problem is that you may be viewed as not entirely up to the intellectual mark.

APPLICATION TIPS

Determining Your Value

Begin by assessing your value to schools. Ask your coaches, rival coaches, and other experts familiar with your abilities how you compare with athletes playing for your target schools. Emphasize that you are seeking their honest, informed opinions. If they mislead you about your value to schools, you may end up missing substantial opportunities, so be certain that they are not sloughing you off with well-intended exaggerations of your worth.

Note that you will be much more valuable to some schools than others. Your value depends on the value the college places on your sport and your ability to help the team win (or at least garner publicity). Colleges tend to value the "money sports," such as football, very highly. Each college also has historical favorites, those sports in which it has traditionally been successful. A look at the past success of the school's teams or a quick chat with a few students will reveal which sports are close to a given school's heart.

As for your ability to help a team win, several factors will be determinative (in addition to your own ability level). First, there is the level of competition at which this team plays: Is it a national contender or a perennial, small-time loser? Second is the importance of your position. A quarterback will be regarded as playing a more important position than that of tight end. Similarly, if you are a sprinter and thus able to run the 100 meters, 200 meters, 4 × 100 relay, and perhaps long jump, you will be considered more valuable than one-event participants such as shot-putters. Third is the availability of substitutes for you. If your school already has a marvelous quarterback, or has a set of them currently applying, your value is proportionately lower.

Coaches have the ability to influence a number of admissions decisions. Depending on the sport and the school, a coach can choose a certain number of top recruits each year. The higher you are on the coach's list, the more impact it will have on the process. Note, however, that if someone above you on the list plays your same position, your fate may depend on whether that person decides to attend the school. Try to find out from the coach where you stand overall and as to your position. Realize, however, that coaches are notoriously less than candid with applicants, wanting to please them and to keep them interested in their programs in case they need "backups." If a coach is not actively pursuing you with numerous phone calls and emails, be honest with yourself about the fact that you are probably not very high on his or her list.

POSITIONING YOURSELF

Unless you are a consensus all-American, you are likely to need to market yourself rather than simply respond to schools' recruiting efforts. The first step is to make sure that you come to the attention of your chosen schools. You can do this by participating in very high-profile tournaments or attending high-profile sports camps. You will also need to contact the schools directly.

The appropriate way to initiate contact is to send a package of materials about yourself to the coaches at your chosen schools. You can send your materials by email or regular mail. They should include:

- A cover letter, explaining your interest in the program (and the coach) and the school.

- A sports résumé, with a brief look at your academic record (including test results), extracurricular and outside of school achievements, and your athletic accomplishments. Include your height and weight, key statistics, and honors and awards.

- Recommendation letters from your coach, an opposing coach, or another expert, focusing on your ability, attitude, and potential.

- Clippings from newspaper coverage of you.

- A schedule of your upcoming competitions, in case a coach or interested alum will be able to see you perform. Similarly, note any sports camps you plan to attend.

- An offer to send a video of your performance.

Have your high school coach contact the coaches at colleges of interest to you. Brief him or her in advance so that he or she knows what to emphasize, including how you will fit into a given school's program. In addition, be sure to visit the school and arrange (in advance) to meet with the relevant coach or coaches.

SELECTING AN APPROPRIATE PROGRAM

Athletic programs are by no means uniform. There is a world of difference between an average Division I program and a Division III program. There is even a large difference between athletic conferences. And, of course, any given program tends to reflect its coach to a large extent. Given the immense amount of time you are likely to be in contact with him or her, make sure you will be able to get along easily. Given that you will spend many hours a day on your sport, in season and out, you owe it to yourself to be sure that a given program fits your needs and interests particularly well before committing to it.

**SHOULD YOU TRADE DOWN IN SCHOOL
QUALITY FOR A SCHOLARSHIP?**

It is easy to take a full scholarship to play basketball at Stanford or Duke rather than attend Swarthmore or Williams, given that the former are both among the academic (as well as the athletic) elite. The harder question is whether to take an athletic scholarship to play for a much lesser academic university. Given that few can earn a living playing basketball or any other sport, the question for most applicants should not be whether a given athletic program will maximize their chances of making it to the "big leagues" or onto the professional circuit. Instead, the question is whether the scholarship money warrants giving up the better education.

Note, however, that there is an additional drawback to accepting an athletic rather than academic scholarship. Your time may be more your coach's than your own at many schools. Partly due to this, the graduation rates of athletes (particularly in the "money sports," such as basketball and football) at some schools are low. Thus, all too often athletes get a second-class education even at schools that are otherwise highly regarded.

ADMISSIONS DIRECTORS DISCUSS RECRUITED ATHLETES

HOW MANY ATHLETES ARE GIVEN SPECIAL CONSIDERATION?

It depends completely on the sport and on a team's needs in any given year. A football coach, or a swim coach recruiting in many different events, will need to recruit more athletes than a tennis or crew coach will. If a team will be losing a large number of seniors to graduation in a given year, the coach may well need more new students the next year than he or she did the previous year. A coach may list two students on the "final" list of prospects for the admissions office one year and seven the next, or seven one year and fifteen the next. What ultimately happens to those applicants in the admissions process depends on how strong they are as students and athletes and how selective the admissions process is. *Margit Dahl, Yale*

WHAT CRITERIA ARE MOST IMPORTANT IN EVALUATING RECRUITED ATHLETES?

We look for three things: academic qualifications, athletic ability, and whether this will be a comfortable fit for them overall. First and foremost, they need to be comfortable as students. They have to have a broad-based curiosity about learning in multiple disciplines. If an applicant says he only wants to study business—not understanding the value of learning a foreign language, studying history, and so on—he won't be a good fit here.   *Paul Thiboutot, Carleton*

Reviewing the applications of recruited athletes is a process of balancing the level of athletic ability with the strengths and/or weaknesses presented in the rest of the application. We look for the same kind of qualities in a student-athlete as in all other applicants, but with the knowledge that athletics is a particular area where the student would contribute at Yale. We also look carefully at the overall academic profile to see how the applicant has handled the time commitment of schoolwork and serious athletic activity. In the final analysis, it is the coach who assesses the level of a student's athletic talent, and the admissions office that includes that assessment in the overall evaluation of the candidate. Coaches do not read the admissions files of their recruits.   *Margit Dahl, Yale*

WHAT SPECIAL POSITIVE QUALITIES DO ATHLETES EXHIBIT?

Recruited athletes have a drive and motivation to be the best they can that comes from their own discipline and organization, derived from their athletic participation, which will serve them well in academics. What we hope doesn't happen is that they separate into cliques consisting of members of their own teams selecting courses as a group and sitting in the back of these courses as a group—instead of engaging in the spirit of expanding friendship and inquiry of a liberal arts education.   *Paul Thiboutot, Carleton*

THE MOST COMMON MISTAKES RECRUITED ATHLETES MAKE

I think some recruited athletes, or their parents, think that a coach has the decisive role in the admissions process when that is not the case. At Yale the coach does the athletic evaluation and makes recommendations to the admissions office based on the applicant's athletic ability and capacity to contribute to their program. But that information must be considered along with essays, transcripts, and recommendations that the coach does not see, and the final decision rests with the admissions office. It's important for students and families to remember that, regardless of the "promises" that the coach may seem to be making.   *Margit Dahl, Yale*

Recruited athletes have devoted a great deal of time and energy to developing their special talents, which has required that they focus on their sport. However, we are bringing students to a much broader community and looking to understand the ways in which they will impact that community. Athletes often don't share things they will bring here beyond the athletics. Thus, we don't get as broad a picture as we'd like of them through their essays. They should keep in mind that we're admitting them to the Dartmouth community, not just to an athletic program. *Maria Laskaris, Dartmouth*

Recruited athletes often tend to submit written responses that are too short. It is difficult to determine context when there is not much substance in their short answers and essay. *Theodore Spencer, Michigan*

Applying to a Division III small liberal arts college is about more than just registering with an athletic recruitment agency that will forward their vital statistics to colleges and coaches. The résumé format some agencies use emphasizes simple data, but an applicant needs to be represented by more than athletic data or a GPA or SAT score. Athletes also have to recognize that getting in requires more than a coach showing interest in them. They should explore classes, meet current students, and meet with admissions officers. Liberal arts colleges still have at least the ideal of having student athletes. *Paul Thiboutot, Carleton*

We find that applications from recruited athletes are often late. Athletes will wait for a cue from the recruiting coach before they apply. My advice is to apply on time and notify the coach that you have done so as well as the admission dean who is the liaison with the coaches. That way, if the coach gives you the nod, the process is smoother and quicker for you, the student. Orientation mailings, health forms, etc., can be sent and completed in a timely manner. I would also recommend sending the application directly to the office of admission versus handing it to the coach. *Kimberly Van Deusen, William & Mary*

It is critical that recruited athletes make sure they know the curriculum requirements of the university. *Theodore Spencer, Michigan*

A common mistake that athletes make is not holding onto what they want a college to be academically and socially. They see athletics as the be all, end all. Then, once they get to college, it hits them how important these other factors are to their happiness. Another mistake athletes make is having too few points of contact in the admissions process. Don't just talk to the coach. Talk to admissions officers, to professors, to students. Try to get a full picture of the place and whether it's somewhere you would like to be when you're off the field. *William M. Shain, Vanderbilt*

Many students assume a greater degree of interest on the part of the coach than actually exists. They often misread what coaches are saying and believe they are stronger candidates than they actually are. Students should make sure to have their parents or counselor help them understand exactly what a coach has said to them. *Maria Laskaris, Dartmouth*

TRANSFER APPLICANTS

SPECIAL CASE STATUS

Transfer applicants are handled a bit differently than are regular applicants for admission to the freshman class. If you are a transfer candidate, your application is not evaluated along with the freshman applications but is placed in a pool of other candidates wishing to transfer to the college from another school. You compete only against other transfer applicants. Because there are fewer transfer applicants against whom one must compete, it is in one sense easier for transfers to make a strong case for themselves. On the other hand, the transfer pool is a bit more diverse than the regular pool, including older applicants who have had substantial careers before going back to college and students from a wide variety of other personal and educational backgrounds. This means that, in another sense, it is more difficult to make oneself appear unusual or unique as a transfer applicant.

At most colleges, the set of criteria by which transfer applicants are evaluated is slightly different from that by which regular candidates are examined. There is much more emphasis on a transfer applicant's college performance than on his high school performance (at some colleges a high school record is not even required for a transfer application). Students who do well in college can apply to transfer to colleges that may not have taken them for freshman admission based on their high school records. Transfers have another great advantage in that they can generally get by with lower standardized test scores than can regular applicants. The test scores of transfer students are not considered in the calculations of incoming class averages that become part of a college's profile (to be publicized in books, magazines, and other written materials). This means that colleges are much more willing to accept transfer students with low standardized test scores than to accept regular applicants with poor scores.

PERCEIVED STRENGTHS OF YOUR POSITION

If you are applying to transfer into a college from a four-year institution or a community college, you have several things working in your favor. First, taking the bull by the horns by applying to transfer to a different college rather than simply accepting your lot requires the kind of initiative that colleges find appealing. (Simply applying to college as a senior, an act that many students perform simply because it is expected of them—a "given" in the life of a high school senior—does not require as much self-awareness and initiative.) Second, transfer students have the benefit of more life and academic experience, which generally allows them to show that they have a good idea of what they want to do in college and beyond. Having a wealth of self-knowledge and the ability to lay out a life plan is always to your advantage.

PERCEIVED WEAKNESSES OF YOUR POSITION

There are not any significant weaknesses inherent in a transfer's profile. If a transfer student is applying to move from a college that is severely inferior to the one she desires to attend, the quality of her collegiate education thus far may be perceived as a weakness by the admissions committee. If a transfer applicant is applying from a college that is radically different from the target school (which is often the case), there is the possibility that the admission committee might be tempted to consider the candidate a poor judge of his own needs for having selected that college in the first place. This is easily rectified, though. Transfer applicants can simply acknowledge the poor judgment call made in youthful ignorance and use the difference in philosophy or style of education to their advantage by highlighting the need for transferring and the suitability of the target school.

APPLICATION TIPS

First, even if it is not explicitly asked of you, you must discuss in your application why your current college is not right for you as well as why the target school is a much better fit. Be as specific as possible to convince the committee that a move to its college is right for you. Acceptable reasons for applying to transfer to a college include the desire for a different academic orientation or curriculum, teaching methods, educational philosophy, location, size, or campus atmosphere. All transfer applicants should find some academic basis for the transfer, even if other nonacademic reasons are cited as well. Proximity to a girlfriend and better cafeteria food are not acceptable reasons for wanting to transfer.

If you originally applied to the target school, were accepted, and declined the offer, it is even more important that you show why your original choice of schools was not right. Acknowledge that you made a mistake the first time around. If you originally applied to the target school but were not admitted, take advantage of this by showing the school that it had interested you all along. If possible, discuss your original application with an admissions officer to get feedback on what went wrong and how you can avoid the same mistakes this time.

Take advantage of the perceived benefits of your status. Use self-awareness and initiative as some of your defining personal characteristics. Show that you now have a better and more complete education plan than you did when applying to colleges as a high school senior. Be as specific as possible about how you have come to realize you need a change and in showing how the target school's curriculum, academic and nonacademic offerings, philosophy, personality, atmosphere, and location match your personal and career needs.

If you are applying from an institution with much lower academic standards (in which case you will have had to receive stellar grades in order to be accepted at the target school), show that you have taken advantage of every opportunity possible to extract the most value from it. Try to show that you have studied the most difficult curriculum or been taught by the best professors there.

Take advantage of any special programs, research opportunities, internships, or other offerings that you can before applying to transfer. Such experiences will allow you to provide evidence of your initiative and success in college, as well as give you a forum in which to develop more meaningful relationships with professors for recommendation purposes. If possible, take small seminars and try to develop substantial relationships with professors so that your recommendations will be as meaningful as possible. Getting the most from recommenders can be trickier for college students than it is for high school students because they generally have less contact with faculty than do high schoolers.

Last, retake standardized tests if you need to in order to be competitive with the college's applicants, remembering that transfer applicants are often accepted with lower scores than are freshman admits. If you are sure that you cannot do any better on your tests, and your scores represent the college's average or not far below, you can probably assume that they will not keep you out of the school.

WHAT ADMISSIONS DIRECTORS SAY ABOUT
TRANSFER STUDENTS

WHAT CRITERIA DO YOU EVALUATE FOR TRANSFER ADMISSION?

The standards that we maintain for transfer student admission are indistinguishable from those we use in freshman admission. *Marlyn McGrath Lewis, Harvard*

When we look at transfer applications, a very important factor is how they are doing academically at their current school. We take a look at the types of courses they have chosen and whether they are challenging themselves. If the transfer applicant has only one semester of college when applying, we'll look at the high school record. Beyond academics, we also look to see how the applicant has contributed to their campus. *Douglas Christiansen, Vanderbilt*

We do require test scores for transfers. Standardized test scores are relatively less important for them than they are for regular freshman admits, but transfer applicants can take tests again if their scores are low.   *Sheppard Shanley, Northwestern*

The most important criterion in evaluating transfer applications is their intended area of study. Assuming they are excellent academically, we will admit the student only if there is room in the academic area they specify. A 4.0 won't help a transfer applicant who wants to go into a college or academic area that is not able to admit students.   *Daniel J. Saracino, Notre Dame*

We're looking for students who have high achievement in a strong liberal arts curriculum. While we look at high school performance, how students perform in college-level courses is much more important. Faculty recommendations also carry a great deal of weight. The recommendations tell us what the student is like in the classroom: intellectual ability, response to setbacks or criticism, inquiring attitude, perseverance, interest in sharing ideas, creativity.   *Debra Shaver, Smith*

In the transfer admission process, we often accept students who we did not accept for freshman admission—but we also reject students we originally accepted for freshman admission, so it can work both ways.   *Michael Goldberger, Brown*

What Kinds of Applicants Show Up in the Transfer Pool?

We have a large transfer program, taking about 500 students each year. Many have applied to UVA for freshman admission, were denied, and attend another school for a year before reapplying.   *John Blackburn, University of Virginia*

Our transfers can basically be divided into three sets: those from larger universities, often prestigious ones—the students feel they are missing out on faculty interaction; those from women's colleges; and those who were originally on our waitlist but didn't get off of it to come here freshman year.   *Richard Steele, Bowdoin*

Transfer application is extremely competitive—we get about 150 applications for about five spots. Some years we take none because we have no room.   *James Bock, Swarthmore*

Generally, we will only admit transfer students for the fall semester. We will typically take around 100–150 transfer students out of about 550 applicants (although these figures vary year to year).   *Douglas Christiansen, Vanderbilt*

What Is Most Noticeably Different Between Those Admitted Straight from High School and Those Admitted as Transfers?

Transfer applicants' interests are more targeted. We can get a better sense of what they'll bring—their athletic or performing arts abilities, for example, are better documented.   *Dan Walls, Emory*

Transfer students come with more maturity about the process and what they really want from the college experience. At Smith, our transfers are not necessarily running away from a bad college experience as much as wanting more from it. They are more sophisticated about the college search the second time around and are very clear about what they want. In addition, transfers don't apply to eight to ten schools, but more like three or four. *Debra Shaver, Smith*

REASONS TO TRANSFER

An important factor is having good reasons for transferring. And there is a thin line to be walked: a candidate needs to have a good reason to transfer but can't be too negative about where they are now. You certainly don't want to convey a sense that you are someone who always considers the grass to be greener somewhere else. In considering what a candidate would add, we may also consider what sort of opportunity transferring to Haverford represents to a candidate; it may be tougher for someone from another small liberal arts college, because Haverford may not represent a different kind of opportunity for him. *Jess Lord, Haverford*

The best transfer candidates are those that apply because they recognize they made a poor choice and can demonstrate compellingly why Tufts is a better fit for their academic interests. *Lee Coffin, Tufts*

My advice to transfer applicants is to be very up-front about why they are transferring. If the first school wasn't a good fit or somehow didn't work with your goals, it's okay to just say so. It's the big pink elephant in the room, but it doesn't have to be. Just be honest in your application about why it didn't work out. Even if it isn't earth-shattering (for example, you would like to be closer to home), that's okay. Just tell us. *Douglas Christiansen, Vanderbilt*

We ask transfer applicants to tell us why their current school isn't working out. Transfer applicants must give us a good reason—it can't appear that they are just hop-scotching from one college to another trying to find happiness. Occasionally, very strong transfer applicants fail to supply a good reason and this gives us real pause. *Robert Clagett, Middlebury*

The two most important factors in evaluating transfer candidates are the academic record at the previous institution and the reason for transferring. Compelling reasons include wanting a different type of school, a different academic offering, family circumstances, etc. Less compelling are statements that students simply aren't happy where they are, or ones that are blatantly negative about their current institution. *Jennifer Rickard, Bryn Mawr*

WHEN TO APPLY: AFTER FRESHMAN OR SOPHOMORE YEAR?

For transfer applicants, we are looking to see if they are capable of excelling in college. If you have a poor high school record, you may need a few years of seasoning at the college level before you are an attractive candidate. *Stephen Farmer, UNC Chapel Hill*

For those trying to transfer during their freshman year, their high school records will matter more than for a sophomore transfer candidate because we'll only have one college semester's grades to examine. And frankly, the first semester grades are not always the best indicator of how someone will do over the course of their entire college career. Someone with a somewhat rocky high school record—i.e., one that would have kept him from being a competitive candidate for Haverford coming out of high school—should not apply until he has had at least a full year of college. *Jess Lord, Haverford*

THE MOST COMMON MISTAKES TRANSFERS MAKE

A common mistake that transfer applicants make is to assume that each year there is a robust transfer option at their target school. This is not always the case. At Tufts, the number of transfer spots varies year to year. One year we may literally have none; another it could be 100+. *Lee Coffin, Tufts*

Appendix IV

MISCONDUCT

Some applicants to college are faced with the potentially difficult challenge of overcoming past misconduct. Examples of misconduct that can affect admissions decisions include being disciplined by a school or by the judicial system. (Misconduct, in this sense, does not include getting poor grades at some point in your academic career.) The range of possible misconduct is great: from being put on school probation for playing a mild prank or disrupting a class to being convicted of assault and battery, or worse.

Admissions committees are seldom concerned about a single minor incident that occurred some time ago. Their worry increases with:

Recency. Whatever you have done is of less concern if it occurred early in high school (or before high school). If you have a record of good behavior since your misconduct, any minor episode is likely to have very little if any impact on your chances of admission. If you did something wrong a few weeks ago, however, an admissions committee may worry that you have gone off the rails (even if just recently) or have always been off the rails but have never been caught until now. Even if the committee's fear is unfounded, you may not be able to demonstrate that you actually are a solid citizen.

Frequency. One indiscretion is likely to have little impact on your chances. Four or five episodes are a different matter, even if each one is a minor matter on its own. A pattern of misconduct suggests that you have an underlying problem.

Severity. Matters that strike at your *integrity* are more serious than those that are a matter of carelessness or high spirits. Academic cheating—whether on the SAT, course exams, papers, or otherwise—automatically puts an applicant's integrity at issue. Similarly, actions that *threaten* or *harm* others, especially if undertaken deliberately, are of grave concern. Even one armed robbery conviction, for instance, however long ago it may have occurred, is likely to be disqualifying.

Meanness. Even a minor incident that shows you to be truly mean-spirited can affect your chances. Mocking or playing a prank on a disabled classmate, for instance, may disqualify your candidacy even if you were never formally disciplined for it.

Nondisclosure. Failure to admit your misconduct can be much more serious than the initial misconduct. Even a trivial misconduct episode, if concealed, raises issues about your integrity. Some applicants think that they can (or must) hide misconduct only to have a school discover it anyway.

Note that high schools and colleges do not necessarily treat a matter of misconduct in the same way. One of the authors was an expert witness in a case involving the circulation of risqué photos of a classmate. The high school reaction was severe: despite many mitigating circumstances, all of the students involved were dismissed. Many colleges, apprised of the full details, would be happy to have various of these students attend their schools.

Colleges increasingly do spot checks on applicants' records, particularly when they encounter something that seems a bit odd. This often involves calling high school counselors and teachers. (Students should understand that there is a considerable grapevine operating between admissions officers at various colleges and high school guidance counselors and teachers.) Another common means by which colleges learn about misconduct is from the parents of high school classmates—perhaps applying to the same colleges—notifying them.

SUGGESTIONS FOR HANDLING MISCONDUCT ISSUES

If you are an applicant with a record of misconduct, by all means:

- Disclose anything even arguably relevant to the ethics/misconduct questions colleges ask in their applications
- Acknowledge your fault rather than blaming others
- Apologize to those affected (and make restitution as appropriate, to individuals, the school community, or society as a whole)
- Show that you have dealt with any underlying problem
- Demonstrate in as many ways as possible what you have learned from the experience and how it has affected your personal development since; show at a minimum that you have learned your lesson and moved on
- Address the problem frankly, in detail, in your application; consider adding a separate addendum to do so
- Give schools a reason to accept you by excelling in every other way you can

ADMISSIONS DIRECTORS DISCUSS MISCONDUCT

NATURE OF THE MISCONDUCT

In terms of which types of misconduct might trouble us, it tends to center on whether the conduct was malicious. *Stuart Schmill, MIT*

Some offenses such as stealing, plagiarism, assault of any kind, are less likely to be forgiven in an admissions context. *Paul Marthers, Reed*

Most people making decisions here have kids in their lives and are generally understanding—unless the issue involves harm to self or others or very recent issues of academic honesty. Boarding-school students should understand that we're also good at distinguishing between what is and is not parental in nature. Kids in boarding schools can be disciplined for something that for other kids would be handled by their parents (and therefore would remain unknown to us). We're reluctant to punish kids for such parental types of situations. *Rick Bischoff, Cal Tech*

We take any disciplinary issues extremely seriously. Obviously, behavioral issues that recur or that are of a certain level of gravity are a major problem—we are a small community and we are looking for people who will contribute in positive ways, inside and outside the classroom. At the same time, we do not wish to punish people inordinately for honest mistakes. We always look at everything on a case-by-case basis. The key is to be forthcoming and to take ownership for your actions. *Ken Himmelman, Bennington*

We have an honor code here, so we find plagiarism to be very worrying. The same is true for things that negatively affect the greater community, and multiple infractions of the same kind that suggests a pattern of misconduct. *Rick Bischoff, Cal Tech*

HOW CAN A STUDENT HELP REPAIR THE DAMAGE?

For applicants with an infraction in their past, we look for evidence of learning from the experience. Evidence can come in many forms: the way the applicant describes herself before and after the event, an additional recommender who can verify lessons learned, a forthright explanation and demonstrated strength in facing the problem, etc. We are looking to see if the applicant is taking active responsibility for their actions. *Jennifer Rickard, Bryn Mawr*

As long as a student is honest and penitent about the offense, he or she will generally be okay in the admissions process. Tell the truth, help us see how much you have learned from your mistake. If you are blaming others or making excuses, admissions officers will not be impressed. *Paul Marthers, Reed*

Even great citizens make mistakes, we understand that. But we want to make sure we are not endangering our community. To assure us, tell the truth in the application. Do not make excuses for things that are your fault. Explain what you have done to make up for what happened. *Stephen Farmer, UNC Chapel Hill*

When students have infractions in their past, we look for candor and self-introspection. Give us a clear explanation of what happened and what its legacy has been. If you are otherwise a compelling candidate, we do not want this to ruin your chances any more than you do. Show us that you have learned from it; be reflective about it. *Lee Coffin, Tufts*

Parents and students should realize that admissions officers have long-standing relationships with high schools and other colleges. Far better to be forthright about disciplinary issues than to have the school find out through the grapevine about a withheld offense. *Paul Marthers, Reed*

We expect students to be honest with us about misconduct issues. We want them to explain what happened and tell us how they have moved past it. One of our essay questions involves telling us about a time when something happened that felt, at the time, like it was the end of the world. We ask this because we want to see that applicants, even through difficult experiences, have the resources within them to build and move forward, to bounce back. *Stuart Schmill, MIT*

COMMUNICATING WITH THE COLLEGE

For students with infractions in their past, we expect a sincere letter of explanation from the student detailing the offense and what he or she has learned from the experience. Information provided by a teacher or counselor in their recommendations carries a lot of weight in our review of these situations. *Theodore Spencer, Michigan*

Most explanations go on much too long and make a bigger deal of things than required. Simply tell us what happened and what you learned from it. *Rick Bischoff, Cal Tech*

Do not write an essay about a past infraction. Write about something you are proud of. Use another venue to tell us about what happened and what you learned from it. *Thyra Briggs, Harvey Mudd*

For us, facing the student eye to eye is an important part of gauging an applicant with a past infraction. If it happens after the student has applied or been admitted, we may require the student to come to campus to discuss the matter, and will even pay for students to come who cannot afford the trip. *Steve Thomas, Colby*

I've encountered just about every sort of bad conduct, including drug and alcohol abuse, stalking, and a lot of plagiarism. . . . The best thing to do is to be up-front from the beginning. It's best that we hear of the infraction from the student, not from the counselor or the school. When a student is forthright, it helps. . . . We follow up with the school—as well as the student—to understand the context. We look to understand whether it was a one-time stupid thing to do or there is a history of such behavior. . . . As part of the application process, we require parent signatures as a release for information about academic or behavioral conduct from the school. This helps counselors provide us with information that they might otherwise worry about providing [due to the possibility of a lawsuit]. *Dan Walls, Emory*

Don't make colleges come back and beg for the information. If we ask you if there has been an infraction, don't just say "yes." Be up-front from the start. Tell us in detail what happened and what you learned. *Chris Gruber, Davidson*

We want to hear from the student, in his or her words, what happened and what he or she learned from the experience. Honesty is the best policy, and sincerity works better than defensiveness. *Kimberly Van Deusen, William & Mary*

Appendix V

DEVELOPMENT CASES

Alumni often try to get their children an admissions boost, the size of which is likely to depend on the importance of the alumni to the college—their involvement in the college's admissions and recruiting efforts as well as their history of giving to the college. (See Chapter 7 for a full discussion.) The tricky part, however, comes in trying to assess how much needs to be given to guarantee admission. This is difficult for an alum to figure out, but even more difficult for someone unconnected to the college. (Yes, most schools will bend their admissions standards as much for non-alumni families as for alumni.) Applicants who need this sort of admissions boost are genteelly termed "development cases."

N.B. Neither of the authors is a fan of this non-meritorious route into college. By shedding some light on colleges' dirty little secret, however, perhaps its importance will be lessened.

CHILDREN OF CELEBRITIES

It is not just families offering money, or being sought for their money, who may be extended admissions benefits. Children of celebrities (or, indeed, child celebrities) are often given preferential admissions treatment, too. The reason is that the celebrity generates publicity (think of the hoopla surrounding a president's daughter or famous movie actor's kids attending Ivy League schools) and can host fund-raising events or sponsor internships at his or her company for a college's students and graduates.

DEVELOPMENT CASES ARE NOT UNCOMMON

Colleges are understandably shy about discussing the number of development cases they consider, but occasional revelations make it clear that they are by no means uncommon. For instance, a senior University of Virginia official recently commented that twenty-five or thirty students are admitted each year "because of the gifts the family has made to the university." This may not sound like a lot, but note that this is a public university (traditionally much less given to such fund-raising-driven favoritism than are private schools) and his figure does not include those admitted because of the expectation of future gifts. At many private schools the figure would be about 10 percent of the incoming class.

UNDERSTANDING THE GAME

The amount of payment necessary to get into a leading school varies according to the qualifications of the applicant and the (financial) standing of the school. The closer the applicant is to meeting the normal admissions standards, the smaller the payment can be. Similarly, it is much easier to get into a less well-endowed school than into a well-endowed one. (During economically difficult times, it is also generally easier to get into a school.)

The standards (as such) are vague. In my (Richard Montauk's) experience, at liberal arts colleges outside of the top dozen or so, the necessary figure has been from $50,000 and up as an initial amount, with the expectation that this will be repeated several times at least. At the leading liberal arts colleges and all but the elite universities, the figure has often exceeded $100,000. At Ivy League and peer schools, however, the minimum has been closer to half a million dollars—and at the very top schools, a substantial seven-figure amount. The extent to which changing financial circumstances for both applicants and schools will alter these figures is not yet clear as of this writing, but they are likely to drop considerably.

TARGETING SCHOOLS

An analysis of per-student endowments at rival schools suggests those most likely to be tempted. Within the so-called Little Ivies, for example, Wesleyan's per-student endowment is only about one-third those of Amherst and Williams. The same is true of Bates relative to Bowdoin and Middlebury; Mt. Holyoke relative to Wellesley; and Penn, Brown, and Columbia relative to Princeton, Yale, and Harvard. (In fact, in the last case, the ratio is nearer one-to-six than one-to-three.) Other schools—such as Georgetown and Tufts—are readily characterized as poor relative to their fame (and their ambitions), whether or not they have obvious traditional rivals.

MAKING THE APPROACH

Every bit as important as the amount to be given is the method of approach. It is potentially fatal to approach the admissions office, given that admissions officers tend to loathe the practice of buying a place in the class. Instead, the focus will ordinarily be on the development office. In general, it is best if the family has a trusted adviser—generally an experienced admissions consultant or, better yet, a friend on the college's board of trustees—make the approach. And, of course, nothing will be agreed in writing. Instead, just as with political bribes (otherwise known as large campaign contributions), the two parties will come to an understanding of what each expects of the other, without anything formal drawn up. (And, as noted above, the college may value the prospect of non-monetary benefits such as internships at a fancy private equity fund, for instance, more than money. It is up to the go-between to assess what is likely to be most highly valued by the school.)

It helps if the family has a substantial history of donating, whether to this school or another, or even to charitable institutions far removed from the university sector. Being considered a reliable donor is important, given that schools resist explicit quid pro quo promises and must depend on the family living up to its part of the bargain just as the family depends on the school living up to its. This is one reason that most payments are multipart, with some portion given before a student applies, and some given after his matriculation (and on and on, in many cases).

HOW MUCH OF AN ADMISSIONS BOOST IS POSSIBLE?

The admissions standard for the children of the rich and celebrities varies according to the factors discussed above, but for top development cases can be very low. Rather than having to be among the best in the applicant pool, the only question concerning major donors' children is whether they have a reasonable chance of graduating. Most schools consider that a substantial majority of their applicants could successfully do the work at the school. Thus, even for schools that accept 10 to 15 percent of their applicants, this means that development cases in the bottom half of the applicant pool may well be accepted.

THE ADMISSIONS AND DEVELOPMENT PERSPECTIVES CONTRASTED

Admissions officers tend not to like this non-meritorious practice, which goes against the grain of their seeking to enroll the most talented class possible. They see two potential problems: one is that you will fail to perform academically, thereby wasting a valuable (and how!) seat at the school; the second is that the questionable admission will become known as such, which will embarrass the school. In fact, they generally consider the practice barely ethical. Development

---

**AN ADMISSIONS—NOT A DEVELOPMENT—DEAN DISCUSSES
DEVELOPMENT CASE APPLICATIONS**

You need to do everything you can to make your application stand on its own.
You can normally be guaranteed that someone will take notice of your connections along the way in the admissions process without your referring to it all
over your application. Admissions people don't want constant reminders of
how important your family is. Gratuitous mention of these matters can very
much work against you. We care first and foremost about you as an individual.
Thyra Briggs, Harvey Mudd

---

officers, on the other hand, tend to view this as a normal way of doing business.
Their sole charge is to raise money—and this is one of their most effective tools
for doing so. The admissions perspective is evident in the quotation above.

8

ACQUIRING STRONG ACADEMIC CREDENTIALS

— KEY POINTS —

Both components of your academic credentials are critically
important at the top colleges:

—Your high school record

—Your standardized test scores

It is essential to understand that a good high school record consists
of more than good grades

—The strongest candidates are those who take the most challenging
courses, especially in the "solid" subjects

—Advanced Placement (AP) offerings, honors classes, and International
Baccalaureate (IB) curriculums represent ideal selections

Understand your standardized testing options as well as the ways
you can best prepare for them

INTRODUCTION

Your academic profile consists of two parts: your high school record and your performance on standardized tests. These data together function like a key that can open the gateway of possibility for admission to a college. There is no way of getting around the fact that for almost all candidates, intellectual ability is the most important criterion on which you will be evaluated for college admission.

Selective colleges are looking for students who bring a lot more than just brains to their campuses, of course. But academic potential, except in special admissions cases such as recruited athletes, is still the number one concern of admissions officers at most schools. The way to prove one's future academic potential is, quite obviously, to provide evidence of superb past academic performance. Admissions committees generally examine the hard facts first, and anyone who passes muster on his or her academic credentials is then passed through the entryway in order to be investigated at closer range as a potential student. If you do not satisfy basic academic expectations, then (in most cases) you will not be considered for admission based on your other characteristics and strengths.

WHICH IS MORE IMPORTANT, THE HIGH SCHOOL RECORD OR STANDARDIZED TEST SCORES?

Colleges generally consider both academic indicators—the high school record and standardized test scores—important. Furthermore, the most competitive schools have so many fantastic applicants that they do not need to make compromises by accepting students who have excelled in one or the other, but not both. Still, the top colleges differ slightly in their messages, contained within their procedural methods, about which is *more* crucial, a great high school record or great test scores. The basic story from all of the most competitive schools is that you cannot completely override poor SAT or ACT scores with a great high school record, just as you cannot completely compensate for a poor high school record with good scores. Both count for something, and depending on which schools you apply to, they vary in their value.

Most schools prefer to see great high school records rather than great standardized test scores. Strong test scores and a poor high school record suggest that, though a student might be intellectually gifted, she is lazy and lacks determination to succeed. On the other hand, poor test scores and a strong high school record suggest that a student can succeed when he works really hard and that he is indeed willing to work really hard. He might not be an intellectual powerhouse, but he has proven that he can do well by applying himself. Colleges generally reason that students who are lazy in high school will continue to be so in college and that hardworking high schoolers will continue to work as diligently in college. Therefore, in many cases they prefer good high school performers over good test takers.

At the same time, there are limits to the extent that colleges will overlook test scores. For one thing, SAT scores are considered evidence of an applicant's intellectual firepower, and no school wants students who will have to struggle to do the academic work it requires. For another, a college knows that the public perception of its caliber and quality rests on several important factors in its profile, one of which is the SAT scores achieved by its incoming freshmen. Along with a low admission rate and a high yield on accepted applicants, colleges want to show that their students have the best SAT scores because this helps them gain a more favorable impression in the public eye. For both these reasons, high SAT scores are inevitably important to the colleges.

Many schools, in fact, use academic ranking methods that systematically take test scores into account. Applicants with better test scores thus receive a better academic ranking than those with worse scores, all other things being equal. So even if the admissions officers at these schools "like" what they see in your file despite less-than-optimal scores, and believe you to be a candidate worth accepting, your academic ranking (based on your test scores) might prevent you from winning out over another candidate with better scores.

THE HIGH SCHOOL RECORD

Having a strong high school record is not as easy as simply having a high GPA—even the minimally talented could manage a high GPA, taking the easiest courses available at a noncompetitive high school. Colleges look closely at the rigor of the school you attend; the classes you have taken over the past four years, including the number of honors or accelerated courses you have opted to take; and where you stand in relation to your classmates. Some schools, as indicated previously, indeed use formulas that plug a candidate's

GPA and test scores into an equation in order to compare him or her academically against other applicants. But schools will alter the GPA portion of your equation if they have reason to believe that it is not a true representation of your performance.

THE HIGH SCHOOL PROFILE

Candidates are evaluated alongside a high school profile, which gives college admissions officers important information about the school you attend. The profile gives detailed information about your high school's curriculum, lists all classes available to students, explains how the grading and grade point average system work, and sometimes provides average or median grades for each class. The profile also tells admissions officers what percentage of the previous year's graduating class went on to attend a four-year college and what colleges recent graduates attend, to provide a picture of the context in which you were educated.

The high school profile makes it difficult for you to fool admissions committees into thinking that you are a better student than you really are. You cannot, for example, trick the admissions committee into thinking that you are brilliant and ambitious (because of your straight-A record) if you have taken only the easiest classes available at your school. The high school profile also provides a fair playing field for those operating in strenuous high school environments or challenging themselves with the toughest options.

Admissions officers will know from your high school profile whether or not you have taken the most challenging courses available to you. If you are a very good student who has opted to take no honors classes despite their existence at your school, then a college may assume you are not intellectually motivated. A college will know not to penalize you for the lack of advanced or AP courses on your transcript if your high school does not offer any. A high school profile lets admissions officers know whether or not the high school calculates weighted or nonweighted GPAs. If your high school "weights" more advanced classes by increasing their grade assignment before calculating a GPA, then a college knows that your numbers account for the fact that you have taken difficult classes. On the contrary, if your high school explains that it does not weight classes when calculating GPAs, a college might decide to boost your GPA when it sees that your courseload has included some really tough classes that have likely handicapped your GPA.

The rigor of your high school and the context in which you were educated can tell an admissions officer a lot about you. Admissions officials recognize that a mediocre student at a very tough high school will probably be more academically prepared than a top student at a very easy high school. Likewise, however, they recognize that if you have performed extremely well and pushed yourself at a high school where only 10 percent of the graduating class goes on to college, you must be particularly determined and goal-oriented, possessing real strength of character. They recognize that it is far easier for a student from an affluent suburb, where life is fairly easy and everyone is *expected* to go to college, to keep her head in the books than it is for an inner-city student who has had to overcome the norms of her neighborhood's teenagers—criminal behavior, dropping out of school, teenage pregnancy—to stay focused on academics.

Because admissions officers are looking for students from a variety of backgrounds, it is not imperative that you attend the best public or private high school available in order to be admitted to a good college. Admissions committees recognize that money and location often prohibit students from attending strong college preparatory schools. The colleges generally want to see that you have taken advantage of those opportunities given to you, but will not penalize you for not having had the same opportunities as others.

IS YOUR HIGH SCHOOL'S PROFILE HELPING OR HURTING YOU?

Most students never see their high schools' official profiles, nor do many even know such a thing exists. The profile is a document full of public information and should be available to you upon request. Ask to see it! This piece of evidence will accompany your applications to colleges, and you certainly have a right to know what your high school communicates about itself. There may even be omissions of information that could greatly help your case—especially if you attend a high school that does not send many students to selective colleges.

For example, if you have taken classes called Track 2 at your high school, yet your high school profile does not explain that Track 2 is accelerated while Track 1 courses are standard options (colleges are likely to assume the opposite is true), your high school profile might be hurting you! Or perhaps you took a science class during your sophomore year called Marine Biology as an alternative to regular Biology. Colleges will assume that this is the easier "fluff" biology course in your school, taken by those who fear the rigors of regular lab sciences. If Marine Biology is actually considered an advanced class with one of the toughest teachers in the school—a lab science just as rigorous as regular biology and not its simplistic cousin—then colleges need to know this. If this information is not communicated on your high school profile, then you need to do something about it.

Review the example of a thorough, well-crafted high school profile starting on page 249. If you recognize that your school's profile does not measure up because it is misleading (in ways that might hurt you) or lacks important information, you have two options:

1. You can schedule a meeting with your school's college counselor and bring your concerns to his or her attention. Ask if the situation can be remedied by explaining your circumstances on your Secondary School Report or in a letter of recommendation.

2. Option one is usually the best one because, coming from the high school itself as part of its academic profile, information seems more objective and will be taken at face value. But if your high school does not comply with your wishes, you can always write a note to colleges, citing the information you wish to convey as simply and concisely as possible. The nature of your note is important. Make your point in one or two sentences and do not blame or criticize your high school for its omissions or errors.

FOLLOWING A SOLID CURRICULUM

It is absolutely imperative that you take the strongest curriculum possible at your high school in order to gain admission to one of the top colleges. College admissions officers know that although you may not be able to control your ability to attend the best schools available, you at least have access to all the courses offered at your high school. The most selective colleges maintain standards that are far higher than most high schools' graduation requirements.

In fact, they want you to take mostly honors and AP classes. Note, too, that they strongly prefer that candidates get a mixture of A's and B's in demanding courses rather than straight A's in less-demanding courses. So do not expect to take what is minimally necessary for graduation at your high school and still get into a stellar college.

A strong high school record shows four years each of the five "solid" courses. Academic solids are classes that prepare you for college in the following subjects:

- English
- Math
- Sciences
- Foreign languages
- Social sciences

NOBLE AND GREENOUGH SCHOOL

10 Campus Drive, Dedham, Massachusetts 02026-4099
781-320-7250 FAX: 781-251-3375
www.nobles.edu
C.E.E.B. Code: 220-680

2008 – 2009 PROFILE

DESCRIPTION: Founded by George Washington Copp Noble in 1866, Noble and Greenough School is a co-educational, non-sectarian day and boarding school for students in grades seven (Class VI) through twelve (Class I). Co-educational since 1974, Nobles has grown to a current enrollment of 567 students - including 282 girls and 285 boys, 50 of whom are five-day boarders.

- Diversity – Nobles is committed to creating an inclusive community, broadly defined. Current enrollment includes 149 (26%) individuals who are self-identified students of color.

- Admit Rate – Nobles had a 23% admit rate in 2008; 195 students were accepted from an applicant pool of 832.

- Financial Assistance – Nobles has awarded $2.8 million in need-based financial assistance.

Robert P. Henderson, Jr.
Head of School

Michael K. Denning
Director of College Counseling
Michael_Denning@Nobles.edu
781-320-7251

Katharine D. Coon
Associate Director of
College Counseling
Kate_Coon@Nobles.edu
781-320-7252

Kate B. Ramsdell
Associate Director of
College Counseling
Acting Dean of Students
Kate_Ramsdell@Nobles.edu
781-320-7253

Meghan C. Hamilton
College Counselor
Meghan_Hamilton@Nobles.edu
781-320-7054

Thomas S. Resor
College Counselor
Tom_Resor@Nobles.edu
781-320-7156

Mary Donahue
Administrative Assistant
Mary_Donahue@Nobles.edu
781-320-7250

DIPLOMA REQUIREMENTS: The standard and expected academic load of every Nobles student is the equivalent of five credits in each semester. There is a petition process by which students may be granted permission to take a sixth full credit course. Please refer to our online Curriculum Guide for comprehensive course descriptions.

DISCIPLINE	MINIMUM REQUIREMENTS FOR GRADUATION	HONORS AND ADVANCED PLACEMENT
English	Eight semesters	No designated Honors or AP sections
Mathematics	Six semesters (through Class II)	Honors Algebra, Geometry, Precalculus; AP Calculus (AB, BC), AP Statistics, Advanced Topics in Mathematics
Languages	Completion of level III: Chinese, French, Japanese, Latin, or Spanish	Honors French II, III, IV; Honors Spanish II, III, IV; AP French Language, AP French Literature AP Japanese, AP Latin Vergil, AP Latin Lyric, AP Spanish Language, AP Spanish Literature
Science	Four semesters: two in Biology and two in either Chemistry or Physics	Biology, Quantitative Chemistry and Quantitative Physics; AP Biology, AP Physics, AP Chemistry
Computer Science		AP Computer Science
History and Social Science	Four semesters: two in U.S. History and two in History of the Human Community	No Honors Sections; AP European History
Visual and Performing Arts	One credit each in Visual Arts and Performing Arts	AP Studio Art AP Art History
Service Learning	Eighty hours	

AP COURSES

Nobles offers AP courses in AB Calculus, BC Calculus, Computer Science, Statistics, Biology, Japanese, Chemistry, Physics, French Language, French Literature, Spanish Language, Spanish Literature, European History, Studio Art , Art History, Latin Vergil, and Latin Lyric. Many Nobles students also take AP exams in English Literature, US History, Microeconomics and Macroeconomics even though Nobles does not have AP-designated courses in these subjects.

Since the majority of AP courses are offered only in the senior year, after completion of the standard curriculum, students are normally able to take <u>a maximum of five AP courses</u> while at Nobles.

THE ARTS

The arts are a vital aspect of the Nobles curriculum. Arts courses are considered to be major academic courses. They meet as often and are as demanding as the "traditional" core academic courses. Most students in the Class of 2009 will pursue courses in the Visual and Performing Arts beyond the one-credit requirement. In recent years, student work has been purchased for the Massachusetts State House and by local businesses and collectors; it has also won acclaim in local and regional competitions such as the Silver Key Award and AANEPS (Art Association of New England Preparatory Schools). The Visual Arts faculty has exhibited widely in the area and holds appointments at prestigious summer arts workshops. In the Performing Arts, several students have been selected for the New England Districts (Vocal and Instrumental), the Boston Youth Symphony Orchestras, and the New England Drama Guild competition. Students in recent years have been selected to attend the Eastman Conservatory of Music, RISD, the Pratt Institute and the University of Miami's and American University's conservatory programs in Musical Theatre.

STUDY AWAY

Many students spend at least one semester studying in a Nobles-approved program away or abroad. Programs include: CITY Term, Maine Coast Semester, The Mountain School, School Year Abroad (France, China, Italy, Spain), The Cape Eleuthera Island School Program, Semester at Sea and Class Afloat. In addition, Nobles students in recent years have participated in study, homestay and service-learning trips sponsored by Nobles in Ghana, Romania, Chile, Hungary, Ecuador, Poland, Vietnam, South Africa, Cuba, Spain, Ireland, Senegal, France, Italy, Japan, Thailand and Panama. Domestically, they have participated in service opportunities in Montana, New Orleans, and the greater Boston area.

· ·

GRADE DISTRIBUTION CLASS OF 2009: ENROLLMENT 111

Distribution for Class of 2009 of six-semester unweighted cumulative averages as of June, 2008.

Ranking System: Nobles uses no form of Class Rank and no differential weighting of courses.

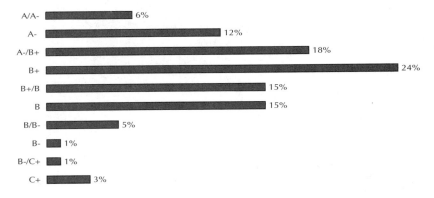

A/A-	6%
A-	12%
A-/B+	18%
B+	24%
B+/B	15%
B	15%
B/B-	5%
B-	1%
B-/C+	1%
C+	3%

STANDARDIZED TEST PERFORMANCE SUMMARY, CLASSES 2008 and 2009, THROUGH JUNE, 2008

SAT Reasoning Test	Middle 50%	Mean	Students Tested
Critical Reading	610-720	661	
Math	610-740	669	
Writing	620-730	672	
Total	1880-2160	2001	213

SAT Subject Tests			
Biology-Ecology	620-710	662	82
Biology-Molecular	590-750	683	9
Chemistry	670-770	717	61
English Literature	590-710	647	79
French	520-680	607	11
French with Listening	750-750	750	1
Japanese with Listening	690-690	690	1
Math Level I	590-710	642	66
Math Level II	650-770	708	123
Physics	690-770	732	32
Spanish	620-740	689	21
US History	570-690	647	19

AP Exams – Classes of 2008 - 2009

Subject	5	4	3	2	1
Art History	2	2	2	0	0
Biology	12	14	8	7	1
Calculus AB	16	5	5	0	0
Calculus AB Subscore	29	7	0	0	0
Calculus BC	30	6	1	0	0
Chemistry	15	8	4	0	0
Chinese Language and Culture	2	0	0	0	0
Computer Science A	0	1	0	0	0
Computer Science AB	1	0	0	0	0
English Language	0	0	1	0	0
English Literature	24	24	11	2	0
European History	26	22	29	3	3
French Language	4	1	3	2	0
French Literature	2	2	1	0	0
Japanese Language and Culture	1	2	1	0	0
Latin Literature	1	1	3	0	0
Latin Vergil	4	3	5	2	0
Macroeconomics	6	9	3	1	0
Microeconomics	4	7	4	2	0
Physics C (Electricity and Magnetism)	5	1	1	0	0
Physics C (Mechanics)	7	4	0	0	0
Spanish Language	14	11	0	3	0
Spanish Literature	3	1	0	0	0
Statistics	5	3	0	0	0
Studio Art	0	0	0	1	0
Studio Art (2D)	3	2	3	0	0
Studio Art (3D)	0	2	3	1	0
Studio Art (Drawing)	0	1	1	0	0
U.S. Government and Politics	0	0	2	0	0
U.S. History	8	13	2	1	0
Total Number	**224**	**152**	**93**	**25**	**4**

Classes 2008 and 2009
Number of students who have taken an AP: 162
Total number of AP tests: 498
% of students scoring 4 or 5: 76%
% of students scoring 3 and above: 94%

Class of 2008
Number of students who have taken an AP: 90
Total number of AP tests: 360
% of students scoring 4 or 5: 78%
% of students score 3 and above: 94%

Class of 2009 (as of June, 2008)
Number of students who have taken an AP: 72
Total number of AP tests: 138
% of students scoring 4 or 5: 70%
% of students score 3 and above: 95%

During May, 2009, members of the Class of 2009 will take approximately 225 additional AP Exams.

MATRICULATION LIST 2004-2008

The following institutions have enrolled 2 or more Noble and Greenough students in the last five years.

Brown University	32	College of the Holy Cross	7	Brandeis University	2
Boston College	30	Dartmouth College	7	Bryn Mawr College	2
Harvard University	22	Hamilton College	7	Bucknell University	2
Bowdoin College	21	Wellesley College	7	Clark University	2
Duke University	21	University of Michigan	6	Colorado College	2
Georgetown University	20	Vanderbilt University	6	University of Connecticut	2
University of Pennsylvania	20	Babson College	5	Dickinson College	2
Tufts University	18	University of Southern California	5	Franklin & Marshall College	2
Princeton University	16	George Washington University	5	Hampshire College	2
Middlebury College	15	University of Richmond	5	Lehigh University	2
Colgate University	14	Amherst College	4	University of New Hampshire	2
Columbia University	13	University of Chicago	4	Northwestern University	2
Trinity College	13	New York University	4	Rhode Island School of Design	2
Williams College	12	Syracuse University	4	Roanoke College	2
Cornell University	11	Union College	4	Sacred Heart University	2
Yale University	11	Boston University	3	University of Saint Andrews	2
Colby College	9	Davidson College	3	St. Lawrence University	2
Wesleyan University	9	Emory University	3	Smith College	2
Connecticut College	8	Johns Hopkins University	3	University of Vermont	2
Santa Clara University	8	Northeastern University	3	Wake Forest University	2
Stanford University	8	Pomona College	3	Washington University in St. Louis	2
University of Virginia	8	Providence College	3	University of Wisconsin	2
Barnard College	7	University of Rochester	3		
Bates College	7	College of Wooster	3		

One to each of the following:

University of Aberdeen, University of Arizona, Bennington College, Bentley College, University of California-Berkeley, University of California-Santa Cruz, California Institute of Technology, Carleton College, Carnegie Mellon University, Catholic University of America, University of Colorado-Boulder, University of Edinburgh, University of East Anglia, Fairfield University, Gettysburg College, Goucher College, The Hotchkiss School, Howard University, Kenyon College, Lawrenceville School, Lewis & Clark College, Macalester College, Manhattanville College, Marist College, Massachusetts Institute of Technology, University of Miami, Morehouse College, University of Notre Dame, Oberlin College, Pitzer College, Regis College, Saint Anselm College, Scripps College, Simmons College, Skidmore College, Southern Methodist University, Stonehill College, University of Texas-Dallas, Tulane University, The United States Naval Academy, Vassar College, The College of William & Mary

Policy On Disclosure

Noble and Greenough School has a policy of nondisclosure regarding discipline matters. On applications where a student is specifically asked to disclose, we counsel the student to report this incident, informing them that failure to do so would be a violation of our community principles. When released to do so, we supplement the student's statement with documentation from our office.

Should you have any questions about this policy, please do not hesitate to contact Michael Denning, Director of College Counseling.

You will likely apply to a variety of colleges. Therefore, you should not decide as a sophomore to stop taking Spanish just because the college you think you most want to attend does not require more than one year of foreign language preparation. It is best if you follow the standard menu of four years of five solids through senior year, since you will likely be applying to colleges with different prerequisites.

BEYOND THE SOLIDS

Semisolids are courses that are related to the solid curriculum but are not necessary as preparation for college-level work or are supplemental to the regular high school curriculum. Courses in psychology, religion, ethics, journalism, or art history are considered semisolids. An earth science or astronomy course, rather than regular senior year physics, would also probably be considered semisolid work.

On top of the solids and semisolids are electives such as art, music, dance, wood shop, home economics, and computer science (this is sometimes considered a semisolid rather than an elective, depending on how rigorous the course is). Colleges do not generally request that their applicants take electives, nor do they ask for specific electives, but they play an important role on your transcript by showing that you have outside interests and differentiating you from other applicants. Electives and semisolids can help you develop special talents or extracurricular passions, so you should not decide to let them go in lieu of concentrating on your grades in solid courses.

WHICH YEARS OF HIGH SCHOOL ARE MOST IMPORTANT?

Generally speaking, colleges will overlook mistakes made during the freshman year of high school as well as pay attention to overall growth and development rather than viewing each year individually. For most colleges, it is the overall trend and growth over four years that is most important, with most of the emphasis placed on the junior and senior years.

Admissions officers disagree a bit on which year—junior or senior—is really the most crucial. Some colleges weight the junior and senior years heavily and lean especially toward performance during the senior year. Other schools, however, contend that the junior year is generally most important in terms of your academic performance. Either way, do not think you can glide once junior year is over. Most colleges you apply to will indeed receive your senior fall grades before evaluating you, and you cannot afford to let your performance drop. Even colleges that admit you Early or under a Rolling Admissions policy will receive senior year grades and have the right to revoke your admission.

PURSUING THE MOST CHALLENGING OPTIONS AVAILABLE

On top of maintaining a high school transcript that is full of solid courses (as well as the right balance of semisolids or electives), you must also show colleges

CHAPTER 8

WHAT ADMISSIONS DIRECTORS SAY ABOUT THE ACADEMIC PROFILE

Everything is a trade-off. If a student is academically weaker than the majority of those we admit, he'll have to compensate for it in another area. *Christoph Guttentag, Duke*

Success in the classroom and the rigor of the courses a student takes is still the foundation on which our decision rests. The academics are the most important part of the overall picture. *Rick Shaw, Stanford*

Our choices are made very much on the basis of academic potential—but other factors come into play as well. *Maria Laskaris, Dartmouth*

When I counsel students, I tell them that if there are hiccups in the record—whether it be a bad semester or year, or something else—to address it somewhere in the written application. A student should speak to any obvious weakness or aberration in the record so that we know what happened. *Nancy Hargrave Meislahn, Wesleyan*

WHICH YEARS OF HIGH SCHOOL ARE MOST IMPORTANT?

Senior fall is the best predictor of the kind of work a student will do here at Amherst if accepted. We look at it very closely—it is absolutely critical that a student do well senior fall. *Katie Fretwell, Amherst*

We weight the junior and senior years very heavily. *Eric Kaplan, Penn*

We look at a student's high school years in total. That said, we do look at trajectory, meaning more recent is more relevant. Ninth grade is farther away, and therefore less telling about who the applicant is now. *Stuart Schmill, MIT*

ALL! We will look closely at the trends in terms of increasingly rigorous coursework and the grades achieved in them. We expect that students will take four years of a foreign language, three lab sciences, math through calculus, or the equivalent in their high school. *Nancy Hargrave Meislahn, Wesleyan*

Senior year is extremely important. What you are doing as you are applying is a good indicator to us of how you will do in college. In part for this reason, we don't make a decision unless we have senior year first semester grades. *Thyra Briggs, Harvey Mudd*

We focus a lot of attention on what happens junior and senior year. For example, a student may have met their high school's requirements, but are they taking classes their senior year that continue to challenge them? We learn a lot about students' intellectual curiosity and drive by looking at curricular choices made their senior year. *Chris Gruber, Davidson*

How Important Is a Challenging Curriculum?

When we look at the high school record along with the profile, we are disappointed if we see a student is not really challenging him- or herself. *John Blackburn, University of Virginia*

You need to take the appropriate level of courses to be challenged but still have the time to be intellectually engaged by your courses. For example, many kids figure that taking seven AP courses is automatically better than taking four AP courses. That's untrue if taking seven means you can't really devote yourself to each of them. Teacher recommendations distinguish very well between students who are just getting the grades and those who are really engaged in the subject. Teachers let us know that it's harder to teach on the day that the engaged student is absent from class. *Rick Bischoff, Cal Tech*

The high school curriculum is probably the least understood part of the application process by college candidates. Students don't understand that a good GPA isn't all there is. *Dan Walls, Emory*

One thing I see applicants doing wrong all the time is not continuing with a demanding curriculum during their senior year—blowing off math or science or foreign languages. We see a lot of senior programs that are fluffy. The strength of the program all the way through senior year is critical. *David Borus, Vassar*

that you have pursued the most rigorous options available to you. The most competitive schools expect that you will choose challenging options over standard classes in all or most cases in which you have a choice. This means taking any courses that are labeled "honors," "accelerated," "advanced," or "Track 1" ("Track 2" if your school assigns the higher number to the more rigorous track) courses, as well as Advanced Placement (AP) courses. Following an International Baccalaureate (IB) curriculum is another way of pursuing the most challenging option, if it is available in your community.

Advanced Placement (AP) Courses

AP courses are those sponsored by the College Board, allowing advanced high schoolers to take college-level classes. Students can take just one AP course if they so desire, or they can take a plateful of AP courses (if their high schools permit them to do so). Students are encouraged to take the AP exam in their subject after completing a course in order to provide evidence of accomplishment and learning; in fact, many high schools require that students taking an AP course also take the exam. AP exams are offered every May and are graded on a scale of 1 to 5, with a 5 being the best score. Most colleges regard only 4 and 5 AP scores as significant indicators of advanced learning. Some colleges give college credit for classes in which AP exams have been taken (with scores of 4 or 5). Such credit can allow a student to place out of requirements, thereby having more time to pursue other academic interests, or sometimes even graduate from college a semester early.

Some students opt to take AP tests in subjects in which their schools do not offer AP courses. They generally get a teacher's help in designing a program of additional study, which often includes test prep materials. By doing this, these students not only show real initiative and determination—not to mention love of learning—but they also are likely to get a strong recommendation from this teacher. (Other students, lacking a suitable AP course, take a college-level course at a local community college.)

International Baccalaureate (IB) Offerings

More common in other parts of the world, International Baccalaureate (IB) programs are becoming more prevalent in American high schools. The IB curriculum was originally created to prepare American students for study at universities across the globe and was thus offered mostly overseas, at American high schools, for the children of diplomats and other expatriates.

The IB is a rigorous two-year curriculum designed to meet the requirements of higher institutions of education throughout the world. Unlike AP courses, which can be taken individually, the IB is a single curriculum covering a range of subjects. Students who opt for it follow the entire program, not just a course here and there, taking distribution requirements in each of six general subject areas: Language A1 (courses in the student's first language); Language A2 (a second modern language); Individuals and Societies (includes history, geography, philosophy, etc.); Experimental Sciences; Mathematics and Computer Sciences; and the Arts. In addition, a student must fulfill two special IB requirements: Theory of Knowledge (TOK), an interdisciplinary course that teaches critical reflection, and Creativity, Action, Service (CAS), which requires immersion in extracurricular events. All students must also undertake original research to write an extended essay in order to graduate from the IB program.

Students who have taken the IB curriculum take six (sometimes seven) IB exams, three of which are preliminary tests, called standard level (SL), and three or four of which are higher level (HL) exams. The exams are graded on a scale of 1 to 7, with 7 being the highest score. The six scores are then added together, with three extra points available for completion of TOK, CAS, and the essay, for a total of 45 possible diploma points. Individual subject scores of 6 and 7 are generally considered worthy of recognition by selective college admissions offices. Again, some colleges recognize IB exam achievement with college credit.

AP and IB curriculums (and their test results) provide evidence that a student is serious and willing to challenge himself or herself, as well as capable of handling college-level work. Furthermore, the higher the student's scores on

AP and IB exams, the more inclined an admissions officer will be to dismiss lower scores elsewhere. These tests are generally considered truer measures than SAT scores of a student's intelligence, knowledge, and ability to perform critical thinking and reasoning skills.

FOR MORE INFORMATION ON THE AP CURRICULUM AND EXAMS

The Advanced Placement program is administered by the College Board. The Board oversees the curriculum and teaching of AP-designated college-level courses in a variety of subjects in high schools around the country, as well as the administration of AP exams in the subjects. For more information, see your high school guidance counselor or contact:

The Advanced Placement Program
The College Board
45 Columbus Avenue
New York, NY 10023
(212)713-8000
www.collegeboard.com

FOR MORE INFORMATION ON THE IB CURRICULUM

For more information about the International Baccalaureate, contact the International Baccalaureate Organization at its headquarters in Switzerland or the North American regional office:

Organisation du Baccalaureat International
Route des Morillons 15
1218 Grand-Saconnex
Geneva
Switzerland
Tel 41 22 791 77 40
Fax 41 22 791 02 77
www.ibo.org

International Baccalaureate North America
475 Riverside Drive
16th Floor
New York, NY 10015
Tel (212)696-4464
Fax (212)889-9242
IBNA@ibo.org
www.ibo.org

**ADMISSIONS DIRECTORS TALK ABOUT AP
AND IB PROGRAMS AND TEST RESULTS**

AP results are really a very minor element in our admissions process. Not every student has access to AP courses—we want to see that a student has taken the toughest courses, so we like to see APs and IB curriculums on a transcript. But not everyone has the opportunity to take these kinds of classes. *Maria Laskaris, Dartmouth*

We certainly hold these sorts of curricula in high regard for the way in which they present and process material in a way that often parallels the small college seminar format that we run here—reading primary material, discussion-based classes in which students learn from each other as well as faculty, emphasis on analysis and written work, and so on. Of course we appreciate IB and AP courses for different reasons than many students do—many students see these courses simply as a means of lowering the price tag for college or shortening their college career. *Stephen Schierloh, Sarah Lawrence*

We absolutely look closely at AP and IB results. But we don't penalize students who don't present them because not everyone has access to AP or IB courses. *Katie Fretwell, Amherst*

It's an advantage, but we try to neutralize advantages individual applicants have, and usually those who do very well on APs or SAT subject tests come from the best schools and the most advantaged backgrounds and have the best opportunities, so we try not to let this make a big difference. We try to keep a level playing field. *Charles Deacon, Georgetown*

IMPROVING YOUR HIGH SCHOOL RECORD AFTER THE FACT

If you have any truly egregious gaffes on your high school transcript, you might want to think about doing something to compensate for them before applying to college. Although your options will not remedy your high school GPA, your efforts and results can show admissions officers that you care about improving yourself and that you are more capable of doing good work than your high school record shows.

The way to partially overcome a particularly poor grade is to retake the class (or a very similar one) to improve your performance. Chances are that your high school will not allow you to retake a class (and that you will not have time to do so during regular high school hours because of other solid curriculum requirements). What you must do instead is look into summer schools or night and weekend classes at community colleges.

To achieve the maximum benefit of retaking a class, you need to commit yourself to getting a good grade. You should not waste time that could be spent concentrating on your current academic commitments with a duplicate class unless you know that you can do well. If you had extreme difficulty with chemistry, for example, and your poor performance did not result from personal problems or lack of effort, you might consider whether or not a retake is worth your time. You might decide that your performance in chemistry is simply a weakness you should contend with by performing especially well in English and the humanities—especially if strength in the sciences is not one of your positioning points anyway. Or, if you do decide to retake the class, you might want to consider hiring a tutor for extra help so that your effort pays off in the end.

STANDARDIZED TEST SCORES

Standardized test scores make up the other half of the academic profile. Standardized test scores provide admissions officers with a standardized measure to use in assessing all candidates. Although the tests are imperfect, they help officers compare students from different educational backgrounds and assess those from backgrounds about which they know very little.

SAT and ACT scores remain important pieces of the admissions puzzle at most schools. There are, however, some schools (even some very selective ones) that do not require applicants to submit any standardized test scores. These include Bowdoin, Bates, and Hampshire colleges.

Most colleges will tell you that standardized test scores are not quite as important as the high school record. This is indeed usually the case when officers are looking subjectively at a candidate's overall application. However, as mentioned in the beginning of this chapter, a college's reputation depends on the strength of its profile, which includes the SAT scores achieved by its incoming freshmen. Many admissions committees are thus compelled to take students who have earned the highest SAT scores. It is for this reason that some schools' academic ranking formulas rely more on standardized test performance than they do on the high school record.

Less selective colleges generally require only the SAT Reasoning Test or the ACT. The majority of the selective colleges require applicants to submit either SAT Reasoning Test scores and two SAT subject test scores *or* ACT scores (in place of both SAT tests), or SAT Reasoning Test scores and two SAT subject test scores *or* ACT scores and two SAT subject test scores. Note that with the advent of the "new SAT," many colleges' testing requirements are in flux.

Although the SAT subject tests do not provoke as much anxiety and discussion as does the SAT Reasoning Test, do not underestimate their importance in the admissions process. As mentioned earlier, the SAT subject scores are often factored into colleges' academic rating formulas. Furthermore, many admissions officers consider them the foremost indicator of academic potential.

Be aware that some colleges require or prefer certain SAT subject tests over others. Since each program has its own SAT subject test requirements, you should be sure to look into individual college and program requirements as early as possible so that you can be prepared to take all necessary SAT tests at the proper time in your high school career.

THE SAT REASONING TEST (AND THE PSAT)

The SAT Reasoning Test, created by the College Board, is administered on seven Saturdays throughout the academic year at high schools across the country and worldwide. The SAT has recently undergone major changes, transforming itself from what was originally more of an "aptitude" test to one that is now more aligned with high school curriculums, testing critical reading, writing, and mathematics skills. Thus, you may hear reference to the "old SAT" and the "new SAT," introduced in March 2005, which eliminates the often-feared "analogies" but includes a writing section (including an essay), more reading comprehension, and advanced math concepts.

Each administration of the SAT is broken down into nine sections, each separately timed: two 25-minute reading sections; one 20-minute reading section; one 25-minute essay section; one 25-minute writing section; one 10-minute writing section; two 25-minute math sections; one 20-minute math section. The essay is always the first section administered, and the 10-minute multiple-choice writing section is always the final section of the test. The other sections may come in any order. Each administration of the SAT also includes one 25-minute unscored "wild card" section. This unscored "wild card" section can be of any variety—it does not count toward the final score, but is used by the College Board to try out new questions for future editions of the test.

Each of the three areas tested on the SAT is further broken down as follows:

Critical Reading	Reading comprehension
	Sentence completions
	Paragraph-length critical reading
Writing	Grammar
	Usage
	Word choice
	Essay
Mathematics	Number and operations
	Algebra and functions
	Geometry
	Statistics, probability, and data analysis

The essay section asks students to write in response to a prompt, using reasoning and evidence based on their own experiences, readings, history, or observations to support their ideas. The essay score can range from 2 to 12, with 2 being the lowest score and 12 being the highest. This is the sum of two trained readers' ratings between 1 and 6 for the essay.

The entire SAT takes 3 hours 45 minutes (4 hours and 30 minutes with scheduled breaks). Each overall section of the SAT is scored on a scale of 200 to 800, 800 being the best score. Thus, the entire SAT, with its three components, is scored out of a total possible 2,400 points.

Scores on multiple-choice sections are totaled by calculating one point for each correct answer and then subtracting a fraction of a point for each incorrect answer. (One-fourth of a point is subtracted for questions that offer five choices; one-third of a point is subtracted for questions that offer four choices.) No points are gained or lost for unanswered questions, nor are any points gained or lost for incorrect answers in the student-produced response area in the mathematics section. Thus, students who can identify one or two answers as definitely wrong are generally encouraged to make educated guesses.

FOR MORE INFORMATION ON THE SAT OR PSAT

To obtain further information on tests developed by the College Board, contact the following:

The SAT Program
(609)771-7600
sat.help@info.collegeboard.com

The PSAT Program
(609)771-7070
psat@info.collegeboard.com

The College Board
45 Columbus Avenue
New York, NY 10023
(212) 713-8000
www.collegeboard.com

The PSAT (Preliminary Scholastic Assessment Test) is merely a practice exam for the SAT. It mimics the format and scoring of the SAT minus the essay section, but scores do not count toward college admission. The PSAT is typically administered to sophomores and juniors so that they can prepare for the

SAT under realistic conditions and test-taking circumstances. It is given only once a year, in October. The PSAT-NMSQT exam is the same exam as the PSAT (although it is restricted to juniors only) but is also the National Merit Semifinalist Qualifying Test. Performance on this particular PSAT determines the National Merit Semifinalists from each state (the top one-half of the top 1 percent of performers in each state qualify as National Merit Semifinalists). National Merit Finalists are then selected from the Semifinalist pool based on an application and a student's academic record.

FOR MORE INFORMATION ON THE NATIONAL MERIT SCHOLARSHIP PROGRAM

To obtain information on the National Merit Scholarship program, contact:

National Merit Scholarship Corporation
1560 Sherman Avenue, Suite 200
Evanston, IL 60201
(847)866-5100
www.nationalmerit.org

THE ACT (AND PLAN)

The ACT is administered by the American College Testing Program and is quickly becoming nearly as popular as the SAT. The ACT consists of subject-based tests that measure a student's knowledge, understanding, and skills acquired throughout high school. There are four sections—English, math, reading, and science reasoning—and the optional section, Writing. Because the ACT is subject-based, just like the SAT subject tests, in-school preparation is key for success.

The optional ACT Plus Writing is an extra thirty-minute section in which students write on a given essay topic, similar to the SAT writing section. The ACT Plus Writing provides students with two additional scores beyond what they receive if they take only the ACT multiple-choice tests. First, they receive a Writing Test subscore, which can range from 2 to 12, with 2 being the lowest score and 12 being the highest. This is the sum of two trained readers' ratings between 1 and 6 for the essay. The essay is graded holistically based on its ability to express judgments by taking a position; maintain a focus on the topic; use logical reasoning; organize ideas in a logical way; and use language clearly and effectively. Test takers also receive positive and constructive comments on the essay from their graders. The Combined English/Writing score is then created using a formula that weights the English Test score two-thirds and the Writing Test score one-third to form a combined score. This combined score is then reported on a 1–36 scale, as with the other sections of the test.

Each section of the ACT is broken down into subsections as follows:

English	Usage/Mechanics
	Rhetorical Skills
Mathematics	Pre-Algebra
	Elementary Algebra
	Intermediate Algebra and Coordinate Geometry
	Plane Geometry
	Trigonometry
Reading	Social Studies
	Natural Science
	Prose Fiction
	Humanities
Science Reasoning	Data Representation
	Research Summaries
	Conflicting Viewpoints
Writing	Writing

Each section of the ACT is scored on a scale of 1 to 36, with 36 being the best score. The scores are then averaged to produce an overall score between 1 and 36. Only correct answers count toward the score, and students are not penalized at all for wrong answers. Thus, on the ACT, even random guessing is better than leaving answers blank.

The PLAN Assessment test is the preliminary test drive for the ACT, much like the PSAT that prepares students for the SAT. It is identical to the ACT except that its scores do not count toward college admission.

FOR MORE INFORMATION ON THE ACT AND PLAN

To find out more about these tests, contact:

ACT Registration
P.O. Box 414
Iowa City, IA 52243-0414
(319) 337-1270
www.act.org

SAT-ACT EQUIVALENCE TABLE

SAT TO ACT		ACT TO SAT	
SAT SCORE VERBAL AND MATH	ACT COMPOSITE SCORE	ACT COMPOSITE SCORE	SAT SCORE VERBAL AND MATH
1600	36	36	1600
1560–1590	35	35	1580
1510–1550	34	34	1520
1460–1500	33	33	1470
1410–1450	32	32	1420
1360–1400	31	31	1380
1320–1350	30	30	1340
1280–1310	29	29	1300
1240–1270	28	28	1260
1210–1230	27	27	1220
1170–1200	26	26	1180
1130–1160	25	25	1140
1090–1120	24	24	1110
1060–1080	23	23	1070
1020–1050	22	22	1030
980–1010	21	21	990
940–970	20	20	950

SHOULD YOU TAKE THE SAT, THE ACT, OR BOTH?

Most students should start by taking the SAT once, at a minimum, or taking both the SAT and ACT once, if they are both required or strongly encouraged by your high school. But after a first shot at both exams, do not continue to take both. Following a course where you are gearing up for both the SAT and the ACT is not wise, as preparation for each takes considerable effort for most students, and you do not want to be spending all of your time preparing for standardized tests—you have other equally important things to accomplish at this time!

If your performance on your first administration of the SAT is fairly strong, and likely to improve with review and practice, then there is no reason to continue taking the ACT as well. Though most colleges happily accept either score, there may still be some miniscule preference for the SAT at super-selective schools. And many colleges convert ACT scores to the SAT scale (see prior table), so if you are doing well on the SAT, you might as well stick with it.

If you have done poorly on the SAT, though, especially if your performance registers well below what your academic performance in school would suggest, then you should at least try the ACT. The ACT, as a curriculum-based test, is still probably a better measure of the knowledge you have gained in school than the SAT. Nearly all schools will accept the SAT or the ACT, and you should pursue the test on which you can achieve the highest relative scores.

There are several other issues that might point you toward the ACT rather than the SAT. First, if you are following an International Baccalaureate (IB) at school, the SAT subject tests may not align well with your subject matter at school; taking the ACT may behoove you, especially if you can submit your score in lieu of both SAT and SAT subject test results for your target colleges. If you are strong in the sciences, your performance on the scientific reasoning section of the ACT could boost your overall score significantly. If you are weak in retaining vocabulary, the ACT is a better test for you because there is no direct testing of word knowledge, as with the SAT's sentence completions. And if you are a poor writer, then you can take the ACT without the optional writing section (as long as it is not required by any schools to which you are applying) to avoid the essay.

Thus, students who will likely be better served by the ACT than by the SAT include:

- Those who perform well in school but poorly on most standardized tests
- Those who are following an International Baccalaureate (IB) program
- Those with minimal ability to retain vocabulary
- Those who excel in the sciences
- Those who are poor writers (by taking the ACT without the optional writing section)

THE SAT SUBJECT TESTS

The SAT subject tests, once called Achievement Tests and then called SAT IIs, are developed by the College Board and administered by ETS. These one-hour exams measure academic achievement in a variety of subjects; in other words, they test a student's learned knowledge of a subject. SAT subject tests are administered across the nation on six different Saturdays each year. Note that students cannot take both the SAT and SAT subject tests on the same day, but can take up to three SAT subject tests on a single test day. Not all SAT subject tests are necessarily given at all locations on all dates, so you should be careful when registering for the exam, especially regarding foreign language subjects.

The SAT subject test should generally be taken immediately after a student has finished a course in that subject. (Tests in foreign languages are best taken at the end of junior year or partway through senior year, assuming you are still following the subject at school.) SAT subjects include Art History, English Literature, Math Levels I and II, Statistics, Computer Science, United States History, World History, Biology, Chemistry, Physics, certain "reading-only" language exams (French, German, Modern Hebrew, Latin, Italian, Spanish), and certain "reading and listening" language exams (French, Chinese, German, Japanese, Korean, Spanish). Note that most colleges do not accept Math Level I because the concepts tested are so similar to those found in the math portion of the SAT Reasoning Test.

The SAT subject tests are scored similarly to the SAT Reasoning Test. Correct answers receive one point, and a fraction of a point is subtracted for incorrect answers. (One-fourth of a point is subtracted for questions that offer five choices; one-third of a point is subtracted for questions that offer four choices; and a half of a point is subtracted for questions that offer three choices.) No points are gained or lost for unanswered questions. Like on the SAT, students who can identify one or two answer choices as being incorrect are encouraged to make educated guesses. The raw score is then changed into a "scaled" score, on a scale of 200 to 800, with 800 being the best possible score.

TOEFL, TWE, AND SAT II: ELPT (FOR FOREIGN STUDENTS ONLY)

The TOEFL (Test of English as a Foreign Language) is a test administered to nonnative English speakers to measure English proficiency. TOEFL is administered by Educational Testing Service (ETS), the same organization that administers the SAT tests. Most colleges require a TOEFL score from overseas students (except native English speakers) and those who have lived in the U.S. for fewer than a given number of years. If you are a nonnative English speaker but are not required by a particular college to take the TOEFL, you should take it anyway if your SAT Verbal score is low. Colleges know that nonnative English speakers tend to score lower on the Verbal portion of the SAT, so admissions officers will look for other indications of English ability. If an admissions officer sees a high TOEFL score, he will be much more inclined to disregard a low Verbal score on the SAT.

The current electronic TOEFL format tests all four language skills: reading, writing, listening, and speaking. Five scores are given:

Reading	0–30 points
Writing	0–30
Listening	0–30
Speaking	0–30
Total	0–120

The most selective colleges are generally looking for a minimum total score of 100, but higher scores are preferred. (The equivalent of a 100 on the older versions was 250 on the computerized exam or 600 on the paper exam.)

FOR MORE INFORMATION ON THE TOEFL

To find out more about the TOEFL exam or register for it, contact:

TOEFL
Educational Testing Service
Rosedale Road
Princeton, NJ 08541
USA
(609)921-9000
www.ets.org

GENERAL TIPS ON PREPARING TO ACE STANDARDIZED TESTS

- Read, read, read. The only sure way of preparing for the reading and writing sections of the SAT and ACT is through lifelong reading of fairly serious literature. This does not mean that you need to read *only* National Book Award or Booker Prize–winning novels or nonfiction from Pulitzer Prize contenders, though trashy novels, self-help books, and pedestrian magazines will not usually provide the necessary rigor. Any semisophisticated adult literature—fiction, nonfiction, good journalism—will do.

- Familiarize yourself with the tests by taking preliminary ones (PSAT, PLAN) and plenty of practice tests, taken timed and under realistic conditions. Review the answers that you miss. Make sure that, at the very least, you know exactly what to expect in terms of a test's format—what each section asks you to do, how long each section is—before going in. That way you will not waste time reading directions or panicking, and will be able to concentrate on your performance.

- After taking the PSAT or PLAN, be sure to contact the testing company to get your actual test back with the correct answers so that you can review better for the real thing.

- Take care of your health and get enough rest for at least two nights before taking standardized tests.

- Be organized on the day of the test. Be prepared to bring number two pencils and a calculator to the exam site. If the site is not familiar to you, be sure that you have precise directions to it and know exactly how long it will take to get there, allowing for traffic or unexpected delays. Arrive at the testing site ten minutes early so that you have time to go to the restroom and calm down.

■ Be prepared to take a test more than once, continuing to prepare and review before the second (or third) shot.

■ Take SAT subject tests at the most opportune time. Any subject exam should be taken as soon as the subject has concluded or as soon as you have the most advanced knowledge of a subject (i.e., during your fourth year of a foreign language rather than after the second year).

■ Make vocabulary lists and notecards with basic math principles to take with you for reviewing whenever you have a spare moment.

■ Buy test prep guidebooks and CD-ROMs if you need practice.

■ Take a test prep course or hire a tutor if you are not disciplined enough to practice on your own. (See page 270 for more details on test preparation courses and tutors.)

SHOULD YOU RETAKE A TEST? HOW MANY TIMES IS TOO MANY?

If your initial round of scores on the SAT or ACT are superb, do not bother to take it again, hoping to reach perfection. You get no brownie points for having taken a standardized test more than once. Furthermore, you risk your score decreasing (it happens all the time), and all scores will be reported to the colleges. Although they will still officially consider only your best score, they will nonetheless see all of them.

If your standardized test scores will not help get you into a college of your choice, however, then you will need to retake them. Review your PSAT or PLAN results and your practice tests again to determine where your weaknesses are. Then work on those specific weaknesses; for example, if it is clear that a limited knowledge of vocabulary has hurt you, work extra hard on that. Buy practice books and put yourself on a self-induced study schedule or enroll in a test prep course if you need to.

Do not take the SAT or ACT more than three times. Two (or three) times is ideal. Although studies show that students perform better on admission tests when taken more than once, admissions officers start to look skeptically at applicants who submit too many scores. These same studies show that students who take a test more than three times seldom increase their scores, and taking the test over and over will cause you to dissipate energy that could have been better spent in other ways.

HOW TO OVERCOME BAD TEST SCORES

There are a few things you can do to overcome poor standardized test scores when applying to college. These will not, of course, erase your standardized test record, but they can help you boost your chances of admission if your record contains scores that are less than optimal. Your options include:

■ *Counter a bad score on the Verbal or Math portion of the SAT or ACT with strong performances on the SAT subject tests, AP exams, or IB exams.*

If you do poorly on the Verbal or Math section of the SAT or ACT, a strong score on the English Literature or Math SAT subject tests, respectively, will indicate to admissions officers that you are academically capable in these areas and make them more inclined to disregard poor scores in either section. You can also help your cause if you do well on an AP or IB exam that tests the area in which you are weak on the SAT or ACT. If SAT scores go into a formula that calculates your academic ranking, then your bad score will still harm you, but admissions officers can override what the numbers tell them if they see information that sways them in another direction. Schools that do not use formulas for calculating academic ratings are even more apt to view your SAT subject test (or other) scores with generosity when SAT or ACT scores are not ideal.

■ *Counter poor scores in one area by positioning yourself in a way that does not require those particular strengths.*

Do not position yourself in a way that requires strengths you clearly do not possess. If your scores on the Math section of the SAT are weak, for example, you will benefit by positioning yourself as something other than a math wizard or future engineer. You want your profile to match your strengths and weaknesses on the standardized tests so that admissions officers are inclined to believe that a deficiency will not minimize or harm your future contributions to the college or society. If you are pushing yourself as a future journalist or poet whose talents lie in the humanities, a college will not need to worry that poor math skills will prevent you from reaching your potential at college or meeting your future career goals.

■ *Apply to some schools that do not require standardized tests or that abide by the FairTest policy.*

The FairTest policy was developed for candidates who need to minimize the weight of SAT or ACT scores in order to do well in the admissions process. Most of the very selective colleges do not subscribe to the policy, but a growing number (including Bates, Bowdoin, Middlebury, and Mount Holyoke) do. Look into applying to a college that recognizes FairTest if you feel your scores will hurt you. There are five categories within the FairTest policy:

1. SAT/ACT used only for placement and/or academic advising.
2. SAT/ACT required only for out-of-state applicants (at public state universities).
3. SAT/ACT required only when minimum GPA or class rank is not met.
4. SAT/ACT required for certain programs only.
5. SAT/ACT not required, but SAT subject tests required.

Middlebury, for instance, requires that applicants submit standardized tests in at least three different subjects, but offers several options for doing so:

1. The ACT, preferably with the Writing Test
2. The (three-part) SAT
3. Three tests in different subject areas chosen from the SAT II, Advanced Placement, and International Baccalaureate exams

---

ARE TEST PREP COURSES AND TUTORS WORTH THE MONEY?

Many college applicants wonder whether or not a test preparation course or tutor is worthwhile. Courses can be beneficial for the right student, but are neither ideal nor necessary for everyone. Students need to examine their own studying and learning techniques, as well as be honest with themselves about how motivated they are to obtain better scores. Any student can prepare on his own just as well as he can in a course that costs a minor fortune. The learning materials are easily obtained without attending a special class (identical practice tests, vocabulary lists, and the like are available in many different kinds of test prep books you can buy in your local bookstore), the prep methods are not difficult to master, and the test prep instructors are often undertrained anyway. The benefits to preparing on your own are that it is low cost, offers you complete scheduling flexibility, and allows you to tailor your preparation to suit your own particular needs.

The problem is motivation. Students who are organized, diligent, persistent, and determined will do just as well on their own—no course needed. You just have to be able to set aside the right number of hours per week (perhaps six to eight hours a week for eight weeks) and stay on yourself to keep up with the work.

On the other hand, it is much easier to follow through with SAT preparation work when you are forced to go to a class and follow someone else's instructions, especially when you feel guilty about all the money your parents are spending to help you. A test prep course forces you to start preparing early, offers you a resource (although not always an expert one) on call when you have questions, and gives you an opportunity to study with others who are serious about doing well. A tutor also forces you to prepare early, gives you a resource for whatever questions you may have, and helps you focus on your personal weaknesses. The price and inconvenience are often outweighed by the higher scores test prep courses and tutors will produce.

You have to decide for yourself whether you have the motivation and the confidence to teach yourself the techniques or whether you would benefit from being under the watch of a supervisor who could better whip you into shape. The appropriate choice for you will depend on the kind of person you are, your study habits, your financial resources, and your goals. Those who should probably think about taking a test prep course or hiring a tutor if it is possible include:

- Those who tend to score below their ability level on standardized tests.
- Those who lack the self-discipline necessary to do basic preparations and review trouble spots.
- Those who need substantial help on more than one aspect of the exam.
- Those who do better when forced by peer pressure to keep up in the classroom.

If you cannot afford a course or a tutor, take advantage of the many complimentary sample test administrations, writing workshops, and the like that many test prep outfits offer on a regular basis.

CHOOSING A TEST PREP COURSE OR TUTOR

Test prep courses and tutors tend to cost a lot of money, so be sure that you will get what you pay for. The best value, and best instruction, may not come from the nationally known firms and their instructors. Look carefully at their smaller competitors before handing over the $1,000 or more that the name-brand companies demand.

There are several reasons to look at the full range of test prep companies and tutors rather than opting for the default choice of one of the famous providers. First, the major companies' claims that they have ultrasophisticated materials, embodying the otherwise unknowable secrets of the exams, are spurious. The fact is that employees of each company, large and small, monitor the efforts of their competitors and readily incorporate their best ideas. Thus, courses are more alike than different. Second, although the major companies can boast enormous libraries of materials on which to practice, few students utilize more than a modest fraction of these materials. Third, the major companies inevitably (given the huge numbers they employ) take on many instructors of average intellect and test-taking talent (including out-of-work actors, waiters, and so on), provide limited training, and suffer from high instructor turnover. The best of the smaller companies and individual tutors can avoid this difficulty. It is likely that there exists an underdog test prep organization or a highly regarded local tutor who can best prepare you for standardized tests. If you do opt for one of the major firms, be careful to select the specific course on the basis of the instructor teaching it. To do so, inquire of others who have already taken courses there and check with the firm's clerical staff, too; you are likely to hear that one or two of their instructors are highly sought after.

ADMISSIONS DIRECTORS TALK ABOUT STANDARDIZED TESTS

HOW IMPORTANT ARE STANDARDIZED TEST SCORES?

The *last* thing we look at is standardized test scores—no one believes this, but it's true! Our students have high test scores because they are great overall applicants, but their scores are really the least important component of the academic record to us. We just don't look at them as heavily as other schools do.
Michael Goldberger, Brown

Test scores are only one measure among many. We do find some predictive value in test scores—if we didn't, we wouldn't use them—but we realize they are just predictive, not determinative. We publish admit rates at different bands of test scores on our website, not because we have cutoffs or minimums, but because applicants appreciate seeing the ranges. We recognize that test scores are context-based, and that's always on our minds when we evaluate candidates.
Stuart Schmill, MIT

Scores don't count as much as students think. There are no students who are admitted solely on the basis of high test scores. There are a few students with quite low scores who might be rejected on that basis. However, most students are within a range that suggests they would succeed here academically. Once you are in that range, scores become a neutral factor. We are far more interested in your day-to-day performance, not just how you did on one particular Saturday morning. *Robert Clagett, Middlebury*

Students and colleges both benefit from the student attaining the highest score possible—the student for entrance purposes and the college for statistical purposes. That said, students should not overemphasize the importance of the test. It is only one factor in the application. In our review process, test scores are the last thing we come to. You will never be dismissed from our process at the get-go because of your scores.   *Chris Gruber, Davidson*

It's the only consistent piece of quantitative information we have, so it's important to use it and use it wisely. We often use it as a complement to the student's academic experience. The most important piece of information we have about students, and to which we give the greatest attention, is the student's academic program and profile: how a student has chosen to challenge herself within the context of her high school experience, the risks that she has taken, the extent to which she has pushed herself to take advantage of opportunities.   *Jennifer Desjarlais, Wellesley*

High school grades are much more important in our process than SAT scores. We feel that SAT scores are used appropriately in the process only if they are used in concert with other factors.   *Ingrid Hayes, Georgia Tech*

What Are the Standardized Test Requirements or Options?

We look only at a student's best scores, even though we are given access to all of them.   *Maria Laskaris, Dartmouth*

We do not require specific SAT II tests. Despite this, we do have a high portion of students who have participated in a lot of SAT IIs.   *Douglas Christiansen, Vanderbilt*

Wellesley requires that students take two SAT subject tests. We leave it up to the students to determine what the two will be. Clearly, if a student has an interest in studying in the sciences, say, it would be our expectation that the student would take at least one quantitative exam. It seems only natural that they reflect a student's interest areas.   *Jennifer Desjarlais, Wellesley*

Any three (subject tests).   *Charles Deacon, Georgetown*

If You Allow the ACT or SAT Tests, Who Should Take the ACT?

We have historically had a preference for the SAT over the ACT. Now we're concerned that as the SAT tries to be a popular test and dilutes itself, most recently with the addition of the writing sample and so on, it becomes less and less useful as an aptitude test and more like an achievement test, in which case we'd look at the ACT, which is more achievement oriented, as being a valid competitor to the SAT today. We now consider them both equally. *Charles Deacon, Georgetown*

We have no preference. *Jennifer Desjarlais, Wellesley*

CAN STRONG SCORES ON ONE TEST OFFSET WEAK SCORES ON ANOTHER?

AP and IB results *can* offset poor standardized test scores. I think evidence from four years of work is often more compelling than evidence from three hours of work! *Christoph Guttentag, Duke*

AP scores don't really have the ability to offset poor SAT or SAT subject test scores. *Maria Laskaris, Dartmouth*

There's a lot of balancing that goes on when we look at test scores. We do use test scores; we think they're important. Highly selective institutions have an expectation that most testing patterns will be strong and this begins with SAT or ACT. If you've done well on your SAT subject tests, or AP exams, even New York State Regents or AIME test or IB exams, then that is an added indication of the strength of your academic preparation. *Rick Shaw, Stanford*

An SAT subject test is a different test than the SAT, so it doesn't replace that, and yet it's another piece of information that adds to the composite of the student's academic program, profile, story, collection of credentials. *Jennifer Desjarlais, Wellesley*

Only in some very specific areas such as in science and math where a very high score could make a difference. But in general we much prefer people who have balance in those scores. *Charles Deacon, Georgetown*

DOES NATIONAL MERIT FINALIST DESIGNATION HELP A CANDIDATE IN COLLEGE ADMISSIONS?

We don't even record whether or not a student is a National Merit scholar—we see it on practically every other application we receive. It's too common to be a distinctive factor in our decision. *James Bock, Swarthmore*

HOW MUCH DO LOW TEST SCORES HURT AN APPLICANT?

We don't have test score cut-offs, but we start to worry if we see a verbal score under 600. If there is a reason for it—if English is a student's second language, for example—then we understand, but otherwise we would be concerned about a student's ability to perform at Amherst, which is a very verbal place. *Katie Fretwell, Amherst*

Low test scores will be just one variable in the evaluation process. People get hung up on test scores, but in reality it's just one of many factors. *Douglas Christiansen, Vanderbilt*

We are one of only a handful of selective colleges that doesn't factor in standardized tests at all in our admissions process—we don't even make testing optional. We found it simply isn't an accurate predictor of how an applicant will fare in a writing-intensive college such as ours. *Stephen Schierloh, Sarah Lawrence*

If a student were interested in engineering and had low scores and skills in math, that would be a problem. But this rarely occurs, because most students' interests lie in their strengths. *Eric Kaplan, Penn*

How Do You Regard Applicants Who Take Tests Many Times?

We feel sorry for the student who takes the SAT eight times. We also note the student who scores a 1580 the first time and takes it over again three times trying to do better. That's putting your priorities in the wrong place. *Dan Walls, Emory*

We see nothing wrong with students retaking a standardized test. We will take the highest combination. That said, scores don't tend to rise much after the second attempt. *Daniel J. Saracino, Notre Dame*

If an applicant has taken the SAT more than three or four times, it looks odd. But we wouldn't really hold that against him or her. *Eric Kaplan, Penn*

Does an Optional Testing Policy Suggest That a School Does Not Care about Standardized Test Scores At All?

Some students jump to the conclusion that we don't care about how a student does on standardized tests since we don't require score results. That's a leap they shouldn't make. Test scores certainly help students who do well on them. We now even recognize National Merit scholars, partly to signal that we *do* care about test scores. We do not require them, however, and we know we can make informed decisions by evaluating applications, transcripts, and recommendations carefully. *Richard Steele, Bowdoin*

What Do You Think about Applicants Who Take Test Prep Courses?

We assume these days that many of our applicants have taken [test prep courses]. We make allowances for kids from poorer socioeconomic backgrounds when we're looking at their test scores—we might assume that their scores would be a bit higher if they had an opportunity to take a prep course as many other students do. We would never, however, let the test prep assumption work negatively on a candidate from a background full of opportunities. *Michael Goldberger, Brown*

Students with scores in the lower ranges might indeed benefit from a test preparation service. But it's important to note that it's easier for student to use test prep services to move a score from the 500s to the 600s. Students trying to move up from the 700s may find these types of programs less helpful. *Robert Clagett, Middlebury*

For me, test prep classes are fine. We have heard it helps students figure out what to expect, which can reduce anxiety. That said, my advice is always that you cannot cram for these tests. You need to be preparing in school by taking challenging classes, reading novels on your own, reading the newspaper every day, and so forth. You need to be able to read and absorb information quickly. This is a skill that takes years of practice to master and that no short-term test prep course will teach. *Douglas Christiansen, Vanderbilt*

9

SHAPING YOUR NONACADEMIC PROFILE

— KEY POINTS —

■

Few candidates will be accepted at the top colleges on the basis of academic credentials alone
—What you do outside of class is critically important

■

There are five areas of nonacademic involvement:
—Intellectual pursuits outside of the classroom
—Extracurricular (school and outside-of-school) activities
—Community service
—Work experience
—Summer experiences (which might include any of the above)

■

Commitment and depth are more important than the number of activities you pursue

■

Your nonacademic pursuits thus become a critical part of your positioning effort

INTRODUCTION

By now most smart high school students know that academics alone will probably not get them into college. As explained in Chapter 8, an excellent academic record will put you in the running for admission at college. It is usually the rest of the material presented in the application, however, that determines whether or not a prospective student is actually admitted over others with similarly impressive academic records at the very best schools. This chapter explores the five main facets of a student's overall nonacademic profile: (1) intellectual pursuits outside of the classroom, (2) extracurricular (school and outside-of-school) activities, (3) community service, (4) work experience, and (5) summer experiences.

Colleges are not looking for the proverbial well-rounded student. Colleges want well-rounded or diverse *classes* of students, not students who themselves are well-rounded.

A strong and diverse class of students requires that each student be exceptional, but perhaps only in a few areas. It is basically impossible for one person to excel to the greatest degree possible at many different things—after all, there are only so many hours in the day to dedicate to one's endeavors. Aiming toward becoming well-rounded will lead to mediocrity rather than excellence. If a student is accomplished academically, then he or she may only need to stand out in one or two nonacademic arenas in order to be competitive at the top schools.

Many students fail to realize that a lack of strength in traditional extracurricular activities may not hurt them if they have spent time outside of school doing other worthwhile things (e.g., working at a paid job, performing community service, or caring for siblings or elderly relatives). In other words, college admissions committees want to see that you are spending your time wisely, but they do not expect miracles. If you have had to work at nights and on weekends to help make ends meet for your family, a college will not blame you for failing to dedicate the fifteen or more hours a week necessary to play a varsity sport. If you have helped to take care of your elderly grandparents after school, that counts for something—it is not lost or wasted time as far as college applications go.

Your nonacademic record becomes a large part of your overall positioning effort. The way in which you spend your free time, the talents and skills you have developed, and the personality traits you exhibit through your nonacademic activities all contribute heavily to your overall profile. You need to tailor your pursuits and the way you present them to colleges in a way that will add to (rather than detract from) your main positioning efforts.

Remember that the placement of the material that makes up your nonacademic profile does not matter too much. You can choose to include your community service under an application's "Extracurricular Activities" list or "Work Experience" list; it is up to you to determine whether you want to discuss your summer enrichment experience at a physics camp under "Summer Experiences," "Extracurricular Activities," or "Coursework Conducted Outside of the Classroom."

The important thing is to include everything that will help you improve your presentation and to do so in a way that makes you appear to be focused, yet also not deficient in any important area. Thus, if you have never worked for pay and have plenty to discuss under "Extracurricular Activities," you will want to place your volunteer service in the "Work Experience" category—to avoid appearing as if you have never lifted a finger or exerted yourself in labor.

INTELLECTUAL PURSUITS OUTSIDE OF THE CLASSROOM

There was a time when it was not very common to hear of students participating in academic pursuits outside of regular classroom learning. Now, however, there are many opportunities for high school students with special interests to get beyond the basics learned in high school, prepare themselves for future training in a subject, or explore possible college majors and career options ahead of time.

Colleges have always liked to see that students show particular affinity for learning by finding ways to supplement their classroom education. Admissions committees have for a long time looked hard to find students whose teachers say that they enjoy "learning for learning's sake" and show evidence of special intellectual interests. But recently this trend has become even more pronounced, especially at very competitive colleges. With growing numbers of high-quality applications, colleges are constantly thinking about how to make admissions decisions when there are too many desirable candidates in the pool.

It has in fact become nearly imperative to show special intellectual prowess beyond classroom participation to be admitted to some of the top schools. MIT, for example, rates all applicants on a scale of 1 to 5, with 5 being the best rating, in four separate areas: Academics, Cocurricular Activities, Extracurricular Activities, and Interpersonal Skills. Cocurricular Activities are described as "learning-oriented activities that take place outside of the classroom." Applicants must be able to show that they participate in academic pursuits beyond what is required of them at school in order to stay in the running for admission at MIT.

Back in 1998, Stanford added a component called Intellectual Vitality to its original two areas in which every candidate is given a numerical rating, Academics and Nonacademics. Stanford's decision to create this category was based on the fact that most applicants they see have excellent grades, high test scores, and impressive talents. The school needed to develop a way to differentiate between strong candidates and stellar candidates. The admissions officers thus made it a priority to select candidates who have demonstrated special intellectual passion and commitment beyond regular expected classroom participation.

ADMISSIONS DIRECTORS DISCUSS THE IMPORTANCE OF INTELLECTUAL PASSION

Ask your friends, teachers, and parents how they know you love math, science, or engineering. Be sure you capture that in your application. *Rick Bischoff, Cal Tech*

A demonstration of intellectual depth is critical—some evidence that students have been actively engaged in the process of learning, that they've made contributions to their classroom experience and learned from others around them as others have perhaps learned from them. That's an important element, because it's our expectation that students are going to take an active role in their educational experience here at Wellesley. It's a dynamic classroom environment. Our faculty is dedicated to teaching undergraduates so it's important that students can demonstrate academic initiative and intellectual engagement. *Jennifer Desjarlais, Wellesley*

Intellectual passion does play a role in admissions decisions inasmuch as it manifests itself in a student's performance academically and in extracurricular participation. You need a passion for knowledge to be successful in college. *Ingrid Hayes, Georgia Tech*

We conducted a study with our faculty, asking them to pick their three favorite students and describe what they like about them. Far above intelligence was "enthusiasm for learning." This is what we are looking for—students who are not particularly engaged in learning shouldn't be at Bowdoin. *Richard Steele, Bowdoin*

We thus highly recommend that you pursue some outside learning in an academic activity with special meaning for you if there are opportunities available. If there are not opportunities readily available, try to create them yourself. In fact, creating these kinds of opportunities yourself is what "intellectual vitality" is really all about. Expand your thinking and do not feel limited by what has been done before in your school or community. Just because your community newspaper has no student contributors at present does not mean that it would not welcome an opinion piece from you. Academic pursuit is often conducted alone rather than in groups, so do not feel that you have to "become part of something" in order to show your spark.

HOW TO PURSUE INTELLECTUAL INTERESTS OUTSIDE OF THE CLASSROOM

- Participate on a model United Nations team.
- Participate on a debate team or a mock trial group.
- Write an editorial (or a regular editorial column) for your town's newspaper.
- Contribute to a newspaper or website on a topic that interests you.
- Conduct special projects for submission to science contests and fairs.
- Submit original fiction, poetry, or drama to writing contests.
- Write a play and then direct it.
- Take classes at a community college or in an enrichment program.
- Take classes at a special performing arts or technical school.
- Attend a special summer program at a boarding school or college to pursue subjects of interest to you.
- Attend a writing workshop.
- Start a Web magazine or journal.
- Conduct a special research project under the supervision of a teacher.
- Take part in Civil War reenactments.
- Organize an event at school to celebrate and teach others about a person or topic in which you are particularly interested. For example, if you are interested in Oscar Wilde, ask a teacher or school administrator whether you can hold a special event on his birthday.

EXTRACURRICULAR (SCHOOL AND OUTSIDE-OF-SCHOOL) ACTIVITIES

Extracurricular activities include everything from playing on high school sports teams to taking part in religious festivals. It is here where most college applicants fail in presenting themselves. A college would much rather see that you have put many hours of valuable work over several years into two activities than joined every club in school, playing very limited roles. Quality matters much more than quantity. In fact, a long list of activities merely dilutes the overall impression that your extracurricular profile gives an admissions officer.

Remember that anything and everything can "count" as part of your profile here—it does not have to be sponsored by your high school. Let us assume, for example, that you are interested in a certain period in American history and have spent time at antique shows and auctions augmenting your collection of stamps from the era. This way of spending your Saturdays can certainly become fodder for extracurricular material, whether it be merely mentioning it on an activity list or incorporating it into your essays somehow. Be sure to put an appropriate interpretation on whatever you are claiming as an activity. In other words, it is better to present the collecting as part of your interest in a certain period (especially if history is a strength that you are positioning) than as a mere "shopping habit." Likewise, if you read philosophy to your grandfather and his roommate at the nursing home once a week, you would want to present it as something more serious and meaningful than just "visiting Grandpa."

Extracurricular activities are important to admissions officers for many reasons. They show how you choose to spend your time away from school; demonstrate special talents and skills; provide evidence of personality and character traits; and complement ideas presented within your academic profile. In sum, they give admissions officers an idea about how you might contribute to the college environment if accepted.

The admissions officers are not looking for any particular activities on a student's palette of extracurricular involvements. Except in cases in which a special talent is a selling point for a candidate, they do not much care whether you are editor-in-chief of the yearbook or director of your school's environmental and recycling team. They are, however, looking for students who have been involved in a few activities for a good length of time, showing commitment and passion. A bit of a balance is usually ideal, so that a student does not appear one-dimensional, but in general showing commitment and focus is better than being the "all-around" kid.

Extracurricular activities help to show your personal qualities. Admissions committees at the top schools tend to look for students who have taken on substantial responsibilities within their organizations, demonstrating (most importantly) leadership, initiative, and a positive "can-do" attitude. Dartmouth likes to see evidence of "adventurousness, a willingness to take risks, and curiosity"—along with the other usual traits of commitment and leadership. Amherst likes to see "perseverance and follow-through" evident in extracurricular activities.

Although it does not really matter what activities you choose, keep in mind these important points about your extracurricular record:

■ *Depth of involvement:* Show that you have been committed to one or more activities for a length of time, preferably three or more years. Show that you have advanced within at least one activity and consistently devoted substantial time to it over several years.

■ *Leadership:* Show that you have taken on an important leadership role in at least one activity. This means founding a club or group, becoming an appointed or elected high officer of a group, or directing a group's efforts in one area. Show that you can motivate others around you to contribute their best efforts to a common cause.

■ *Something unusual:* Not everyone has the talent or resources to do something really out of the ordinary. But everyone can find a way to use his or her abilities to get involved in something that stands out from the usual student council, yearbook, and varsity sports activities that show up on college applicants' rosters. Doing something a bit unusual can be beneficial because it will expand your own mind, exposing you to something you might not have run into without special effort, as well as make you a bit more memorable to college admissions officers. Training Seeing Eye dogs, leading nature hikes, participating in a community choir, becoming a glassblower, joining a Neighborhood Watch association to fight crime, or playing in a Korean drumming ensemble are examples of activities that are distinctive but within reach of high school students with the right ambition and prerequisite skills.

■ *Possession of at least two dimensions:* You want to present yourself as a focused individual with a memorable profile, not someone who dabbles in everything without much commitment to any one particular activity. But avoiding the tag of "well-rounded student" does not mean you should become one-dimensional. Be sure that there is at least one activity you can point to that stands out as not fitting into your main positioning effort. For example, if you are presenting yourself as a future biologist who is strong in the sciences, works at the city aquarium, and leads children's nature hikes at a nearby park, make sure to get involved in at least one activity that is completely unrelated to your interest in the biological sciences—painting classes at an art institute or playing on the tennis team, for example.

WHAT ADMISSIONS DIRECTORS SAY ABOUT
THE NONACADEMIC PROFILE

How Important Is an Applicant's Nonacademic Profile?

After we determine there is a match between a student and Harvard in terms of academics, then we're basically looking to find out who you are, what makes you tick—to flesh out the other sides of you. *Marlyn McGrath Lewis, Harvard*

We want to see what kind of recognition a student has received from the community, school, or peers for his or her various contributions and activities. Looking at "recognition" allows us to feel a candidate's real impact on those around him or her. *Christoph Guttentag, Duke*

In looking at how a student spends her time outside of class we're also trying to assess why a student has been involved with a particular activity or organization or volunteer work or work experience—and what this has meant to the student. So beyond just a laundry list of activities, what a student takes away from that experience and what a student contributes to that experience demonstrate a great deal about who that student is. It reflects a great deal about her character, her values, her maturity, her leadership ability, and her initiative. So what she chooses to be involved with says a lot about who she is personally. *Jennifer Desjarlais, Wellesley*

We assign an extracurricular rating using an A-B-C scale. A's are those who are really stars at something. B's are good, well-rounded students—maybe a president of a club or a captain of a team. C's are those who sit inside playing Dungeons and Dragons all day. *David Borus, Vassar*

What Activities "Count" as Part of the Nonacademic Profile?

People really overestimate the importance of summer programs at colleges and prep schools. I do not like the idea that students and parents see them as a stepping stone to the college of their choice. Some families believe that if you go to these programs you will have a significantly better chance of being accepted into the best colleges. These programs are fine, but students should feel empowered to focus on a single activity, go to computer camp or music camp, or work for community outreach programs (domestically or internationally) in a sustained way. *Rick Shaw, Stanford*

All activities "count." Often students think we're not interested in activities outside of school, but we are! It's important that students tell us about their experiences in scouting or community service or work with their churches or synagogues. Also, after-school jobs or caring for younger siblings after school are also important activities. I don't care what students are involved in, but that they are doing something that they care about, something that occupies their minds and hearts in a different way than school. *Debra Shaver, Smith*

It's clear that students thrive when they are most engaged and passionate. They shouldn't do something just to impress colleges—in the end, that probably won't serve them well. Students need to be able to tell us *why* something is important to them, what value it has had for them. *Eric J. Furda, Columbia*

WHAT PERSONAL QUALITIES, EVIDENCED THROUGH THE NONACADEMIC PROFILE AND ELSEWHERE, DO ADMISSIONS OFFICERS MOST LIKE TO SEE IN CANDIDATES?

Passion, maturity, civic-mindedness. These are some of the things we look for. *John Blackburn, University of Virginia*

We are committed to finding students who show adventurousness, willingness to take risks, and curiosity. *Maria Laskaris, Dartmouth*

Perseverance and follow-through are important. Quality over quantity of activities is also key. *Katie Fretwell, Amherst*

We have stressed maturity quite a bit in our admissions process. We give our students quite a bit of freedom here, and we want to know they can handle it. Honesty is also a big factor for us because of our honor code. *Richard Steele, Bowdoin*

I am looking for someone who knows who they are, someone who is self-aware. I like candidates who understand their strengths and weaknesses and view this knowledge as a source of confidence, as opposed to applicants who try to hide from this information. *Douglas Christiansen, Vanderbilt*

Some of the personal qualities we look for in candidates include curiosity, self-motivation, initiative, adventurousness, willingness to take risks, strong sense of community, and being a bridge builder. *Robert Clagett, Middlebury*

We have a real commitment to Philadelphia here so we need students who will be able to contribute, who have shown real involvement in the community. *Lee Stetson, University of Pennsylvania*

Curiosity! I am relentless in my search in an application for evidence of a student's curiosity: about the world, your place in it, the impact of your decisions on your community. *Nancy Hargrave Meislahn, Wesleyan*

Part of what we're looking for is passion and commitment, and how these things have developed. Leadership, character, integrity also come into the mix. *Nancy Hargrave Meislahn, Wesleyan*

Duke's admissions committee often uses the word "impact" when discussing candidates for admission. We look for evidence of impact and having made a difference. We ask ourselves, What has this student done with the opportunities given to him? *Christoph Guttentag, Duke*

How Important Is It to Show Commitment and Follow-Through?

It's not about joining, it's about what you do with your involvement. Having a sustained commitment to something is important. We're looking for depth and passion. *Rick Shaw, Stanford*

"Significant follow-through" is a term coined by my colleague Phil Smith at Williams. This is very important to us. We don't care if a student does piano lessons or wrestles or sits on the student council, but we want to see a student pursue something and stick with it. Success in life requires diligence, cooperation, the ability to stick with something—we like to see evidence of this. *John Blackburn, University of Virginia*

Which Is Better, Breadth or Depth?

Level of commitment is very important, but that doesn't mean that students shouldn't experiment a little and make changes in their extracurricular schedules when it's appropriate. We expect that there will be growth in many different directions. *Eric J. Furda, Columbia*

Some versatility is advisable. This doesn't mean that we don't like someone of Olympic stature who does nothing else but train in his or her spare time. But for the most part we like students who are focused, yet still somewhat versatile. *Sheppard Shanley, Northwestern*

Depth is always more important. I like to see that students have committed to a certain activity and grown with it over a period of time. It's this kind of passion outside the classroom that shows another important characteristic of the student. *Debra Shaver, Smith*

As between breadth or depth, we tend to pick depth. We like to see students apply themselves to something they are interested in. *Thyra Briggs, Harvey Mudd*

We really want to see depth and focus in extracurricular activities. *Eric Kaplan, Penn*

It is generally better to have breadth academically but depth extracurricularly. Showing that you do not have blinders on intellectually and are interested in a wide range of academic pursuits is a plus. On the extracurricular side, however, many applicants spread themselves too thin. We like to see fewer areas of specialization in the extracurricular realm, but great passion for those that are undertaken. *Robert Clagett, Middlebury*

What About Showing That You Have Taken Advantage of the Opportunities Around You?

The question behind the question about extracurricular activities is, "In what have you invested yourself?" We're also getting at whether or not students have taken full advantage of the opportunities given to them.   *Nancy Hargrave Meis-lahn, Wesleyan*

All of what we see in the nonacademic record is tempered by the fact that we realize not everyone has the same level of opportunity. Some students have to work after school. Children in military families move around so much that it's hard for them to sustain commitment to anything. We care deeply about context and we pay attention to what opportunities are or are not available to the student.   *Rick Shaw, Stanford*

COMMUNITY SERVICE

Most college applicants should be sure to have some sort of volunteer or community service to show for their four years in high school. As an exception to this general rule, those who come from very low-income families or are required to work a great deal to help support the family should not feel that they need to add community service to their high school activity lists. If it is clear that you spend a substantial amount of energy working for wages necessary for your or your family's survival, you will not be expected to have donated your limited free time to charity work.

Other college applicants, however, should at the very least have on their activity lists (or work experience lists) a mention of running an event at a Special Olympics function or raising money for a local charity. As with other areas of one's nonacademic profile, more depth in a community service project is always better than these kinds of single instances of volunteerism. Thus it is much better if you can show that you worked for a cause for a length of time rather than showing up for one Saturday or participating in a single campaign.

WHAT KIND OF COMMUNITY SERVICE?

Again, as with other kinds of activity, it is not particularly important what group or cause you help with your time and effort. An admissions committee will be impressed whether you have helped blind children learn Braille, contributed to an effort to save the seals, or served meals to hospice patients with AIDS. You should try to be as directly involved in your cause as possible rather than performing work that is only attached to the cause indirectly. Volunteer to work with patients at a hospital rather than shuffling papers in the administrative office, for example. Being directly involved with the people who need your help or in fashioning efforts to solve a community problem will teach you much more (in terms of both hard skills and life lessons) than raising money to support a cause or doing office work for a community organization. These other indirect tasks might become part of your job, but try to allot at least some of your time for hands-on experience with the "service" component of the work.

Community service can also be used to show leadership, initiative, drive, creativity, or an entrepreneurial spirit. Your volunteer efforts in a service project will be that much more powerful and useful to you in college admissions if you can go beyond the standard effort to contribute more meaningfully to a cause. For example, rather than merely joining a group that protects the natural habitat in your community's park systems, you might consider going one step further by spreading the group's efforts to the next town, thereby becoming the head of the task force for another community. Or you might create a new program for the existing service organization—perhaps a monthly educational meeting for community residents or a kids' task force, to encourage young children to join the service. You might even create an entirely new organization by yourself. One upstart we know founded an organization to teach senior citizens how to use email to contact their grandchildren.

What counts most with community service is that you prove your commitment to caring about something other than yourself. Some schools look particularly carefully for evidence of volunteer service. The University of Pennsylvania, for example, looks for students whom it can depend on to contribute to volunteer functions because the school is committed to improving Philadelphia and the surrounding community. Personality traits that are attractive to college admissions officers can show up through volunteer service as well. Involvement in community service can help demonstrate compassion, appreciation for one's own fortunes, maturity, special talents, leadership potential, and responsibility for others' well-being.

IMPORTANCE OF COMMUNITY SERVICE FOR ADVANTAGED APPLICANTS

Community service is especially important if you come from a wealthy or even moderately well-off family and have never had to work for wages. If it is evident that you have enjoyed many advantages in your life, you should make an effort early in your high school career to find a service or cause that excites you and devote substantial energy to it over the next few years. When it comes time to apply to colleges, try your best to provide evidence that you have contributed your energy to something that helps those less fortunate than yourself or serves community interests in some way.

In the case of the advantaged applicant, something in the way of volunteer service is usually better than nothing at all. There are instances, however, when a tiny contribution to community service—when viewed in comparison to energy spent on other activities—might seem crass rather than admirable. For example, if a student from an extremely wealthy family were to throw in a mention of a one-day commitment to United Way after including loads of information about numerous travels abroad with the family, expensive soccer camps, and special summer programs, he might come across as disingenuous to an admissions officer.

WORK EXPERIENCE

Many candidates for college discount the value of the experience they have gained working for wages—often because the jobs high schoolers have might not seem to be worthy of discussion in an application to a top college. Candidates may think, "How can I prove that I'm Princeton material when I flip burgers for a living?" Yet the truth is that work counts for a lot in college admissions, and it often does not matter what kind of work is being performed.

WHAT KIND OF WORK "COUNTS"?

All schools, quite obviously, value the basic ideas of "work" and "responsibility" that come with paid labor. But some schools admit they maintain a double standard with respect to the value they place on the nature of paid work experience. All colleges report that for students from low-income backgrounds, it absolutely does not matter what the paid work experience is. If a student is working because he has to in order to support himself or his family, no thought is given to whether or not the job is particularly worthy, meaningful, or enlightening. For students who come from upper-class or upper middle-class backgrounds, and can choose whether they want to work or spend their time doing something else, the nature of the work generally matters to admissions officers.

If you come from a disadvantaged or low-income background and must work to support yourself or your family, do not worry about what job you are performing. Take the job that will best contribute to your expenses—and then do the best you can to stick with it long enough so that you can move up in your role or take on added responsibility. The more you can show colleges that you have utilized your work experience to the best of your potential and extracted all you can out of the experience, the better off you will be. Be sure to explain thoroughly on your college applications why you work, how much you contribute to your own basic needs or those of your family, and the reason you took the job that you did.

Admissions officers prefer that someone who does *not* have to work take advantage of the best opportunities for success rather than work in an unskilled job for cash. Schools would rather see a student in a leadership position or doing something that will enrich him than working at a job that will contribute little to personal growth. This often means that leadership activities or substantial internships count more in college admissions than do "meaningless" paying jobs for those candidates who do not have to work.

For those who do not have to work for pay but choose to do so, be careful about the choices you make. It is not unwise to work for pay, but if you have the leeway to be picky about what you do, take time to be sure you are getting all you can from your paid job. Ask yourself these questions to ascertain that the job you choose will not only contribute to your bank account but also contribute to your overall growth and the record you are building for college preparation purposes:

- What kinds of responsibilities and skills will I gain from the job?

- Is there room for growth and development within the job once I master my original tasks?

- Will my performance and learning contribute at all to my future academic and career plans?

- Will this job help me make crucial decisions about the direction of my academic focus or future career?

- Will I gain valuable contacts in this job to help me in later life?

You should choose a job that balances the best pay and the most enjoyment with positive contributions to your future.

**WHAT ADMISSIONS DIRECTORS SAY
ABOUT WORK EXPERIENCE**

Paid work experience shows energy and commitment—and also helps to tell us what a person does with his or her time.   *Marlyn McGrath Lewis, Harvard*

All work experience—even if it's working in a convenience store—is life experience and involves responsibility. We value all of it—and wouldn't expect as much extracurricular involvement from a student who has to work.   *Maria Laskaris, Dartmouth*

I think that students can learn a lot from almost any work experience. You learn to work on a team, to work with people who are different from you, to work toward a common goal. It's not so much *what* you're doing but what you're learning or taking away from that experience.   *Debra Shaver, Smith*

We find that students who have worked often have an enhanced chance to have a good work ethic and good time-management skills. But you can get those same skills and values through participation in a club or sport or by volunteering. It's all driven by what you accomplish in whichever setting you choose to apply yourself.   *Chris Gruber, Davidson*

The way we look at work experience depends on the context. Internships can be great, but they are often handed down by a friend of Mom or Dad—and sometimes don't amount to much substance.   *Lee Stetson, Penn*

Work is evaluated in a contextual way. For someone who doesn't have to work but still chooses to work twenty hours a week, the job should have some sort of cumulative effect. If it doesn't, we'll wonder what moves this person. We want to see how a student establishes priorities outside of school.   *Sheppard Shanley, Northwestern*

Anyone who has to work should not feel badly about this or worry about what it will do to his extracurricular profile. But again, like other nonacademic activities, work is an opportunity. We want to see what a kid has done with this opportunity, whatever it may be.   *Christoph Guttentag, Duke*

Work experience often demonstrates the same qualities we would look for in any extracurricular activity: motivation, self-discipline, and independence. *Robert Clagett, Middlebury*

One of the first factors we look at when looking at the nonacademic profile is if the student is working.   *Richard Steele, Bowdoin*

It's one thing if the student has to work, it's another if he just wants gas money for his Mustang.   *David Borus, Vassar*

For us the commitment to a job is more important than what the job is. If you've had a newspaper route for seven years, I'm impressed. If a job just began six months ago, it probably won't matter that much on the application. *James Bock, Swarthmore*

SUMMER EXPERIENCES

Summer experiences, especially what you choose to do between your junior and senior years, can become significant contributors to the nonacademic profile you create for your college applications. The summer experience is not really a new category of nonacademic involvement, but is another way in which to include one of the first four categories of nonacademic activity on your high school record. In other words, a summer can be spent pursuing intellectual endeavors outside of the regular high school classroom; immersing yourself in an extracurricular activity; doing a community service project; or working for pay.

Although it is hardly necessary that you spend your first summer in high school doing something impressive, your summers should include something substantive the closer you get to the college application process. This does not mean that you need to attend expensive private institutes each summer or travel the world in search of meaning. A meaningful summer can consist of working part-time for pay, or doing volunteer community service along with training intensively for your sport. Participating in an enrichment program in an academic subject, attending a camp to improve a special talent, or going on an organized trip in the United States or abroad are other ways of spending your summers wisely. The specific content of your summers does not particularly matter, but be sure that at least part of one (and preferably two or all three) of your high school summers is spent doing something that a college admissions officer would call "worthwhile." See the first four sections of this chapter to learn more about how your choices will affect your overall application and how you should best plan your time during the summer months.

TAKING ADVANTAGE OF SUMMER

Summer activities should offer something not readily available to you during the regular school year—even if that just means unwinding from school stress.

Reasonable goals, if you have the luxury of choice, might include one or more of the following:

- Taking a course of interest that your high school does not offer
- Learning what college life is like—and what size and location of college (and environment) is appropriate for you—by attending a college summer program
- Trying out an arts program to determine whether this offers you a better option than a traditional university

- Experiencing a different—and perhaps more heterogeneous—school and/or community
- Coming to the attention of college athletic coaches, theater directors, and so on
- Exploring possible college majors or career interests
- Tackling a demanding job, internship, or volunteer position to develop your skills
- Volunteering for a group of underserved people (in a seniors' home, hospice, or prison, for example), determined to have an outsized impact upon their welfare

Focusing on either personal or intellectual growth would be ideal. If your family's financial circumstances require that you work, however, keep in mind that this is one of the most impressive things you can do during the summer. The discipline, determination, and teamwork you can demonstrate thereby greatly appeals to admissions directors.

The less you appear to be engaged in a frenetic bid to get into college, ironically enough, the more appeal you will have.

ADMISSIONS DIRECTORS DISCUSS SUMMER EXPERIENCES

To be honest, we don't take that much stock in what a student does during the summer. In fact, it can sometimes be a concern if we learn that an applicant has spent summer after summer at a pre-college academic program. We like to see that students have taken a break. *Robert Clagett, Middlebury*

We look for students who have done something engaging during their summers. It can be anything from working at the local grocery store to taking advanced courses in math or science. Students get in trouble by looking for something to do over the summer that "looks good" without thought to whether it fits their interests. This can make for an incoherent application. *Stuart Schmill, MIT*

The most important thing kids can do over the summer is something to give them energy for the coming fall—something that challenges them and excites them. By this I do not necessarily mean an academic challenge. For some students academic programs are great, but others really need and deserve a break. We love to see students who work, for example. Working at a store or a restaurant can be challenging in different and important ways. Above all, we want to see that students have been keeping busy over the summer. *Thyra Briggs, Harvey Mudd*

10

COMPLETING THE WRITTEN APPLICATIONS

— KEY POINTS —

Choose whichever type of application is best for you:
—Standard printed applications
—Downloaded applications
—Online applications

Take advantage of the Common Application where feasible

Although the essays are the most critical part of the written application, you cannot afford to be lackadaisical in putting together the rest of your materials

—Sloppiness says you do not care about the application

—You need to take advantage of all opportunities to fully support your positioning effort

—This is a unique opportunity to paint a complete picture of your high school career, since your essays will focus on no more than a couple aspects of your candidacy

Supplemental materials can be of great value to some applicants, especially those with special talents in the performing and visual arts

Avoid gimmicks

INTRODUCTION

Although the essays are inevitably the most important (and worrisome) part of the written application, you must also be cautious when filling out the other portions. Completing the other parts of the written application requires attention to detail as well as attention to your main marketing and positioning efforts. This chapter discusses how to organize and complete your applications most effectively.

CHOOSING YOUR APPLICATION FORMAT

First you will have to decide what method you will use for submitting each college's written application. Whereas a decade ago applicants had no choice but to file a standard printed application form obtained from the college's admissions office, there now exist several different kinds of computer-based application formats.

The application formats currently available are:

- *Standard printed application.* You obtain the printed application from the college's admissions office and fill it out with pen and/or electric type and mail it to the college.

- *Downloaded application.* You download the application from the college's website and, after filling it out on your computer screen, print out a hard (paper) copy and mail it to the college.

- *Online application.* You fill out an online application produced either by the college itself or by the Common Application organization and submit it electronically to the college.

Each application filing approach has advantages and disadvantages. Factors you will want to consider when looking at your options include:

- *Cost.* Each college requires a nonrefundable fee for filing an application, but some colleges waive the fee if you apply online. Sending applications by mail (particularly if you know you are a procrastinator and will be doing so at the last minute) can be quite costly.

- *Overlap usage for other colleges.* Filling out each individual college's application will require you to complete similar yet not identical forms many times over. When using the Common Application, however, you will need to enter basic pieces of data into the database only once.

- *Ease of filling out the forms.* Some application methods require more work than others. Each method varies in terms of the amount of information you must provide on the application form and the user-friendliness of the forms. Look at each method to decide for yourself if the directions are easy to understand, if there is enough space allotted for the answers, etc.

- *Flexibility and adaptability.* Whereas you can always make a standard printed application conform to your own needs by adding sheets of paper or writing outside of the boxed areas provided, some of the online applications will not allow users any additional space for answering questions.

- *Readability.* You want to be sure that what you submit to colleges is presented well (i.e., that it is neat, legible, and well-organized). If you fear that you will not do a good job filling in standard printed applications neatly, you should consider using one of the downloaded or online options.

THE COMMON APPLICATION

The Common Application is a single application that is accepted by a substantial number of schools in lieu of their own applications. In other words, you can fill out this one application and use it to apply to a number of colleges. It allows for a simpler, more manageable application process. Each school's application materials will let you know whether it accepts the Common Application or not.

Some colleges use *only* the Common Application (often with a special supplement), whereas others offer it as an option to their own individualized questionnaires. All schools that have their own applications but also accept the Common Application should give the latter equal weight in the admissions process. Some admissions officers admit that they believe the most interested applicants go the extra mile and complete the college's own particular application. If a college is at the very top of your wish list, you might be better off taking the extra time to fill in its own application forms. This is a strong signal of "demonstrated interest" in the college. Likewise, if you use the Common Application, be sure you have had other, previous contact with the school to show your enthusiasm. But generally speaking, it is wise to use the Common Application because it will greatly streamline the application process for you. When you fill out the Common Application rather than a school's own form, *always* complete any optional supplemental essays or questions provided.

COMPLETING THE BASIC DATA FORMS

PREPARING THE MATERIALS AND PAYING ATTENTION TO THE BASICS

No matter what format you use to fill out your applications, you should take the following initial step before doing anything else. Use a spare application or a downloaded Common Application and use it as your master list for recording the stock information (name, address, Social Security number, parents' occupations, etc.) you will be asked to fill in on all the applications. Make sure when producing your master list that all your information is accurate and that spellings are correct—if you get it wrong here, it will be copied incorrectly onto everything you turn in. Have your parents check it over for accuracy. You will refer to this master list as you fill in each application form.

If you are filling out a standard printed paper application by hand or electric type, by all means make at least two copies of the blank form before beginning. (Similarly, if you are downloading an application from a website, print out a few copies of the form.) Making extra copies will ensure that if you make mistakes in the application process, you can use another clean page to start over again.

Remember when filling out your applications that neatness counts. An application's appearance is called "self-representation" in college admissions lingo, and it symbolizes an applicant's interest in the institution and care for the application process. A poorly planned presentation, misspellings, grammatical errors, or a failure to follow directions make admissions officers think that a student is little concerned about an application.

It is still acceptable to fill out the basic data portion on a paper application in your own handwriting, but if you take this route, be sure your handwriting is neat and legible. Never use pencil; use only black or blue pens, and stay away from ink that will smear. Longer answers and essays should be typed or computer-generated if at all possible, even if the application says that you can do them by hand. It is difficult for a tired admissions officer to read even the most legible handwriting for any extended period of time.

Be consistent. Use the same pen and color of ink, and do not mix handwriting styles. Your name should be written the same in each entry (and should be the same name that appears on your standardized test scores and transcripts). Do not mix "William" and "Bill," for example, even if you go by both names in your personal life. Refer to school names, clubs, and the like consistently. Readers will not know that your school often refers to the "Big and Little Sister Program" as "Sibs" if you do not explain.

ADMISSIONS DIRECTORS TALK ABOUT THE IMPORTANCE OF THE WRITTEN APPLICATION'S APPEARANCE

The written application's appearance—we call this "self-presentation"—can be pretty important. It can represent a student's interest in the institution and care for the application process. *Eric Kaplan, Penn*

Failure to follow directions is a real turn-off. If an applicant staples a résumé of activities instead of answering our question about what activities are most important to him, we've got to make the assumption that he just doesn't care about this application very much. *Michael Goldberger, Brown*

A written application's appearance is very important. Just as you should not show up to an interview in tattered blue jeans and no socks, your application should be neat and easy to read. It is a reflection of you before the committee. *Daniel J. Saracino, Notre Dame*

The appearance of an application is important. It is important that it be legible. And this is not the time to pull out your purple pen—we want it to be readable. *Thyra Briggs, Harvey Mudd*

ANSWERING THE QUESTIONS

Most of the questions on the data forms are fairly straightforward. You do not have very many decisions to make before you get to the extracurricular activity and award lists or short-answer portion of the application. Your answers on the basic data forms matter, so give some thought to what you are doing.

For example, if you are asked to state your intended major, be keen but reasonable. Do not write down the first interesting idea that pops into your head. Instead, remember your positioning strategy when answering questions about what you will study at the college. You will want your answers to the basic data sheet questions to remain consistent with your general profile. It is often a good idea to list a major that is consistent with your previous achievement and success in that field, whether you think it will be your actual field of study or not. (Refer back to Chapter 6 for more specific information on positioning yourself.)

If you are considering several possible majors, be strategic about which one to list. Remember that a school with a particularly good reputation in one area most likely maintains especially high standards with regard to applicants interested in that field. You will not be held to what you state as your intended major on the application if you are admitted to the school, so you can always change your mind later on. If you know that a college has put a lot of effort into recruiting good students for its anthropology major over the last few years and this response fits with the rest of the information you provide on the application, there is no reason you cannot write "Anthropology" even if you are not sure that is what you will major in. On the other hand, if you have never taken Greek or Latin and are not strong in languages in general, do not write "Classics" just because you know that the college is looking for classics majors. Do not worry if you have no clue as to what major you want to follow. Admissions directors note that writing "Undecided" in no way harms your application.

ADMISSIONS DIRECTORS DISCUSS SPECIFYING A MAJOR

Generally we don't put a lot of stock in what they say. It tends to be a matter of what their parents want them to say [to impress their friends]. In fact, as a liberal arts college, we tend to feel that students get more out of their education if they come here open to possibilities. . . . When someone specifies an exotic major, we check for validation of it. Otherwise, we regard it as possible gamesmanship. *Dan Walls, Emory*

What major you specify does not influence our selection process or affect your chances of admission. We do ask what you want to study in the application, but we do so knowing that about half of the students will change their minds before declaring a major and ultimately major in something else. *Stuart Schmill, MIT*

COMPLETING EXTRACURRICULAR ACTIVITY AND OTHER LISTS

REMEMBER YOUR POSITIONING EFFORTS

When filling in lists of extracurricular activities, jobs, awards, and the like, be sure to read the college's directions. Most schools ask you to list activities from most important to least important (rather than chronologically). Although you should be honest, you also need to make sure that your answers support your positioning efforts. If in your heart you enjoy playing on the soccer team more than anything else but have played for only a year, serve no supplemental roles on the team, and are not a very good player, then soccer should not be listed as your "most important" activity. If your long-term commitment to community service on an AIDS hotline is a crucial piece of your positioning effort, then this might be what you list first instead. Activities in which you have evidenced serious leadership (through your particular role or position) or time commitment (in terms of both length of involvement and hours of dedication per week or month) are generally those that should be listed first.

QUALITY OVER QUANTITY

Because quality over quantity is what counts when listing your activities, being part of twelve different groups or teams will not mean a thing to the admissions committee if your involvement in each is minimal. Admissions committees frown upon "serial joiners" who do not amount to much in any of their organizations. Instead you need to show that you play an important role in what you do.

Do not feel the need to mention every committee you are part of here, even if you think that the strength of your most important activities will make up for the weakness of the stragglers at the end of the list. Too long a list will merely dilute your message. Include things that might bear relevance to your positioning efforts (if you state that your intended major is physics and talk about it as being your favorite subject, you might want to tack on your involvement in the Science Club, even if the club's presence in your school is minimal)—but consider leaving off other unimportant involvements. There is no reason the college needs to know that you show up for French Club meetings once a month to get the *pain au chocolat* served or helped wash cars for an hour last spring to raise money for the school's foreign exchange program. By the time the reader gets to the bottom of your long list, he will have forgotten all about your first entry mentioning your impressive role as founder of the school's Writing Resource Center.

Grouping related activities together under a category heading, such as "Athletics" or "Environmental Efforts," can be very helpful for your positioning efforts. This is an especially beneficial way of listing items if you want to include many minimally important activities on your list, because it will allow you to create focus and order out of what would otherwise appear haphazard. If you choose this option, list the category headings (rather than the individual activities) in order of importance to you.

A student might, for example, first list "Literary Activities" (which would include her position as editor-in-chief of the school's fiction and poetry magazine, her attendance at a special by-invitation-only writing camp, and her job as a writing tutor at a neighborhood grade school), "Religious Activities" (which would include her position as an adviser for bat mitzvah candidates at her synagogue and her role as an editorial writer for a local Jewish community newspaper), and "Athletic Activities" (which would include her position as a coxswain on the women's crew team as well as a cocaptain position on a coed Ultimate Frisbee League team). Note that the position as contributor to the Jewish paper could be listed under "Literary Activities" or "Religious Activities." This particular student would be wise to include it in the latter in order to "create" another positioning tag for herself as someone dedicated to learning about and studying Judaism.

Remember that anything and everything is fair game here, as long as it is an activity to which you devote time and effort. Do not forget to list volunteer work or community service; service as an acolyte or teacher at your church, temple, or religious group; and employment (if there is no separate space for its inclusion). Be sure to provide a brief (one phrase or sentence is usually sufficient) description of any activity, award, or program whose meaning will not be obvious to someone outside your school or community. For example, if you say you are a "member of the High Rollers" without elaborating, the admissions committee will never guess that you are the tenor in a six-man a cappella singing group chosen from over 200 auditioners in your high school each year. You will have lost a real opportunity to say something about your unique talent, your passions, and how you spend your time. Give meaning and detail to awards so that their significance is clear. Instead of simply listing "Recipient of the Firestone Award," which will not tell admissions officers anything, explain: "Recipient of the Firestone Award. Award given annually by faculty to one junior who exhibits highest commitment to improving the community. Cited for excellence in directing the High Hopes literacy program and running an environmental awareness colloquium on Earth Day."

WHAT ADMISSIONS DIRECTORS SAY ABOUT EXTRACURRICULAR ACTIVITY LISTS

Serial joining is certainly not what we're after. We want to see that applicants have invested themselves in a few activities rather than joined a bunch of organizations on which they've had only a marginal impact. *Marlyn McGrath Lewis, Harvard*

I see so many résumés where students list the places they have visited on family vacations—long lists of the names of the cities and countries. I have never been able to understand how this information is supposed to be factored into admission decisions. Admission processes respond to experiences that lead to something, that make a lasting impact over time or change you in some way, which cannot be told from a single line on a résumé. That you went to Zimbabwe is in itself of no interest. *William M. Shain, Vanderbilt*

The activity list is not a scorecard—one activity or work experience is not worth more points than another. *Dan Walls, Emory*

All too often we see little boxes filled out but not enough explanation as to what those activities or jobs mean. This type of information is important—candidates need to provide as much supporting information as possible so that we can best understand their nonacademic side. *Richard Avitabile, NYU*

SPACE CONSIDERATIONS

Sometimes the space that colleges give you for making extracurricular lists and answering short-answer questions is limited. If you need to, you can certainly attach an extra sheet of paper where necessary or complete the entire answer on a separate attachment. Be sure that wherever you do this, you indicate in the space provided where the supplemental material can be found. Simply write, "Please see attached page, headed 'X'" or "Continued on attached page." In addition, head all attachments with appropriate titles or response numbers and always remember to put your name and Social Security number on every piece of paper attached, just in case they become separated from your application.

RESPONDING TO SHORT-ANSWER QUESTIONS

When responding to short-answer questions, take the time and effort to polish your material. These short-answer responses can be as important as the essay questions in helping readers gain a sense of who you are and how you compare to others in the admissions pool. Write drafts just as you would for lengthy essays. You will want to be sure that the various short and long answers are tightly integrated so that together they form the best application possible, with constant themes but no redundancies. See Chapters 11 and 12 for more detailed information on how to address various essay topics and how to write effective essays.

AN ADMISSIONS DIRECTOR DISCUSSES THE IMPORTANCE OF THE SHORT-ANSWER QUESTIONS

The short-answer questions on our application are fairly important. We can determine what a student's focus is from them, and gain insight into the student. They also give an applicant the opportunity to add insight to his academic profile. *Maria Laskaris, Dartmouth*

SUPPLEMENTARY MATERIAL FOR SHOWCASING SPECIAL TALENT

Sending in supplementary material for evaluation is generally fine *if you are certain that your talent is significant and will help your chances of admission.* Most schools advise that you should not send in "ordinary" work such as writing samples, poetry, research papers, projects assigned at school, or computer programs you have designed. Stanford states in its admissions materials, "We would prefer that you and your recommenders describe your special academic pursuits and talents on our application forms." But if your work has won an important award or you have reason to believe it demonstrates extraordinary talent, it will not hurt you to send it in.

Do not go overboard. Choose one piece that best showcases your talent rather than sending in multiple pieces. The admissions officers will only be exasperated and annoyed if they are buried underneath a stack of poetry you have composed between the ages of five and seventeen. If you send them too many pieces, they may never even get to your best work in order to examine it. Do not expect the admissions officers and their faculty colleagues to sort through your material—you need to make their task as simple as possible and show that you have the sense and talent to spot your own best work. Furthermore, as mentioned in the section on activity lists, a large number of items often dilutes what could have been a strong message.

Most schools list specific guidelines for submissions of extra materials to demonstrate fine arts (art, music, drama, or dance) talent. If you are an extraordinary artist, you should by all means submit slides or prints of your work (most schools specifically ask candidates to refrain from sending original work); an extraordinary musician, a recording of your work; an extraordinary actor or dancer, a videotape or résumé of your training and performances. If you are an extraordinary athlete, it is sometimes appropriate to send in a videotape of your performance (with a data sheet describing your skills and record or a letter from a coach). (See the section for Recruited Athlete Applicants in Chapter 7.) It is likewise sometimes appropriate for you to send in evidence of original scientific research. Your supplemental material should showcase *your* talent, not someone else's. Do not, for example, send in recordings of your school's forty-piece orchestra simply because you are one of the percussionists. Nor should you send in anything of less than exceptional quality, just to prove that you are involved in an activity. This is a waste of the admissions committee's time and will only hurt your chances of admission.

You should follow each college's instructions when submitting supplemental admissions materials. Most colleges publish guidelines in their application instructions. If you are uncertain about a college's policy, call the admissions office and ask where to send your supplemental materials (you might be asked to pass them directly on to an appropriate faculty evaluator). Do not send anything directly to a department or faculty member unless you are told to do so by the school. Be sure to label every piece you send in with your name, Social Security number, and a brief description of the material.

WHAT ADMISSIONS DIRECTORS SAY ABOUT APPLICANTS WITH SPECIAL TALENTS

We ask that candidates send their supplemental materials to the admissions department first so that we can pass them on to the appropriate faculty members for professional assessment. *Katie Fretwell, Amherst*

We receive a lot of videotapes, website locations, and CD-ROMs from applicants—many of which just aren't necessary or helpful. It's true that the basic application is geared toward people who can articulate what they need to say in *writing*, which may not seem particularly fair to those who can't express their talents well in this medium. But it's really only appropriate for those with *extra special* talents to be sending us videos or cassettes. *Eric J. Furda, Columbia*

Make sure the admissions committee knows about the talent. Some places would have auditions or require portfolios; we don't require these things, but someone who is very talented could submit something like that to illustrate their talent. We will look at everything. And perhaps, if they can make their way to the relevant department to get to know someone on the faculty who can represent their talent to the admissions committee, that would make a difference as well. *Charles Deacon, Georgetown*

It's very important students ask each college in which they're interested how that talent will be evaluated. In so many cases colleges are really not interested in having additional information or materials submitted because they can't handle the volume or dedicate the expertise to a careful review of special talents in the arts or music. So it's important for students to wade carefully through what a school would expect or require. *Jennifer Desjarlais, Wellesley*

If you are strong enough in a specific talent that you think it could make a difference, send us a sample of your work. You should send the sample to the admissions office—not to faculty in a specific department. Remember that not all colleges are equipped technologically to view various formats. We get lots of material from applicants that no one here can open. *Robert Clagett, Middlebury*

We invite students to submit supplemental materials in art or music, but we ask them to think very carefully about whether or not they would like that talent evaluated. Their submission will be evaluated by a faculty member from the appropriate department, and that evaluation will then be shared with the admissions committee. If a student has contributed significant time to an art program or musical group and that's an important part of her extracurricular life, it's important for us to know that. If a person has significant talent in that area and would like to pursue further study in it, that's a separate kind of evaluation. *Jennifer Desjarlais, Wellesley*

Candidates with special talents must first decide how they plan to pursue them in college. If you hope to major in a related field, you'll want to make sure the college you choose has a strong program. If you plan to pursue the talent in an extracurricular setting, research how developed activity is in that area to make sure you can tend to your needs outside the classroom. *Ingrid Hayes, Georgia Tech*

We try to discourage kids from sending us too much material for their files. We try to give everything in the file at least a cursory look, though, and we send special talent contributions to the appropriate faculty members for evaluation. *Rick Shaw, Stanford*

We're a little different in how we deal with special talents here. I recommend that students applying here correspond via email or phone with an appropriate person on the faculty. Faculty on campus can become real advocates for students in admissions. *Dan Walls, Emory*

ADMISSIONS GIMMICKS

It is difficult to cite a hard-and-fast rule about admissions gimmicks and quirky efforts at catching the attention of the admissions committee. The problem is that over the years, the admissions committees have seen it all: chocolate cakes with "Admit Me!" messages on them, blow-up life preservers that read "Keep Me Afloat!" from applicants on the waitlist, and so on. In addition, glossy, lavishly produced admissions materials do absolutely nothing to help a candidate's chances of success. Do not bother making your application stand out aesthetically. This is not what counts in college admissions. The effort will only make it seem as if you do not stand out enough on your own merits and are trying all too hard to make up for that fact.

When there is real creativity at work *and* the admissions folks have never seen the idea used before *and* the effort contains something more valuable and meaningful than just a clever "Please admit me" message, a quirky gimmick *might* work. It will never change the committee's mind about a candidate who would otherwise be rejected, but it can push a borderline applicant into good favor or make an already "in" candidate especially memorable.

For example, a candidate to Dartmouth worked as a painter at an original fabric design company. She asked the owner of the company to write her a "recommendation" on the back of one of her originally designed shirts. The message praised the applicant's responsibilities as one of the young entrepreneurs at the company. More important, it noted her talent and craft, saying that she would be a wonderful ice sculptor at Dartmouth's Winter Carnival in the coming years. It was most likely not this gimmick that got the candidate admitted to the school, but it made sense as an admissions effort because it did more than just show the applicant's ability to think of something cute. It showcased a talent and made a highly specific connection between the candidate and the college.

ADMISSIONS DIRECTORS DISCUSS GIMMICKS

I don't like gimmicks at all. It's detrimental to the application. We are looking for balance, reason, and reflection. We don't admit people who "rise to the top of the pile" because of a gimmick. There are certainly ways to be creative in your application. But you should be creative in an application only if you are a creative person at heart—not because you are trying to be someone you are not. In general, it's a bad idea to use a gimmick because you might end up in a place where you don't fit.   *Douglas Christiansen, Vanderbilt*

Don't try gimmicks. There is a role for humor, but "cute" is not something I would advise.   *Daniel J. Saracino, Notre Dame*

If you want to be creative in preparing your application, make sure it does not detract from the substance. When I was at Sarah Lawrence, we had an amazingly creative applicant who made us a pop-up book. She included a substantial amount of writing that showed she had the stuff, plus it was small enough to fit in the application—two essential elements of any creative approach.   *Thyra Briggs, Harvey Mudd*

THE FINAL STRETCH

As with every other piece of your application, you should have a third party read your data and short-answer sheets before sending them off. The data sheets and short-answer questions need to be examined carefully to catch mistakes of all sorts (typos, grammar problems, spelling errors, inconsistencies) and to ensure that everything is readily comprehensible. Before slipping all the pieces into an envelope to send to the admissions committee, or pressing the Enter button on your keyboard to transmit them electronically, read over the college's application checklist to be sure that you have included everything and not misplaced anything.

Get the application in on time. Some sources will tell you that colleges receive so many applications near their deadlines that they cannot possibly know which reach the campus on time and which are a few days late. But at some schools, administrative assistants do record arrival dates on packages or make a note on folders that arrive late. Though a day of tardiness will probably not matter, you should not risk your college career on a silly mistake.

AN ADMISSIONS DIRECTOR OFFERS GENERAL ADVICE ABOUT THE APPLICATION

Follow instructions and get your application in by the deadline. Not doing so takes you out of the game before you've gotten a chance to play. *Kedra Ishop, Texas*

BASIC RULES FOR COMPLETING WRITTEN APPLICATIONS

1. Neatness counts.
2. Be consistent in your positioning efforts, descriptions, and style.
3. Make copies of all blank forms before filling them in.
4. Follow each school's directions carefully.
5. Remember your positioning effort—it is important not only in writing essays but also in completing data sheets and short-answer responses.
6. Treat short-answer responses seriously. Make drafts and plan out your entire application before finalizing any answers.
7. Make copies of all pieces of your application before sending it in.
8. Get the application in on time.

11

UNDERSTANDING THE
KEY ESSAY TOPICS

— KEY POINTS —

■

Familiarize yourself with the topics you need to address

■

You will be evaluated on your choice of topic as well as your writing style

■

Be leery of the approaches that are all too common

■

Be sure to use the essays to further your positioning effort

THE IMPORTANCE OF YOUR ESSAYS

Yale explains the importance of the college application essays in the following way: "There are limitations to what grades, scores, and recommendations can tell us about any applicant. Please use the following two essays to help us learn more about you. We hope that in writing these essays you will reflect on your attitudes, your values, and your perception of yourself." That last line sums up well what most colleges are looking for when they read your essays. They do not want regurgitations of information about your academics or awards that can be found elsewhere in the application. They are seeking to discover more about *who you are*.

The essay portion of the written application offers you the chance to show schools who you really are as well as to demonstrate your writing ability. The essays will, after all, be evaluated for both content and writing style. Take advantage of this opportunity and use it to further your positioning efforts. Do not write what you think the committee wants to hear or go for a "safe" topic—such approaches usually produce tired and stale essays that sound like thousands of others the admissions officers have read. You need instead to tell your audience something special and particular about you. You do not have to come across as the smartest, most talented, or most glamorous applicant in doing so—an essay about looking for shells on a beach with your little brother can be as telling and enlightening as one discussing an immigration journey from Guatemala to the United States.

It is crucial that you use the essay portion of the written application—the first of the three positioning vehicles available to you in the application process—to do things that the other two vehicles cannot. Recommenders can show only a part of who you are, since most recommendation writers are teachers or other adults who know you in a single context. Similarly, interviews are not under your control to the same extent that essays are. Essays can be created over time with great thought poured into them. They can be rewritten and reexamined to make sure that "the real you" (as well as "the best you") is presented.

This is your chance to choose which parts of yourself to highlight, and to determine how people should view them. This is also a precious opportunity to color the reader's interpretation of all the objective criteria included elsewhere in the application. Your essays should thus present a clear picture of who you are, but they do not need to tell all. Sketching in the critical main points with appropriate stories full of detail—rather than covering every possible point with little supporting narrative—is always the best solution. Whenever possible, try to tell a story rather than write an essay. The task will seem lighter, more enjoyable, and easier to accomplish.

Furthermore, visualize your audience in a way that encourages you to be forthright and creative rather than in a way that frightens you into creating something commonplace and cliché. Imagine that a pleasant man or woman is sitting down with a cup of hot tea in an easy chair examining your essays, hoping to find something that distinguishes you and makes it possible to know you, even without having met you. That more accurately describes how your audience will approach your essays than the nightmarish visions (perhaps a stern librarian-like figure with reading glasses peering down at your application with disdain) you have likely conjured up for yourself. The admissions officers want to find reasons to admit you rather than reasons to keep you out of their college. They bring a feeling of hope and a genuine love and understanding of students your age to the table when reading your application materials.

This chapter analyzes the most common essay questions, including the Common Application options. The next chapter will show you how to go about writing the essays. There are also thirty-one examples of actual student essays to the top colleges in the back of this book, in the section entitled "Application Essay Examples."

If you need individualized assistance, however, feel free to contact us. See page *xiii* for contact information.

GENERAL RULES FOR APPROACHING ANY ESSAY

A thoughtful approach is required when confronting any essay. Remember that a question does not exist in a vacuum. Instead, it is part of the whole application and should be answered in the context of how you wish the whole package to read.

Although there are dozens of possible essay questions, every one of them is aimed at the same goal: helping the admissions committee understand who you are. As a result, no matter what essay topic you choose, keep in mind several key principles:

- Make sure every essay reveals something important about you (and what you value), particularly things not covered elsewhere in the application. Look to further your positioning effort to whatever extent you can.

- Make the essay interesting and unique through the use of specific examples and details.

- Try to avoid commonly chosen topics.

- Don't contradict anything else in the application (including information pro-vided in a recommendation).
- Stay positive, constructive, and forward looking.
- Don't think you need to sound like a fifty-year-old. You don't. Be yourself.

Consult Chapter 12 for in-depth advice for producing the most effective essays possible.

THE COMMON APPLICATION QUESTIONS

The Common Application asks students to submit a personal statement of 250–500 words on one of five suggested topics or a topic of their own choosing.

QUESTION

Please write an essay on a topic of your choice or on one of the options listed below:

1. **Evaluate a significant experience, achievement, risk you have taken, or ethical dilemma you have faced and its impact on you.**

2. **Discuss some issue of personal, local, national, or international concern and its importance to you.**

3. **Indicate a person who has had a significant influence on you, and describe that influence.**

4. **Describe a character in fiction, a historical figure, or a creative work (as in art, music, science, etc.) that has had an influence on you, and explain that influence.**

5. **A range of academic interests, personal perspectives, and life experiences adds much to the educational mix. Given your personal background, describe an experience that illustrates what you would bring to the diversity in a college community, or an encounter that demonstrated the importance of diversity to you.**

6. **Topic of your choice.**

WHY THE QUESTION IS ASKED

The Common Application question, like the essay questions on many schools' own individual applications, is open-ended. Even the five topical suggestions offered are exceedingly vague. The colleges are being deliberately inexplicit because they want you to provide them with what they call a "personal statement." They want you to write something that best speaks to who *you* are, something that will allow readers to know and want to admit you to their colleges. All college applicants are different, and therefore most college application questions are fairly broad, allowing each responder ample opportunity to develop an essay that is personal and meaningful.

Thus, vague questions do not and should not command vague answers. Your responses to the Common Application question and others like it should be as detailed and specific as possible, offering plenty of poignant and unique information about you. Essays having a narrow focus are nearly always more effective than those that are broadly construed, even when answering a question that lacks specificity.

Since all of the topics suggested in the Common Application deserve individual attention, we treat each one separately in the pages to follow, under "Frequently Asked Essay Questions." The Common Application topics are covered first. Note that the various possible topics for Common Application choice 1 are broken down and treated separately.

QUESTION

Evaluate a significant experience and its impact on you.
(Part of Common Application question #1)

WHY THE QUESTION IS ASKED

One's personal character and outlook on life are often shaped by pivotal experiences. Such experiences can make for interesting narratives, if retold convincingly. Admissions committees are hoping that applicants are capable of the kind of self-reflection required to think back on their lives and identify meaningful moments. Being able to do so indicates maturity as well as self-knowledge. Admissions officers also ask this question because they want to see what your values are. By identifying something that has had meaning for you, you are pointing to a personal value.

You have several major options in answering this question. For example, you can answer it by identifying any one of the following: an epiphany, an immersion in the unknown, an achievement, a risk taken, a leadership experience, or even a failure. (Note that essays concerning the last four possibilities—achievement, risk, leadership, and failure—are dealt with separately in the following pages.)

AN EPIPHANY: THE TYPICAL APPROACH

Describing a life-changing experience or realization can be an effective way to get at one's character and current state of being. The problem with this approach is that describing an epiphany can often sound contrived and theatrical rather than honest and forthright. The applicant who describes a single moment in his life that suddenly and unexpectedly changed his entire course or perspective on something is seldom believable. The story may seem too convenient or too dramatic to be true. Applicants who describe a single event as being life changing without backing up the statement with plenty of convincing detail risk appearing dishonest.

A BETTER APPROACH

An epiphany can be an ideal way to bring up the story or anecdote you have otherwise been unable to fit into your application if you go about it the right way. Treat the experience intelligently but lightly. Keep it in perspective. Do not resort to dramatic overtures or exaggerations of impact. A single event rarely changes everything all at once. Do not, for example, claim that as an affluent white you never realized what it is like to be a minority in this country until reading Richard Wright's *Black Boy*, after which you forged an identity with the black man, thus changing your outlook on social injustice. A book can change lives, but it seldom does so on its own or all in one sweep. Instead, you might discuss how the initial reading of the book got you thinking about race relations; as you discussed what you read with others, your ideas solidified further, eventually allowing you to approach your relations with minorities differently; you now continue to examine your new perspectives through other readings and activities to educate yourself further.

This approach to describing an epiphany allows you to use a poignant yet perhaps not particularly exciting event (such as reading a book or taking care of an ailing parent) to make yourself better understood.

CRIB SHEET

- Avoid overdramatization or exaggeration.
- Discuss something that is personally poignant, with sufficient detail to help your reader understand its significance to you.
- Note that the epiphany need not be earth shattering; it just needs to matter mightily to you—and you must be able to describe effectively why it matters.

AN IMMERSION IN THE UNKNOWN: THE TYPICAL APPROACH

An immersion in the unknown is a convenient way for applicants to answer a question about a significant life-altering experience while also revealing what makes them unique and different. It often allows applicants to tell compelling or humorous stories. This topic is ideal for students who have lived, studied, or perhaps just traveled in foreign countries; conducted community service projects in environments previously unfamiliar to them (such as the inner city); or experienced things that many others have not, such as undergoing potentially life-threatening surgery or working on a vineyard for a summer.

The problem here is that many applicants *think* they have done or discovered something really special, yet the written effort conveys something far from unique. Too many students say they "learned how to appreciate other cultures" by traveling or "learned to value human life and not take things for granted" after having experienced serious health risks. Such statements are trite and unsophisticated. (Of course you learned to appreciate other cultures while traveling around the world! Of course you value your life more after nearly losing it!) This kind of essay will seem superficial if you cannot discuss your immersion in the unknown with particular detail and engagement and make it unique to you, not like everyone else's immersion in foreign territories.

A BETTER APPROACH

Use this topic only if you can penetrate it and go beyond the superficiality of "experiencing something new." We all experience new things all the time, but that does not mean they are worth discussing in a college essay. Talking about new and unexpected situations is meaningless if you cannot bring real insight to the topic. Consider the differences between what a high school classmate might say about a summer trip he took and what a good travel essayist might do with the same trip. Your classmate might say that the trip was "awesome," but would give you little actual description of what he saw or experienced. A good travel essayist would not only paint vivid pictures of what he encountered but also provide unexpected insight into the regions or people encountered and the effect his experience had on him.

CRIB SHEET

- Write about something unique, if at all possible. If you do choose a commonly selected subject, make it your own. Incorporate sufficient detail to distinguish it from everyone else's essays; highlight your own perspective.

- Show appealing personal characteristics such as adventurousness, curiosity, and willingness to take calculated risks.

■ Probe thoroughly the impact this experience has had on you in order to show important, nonobvious aspects of your character, including your ability to reflect in a meaningful way on your experience.

QUESTION

Evaluate an achievement and its impact on you.
(Part of Common Application question #1)

WHY THE QUESTION IS ASKED

This question allows you to tell the college something you are proud of, which gives the school insight about what is important to you. It also allows you to show how you might contribute to the life of the college, based on your past performance. Just as importantly, it allows colleges to learn how you have changed as a result of this performance.

THE TYPICAL APPROACH

Most applicants use the whole of the essay to demonstrate that their accomplishments are impressive. They focus on their accomplishments and not on themselves. The achievements discussed by most applicants tend to be commonplace: making the high school basketball team or being elected to student council, which can be learned by taking a brief look at the applicant's data sheets. Another mistaken tendency is to list a string of accomplishments rather than explain one accomplishment, and its impact, in detail.

A BETTER APPROACH

This question obviously gives you the chance to "toot your own horn." You can brag a bit about what you have accomplished, but what is more important is that you put your own spin on what you have done. A particular accomplishment is all the more impressive when you explain the obstacles you have had to overcome to succeed. That you were the captain of your cross country team is much more interesting and compelling if you became captain despite being the team's slowest runner. You should be sure to give the full context of your accomplishment so that its importance comes to life for your readers.

Some accomplishments are of obvious significance. Other accomplishments are much more personal in nature. It is perfectly fine to discuss an achievement that may not be obvious to others. For example, if you stuttered as a youth and finally overcame the problem during high school after resorting to a strenuous program of speech therapy, this might be an extremely significant event for you personally. Besides, it is not something that is mentioned on your data sheets, so the essay can add new information and a whole new dimension to your application. You will want to talk about your achievement as an example of your determination and desire to improve yourself, as well as describe all the work that went into achieving your goal of stutter-free speech. Even if you just discuss accomplishments of a more public nature that can be discerned from other parts of your application, be sure to personalize them in such a way that they take on greater significance than they would as one item on a list.

The first step is to determine which accomplishment you will discuss. Choose one that furthers your positioning effort, highlights something unusual, and is interesting for admissions committees to read about. An achievement in which you can discuss your values (as part of the explanation of its importance to you) will also benefit you. You may also want to choose an example that meets one or more of these criteria:

- You had to overcome major obstacles, showing real determination in doing so.
- You learned more about yourself.
- You used real initiative, perhaps by pushing a bureaucracy to respond or bypassing one altogether.
- Your success was unexpected.
- Your impact on others can be seen clearly.

Go into sufficient detail to bring events to life, but do not stop there. Discuss why you consider this a substantial achievement, why you take pride in it, and its impact on you and others. Did you change and grow as a result? Did you gain confidence in yourself? Did you find that you approached other matters differently after the event?

CRIB SHEET

- Do not recite achievements without discussing in depth their impact on you.
- Consider subjects unlikely to be listed on your data sheets or mentioned by your recommenders. Use the essay as an opportunity to reveal more of the real you.
- Show both the effort required for your success and the positive impact it has had on you (and others). Ideally, your essay will show how you have overcome challenges as well as achieved something useful.

QUESTION

Evaluate a risk you have taken and its impact on you.
(Part of Common Application question #1)

WHY THE QUESTION IS ASKED

Colleges know that young people take risks—some calculated and some irrational—and they know they will get some interesting stories here. What they hope to discover about their applicants is that they can learn from previous "difficult" situations, and that they can evaluate their options in an intelligent manner. Discussing a risk taken is also an opportunity to demonstrate that you are curious or ambitious to an extent that impels you beyond the safe and easy.

THE TYPICAL APPROACH

Many applicants worry that they should not show themselves as having taken any risks at all, so they choose a topic that does not actually involve any risk. Almost anything can be said to have a possibility of not working out, but a real risk involves the potential for dire consequences. For example, asking your basketball coach to name you as a cocaptain of the team may fail: He may turn you down. This is hardly an example of taking a risk, however, because the consequence—being told no—is hardly dire.

Other applicants do the exact opposite and use stories that show extremely irrational or even unethical risks—cheating on a test when a teacher is in the room, for example. Such a topic can hardly do one any good in the application process.

A BETTER APPROACH

You have many options here. For example, you can discuss a physical, emotional, academic, or personal risk—learning how to skydive if you are afraid of heights, searching for your biological mother if you are adopted, becoming the first junior in your school to take AP European History, or doing a guitar solo at the five-school talent show if you are shy. You can show that the risk you chose to take was or was not the right thing to do, depending on the outcome. Do not shy away from using a situation that did not turn out to be a good idea—here is where the greatest "learning" can be found, the best way for you to show your growth and development. For example, if your stab at taking AP European History brought you your first C in high school, this would be a good way of explaining your decision and what you learned from the challenge. Colleges want young people who can take risks, and know that not all of your youthful risks will have been prudent ones.

No matter your subject choice, you can do one of two things. You can show that you weighed each of your options (in terms of their level of risk versus their possible benefits) against one another and took a risk based on some sort of judgment criteria. Or you can show that you failed to do this but have since learned your lesson. In the latter case, it is helpful to mention a later example of being more prudent in light of your prior mistake.

CRIB SHEET

- Write about taking a real risk where dire consequences were either realized or avoided.

- Discuss your reasoning (if any) in taking the risk, and analyze its impact on you.

- Show the passion that drove you to take a risk, but if this was once out of control, show that you have since learned your lesson.

QUESTION

Evaluate an ethical dilemma you have faced and its impact on you.
(Part of Common Application question #1)

WHY THE QUESTION IS ASKED

Educational institutions are invariably concerned with ethics. Colleges are, after all, attempting to educate their students not only in academic subjects but also in life itself. Thus, this question is generally a sincere attempt to understand your moral grounding. The question helps admissions officers evaluate your level of honesty and maturity. Sometimes, though, the question is less about ethics and more about finding out what makes you tick. Readers can learn more about your thought processes and how you relate to the greater world around you through your answer to this question.

THE TYPICAL APPROACH

Most people have trouble finding something to discuss here, so they end up choosing something trivial. In discussing it, they think that a question about ethics must call for a holier-than-thou stance, so they end up sounding disingenuous, or like the leaders of a New Age conference. Another common mistake, which could single-handedly kill your chances of admission, is to describe a situation in which you made a very serious moral transgression or in which you seriously considered doing something terribly wrong. For example, you would not want to discuss stealing of any kind or the serious consideration you gave to helping your friend blow up the principal's office.

A BETTER APPROACH

The toughest part of this essay is finding something suitable to discuss. Here are some possible topics:

- *Personal gain versus community benefits.* Discuss a situation in which you had to choose between gaining a reward for yourself versus helping a group achieve a reward. For example, perhaps you once agreed to work with four classmates in a science competition that requires teams of five. After two weeks working on the project, with only one more week left to go until judgment day, a different group asks you to join them, and you believe its project has a better chance of winning first prize. You need to decide whether to honor your commitment to the first group (who will not have enough time to find a fifth partner if you bail out on them, thus losing a shot at the prize) or whether to sign on with the second group, in which case you might win big.

- *Loyalty to a friend versus loyalty to an ideal.* College admissions officers value loyalty to friends, but they also want students of high moral integrity. It is therefore appropriate to discuss a situation in which a good friend asked that you lower your moral standards in order to help him or her out. For example, perhaps you see your best friend, who has trouble in math classes, cheating on a geometry exam. You need to decide whether to remain loyal to your friend but act against your school's honor policy, which requires students to report one another when transgressions occur, or to uphold the honor policy and betray your friend.

- *An opportunity to take advantage of someone else's weakness.* You can discuss a situation in which you stood to gain from someone else's problem, lack of knowledge, or lack of ability. Perhaps, for example, a wealthy customer of your landscaping company asks to purchase a fertilizer treatment that you know is bad for the long-term health of her lawn. You need to decide whether to sell the product to an unsuspecting customer who is willing to fork over a lot of money, at a substantial profit for your company (and yourself), or to tell the customer the truth about the product, thus sacrificing financial gain.

Remember that the situation you describe must be a "dilemma," which means that, although you may have eventually managed it well, there was no clear-cut answer or surefire way to handle it. You cannot describe a situation and then claim that you never hesitated about doing the right thing, because then it could hardly be described as a dilemma. You will probably want to show that you explored and investigated the nature of the problem, turning it around in your mind, since you were no doubt reluctant to make a snap decision when it appeared that any decision would have generated adverse consequences. You will want to show that you explored every option and did your best to minimize the negative impact, whatever your decision.

The tone of this essay must be just right. If you sound like an innocent child who believes it is always wrong to exaggerate or lie, you will not seem believable. You will also not appear tough enough to handle the real world, where people constantly have to make hard decisions with rotten consequences for some. On the other hand, if you sound like a Machiavelli, for whom the only calculus depends on personal advantage and for whom the potential suffering of other people is irrelevant, you will be rejected as a moral monster. You need to be somewhere in the middle, someone who recognizes that the world and the decisions it requires are seldom perfect, but that it is appropriate to try to minimize adverse consequences as best one can.

CRIB SHEET

- Find a subject that presents a real dilemma and one into which you can sink your teeth.

- Explore your subject in depth, examine it from different angles, and then weigh the options.

- Show the reader who you are as a person and how your values affect your decision making both at the time and going forward.

QUESTION

Discuss some issue of personal, local, national, or international concern and its importance to you.
(Common Application question #2)

WHY THE QUESTION IS ASKED

Colleges want students who are intellectually engaged, not just grade-grubbers who do only what is necessary to get an A in class. One way of testing this is to see whether they have become interested in an issue that is not necessarily a classroom subject. Besides, students who are interested in the world around them are themselves interesting and thus good to have in a classroom or dormitory.

THE TYPICAL APPROACH

Most people discuss the most headline-grabbing item they can think of. In recent years, these subjects would have included global warming or ethnic cleansing of any one of numerous groups of people around the world. Most applicants' discussions, moreover, tend to resemble the headlines of tabloid newspapers: "Global disaster forecasted! Major changes needed immediately!" No research or analysis informs the essay, and it is full of broad moral imperatives. The other bad approach is that of too obviously cribbing from a recent lead story in an issue of *Newsweek* or some other newsmagazine. This makes it seem as if you have no original opinions and can only regurgitate common ideas on the matter. Both of these mistaken approaches also usually fail in that they provide no clue as to why the topic is of importance to the applicant, thus not helping to develop her profile or make a case for her admission. As with most essays, keep in mind that colleges are more interested in learning about you than about the particular topic you choose.

Some feel obligated to choose this topic to demonstrate that they are not ignorant of the world. The temptation then is to try to show all you know about the topic, which may dispel the mistaken notion of your ignorance but fails to show much about you.

A BETTER APPROACH

If you have firm beliefs to discuss, especially if they at all relate to your positioning effort, do so. For example, if you are pitching yourself as both a feminist and a future doctor, you might want to discuss the need to introduce better women's reproductive health clinics as part of a greater health-care movement, either here in the United States or elsewhere in the world.

Most applicants do not have such a clear-cut opinion on any issue. Instead, they have some not overly informed opinions about a handful of topics, any one of which could fit well here. If this is your case, choose the topic that shows you to best advantage. It should enable you to express sensible but not blindingly obvious ideas, enhance your positioning, show you to be intelligent and analytical, demonstrate your interest in societal matters, and provide evidence that you care about people other than yourself. You may not be able to satisfy all those criteria at once, but aim for as many as possible.

Does it matter what topic you choose? Yes and no. It matters that you choose something that strikes admissions committees as reasonably important—at least after you have explained why it is important. It is also helpful if the topic is not likely to be chosen by the bulk of applicants; it is more difficult to stand out when your essay is one of hundreds on the same topic. But what is likely to matter more is how you discuss the topic you have chosen.

When discussing any topic, remember to follow the usual rules: Be as specific as possible and be upbeat rather than defeatist. Instead of looking at the negative side of change, try to look at the issue from all angles. Analyze the opportunities and challenges that might follow in the wake of change, whether it is negative or positive. You should be able to give a sophisticated treatment of your subject, but this may be the case only after you have bolstered your knowledge with additional reading. Look at issues of respectable magazines or books to find out more about the issue. Be careful in this regard, though, because an essay drawn from textbooks and magazines will prove less revealing of your own thoughts and values—which is what admissions officers look for—than writing from your own observations and experience would be.

CRIB SHEET

- Be careful if you choose a mainstream topic. Make sure you can make it personal and that you are able to use it to demonstrate something unique to you.

- Show that you have given real thought to a complex matter in light of your own values and interests.

- Use this opportunity to demonstrate that you are engaged in the world around you.

QUESTION

Indicate a person who has had a significant influence on you, and describe that influence.
(Common Application question #3)

WHY THE QUESTION IS ASKED

This question allows colleges to discover more about your personality, your values, and how you interact with others. Colleges like to know that the students who will populate their campuses are capable of sustaining meaningful relationships, working with other people, and learning not only inside the classroom but also outside of the classroom, through life experiences.

THE TYPICAL APPROACH

Many candidates use relationships with others to demonstrate their personal values or show an important life lesson they learned through interacting with someone else. The problem here, especially for those who choose to discuss a relationship with a mentor or a special relative such as a grandparent, is that they often end up discussing the other person much more than themselves. Candidates often write entire essays praising and eulogizing those they admire, but end up failing to show anything important about themselves in the essay.

A BETTER APPROACH

Remember that *you* are applying to college—not your grandfather, your older sister, or your football coach. When answering any question on a college application, even about a relationship, the focus on the discussion needs to be on you. That is not to say you should take a self-important attitude, shouting "me, me, me" in all your discussions of interactions with others. However, the impact of all activities and situations on you must be at the center of what you write. It is imperative that you use the other person as a foil in this case—the person should ideally reflect what is most impressive or helpful about *your* interests, *your* values, *your* achievements, and *your* goals.

CRIB SHEET

- Be sure the heart of this essay, although technically about someone else, reveals important information about you.

- Demonstrate how you find others' lives relevant to your own. Show you are mature and receptive to others' knowledge and input.

- Show what you have learned from the person you discuss.

QUESTION

Describe a character in fiction, a historical figure, or a creative work (as in art, music, science, etc.) that has had an influence on you, and explain that influence.
(Common Application question #4)

WHY THE QUESTION IS ASKED

As with many other questions, this question is meant to probe your values and discover how you react to the stimuli around you. Colleges also want to see that you can provide an intelligent analysis of history, a piece of art, or a work of fiction.

THE TYPICAL APPROACH

All too many applicants make the lazy mistake of tracking down an essay written for a history or English assignment and trying to make it work here. But this should be avoided; colleges want to see some analysis, but most of the focus here needs to be on you and how the piece has altered your thinking or changed you in some way. You can certainly choose as a topic something that you have studied in-depth in school—that way, you are sure to know the subject matter—but start fresh with your approach to the topic for these purposes. The other problem with this tactic is that you don't want to sound overly academic—again, you want some detail, and to show you know how to analyze a work of fiction or history, but the piece must be very personal and self-reflective.

A BETTER APPROACH

This is a license for creativity if ever there was one. But that does not mean your answer must be bizarre. It is perfectly fine to select a character or passage from Jane Austen if you so choose, but be sure you provide ideas or a viewpoint that is yours alone rather than a redigested version of some other source's analysis. Admissions officers do not want to read one more standard analysis of Holden Caulfield or Van Gogh's *Starry Night.* Moreover, be sure to place most of the emphasis on the influence this piece has had on you—this, more than in your analysis of the work of art, is where the admissions committee will learn something truly valuable about you.

If possible, heed your positioning efforts in your choice of topics. Note that this can mean either using a topic that would aid your pitch, if it needs a boost, or choosing a topic that would be somewhat "unexpected" from you, if you fear appearing too one-dimensional. For example, if nearly all your materials refer to your political ambitions and your desire to be a future president of the United States, then you may not want to write about Abraham Lincoln.

Keep in mind that this is a very difficult essay to write without seeming corny. Relatively few applicants will have actually been influenced in a substantial fashion by a creative work or historical figure. Rather than pretend to have been so influenced, you are almost surely better off choosing a different topic.

CRIB SHEET

- Show you are a capable analyst by your discussion of your chosen character, figure, or work.

- More importantly, analyze your topic in a way that says something about you. Don't forget that the question asks you to discuss an influence on you, not simply the character or work itself.

- Consider using this essay to show something about yourself that the reader may not see elsewhere in your file.

QUESTION

A range of academic interests, personal perspectives, and life experiences adds much to the educational mix. Given your personal background, describe an experience that illustrates what you would bring to the diversity in a college community, or an encounter that demonstrated the importance of diversity to you.
(Common Application question #5)

WHY THE QUESTION IS ASKED

Schools want to know that if they admit you, you will bring something special to the campus. They want to know that you will benefit from the college, but they also want to be assured that the college will benefit from you. Colleges are concerned about the composition of the class as a whole: they want a good mix of skills, strengths, backgrounds, and experiences represented, to maximize the potential learning of their students. This essay is your chance to show what you bring to the mix.

THE TYPICAL APPROACH

Many applicants see this as a very broad question and give a very broad response in return. They try to tell their whole life stories, or give a résumé-like recounting of their accomplishments. The other typical approaches vary by type of applicant.

All too often a nonminority applicant focuses on ethnicity, which can easily fall flat. If he is one-quarter Romanian, for instance, he will play up the limited contact he has had with his Romanian grandparent—this despite the fact that he doesn't speak Romanian; has never spent time in Romania; and has only the smallest scattering of knowledge about Romanian life, culture, and history. At best, he might paint a nice portrait of his grandparent, although this clearly does not advance his own candidacy insofar as it tells us nothing about him.

A minority applicant, on the other hand, may write a complaint about the continuing injustice of American society rather than focusing on a specific personal experience. This general complaint does nothing to advance her candidacy because we learn little of substance about *her*. Furthermore, it risks alienating admissions officers because of its negative tone. Well-to-do minority applicants are at particular risk of alienating admissions officers if they pretend to have grown up in dire circumstances, thereby exaggerating any hardships they may have encountered.

A BETTER APPROACH

The main goal here is to discuss an experience or encounter that will show how you would add something valuable and unique to the operations of the school. You can emphasize perspectives that will be important in or out of class. If you are uncertain of what might qualify as both unusual and valuable, consider discussing an experience or encounter that demonstrates:

■   *A different perspective.* If you are from an unusual part of the world (or country) compared to most of the student body, discuss this. If you are a member of a racial, ethnic, or religious minority not well represented on most campuses, discuss this. Perhaps you have had an unusual personal history (for example, if you grew up sitting in the front of a taxicab with your dad while he drove the streets of Chicago). Note that what you might consider ordinary may strike admissions officers as anything but ordinary. For instance, growing up in a small, tight-knit community in which everyone is a member of a nonmainstream religious organization would certainly qualify as unusual.

- *Knowledge of an unusual academic field.* If you have done extensive research in quantum physics or have studied African cultures, you can explain how your expertise will benefit others in the classes and activities you intend to pursue.

- *Specialized outside interests.* A person who has started her own business, has published her written work in a national magazine, or is a superb jazz musician can readily discuss how her experience or knowledge will be of use to others on campus.

Whichever perspective you choose, limit your focus. Develop one idea only, not a litany of possible perspectives.

Those who are writing from the perspective of having suffered, whether as a result of their race, ethnicity, religion, or poverty, are advised not to overplay their experience. Any of these perspectives can be extremely valuable for admissions purposes, but wearing your difficulties lightly is highly advisable. You will seem the bigger person for not having had your spirit overwhelmed by your experience. Also, you won't take the risk of alienating admissions officers by seeming to exaggerate your experiences or by playing for sympathy. The best tone for your essay is therefore a flat, nearly neutral one.

The last component of the essay is to show that you are the kind of person who will share knowledge with others at school. You should try to show that you are accustomed to interacting and exchanging ideas with others. Demonstrate that you are able to work well on a team, within an organization, or with a project group. To the extent that you are comfortable working across cultural boundaries with people not entirely like yourself, show that this is the case. Of course, the best way to validate that the perspectives you have mentioned will have value for your future college classmates is to demonstrate that you have already influenced peers at high school or in your community.

CRIB SHEET

- Help the reader understand what distinguishes you from other applicants and why the admissions committee should choose you over other, similarly credentialed applicants.

- Think broadly about what is unusual in your background and experience, but write specifically. Choose one or two themes and stay focused.

- Make sure the experience or encounter you discuss is not based on a superficial or relatively unimportant aspect of who you are.

AN ADMISSIONS DIRECTOR DISCUSSES THE MOST COMMON PROBLEM WITH COMMON APPLICATION ESSAYS

The biggest problem with responses to the Common Application essays is a student's failure to relate what they are writing about back to themselves. We want to be able to put the application down and say, "Here's who this person is, here's what they stand for," etc.   *Chris Gruber, Davidson*

FREQUENTLY ASKED QUESTIONS

QUESTION

What has been your most significant leadership experience?

WHY THE QUESTION IS ASKED

Top schools expect to produce society's future leaders in all fields. They are looking for applicants who have already distinguished themselves as leaders, since past performance is the best indicator of future performance. Learning about your leadership skills also allows a committee to see how you interact with others, whether or not you are effective in group situations, and how determined you are to succeed.

THE TYPICAL APPROACH

All too often, applicants discuss being part of a group that achieved something noteworthy without making it clear that they themselves were leaders in the effort. Other applicants, seeing this question as similar to the substantial accomplishment essay, focus on the end result or achievement rather than honing in on the leadership aspect. Other applicants discuss roles in which they were designated as leaders through a title (such as captain or editor-in-chief) but then fail to show how they approached the role and that they did a good job with the task. Claiming a leadership title and doing something significant with that role are two different things.

A BETTER APPROACH

This question is deceptively similar to the substantial accomplishment essay. The leadership essay, however, is not looking so much for an achievement as it is for an understanding of how you led an effort to reach the end result. In other words, your emphasis should be on your leadership of other people rather than on the accomplishment itself.

To write this essay, you must grasp what leadership is. One obvious example is managing or guiding others in a group effort when you have a formal title (such as captain or editor-in-chief) that identifies you as the leader. Less obvious examples involve pushing or inspiring nonsubordinates to do what you want done. This can be done through leading by example, relying on your influence as a perceived expert in something, relying on others' respect for you, influencing through moral suasion, or influencing through personal friendship. Whether your leadership was formalized or influence-based, you should describe your methodology in depth. What was your approach, and what strategy did you employ? Why? You may not have been deliberate or extremely self-aware in your actions, of course, in which case you might wish to discuss what you learned from the effort and how you would use those same newly found leadership skills again. What problems did you confront? What other strategies have worked? Have you developed a philosophy of leadership as a result of the effort?

Your leadership qualities should be those of a mature adult leader: thoughtfulness, sensitivity to others, empathy, determination, valuing other people's input, the ability to influence or communicate with different kinds of people, the ability to integrate disparate parts into a unified whole, honesty, and personal integrity. Enthusiasm is a fine trait, but it is unlikely to be a sufficient explanation for your leadership success.

CRIB SHEET

- Demonstrate your understanding of what it means to be a leader and how you have personally fared in this role in a specific instance.

- Describe a situation in which you actually led—not simply an instance in which your organization succeeded.

- Show why leadership is important to you, how this experience affected you personally (and perhaps in terms of how it changed or developed you as a leader), and what it means to you going forward.

QUESTION

What has been your greatest failure? Why do you consider it a failure, and what did you learn from it?

WHY THE QUESTION IS ASKED

This question is basically asking whether or not you are mature enough to admit that you will make mistakes and whether or not you can extract meaning from past errors. The question also helps admissions officers see how you have changed and grown in recent years.

THE TYPICAL APPROACH

Many admissions officers like to see applicants write about failures or weaknesses, as long as they are treated in the right way. If you choose to discuss a failure voluntarily without being required to do so (for example, if you talk about a failure in your answer to the first topic suggestion in the Common Application), you must be especially certain that the story is going to work for you. After all, it if does not do a superb job of showing positive qualities and expressing thoughtfulness, then you might as well avoid it altogether and discuss an achievement, if given the choice.

The problem is that many applicants write about failures without being able to show how the event has turned out to be helpful in their growth or development. Applicants often talk about failures by simply retelling the story of what happened. They focus more on the mistake than on what they learned from it. The typical applicant does himself a disservice by not analyzing *why* he failed, what he could have done differently, what he learned, and how he would approach the situation if faced with it again. Other applicants discuss trivial failures that are incapable of instilling life-changing thoughts or feelings, such as forgetting to mow the lawn or arriving late to a test. (Failing to find the perfect prom dress would certainly constitute a poor choice of topics.) This merely shows admissions committee members that you are hoping to convince them you have never had any great failures in life—something they know is not true.

A BETTER APPROACH

Whenever you are discussing a failure, but especially when doing so voluntarily rather than because you are explicitly asked to talk about one, you must use an experience that you can show has affected your subsequent actions and decisions. It should be a failure to which you can attach a story of another incident to demonstrate that, when presented with a similar situation a second time, you succeeded. One implication of this is that the failure probably should be something that occurred not last week but at least many months ago. We generally need time to learn from our mistakes.

A sensible approach to the statement about a failure places an emphasis on your development. We learn more from our mistakes than we do from our successes, which is why it is legitimate to discuss failures, even when not asked to do so. A willingness to admit mistakes is one sign that you are reaching adulthood. Even the best students are sure to suffer some failures at a demanding college—admissions officers like to know that admitted students are prepared to handle such challenges and can benefit from mistakes rather than being sunk by them.

Do not, however, belabor a description of the failure itself. Although details always make a story more interesting, in this case too much detail might make you look bad. Remember that it is what you learned from the failure that is critical here, not the situation itself. Consider what you learned from the experience concerning yourself, your education, your work ethic, your opinions, or your relationships.

CRIB SHEET

- Include a thoughtful discussion of what you learned from the failure you described.

- Keep the discussion of the failure short. Focus instead on its impact and lessons learned.

- The most effective essays of this ilk discuss a real failure—not, for instance, receiving an A- rather than an A in some class. Choose an event that affected you substantially.

- Pick a topic you can discuss constructively and demonstrate its positive effects on who you have become.

QUESTION

Describe the impact that a secondary school teacher has had on your intellectual development.

WHY THE QUESTION IS ASKED

Colleges, especially small ones where students have the opportunity to receive much individualized attention from professors, want to know that you will take advantage of all the learning resources made available to you. They want to know that you appreciate your teachers, interact with them on a regular basis, feel grateful for all that they have done for you, and are prepared to forge meaningful relationships with faculty at the college you hope to attend.

THE TYPICAL APPROACH

Many applicants start with a trite "My favorite teacher is . . . " Although it is fine if the teacher you discuss here happens to be your favorite, the more important focus should be on the impact the teacher has had on you. This essay can just as well be on a teacher whom you once disliked, especially for his challenging nature, but then grew to respect because of the way in which he forced you to expand your mind. The other mistaken course that many applicants take is simply to list all the wonderful things the teacher has taught them without explaining *how* they have been taught, the methods the teacher uses, or in what way he has been so effective. Other applicants write about a teacher whom they value because they particularly enjoy the subject matter learned in the class. Although intellectual content can certainly be a part of this essay, the emphasis should be on the teaching skills and methods and your interaction with the teacher.

A BETTER APPROACH

First remember that this essay does not have to involve the nicest teacher in your school, or the one who has given you the best grades, or even the best faculty member. It should focus on someone whose unusual teaching habits, approach to his subject, or philosophy of education has changed or inspired you the most. Think about the secondary school teachers you have had and choose one for whose special teaching you can provide anecdotes and supporting evidence.

It is ideal, although not absolutely necessary, if you can show that this teacher has affected your development inside and outside the classroom. In other words, if at all possible, show interaction with the teacher on an intellectual or academic level and on a personal level. Remember to focus on how he teaches, not what he teaches. As mentioned previously, it is often appropriate to discuss a teacher you did not (or still do not) even like that much. By demonstrating that you learned a lot and gained respect for someone you did not particularly like, you will show outstanding maturity. If you take this approach, however, remember to temper your opinions and not sound too negative about the teacher.

CRIB SHEET

- Discuss a teacher who had a real impact on you.
- Describe the way in which your intellectual development has been different than otherwise would be the case as a result of this teacher.
- Have your discussion teach the reader about you and what you value in the student-teacher (or mentoring) relationship.

■ Show your passion for learning and appreciation for those who devote their lives to teaching.

QUESTION

What academic areas interest you most? Why?

WHY THE QUESTION IS ASKED

It is fairly obvious why admissions officers ask this question. Although they can see the list of classes you have taken and the grades you have gotten from the rest of the application, they also want to know what most interests you. They want to know that you are intellectually engaged, that you do not just perform well in school because you want to get good marks, and that your interests are such that you will be able to continue them at (their) college.

THE TYPICAL APPROACH

Many applicants make the mistake of discussing academic strengths here, merely recounting grades and academic accomplishments instead of piercing the heart of the matter. Your strengths in an academic subject may come into play here, but that is not the point. Too many applicants also make trite remarks that could easily be made by anyone possessing even remote familiarity with the subject matter discussed. For example, an applicant might write something such as, "I love math because I am obsessed with numbers. I like the challenge of looking at an equation and having to work through it until my response works." This kind of thing tells the admissions officers little about what makes you tick, nor does it hint at what you might do with your academic interests once you get to college and thereafter.

A BETTER APPROACH

First, be sure that your choice of subjects matches your positioning effort. If you are selling yourself as someone particularly interested in foreign trade and hoping to study at the school's program in Geneva, you might consider discussing French as your favorite subject. Although your academic interest does not necessarily have to match your greatest academic strength, it is a good idea to demonstrate that you are talented in your favorite subject matter. After all, if this is what you are planning to focus on and share with others, then it is more helpful if you are particularly good at it.

Try as best as possible to dig deep into the subject matter here to get at what it is about this subject that most interests you. In other words, the *fact* of loving history does not matter so much as *why* you love history, or what about it is so fascinating to you. Remember that the number of topics that can be discussed here is limited (there are only so many subjects that are studied at the high school level). The admissions officers will receive hundreds of responses based on the same basic subject that you choose to write about. You have to take special precautions to avoid cliché or stale statements, and you need to show that you really know something special about the matter or bring a fresh perspective to your work in the area. If possible, it is always good to allude to how you will continue your study of the subject in college. Similarly, if it has influenced your choice of college, be sure to explain this.

CRIB SHEET

- Do not simply name an academic area of interest. Make sure the reader knows the reasons behind your interest.

- Show you have a unique perspective, that you know something special about or have devoted unique attention to the area you discuss. (Did you participate in a competition, undertake related travel, do advanced research, or take up a related extracurricular activity?)

- Help the reader understand why this subject matters to you, how it relates to your values and passions.

QUESTION

What extracurricular activity is most meaningful to you? Why?

WHY THE QUESTION IS ASKED

As with the similar question about academic interests, it is fairly obvious why admissions officers ask this question. Although they can see the list of activities you have participated in over the years, they want to know more detail about those activities and what they say about you. They want to know that you are stimulated by what you choose to do in your spare time and that you have a balanced life. They want to know that you are someone who will add to the community at the college, not just to the academic atmosphere.

THE TYPICAL APPROACH

Many applicants do not take this question seriously and end up merely listing a few favorite activities, doing nothing more than what they have already done in the activity data sheets. Furthermore, a lot of candidates mistakenly discuss too many activities rather than focusing attention on one. Many applicants also make the mistake of discussing nonacademic strengths here, merely recounting extracurricular accomplishments or pointing out leadership positions instead of digging deeper. Just as with the academic interest question, your strengths may come into play here, but that is not the point.

A BETTER APPROACH

Start by thinking about things you really enjoy. To choose one for discussion, use these guidelines:

- The activity aids your positioning effort.
- Its value is apparent.
- You know a lot about it and can discuss it intelligently.
- You have something distinct and different to say.
- You have listed it at or near the top of your extracurricular activity list on the Common Application and on other applications that request activities be listed from greatest to least importance.

First, be sure your subject matches your positioning effort. If you risk being pigeonholed as an antisocial loner, discuss an activity (even if it is the only one on your list of this type) in which you can point to interaction with others. Although your greatest extracurricular interest does not necessarily have to be one in which you have racked up loads of honors, it is a good idea if you can show promise through your performance. If you are not particularly talented at the activity, at least show that you are working at it for a good reason. For example, you do not have to be preparing to swim the English Channel if you want to discuss swimming in this essay. You could just as well talk about how you have been a rotten swimmer your entire life, a source of real embarrassment to you, but are currently training for a swim-a-thon to improve your skills and raise money for a charity at the same time. You should show that the activity has had some value and meaning in your life.

Since an activity is what you do in your spare time, it should inspire you with special enthusiasm. Try to capture this as much as possible. As mentioned earlier, the *fact* of loving basketball does not matter so much as *why* you love basketball, or what about it is so fascinating to you. The other key to your essay is to show that you are knowledgeable about the endeavor. The more unusual the activity the better, but you can make a discussion of anything at all distinct if you bring a fresh perspective to it.

CRIB SHEET

- Showcase your knowledge of a nonacademic topic.
- Let the reader see what you really care about: how you spend your free time says a lot about who you are as a person.
- Demonstrate that you bring a fresh and personal perspective to the activity. Others may be involved in the same pursuit, but your involvement should tell us something particular about you.

QUESTION

Why do you want to attend this particular college?

WHY THE QUESTION IS ASKED

Colleges ask this question for several reasons. First, they want to see that you have "done your homework" and that you care enough about the school that you have bothered to learn all you can about it. They want to determine whether you are a good fit for the college, and they want to know how you value their school relative to other schools you might be considering.

THE TYPICAL APPROACH

Most applicants make one of several mistakes here. Some make the error of discussing why they want to attend college in general rather than talking about the school that is asking the questions. Other applicants reveal (perhaps unintentionally) that they do not really know what they are looking for in a college experience. This can happen when an applicant discusses very general features of the college, such as the dormitory living environment, which are shared by most other schools as well.

Another mistake is for a student to state a reason for wanting to attend that is simply unacceptable to the college. An applicant might, for example, chalk up his interest to the fact that he has "always wanted" to go to the school. Or he might state "U. Penn. is simply the best" or discuss the prestige factor, neither of which say anything intelligent about the school's appropriateness to the candidate as an individual. Another error is to say that you want to go to a school primarily because your parent is an alum or because a current boyfriend or girlfriend is in attendance. These are, on their own, weak reasons to want to attend a school.

A BETTER APPROACH

Start by discussing your academic and nonacademic goals, desires, and needs, as identified during your college search process. Then relate what you are looking for in a college, showing that this particular school fits your needs. Be specific and detailed, referring to information you have gained from the college's website or publicity materials and, more important, from a visit or discussions with admissions officers, faculty, alums, and students. Show that you want to attend the college because of the educational and nonacademic experiences it will give you, not because of its prestige or the résumé value of attending it. Refer to the discussion in Chapter 3 about deciding where to apply to refresh your memory on how to do this.

This approach will help make it clear that you are serious about college, that you are interested in finding a place that is a good fit for you, and that you have researched the school to find out what it offers. It shows you to be a sensible decision maker for having done your research and made the choice based on your findings. It shows that you value the school and are excited about attending. Your enthusiasm about and valuation of the school can be important for gaining admission since schools are concerned with their yield rates—they want to admit students who they believe will attend the school rather than decide to go somewhere else.

CRIB SHEET

- Tailor your response to the college to which you are applying.
- Use specific examples, highlighting your knowledge of the school and its offerings.
- Demonstrate that you are a sensible decision maker—and that you have researched and reasoned thoroughly.
- Show enthusiasm for the school.

BRIEF NOTES ON OTHER ESSAY QUESTIONS

QUESTION

How did you spend last summer?

This is a fairly straightforward question, but remember to give your answer spark and life. If you spent the summer working, taking classes, traveling, or doing a community service project, you have no legitimate worries about what to discuss. If you traveled, however, make sure to avoid sounding spoiled (an extravagant trip can make you appear less than ideal). Instead, show that you have taken advantage of all the opportunities available to you. If you worked, talk about the job, how it instilled further responsibility in you, and what you learned.

QUESTION

What are you most hoping for in a roommate?

It is pretty difficult to avoid sounding cliché here, but try to make some sort of statement about yourself with this one. You could, for example, talk about the homogeneity of your present school, saying that you are hoping to benefit from the diversity of the college by having an international roommate or someone with a very different background from your own. You could talk, on the other hand, about your best friend and the characteristics that make him or her a fine person. Whatever you say, remember that admissions committee members are looking at your answer to see what it says about your values.

QUESTION

Attach a small photograph of something important to you and explain its significance.

Here is another question that begs for creativity, so use it. The photo obviously needs to be of something tangible, but you can use an object to represent an idea or intangible value if you want. For example, you can use a photo of your town hall to stand for the importance of the community in which you have lived all your life and the value you place on all it has done for you. Whatever you use, even if it is an object you appreciate for what it is, you must also talk about why it is important to you. You need, in other words, to say something about your values here.

QUESTION

Create your own college application question and answer it.

This is another chance for you to stretch your creative limbs. Many applicants simply substitute a question they have had to answer for another college's application to save themselves the task of having to do extra work. If the question you are using is very common or broad, this is usually fine—it will legitimately seem to be something you consider important to ask college candidates. Avoid using a question that is too specific to another school. It will be obvious you are being a bit lazy and may appear crass. If you desperately want to use an essay you have written for another school because you think it is particularly good, disguise the question a bit and modify the essay appropriately. Whatever you do, make sure your own answer matches your positioning efforts. Use this question to include the material or anecdotes you have not yet been able to discuss elsewhere in the application.

QUESTION

You have just completed your autobiography. Please submit one page of it.

Be creative yet thoughtful here. You want to do something catchy but also express something important about yourself. One good idea is to use this essay to discuss a future goal, here discussed as something that occurred in the past. It might even be something that happened during college. Remember that pages in books do not necessarily begin at the beginning of a paragraph and end at the end of a paragraph. Your page may well begin in the middle of a sentence.

WHAT ADMISSIONS DIRECTORS SAY ABOUT CHOOSING ESSAY TOPICS

WHAT TOPICS SHOULD APPLICANTS AVOID WHEN WRITING THEIR ESSAYS?

Don't talk about someone other than yourself in the essay! And no sexual experiences; those usually don't work. *Michael Goldberger, Brown*

Applicants should avoid writing autobiographies, travel logs, or about national or international issues (unless the applicant has been directly affected by them). *Robert Clagett, Middlebury*

It's difficult to cite a hard-and-fast rule about what essay topics to avoid. Insightful applicants and good writers can craft wonderfully effective essays from seemingly dull or inappropriate material. *Marlyn McGrath Lewis, Harvard*

I usually say that there are no bad topics, only bad essays. However, there are some topics that almost never work: winning or losing the big game, boyfriend or girlfriend problems, journaling, not seeing beyond high school (the pressures of planning the prom!). *Debra Shaver, Smith*

Students should not write an essay they think admissions will want to see. Instead, write about yourself, your life, your strengths, and what you would contribute. Write about something you want to write about, not what you think we are looking for. *Paul Marthers, Reed*

The most important thing in answering an essay question is not the topic but the way you approach it. Any topic that genuinely engages you and allows you to show your ability to put ideas together, and that gives us a sense of you as a person, is a good choice. *Ken Himmelman, Bennington*

Students should avoid writing about anything they would not want published in a newspaper about them. This is to say, it's possible to be too personal in an essay without conveying who you really are. *Jennifer Rickard, Bryn Mawr*

Lots of essays focus on the same topics—international travel, community service, outward bound . . . They may be well written, but they are telling me the same thing. The best essays, in addition to demonstrating talent in written expression, give us a new and unique way of understanding who you are. *Lee Coffin, Tufts*

An average writer should avoid topics that will be addressed by many seventeen-year-old applicants. *Kimberly Van Deusen, William & Mary*

You don't need to discuss your most traumatic experience. Some students feel they're at a disadvantage if they haven't had a traumatic experience, but this is not the case. In fact, some of my favorite essays have been about a favorite teacher, coach, or family member. *Janet Lavin Rapelye, Princeton*

Don't choose topics outside your comfort zone. If you are considering writing about a topic that will require you to do research rather than being able to address it with what you already know, you are probably headed in the wrong direction. You should choose something you can address and that shows us something important about you. Essays should be about you. *Kedra Ishop, Texas*

IS IT EVER APPROPRIATE OR BENEFICIAL FOR AN APPLICANT TO DISCUSS A WEAKNESS IN AN ESSAY?

Discussing a weakness in an essay can be a good thing sometimes—it demonstrates "taking a risk," a quality we highly value. *Maria Laskaris, Dartmouth*

I have advised students in the past to discuss weaknesses when appropriate. We want information, though, not excuses or whining. *David Borus, Vassar*

It is always appropriate to write about a weakness—no one is perfect. However, consider offering context for those weaknesses (e.g., poor grades, low scores) in an addendum to your application. It's unwise to use space in the essay for doing so. *Robert Clagett, Middlebury*

Everyone sitting around the committee table has a weakness. We understand that students have weaknesses, and essays about this kind of thing can be wonderfully expressive. *Eric Kaplan, Penn*

WHAT ARE THE MOST COMMON MISTAKES APPLICANTS MAKE IN CHOOSING TOPICS?

Students commonly make the mistake of failing to read the question or trying to overanalyze the question to find the "right answer," which of course doesn't exist. *Theodore Spencer, Michigan*

Sometimes essays are about interesting topics, but they fail because they do not reveal enough about the applicant. *Paul Marthers, Reed*

I think one of the most common mistakes applicants make is that of choosing a topic they think the admissions office will think is a good topic rather than one that genuinely means something to the student. A good topic does not necessarily make a good essay. I have read many essays about theoretically interesting topics that fall utterly flat because they never go below the surface level. I have also read many essays about "ordinary" topics that are wonderful—personal, full of life and reflection and a strong sense of the person behind the words. As an admissions officer, I don't want to read about any particular subject. I want to hear the applicant's voice in an essay that seems personal and lets me get to know them. *Margit Dahl, Yale*

WRITING EFFECTIVE ESSAYS

— KEY POINTS —

Keeping your positioning efforts in mind, sift through your possible topics and choose those that will allow you to establish your most effective themes

Plan before writing: think about, outline, and draft your essays before writing them
—When a school requires more than one essay, make sure that they complement one another before finalizing any one of them

There is no excuse for basic foul-ups: misspellings, grammatical mistakes, factual errors, or inserting the wrong school's name into an essay

Remember the tenets of good writing

Allot substantial time for reorganizing, redrafting, and soliciting the input of others: Remember, "There is no such thing as good writing, just good rewriting"

INTRODUCTION

Admissions officers will judge you on the basis of what your essays reveal about your writing ability (including your ability to persuade, structure, and maintain a well-reasoned argument, and your ability to communicate in an interesting and sophisticated manner). They will also look at your essays for revelations about your honesty, maturity, personality, uniqueness, understanding of what the college offers and requires, future contributions to the campus, and thoughts on where you are headed in the future. In fact, the better the school, the more likely it is that the objective data in your file will not determine your fate and that the essays in particular will weigh heavily in the decision.

This chapter is designed to help you actually write your essays. You have learned from prior chapters the types of things you are likely to want to get across in your essays. Now it is time to master how to go about putting what you want to say on paper. In addition to reading this chapter, you can learn about successful essay writing by examining some of the many examples provided at the end of the book.

THE WRITING PROCESS: GETTING STARTED

THINK ABOUT YOUR AUDIENCE AND YOUR OBJECTIVES

Before you start to write, you should consider once again your audience and the admissions criteria, pledging to keep both of these in mind while fashioning your essays. This does not mean, however, that you should forget who *you* are or write what you think "they" want to hear.

Your audience is the set of admissions officers who will read your application. These admissions officers are generally intelligent, astute people who review thousands of college applications from bright and accomplished individuals every year. In other words, you should aim high and be sophisticated. Admissions officers are generally "people oriented" and want to see you in a positive light; they are looking for information that will make you shine, not searching for material that will disqualify you from the game. Therefore, you should be open and honest, even about any apparent weaknesses; if you offer good explanations for them, you will be better off than if you hope your mistakes will rest undiscovered. Admissions officers are dedicated to their jobs and extremely conscientious but also undeniably overwhelmed by the volume of material they need to read each season. You need to make a strong impact with a small amount of material; do not be subtle or vague.

Admissions officers are highly familiar with the determinants of success in college and life after college. They will examine your application for convincing evidence of your intellectual ability, your potential as a leader and contributor to your community, your personal characteristics, and your future goals. They want applicants who clearly value learning and education. You will need to provide evidence that you make the most of opportunities, whether large or small. Remember also to think about what each particular school values when creating your essays (as when putting together the other components of your positioning effort).

Your essays should reveal your true self and convey an honest sense of who you are as a person. Colleges are looking to admit *people,* not numbers. They want to create classes full of interesting, compelling people, not just brains who do well in class or jocks who can perform on the athletic field.

PLAN BEFORE WRITING

It is important to plan your essays before writing a word. Planning—which includes both developing and organizing your material—forces you to think about what you will write before you get tied up in the actual writing process. Too many people take the opposite approach, writing random paragraphs, hoping to be able to glue them together later, or trying to write the whole of an essay before thinking about it.

DEVELOP YOUR MATERIAL

All too many essays sound the same. The poor admissions officer who has to read thousands of essays gains no understanding of an applicant who writes something that could have been written by any of another 500 applicants to the school. Your goal is to develop materials that will help you write stories unique to you, stories that no one but you could tell.

Failing to develop your own material or examine yourself thoroughly will lead to dull generalities and mark your application with a deathly ordinariness. Avoid tired and worn clichés stating the obvious:

- "My travels broadened my horizons by exposing me to different cultures."
- "The experience taught me that with hard work and determination I can reach any goal I set my mind to."
- "Working with a variety of classmates from different backgrounds, I learned the true value of diversity."

Statements like these do not merit space in your essays if you want to dazzle the admissions committee.

The best way to start the process of generating material is to fill out the Personal Profile Worksheets in Appendix III. Try to fill them out over a period of time, because you will be unlikely to remember everything they call for in one sitting. You may want to reread personal diaries or journals to refresh your memory. Looking at family photograph albums, school yearbooks and report cards, as well as any résumés you may have written might also help jog your mind. Consider keeping a notebook or computer handy for jotting down ideas, stories, or details about your past or your goals for the future. When you have completed the Personal Profile Worksheets, you should have far too much material to use in your essays. You should feel that you have a wealth of material from which to pick the most appropriate items.

ORGANIZE YOUR MATERIAL

After you have generated information, you must organize it. You will do so by recalling your overall positioning efforts, as well as determining what other important themes or messages emerge from your material. Then choose the pieces of your material that are most useful for answering the various essay questions posed by your target schools. Determine what your core message in each essay should be. In other words, what key points should you try to make? If you can state these, the next step is to group your supporting material according to the appropriate points.

OUTLINE YOUR IDEAS

To organize your thinking effectively, it is generally a good idea to outline your essay. This will save you time because the outline will make it clear whether you have too much or too little material and will provide a logical means of organizing your material. It will also allow you to make changes early in the process, rather than working on something that does not belong in the essay.

HOW TO MAKE AN OUTLINE

There are several outlining methods commonly used. All follow the same general rule, listing primary organizing ideas against the left-hand margin, with supporting materials indented to indicate their subordination to a larger idea.

I. Primary idea
   A. Subordinate idea
   B. Subordinate idea

1. Sub-subordinate idea
2. Sub-subordinate idea
   a. Sub-sub-subordinate idea
   b. Sub-sub-subordinate idea
3. Sub-subordinate idea
II. Primary idea
   A. Subordinate idea

REVIEW BASIC WRITING AND GRAMMAR RULES

It is usually a good idea, especially for those who are not accustomed to writing a great deal, to review the elements of good writing usage and style. We suggest perusing Strunk and White's *Elements of Style*, paying special attention to the principles in Chapters 1 and 5. It is a good idea to have a book like this on hand as you write and rewrite, in case you need to check up on your grammar or word usage. Another good grammar and usage reference is Patricia O'Conner's *Woe Is I*, which also happens to be a fairly entertaining read. William Zinsser's *On Writing Well* is an excellent guide to developing good writing style—it elaborates on many of the basic tenets set forth in this chapter. You should definitely have someone with the requisite knowledge of the English language (an English teacher or college counselor) review your essays before sending them off, no matter how polished your grammar and writing skills.

THE TENETS OF GOOD WRITING

- *Simplicity.* Every sentence should be stripped down to its basic components. Every word that is redundant or does not add meaning should be removed.

- *Show rather than tell.* Rather than tell readers what a situation is like, show them the situation (i.e., describe it in detail), and they will sense on their own what you want them to feel. For example, do not tell readers, "I was very sad and lonely when my older brother left for college." Instead, describe the twisted feeling you had in your stomach as you sat on his bed while he packed his things; recall the last few minutes of nervous conversation the two of you had before he slipped out the back door; describe the tears you shed as you watched the car pull away; talk about sitting at the breakfast table all alone with your parents for the first time; explore the feelings of abandonment you sensed when he called home but never asked to speak to you. By showing the situation, you will more powerfully convey to your readers how lonely and sad you really were.

■ *Choose your words carefully.* Avoid clichés and common phrases whose "understood" meanings could be conveyed more effectively using different words. Clichés will dull your reader and make you sound unimaginative or lazy.

■ *Stick to one style and tone.* Decide before writing what kind of style and tone you will employ and stay with it throughout the entire essay. If your tone at the beginning of an essay is light-natured and humorous, do not switch to a somber or stern voice midway through the piece. If your essay is meant to be fashioned as a personal diary entry, do not suddenly start preaching to an outside audience.

■ *Alter the lengths, styles, and rhythms of your sentences for variety.* Your writing should contain some very long sentences as well as some especially short ones for greatest effect. You should not rely too heavily on any one or two types of sentence construction, but weave many different sentence forms and structures into your essays.

■ *Forget what you learned in grade school.* Every essay does not have to have the kind of "introduction," "body," and "conclusion" that you learned about as a kid. Your writing *does* need to be organized and unified, but organization and the development of ideas take on more sophisticated meanings once you have mastered the basics of writing. Your introduction does not have to have one single "topic sentence," nor does it have to summarize everything that will follow in the body of the essay. Your conclusion does not have to restate the topic sentence. Using the first person ("I") is entirely appropriate and necessary for college essays. Throw out the old rules of thumb if you have not already done so.

THE WRITING PROCESS: PEN TO PAPER

WRITING THE ROUGH DRAFT

The next step in the writing process is to produce a rough draft. Be sure that you are not too demanding of yourself at this point. Even though you want to do a good job, perfection at this point can be your worst enemy. Limit your goal to that of producing a rough draft that incorporates most of the basic points you want to make. Do not be concerned if the order you had planned to follow no longer seems to work well, or if you cannot quite express your thoughts, or if your word choice is awkward. Get something reasonable down on paper as a starting point.

GET YOUR CREATIVE JUICES FLOWING

The difficulty with college essays is that they fall somewhere between "fact" and "fiction" in terms of the stylistic approach you must use when writing them. On the one hand, you must be truthful because these are meant to be honest expressions of who you really are. The "facts" must be solid and accurate. On the other hand, you want your writing style to be compelling and your language energetic; you want to come across as creative and perceptive. This is not like writing a chemistry lab report! You must therefore balance the facts with fresh prose.

REVISING YOUR ROUGH DRAFT

Remember that "the only good writing is rewriting." When you start to edit your rough draft, you are embarking on the first part of the crucial revision process. Even the very best and most practiced writers rewrite and revise over and over before reaching a finished product that is acceptable.

One of the most important aspects of the editing stage is its timing. Neglecting to take a break between the drafting and the editing stages will limit your insight into the flaws of the first draft. If you can take a break—preferably at least a few nights, better yet a week or a few weeks—you will be better able to read your draft from the perspective of an outsider.

Make sure that you have edited your draft for substance—for what points will remain and what points will be eliminated—before you start editing the language. Otherwise you will devote time and effort to polishing the wording of material that might be discarded. (And, even worse, you are likely to keep the unnecessary pieces in your draft if you have gone to the trouble of making them at least sound good.) If you are a good writer and have taken the time to think through an essay before doing your first draft, you might well need to edit only once or twice. By the same token, if you are struggling with an essay, it might require more than three revisions to sort out problems.

One very important warning: Do not view editing as taking the life out of your essay. Editing should clear out the dead wood, simplify your statements, and make your important points stand out, in effect adding more energy to an essay. Editing should not, however, necessarily make your writing more formal, serious, journalistic, or adult-friendly. In other words, do not think that the rules for creating a unique and personalized essay—one that really speaks from your heart—should suddenly be discarded during the editing process.

Your revisions to the rough draft should focus on the following:

- *Revise to accomplish your objectives.* Make sure that your essay directly answers the question and that your main ideas are clear.

- *Revise for content.* The typical rough draft may have too little and too much material, all at the same time. It might have just touched the surface of some portions of the essay without providing explanation or convincing detail. At the same time, it may have discussed things that do not contribute significantly to your major points. A good essay eliminates extraneous material while including all of the information necessary to make your point. Your reader needs sufficient evidence to accept what you are saying, so be sure that you have adequately developed and supported your main ideas. Avoid belaboring the obvious (an admissions officer knows what the catcher on the softball team does) but do not assume that readers have any more technical knowledge than does the general public about certain less popular activities.

- *Revise for organization.* A well-organized essay will group similar ideas together and put them in the proper order. To be sure that your draft is in appropriate order, try to outline it from what is written. If it is easy to produce an outline from the draft and there is a clear logic to the flow of the material, you can be reasonably certain that you have a well-ordered essay.

- *Revise for length.* Be sure that your essay is approximately the right length. It is always best, of course, if an essay is under the prescribed word or page limits. If it is substantially longer than the stated word or page limit, then consider how to reduce the supporting material without losing exciting detail or life. If it must go beyond the limit, a good rule to follow is to avoid lengths 10 percent more than the stated limit. In other words, if there is a 500-word limit, try not to write more than 550 words. If your essay is shorter than the allowed length, consider whether to leave it be (which is always the right thing to do if the essay successfully communicates your main points) or to expand it by making additional points or providing further supporting material. If the essay is very much shorter than the suggested length, you probably need more depth to your answer. If you feel you have nothing more to say, consider rethinking your choice of topic.

- *Revise for flow.* Even when you have well-written paragraphs placed in the right order, your writing may still be difficult to read because it lacks suitable transitions between ideas or other means of showing how the ideas relate. Use transition words or connect paragraphs, making the beginning of one paragraph follow directly from the end of the prior paragraph.

■ *Scrutinize your introduction.* Make sure that it not only introduces your subject but also grabs the audience as much as possible. A good introduction is interesting as well as successful at conveying your main points or a notion of how you will be answering the question. In other words, it does not have to be an "introduction" of the variety learned in sixth-grade writing class (in which you write a topic sentence followed by a list of the main points you will make in the body of the essay, followed by a restatement of the topic sentence), but it should at least hint at the direction in which your essay will lead.

For example, let us assume you are answering the question, "What is your favorite hobby and why?" You do not need to open with the following kind of all-in-one-breath statement to summarize your entire essay: "Fly-fishing is my favorite hobby because . . ." Your essay would be far more compelling and meaningful if it were to lure in the reader at the beginning with a hint of what is to come, saving some of the exciting detail for later in the story. For example, your introduction could read, "On the morning of my seventh birthday, Grandpa Carl handed me a miniature fly-fishing rod and a brown paper lunch sack, and drove me out to the Flathead River for my first lesson."

Your introduction should appeal to the reader and set the tone for the whole essay. There are many effective ways to open an essay. You can state an interesting and relevant fact, refer to something currently in the news, lead in with a historical event, or discuss a personal experience. You can use an introduction to shock, disturb, or humor your reader. You may compare or contrast two different situations, present a paradox, or ask a compelling and thought-provoking question. You can also start an essay by simply beginning a story. A narrative naturally builds on itself; as long as the first sentence is strong and the next few are equally compelling, it does not matter whether the lead statement is all-encompassing or merely a passageway into the real heart of the matter.

Do not restate the original question; it wastes valuable space and is a weak, plodding way to begin. Similarly, rarely should you use a quotation from someone famous to begin your essay. Mark Twain and Martin Luther King Jr. both said a lot of very interesting and valuable things, but the admissions officers know that as well as you do. There is no reason you should quote them in your college essays. Unless the quotation, the speaker, and the context in which the remark was uttered all directly relate to the point you are making in your essay, you should not consider beginning an essay with the words of someone else. This is *your* application to college; the admissions officers want to read what you have to say for yourself.

■ *Scrutinize your conclusion.* A good conclusion does one or more things:

—Pulls together different parts of the essay.

—Rephrases a main idea (without repeating anything word for word).

—Shows the importance of the material.

—Makes a recommendation.

—Makes a forecast.

—Points toward the future.

—Gives a sense of completion.

—Brings the story full circle, perhaps by echoing an idea mentioned in the introduction.

The conclusion should not follow a tired and belabored winding down. Your very last sentence should be just as crisp and perfect as your first.

GIVE YOUR ESSAYS TO SOMEONE ELSE TO READ

After you have edited the essays to your own satisfaction (or gotten stuck in the process of editing), hand them to several people whose views on writing you respect and who know you well. They can provide you with an objective view that you may not be able to bring to the essays yourself. They can be particularly useful in determining whether your attempts at humor are working, whether the essays convey a true sense of who you are, and whether you have left out important connections or explanations. Pay attention to their opinions, but do not give up control of what are, after all, your essays, not theirs. Do not let them remove the life from your work.

PROOFREADING

Why proofread your essays if you have been careful in composing the final drafts? No matter how careful you have been, errors are still likely to crop up. Taking a last look at all essays before sending them off is a sensible precaution.

What are you looking for? Basically, the task at this point is no longer to make sure that the structure is correct but simply to spot any errors or omissions. Errors tend to show up most often where prior changes were made. Combining two paragraphs into one, for example, may have resulted in the loss of a necessary transition phrase. Grammatical mistakes can also live on, even after many pairs of eyes have combed over your essays. Be ready to spot any kind of mistake.

As with any editing task, your timing in proofreading is of the essence. Wait until you have already finished what you consider to be your final draft. If you can then put this draft away for a few days, you will be able to give it an effective last look. If not, you risk being unable to see mistakes because you are still too close to the writing. Another useful precaution is to have a friend proofread your essays.

PARTING THOUGHTS ON GOOD ESSAY WRITING

- Give yourself the time to do the essays right. Start early! The results will be better if you take time between steps rather than trying to finish an application in a hurry. Expect to spend ten to twenty hours getting ready for the effort, and then perhaps five to ten hours per essay, with the most difficult (and first) efforts taking longer.

- Answer the question. Do not ever substitute an essay on another topic, even if it was your best essay for another school. The likely result of doing so is points off, either for your inability to do as directed or for laziness.

- Use humor, but only if it works. Even if you are hilarious in person, that does not always mean you can *write* humorously.

- Keep the focus on you. For example, do not get carried away in describing the outcome of your junior class community service project without showing how it relates to you and your efforts.

- Favor a full and detailed description of one incident rather than listing or discussing several incidents briefly. It is generally better to describe one event or accomplishment at some length rather than mentioning a number of them without explaining the full range of details, such as why it occurred, what it meant to you, what the results were, and what you learned from it.

- Be specific. The more detailed you make your writing, the more you personalize it and make it memorable. Generalizations ("I am very determined") without specific explanations and examples are weak and unconvincing.

- Use bold type and italics sparingly. Resist overuse of these effects. Bold print and italics can be helpful for emphasis or in making your meaning clear if used moderately.

- Limit the use of headings, subheadings, or other dividers in your essays.

- Find someone to read and edit your work. Explain what you are trying to accomplish so that your editor can both determine whether you are meeting your objectives and correct your grammar and style. The test of your writing is what the reader understands, not what your intent may have been.

- Do not use your limited space to recite information that can be found elsewhere in the application.

- Do not give superficial answers. Take the essays seriously and remember that they are a crucial part of the college application.

- Do not pretend to be someone other than yourself. Doing so will not be supportable with your own history and will sound insincere or phony.

- Do not lie or exaggerate. Doing so will put all of your assertions into doubt.

- Use an appropriate amount of space. It is generally acceptable to exceed word or page limit by 10 percent, but doing so without good reason suggests you are unable to follow directions. (Sometimes online application forms will not allow you to exceed the limitations at all.)

- Do not use a minuscule type size or tiny borders to shrink an essay so that it fits a prescribed length or limit. Remember that your readers have to read thousands of essays and will not appreciate this inconvenience.

- Do not ever refer to the fact that you are writing an essay. For example, do not begin with "In this essay, I will . . ." or state, "When I sat down to write this essay . . ."

- Do not use quotations from famous people unless they are perfectly and directly related to what you are saying. Too many people seem to have been taught to start everything they write with a cute or philosophical epigram, regardless of the fact that it may not fit the subject well and all too often does not match the intended tone of the essay.

- Do not use bullet points, lists, or other ways of conveying information without using full sentences.

- Do not use fancy vocabulary for its own sake.

- Do not preach. Provide support for your viewpoint but do not keep repeating your beliefs or take on a "high and mighty" tone.

REUSING YOUR ESSAYS

Colleges generally want to learn the same things about their applicants, so they tend to ask similar questions. This is good for you in that you can reuse some of your materials and cut down on the amount of work you have to devote to the essay writing process. On the other hand, few things annoy admissions officers more than to receive essays that were clearly first written to answer a question on another college's application (particularly if the other college's name is accidentally left unchanged!). It is possible to recycle your essays, but only as long as you do so intelligently.

Recycling is usually fairly simple to do when the question asked by a college is identical to one you have already answered for another school. Even so, you must remember that there are several situations in which you will have to make more of a change to a previously used essay than simply substituting the new school name:

- If your positioning efforts for the two schools are quite different.

- If one of the schools requires one essay while the other requires several. For the school requiring one essay, you might have packed brief descriptions of many events into one piece. When writing for a school that requires more essays, you may want or have to spread these events throughout different answers. This might also require lengthening your descriptions of individual events. (The reverse process would be appropriate when changing an essay for an application with several questions to an essay for an application with just one essay.)

- If the length limits set by the two schools are different. In this case, you might have to shorten an essay, keeping your major points but reducing your elaboration of them. Alternatively, you might want to consider lengthening an essay if there were points or descriptions omitted from the first version because of space considerations.

Every once in a while, you can successfully recycle an essay to fit a question that is slightly different from the original one. For example, let us assume that in response to one college's question, "What is your favorite class and why?" you have written an essay that discusses your love of American history—because you are interested in human psychology and like to imagine yourself as various characters in the historical dramas you study, gauging your reactions to events from multiple perspectives. To answer a question on another application, "Tell us about a school project you particularly valued," you might recount a history project in which you compared testimony from Chief Sitting Bull, a lieutenant in General Custer's army, and a Montana prairie wife after the Battle of Little Big Horn—discussing many of your previously developed ideas about human psychology and the importance of examining varying perspectives in explaining why you valued the project so much. In this case, just be cautious that you satisfy the demands of the second question. Again, always have someone else read your essay to assess its ability to answer the appropriate question.

ADMISSIONS DIRECTORS REFLECT ON APPLICATION ESSAYS

HOW IMPORTANT ARE THE ESSAYS?

Amherst is a very verbal place—we're very committed to the written word. This means that the essay is of utmost importance to the application. *Katie Fretwell, Amherst*

Absolutely crucial. *Rick Shaw, Stanford*

The essays are very important. We care about an applicant's ability to write, of course. But essays show more than that. They are a way to make a person come alive, a reflection of who you are, how you think, and what you value. *Janet Lavin Rapelye, Princeton*

They can be very important. In an admissions process like Yale's, the vast majority of applicants are strong students and present excellent academic credentials. That's why they're applying to places like Yale. We could fill our freshman class many times over if all we looked at were grades and test scores—we would have a lot of trouble discriminating among students if that's all we had to go on. Because so many students pass this initial academic "threshold," very quickly all the other things in the application play a role. Because the essay is the most personal document in the file, it can play a significant role in bringing the applicant to life in the admissions committee discussion. *Margit Dahl, Yale*

Sometimes when I read an essay I think, "Oh, I love this kid," and that has an amazing ability to reframe an application. Conversely, as with a recent applicant who wrote about getting her teacher fired, some essays leave you soured. *Lee Coffin, Tufts*

The essay portion is huge. A student is going to be embracing a curriculum that is intensive in the area of writing. They need to be able to write in a clear, concise manner that answers the questions put before them. We are looking for them to do the same in the application. *Chris Gruber, Davidson*

Every year, it seems like the gray area of the applicant pool (applicants who are not clear admits nor clear denies) gets bigger and bigger. The more it grows, the more important the essay becomes in helping admission committees distinguish among qualified candidates. *Kimberly Van Deusen, William & Mary*

WHAT RECOMMENDATIONS DO YOU HAVE FOR COLLEGE APPLICANTS IN WRITING THEIR ESSAYS?

I recommend that applicants write an essay more than a month before the application deadline. Put it away in a drawer, don't look at it for a month, then take it out and ask yourself, "Is this me?" *Maria Laskaris, Dartmouth*

It is crucial that applicants allow themselves to be as personal and self-reflective as possible when writing their essays. Avoid writing about something on a superficial level or resorting to a topic that does not reveal anything special about you. *Rick Shaw, Stanford*

Essays that work tell us about the student, not the latest world crisis. *Richard Avitabile, NYU*

Realize that your essay is not a make or break thing—give yourself some freedom to express your personality. It doesn't have to be a certain kind of personality. It just has to be genuine. *Jennifer Rickard, Bryn Mawr*

You should tell a story that's important to you and that only you can write. If you've missed the point that it's meant to be a story, you'll probably write a polemic instead. *Paul Thiboutot, Carleton*

The most important question to ask *before* you put pencil to paper, or fingers to a keyboard, is "What do I want the person reading my application to know about me before they make a decision on my application?" Reflect first, write second. Remember: You are in the driver's seat in this part of the application, and you need to take control. What's most important to you? What do you really love? Just why was that experience so meaningful? How did it change you? Can you get to the heart of why you pursue something so intensely even though you aren't very good at it? What aspects of your personality do you think most define you? Any topic that's approached from a personal perspective like this will serve you better than the perfectly crafted but impersonal essay. *Margit Dahl, Yale*

Write about things you care about. Don't worry about what we want to read. Answer questions you have something to say about—or change the questions. *Rick Bischoff, Cal Tech*

My favorite essay last year was certainly not publishable prose, though it was grammatically correct. It was self-indulgently long. But the student wrote about several things that truly mattered to him. He was sincere, and it was entirely clear that it came straight from his heart—not a committee of essay-writing advisers. *William M. Shain, Vanderbilt*

The topic should be something they've thought about long before they begin writing this essay. The purpose should be to reveal something of themselves, whether that is their thought processes, personality, passion, or what they are about in some other regard. *Jess Lord, Haverford*

The best essays are those that don't bite off too much, and where the writer comes across sounding like a real person. *Stephen Farmer, UNC Chapel Hill*

Applicants should not write essays that are résumés in paragraph form. If you want to give us a résumé, do so. But use the essay to give us insight into who you are beyond what we see in other parts of the application. *Tim Cheney, Connecticut College*

Many candidates who write about traumatic experiences fail to show whether they have emerged successfully from the experience, so we don't know whether they're ready for rigorous academics and residential life. *Janet Lavin Rapelye, Princeton*

Good writing is the first thing a student should accomplish with the essay. Even if the essay isn't effective overall, a well-written essay will count for something. *Paul Marthers, Reed*

The biggest mistake students make is spending the entire essay telling about an experience, but not telling enough about how it changed them. *Thyra Briggs, Harvey Mudd*

What Writing Style and Tone Do You Recommend?

Cynicism doesn't play well in a college essay. *Debra Shaver, Smith*

A faux voice is the biggest mistake a writer can make regardless of the topic of the essay. *Steve Thomas, Colby*

There are two reasons people become admissions officers. They like the school they work for immensely, and they just like high school students in general. The best way to get someone in the latter category on your side is not to write like a forty-year-old. Don't be afraid to be seventeen. *William M. Shain, Vanderbilt*

Overedited essays lose all their personality. Applicants shouldn't have a lot of different people—especially parents—give their input. This can really ruin an essay. *Maria Laskaris, Dartmouth*

Must Applicants Abide by Stated Word or Page Limits When Writing College Application Essays?

With a little wiggle room, yes. There are reasons an admissions office gives a word limit, one of which is to force students to choose the most important details of whatever they are writing about. No admissions officer is going to tear off the page with an overflow paragraph; but neither do you want to annoy your admissions officer. If an applicant completely ignores the word or page limit and writes three times what was requested, the reader will make note of that fact. That being said, there are times when more words are simply necessary to tell an important story, and the admissions office realizes that. *Margit Dahl, Yale*

We don't really care about word or space limits, but one year we received an essay that was forty pages long—an unprecedented situation. It detailed the minutiae of the applicant's life from birth until present. Students should use common sense about these things! *Sheppard Shanley, Northwestern*

If you go above the limits, you need a good reason to do so—the nature of the topic or the quality of your writing. *Paul Thiboutot, Carleton*

When a college application sets page limits, it is asking you to choose your words carefully. It's a good exercise, and the limits should be respected. *Daniel J. Saracino, Notre Dame*

It obviously makes sense to stay as close to the stated page limits as possible. It's important to be respectful of the limitations that are given. That said, if your very best graded paper is seven pages and we've asked for five, send us the seven pages. *Ken Himmelman, Bennington*

If students go over our stated word preference, we might grumble about it, but it isn't going to doom an applicant. That said, I think that if you are having trouble getting your point across in 500 words, tightening up what you are trying to say is time well spent. *Stuart Schmill, MIT*

13

REQUESTING
RECOMMENDATIONS

— KEY POINTS —

Choosing the right recommenders is important

Approaching potential recommenders must be done carefully:
—Give them a chance to say no
—Explain what your goals are and why you are applying to the
target colleges you have chosen
—Explain your positioning effort so that they can do the best job possible
in supporting your case

Consider whether you will benefit from supplemental recommendations

Make your supporters' work as easy as possible

INTRODUCTION

Many high schoolers complain that recommendations are a waste of time because "everyone can find someone to say something good about them." These applicants are right to believe that most people *can* find a supporter, but they are wrong about the importance of the recommendation process.

Recommendations are probably the most overlooked and underutilized aspect of the college application. If someone writes a mediocre recommendation for you, your judgment will be questioned at the very least. It may even be assumed that you simply could not find people who would say something fantastic about you. A mediocre recommendation can be harmful to an application; a bad recommendation, worse. Recommendations play a vital role in the big picture of the application and make up a crucial component of your positioning strategy. A good recommendation, by supporting your pitch with illuminating anecdotal evidence or by addressing critical issues of your candidacy, can be just the right added touch to set you apart from equally qualified, or even more qualified, candidates.

To understand how crucial a recommendation can be, let us compare two applicants, Anand and Cindy. They are both straight-A students in schools with rigorous curriculums. Both have strong SAT and AP scores, and each is the captain of a varsity team. Both have presented solid essays; both are in the running for admission. As is often the case in college admissions, officers might be faced with two such students but one slot for admission. In such a situation, when all else is equal, a recommendation can be the distinguishing factor in an acceptance. Compare and contrast these two letters of recommendation:

TEACHER RECOMMENDATION FOR ANAND

I have had the pleasure of teaching Anand on two occasions: freshman English and senior year AP English. Given two years of experience with him in my classroom, I feel well qualified to address his candidacy to your school. One look at Anand's grades and scores and you will see why he is in the top 10 percent of his class and why I feel so confident in his ability to succeed academically at the college level. His verbal scores on the SAT critical reading and writing sections are proof enough of how strong his English skills are. He has never received below a B+ on a paper in my class, and I am considered one of the toughest graders at our school!

Anand is also quite a soccer player. Although I don't follow soccer very closely (tennis is my thing), I have been to a few games and Anand has always scored a goal. He is also very vocal, cheering on his teammates at all times and showing fine leadership as a captain. Truly, I can't say enough good things about Anand. He is an all-around great kid and would be a wonderful addition to your school.

TEACHER RECOMMENDATION FOR CINDY

A student like Cindy comes around only once or twice in a teacher's entire career. She excels at everything she does—academics, athletics, personal relationships, community service—but more importantly, she brings a real spirit and vitality to her endeavors. Cindy does not just go through the motions, she invests her soul into her studies and activities. When we studied *The Canterbury Tales*, she took it upon herself to check out instructional tapes in Middle English pronunciation from the library to learn how to recite Chaucer correctly.

I will not bother to repeat Cindy's fine scores and grades for you—they speak for themselves. Her A in my class can be partly attributed to her excellence in the basics—she writes, analyzes, and presents her ideas well. But what makes Cindy stand out in class is her insight and her unyielding pursuit of the truth. *Never* does she simply read a text. She is constantly trying to attain a deeper understanding—of human nature, of historical contexts, of her own world and values, of the philosophies held by particular authors. This dedication to discovering the truth makes her written work, as well as her contributions to class discussions, a learning experience for everyone, including myself. It is not uncommon for me to come away from a class discussion or one of Cindy's essays pondering a new dimension of a text I have taught for over twenty years. Just last week, I earned a new respect for Tessie Hutchinson, the rather unappealing and hypocritical lottery "winner" in Shirley Jackson's short story "The Lottery," because of a unique but plausible interpretation of her character that Cindy provided in class. Her boldness of opinion is a refreshing change from the timid conjectures of students who do not trust their own instincts.

If there is a weakness to be had in Cindy's English performance it may be that she is better at offering insight to her own thoughts and feelings "in relation" to a character in a book or an author's message than she is at evaluating her thoughts on their own, without using any comparative measures. While this may be a weakness, I believe part of the reason for this is Cindy's humility—as well as her awareness that she is but one player in a vast and diverse world.

Relating to this idea of Cindy's humility and her awareness of those around her, I would like to share an experience I had as faculty adviser for the "Thanksgiving Dinner for the Homeless" committee, chaired by Cindy and another student last year. I had heard from several teachers that I was lucky to have such a mature, responsible, caring person as Cindy for my student liaison, especially since her co-chair was not known for his sense of responsibility. Inevitably, I focused my attention on Cindy and left it to her discretion to assign responsibilities for the event. During a conversation, though, Cindy politely said to me, "Thank you for having such confidence in my ability to run this event. I think, however, that it would mean a lot to Sam if he were in charge. It just seems that people are often discounting him. I know this would mean a lot to him, and I have other projects in which to develop my leadership skills at the moment—whereas this is Sam's one big chance to prove himself in an extracurricular activity." Needless to say, the event was an astounding success, with Sam as the recognized leader and Cindy doing more than her fair share of the "back room" work. I learned a valuable lesson about mentoring and developing my students.

I do not want to take up more space than I already have. But let me reassure you that despite Cindy's athletic prowess, she fits none of the negative jock stereotypes. She is not shallow or one-dimensional. She is an intelligent, insightful, caring, mature, and balanced young woman who would add to your school in many ways. I feel well qualified to recommend Cindy to you. I recommended two students last year who are now members of your freshman class—even in comparison to these two stellar students, Cindy is a real standout.

Which one—Anand or Cindy—would you select? Cindy wins easily, appearing to be the stronger candidate if we compare the two letters of recommendation. This finely executed recommendation tips the balance well in her favor. While Anand got his recommender to say good things about him, Cindy got a lot more mileage out of this recommendation. She chose the right person—someone who could share classroom as well as personal experiences about her, offer interesting anecdotes, and address her weakness in a sophisticated way. The letter offers insight that goes well beyond regurgitating already known facts and assumptions. The rest of this chapter is dedicated to helping you get your supporters to do the same for you.

WHAT ADMISSIONS DIRECTORS SAY ABOUT THE
IMPORTANCE OF RECOMMENDATIONS

We pay very close attention to them. My feeling is that recommendations are very important in distinguishing between students of similar caliber. *Christoph Guttentag, Duke*

I have to be honest about this—the recommendations are *extremely* important. This is one of the most valuable parts of the application. *Rick Shaw, Stanford*

There can be real strategy involved in recommendations. I don't think enough students realize this. With good, careful preparation, you can get a great recommendation. Bad recommendations are usually the result of poor planning or a cavalier approach to them. I tell applicants to take this seriously because it's important! *Dan Walls, Emory*

We pay quite a lot of attention to recommendations. I'm always fascinated by those from teachers of a class in which a student struggled, if the teacher saw the student overcome challenges and improve. *James Bock, Swarthmore*

Recommendations from teachers and counselors in particular are absolutely critical. In an applicant pool as strong as ours, school recommendations help us distinguish among many students who have equally strong transcripts. Qualities such as intellectual curiosity, energy, leadership, sensitivity to others, or the capacity to contribute to a community are often conveyed in these letters—as are qualities that are less impressive, or that raise questions for the admissions committee. I think many students don't realize just how well their teachers and counselors often know them—these people interact with students daily both in and out of the classroom and observe students interacting with one another, and they tell us what they see. The admissions process at Yale would be dramatically more difficult without the school recommendations. *Margit Dahl, Yale*

We don't use recommendations in our admissions process. I don't know that I have ever seen a poor recommendation. I feel they are a less reliable indicator. *Ingrid Hayes, Georgia Tech*

In some ways, I think teacher and counselor recommendations are becoming more important. Other parts of the application are increasingly generic. Grade inflation makes it harder for us to differentiate applicants on that measure. Test prep companies distort things further. And for that matter, essays are often heavily vetted by people other than the applicant, and therefore may not be revealing of the true student. Particularly when we get multiple applications from the same high school—public and private—we weigh recommendations quite carefully, taking to heart any comparative signals the schools are sending us. *Robert Clagett, Middlebury*

WHAT ADMISSIONS OFFICERS LEARN FROM RECOMMENDATIONS

1. *Your claims are true.* Recommendations are examined first for the extent to which they confirm and support your claims and your positioning. Consistency between what you say about yourself and what recommenders say about you is important.

2. *You have many qualifications.* In looking at the teacher recommendation forms in the Common Application, you will see that teachers are asked to rate you in many areas—creativity, originality, motivation, independence, initiative, intellectual ability, academic achievement, written expression of ideas, effectiveness in class discussion, disciplined work habits, potential for growth—and then expand on these ratings. Recommendations are an opportunity to provide more information about you, preferably in the form of stories and illustrations of general points the recommenders wish to make.

3. *There is more to learn about you than what is covered in the essays.* Because you are limited in what you can include in your application essays, it is difficult to present everything that might make you a desirable candidate. Therefore, your recommendations can fill in the gap.

4. *Your accomplishments have impressed others.* Admissions officers do not look favorably on an applicant who blatantly toots his own horn. This is especially true if a statement about you represents a subjective opinion rather than an objective fact backed up with concrete evidence. Saying you are "the funniest guy in the drama club" or "the one everybody looks up to" will be better received and more credible if offered by a recommender rather than by you. A recommender's positive comments show the admissions office that you have made an impression on others and assure them that your own self-descriptions are valid.

5. *There are special circumstances that influence your academic or extracurricular performance.* Recommendations are a good place for shedding light on certain anomalies or special circumstances that might negatively influence your record. Teachers or guidance counselors can explain that your B– Spanish grade reflects the fact that you landed in the section with the toughest teacher, whose class average is actually a C. They can discuss your performance over time if you are a late bloomer who did not do well during the ninth and tenth grades. They can also enlighten admissions officers on personal issues that might have gotten in the way of your performance, such as learning disabilities, health issues, or family problems.

6. *Information about your school and senior class, which helps to show how you are regarded and how you compare with others in your same environment.* Admissions committees look to the college or guidance counselor recommendation to get a sense of your high school and your class. This recommendation provides a context in which to evaluate you, thus giving admissions officers the ability to better assess you. A discussion of your class rank, the school's GPA weighting policy, the level and breadth of your courses, your impact within the school, and your extracurricular involvement are commonly offered in this recommendation.

7. *You can accurately evaluate others and their perceptions of you.* If you end up choosing someone who writes a mediocre recommendation, your judgment will be questioned at the very least. It may even be assumed that you could not find people who would say something good about you.

CHOOSING TEACHER RECOMMENDERS

Selecting appropriate recommenders involves sifting many factors. Most colleges allow you great freedom to choose your teacher recommenders, while others limit your choice. Here are some general rules to apply when choosing teacher recommenders:

1. *Choose teachers who know you well.* Many teachers have the opportunity to get to know students well in an academic setting (if the class is interactive or if you spend time with the teacher outside of class) and in social or extracurricular settings (if they coach a sport, supervise a club, or perhaps have chaperoned class trips and functions). This serves you well because the better a teacher knows you in and out of the classroom, the more able he is to make the recommendation credible and powerful by illustrating points with anecdotes and lively details, and the less likely he will be to limit the recommendation to a discussion of your grades and scores. If your relationship with a teacher is relegated to the classroom, be sure it is a class in which you are very active and have frequent communication with the teacher.

2. *Choose junior- or senior-year teachers.* Teachers from later in your high school career are better able to give a current and detailed picture of you than are teachers from earlier on. Admissions committees will question the validity and pertinence of a recommendation from a freshman or sophomore teacher unless you have a special reason for asking that person and that reason is made clear.

3. *Choose a recommender who can support your positioning.* If you are positioning yourself as a potential journalism major, for example, it would behoove you to get a recommendation from an English teacher who can attest to your writing ability and perceptiveness. In some cases, the teacher who best supports your positioning is one who can address your weaknesses and put a positive spin on them. For example, if your academic courseload has been unevenly distributed, with more time spent in humanities courses, and you want to shed light on your analytical and quantitative abilities, request a recommendation from a math teacher. If you risk being stereotyped (as "an athlete," "a genius," etc.), you will want your recommendations to address the weaknesses assumed of such types and, even more usefully, why you do not display such weaknesses.

4. *Choose teachers whose classes you enjoy and in which you have worked hard.* These are not necessarily classes in which you have received A grades. In fact, if a B or even a C grade is the result of much determination and enthusiasm, the teacher of the class can probably speak far more favorably about you than can a teacher who says you received an A in her class without having more than that to discuss.

5. *Choose teachers who genuinely like you.* Teachers who like you will take the time to write you a good recommendation and will provide examples to illustrate points made about you. This is impressive in its own right. A recommendation that looks as though it took only five minutes to write suggests that that is exactly how much time the recommender felt you deserved. In contrast, a recommendation that looks carefully written and well thought out suggests that the recommender is committed to helping you.

6. *Choose teachers who can address several of the key qualities colleges look for.* The key qualities include brains, character, leadership ability, and other talents and skills. Each of these qualities can be broken down into many smaller elements.

Brains

- Academic achievement
- Analytical ability
- Quantitative skills
- Originality
- Healthy skepticism
- Imagination and creativity
- Problem-solving ability

- Research skills
- Communication skills (written and oral)
- Effectiveness in class discussions
- Mastery of language
- Insight
- Thoroughness

Character

- Sense of morality
- Dependability
- Motivation and sense of initiative
- Sense of humor
- Perseverance and work ethic
- Independence
- Discipline

- Involvement in relationships
- Sense of social responsibility
- Social skills
- Maturity
- Potential for growth
- Open-mindedness

Leadership Ability

- Managerial skills
- Fairness
- Organization skills

- Respect for others
- Ability to motivate others

Other Talents and Skills

- Artistic talent
- Athletic talent
- Musical talent
- Acting talent

- Foreign language skill
- Technology and computer skills
- Other special talents and skills

In addition to these general rules, two additional criteria may also warrant consideration when looking for recommenders:

1. *The voice of experience.* Many teachers have recommended students before you to the colleges of your choice. Therefore, these teachers—at least those who have successfully helped prior students gain admission!—have a sense of what the colleges are looking for. In addition, they can compare you to those from your high school who are now attending a college to which you are applying. Admissions committees appreciate this kind of insight and will often become familiar with and look favorably on particular recommenders who consistently promote good candidates.

2. *Timeliness.* Choose someone who is reliable and therefore likely to submit your recommendations on time.

ADMISSIONS DIRECTORS GIVE ADVICE ON
HOW TO CHOOSE RECOMMENDERS

Choosing the right recommenders is incredibly important. Go talk to the teachers you are considering asking, tell them what schools you are applying to, explain why you want a recommendation from each, let them get a feel for what you are after. *Michael Goldberger, Brown*

I suggest applicants choose recommenders who know them in more than one dimension if possible. This way, the writer has a greater frame of reference for speaking about the student. Also, make sure to give them enough time to do a good job. *Lee Stetson, University of Pennsylvania*

It's perfectly okay to get a recommendation from a teacher who didn't give you an A. Someone who knows who you are as a person and how you engage in the classroom may have a good deal more to say than the teacher who reports only, "This is a good kid who always gets A's." *Bruce Poch, Pomona*

Choose teachers who you think know you well—not necessarily the one who gave you the highest grade you got last year. The grade will be on your transcript. It's the commentary in the text of the letter, both academic and personal, that will be most helpful. *Margit Dahl, Yale*

You should pick a teacher who knows you well, and ideally someone who has taught you recently (as in not a teacher from grade 9 or 10 unless he or she is also teaching you now). *Nancy Hargrave Meislahn, Wesleyan*

It is wise not to have all of your academic recommendations come from the same department. That may be where you have devoted the bulk of your energies, or had your most consistent successes, but including a recommender from elsewhere shows roundedness. *Bruce Poch, Pomona*

Sometimes teachers approach the recommendation with an attitude of "They're not really going to read this." We even see recommendations that are obviously form letters, with the wrong name substituted in for the applicant's name. Unfortunately, this can really harm the student. Applicants should be sure the recommenders they choose are prepared to do a good job. *Rick Shaw, Stanford*

Candidates ought to choose recommenders who know them well. Also, it's usually best to get a recommendation from a recent teacher. *Maria Laskaris, Dartmouth*

TEACHER RECOMMENDATIONS

You will want to foster close relationships with those teachers who will write you recommendations during your senior year. The more time you spend cultivating a relationship with the teacher, the more likely it is that he or she will have illuminating examples to support the points made about you.

Thankfully, the same things that ensure a good recommendation from a teacher also help make you a good student: class participation, insight into the material, good behavior, diligence, well-executed and timely homework assignments, interest in the subject matter that goes beyond what is expected of you, willingness to assist the teacher, eagerness to approach the teacher on a regular basis (whether it is to chat or to seek help), and the ability to work well with your classmates on assignments.

Depending on the schools to which you are applying, you may have free reign to choose your teacher recommenders, or you may be restricted to recommendations from a math and an English teacher.

To the extent that you are given a choice, you will want to select teachers who will best support your pitch and who will shed light on things that are not already presented in other areas of the application. For example, it does not serve you to choose a teacher in a subject in which you have strong grades and scores if that teacher cannot do more than reiterate your report card. Rather, you will want to select a teacher who knows you well enough that he is going to share insight about you beyond your academic record. Furthermore, you will want to choose teachers in core subjects (i.e., math, science, English, history, foreign languages) rather than noncore electives, such as physical education or typing.

In order to be especially proactive, you should choose teachers who are able to minimize your weaknesses (or at least what admissions committees might view as your weaknesses) rather than merely hoping the college will not notice them. For example, if you did not do well on the math portion of the SAT but have worked hard in your calculus class and know your teacher well, you might request a recommendation from her.

Here is an example of an effective recommendation written by a math teacher.

RECOMMENDATION FOR EMMA

Emma is one of the top three math students I have ever taught. This is an accomplishment in and of itself, but when coupled with the fact that Emma is succeeding despite odds against her (she was diagnosed with a slight learning disability during her sophomore year), her success is that much more impressive. To address her disability briefly, let me assure you that it has affected her analytical abilities hardly at all; the techniques Emma has studied to avoid misreading or reversing numerals have worked well. I admire her for confronting her problem and want to assure you that it should not make you lower your opinion of her academic quality whatsoever.

What makes Emma one of the best math students in my eighteen-year career? You can see for yourself the high achievement she has reached in my class. For the purpose of this recommendation, I will focus on two of her many outstanding qualities.

First, she has the ability to project and utilize mathematical ideas and concepts beyond the confines of the classroom. The following situation occurred earlier this year: An article in our student newspaper reported that the school was contemplating the construction of a new senior parking lot, but due to high contracting costs, the plans had been discarded. After reading the article, Emma approached me and asked if I would supervise her effort to draw up some plans for the project. I myself found this to be a daunting project, but how could I, the teacher, say no? Applying several concepts we had learned in class, as well as concepts she learned in her community college course, Introduction to Engineering, Emma produced a plan for the lot. Not only did it include the sixty spots the school had requested, but it also included five extra spots for the school's sports vans, which to date have been located half a mile from school. She consulted several construction firms to confirm that her ideas were reasonable and even got some very rough estimates from them—estimates that were feasible given the school's budget. Emma presented her plan to our administration and board of directors and the school has now returned to the idea. I cannot say that her exact plan will be used for the construction of the actual lot, but it was an accurate and impressive assessment of and solution to the problem. More importantly, Emma's initiative provided the stimulus necessary for the school to go ahead with the project. And Emma doesn't even have a car! She didn't take this project on for selfish reasons, but merely to confront an interesting question and challenge herself.

Second, Emma's involvement in the predominantly male Math Club is notable. She is one of only three female members and was voted president this year by her peers. Emma has made it a point to invite women who have been successful in the fields of math, engineering, and computer science to the school to speak. Emma feels it is important to expand young women's minds so that they do not buy into negative stereotypes regarding their abilities in math and science. Never one to shy away from a challenge, she is collaborating with our counseling department on a "Women in the Workforce" assembly that will showcase women professionals in our area. She hopes that through this program she will reach a large number of young girls who have abandoned the idea of becoming successful in technical careers.

As Emma has indicated, she is interested in your engineering program. There is not a question in my mind that she will succeed. But more importantly, she will be a positive presence in your department and in your school.

What do admissions officers learn from this letter that makes Emma such an attractive candidate?

- She has a passionate interest in math and learning in general.
- She has drive and initiative.
- She applies knowledge learned inside the classroom to other areas of life.
- She has made an impact at her school.
- She is community-minded.
- She enjoys challenges.
- She is interested in engineering (a major known for its low number of female students).

ADMISSIONS DIRECTORS EXPLAIN WHAT THEY MOST WANT FROM TEACHER RECOMMENDATIONS

The qualities a teacher should address in the recommendation include originality of thought, engagement, personality, how the student reacts to criticism, how she interacts with other students.   *Michael Goldberger, Brown*

Some recommendations are boilerplate—from far too overworked and harried teachers. Then again, some teachers are very helpful and insightful. I wish more teachers would think about critical issues: When the student is presented with new material, how does she react? What is the student's mode of thinking and questioning? What has the development over time been like?   *David Borus, Vassar*

When we have forty applicants from one school—one of our typical "feeder" schools—we're looking for a comparative discussion. We need a way to distinguish between students.   *John Hanson, Middlebury*

If a recommendation doesn't jump out at us because of the praise contained within it, we see a red flag. We're so used to ebullience in recommendations that a tepid one makes us wonder how great the student really is. *Eric Kaplan, Penn*

We are not interested in hearing a teacher regurgitate a résumé or grades. We want to see concise, pointed, colorful commentary that provides examples of what kind of a student the applicant is. We all know that there are many different kinds of strong students—those who float through effortlessly, those who work tirelessly for each and every class, and many who fall in between. We want to learn what kind of student is *behind* the performance. *Stephen Schierloh, Sarah Lawrence*

We're looking for comments that draw distinctions between a student and others in the classroom. We aren't looking for facts or data here—a teacher shouldn't waste space telling us about the student's grades or what he does outside of class. *Sheppard Shanley, Northwestern*

We ask teachers to discriminate, to compare students with others they've had during their entire teaching experience. We want to see outcomes in the classroom and interaction in the classroom. We want to see that there's intellectual depth beyond rote. Most kids get *grades;* we want to see *learning*. And that often comes best from a teacher's response. *Rick Shaw, Stanford*

We're interested in knowing more about who the student is as a student. A teacher recommendation need not include information we are more likely to receive from the guidance counselor (e.g., commitment to activities outside class, etc.). With teacher recommendations, I'm always very interested in the level of engagement a student has had in the classroom. How does she interact with others? Is she a vocal contributor? Is she a quiet contributor? (And both of those things are good and important.) How she contributes in the classroom reflects how she might be in our classroom—what she would contribute here. What does she take away from her learning experiences? Does she get involved in the messy work of learning? *Jennifer Desjarlais, Wellesley*

The teacher has the advantage of having the student for extended periods of time, and one of the things we find most helpful is the teacher can tell you whether this is a student who makes the class interesting or stimulates the discussion or so on. This is particularly valuable because in a classroom of very good students, who are the ones who move the issue along or lead the discussion? That kind of characteristic is something we find particularly interesting. *Charles Deacon, Georgetown*

GUIDANCE COUNSELOR RECOMMENDATIONS

Of all the recommendations, the college or guidance counselor's tends to be the one over which you have least choice. In most schools, students are assigned to a particular guidance counselor, or there is one who acts on behalf of all the seniors. At some schools, students have minimal interaction with their counselor because of his or her caseload. A lack of choice and interaction, however, does not mean you cannot make this recommendation work for you. It does mean that you may have to take some initiative in ensuring a positive relationship with your counselor. Do not worry excessively if you fail to attain a close relationship with her due to her caseload, her arrival at your school in your senior year, or other factors beyond your control. The counselor's recommendation is likely to be based, in large part, on input from your entire faculty and administration, and thus she should be able to do a good job even if circumstances prevent a close relationship.

The purpose of the guidance counselor recommendation is first and foremost to give admissions officers a context in which to place you. Admissions committees are trying to answer the question, "How does this student fit into his high school setting?" On an elementary level, the answer to this question lies within your class rank, a figure requested of guidance counselors. But the most effective counselor recommendations provide a comprehensive picture of you that includes your academic record, your social impact, and explanations of any extenuating circumstances that may have affected your performance.

For example, your class rank may not indicate that you have taken a heavier courseload than students ranked higher than you. Or, maybe your mediocre scores on a particular SAT subject exam are attributable to the fact that you had suffered from mononucleosis for the two weeks preceding the test. A guidance counselor can shed light on a rise or decline in your overall record or explain your lack of extracurriculars. She can explain that your poor performance during a particular semester was the result of the concurrent diagnosis of your mother's breast cancer. On a more positive note, if you are too humble to speak of the success of the food drive you organized at Thanksgiving time, a counselor can sing your praises for you.

Here is an example of an effective guidance counselor letter.

RECOMMENDATION FOR KEVIN

Kevin is an exuberant leader—he zips around like a cartoon character, a man always on a mission—and has worked hard to maintain a spot toward the very top of his class.

Kevin is a member of the Class of 2009 at Marshall Preparatory School. Our rigorous program requires that students think critically, write articulately, and defend their ideas in small discussion-based classes. Please note our difficult grading scale and unweighted GPA, both explained in our school profile.

Kevin is a workhorse. His efforts have paid off with a place in the second decile of his class, despite the fact that his GPA dropped junior year, the result of a much more difficult curriculum. Kevin has challenged himself by taking our most difficult classes, despite a slight learning difference, for which he has never sought special accommodations from us or the College Board, wanting instead to live up to the highest standards. Math is Kevin's best subject, and he flourishes with less effort there. Kevin's calculus teacher says, "Kevin is actively concerned with his performance and comes in often to get extra help. His intuitive math skills are very strong." Kevin's American literature teacher says, "He picked Steinbeck as the subject for his term paper, and struggled with some of the concepts in *Of Mice and Men*, 'The Chrysanthemums,' and 'Breakfast.' But he brought in draft after draft for me to comment on, and kept making appointments with me to come up with a great final product." She says one of her favorite memories of Kevin was his hilarious portrayal of Lady Macbeth—complete with a frilly nightgown and wig—for their Shakespeare unit. Dramatic reenactments definitely come easily to Kevin, who is full of personality and a confident public speaker. His Spanish teacher of four years says that sophomore year he did the best skit in the class with two other students, where they dramatically acted out the poetry of Pablo Neruda. He also says of Kevin, "He is so likeable and a bright young man. He does great work as long as he's not side-tracked by the class clowns." Kevin occasionally has had problems getting distracted in class and channeling his exuberance into appropriate behavior, but these incidents seem to have disappeared this year with maturity. Some faculty also feel that Kevin's goals are at times too shortsighted—that he is often working more for the grade than for the pleasure of learning. I think this, too, may change as he can focus more on his strengths while leaving behind the subject matter that is more difficult for him. These weaknesses are minor ones, as evidenced by the fact that Kevin has won several awards over the years from our faculty.

Kevin really shines when it comes to leading his peers and engaging in the world around him. He is a three-sport athlete, serving important roles on our football, basketball, and lacrosse teams. (He helped guide our basketball team to the league finals last year and was named to the 1st team All-League two years in a row. He recently helped our varsity football team win our league's title, a huge feat for such a small school.) Kevin has always served on our student government in some capacity and this year is our student body secretary. Our Director of Admissions and Student Activities, who has overseen Kevin's involvement in government as well as in the Gold Key Society, where he hosted prospective students and their families, says of him, "He is just an awesome kid on every level. He's the kind of student you always want representing the school. He's also very responsible—I don't think he's missed a single student government meeting in four years, and is always there to help clean up after a dance or drum up excitement for an event." Kevin has also been motivated to seek out internships in various areas of interest to him. He was part of the Philadelphia Young Entrepreneurs Program in the summer of 2002, he worked in the marketing department of a finance company last summer, and he has interned as a production engineer at the Philadelphia area NPR station as part of the Youth Radio program since last spring. Kevin has also done his fair share of community service by coaching the Latino Recreation Center basketball team, mentoring a young boy who lost his father, and other various activities. For his multifaceted commitment and for the upbeat presence he brings to every activity, our Head of School awarded Kevin our prestigious Spirit Award last year.

Kevin's character has been fortified by his family's ups and downs. His parents were hit hard by the economic down turn of the late 1990s, and Kevin has done his part to help weather the storm by holding down paying jobs in addition to his other commitments. Through his parents' recent very tumultuous and public divorce, Kevin found solace in openly talking to faculty members about his emotions and also played a large role in helping his younger brother cope with the situation.

I highly recommend Kevin to your college and know he will continue to energize your community as he has ours.

WHAT IMPORTANT INFORMATION DOES THIS COUNSELOR RECOMMENDATION OFFER ABOUT KEVIN?

- He is a committed worker, dedicated to his studies and determined to excel.

- He has a diagnosed learning difference, but knows how to compensate for it.

- He has an exuberant personality and is a real community leader.

- He is an accomplished athlete and also pursues student government, a range of community service activities, and semiprofessional internships.

- His family circumstances have created hurdles for him in high school, but he has weathered the storm well.

- He holds down paying jobs in addition to his academics and activities.

- His weakness, the ability to get distracted and "clown around" a bit too much, is minor and has lessened with time and maturity.

ADMISSIONS DIRECTORS TALK ABOUT WHAT THEY MOST WANT FROM GUIDANCE COUNSELOR RECOMMENDATIONS

It's very important in providing us a context for the student's experience and performance. I always find it helpful when the counselor can provide a bit more information about the school, especially if it's a school sending us an applicant for the very first time—if they can explain what the student's performance means within the context of that community. Has she achieved well above her peers? Are her accomplishments consistent with others' or do they stand out? The guidance counselor recommendation provides us with a snapshot of the student's entire experience; the teacher's recommendation provides us with a snapshot of the student's experience in one or two subject areas. Each one is part of the whole. They have very separate but important roles to play in our process. *Jennifer Desjarlais, Wellesley*

We want the counselor to put the student in the context of his or her school and/or to tell us about any out-of-the-ordinary circumstances that may have affected the student's development. *Thyra Briggs, Harvey Mudd*

One thing is to talk about how this particular student makes a difference in their community. This could be in any number of different ways. The person could be a star athlete, or a great musician, or someone who gets things done behind the scenes. As a national university, when you walk into a school to discuss students who've applied, you'd like to ask, "Is this person well known in this community and for what reasons?" In the group of a hundred or five hundred, does this person stand out, and in what way? *Charles Deacon, Georgetown*

We ask guidance counselors to explain any anomalies on the record. We also ask that they use tangible examples when possible; we like to see more than opinion on these recommendations—we like to see statements backed up by quotes from teachers. *John Blackburn, University of Virginia*

The best counselor recommendations come from those counselors who take the challenge seriously by starting early, talking with all the teachers, and getting to know the kids personally. *Rick Shaw, Stanford*

SUPPLEMENTAL RECOMMENDATIONS

A supplemental recommendation is one that a student submits in addition to the guidance counselor and teacher recommendations. A supplemental recommendation typically comes from a nonacademic source. This would include coaches, instructors or tutors in nonacademic courses such as pottery or drama, employers, community service supervisors, music instructors, Scout leaders, alumni of the college to which you are applying, religious leaders, or peers.

Often, supplemental recommendations are looked on unfavorably by admissions committees because they do not provide any new information or special insight about the candidate. In fact, there is a saying in admissions offices that shows disdain for useless supplemental recommendations and other unsolicited materials: "The thicker the kid, the thicker the folder."

But a supplemental recommendation can be worthwhile in some cases. First and foremost, you should include an extra recommendation only if someone can offer insight that other recommenders cannot. Whenever possible, it is best to provide as much information as possible through the required recommendations rather than relying on an additional one to do the job, because admissions officers look closely and favorably at the required letters. In some cases, however, a supplemental recommender may be in a better position to offer solid, in-depth information about you.

For example, a guidance counselor might say that you work twenty hours a week at a software company and nothing more. If your interest in computers is a crucial selling point for you, then it would behoove you to request an additional recommendation from your supervisor at the company.

Second, as with your teacher recommendations, select optional and supplemental recommenders based on their abilities to address critical issues. If you have conveyed a penchant for involvement in solitary activities (stamp collecting, playing an instrument, computer programming), your social skills might constitute a critical issue. Therefore it would benefit you to seek a coach, club adviser, or community service leader to write on your behalf, speaking about your team spirit, ability to relate to others, or the like.

A common mistake made by applicants is requesting a recommendation from an alumnus or a well-known person for the sake of impressing the college with her connections. Unless this person knows you well and can offer real insight, the only thing that you will impress upon the admissions committee in this case is your poor judgment. Do not seek letters of support from alumni or important people *unless there is a reason apart from their status* that supports their writing on your behalf.

When should you consider soliciting a supplemental recommendation?

- If you have an extraordinary accomplishment such that admissions officers might not appreciate its significance because of lack of familiarity with it, you should ask someone equipped to convey the importance and prestige of such recognition to write a recommendation. Here we mean genuinely "extraordinary"—admissions officers already know what it means to be named an All-American or Eagle Scout.

- If you have a unique dedication to an activity, such as religious instruction or community service, that goes beyond the regular student's commitment, select a recommender who can convey the depth of your commitment.

- If you have changed significantly over time (for example, if you have matured from a shy, reserved wallflower in the ninth grade to student body president in your senior year, or were once a self-absorbed prima donna who now uses her opportunities to benefit others), then request a recommendation from a person who can attest to this growth and transformation.

- If you have a close relationship with someone who knows well the college to which you are applying (an alum, professor, or trustee), then request a recommendation that will explain why you are such a good fit for the school.

- If you have been limited to math and English teacher recommendations but your greatest strength lies in a different academic subject, request a recommendation from a teacher in that subject.

- If a family or personal situation has affected your high school experience or performance, request a recommendation from a family friend, psychologist, spiritual leader, or someone else who can shed light on the situation and its repercussions.

Keep in mind that in most of the aforementioned circumstances, a college or guidance counselor is capable of addressing the issue. Request a supplemental recommendation only if such a recommender can offer new information about you or if he will do a significantly better job of demonstrating your strengths and minimizing your weaknesses than a guidance counselor would.

A NOTE ON PEER RECOMMENDATIONS

Some colleges require a recommendation from a "peer," meaning a friend or acquaintance of the candidate, generally someone of approximately the same age. Dartmouth, for instance, asks that this recommender provide information about the candidate's personal and academic qualities, especially his or her maturity, ability to work with others, interests, special talents, and experiences. A candidate can choose a good friend or someone he or she knows through an activity or class (a soccer teammate or lab partner, for example). Follow these guidelines if you are required to select a peer recommender:

- Choose someone who knows you well and can tell interesting stories and anecdotes to support his or her comments.
- Choose someone who possesses superior analytical thinking and writing skills.
- Ask that the writer submit his recommendation to a teacher or guidance counselor for critique and review.

A NOTE ON PARENT RECOMMENDATIONS

Some colleges now ask for a statement from a parent of each applicant. Colleges that ask for such a statement are primarily looking for extremely personal information, material that only a loving guardian who has known the applicant for seventeen or so years could provide. Applicants should not worry too much about a parent's analytical thinking or writing skills, nor should they worry about a parent's English language skills or sophistication. As you have learned from reading other sections of this book, college admissions officers are often very attracted to candidates from low-opportunity households or situations. Thus, a recommendation from a parent who is not college educated, does not possess solid English writing skills, or cannot create a sophisticated letter will not necessarily harm you—such a letter may even benefit you substantially because it will help the admissions officers see how well you have succeeded given the situation in which you have grown up. An applicant should simply ask his or her parent to provide an honest statement with as much detail as possible, perhaps highlighting the applicant's desire to attend the particular college or passion in pursuing his or her dreams. Other helpful areas for parents to address include weaknesses that the child has overcome, family problems or circumstances that may have affected the child's performance and outlook, and areas in which the child has matured or grown in recent years.

ADMISSIONS DIRECTORS DISCUSS
SUPPLEMENTAL RECOMMENDATIONS

WHAT OTHER RECOMMENDATIONS, BESIDES THOSE FROM
TEACHERS AND GUIDANCE COUNSELORS, DO YOU REQUEST?

The peer recommendation is very important to us. These tend to have a real freshness to them. We get to know a student on human terms, as a person. They're very valuable. The peer recommendation often crystallizes the whole case for me—I'm often in a position where I'm fairly certain I want to accept a student, then I read the peer evaluation and it does wonderful things for the candidate, making admission the clear decision in my mind. *Maria Laskaris, Dartmouth*

IS IT OKAY FOR APPLICANTS TO SUBMIT EXTRA RECOMMENDATIONS?

An extra recommendation is fine, as long as the applicant has thought about it. A candidate should ask himself, "What new dimension is being added here?" before submitting extra letters of recommendation. *Eric J. Furda, Columbia*

We've seen excellent recommendations from employers—some of the best recommendations have also come from parents who have employed their own kids. Because we don't generally interview, the recommendations become very important. *Richard Avitable, NYU*

Only when there is a special arts talent do we recommend that an applicant get an extra recommendation. *Katie Fretwell, Amherst*

It is fine to submit extra recommendations as long as they are from people who know the applicant well and can say something that other recommenders have not said. Letters from friends of parents, congressmen, sport stars, and the like who do not know the applicant well have no impact on our decision. *Robert Clagett, Middlebury*

Extra recommendations are always fine. We like and welcome them, but students need to be judicious. An extra recommendation should have a purpose, make a contribution, and not reiterate what others have said—and always be from a person who knows the student well. *Nancy Hargrave Meislahn, Wesleyan*

If you provide an additional recommendation, make sure the person is supplying new information—something that's not already in your file. *Tim Cheney, Connecticut College*

We don't discourage additional recommendations. We like them; we're not fussy on this issue. *Richard Steele, Bowdoin*

Students should follow directions when applying to colleges. If the admissions office asks for three recommendations, send three. If the admissions office suggests only one letter, submitting twenty will not send your file to admit-land. *Kimberly Van Deusen, William & Mary*

Not many. Someone who knows you well, through an internship you've done or a work experience, would be potentially beneficial because they would have immediate, firsthand knowledge of you. If they also have some connection to the university community, an alumnus or someone like that whom we might know already, that would be an additional advantage. But in general we don't seek outside recommendations unless they're really going to add something significant to the file. *Charles Deacon, Georgetown*

Who Else Can Be a Helpful Recommender?

Alumnae recommendations can be very helpful when they know the student well. We take them in the spirit in which they're given. Clearly they aren't giving an academic recommendation, but rather a character reference. The key is that they provide some additional information about who that student is and how she might be an appropriate match for Wellesley. *Jennifer Desjarlais, Wellesley*

The recommendations I find less helpful are those from someone who has a tangential connection. These recommendations rarely reveal anything new or helpful about a student's candidacy; they are superfluous and can simply clutter up a student's file. *Jennifer Desjarlais, Wellesley*

Recommendations from bosses or employers can occasionally help a student, but letters from friends of family don't help. *Michael Goldberger, Brown*

HOW TO APPROACH A RECOMMENDER

The typical high school student's approach to a potential recommender involves a hurried interaction in the hallway or after class in which the student does little more than make a squirmish plea for a recommendation ("I'm wondering if maybe you could do me a big favor?"). (And sometimes then a sigh of relief from the student before she dashes off, late to field hockey practice!) This represents at best a completely wasted opportunity.

THE MOST IMPORTANT GENERAL RULES TO KEEP IN MIND WHEN APPROACHING A RECOMMENDER

1. Give a recommender an opportunity to decline the request if she does not think she can write you a strong letter.

2. Allow your recommender enough time—one month at the very least—to write a good recommendation.

3. Provide your recommender with enough information to make her job easy and ensure an insightful letter of support.

Ideally, you should start the process two to three months before the recommendation deadline. Begin your request to a potential supporter by scheduling ahead of time a fifteen-minute meeting with the person. The meeting should be face-to-face, not over the telephone, unless a meeting cannot be arranged. Arrive at the meeting well prepared to give information, including:

- What colleges you are applying to and why
- Why you have chosen this recommender
- Your positioning effort, including strengths to be marketed and weaknesses to be addressed

It is best if you come to the meeting with a printout of some basic information that you can give to the recommender, so she can use it to refresh her memory when sitting down to do the task. If the recommender is someone unassociated with your school and/or unaccustomed to writing letters of support on behalf of college applicants (perhaps a religious leader or art instructor), then you might also want to explain what is required in the admissions process, and how important the recommendations are. You of course need to do this carefully, not in a way that would seem condescending to the recommender. No adult wants to be treated as ignorant or less than capable by a high school student!

Next comes one of the most critical pieces of the process, which is often overlooked by high school students who feel desperate about merely finding recommenders rather than ascertaining that they will find the *right* recommenders: Make sure that each recommender is going to write a very favorable recommendation for you. The way to be sure of this is by giving the person an "out" if she feels unable to be highly supportive of your candidacy. Ask her if she believes she would be the right person to write a recommendation for you. If she declines, seems hesitant, or suggests using some-one else, do not press her. You do not want to weasel a recommendation out of someone who is not eager to write one. Thank her for her time and move on.

If, on the other hand, she agrees to write a letter, give her a further brief-ing in both verbal and written form. You might want to tell her in more detail why you are applying to each particular school. Explain how you are trying to position yourself in general, and show her what questions she will need to an-swer about you. Suggest stories and anecdotes she can use. Provide her with enough detail to refresh her memory about the stories. If appropriate, ask her to address a weakness if you think she can mitigate it.

This well-thought-out approach for procuring recommendations will prove helpful in a number of ways. First, it minimizes the chance that you will end up with a lukewarm recommendation. Second, you will have been highly organized and shown a serious attitude about your college applications, always a good impression on the recommender. Third, your organization and effi-ciency will avoid any resentment on the part of the recommender, which some-times is the case with last-minute pleas. Fourth, you know in advance what stories she is apt to tell and in what ways she will support your positioning. This all means that you will retain some degree of control over the admissions process.

TACTFUL WAYS TO PRESENT YOUR POSITIONING APPROACH TO RECOMMENDERS

Here are some suggestions for presenting your pitch without sounding pre-sumptuous:

- "I have been researching colleges and it's clear to me that given the low accep-tance rates at so many of the schools I'm interested in, I'm going to have to dis-tinguish myself. I think that what will really count for me is . . . Similarly, I think my biggest weakness is probably . . . If you agree, I'd love for you to address those issues."

- "I know that, as an athlete (or whatever label), I might be stereotyped by admissions committees as being a 'jock.' I want to set myself apart from other athletes and avoid these stereotypes. I think the best way to do that is . . ."

MAKING THE JOB EASY FOR YOUR RECOMMENDERS

Try to do as much of the work as you can for your recommenders, to make their job as simple as possible. Your recommenders are undoubtedly busy people and probably have many other college recommendations to write, in addition to yours. Allow them plenty of time to write the recommendation (two to three months is about right) and provide them with the following:

- The deadline for each application (and whether it is a postmark deadline or the day it must be in the admissions office)
- Stamped, addressed envelopes for each recommendation
- Several copies of each form, with the objective data about you (i.e., name, address, etc.) already filled in
- A list of the main points the person must discuss to satisfy the recommendation questions for all your target schools if he or she is writing a one-size-fits-all letter (discussed later in the chapter)
- Copies of your own application essays
- A description of your positioning strategy, noting strengths and weaknesses
- Samples of work you have done for the person, such as papers or tests
- A list of your extracurricular activities (including employment) and what you have gained from them (this is especially important for your guidance counselor's recommendation)
- A list of experiences and stories the recommender can use to support your positioning
- A résumé, if you have one

WHAT MAKES AN IDEAL RECOMMENDATION?

The ideal recommendation would show that you are an outstanding individual, one who is an appropriate candidate for a fine college by virtue of having the brains, personality, special talents, and leadership ability such schools are seeking. It would also support your individual positioning strategy. Such a recommendation would meet as many of the following criteria as possible.

- Be well-written. It should be grammatically correct and reflect the thinking of a well-educated person.

- Reflect substantial thought and effort on the part of the recommender. In other words, the writer shows he cares about you enough to spend the time to be as helpful as possible.

- Show the writer knows you well. It should provide highly specific examples to illustrate points. These generally should not be the same examples you use in your own essays or that other recommenders note, although some overlap is acceptable. As with your essays, the use of illustrative stories and examples will make the recommendation credible and memorable.

- Not mention things best handled elsewhere in the application. SAT scores, for example, usually have no place in a recommendation letter, unless the guidance counselor is mentioning them to explain extenuating circumstances that affected your performance.

- Show you to be distinctive. The use of examples helps make you an individual rather than a type.

- Discuss your growth and development over time.

- Explicitly compare you to others who have gone to the college, if possible.

- Show how you meet the requirements of the college and will add to the collegiate community.

Note that there are exceptions to the first requirement for a good recommendation letter, that it be well-written. For example, if you were to ask your student in an adult literacy program to write a recommendation for you, admissions officers would not expect it to contain perfect grammar and punctuation. On the contrary, part of the appeal of such a letter would be that it comes from someone outside the league of those with college-application know-how and that you are involved in helping that person, thereby improving your community. Similarly, if you were to ask an Outward Bound instructor to write you a recommendation, grammar mistakes and other imperfections would not be frowned on by college admissions officers because the purpose of this letter would be to address qualities not directly related to academics.

CAN RECOMMENDERS WRITE A ONE-SIZE-FITS-ALL RECOMMENDATION?

It is fine for a recommender to write a single letter of recommendation and attach it to the recommendation form for each school, *as long as it answers all of the questions that a school poses.* In other words, recommenders should not feel that they have to reinvent the wheel for each of your target schools, but they must be thorough and complete in performing their task. It is important that all recommenders realize the importance of explicitly answering all questions asked by each college. They must also fill out any required grids or checklists (concerning your qualities and abilities) that a school provides as part of its recommendation form if they choose to attach a one-size-fits-all recommendation letter.

In addition, there may be special cases in which a particular school should receive a slightly modified or amplified version of a recommendation letter. For example, if your recommender herself attended one of your target schools, she will want to make note of that in the recommendation.

LENGTH OF RECOMMENDATIONS

Colleges afford recommenders some latitude in choosing how best to write a recommendation. It is generally acceptable for a recommender to write more than is required if he feels it is necessary in order to give the best letter of support. Of course, length does not always equal quality, and some ideas are best conveyed concisely. Acceptable length varies with the quality of the letter of recommendation. A recommendation that is a bit too long according to the prescribed standard will not count against you.

TIMELINESS OF RECOMMENDATIONS

The schools can keep you informed as to whether a given recommendation has arrived. If it has not arrived and time is getting short, contact your recommender and ask very politely (not accusingly) how his effort is progressing and whether or not there is anything else you can do to make the process easier. This will tend to prod a recommender into action. Understand that, if you are notified that a recommendation is missing, there may have been a simple mailing or processing/sorting error rather than a failure by your recommender.

THE FOLLOW-UP

Be sure to send your recommenders a nice note thanking them for their efforts and stating that you will keep them informed of your progress. This is simple good manners and the least you can do to show appreciation in return for help in gaining admission to college.

Keep your recommenders informed as to each school's decision. Also be sure to tell them what you have decided to do in the end. At this point it would not be inappropriate to send them a small, inexpensive gift (e.g., flowers, chocolates, a book). Very few people do this and it is certainly not required. High school teachers are generally accustomed to writing recommendations and consider it part of their job—they certainly do not expect students to buy them gifts in return. But a small gesture might mean a lot to them.

Do your best to stay in touch with recommenders as you go through college, even if this means nothing more than dropping a postcard in the mail or sending them an occasional email with news of your progress.

WAIVING YOUR RIGHT TO SEE RECOMMENDATIONS: THE BUCKLEY AMENDMENT

The Buckley Amendment allows every applicant access to a college's files containing his or her recommendations. Admissions committees look more favorably on the recommendations of applicants who have waived the right to see them because they can be confident of the recommender's honesty and openness. Moreover, if you do not waive this right, admissions committees will question whether you have something to hide and doubt the fairness of your recommenders.

We encourage you to waive your right to access your recommendations. Waiving your right does not mean that you cannot ever see your recommendations. The amendment concerns your relationship with the college and its files and has no bearing whatsoever on your relationship with your recommender and the letter he has written. In other words, if the recommender chooses to share a recommendation with you, it is perfectly acceptable and legal for you to see it, even if you have waived your right to access the college's files. Note, however, that most high schools' policies prevent you from gaining access to your official recommendations, for good reasons.

14

INTERVIEWING

— KEY POINTS —

■

Establish your objectives: conveying a good impression, imparting your strengths, demonstrating your knowledge, and gaining information

■

Prepare yourself by:
—Learning the most likely questions
—Knowing yourself and your candidacy
—Knowing the school
—Formulating your own questions

■

Know what to expect from different types of interviewers:
—Admissions officers
—Alums
—Students

■

Practice via mock interviews

■

Familiarize yourself with the do's and don'ts of interviewing

INTRODUCTION

Many colleges interview their applicants. For many readers this is good news, since the interview will give you a chance to personalize your candidacy and present yourself in the best possible light.

Most of the very selective schools view the interview as important and want to interview most or all of their applicants for several reasons. One is the colleges' desire to admit outstanding *people* rather than just names attached to outstanding test scores and grades. An applicant's personality and social skills often "count." A related reason is that interviews offer schools the chance to learn more about applicants. Some things are not readily determinable without a face-to-face meeting. A high school student's interviewing ability can tell an admissions officer quite a bit about his presentation, maturity level, charm, confidence, sociability, and fit with the school. Thus, an applicant with good "paper" credentials will be less attractive to a school if she comes across poorly in an interview. Interviews also provide an opportunity to probe areas insufficiently addressed in the application itself.

A final reason for college admissions officers' love of interviews is that schools can market themselves better by meeting individually with applicants, even if the interview is conducted by an off-campus alum or a current student. This is particularly true for elite schools that compete for the best students each year. These schools welcome any chance to gain a voice through the interview, getting a jump on their rivals by better assessing candidates and promoting themselves to their top choices.

Not all colleges interview their applicants, though. Some do not interview because the size of their applicant pools prevents it; others do not believe the interview to be a sufficiently reliable indicator of future success to warrant the effort.

WHAT ADMISSIONS DIRECTORS SAY ABOUT THEIR INTERVIEWING POLICIES AND THE IMPORTANCE OF THE INTERVIEW

We want to talk to our applicants. Only in a rare case, if we have no alums in the applicant's area, would a student not interview—and even then, we usually try at the very least to do a phone interview.   *Marlyn McGrath Lewis, Harvard*

We especially encourage home-schooled applicants, older or nontraditional student applicants, and other people with special concerns to come to us for an interview. We'd like to talk to applicants with special situations so that we can better understand their cases when it comes time.   *John Blackburn, University of Virginia*

The interview isn't required. It's more of an opportunity for the candidate to get to know Brown.   *Michael Goldberger, Brown*

Bennington places great value on the interview. For us, having a conversation with students about their passions and their work is a critical part of our process—because dialogue is central to a great education. Through that process, students make connections between their interests and the breadth of a liberal arts curriculum.   *Ken Himmelman, Bennington*

It's more valuable for the applicant to learn about a college than for the college to learn about the applicant.   *Paul Thiboutot, Carleton*

At Williams, we do not require an interview. They are offered, but are informational rather than evaluative.   *Dick Nesbitt, Williams*

Interviewing can be very important. It's much harder not to admit a person than not to admit a file. If you have made the extra effort to add dimension to your application (whether through interviewing or through other means) you will have helped your case.   *Jennifer Rickard, Bryn Mawr*

We strongly encourage candidates to interview because it helps us get to know them on a more personal level, to learn more about the intangible qualities on which so many decisions are based.   *Jess Lord, Haverford*

THE NATURE OF THE INTERVIEW

Our interviews are meant to be personal exchanges rather than academic grillings. We try to have as natural a conversation as possible, so that a candidate has a chance to put his best foot forward.   *Jess Lord, Haverford*

We ask our alumni interviewers to try to ascertain candidates' strengths, what they are interested in, and where they have made a contribution.   *Douglas Christiansen, Vanderbilt*

I think of the interview like a conversation. I'm not trying to put the student on the spot. What I really want to know is what motivates her? What makes her happy or sad or angry? What gets her excited? The interview gives me a sense of the student beyond the grades and test scores; a sense of the person as three-dimensional. And while I appreciate this time to get to know the student, I think the interview is just as important for the student to get to know Smith. This is *her* time to get individual questions answered. This is *her* time to find out all she needs to know about the college so that she can make a good decision about fit.   *Debra Shaver, Smith*

We allow individuality to come through on the part of both the interviewer and the applicant. However, we encourage discussing academic interests, nonacademic interests, reading habits, extracurricular activities, career interests, and what they hope to get out of college.   *Paul Thiboutot, Carleton*

We often ask students to describe a project they worked on recently. Our unspoken rule is not to bring up a specific topic unless the student does first. *Thyra Briggs, Harvey Mudd*

GENERAL INTERVIEW ADVICE

Applicants should be themselves; the interview should confirm everything else we read in their files. The interview is not a moment to show off—it's a moment to have a conversation. *Janet Lavin Rapelye, Princeton*

What should students do to prepare for an interview? They should review the things that interest them—this is by and large what our interviewers want to know. How do you explore and pursue the things that interest you? Come prepared to talk about it. You like world politics? Great! How do you get involved? Do you read the newspaper every day? Are you in related student clubs? Say those answers out loud for practice. But beyond this preparation, relax and consider the interview to be simply a conversation about things that interest you. What could be more fun than talking about the things you like? That's all a good interview is. *Stuart Schmill, MIT*

Do your research and come prepared with a list of questions specific to the college. *Dick Nesbitt, Williams*

INTERVIEW PROCEDURES

Just as there is no one uniform interviewing policy, neither is there a singular interviewing procedure shared by the various colleges. Colleges have different systems for organizing and facilitating their interviews.

There are three different types of interviewers used by the colleges. Alums conduct interviews on behalf of colleges in their home locations across the United States and overseas as well. Admissions officers conduct interviews on campus and while traveling across the country on high school visits. Finally, some colleges have recently adopted the practice of using current college students to interview future candidates on campus. Some colleges use only one type of interviewer, whereas others use a combination of resources—alumni, admissions officers, current students—to conduct their interviews.

CONFIDENTIALITY ISSUES

There is no reason to worry about sharing personal information or information contained within your application materials with the two varieties of "unofficial" interview administrators (i.e., alums and current students). The colleges understand concerns over privacy and have generally taken measures to address the issue. Many schools give interviewers nothing more than a briefing on an applicant prior to an interview. In other words, a non–admissions officer interviewer most likely does not have access to your test scores, grades, recommendations, or essays. Other schools have students and alums sign confidentiality agreements to ensure that they do not discuss the cases of the candidates they interview. All interviewers are expected to take the interviewing process very seriously and not to discuss candidates' private issues and concerns with other people.

Schools use interview results slightly differently. The great majority of the colleges give the interview no formalized weight factor in the evaluation process. A few schools assign a rating to each candidate based on his or her interview results. Most colleges place the interview report as the last piece of information in an applicant's folder, so it is the last document a reader reviews in a file. The interview evaluation therefore often takes on the responsibility of sealing a case. At schools where admissions officers themselves interview applicants, the interview has even more power because the interviewer is present at committee meetings to act as an advocate or naysayer on behalf of the applicant. Most colleges confirm that the interview rarely "breaks" a case, but it can sometimes "make" one when a borderline candidate gets a rave review from an interviewer, especially an admissions officer interviewer.

ADMISSIONS DIRECTORS OFFER OPINIONS ON AN INTERVIEW'S ABILITY TO INFLUENCE A DECISION

Interviews are not more or less important than other aspects of the file. No one piece of a file is likely to make or break an application—it's the combination that matters. *Janet Lavin Rapelye, Princeton*

Interviews can be extremely important. If there is a student who is a borderline admit, having made the effort to come interview can make all the difference. If someone makes the trip to see us, that is very meaningful to us. *Paul Marthers, Reed*

I believe 90 percent of interviews confirm what's already in the folder. *James Bock, Swarthmore*

Interviews inform and supplement in an important way, but they are not a deciding factor. *David Borus, Vassar*

The interview is probably the first thing we'd discard in a file—if everything else pointed to a spectacular candidate but the interview was so-so, we'd probably ignore the interview report. *Richard Steele, Bowdoin*

SHOULD YOU INTERVIEW IF GIVEN A CHOICE?

If a school "strongly recommends" or even "recommends" that applicants interview, it is usually a mistake not to do so, as long as an interview can be conveniently arranged given your location or college visit schedule. Failing to interview (or at least to attempt to set up an interview) may be taken as an indication of a lack of interest in the school or a tacit admission that you do poorly in one-on-one situations. Most admissions officers thus agree that it is usually a mistake to decline an interview.

There are often logistical considerations, of course, and schools are aware that it may not be realistic to expect you to travel 3,000 miles for an interview, especially if you are from a low-income background or have already visited the campus. Logistical barriers are rare these days, though, because the colleges that conduct interviews generally send their representatives to major regions on a regular basis and have alums scattered throughout the country and worldwide.

Although it is almost always appropriate to interview, if you are certain you will make a poor impression, either take steps to improve your interviewing skills or maneuver to avoid an interview. The people who should probably avoid interviews include:

- Those who are pathologically shy (not just the ordinary variety of shy)
- Those whose English language abilities will crack under the strain of an interview
- Those who are so contentious that they will inevitably get into a verbal battle with their interviewer
- Obviously anorexic girls (or boys, although they rarely fit into the anorexic stereotype that troubles admissions officers)

The preceding types of college candidates should consider not interviewing if given a choice because their individual problems might get in the way of their performing well in an interview and impressing the interviewer. Those who are desperately shy or whose English language skills might cause problems in a nerve-wracking situation might stumble too much in an interview to do themselves any good. Those whose anger or contentiousness tends to get them in trouble in social situations should avoid personal contact with those involved in the admissions process.

ADMISSIONS DIRECTORS DISCUSS HOW APPLICANTS ARE VIEWED WHEN THEY CHOOSE NOT TO INTERVIEW

Interviews are recommended, but it is not at all a problem if a student doesn't do one. If an interview evaluation is in the file, we look at it. The absence of an interview evaluation in a student's file is neutral, not negative. *Christoph Guttentag, Duke*

We strongly recommend personal interviews. However, we recognize that some are unable to come to campus to have one. If you find yourself in this position, let us know. We may have an alumnus in your area who can conduct the interview, or we might be out your way on an admissions trip. Most important is to communicate your interest to us. *Tim Cheney, Connecticut College*

Choosing not to interview doesn't have a huge impact unless the applicant lives nearby. If they do and don't interview, it looks a little odd. *Thyra Briggs, Harvey Mudd*

We don't penalize an applicant for not doing an interview. What we don't like is if an applicant doesn't show up for one, or if he cancels and reschedules a bunch of times. Alums tell us these things, and this kind of behavior makes us wonder how serious the candidate is about Penn. *Eric Kaplan, Penn*

If you turn down the opportunity to interview, it may be viewed as an expression of disinterest. *Robert Clagett, Middlebury*

Not interviewing doesn't have a negative impact at all. The interview is meant to be a plus—a chance to enhance your application. It can only add; it can't take away from the strength of an application. *Douglas Christiansen, Vanderbilt*

If a student decides not to do an interview after being contacted by our alum, then it's always a good idea to tell us why. Write us a letter to the effect that, "I think I communicated all my information well in the application. I have visited the school, and have no further questions. I'm having scheduling difficulties." If the applicant just doesn't call back the alum when contacted, then that reflects badly on him or her. *Eric J. Furda, Columbia*

PREPARING FOR THE INTERVIEW

The interview is important to the college for the reasons listed earlier. It is important for you, the candidate, as well—because it means that you have the opportunity to pitch yourself. To be a good interviewee, you need to have prepared the points you want to get across, anticipate what questions will be asked, and understand how to enhance your presentation to satisfy your needs and those of your interviewer. In other words, you should analyze what you will confront and then practice performing under realistic conditions. Doing this will help you avoid going blank, letting things you intended not to share slip out, forgetting to mention important points, or being unable to keep the interview flowing in a comfortable fashion.

Some candidates are afraid of the interview and set themselves hopelessly limited objectives for it. They hope to get through it without embarrassing themselves. Or they hope that the interviewer is simply "nice," smiling a lot and seeming to be mildly interested in the conversation. You have the chance to make a very positive impression that will further your application efforts, so it is up to you to seize it. Do not simply hope to survive the interview and extract pleasantries from your interviewer. Set higher goals for yourself: Be determined to achieve positive results. Use the interview to reinforce the positioning efforts you have used in your essays and recommendations.

You already have a positioning strategy in place, so go back to it when you are considering what you hope to accomplish in the interview. If you have positioned yourself as a virtuoso violinist whose talent has led him to an interest in late European music history, for example, this positioning strategy will help you think through the interview and how to prepare for it.

Ask yourself the following questions when beginning your preparations:

1. How do I want the interviewer to think of me? What specific impressions and information do I want her to carry away from our meeting?

2. How can I reinforce my strengths and address my key weaknesses?

3. How can I show that I know a great deal about the school—not only that I am extremely interested in attending the college but also that I am prepared for the interview?

4. How can I learn whatever I need to know to decide what school to attend?

TYPICAL INTERVIEW FORMAT

■ A welcome from the interviewer.

■ A few chatty, basic warm-up questions from the interviewer. These might include questions such as, "Did you find the interview location all right?" or "How are you?"

■ A comment or two from the interviewer about the school, its future, and the admissions process.

■ Detailed questions from the interviewer, which may lead to a back-and-forth discussion. Most interviewers start with some sort of general question, such as asking you to describe your personal background (including where you grew up, your family, etc.) and your high school education.

■ An opportunity for the interviewee to ask questions.

■ An exchange of thank-yous and a good-bye.

THE INTERVIEW FORMAT

A typical interview will last between twenty and sixty minutes. The first few minutes of an interview may not involve substantive discussion, but they are still important in forming the interviewer's general impression of you. Therefore, do your best to appear confident and relaxed when answering initial questions, before reaching the heart of the interview.

THE INTERVIEWER

You can expect different things of an interviewer depending on whether he is an admissions officer, an alum, or a student. Here are some guidelines on what you are likely to encounter with each type of interviewer.

INTERVIEWS WITH ADMISSIONS OFFICERS

An interview with an admissions officer is likely to be the most formal, although not necessarily the most difficult, of the three types of meetings. Admissions officers will conduct themselves in a gracious and poised manner—their job is not only to find out more about you but also to leave you with positive impressions of their school. They are thus likely to consider an interview as much a public relations opportunity as anything else. Admissions officers have plenty of experience interviewing and socializing, so they should not leave you feeling uncomfortable or lead you astray in your discussions. In addition, college admissions personnel are accustomed to dealing with high-school-aged students—they generally like young people and understand teenage modes of behavior and dress, so you probably do not have to be as careful with them as you might with alumni interviewers, who likely do not interact with people your age on a regular basis.

If you have already made an application to the college at the time of interviewing, admissions officers will know more about you and your background than will alumni or student interviewers because they have access to all pieces of information in your file. Therefore, you need to be careful to prepare to expand on or supplement information included in your written application when interviewing with admissions officers in order to avoid boring them with repetitious details.

An admissions officer will be extremely well prepared and thorough. This does not mean, however, that he will spend a great deal of time with you. On the contrary, an admissions staffer's busy schedule will probably keep an interview short rather than allowing it to run overtime.

An admissions officer will want to gain some definite opinions about how your past experience and career goals suit you for his school's program, but that does not mean he will be uninterested in your personal life or in getting a feel for your general demeanor. Do not become a straight-and-narrow bore in front of the admissions folks! Be serious, but not overly so. Admissions personnel are concerned about filling their programs with lively candidates who offer more than just good grades and admirable future goals.

An admissions representative will obviously have the most thorough knowledge of the "official" aspects of the college, such as its opportunities for study abroad and its strongest departments or fields. But he will not necessarily know much about how to get involved in the college's annual animation festival or what life in the dorms is all about. A recent grad doing a stint in the admissions office, though, can be a fantastic resource regarding all aspects of the program—formal and informal, academic and social. She essentially represents all three roles wrapped up in one: admissions officer, alum, and college student.

INTERVIEWS WITH ALUMNI

An interview with an alum is likely to be the most relaxed and easiest of the three kinds of meetings. (Obviously, this is not *always* the case. An occasional alum will approach her role with a hard-nosed determination to let only the best applicants shine.) In most cases, alums who volunteer their time to interview applicants do so because they are personable, friendly types who like to meet new people and are basically interested in promoting their schools.

Alumni interviews generally take place in the alum's home, in the alum's office, or at a public meeting space such as a coffee shop. Interviews that are conducted in an alum's home tend to be more relaxed and perhaps a bit longer than those that take place outside the home. Interviews with alums in their offices might seem more formal because of the setting and the interviewer's naturally more serious demeanor while at the workplace. Some alums, particularly older ones, will be more sensitive to appearance and language than will admissions officers or students, both of whom are accustomed to being around college-aged students, with their sometimes radical dress codes and casual lingo. Err on the cautious side when dressing for an alumni interview—especially if you know ahead of time that the person is older—and be especially careful with your speech and behavior during the interview.

You can assume that the alum will have received some limited information about you, but her knowledge of you and your candidacy is likely to be sparse. She will probably not have seen enough of your application to know what your weaknesses are, and thus will not challenge you on these points. By the same token, she will not know your strengths and positive attributes, so to make a good impression, you might have to talk at length about ideas you have already expressed in your essays and supporting materials. It is certainly fine to ask your interviewer, if she does not offer the information herself, how much background material she has been given so that you know what to talk about and what not to repeat.

Alumni interviewers are instructed to follow certain guidelines, so expect them to ask some crucial questions—but most will not be as meticulous or sharpshooting as an admissions officer or student interviewer. Alums tend to be chattier, more relaxed, and more interested in selling their beloved schools (or recounting their glory days for you) than they are in grilling you or using hardball tactics. An interview with an alum might feel more like a conversation with your mom's friend at a holiday party than the intimidating or stressful experience you might conjure up in your nightmares. It will be unlike the casual conversations you have with friends your own age, yet it might not be scary or uncomfortable.

One drawback of having an alumni interview is that your interviewer will not be present in admissions committee meetings to personally push your case and, furthermore, might not know how to formulate a winning position to support your application. Although schools that use alumni interviewers take their opinions seriously, an alum can convey his opinion about you only through a written evaluation that he sends in to the admissions office after your meeting. Even with a favorable impression of you, if he is not an effective or convincing writer, his evaluation might not exude the necessary enthusiasm to make a serious impact on the admissions committee when they sit down to review your file. He may be relatively unpracticed in the art of admissions and might not know what it takes to push an applicant from reject to waitlist status, or from waitlist to admit status. A professional admissions officer interviewer, on the contrary, not only will know how to convey a proper argument for a candidate, but might also be able to argue her case in person at an admissions committee session.

Another drawback of having an alumni interview is that those who have not been part of the school for some time will know the least about it. In other words, if you are hoping that your interview will provide a great opportunity to learn more about a school's program and how it compares to others, an interview with an alum who has been out of school five years or more might leave you unsatisfied. Even if an alum graduated fairly recently, it is likely that certain aspects of the school have changed since her time or are currently in the process of revision.

INTERVIEWS WITH CURRENT STUDENTS

Student-led interviews are not the norm, but some schools use them. Students compete heavily for these coveted honorary positions on the campus and are thoroughly trained before having contact with applicants.

The schools that use student interviewers believe that candidates for admission regard interviews with students as being easier than other kinds—and that they may thus benefit from feeling "less pressure" in the interview session. But do not be fooled into thinking that an interview with a current student will be a cinch. As rookies, students tend to be less smooth in their interviewing tactics. A student interviewer may have trouble keeping the conversation flowing or thinking of things to say, in which case your job will be that much more difficult. He may even be just as nervous and ill-at-ease as you are. Of course, this is not usually the case. The students admissions offices recruit to conduct interviews of applicants are selected in part for their good communication skills and comfort acting as representatives of the school.

Student interviewers generally have very little access to your application file. Students are not privy to sensitive or confidential materials, so will know little about you going in. You may have more ability to take the ball and run with it rather than waiting for specific questions or prompts.

Students often ask applicants very tough questions. Sometimes they simply do not have enough perspective and life experience to realize what is and is not important. Furthermore, because they are so steeped in the intricacies of the college experience, they naturally have a lot of interview material at their immediate disposal. They know what life at the school is like, and thus can come up with very directed questions, maybe even ones that are so specific that they seem useless for obtaining relevant "big picture" information about you.

But some student interviewers are likely to be as bouncy, friendly, and relaxed as alums—people with whom you will feel at home, with whom you could imagine becoming friends. You are fortunate if this is the case, but remember to be alert and serious; do not let your guard down just because you see a friendly and welcoming face in front of you. You want to match your interviewer's demeanor, but do not forget that this interview "counts," which means that you must promote yourself and why you should be admitted to the college. Selling yourself to a current student is a bit tricky, because you do not want to appear cocky or obnoxious. It is easier to market yourself aggressively to a more official administrator, whose job it is to be impressed with you, than it is to someone on a peer level.

An interview with a student is likely to be the most useful for your own fact-finding purposes. Because students are themselves involved in the day-to-day operations of the school, they will be able to give accurate answers to many of your most detailed questions. You will probably feel more at ease asking them about the nonacademic side of collegiate life as well. But be astute about the types of questions you ask—by the end of the interview, you will probably be able to sense whether or not your student interviewer will welcome the kinds of casual or odd inquiries that you would probably not dare to ask an admissions officer. If a student interviewer, for example, jokes with you about how wonderful he found the Pass-Fail option to be when he realized he was not doing well in an English class, it is probably fine to ask him how many times a student at the college is allowed to use the Pass-Fail option; on the other hand, if your interviewer seems particularly serious about academics or mentions that he thinks the grading scale at the college is too lax, it is not a good idea to ask him this kind of thing.

ADMISSIONS DIRECTORS TALK ABOUT THE VARIOUS KINDS OF INTERVIEWERS

WHO CONDUCTS INTERVIEWS?

We have limited on-campus interviews with admissions staff provided on a first-come, first-served basis. But even if a candidate does one of these interviews on campus, he or she will normally also be invited by an alum in the hometown to do an interview. *Marlyn McGrath Lewis, Harvard*

Our admissions staff will speak informally with candidates, but 100 percent of the formal interviews are done by alumni. *Douglas Christiansen, Vanderbilt*

Here in the office, it's mainly admissions counselors who conduct interviews. There are a few rising seniors who interview during the summer. The bulk of our admissions interviews—75 to 80 percent—is done by alumni interviewers. *Robert Clagett, Middlebury*

HOW ARE STUDENT INTERVIEWERS USED?

We have twelve highly trained seniors who interview for us. I love this aspect of our admissions—the only problem with it is that parents sometimes think it's a second-rate interview, which is not the case at all. It's the real thing. *Richard Steele, Bowdoin*

Using student interviewers seems to put less pressure on the candidate. I think applicants see them as being easier to talk to, and they probably get a much better feel for the school through them. *Maria Laskaris, Dartmouth*

IS THERE ANY ADVANTAGE TO BEING INTERVIEWED BY ONE SORT OF INTERVIEWER RATHER THAN ANOTHER?

We have three different groups of interviewers: admissions officers, college seniors (about ten, who are well trained), and alumni volunteers. There is no advantage to being interviewed by one type rather than another. *Paul Thiboutot, Carleton*

There is no advantage to being interviewed by an admissions officer, a student, or an alumni interviewer. All interviewers work off of the same evaluation form. We try to keep the playing field level on this front. *Robert Clagett, Middlebury*

Here are some generalities that usually apply to interviews with the three kinds of interviewers:

	ADMISSIONS OFFICER	**ALUM**	**STUDENT**
Formality of Interview	High	Medium	Low
Ability to Influence Admissions Decision	Strong	Weak	Medium
Sensitivity to Appearance and Language	Medium	High	Low
Prior Knowledge of You	Access to Entire Application	Little Knowledge	Little Knowledge
Knowledge of School	"Official" Knowledge (i.e., about Student Body, Majors Offered, Strength of Departments, Housing Options, etc.)	Little Knowledge (Unless Very Recent Graduate)	"Official" and "Unofficial" Knowledge (i.e., Info on Quality of Food, Social Options, etc.)

UNDERSTANDING YOUR INTERVIEWING OBJECTIVES

KNOWING THE COLLEGE

Chapter 3, "Deciding Where to Apply," examines many criteria relevant to the decision about where to attend. It also details how to find the information necessary for making a well-informed decision. Now that you are preparing for interviews, it would be a good idea to review the information you put together on each school with which you will interview. In particular, you should be extremely familiar with the information that the college publishes about itself. If you tell the interviewer that you plan to major in business, but the school offers no undergraduate business major, you will look foolish (not to mention looking like a bad fit for the college).

If you are going to interview on the campus itself, try to spend several hours in advance exploring the school and its environment. Talk with students in the cafeteria or student center, paying attention to the attitudes they evince. Are they generally happy there? Do they respect their professors? Is the social life adequate? Do they think the career services center does a good job of counseling students before sending them out into the real world? Are there any major issues, such as campus crime or lack of late-night library hours, that might matter to you? It always impresses an interviewer to see that you have taken the time and effort to examine the school up close rather than just reading some brochures or materials off the Web. Knowing what type of housing is available, or which courses students line up to get into, is the sort of thing that shows you to be determined, interested, and resourceful. It also helps you develop good questions to ask the interviewer without sounding artificial. Even if you are not interviewing on campus, take advantage of any opportunities to visit schools or talk to students by telephone for precisely these reasons.

**THE ADVANTAGES OF KNOWING A COLLEGE
THOROUGHLY BEFORE INTERVIEWING**

- Feeling prepared will enable you to relax somewhat during the interview and feel confident.

- You will be able to ask intelligent questions about the school, thereby impressing the interviewer and helping yourself to further determine the college's suitability for your needs.

- You will be able to convey your "fit" with the college to the interviewer.

- You will show yourself to be highly motivated, concerned about your future, and in possession of the right work ethic.

ANTICIPATING THE INTERVIEW QUESTIONS

You must also prepare for your interview by thinking about what questions you might be asked beforehand. The interviewer is likely to have two types of questions to ask you. One type includes the questions that are addressed to all applicants, such as "Why do you want to attend college X?" The other type includes responses to your file or to your comments during the interview. If you have claimed in your written application to have founded a new successful literary journal at your high school, for example, your interviewer might ask you about this endeavor to find out more or to ascertain that you have not exaggerated. She might ask you, for example, what your greatest barrier to starting the journal was, or what kinds of literature you personally enjoy most. Your interviewer might also want to probe your weaknesses or problems with your high school record. If, for example, you have one remarkably weak grade that stands out on your report card, she might want you to explain your troubles with the class.

If you are prepared to answer the questions listed here, you will be ready for just about anything that can come up. Preparing for these questions, separated into four categories, will force you to think through all the main issues that are of interest to colleges. Some interviewers may spend more time asking you questions about your personal life than about your academic interests; likewise, some interviewers may not ever touch on a certain subject matter, such as your postcollegiate goals.

Academic Life and Interests

- What is your favorite subject in high school? Why?
- What is your least favorite subject in high school? Why?
- What do you like most about your high school?
- What do you like least about your high school?
- How have you grown academically during high school?
- What have you found most challenging about high school?
- Who is your favorite teacher? Why?
- Who is your least favorite teacher? Why?
- What is your greatest academic accomplishment?
- What is your greatest academic failure?
- How do you compare with others in your high school class in terms of academic performance and academic effort?
- Are you more concerned with getting good grades, or do you ever enjoy learning for learning's sake?
- Is your record an accurate reflection of your abilities?
- If you had to start high school over again, what would you do differently?

College and Future Goals

- Why do you want to go to college?
- Why do you want to attend this college?
- What are you most looking forward to when you reach college?
- What are your most important criteria in looking at colleges?
- If you were prevented from going to college, what would you do instead?
- What do you think your major will be in college?
- What are your future career goals?
- How will attending our college help you reach your goals?
- What is most important to you in your life?

Personal Life

- Tell me about yourself, including your family background and where you grew up.
- How would your friends and family describe your personality?
- How would you describe your best and most valuable friendships?
- What is your favorite book? Why?
- What book—not assigned for a class—have you read most recently?
- What book has affected you most? How?
- Who is your favorite author? Why?
- What magazines or newspapers do you read regularly? Why? What sections do you most enjoy?
- What is your favorite movie? Why?
- What is your favorite TV show? Why?
- How do you feel about [certain current events, whatever has been dominating the headlines]?
- If you were the president of the United States, what one issue would you address before any others?
- How do you spend your free time?
- What activity do you enjoy/value most? Why?
- What person has most influenced you in your life to date?
- If you could meet one person, past or present, who would it be? Why?
- Who are your heroes? Why?
- If a genie were to grant you three wishes, what would you ask for?

- What is your greatest personal accomplishment?
- What is your greatest personal failure?
- Why should we accept you?

Extracurricular Activities

- What extracurricular activity are you most committed to? Why?
- What has been your greatest contribution to an extracurricular activity or group?
- Please give an example of an activity in which you have demonstrated leadership.
- Please give an example of an activity in which you have displayed good teamwork and cooperation skills.
- Are you a better leader or follower? How has this changed (if at all) in the past few years?
- Please give an example of a time when you were accorded a large responsibility. How did you handle it?
- What is your greatest extracurricular success?
- What is your greatest extracurricular failure?
- If given a choice, would you choose to join an activity in which you would work alone, with friends, with strangers, or with your family?
- In hindsight, is there any high school activity you wish you had participated in but did not?

THE MOST COMMON INTERVIEW QUESTIONS

- Tell me about yourself.
- What do you envision yourself doing professionally after college?
- Why do you want to attend this particular college?
- Why should we accept you?
- What would you add to our campus and our student body?
- What is your favorite subject in high school? Why?
- Tell me about your extracurricular activities.
- What is your favorite book? Why?
- What do you like most about your high school? What do you like least about your high school?

- How have you grown both personally and academically during high school?
- Who is your favorite teacher? Why?
- What questions do you have?

THE TEN MOST IMPORTANT TIPS FOR ANSWERING THE QUESTIONS

1. Maintain a positive attitude. Avoid complaining, whining, or blaming failures or problems on someone or something else.

2. Use correct grammar (see "Death by Impaired Speech" on the next page).

3. Show that you are committed to learning.

4. If there are glitches in your academic record, show that you have since compensated for those failures and mistakes.

5. If you have changed your academic or extracurricular focus several times (or have no focus), show that you have become serious about one of your recent endeavors to the extent that you plan to continue with it.

6. Discuss leadership experiences.

7. You are certainly not expected to have set your career goals in stone while in high school, but show that you are aware of some professional possibilities, given your current interests and strengths.

8. Remember that it does not much matter what your personal interests are (i.e., whether you like to play field hockey, read science fiction, or play the trombone)—what matters is that you show passion and commitment to your interests.

9. Be sure that you can have a sophisticated discussion about any heroes or historical figures you mention, as well as about any books or authors that you bring up. You should know "the facts," but also have developed your own viewpoint regarding these topics.

10. It is always a good idea to be up on current events when going on college interviews. If you do not already do so, read a good newspaper such as the *New York Times* regularly. Another way of becoming well-versed in current affairs is to read the *Economist* every week, particularly the lead articles in the first few pages of each issue. The *New Republic*, the *Atlantic Monthly*, and the *New Yorker* are some of the other sophisticated and well-written magazines that will help you become more informed and give you provocative material to learn from and reflect on.

DEATH BY IMPAIRED SPEECH

Educated adult interviewers often find their interviewee's speech off-putting. It's bad enough to listen to dreadful mistakes of grammar ("me and George went to Chicago"—rather than "George and I went to Chicago"). Far worse is having to listen to teen-speak nonsense such as:

- Hey or yo (instead of hello, hi, or how do you do?)
- Totally (as in "dude, it was totally great")
- Awesome
- Like (when used incorrectly over and over. Sensible adults assume those using "like" multiple times in an average sentence have double-digit IQs. Of course, they are predisposed to be kind.)
- Wazzup

Make sure to scrub your speech clean of this sort of twaddle well before you get to the interviewing stage.

PREPARING TO DESCRIBE KEY EVENTS

You should be ready to discuss major and minor events and milestones in your academic, personal, and extracurricular life. Some interviewers prefer to ask very general, open-ended questions; part of the test here is to see how well you can develop an organized, intelligent response. In other words, a general, open-ended question should not be answered with the same; your answers should, for the most part, always be detailed and specific. You must color your discussions with detailed incidents and situations, paying special attention to "inflection points," or points of change in your life. These locators along your personal timeline will help you develop narratives about your life that make sense and offer reasonable explanations for success, failure, strengths, weaknesses, preferences, values, attachment to ideas, the development of passions, etc. Your inflection points might include, for example, the semester in which your grades began to improve; the period during which your parents' divorce began to burden you less; the fencing tournament at which you lost your first match; your move to a new neighborhood, which allowed you to attend a smaller and better school; or the year in which your dad lost his job, forcing you to get part-time work and take on more family responsibility. The ability to identify inflection points, explain their causes, and analyze their effects will help create sensible discussions of your life events.

In preparation, it is useful to write down the half dozen or more important incidents you expect to discuss on index cards. Carry these cards with you for reading when you are waiting for the bus or have a spare moment. Learn them well enough that you can produce a well-organized, apparently spontaneous summary of each of them at the drop of a hat, but do not memorize stories by rote.

DOING PRACTICE INTERVIEWS

There are two ways that you can practice your interviewing skills and responses. The first is by doing mock interviews with others who are applying to college or someone else who appreciates what is involved. This is a good first step to understanding what an interview will be like. The quality of the experience will depend in large part on how prepared your interviewing partner is. If you can find someone who is willing to read your application carefully, and perhaps even read this chapter, then you will most likely have a good practice interview. The ideal person to team up with is someone who understands the college admissions process and is willing to be tough with you. A parent is generally not ideal. A parent knows you too intimately to be able to ask useful questions and look at you from an outsider's perspective; furthermore, most parents tend to be either too soft or too demanding on their children in mock interviews. A teacher or adult whom you trust (and whom you feel comfortable asking to help you) is ideal.

Practice interviewing in several different settings or positions: facing your interviewer with a desk separating the two of you; in a comfortable armchair (which is not always so comfortable when attempting to sit up straight and maintain a serious conversation) angled beside your interviewer's chair; at a table in a restaurant. This way you will be able to practice maintaining eye contact in a variety of different positions as well as catch any annoying habits that might not be noticeable from all angles, such as nervously swinging your foot back and forth. Wear your interview outfit (including jewelry and any "extras" that need to pass inspection for their suitability in an interview setting). Practice your entrance into the room, your handshake, your initial greeting, and the chatty conversation that precedes the serious questions. Practice your final questions, your thank-you, and your exit from the room as well.

Your interview partner can evaluate all aspects of your presentation, from the firmness of your handshake to the impact of your answers. She can tell you which responses were convincing and which were not (and why). Force your interview partner to be specific in noting what worked and what did not. After all, it is not what you say but what your interviewer hears that determines the success of your interview. In fact, simply saying things out loud will often cause *you* to hear what is not right. Speaking out loud often makes it clear that you are wandering instead of staying focused, trying too hard to excuse some prior mistake, or pleading rather than convincing.

Tape-recording—or, better yet, videotaping—your practice sessions will help make your interviewing strengths and weaknesses apparent to you as well.

If you can videotape your practice sessions, by all means do so. Your high school might give special permission to you to use videotaping equipment for this purpose if you do not have access to such equipment at home. Seeing yourself in action will help you eliminate extreme gestures and repetitive phrasings. Particularly annoying (and particularly prevalent among high schoolers) is the awful-sounding and inappropriate use of phrases such as "like," "you know," and "whatever." Although admissions officers and students may be somewhat used to teenage habits, your use of these speech patterns will certainly not help your case. Alum interviewers may become altogether turned off by your "teen speak," seeing it as a sign of immaturity, imprecision, or lack of intelligence. Wear your interview outfit on the video to be sure that it passes muster, too.

The second means of practicing is to be sure that you interview first with your safety schools. If you are applying to three "likely" choices, make sure your first interviews are with these colleges rather than the "possibles" or "reaches." This allows you to develop and refine your pitch and get rid of your first interview nerves without having too much at stake.

OTHER INTERVIEW PREPARATIONS

PHYSICAL ENERGY

Be sure to get plenty of sleep the two nights before the day of the interview. It is standard practice for marathon runners and other athletes to get plenty of sleep both the night before a big event and the night before that, in order to maximize the amount of energy and concentration available to them. This same practice can be applied to test taking, interviewing, and other events requiring peak mental performance. It is, for obvious reasons, not a good idea to schedule an interview immediately after an exam or paper for which you know you will be pulling an all-nighter.

APPEARANCE

It is no longer absolutely necessary to wear your fanciest clothes or your most conservative outfit to a college interview. College administrators are by now quite used to the diverse appearances of college-age students and should not penalize you for your dress or personal presentation if it does not meet their taste. As long as you appear respectful and make it clear that you put an effort into looking neat and presentable, you should be fine.

Appearing respectful of the admissions staff and showing that you take the college admissions process seriously basically involve appearing neat and clean and not wearing anything that would be considered inappropriate for obvious reasons. Be sure you have bathed and that your clothes show no stains or rips. Avoid jeans. Do not wear wildly strong cologne or perfume. (It is a good idea not to wear any at all.) You should not wear cutoffs (shorts in general should be avoided), tank tops, baseball caps or sunglasses (indoors), clothing bearing foul or inappropriate language, or sloppy beach-type shoes. If wearing a tie, men should make sure it is centered and the knot is pulled up high and tight at the collar rather than hanging loosely. By no means should women ever wear a skirt that is very short (slightly above the knee is probably the shortest length you should consider) or blouses that are too tight or revealing. Makeup should be tame, not out of control. Boys should always consider bringing an extra tie (in case you get a stain) and girls an extra pair of stockings (in case you get a run) if these are part of your outfit.

LOGISTICAL PREPARATION

Be sure that you have exact directions to the interview site and know where to park. Parking can be a big problem on college campuses (and many urban off-campus locations), so you should inquire ahead of time so you do not waste time (or get a parking ticket) when you get there. Arrive at the site slightly before the scheduled interview time so that you can find the restroom to check your appearance, go to the bathroom, and generally gather your thoughts and compose yourself.

You should take with you a copy of the college's brochure as well as copies of your application (to review or give to the interviewer) and a résumé. You might also want to bring along index cards with interview notes on them to review before going in to the discussion. Also be sure to bring the name and telephone number of the admissions office or of your off-campus interviewer so that you can call if you have a travel emergency.

STAY RELAXED!

A modest degree of nervousness is good because it gives you the energy to perform at your best. If you tend to be too nervous, try one of these techniques to keep yourself calm.

- Remind yourself that you have prepared thoroughly (assuming you have followed the directions in this chapter) and that this preparation will see you through.

- Remind yourself that college admissions interviewers are aware that for many high schoolers, the college interview is the first interview they have ever experienced, and that they will excuse your jitters.

- Acting positive, by using the appropriate body language, will help you to feel the way you are acting. Keep your head up, your shoulders square, your back straight, and your eyes forward. Do not wring your hands or make nervous repetitive gestures. Your body should be still (avoid swinging a leg or drumming your fingers on the table) but not stiff.

- While in the restroom before the interview, take a deep breath and close your eyes for a minute to compose yourself.

DURING THE INTERVIEW

Your goal is to answer the questions thoroughly, support your profile, and appear interesting as well as interested in the college. College admissions officers (and most alums and students who partake in the interview process) are aware that nervousness is common. They know that getting into college means the world to you and that you may not be practiced in interviewing techniques. So remember that you do not have to appear to have the confidence of Humphrey Bogart when you walk in the door. Still, you should try your best to remain poised and thoughtful throughout the interview. Even though the standards are not particularly high, you will certainly get good marks for being a pro. Follow this good advice, no matter what kind of interview you are preparing for:

General Appearance and Demeanor

- Greet the interviewer with a smile, an extended hand, and a firm handshake (match the interviewer's pressure, but do not use a death grip).

- Look the interviewer in the eye upon greeting him.

- Do not sit down until you are invited to do so and told where to do so.

- Do not put anything on the interviewer's desk.

- Do not smoke, or eat or drink anything awkward to handle.

- Remain physically at ease, without fidgeting. Do not fiddle with jewelry or belongings. Refrain from twirling your hair, drumming your fingers, bouncing your leg up and down, or picking at a part of your body or clothing. Many people have a tic of which they are completely unaware. Use your mock interview partner or videotape to determine if you have one, and then work on putting an end to it in the weeks before your interview.

- Do not chew gum or play with orthodonture.

■ Maintain a moderate amount of eye contact throughout the interview, but do not stare.

■ Gesticulate moderately to make points, but do not go overboard.

■ Maintain good rapport with the interviewer by being warm and smiling often. Do not, however, smile without stopping throughout the entire interview!

■ Sit up straight, but not too rigidly, and lean forward slightly, rather than slouching. This shows that you are serious, are interested in what the interviewer has to say, and are excited about conveying your own thoughts.

■ Avoid crossing your arms in front of you or folding them up above your head.

■ Keep your voice well-modulated and lively. Speak at a normal speed. Do not rush—this generally indicates nervousness or a lack of confidence.

Attitude and Presentation of Ideas

■ Be upbeat and positive. Be sure to emphasize your strengths.

■ Do not complain or whine about anything.

■ Do not criticize others. You may be viewed as a chronic malcontent or worse.

■ Assume that any interviewer who is not an admissions officer has not had access to your entire file of information.

■ Be truthful. Do not lie in answering questions. Being honest, however, does not mean the same thing as being blunt, so do not volunteer negative information if it can be avoided.

■ Be yourself. Do not pretend to be someone other than yourself to impress the interviewer. Very few people are able to act well enough to carry this off successfully. Focus instead on presenting the best aspects of your own personality.

■ Do not try to take over the interview, but take advantage of opportunities to make your points. Interviewers want to feel that they are in charge of an interview, since they are likely to make decisions based on the information they get about you. They need to feel confident that they will be able to get information relevant to their decision making, which may happen only if they are able to direct the interview. Taking over the interview may allow you to make the points you want to make, but the risk is far too great that your interviewer will react negatively to this and resent your aggressiveness. Use of polite phrases in a confident tone of voice can keep your interviewer from fearing that you are trying to take over the discussion:

"Perhaps you wouldn't mind my sharing . . ." or "Would it be helpful if I were to expand on that last point?"

- Flatter the interviewer, but only subtly. Although a good interviewer will have you speaking 75 percent of the time, that does not mean that you will be excused for not having listened to him. Appear interested in what he has to say.

- Adopt an attitude similar to the interviewer's. If your interviewer is deadly serious, avoid joking. If your interviewer is lighthearted and jocular, do not sit deadpan. In the first instance, jocularity will make you seem unsophisticated and unserious, whereas in the latter instance, seriousness will make you seem unintelligent and lacking spark.

- Treat the interviewer respectfully, but do not overdo it. Give the interviewer due respect, especially if he is an adult, but do not be overly submissive. Do not use the interviewer's first name unless instructed to do so.

- Relax and try to enjoy yourself. The relatively few people who enjoy interviews are those who view them as a chance to discuss important matters with someone with similar values and interests. If you are nervous, it may help to say so to your interviewer. It is perfectly acceptable for a college applicant to do so, and it will probably make both of you feel better if you get it out in the open lightheartedly.

- Have a conversation. The best interview is an intelligent back-and-forth conversation. If there is a pause in the conversation, consider whether you have answered the question fully enough. If you suspect not, ask whether the interviewer would like you to add more, or consider whether you should follow up with a question of your own related to the same subject.

- Avoid sounding like a robot. It is good to sound prepared and confident about your answers, but not as though you have memorized answers to expected questions.

- Look interested. Do not look at your watch or appear bored, no matter how long the interviewer has gone on speaking.

- Do not ramble. If your answer has gone on too long, cut your losses by briefly restating your main points. You can tell if your interviewer believes you are rambling if he hurries you through an answer or interrupts you with comments such as, "Let's move ahead quickly—we're running out of time."

Other Rules of Thumb

- Do not ask your interviewer how you did at the end of the interview. This will put him on the spot and make you seem immature, lacking tact, or unable to wait for a decision to be made in due course. It will not do anything to improve your chances of success.

- Assume that anyone at the office may be an informal "interviewer." Therefore, never be less than highly courteous and friendly to the staff. The staff is generally in charge of all logistical elements of your candidacy, so do not alienate them. Furthermore, though not part of the formal decision-making apparatus, the staff are certainly free to share their opinions of you informally with their coworkers. The admissions officers may even ask them to give their impression of you, so make sure it is a positive one.

THE END OF THE INTERVIEW

You will almost always be asked if you have any questions at the end of an interview. A failure to ask questions if invited to do so risks leaving the impression that you either did not do your homework or do not particularly care whether the school admits you. Asking questions gives you the opportunity to show how knowledgeable you are about the college as well as that you are taking a proactive approach to your educational future. Furthermore, the question, "Do you have any questions?" is generally the easiest question to prepare for. You should be ready with two to five questions that reflect your concerns about the school.

Do not ask questions that can be answered with a simple glance at the college's publications or brochures. In addition, try to avoid questions that require a simple yes or no response. Your questions should, for the most part, require an analysis or opinion from your responder. See page 416 for the kinds of questions you should ask.

Do not try to baffle your interviewer by asking questions you know he will not be able to answer. If he is an alum of the college, for example, he probably will not be privy to the school's rationale for its recent decision to deny tenure to a certain professor. Being asked if you have questions is a genuine offer but also signals that the interview is coming to an end—so do not take too long.

If you have not yet had the opportunity to present all of your key points when the interviewer asks if you have any questions, do not rush into asking them. Ask instead if it would be acceptable for you to go back to an earlier question or add to a previous discussion. Even if these points are unrelated to any prior question, feel free to say, "I am glad to have the opportunity to ask you some questions, but I hope you will forgive my wanting to mention two things that I haven't yet addressed in our discussion." Briefly make your points, and then go on to your questions.

If you think the interviewer harbors major objections to you, try to get a sense of what his concerns are so that you can address them if you have not had the opportunity to do so. This requires tact, of course, so as not to offend your interviewer or sound crass. You might, for example, say, "Are there any major issues concerning my candidacy that you think I could usefully address before leaving?"

At the end of the session, be sure to smile at the interviewer, shake hands, and thank him for seeing you.

INTELLIGENT QUESTIONS TO ASK YOUR INTERVIEWER

- In your opinion, what makes this college unique?

- Can you tell me a little bit about the relationship between the college campus and [the city or town in which it is located]? Is the town dominated by the college or is it the other way around? Are relations between "town and gown" generally friendly?

- In terms of improvement to or changes at the college, what are the administration's top priorities at the moment?

- If you had the chance to make one improvement to the school, what would it be?

- Do you think the character or personality of the college campus has changed at all in recent years? How?

- What is your opinion on [a recent campus debate or issue, such as the elimination of alcohol on campus or the administration's treatment of a racial incident]?

INTERVIEW WRECKERS

- Overly criticizing your teachers, school, or parents

- Being too nervous to answer questions confidently

- Appearing blasé about attending the school or about life in general

- Appearing too cynical or negative about life in general

- Asking no questions

- Whining or complaining, especially about grades or standardized test scores

- Blaming others for a weakness in your profile

SPECIAL INTERVIEW SETTINGS

RESTAURANTS

- If you arrive first, wait patiently in the entryway for your interviewer rather than taking a seat at a table.
- Do not sit until the interviewer invites you to be seated.
- Do not consider the menu until the interviewer invites you to. Do not order too much and do pick something midpriced. Do so without lengthy deliberations—the point of the meeting is for you to stay focused on your presentation, not to have a gourmet feast. Make sure that you choose something familiar and easy to eat. Avoid things that splatter or require eating with your fingers (unless it is a sandwich or something else benign).
- Do not take any alcohol, even if the interviewer tries to buy it for you.
- Do not criticize the food, the décor, or the service.
- Treat all waitstaff very politely.
- Wait for the interviewer to begin the interview. She may prefer to wait until after drinks arrive or the first course has been consumed.

YOUR INTERVIEWER'S HOME OR OFFICE

- Do not wander around or snoop if you are left alone before the interview begins.
- Do not sit until the interviewer invites you to be seated.
- If you are offered a drink or a snack, be modest in your consumption.
- Since this is your interviewer's private space, an honest (not convoluted) compliment or observation about the surroundings might be appropriate. ("I see from your photos that you visited the Great Wall with your family— what year were you there?" or "I love this area of town—my uncle's building is just down the block.")
- Treat anyone who helps to escort you or serve you very politely.

HOW TO DEAL WITH AN INCOMPETENT INTERVIEWER

What marks an incompetent interviewer? Talking too much, going off on tangents, failing to maintain control of the discussion, dwelling on inconsequential

matters, or failing to pay attention. Here are some tips for dealing with the
most common problems:

- *If he talks too much:* The more an interviewer talks, the less information he
  can get about you. Build rapport with him by providing nonverbal encouragement. You do not want to offend him or be rude, but you want to get
  your points across before your time is up. Do so by appearing to agree with
  him, following up on one of his comments by immediately saying something
  like, "In fact, one of the things that first got me interested in your school
  was . . ." And, of course, take advantage of his offer at the end of the interview for you to ask your own questions. Frame the statements you want to
  make as questions, but make sure they are really advertisements about yourself. For example, "Can you tell me a little bit about how I can incorporate
  my commitment to the study of modern dance into my curriculum here?"

- *If he goes off on tangents, dwells on inconsequential matters, or constantly inter-*
  rupts: If you want to get the discussion back on track, use such phrases as,
  "Let me be sure that I listed all my points to you earlier" (and then repeat
  your main points briefly); or "Could we go back to your previous question,
  so that I can tell you a little bit about my cultural background?"; or "In our
  remaining time, I hope that we will have the chance to touch on some
  points that I feel are particularly relevant to my application. . . ." Be very
  friendly and nonconfrontational, showing that you are not trying to take
  over the interview but are instead trying to take advantage of the opportunity to learn more about the school and sell your own abilities. He will be
  impressed that you have kept your focus while he was losing his.

- *If he fails to pay attention:* Try to bring him back in, but do not be rude. For
  example, say something like, "It looks like I've lost you—maybe I am not
  being clear. Let me try to explain it differently. . . ."

AFTER THE INTERVIEW

There are several brief steps you should take after the interview is finished.
First, debrief yourself regarding what went well and what went poorly and
why. This will help you with later interviews for other schools; you will be able
to anticipate what you might be asked concerning an apparent weakness.

Second, send a brief thank-you note to your interviewer. This can be
handwritten (still a nice gesture) or emailed. Note something that occurred
during the interview or something specific she said that enlightened you to
make it clear that this is not a form note. You can mention, for example, that

you were glad to learn more about the administration's current debate regarding the campus alcohol policy. The one absolute requirement is that you spell your interviewer's name correctly. Be sure to get a business card from your interviewer or ask a staff member (you can always call the office later if you need to) for the correct spelling of his name.

SPECIAL CONCERNS FOR INTERNATIONAL APPLICANTS

Interviewing in a nonnative language is not easy, especially when you are under substantial performance pressure. This is precisely when your worst verbal tics are likely to show up. Similarly, normal manners of speaking in your own language can be bothersome to others. Highly educated French speakers are accustomed to using a large number of "uh"s and, if anything, seem to gain respect for doing so in their own culture. To English speakers, this same trait when expressed in English can be highly annoying. You certainly want to retain your unique cultural identity in your interview—and will generally be excused any foreign mannerisms—yet you do not want to inadvertently annoy or distract your interviewer. Check your performance under realistic conditions and go the extra step of asking a native speaker to help you eradicate any verbal mannerisms that seem strange when placed in an English-speaking setting.

Cultural differences manifest themselves at many points in interviews. The physical distance people maintain between themselves, the amount of eye contact that is considered polite, and many other similar behaviors are culturally defined. Give some consideration, and some practice time, to incorporating some American norms into your interview performance. Again, the point is not to rob you of your own cultural identity but to avoid distracting or alienating your interviewer. The best way to prepare for a cross-cultural interview is, of course, to speak the appropriate language frequently and spend time in the appropriate setting for as long as possible immediately prior to the interview.

Part III

ON THE ROAD TO COLLEGE

15

RESPONDING TO ACCEPTANCES, DEFERRALS, WAITLIST PLACEMENTS, AND DENIALS

— KEY POINTS —

▪

Take the necessary steps to secure your place at your chosen school

▪

Do not panic if the first college you hear from denies you admission
—Assuming that you have chosen your schools appropriately (balancing "reaches," "possibles," and "likelies"), you can expect better news in the future

▪

Recognize that few waitlisted students are admitted at most schools
—To optimize your chances of being accepted from a waitlist (or after being deferred), bring relevant new material to the attention of the admissions office

▪

If you are not satisfied with your options, several paths remain open:
—Reapply after a year or two off
—Transfer after one or two years at another school
—Attend the school of your dreams as an exchange student
—Attend the school of your dreams as a graduate student
—Fall in love with the school you do attend

INTRODUCTION

Colleges will render one of four possible responses to your application: (1) A college can accept you, in which case it will also provide details regarding how to respond to the decision and the deadline for your decision. (2) If you have applied Early Decision, Early Action, or to a school with a Rolling Admissions process, a college can defer you. This means that the college neither accepts nor rejects you but will wait to make its final decision in a later round of application evaluations. (3) A college can place you on the waitlist, in which case there is a small to moderate chance that you may still be admitted to the school at a later date. (4) Finally, a college can deny you admission. If denied admission, you can always reapply for admission to the freshman class (if you decide to take a year or two off) or as a transfer student in a future year. This chapter tells you how to deal with each of these possibilities.

If you have followed this book's suggestions, you have applied to approximately eight colleges, at least two of which are almost certain to admit you and at least two more of which are fairly likely to admit you. Likewise, if you have followed our approach (introduced in Chapter 3), you have also maintained enthusiasm for all your schools rather than setting all your hopes on attending one particular reach school. If you have consistently tried to picture yourself enjoying your college career on many campuses, then you should not suffer overwhelming bouts of disappointment if you are deferred, waitlisted, or denied admission by one or several of your reaches.

RESPONDING TO AN ACCEPTANCE

If you are accepted by one of your top-choice colleges, congratulations. You should be sure to send in your confirmation of acceptance as well as your deposit, which reserves your place, in a timely manner. The response and deposit deadline is quite important (the Candidates' Common Reply Date, followed by most colleges, is May 1). In recent years, many colleges that have been oversubscribed have used a student's tardy deposit as an excuse to bar her from coming to the college—a convenient way to trim class size if necessary. You must get your deposit in to the college by May 1 (not postmarked May 1) or you risk losing your place at the school. Your acceptance letter or other materials will give you instructions on how to do so.

Likewise, as soon as you respond positively to one school, you should notify all other colleges to which you are accepted of your decision to decline their offer. Your acceptance letter will tell you how to go about notifying the college of your response. Do not begin to decline offers, however, until you have received an offer you prefer—even if you feel certain that you will be admitted to a college whose response you have not yet received. Furthermore, if there is any doubt in your mind about which college to attend, you should do some more research (see Chapter 3, "Deciding Where to Apply"), most importantly by visiting the colleges. Many colleges now have special weekends for admitted students. These events are designed to help you better assess a college before firmly deciding to attend.

The scenario becomes complex when you are accepted by a second-choice school and waitlisted at a preferred institution. It is important that you recognize that being on the waitlist is nowhere near certain future acceptance. Most of the very top colleges, in fact, put hundreds of kids on their waitlists each year and take only a tiny fraction (if any) of those students in the end. (See page 426 for more detailed information on waitlist offers.)

Since you may never be admitted to a school at which you are waitlisted, you must choose another institution to attend, thus sending in a nonrefundable deposit. You will forfeit this amount of money if, in the end, you get into the first-choice school from the waitlist and decide to attend it instead. You and your parents must decide if this is a feasible and reasonable option for you. Most colleges require initial deposits of about $500–$1,000; it is usually worthwhile to forfeit this small amount of money (in relation to the total amount you will spend over the next four years) to attend a college that is an obviously better fit.

FOR INTERNATIONAL STUDENTS ONLY

As soon as you have heard from all of your schools and made a decision to attend a college in the United States, you should begin the student visa application process. This means getting a Certificate of Eligibility (I-20) form from the school you will attend, which verifies that you have the appropriate credentials, language skills, and financial resources to attend the program. This form, along with the accompanying financial documents, must be submitted to the U.S. consular office to request the actual visa. The visa you will receive for full-time study in the United States is referred to as an F-1 student visa. The visa application process is often delayed by one party or another, so it is important to begin as soon as possible.

RESPONDING TO A DEFERRAL

A deferral means that a college neither admits nor denies you but rather postpones its decision until a later round of admissions. When Early Decision and Early Action applicants are deferred, it means that the committee will wait to make its decision until the regular admissions process gets under way. (Note that for Early Decision applicants, a deferral means that you are no longer under an obligation to attend the college if admitted in the spring.)

Being deferred is not the end of the world. What you should realize, however, is that the great majority of deferrals are actually prolonged rejections. In some cases, however, the college defers an applicant because it wants to wait for another piece of evidence before making a positive decision. In other words, you are under the gun. The college may be waiting to see your next set of grades or standardized test results, the outcome of your athletic or other extracurricular endeavors, or confirmation that you have resolved any disciplinary issues raised heretofore. It may also be waiting to see what the entire admissions pool looks like (i.e., how you compare to others in the pool) before making a decision.

If you are deferred, you should not wait quietly to see what happens. You should follow the general guidelines for waitlisted students by letting the school know of your continued interest in it as well as notifying the admissions committee of further evidence to support your candidacy. Read the next section, "Responding to Placement on a Waitlist," for more details on how to improve your chances of being admitted after being deferred.

RESPONDING TO PLACEMENT ON A WAITLIST

HOW COLLEGES USE WAITLISTS

Being placed on the waitlist means that you might be admitted to the program only if enough accepted candidates decide to go elsewhere, thus freeing up space in the freshman class. Colleges know that a certain percentage of their admitted students will choose other schools, so they routinely admit more candidates than they can realistically take in the freshman class. The excess number admitted, however, is often not sufficient to make up for all those who decline the offer of admission. The waitlist is used to manage this situation.

Many of the students placed on the waitlist are legitimately put there because a college would like to be able to reevaluate their applications should it need to accept more students for its freshman class in the future months. A student, however, can also be granted waitlist status out of courtesy rather than because of the college's sincere desire to reconsider his application. For example, legacy applicants and applicants from high schools with strong relationships to the college are often waitlisted.

When a college finds itself with a number of empty spots for the freshman class after many admitted students decide to go elsewhere, it goes to the waitlist to offer places to additional candidates. In other years, colleges find themselves in trouble because more candidates than expected accept the offer of admission—thus causing freshman housing and course availability problems. During these years, colleges do not accept anyone at all from the waitlist because the incoming class is already too full. Some schools intentionally leave room to go to their waitlists each year, using the waitlist to make the final changes that shape the freshman class.

Most colleges, however, go to their waitlists only on an as-needed basis, so the number of students accepted off waitlists at most institutions varies tremendously from year to year. A college might not even go to the waitlist one year, then the next year take over 100 candidates. The chances of being accepted from the waitlist lineup are slim when you consider how many students sit on the list. Most of the top schools place anywhere from 400 to 900 candidates on the waitlist each year. Generally speaking, half of the waitlisted students choose to remain "active," meaning that they notify the school that they would like to remain on the list for consideration should any spots in the freshman class become available. All other students are considered "inactive" once they either fail to respond to a college's waitlist offer or notify the college that they have made a decision to attend another school. At the very top schools, the maximum number of students accepted from the waitlist in recent years has been about 100. At best, you might have a one in four chance of being admitted this way, but chances are usually much slimmer than that.

As you can see, being placed on the waitlist is a bit like being put in purgatory indefinitely. An additional problem with being waitlisted is that even if you are eventually admitted, it might not be until very late in the game. (Note also that those accepted off the waitlist are not generally allowed to defer their acceptance until a later year. You must agree to come to the college right away, rather than a year or two later.) It is not uncommon for a college to notify a waitlisted student only days before classes begin in the fall—or, sometimes, even after the start of school!—that she is accepted. Many candidates like to save themselves the anxiety that can come with remaining on a waitlist by deciding to attend another college.

WHAT THE ADMISSIONS DIRECTORS SAY ABOUT THE WAITLIST

How Does the Waitlist Work?

At Wesleyan, we expect to use our waiting list every year; we plan for that when we make our offers in early April. When we choose candidates from the waitlist, we're basically looking to balance the class. If the yield from California applicants is a bit low, we take more Californians. The purpose of the waitlist is to shape the class at the final hour.   *Nancy Hargrave Meislahn, Wesleyan*

We don't always use our waitlist, although we like to use it a little if we can. We don't rank the candidates on the list. We basically sit down again in committee to review the applicants on the list, usually relying heavily on senior spring grades and scores to make our decisions.   *John Blackburn, University of Virginia*

The number we take off the waitlist for regular freshman September entrance varies—some years it's one student, in rare years close to 100. Each year we also take around twenty to twenty-five kids from the waitlist for January admission as well.   *Michael Goldberger, Brown*

We don't use our waitlist like some schools do. We don't put people on there as a polite way of letting them down.   *Richard Avitabile, NYU*

If we use our waitlist, we go back to committee all over again and look at everyone on the list.   *Maria Laskaris, Dartmouth*

How Is the Waitlist Used?

The waitlist serves a variety of purposes. The most important thing it does for us is allow us to come in on target. We have a very specific enrollment goal; we can't be over that number. The only way we can get the right number is by underestimating a little and filling in with the waiting list. Secondly, it allows us to fill in gaps. If we come in short in biologists, for example, we can fill in with biologists. It allows us to round out the class with some diversity not initially reached with the original class. Finally, it provides some candidates who are unusual but don't stand out in the regular pool the opportunity ultimately to stand out.   *Charles Deacon, Georgetown*

Pomona has an incredibly strong pool of applicants, and there really is no "spin" to why we place students on a waiting list. Sometimes when we waitlist a student it's just simply a matter of us saying we really can't admit everyone we wish we could. Waitlists serve both colleges and students well. They can serve students well if space does open up, and they do serve colleges well by assuring a talented group of students who will enable a college to open with a full enrollment.   *Bruce Poch, Pomona*

WAITLIST NUMBERS

We put several hundred kids on our waitlist. Some take lovely offers elsewhere, while some remain on the list. It's impossible to predict what we'll do. We have taken as few as zero (this year) or as many as ninety-nine (last year) or some number in between. *Janet Lavin Rapelye, Princeton*

We admit about 20 percent of our applicants, to enroll about 10 percent. In other words, we get 15,000 applicants, offer places to about 3,000, and enroll about 1,500. We offer another 1,500 a place on the waitlist. Of that 1,500, about 1,000 say, "Keep me on the waitlist." When we go to the list, starting May 1, that number is down to about 400–500. We take anywhere from fifty to one hundred from the waitlist. *Charles Deacon, Georgetown*

We offer waitlist spots to a couple thousand applicants. . . . After May 1, the waitlist shrinks daily, even hourly, as people make final decisions about where to go. . . . About 700–800 are active, of whom we take anywhere from none up to 100, depending on the year. *Dan Walls, Emory*

Last year we had about 350 active waitlist candidates. We enrolled about 40 students from the waitlist. The number admitted will vary from year to year. *Jennifer Desjarlais, Wellesley*

This year we waitlisted a few more than we normally do. Generally we try to waitlist fewer than 500 students, but this year we waitlisted slightly over 700. We did so because there was an unusual amount of unpredictability in response to several of our peer institutions eliminating their Early application programs; many of us also made changes to our financial aid policies. These factors affected our ability to predict yield—the number of students accepting our offer of admission. In the past three years we've been taking around twenty to forty students off the waitlist. In the three years before that, we did not go to the waitlist at all. *Stuart Schmill, MIT*

We get many applications from strong students who could probably do very well at Georgia Tech but for whom we simply don't have the space. That is when the waitlist comes into play. How many students come off the waitlist varies greatly year to year. One year it may be 10, the next year it may be 100. *Ingrid Hayes, Georgia Tech*

WHAT TO DO IF YOU DECIDE TO REMAIN "ACTIVE" ON THE WAITLIST

If you decide to remain "active" on a waitlist, you should not wait in silence. There are three tasks you must complete if you want to improve your shot of getting into a college off the waitlist:

1. Write the college a letter to convey your interest in the school (along with sending in a confirmation card, if the college has provided one, declaring that you wish to remain "active" on the waitlist). It is best if you convey to the school that you will definitely accept if admitted. Obviously, you cannot say this to more than one college.

2. Augment your profile with updated information that will reflect positively on your candidacy.

3. Keep your college counselor up-to-date on your waitlist status and your desires.

The first task, writing the admissions committee a letter stating your continued interest in the school, is extremely important. Although many college admissions officers say that a candidate's interest in the college is not that relevant in the original admissions process, virtually all of them regard proof of interest in the school as practically mandatory for those who want to be admitted off the waitlist. Waitlisted applicants should not just confirm their place by sending in a form but also write a letter of real enthusiasm. It is also important that you keep your college counselor informed of your enthusiasm for colleges at which you are waitlisted, since he or she will also likely be communicating with the college.

There are two reasons why you must show your commitment to attending a college to be admitted off the waitlist. First, the admissions committee has some difficult choices to make in admitting just a small fraction of the waitlisted students. The admissions people know how anxiety-ridden it can be for students to remain on a waitlist and feel badly that they cannot offer admission to every candidate. Committee members naturally feel better about accepting those who seem particularly enthusiastic about the college.

Second, and much more important, there is a practical reason for the committee's need to see some real interest from waitlisted candidates. By the time a college goes to its waitlist, it needs to finalize the list of incoming freshmen. Every college needs to meet its minimum size for each class, and a college's administration starts to get nervous if things are not settled and firm as the summer rolls by. Therefore, the admissions officers want to admit students whom they know will accept admission, so that they can be done with the admissions process as quickly as possible.

The second task—updating the admissions committee on your successes and positive record—is as important as letting them know that the school is your first choice. You need to give the committee as much ammunition as possible to decide to admit you over other students on the waitlist. Providing them with updates about your accomplishments and other happenings throughout your senior year of high school reminds them not only of your interest in being accepted to the college but also that you are a candidate worth admitting.

The information you will want to impart to the admissions officers might become available at different times. It is all right to send them more than one update for your file, but it is wise to limit your contact to two (at the most three) instances, unless you know for certain that they welcome your constant attention. Find out from the school at which you are waitlisted how it suggests that you carry out your contact—whether it wants to receive one or two notices from you or whether it enjoys continuous updates and inquiries from its waitlisted students.

What new information will be relevant to the admissions committee? Colleges generally require that you send them your updated transcript if you are to remain on the waitlist. You should also notify them of any academic awards or honors you receive, as well as any enrichment classes you enroll in for the summer. You should tell them about athletic achievements if they are significant, as well as any nominations to leadership positions that occur after your original application, such as an elected position as captain of the spring lacrosse team. Notify the committee of any positive changes in status or role regarding your job, community service work, or other extracurricular commitments. You can let them know about a summer job if it is especially impressive or significantly adds to your particular marketing efforts.

ADMISSIONS DIRECTORS DISCUSS WHAT WAITLISTED APPLICANTS SHOULD DO TO IMPROVE THEIR CHANCES OF ADMISSION

Being patient is a requirement for those on the waitlist. Schools have waitlists because we're not sure how seventeen- and eighteen-year-olds will decide in April. Our actions depend on the returns we get from our initial offers. Kids on the waitlist are welcome to write a letter expressing their continuing interest. After that, they should just sit tight. *Janet Lavin Rapelye, Princeton*

A lot of students forget a critical step: they forget to inform us that they wish to stay on the waitlist and remain interested in attending. It seems like we're either being barraged by students calling every day or as if we have fallen off the waitlisted students' radar. Somewhere in between is preferable. *Thyra Briggs, Harvey Mudd*

You need to make noise if you are waitlisted, but you should figure out how to make just enough and not too much noise. There is a fine line. If you walk it well, if you are savvy in handling yourself as a waitlist candidate, this may impress us. *Steve Thomas, Colby*

Waitlisted students absolutely should let us know that they're interested in coming here. They should not just confirm their place with a "Yes, keep me on the waitlist," but write a real letter of enthusiasm. *Eric Kaplan, Penn*

If you are waitlisted and Middlebury is in fact your first choice, it's a good idea to let us know that you'd matriculate here if we admitted you. It's also good to send along any updated information. *Robert Clagett, Middlebury*

Waitlisted students should correspond with our office at appropriate intervals. I don't want a pen pal. I don't want to know that you aced your history quiz today. I do want to know when grades come in and are officially posted, or if you receive an award. *Chris Gruber, Davidson*

There is a fine line between waitlisted students showing sincere interest and being obnoxious. Just follow directions stated in the letter. Follow up with a good letter stating your continued interest and submit any additional academic information. No more is needed. *Daniel J. Saracino, Notre Dame*

You should make yourself known if you are waitlisted, but going overboard can be shooting yourself in the foot. *James Bock, Swarthmore*

Applicants on the waitlist should send us updates, but be reasonable. Send us the important information, and do not overload us with letters and emails every day! *Rick Shaw, Stanford*

Anyone wanting to get in off a waitlist should send us updates on performance. Any supplements to the original application are good as long as they add to the profile. They should also show that they *really* want to come here. *Maria Laskaris, Dartmouth*

RESPONDING TO DENIALS OF ADMISSION

Most denials of admission require and necessitate no official response. For most college-bound students, there is no benefit to analyzing your rejection too closely. As you know by now, colleges have to make very difficult decisions about whom to admit and deny, and many qualified candidates are denied admission. Unless you are seriously thinking about putting off college for another year in order to reapply, or have real reason to think that an error has been made, you should simply try as best you can to shrug off the rejection as one of many more to come in your life, and start putting all your energy into preparing for the college you will attend.

If, after receiving responses from all schools, you decide that your best option is to take a year or two off and reapply to college, then it may be beneficial to attempt to understand a college's decision. (Note that you should not jump quickly to the conclusion that reapplying is a good idea—especially if your aim is to be accepted at one particular school. Many applicants cannot significantly improve their candidacy during a "year off.") The first step to take in this case is to analyze why you were rejected. You may already know the reason, of course, if you were aware of one or two specific aspects of your application that were likely to keep you from being admitted. If you are not sure, you can try to contact the school's admissions office to get the committee's view on the matter. Some colleges are willing to discuss a rejection. The schools most likely to do so are the smaller ones that have relatively fewer applications. Colleges are most receptive to such inquiries during their slow periods, especially during the summer. They will generally refuse to discuss the matter during their busy periods.

Remember that any school that takes the time to discuss your denial is doing you a real favor, so be ultrapolite in dealing with the admissions representatives. If you are defensive or hostile, natural reactions to being told that you are less than perfect, you will elicit less useful information and even less sympathy.

WHAT IF YOU ARE REJECTED EVERYWHERE?

If your strategy, or its execution, has failed and you are rejected by all the schools to which you applied, you have three basic options. You can:

- Apply to one of the (probably less competitive) colleges that keeps seats open for those in this circumstance. Check with your high school counselor for the names of those likely to be of greatest interest to you. You can look to transfer at the earliest opportunity if the school proves a poor choice. See Chapter 7 for a discussion of transfer applications.

- Take time off and reapply next fall, being sure to correct the errors you made last time around. See Chapter 17 for a thorough discussion of this option.

- Apply abroad. Many universities in Canada and elsewhere have much later deadlines than American colleges do, thereby giving you the potential option of attending a top school immediately after high school, rather than waiting a year or more to do so (as the first two options imply). See Chapter 19 for an analysis of this option.

SHOULD YOU EVER APPEAL A REJECTION?

Only if you think that a true error has been made should you consider appealing a rejection. A college will listen to your appeal of its decision, but rejections are almost never appealed successfully. Only in cases where there has been a computer or other serious error made in evaluating the student's file has a decision been overturned.

If you have no extremely strong conviction that the committee somehow made its decision based on erroneous information, do not raise your blood pressure and that of the committee members by appealing a rejection. Admissions committees go to great lengths to give all applicants' files a sympathetic and fair reading, so you can count on the school's having considered your application material fairly, as long as the information presented to them was correct.

If you have reason to believe an error was made and you present your case firmly and calmly, you will at the very least get the attention of your audience. If your high school registrar notifies you, for example, that he accidentally sent the transcript for your classmate Emilia Power rather than for you, Emily Power, to your target colleges (and Emilia's record is inferior to yours), then you have reason to call this error to the attention of an admissions committee. Contact the admissions office by telephone or by letter, politely explaining your situation as best as possible to inquire if the committee will review the case. Never, ever accuse the admissions office of wrongdoing. If the committee believes it has reason to entertain your appeal, bring all evidence or new information to them and reiterate your desire to attend the school.

Recognize that appeals are not generally welcomed by admissions committees. No college will change its decision if you (or your parents) appeal because you were not accepted while your neighbor with a lower GPA was given a place in the class. You must trust that the admissions committee has its reasons for admitting other students over you.

WHAT ADMISSIONS DIRECTORS SAY ABOUT APPEALING DENIALS

Sure, denied students can appeal. It's not a very smart use of time, though. We've never revised an offer yet. *Katie Fretwell, Amherst*

No appeal on an admissions decision has ever been successful. Every once in a while there's been an erroneous piece of information submitted as part of someone's file. If this is called to our attention after we have denied a candidate admission, we'll return to committee to look at it again, but in my memory never have we actually changed our decision. *Marlyn McGrath Lewis, Harvard*

Denied applicants should appeal if the committee had incorrect or incomplete information. If there was an error on your transcript, let's take another look. However, appeals do not make sense if the applicant simply wants us to see additional information, such as another recommendation. *Chris Gruber, Davidson*

There are lots of students these days who call to appeal a denial—this has probably been precipitated by the movement toward making appeals for financial aid. Once in all my years we changed a decision—but it was only because we had actually misread a transcript. It was an international student whose record was difficult to understand. *Nancy Hargrave Meislahn, Wesleyan*

If you are denied admission, there is no reason to appeal the decision unless we made the decision based on inaccurate information (for example, ETS reported the wrong standardized test score). Updated information (spring grades, etc.) are not a basis for appeal. *Robert Clagett, Middlebury*

The only situation in which I might recommend a student ask a college to check its records is if the student has a very common name—"David Kim," for example. Then there's always the possibility that there were two applicants with the same name, and misfiling might have occurred. Otherwise, there's really no reason for anyone to appeal a denial or double-guess a college's decision. *Sheppard Shanley, Northwestern*

SHOULD YOU REAPPLY IN THE FUTURE?

REAPPLYING AFTER TAKING A YEAR OR TWO OFF

The question of whether or not to reapply is, of course, a complicated one. If you were accepted at one of your top-choice colleges, it would be foolish to decide to wait a year to reapply to your very favorite school, hoping that you would be successful the second time around. If you have followed the advice in this book and applied to approximately eight schools that are good fits for you, chances are that you will be accepted somewhere that will make you very happy. A year or two off can be beneficial but in many cases does not radically change a student's profile, at least not enough to justify waiting an entire year in the hope that you can get into one particular college.

The situation is more difficult if you have gotten into your eighth-choice college and not into any of the seven colleges about which you are more enthusiastic. If you realistically think that you will be a better candidate after another year, during which you will have to do something extremely valuable in order to convince an admissions committee that your year off has made you a better candidate for their college, then it might be a good idea to wait and reapply.

The important thing here is to do some serious research on your "year off" options and then decide whether or not you will or could be a stronger candidate with this experience under your belt.

Cast a critical eye over your file and talk to some guidance counselors. If you have a real weakness, can you improve it within the next year or two? For example, if you come from an obviously privileged background and have never performed any community service, you might consider that this was a significant detracting factor on your college applications. Spending a year volunteering in India at a free health service could really change the way that admissions officers view you in the future. Something like this could be doubly valuable if you are trying to pitch yourself as a premed candidate with a commitment to medical and health issues or as someone who is interested in studying the developing world. Or maybe you are one of those students whose freshman and sophomore grades really detracted from your overall high school record. Spending a postgraduate year at a tough prep school (and doing extremely well there) will give admissions officers more confidence that you have truly overcome your earlier difficulties. They will thus be more inclined to admit you than they were when looking at two rather than three years of solid work. Similarly, if you have just come to grips with a learning disability or have finally overcome a family tragedy that affected your school performance, another year or so of stellar academic performance can change how colleges view your potential.

If, on the other hand, you know that your academic profile is simply not as strong as that of the average admitted student at the school (if your standardized test scores and GPA are well below the college's published averages, for example), then there is little reason to think that you will be admitted next year. Ask yourself whether you are being realistic in thinking that you can change your profile significantly before next year.

REAPPLYING AS A TRANSFER STUDENT

Remember that there are a lot of very good colleges out there. The ones you were admitted to can probably give you an education that is just as good as (maybe even better than) the one you think you want to attend so badly. Still, if your heart is set on one school or you think it is the best fit for you, there is always the possibility of reapplying as a transfer student to your target college after one or two years attending another school. Many of the top colleges report that some of their successful transfer students each year are students who applied unsuccessfully for admission to the freshman class. Of course, you may ultimately decide not to try to transfer because you like the college in which you initially enrolled so much.

If you do go ahead to college with the plan that you will reapply as a transfer student to another particular school in one or two years, check that your future target school actually takes transfer students and investigate its transfer program thoroughly before setting your sights on it. You will want to know exactly what that college will expect of you as a transfer applicant before putting together your first- and second-year academic schedules. You will also want to begin preparing to market yourself as a transfer student early on. (See Chapter 7's section on "Transfer Applicants" for more information on how to prepare to market yourself as a transfer student.) Be careful, however, not to waste your time at the first school you attend by going in with the feeling that it is only a halfway house. Do not "check out" of collegiate life just because you plan to leave within a year or two. Get everything you can out of a college—its academics, its resources, and its social atmosphere—no matter how long you plan to stay there.

REAPPLYING AS AN EXCHANGE STUDENT

Most colleges have flexible exchange programs that allow you to spend a semester or two at another school. If you failed to get into a school you desperately want to attend, you can check into the possibility of studying there as a visiting student in the future. This will give you much of the social and intellectual experience of attending the school, as well as letting you tap into its network and list it on your résumé. If you plan to follow this route, examine the various exchange possibilities at your potential colleges of attendance before deciding where to go.

REAPPLYING FOR GRADUATE SCHOOL

Finally, remember that there is always graduate school. Some of the colleges with the most prestigious names provide much better educations to their graduate students than they do to their undergraduates. You never know—you just might end up going to your favorite school after all.

16

Preparing for College Life and Academics

— KEY POINTS —

▩

Maintain a strong academic performance during your senior year
—Colleges can and will revoke an offer of admission for dismal grades
or bad behavior

▩

Performing your best through the end of high school offers
you the best chance of:
—Beginning college courses ready for their rigorous academics
—Fulfilling college requirements via Advanced Placement (AP) exam results
or SAT subject tests
—Impressing future employers with honors and awards
as well as a strong final GPA

▩

Upgrade your skills (especially in writing and research) in order to be able to
compete effectively in your new college environment

▩

Make the proper logistical, social, health, and emotional
preparations for college

INTRODUCTION

Once you have finished the college application process, you will probably feel that you deserve to celebrate and take a break from the strains of your senior year. You should indeed congratulate yourself on a tough job out of the way, but you also need to remember that it is not yet time to "check out" of your high school existence. You need to maintain your focus in school as well as begin to prepare to leave home and enter your adult life at college.

In addition to reading this chapter, you may want to consult other people about how best to prepare for entering college in the fall. Contact friends who are already in college and ask their advice about what to bring and how to prepare for the changes ahead. Friends who are already attending your particular college are especially good resources.

MAINTAINING YOUR FOCUS DURING THE SENIOR YEAR OF HIGH SCHOOL

It is very important that you maintain focus and avoid "senioritis" during your final months of high school. This is true at all points during the senior year, whether you have been accepted to your college of choice Early Decision, accepted to a school during the Regular Admissions round, or waitlisted at any of your top-choice schools. There are several reasons you will want to keep on top of your academics and overall performance during the latter portion of your senior year:

- Colleges request final high school transcripts of all accepted applicants. Colleges retain the right to withdraw an offer of admission to a previously accepted applicant if academic performance or general behavior during the senior year is unacceptable. Most schools report that they indeed exercise this right, some in numerous cases each year.

- If you are waitlisted by one of your top-choice colleges, admissions officers will want to see last-semester grades before finalizing their decision. An impressive senior year record will make all the difference between staying waitlisted and getting in.

- If you decide to transfer to another college after your freshman or sophomore year, your total high school record will be evaluated in addition to your collegiate record.

- Falling out of good study habits during your final high school semester might lead to greater difficulty coping with the heavy workload in college.

- Much of the information learned during the senior year, especially in math and science courses, is bound to be of direct use in college. You should make sure to digest as much of the material as possible before moving on.

- Maintaining a strong performance during the latter half of your senior year will ensure that any awards or honors for which you are under consideration will still be available to you. You should aim to finish the year well so that your permanent academic record remains as impressive as possible. This will be important for résumé purposes, especially when applying for job opportunities during or immediately after college. Major awards received at the end of high school can be relevant far into the future, even mentioned on graduate school applications.

ADMISSIONS DIRECTORS DISCUSS REVOKING OFFERS OF ADMISSION

We have revoked offers of admission after the spring grades come in, as well as for significant behavior problems that occur after our offer of admission was made. *Marlyn McGrath Lewis, Harvard*

We do occasionally revoke an offer of admission—if the spring grades are truly deplorable. *Katie Fretwell, Amherst*

We review all the final transcripts of our incoming freshmen in June. If one of our incoming student's grades are truly deplorable—a terrible case of senior slide—we ask the student to write us a letter explaining what happened. In the truly egregious cases, we will withdraw our offer of admission after reconvening the entire committee for a reconsideration. *Nancy Hargrave Meislahn, Wesleyan*

If someone's grades have dropped significantly, or there is a reduced course level (relative to what we were led to expect), we will consider whether to withdraw an acceptance. *Dan Walls, Emory*

The most common reason is a precipitous drop in grades. The letter of admission comes with a reminder that the decision is contingent upon successful completion of the senior year. We have revoked at least one decision each year for the past three years. *Dick Nesbitt, Williams*

For disciplinary problems, we do not automatically withdraw our admission offer, but we do ask for a written explanation from the student, and sometimes require an interview to discuss the circumstances. In some cases, where it is just a small slip or hiccup with one course, I will write the students with a "slap on the wrist" or wake-up call to remind them what they need to do to be successful at Wesleyan. *Nancy Hargrave Meislahn, Wesleyan*

ACADEMIC PREPARATIONS FOR COLLEGE

We certainly do not advocate that seniors headed for college in the fall cram their summers full of rigorous academic work! This is your time to relax a bit before heading off on your own. There are, however, several tasks you should take care of in order to ensure that you arrive on campus ready for a strong start.

Starting college well prepared is key. The student who is poorly prepared will find it difficult to succeed. The poorly prepared student is highly likely to struggle in the first term and barely get through the first set of courses. As a result, he will be perceived by his professors and fellow students as someone who has little to offer. As you may have witnessed of poor performers during high school, reputations have a way of following people around. The students who perform well initially pile up points with professors from the very beginning, demonstrating that they are committed scholars and learners.

Furthermore, a common complaint shared by graduating college seniors is that they did not have enough time to explore all of the things (academically and extracurricularly) in which they were interested. Because many spend the first one to two years in college coping with academic weaknesses or problems and trying to figure out where their interests lie, they are left with less time to pursue these interests. To the extent that you can remedy any academic sore spots as well as determine your interests and possible pathways before entering college, you should do so. The sooner you become involved in those things about which you are passionate, the more rewarding your college experience will be.

Here are our recommendations for ensuring that you arrive on campus as academically prepared as possible:

Before Arriving on Campus

■ Take final AP tests and SAT subject exams at the end of your senior year if your college will give you credit for your scores. Your college's course offerings catalog will tell you about its policies regarding incoming credit for classes and placing out of requirements. If you have questions, call the admissions or academic advising office to find out more.

- Ensure that your writing, research, and note-taking skills are up to par. Take a writing course if you are not entirely confident of your writing and/or research skills. Be sure that you know how to state, develop, and support a thesis and that you command a firm understanding of the mechanics of various forms of writing: an analytical essay, a lab report, a research paper using primary and secondary sources. You will have little time and energy once you start classes to hone these crucial skills for succeeding at the most competitive colleges.

- Hone your word-processing or typing skills. You will write constantly during college and cannot afford to waste time with the hunt-and-peck typing style that got you through high school. Typing speed can be a huge advantage when taking exams (often written on laptops rather than in "blue books" these days).

- If you have extra time over the summer to take a class at a community college or nearby university, determine whether there are any core curriculum requirements you can get out of the way before entering school.

- Determine whether you are interested in any freshman seminars or honors programs offered by your college. Such programs usually require separate applications during the summer before college entry. Particularly at larger schools, these programs give students a rare opportunity for student-professor interaction in an intimate classroom setting.

- Consult the past year's course catalog (or the current one, if it is available) and start considering your curriculum. Even though you will probably be assigned an academic adviser, such advisers can only be as helpful as you allow them to be, given your own ideas and input. It is better that you have a sense of what you want to do and how you can do it before arriving on campus. Also give thought to possible research or independent study you could do in college. If you have no idea what academic path you want to take in college, go through the catalog and highlight all courses that sound remotely interesting to you, then analyze them for any recurring themes or interests.

Before or After Arriving on Campus

- Get acquainted with the various services (tutoring, career advising, writing resources, etc.) offered at your college to help with academic problems as well as academic and career planning. Doing this early on will ensure that you will be ready if a problem arises to tackle it as efficiently as possible.

- Make an appointment with your college adviser. Your school will most likely require that you meet with your adviser at the beginning of the year, but even if it does not, be certain to acquaint yourself with this person and solicit his or her advice. At most schools, professors, administration faculty, and other members of the campus community serve as advisers. Their job is to support and guide advisees to the right resources; they do not usually have all the answers themselves. In other words, do not assume that your chemistry professor adviser will know exactly what freshman writing seminar you should take in order to ensure entry into an upper-level creative writing class. He should, however, be able to direct you to the right places to find the answers you are looking for. If, over time, you do not feel comfortable with your adviser or find other faculty members who can better serve your needs, you can either change advisers officially or simply use other people for advice as needed.

LOGISTICAL PREPARATIONS FOR COLLEGE

When your senior year is over and the summer sets in, you should start thinking about the many logistical preparations you will need to make during the next five months or so. Some logistical preparations are best taken care of ahead of time, whereas some are best left until you arrive at your new location. This is apt to be a period of growth for you because you will be performing tasks that have probably not been within your jurisdiction during your life so far. But growth is often accompanied by frustrations, so you should expect to feel both exhilarated and exhausted by completing the necessary tasks. Here are some of the preparations you should make before leaving for college:

- Take care of all housing details to ensure yourself a place in a dormitory or other housing option. Most colleges send out freshman housing information and registration materials soon after they receive your notice of acceptance at the college. Check to see whether your college's housing lottery operates on a first-come, first-served basis; if so, be sure to get your materials and deposit in as soon as possible to ensure the best treatment.

- Ensure that you have selected and registered for a proper meal plan, especially if you have special dietary restrictions.

- Purchase the clothing and other goods you will need at college.

- Learn to do your own laundry and ironing. Take a mini home economics course from one of your parents if you are unsure how to do daily chores such as washing your clothes or cooking basic foods.

- Be sure you know the basics about managing money. You should know how to write checks, withdraw and deposit funds, and balance an account.

- Compare long-distance or mobile phone services and sign up for one.

- Research airlines and transportation services to your college location to determine which offers the best student rates.

- Find out about and purchase parking permits if you are bringing a car to campus.

- Talk to your parents about their expectations of you while you are away at college. Having a somewhat formal discussion about their ideas as well as your own guarantees that everyone in the family is in agreement on certain issues of mutual concern before you leave. Discuss finances: What are you responsible for financing yourself? What expenses will they pay? How will money be transferred to you? How often will money be transferred to you? Are there any conditions they expect to be met in order for them to continue financial support throughout college? Discuss vacation time: How often will they expect you to come home? Who will pay for trips home? Will they visit you on campus? Discuss academic issues: Do they expect you to share your grades with them? Are they comfortable with the idea of your switching fields? Are they open to the idea of your transferring if you are unhappy? What are their feelings about programs abroad?

SOCIAL PREPARATIONS

Before leaving for college, try your best both to keep up old ties with the people who have been important in your life thus far and to begin forging relationships with the people who will surround you at school.

Before Arriving on Campus

- Maintain correspondence with teachers, classmates, school administrators, coaches, and employers. You should do so out of respect and also in order to ensure the best treatment from these people down the road. (You never know when you might need their help for recommendations or career purposes.) Send an initial note and vouch that you will do the same at least once a year in the years to come. Put a reminder note in your agenda so that you will remember to do so.

■   Contact your future roommate or roommates to introduce yourself as well as to discuss what you will need for your room and other logistical details.

■   Contact any professors or special instructors with whom you would like to speak before arriving on campus. An early call or email to inquire about a course's curriculum or discuss your interests and needs over the summer can make a good impression on a professor. In addition, contacting a professor over the summer ensures you will receive adequate attention, whereas if you wait until the school year begins, you risk losing faculty attention to other pressing matters.

HEALTH PREPARATIONS

Whether you are perfectly healthy or have significant health problems, do some research on health-care policies and take care of any necessary doctor visits before arriving on campus.

Before Arriving on Campus

■   It is unlikely that you will have the time or the inclination to make a doctor's appointment while in school, so it is best to visit your physician and get a checkup before heading to college. Some schools require a record of this visit (proof that you have had various immunizations—e.g., for measles, mumps, rubella, hepatitis B) before registering for classes freshman year.

■   Compare health-care coverage plans and sign up for one. Most colleges offer decent, affordable student health insurance, but you should also investigate the possibility of remaining on your parents' plan as a dependent or taking out a different form of coverage. This is especially true for those with considerable health risks or preexisting conditions, because certain forms of health insurance might offer better services and more coverage for those services than what you would receive under a campus plan. Learn as much as you can about your health-care policy, even if you plan to remain on a parental plan—you will need to understand its policies and limitations yourself, since your parents will not always be with you when you visit doctors.

Before or After Arriving on Campus

■   It is usually a good idea to select a primary care physician upon arriving on campus, whether you are utilizing the college's health-care plan or an alternative one. You will probably need assistance or advice from a primary care physician at least once during your four-year stay, if not quite a bit more. Most special health needs also require an initial referral from a primary care doctor, so it is often best if you select one person to oversee your care—someone who will know your history and make the best recommendations for you over the years.

- Familiarize yourself with the college's emergency health procedures. Post emergency numbers on or near your dorm room phone, and memorize them as well. Know where the nearest emergency room is (often at a campus-based hospital).

HELPING OTHERS PREPARE FOR YOUR LEAVING HOME

For many people, entering college is the first definitive step toward adulthood and independence. While monumentally significant in *your* life, this transition is also significant in the lives of your family and friends. Parents fear losing you to your new independent lifestyle while friends fear that you will begin new relationships and forget about them. Being sensitive to these concerns can help those around you make the transition with you.

Spend a lot of quality time with both family and friends (even though you will probably be more inclined to spend time with friends) over the summer. Do not forget grandparents and other relatives who might be anxious about your move away from home and into adulthood. Having meaningful interactions with family and friends over the summer will reassure them that they are important to you.

Part IV

OTHER OPTIONS

TAKING TIME OFF BEFORE COLLEGE

— KEY POINTS —

■

Some types of students benefit substantially from taking off a year (or even two) before college

■

You can apply to college before *or* after the year off

—Many colleges encourage successful applicants to defer entry for a year or two in pursuit of personal interests

—Taking time off before applying to college can make all the difference in turning dull or otherwise underpowered candidates into desirable admits

■

Time off can be spent:

—Studying, working, volunteering, traveling, or some combination of these activities

—These can be done at home, elsewhere in the U.S., or abroad

■

Potential benefits to taking time off include:

—Becoming a stronger college applicant

—Gaining knowledge of yourself and the world, enabling you to make better choices regarding which college to attend, course to pursue, and career to enter

—Developing increased maturity, confidence, focus, and skills

INTRODUCTION

Most people who attend top colleges start right after graduating from high school. That does not mean, however, that it is always a good idea to plunge into college without taking time off first. There are plenty of people who would be much better off spending a year (perhaps even two years) pursuing other interests and gaining some additional maturity and perspective before heading off to college.

People with a variety of interests and needs may find it beneficial to spend time doing something other than full-time, formal education. They include those who:

- Are not yet ready to get the most out of their (expensive) college education

- Can substantially improve their chances of getting into a top college by waiting a year to apply

- Are considering British universities, which place a premium on maturity and course and career focus, and necessitate living far from home in a different culture (see Chapter 19)

- Are fed up with school or simply burnt out

- Want to acquire specific skills or experience

- Want the opportunity to sort out career and/or study options

- Are filled with wanderlust

- Can benefit in study or career terms by improving language skills or cultural knowledge abroad

Anyone who can see how a year off will benefit her should consider the opportunities available, and weigh the advantages and disadvantages of pursuing one or more of them before going to college.

TIMING ISSUES: DEFERRING COLLEGE OR WAITING A YEAR TO APPLY

If you intend to take time off before college, you have a choice between applying to college during your senior year—and, upon acceptance, seeking a year's deferment—or waiting until a year later and applying during your year off. The two approaches are not mutually exclusive, of course, insofar as you can try to get into your chosen college(s) during your senior year and, if you succeed, defer at your chosen school. If you fail to get in, you can try again during your year off.

DEFERRING COLLEGE

There are substantial advantages to applying while a senior and simply deferring after being admitted. One is that you will have the peace of mind of knowing that you are indeed guaranteed a seat at college whatever you manage to do or not do during your year off. Another advantage is that it is generally much easier to apply when in high school than when you are out of school. High schools are set up to deal with seniors applying for college. More than that, you are in a milieu in which you can get things done: you are probably in the same town as those who will recommend you, for example. If you are working in Paris, doing a succession of scientific projects in Latin America, or just traveling a thousand miles from home in the United States, it can be very difficult to get documents (such as transcripts or old recommendations), sign up for and take SAT or AP exams, discuss your preferred positioning strategy with recommenders who are still back in your hometown, and so on.

WAITING TO APPLY

If you apply during your year off, on the other hand, you have the possibility of improving your chances via each of the following:

- You can take your standardized exams when you are better prepared to score well on them. You may do better on the SAT because you will have had more opportunity to study and take practice tests. Similarly, you can expect to do better on the SAT subject tests with the appropriate coursework under your belt. (If you are spending your year off abroad and/or taking language classes, you can certainly expect to do better on the relevant SAT language exam [and AP test] too.)

- You may be able to present a much more impressive array of AP results.

- Your recommendations can be stronger. First, you will be able to offer recommendations from your senior year teachers based on a full year rather than a half-year of work. Second, you may be able to offer a supplemental recommendation from someone who has supervised you in the work world after high school.

- You can look more interesting as a result of having done something unusual during your time off.

- You can reinforce your positioning effort (see Chapter 6 for an in-depth discussion of this critical concept) by what you do after high school.

■   You can look more mature and focused than you did a year earlier. This is especially significant for those whose freshman and sophomore academics look weak or those who encountered disciplinary difficulties early in high school. The passage of time, coupled with good academic results and a showing of seriousness, can relegate the earlier problems to the dustbin.

■   You can reduce or eliminate most weaknesses by devoting yourself to the right activities after high school, whether they are personal, academic, or extracurricular in nature.

The key is to choose activities that will be most helpful to your chances of admission, something that depends entirely on your own starting point. For example, if you suffer from the perception of being rather frivolous and not particularly interested in academics, you might be helped by a year spent working in an analytically demanding job and taking some courses at night; this particular problem is unlikely to be overcome, however, by a stint as a cruise ship entertainer. On the other hand, if you are trying to position yourself as an environmentally driven scientist, you may be able to help this positioning by working for a time in an organization that does interesting conservation work, or taking time off to pursue several Earthwatch projects around the world, but you would not be helped to the same degree by a stint as a chambermaid in a local hotel.

The question of when to apply is likely to be a matter of trading off the potential improvement in your value to top colleges with the increased difficulty of applying when out of school.

YOUR OPTIONS

The activities you might choose to pursue during a year off include those in the following categories:

Working in the United States. You can work part-time or full-time, in your hometown or elsewhere. You can use your year off to make money (or in an unpaid internship), to develop skills for college or future jobs, to investigate careers that interest you, or simply for the fun of the job—or the fun of being where the work is (e.g., a ski resort).

Working abroad. The primary differences between working in the United States and working abroad are that in the latter case, you will face even greater difficulty getting an appropriate job, but the potential rewards (such as improving a language, learning another culture, and so on) are all the greater.

Volunteering in the United States. The range of organizations (local, national, or international) and the focus of their efforts (at-risk kids, the homeless, conservation, the environment, crime prevention, culture, and so on) are virtually limitless.

Volunteering abroad. As with volunteer organizations in the United States, the possibilities are endless. The difficulty is to find something that fits you, and a responsible organization that will meet your needs (not just those of its intended beneficiaries).

Traveling (in the United States or abroad). Only your imagination, wallet, and sense of adventure limit the possible destinations.

Pursuing short courses. You can study academic or nonacademic subjects, including cooking, a language, furniture repair, office skills, culture (art history, decorative arts, sculpture, et al.), sports, acting, or anything else that you believe would prepare you to make money during your year off (or at college or later on), allow you to explore a subject (before choosing a major for college) or career, or further your personal interest in a field.

Pursuing a postgraduate year of study. (See the box below.)

POSTGRADUATE YEARS

Spending an extra, thirteenth ("postgraduate" or "PG") year in high school is another way to improve credentials and thereby impress college admissions officers. Traditionally, however, only three categories of students have taken advantage of this opportunity. Recruited athletes whose academics are not up to snuff have often been urged by their prospective college coaches to put in an extra year of high school either to improve their skills and strength or to prepare to survive college classes—and to demonstrate to skeptical admissions officers that they can do so. International applicants sometimes use a PG year to develop their English language skills, (re)take the SAT, and get used to American-style classes. A handful of kids have also taken the opportunity to demonstrate that they are more mature, newly serious about academics, or have put discipline problems behind them.

One reason for this not being a popular choice is that it requires money: essentially only private high schools offer a PG year, and the price can be equal to a year at a private college. A second reason is that it delays the ultimate graduation date from college by a year, something that has prevented most students (and their parents) from considering a break of any sort between high school and college.

On top of all this, it can be difficult to perform well in the PG environment. Going to a new school requires adapting to a new environment and, in most cases, a new system. It is not easy to adjust quickly enough to get top grades in the first term (the only one that colleges will see when making admissions decisions), without which the effort is likely to be wasted.

As a result, many applicants will be well advised either to make more creative use of a year off before college—i.e., to consider one of the other categories of activities listed above—or to go to a less desirable college and plan to transfer once a solid collegiate academic record is in place.

If you decide to pursue a PG year, note that you do have several options. One is to go to a private high school in your area that offers a postgraduate year. Another is to go to a boarding prep school in another area; many of the most famous, long established schools (especially those in the Northeast, such as Phillips Exeter, Deerfield, and Hotchkiss) offer PG years. Yet another option is to go overseas. British and Swiss schools are obvious possibilities. The former offer a thirteenth year as a matter of course because the British secondary school system is predicated on a thirteen-year (rather than twelve-year) program. The Swiss private schools have long catered to those who need extra help and have the money to pay (well) for it.

HOW TO CHOOSE THE RIGHT ACTIVITIES FOR YOU

The possibilities of what you might do are so numerous that you risk being overwhelmed by choice. Knowing why you want to take time off, and what you hope to gain from it, will help you select activities that will maximize your experience. If you are weighing numerous possibilities, or unsure of how to think about which activities will provide you with the greatest benefits, consider the following criteria:

- What personal skills and experience will you gain? For example, dealing with the public, supervising other workers, negotiating with people, learning how those from different socioeconomic or ethnic/racial backgrounds live, and so on
- What practical skills and experience, qualifications, and contacts will you gain?
- Will you be able to do something similar at college? Or, during vacations?
- Will it prepare you for other, better work at college?
- Will it help prepare you for work after college?
- Will you impress potential future employers with the nature of this job or your performance on it?

▪ Will you be able to explore potential career (or college study) options?

▪ Will it help you get ready for college coursework?

▪ Can you do it in conjunction with other activities you would also like to undertake?

▪ How much will you learn about yourself and others, about your community or another part of the world?

▪ What level of satisfaction (and fun) will you derive from doing this job and doing it well?

The questions listed above are relevant whether you intend to take time off after having deferred entry to your chosen college or, instead, intend to reapply to schools during your year off. In the latter case, however, two additional questions should be considered:

▪ Will your planned activities enhance your college application positioning effort (see Chapter 6)?

▪ Will you make yourself more interesting, more unusual, and saddled with fewer negatives than you currently are?

The two stories at the end of this chapter illustrate the different situations faced by those who need to improve their chances of being admitted by top colleges via their year-off activities, and those who have already been deferred by their chosen school.

START THE PROCESS EARLY

The most likely trouble you will encounter is failing to plan your year off and ending up wasting it. Many of the useful things you might do require substantial advance planning. For example, if you intend to travel or work abroad, you may need to arrange for visas, some of which will take weeks or months—not days—to obtain. There is the same need for advance planning for courses you wish to take, jobs you hope to obtain, volunteer work you wish to do, and so on. Remember that although admissions officers and employers value the additional experience, maturity, confidence, and perspective that a year off can add, they are suspicious of those who have failed to take advantage of the possibilities a year off offers.

YOUR OPTIONS AT A GLANCE

The chart below is a quick-and-dirty guide to some of the likely potential advantages and disadvantages of different types of activities. The specific activity chosen will, of course, determine the actual benefits (and costs) you derive.

EVALUATING YEAR-OFF OPTIONS

OPTIONS:	PAID JOB		VOLUNTEER		TRAVEL		COURSEWORK	
	U.S.	ABROAD	U.S.	ABROAD	U.S.	ABROAD	SHORT	PG YEAR
Potential Advantages:								
Earn money	++	+						
Contacts	+	+	+				(+)	
Job-specific skills	++	+	+	+			+	
Transferable skills*	+	+	+	+			(+)	
Learn about life	+	++	+	+	+	+		
Explore possible careers	+	(+)	+	(+)			+	
Learn language/culture		+	(+)	+		(+)	(+)	(+)
Demonstrate independence	+	++		+		+		(+)
Help others			+	+				
Academic learning							+	++
Potential Disadvantages:								
Hard to find/arrange	+	++						
Costly				+	+	+	+	++
Snobbish image			(+)	+		++		++
Homesickness		+		+	(+)	+		(+)
Emotional exhaustion			++	++			**	
Danger			(+)	+	(+)	+		

*Such as communication, negotiation, leadership, or time-management skills
**Can feel like you never left school if the course is too long or too academic

COMBINING PURSUITS

Fifteen months—the period between finishing high school and starting college a year later—is a long time, offering you the opportunity to do more than just one thing. One common approach is to travel in a relaxed fashion for the first month or two out of school, in order to wash high school out of your hair, then settle down for a time to study, work, or volunteer (or some combination thereof). It is fine to leave certain periods unspecified and unplanned for, such as designating a six-week period for loose-jointed travel in whatever direction the first train takes you, but be careful not to leave the whole effort unplanned. The greatest risk of wasting a year is by waiting until graduation without having planned anything with the expectation that "something will turn up."

FUNDING YOUR YEAR OFF

It is important to budget for your year off very carefully and realistically. Some efforts may not require funding—working and living at home, for instance—but others will require more money, or at least more money up front, than you may have assumed. Thus even if you have a job lined up in another city, whether in the United States or abroad, you can expect to need money to get under way. Just getting there, arranging for a place to live, and paying for food until your first paycheck arrives are likely to require more than you might expect if you have never done something comparable.

Work out a sensible budget for your planned year. The following chart may help:

	RANGE OF ESTIMATES	
	HIGH	LOW
Expenses		
Travel (to and from)	____	____
Room	____	____
Board	____	____
Entertainment	____	____
Local travel (bus pass, e.g.)	____	____
Holiday travel	____	____
Fees (for volunteer projects, courses, etc.)	____	____

	RANGE OF ESTIMATES	
	HIGH	LOW
Other	____	____
Subtotal	____	____
Sources of Cash		
Savings	____	____
Earnings between now and starting	____	____
Earnings during year off	____	____
Contributions	____	____
Subtotal	____	____
Total	____	____

Whether you need a little or a lot of money will probably determine how you try to raise funds. The following is a brief look at the possibilities:

You can pitch your parents (or grandparents, or favorite aunt and uncle, and so on). Do not take their financial support for granted. They will respond best if you have a carefully thought-out plan and budget to present to them, complete with well-stated rationales for undertaking whatever you propose. Two cautions: first, be clear as to the precise amount you want from them, so that they do not feel that they are going to have to contribute endlessly if they make this initial payment. Second, be sure to ask at an appropriate time, when your parents can think calmly and clearly about your proposition.

Work hard senior year and/or immediately upon graduation. Funding yourself will give you a great deal of pride in your own abilities; it will also impress college admissions officers and potential future employers.

Arrange sponsorship with a local business or charity. Local businesses may be willing to put up some money for you if they can be persuaded that you will provide them with a worthwhile marketing or publicity opportunity. For example, if you plan to hike the Andes, consider approaching a camping equipment company to help you based on the newspaper coverage you will get, the stories you will write for publication in specialist magazines, and so on. They may donate the equipment you need and even provide you with flights to and from Latin America. A similar approach could be made to a large, local sporting goods retailer or camera shop. If you were hiking to publicize the plight of a certain species of bird in the Andes, you might be able to get an American birding organization or wildlife charity to contribute to your expenses.

A NOTE FOR PARENTS

Taking time off before college is not for everyone. Too few people in our experience, however, take advantage of an opportunity to explore the world and themselves at a time when the costs of doing so are quite low—when they have no mortgage payments to make or careers that cannot be interrupted—and when the rewards are potentially immense. College admissions officers, especially those who have been in the business for a substantial period of time, strongly believe that time off, when pursued constructively, is beneficial for virtually all who try it. Separating the process of becoming a (somewhat) independent adult from that of starting college can be useful. The personal growth of those taking time off helps prepare them to get the most out of their college experience. They are more inclined to pursue their college studies with a purpose and less likely to be distracted by the frivolous (and even the potentially dangerous) aspects of college than they would be had they gone straight from high school.

"YEAR OFF" SUCCESS STORIES

APPLYING TO COLLEGE AFTER HIGH SCHOOL: JOSH'S STORY

Josh started interning (without pay) at a local political consulting firm after his junior year in high school. He filed, copied, input data, and so on. As he became more and more interested in what he saw the senior consultants doing, he decided to pursue political consulting as a possible career.

Following the senior consultants' advice, he took every math course he could during his senior year: calculus, statistics, and math for computer science. He also enrolled in a data analysis course at his local community college. As his understanding of relevant mathematical techniques and computer programs progressed, he was allowed to do more and more of the initial data analysis for clients.

DECIDING TO REAPPLY TO COLLEGE

Because he had goofed off during his early years of high school, Josh was unable to get into his top college choices. He decided that rather than go to his backup choice, which failed to inspire him with enthusiasm, he would reapply the next fall. He reasoned that he would look like a much more interesting and accomplished applicant at that point, with his budding political consulting career being further advanced, and another year of strong academic effort under his belt.

He pitched his parents and was delighted to find out that they were in agreement. They did, however, condition their acceptance of his plan on his commitment to attend college a year later. Josh next arranged an offer of full-time work after high school; his firm was pleased to have him, given the good attitude he had demonstrated in addition to his on-the-job growth.

GETTING THE MOST OUT OF SECOND SEMESTER SENIOR YEAR

Josh got recommendations from his favorite math teacher at the end of the year, when his teacher had the time to do a particularly careful job and after the teacher had seen him perform very well in several courses. Josh had recognized the value of these courses and worked hard in them; his work in the political consulting realm meant that he had wonderful real-life examples that he could use in doing class projects. He had presented his results to each class with real enthusiasm. This performance was, of course, much more impressive and far more interesting than that undertaken by any of his classmates. His teacher was therefore able to recommend him extremely enthusiastically, with detailed stories about the work he had done, the way he had enjoyed presenting it to his classmates, and their positive response to his enthusiasm.

JOSH'S WORK EXPERIENCE AFTER HIGH SCHOOL

Josh worked hard for his consulting firm, and also took several related community college courses. As Josh developed his understanding of the business as well as his technical skills, he was given increased responsibilities. For example, he frequently did background research on the needs of potential clients; he also did the initial "situation assessments" for new clients. He eventually attended client meetings to be available to answer clients' requests that depended on in-depth knowledge of the statistics and methodologies underlying the firm's presentations.

Josh also took AP tests in subjects he had enjoyed his senior year, such as calculus and statistics. He scored well in all four he took, further strengthening his academic profile.

APPLYING TO COLLEGE THE FOLLOWING FALL

Josh had learned a great deal about what he wanted in a school. He knew that he wanted a school with strong political science and statistics departments, with a chance to double major in the two subjects. He wanted the opportunity to take highly quantitative courses within the political science department and to write a thesis under the supervision of a recognized authority on applying quantitative methods to political science issues.

Josh took advantage of his year off to bolster his positioning. He became clearly identifiable as "the politico." He contacted political science professors teaching American politics or data analysis courses, explained what he was doing, and discussed at length with them how their courses could be of benefit to him. In several cases, they ended up marketing their respective schools to him, going so far as to write strong letters on his behalf to their admissions directors. Josh also got a very strong supplemental recommendation from his boss, who had never before had a high schooler make such an impact. Josh was further helped by the fact that his senior year grades were good, as were his community college grades during and after his senior year.

Armed with his improved credentials and positioning, Josh got into two of the schools that had previously rejected him and two others to which he had not previously applied. He went to one of the latter, and enjoyed remarkable success there; this included capitalizing on his political consulting experience both in and out of the classroom.

Working During College

Josh began by working as a pollster for his college newspaper freshman year, producing biweekly articles (always with his own byline). He ultimately managed to "quintuple dip," that is, get five benefits from his efforts. He got the credit for his newspaper articles, which turned him into a well-known figure on campus by the end of his first semester. Second, he published only some of his data, thereby creating the opportunity to sell some of his insights to student politicians running for office. Third, he contributed modified versions of his campus writings to the city newspaper nearby, for which he was also paid. Fourth, he eventually started consulting to politicians interested in attracting the student vote at his campus. He was a more credible source of information for them about students than were their usual consultants. And fifth, he generally managed to use his survey data for political science and data analysis courses he was taking.

Long before he graduated, Josh was working nearly full-time as a pollster and consultant. He had the choice, upon graduation, of further developing his own consulting business or of joining an established firm as a junior partner. (Had he wished to go on to graduate school immediately he would have found doctoral programs in political science—and quite possibly leading MBA programs—keenly interested in him.)

DEFERRING COLLEGE: FABIANNA'S STORY

During her senior year, Fabianna had been admitted to an Ivy League college. She had intended to go straight to college, but had been convinced to take time off beforehand. Her parents and grandparents were concerned that she was too serious about everything, had pushed herself too hard in high school, and had not yet seen enough of the world or learned enough about herself to head straight into an academic pressure cooker. Her maternal grandparents, both born in Tuscany, suggested that she spend time in Italy getting to know her relatives.

Fabianna liked the idea of improving her rather poor Italian, which she generally spoke only with the two of them. She also proposed that she pursue a new interest of hers—cooking. She investigated the possibilities in Italy and was delighted to learn that several well-regarded schools offered cooking instruction in English. She figured that she could at least start in such a school while she improved her Italian, then switch to an Italian language cooking school.

During the summer following high school, Fabianna lived with one set of her relatives while attending cooking school and taking Italian language lessons at the local university. By September she felt ready to step out on her own. She moved to Rome to enroll in a cooking school that offered courses solely in Italian. She took classes for two months, then spent several more months interning in a local restaurant, a position that the school arranged for her. After that she spent the winter working as a cook at a ski chalet in Cortina, in the Dolomites (in the Italian Alps). During the late spring and summer, she worked as a chef aboard a yacht in the Mediterranean. In between each of these efforts, and on many of her weekend breaks, she spent time traveling around Italy with the people she met studying or working.

FABIANNA'S RESULTS

At the end of her year off, Fabianna knew that she could celebrate several accomplishments. Her command of Italian had soared, going from poor to native in fifteen months, as had her knowledge of Italy. Equally important, she had become a truly professional cook, able to put together a very wide range of meals at a moment's notice, to work as part of a team of professionals in a restaurant kitchen, to design a menu to various cost and taste specifications, and to supervise lesser skilled helpers in cooking for private parties. During college she would of course be able to work part-time (and on an emergency fill-in basis) for excellent wages at any of the Italian restaurants in the area. She planned to investigate setting up her own catering business as well. During holidays she figured to work again as a private chef in ski or summer resorts, except this time she would be able to command a higher salary, given her demonstrated skills and experience (along with the recommendations she had from her prior employers). As a result of this year, Fabianna knew full well that she would be able to make her own way in the world wherever she found herself. A bonus was that she had also greatly improved her skiing and learned a great deal about sailing, thereby advancing two hobbies.

Fabianna's parents and grandparents were relieved that she had started to view life as more than an academic exercise. They believed that she would be less likely to overcommit herself prematurely to a career path in her freshman year. They figured that she would instead be more inclined to sample different educational and career possibilities, given her greater self-awareness and broader base of experience on which to draw. As a result of this—and of her having gotten to know some of her relatives and having had a delightful year—they considered their money extremely well spent.

ADMISSIONS DIRECTORS TALK ABOUT TAKING TIME OFF BEFORE COLLEGE

WHAT IS YOUR OPINION ON TAKING TIME OFF BEFORE COLLEGE?

We think it's a good idea if *the candidate* thinks it's a good idea.   *Michael Goldberger, Brown*

I think it's great. There's no reason you have to go to college right after high school, just as there's no reason you have to go for four straight years.   *Dan Walls, Emory*

We think it's a great idea! For perhaps a decade we've been putting a statement into the admit letter to the effect that "We hope you'll consider taking a year off before coming to Harvard." We really do want students to think about it—we believe it's in their best interest. We also want parents to see that we think it's not only okay, but even a very good thing, supported by the college. We don't want parents discouraging their children from taking time off before college.   *Marlyn McGrath Lewis, Harvard*

I really admire students who defer their college enrollment right out of high school out of a recognition that they are not yet ready for college.   *Daniel J. Saracino, Notre Dame*

I honestly think a good portion of students would benefit from taking time off before college. So many students reach a level of academic burnout by the end of high school that they would really benefit from a year of non-academic rejuvenation. Families often worry that students will get off track if their son or daughter stops school temporarily. However, we almost never see this as a result of students deferring for a year.   *Thyra Briggs, Harvey Mudd*

Not that many students defer, somewhere around ten to twenty a year. I'd be happy to see it happen more. Deferring gives you time to mature and learn more about yourself. The more you experience prior to college, the more you will benefit from college. *Stuart Schmill, MIT*

What Are the Benefits of Taking Time Off Before College?

The need to simply reinvigorate before diving into college is a very good reason to take a year off. Students develop a level of maturity, which contributes to their desire to engage the learning environment. *Rick Shaw, Stanford*

Taking time off before college can be a great thing to do. There is such a variety of things you can do that could help you focus your attention on what you might want to study in college as well as give you a base of experience that you'll draw on in college. *Paul Thiboutot, Carleton*

The benefits of taking time off before college depend on what the student chooses to do during that year. Students who decide to work will gain skills in managing their time, being resourceful, and being responsible. Working will really help them figure out how to handle themselves. We find that students who have worked before college get really good at problem-solving and come to us as stronger community members and stronger students. *Thyra Briggs, Harvey Mudd*

All of us wish more students took time off because it lets students step off the treadmill and take stock of their education. Virtually all students get more out of college—and bring more to it—for having done so. It might be wise to go through the application process while still in school, but by all means consider deferring admission. *Robert Clagett, Middlebury*

We have a strong viewpoint on the idea of taking a year off. First, it's better to be more mature and focused when arriving at this demanding place. We also think being older by a year, in and of itself, is usually beneficial—an extra year before you start college can only be a good thing. We also encourage students to take time off from college while they are here. *Marlyn McGrath Lewis, Harvard*

When Is It Beneficial for a Candidate to Wait Until After Graduating from High School, During a Year Off, to Apply to College?

Applicants who take time off and then apply to college can be very appealing—they've often done very interesting things during that year off. But making yourself more interesting won't make up for a so-so high school record—applicants should keep that in mind. *Maria Laskaris, Dartmouth*

I suggest students apply here while in high school and then, if admitted, defer a year before entering. Very seldom does a year off change one's chances of being admitted to a school like ours. The fundamentals are the high school grades and the test scores, and those won't change during a year off. Occasionally doing something really phenomenal during a year off can change a student's perspective or give her something exciting to present in the application, but it's rare it might influence our decision. *Rick Shaw, Stanford*

I'd encourage students to apply while in their senior year of high school, while they still have access to teachers and counselors for recommendations, and institutions for required documents. Otherwise, if they will be out of the area, they'll need to know in advance what documents they'll need and how to get them—or they need to have a mom or dad willing to act as their secretary, particularly if they're abroad. *Paul Thiboutot, Carleton*

Under What Circumstances Is a Postgraduate (PG) Year Beneficial?

A PG year *can* be beneficial but this one year does not erase the rest of an applicant's high school record. It can only do so much. It's usually helpful for those who got a late start in terms of performing academically or for potential athletic recruits who need more college preparation and a slightly better record. *Maria Laskaris, Dartmouth*

A PG year can be good if students are going to *do* something with it. They really need to be able to hit the ground running, though. They need to be able to adjust quickly to a new academic and social life. Students should put a lot of thought into doing an extra year of high school—don't do it thinking that it will be easy to boost your chance of admission, because that's not always the case. *Eric Kaplan, Penn*

Often a PG year is a benefit for students who need to boost their academic profile or for those who could do with another year of maturing emotionally. *Thyra Briggs, Harvey Mudd*

Is It Generally More Difficult for a PG Student Than a Regular High School Student to Gain Admission?

A PG year doesn't drastically increase a person's attractiveness—but it's also not looked at negatively if there was a reason for doing it. *Maria Laskaris, Dartmouth*

This has largely to do with why they have done the PG year. Lots of times, students do PG years for athletic reasons. Most colleges understand and are sympathetic to this reason. For the PG year student who chose this route for other reasons, you just need to clearly explain in your application why you chose to do it and how you have benefited from the experience. *Thyra Briggs, Harvey Mudd*

PG students usually have a harder time being admitted because if they're doing a PG year in the first place, there's probably a reason for it—a weakness of some sort in their regular high school record. *Eric Kaplan, Penn*

Legitimate Reasons for Allowing Someone to Defer Matriculation

I think it's great when students want to take a year off before college. Those who apply here and defer can do anything except go to college somewhere else for that year. They can take courses somewhere—at a college overseas, dance classes, language classes, whatever—they just can't go full-time for regular college credit. *Christoph Guttentag, Duke*

Our expectation is that the student has a plan—a reason for the year off. As long as this is the case, we say go ahead. We see these students with real-world experience as bringing another element of diversity to the classroom. *Nancy Hargrave Meislahn, Wesleyan*

Deferring a year to "hang out" is not a good idea. I don't consider that a legitimate reason for taking time off. There should be a plan on how you intend to spend the year, and it should be something that will contribute to your overall development. *Rick Shaw, Stanford*

We readily grant deferrals for those who want to take time off before enrolling. The only condition is that they not enroll in full-time, graded college courses. (If they do, we want to see the results, because this makes them into transfer applicants, in effect.) *Dan Walls, Emory*

Almost any reason for deferring is legitimate. We find that a year away makes students better participants in the college experience. The only problematic reason for deferring is if a student doesn't have a clear plan. *Thyra Briggs, Harvey Mudd*

There are many legitimate reasons to defer matriculation, including opportunities to travel, community service opportunities, etc. We are looking for positive reasons, not reasons that hinge on the negative, such as "I'm not sure Davidson is the school for me." *Chris Gruber, Davidson*

IMPACT ON FINANCIAL AID

The initial aid offer is good only for the year it is made. After that, families' circumstances are likely to have changed, so students need to reapply for aid. We do generally hold merit scholarships for the year, though, so students should not worry about losing them. (We grant 150 each year.) *Dan Walls, Emory*

If a student decides to defer for a year, we may be able to defer scholarship money. However, the need-based portion will depend on income figures for the following year. *Douglas Christiansen, Vanderbilt*

18

ATTENDING A UNITED STATES SERVICE ACADEMY

— KEY POINTS —

■

The five U.S. service academies are different from civilian colleges
—The curriculum is narrower and more fully prescribed
—The emphasis is on developing leaders more than on developing scholars

■

The application process is also different than that at civilian colleges
—Nominations from congressional representatives and the like are needed at most of the academies
—The evaluative criteria greatly emphasize leadership

■

The service academies offer wonderful value, but are not for everyone
—Only those determined to be military officers should consider them

■

Alternatives to the U.S. service academies are also available
—These include state military colleges and dedicated preparatory schools

INTRODUCTION

America's five federal service academies are different enough from other colleges to warrant their own chapter. The differences include a more focused curriculum, driven by the mission of training military officers; an emphasis on physical fitness; conscious efforts to develop leadership skill and experience; and, not least from our point of view, a radically different application procedure.

The five academies, all of which are discussed throughout this chapter, include:

- United States Military Academy, also known as West Point or Army
- United States Naval Academy, also known as Annapolis or Navy
- United States Air Force Academy
- United States Coast Guard Academy
- United States Merchant Marine Academy, also known as Kings Point

WHY APPLY TO SERVICE ACADEMIES?

Applicants to the service academies are similar to those applying to selective civilian colleges: successful high school students looking to attend the college that will help them achieve the most they can in life. The main feature that sets these students apart is their ambition to be military officers after college. Although service academies offer students an excellent education, they are no place for someone looking for a good education as an end in itself. Developing the best possible officers for the military is the driving force behind every aspect of service academies' curricular and extracurricular programs, making them a suitable choice for would-be officers but not for others.

The desire to serve as an officer is, of course, only part of most candidates' motivation for applying. Other common motivations include a desire to:

- Lead others and bear responsibility, beginning early in a career
- Be challenged (physically, academically)
- Receive a top-flight education free of charge
- Shoot guns, fly planes, navigate big boats, and so on
- Be in a structured environment
- Follow in footsteps of mentors or family members

- Continue previous military career/experience
- Gain the prestige of graduating from a service academy
- Ensure career stability

DECIDING WHETHER A SERVICE ACADEMY IS RIGHT FOR YOU

As this chapter discusses, the service academies differ from civilian colleges in important ways. Similarly, a military career—to which attendance at a service academy (with limited exceptions) will obligate you—is also likely to be extremely different from a civilian career. This means you are being called on at age eighteen to make a highly consequential decision. Do not do so lightly.

You need to:

Learn about the service academy. What is life like for a student in the first year? In the following years? What do people love about it? Hate about it? What types of people are happiest at it? And so on. Read about the academy. Talk with the academy's representatives, but most of all talk with current students and alums. And by all means visit the academy.

Learn about the service itself. Understand what you will do as a junior officer in peacetime and in war. Read about it. Also, be sure to talk with a wide range of serving and retired officers, not just recruiters.

Understand your own motivations and psychology. Be sure you are the one who is dying to go, not your mom, dad, or Uncle Bob. Understand why you want to go. Consult the list above to see what describes your motivation. Be honest with yourself. If you want to attend because of the glamour or a lack of anything else to do, you are headed for trouble. Assess whether you are sufficiently determined to overcome the demands and stress that will be placed on you over a long time period.

ALTERNATIVES TO SERVICE ACADEMIES

Those unable to gain admission to a service academy should take heart: other options for becoming a military officer are available. State military academies are one. They also offer a military style education, but are easier to get into. Prominent state-supported military universities include places like the Citadel and the Virginia Military Institute. If you are interested in a military education but want to attend a "regular" university, there are several civilian universities with established military cadet corps, such as the Virginia Tech Corps of Cadets and Texas A&M's Corps of Cadets. (Yet another route is to go to a civilian college and enroll in ROTC (Reserve Officer Training Corps) in order to prepare to be an officer.)

COMPARISON OF SERVICE ACADEMIES AND TOP MILITARY COLLEGES

	U.S. MILITARY ACADEMY (NY)	U.S. NAVAL ACADEMY (MD)	U.S. AIR FORCE ACADEMY (CO)	U.S. COAST GUARD ACADEMY (CT)	U.S. MERCHANT MARINE ACADEMY (NY)	THE CITADEL (SC)	VMI (VA)
Total Enrollment (approx.)	4,000	4,000	4,000	980	950	2,000	1,300
Admissions Per Year (approx.)	1,150–1,200	1,200	1,300	300	285	1,300	420
Acceptance Rate	15%	14%	19%	24%	28%	75%	57%
% Female (approx.)	14	19	18	28	14	7	8
Graduation Rate	85%	87%	79%	68%	73%	69%	73%
Degree Conferred	Bachelor of Science	Bachelor of Science	Bachelor of Science	Bachelor of Science	Bachelor of Science	BS or BA	BS or BA
Rank upon Graduation	Second Lieutenant	Navy-Ensign Marine Corps—Second Lieutenant	Second Lieutenant	Ensign	Licensed as a Merchant Marine Officer (issued by the U.S. Coast Guard); Reserve duty; civilian service in Maritime Trans. Industry	Core Cadet; can earn rank if you go on to military service as Ensign or Second Lieutenant	Second Lieutenant

State military institutions offer many benefits for those interested in a military education. Graduates of these institutions have flexible career options—unlike graduates of service academies, they have a choice of careers in either the military or the private sector. Employers, enticed by the discipline and leadership qualities of military school graduates, value them highly.

Applying to state military schools is similar to the service academy process—they have physical and medical requirements not found in a civilian application, yet applications to state military institutions do not require a nomination from a politician (see below). State military colleges do not have service requirements upon graduation (unless students have signed a contract as part of a military scholarship like ROTC). However, many state military school graduates go on to serve. At the Virginia Military Institute, about 50 percent pursue military careers. At the Citadel, approximately 35 to 40 percent go on to careers in the military. Graduates of the Citadel and VMI earn a Bachelor of Arts or a Bachelor of Science depending on their academic focus. They have the rank of second lieutenant or ensign if they proceed to a military post.

WHO SHOULD NOT APPLY TO SERVICE ACADEMIES

Many people should not consider applying to service academies. Certain kinds of applicants are barred outright. Due to the rigors of academy life and military service, applicants must meet certain physical and medical standards, laid out in this chapter. In addition to these prerequisites, service academies will not admit persons who:

- Are married
- Are pregnant
- Have legal dependents (if cadets become married or a parent during the course of their studies, they are expected to resign)
- Are not U.S. citizens (although the service academies typically take a very limited number of foreign applicants, pursuant to operating agreements with specific foreign countries)
- Are not between the ages of 17 and 23 (by July 1 of the year admitted)

Although these characteristics will disqualify you from attending a service academy, there is another subtle but critical factor that must be weighed to determine whether a service academy is right for you: it has to be in your heart.

Service academies frequently see students matriculating only to please a parent. Being at a service academy must be something you want for yourself—it's simply too difficult and too big a life decision to do just for someone else's benefit. If you question whether you will be able to handle the rigors of the experience, sign up for one of the service academies' short summer programs (available the summer between your junior and senior years of high school), during which you will have a sneak peek at what the experience entails. If you question whether you want to go, find a way to resolve that question before you apply.

If you end up at a service academy only to realize that you have made a mistake and you really want to be an elementary school teacher or a sculptor, be forewarned that depending on the timing of your epiphany, there may be no way out. At most service academies, the minute you begin your third year of study, you are on the hook for years of service commitment after graduation (discussed below).

THINKING TWICE

In fact, graduating from a service academy is not a foregone conclusion once you matriculate. Whereas civilian schools often bend over backwards to increase or maintain their retention rates (in part because this is a key factor in the *U.S. News & World Report* ranking), service academies are not as determined to keep cadets who are not interested in continuing. Service academies are looking for people who are in it for the long haul—they depend on their continued commitment long after graduation. The first few years of any service academy education is focused, in part, on weeding out those individuals who lack sufficient determination and drive to become officers.

Service academies give conflicted students a chance to bow out if they determine, after giving it a fair shake, that the military is simply not for them. At each service academy (except for the Coast Guard Academy), a student may withdraw from school *without incurring a postgraduate service obligation* any time within the first two years of school. As soon as the student begins third-year courses, however, the opportunity to back out disappears and the full service commitment obligation kicks in. At the Coast Guard, even if a cadet leaves during his or her fourth year, no service obligation is incurred (although this happens extremely rarely).

The chart below shows how often cadets fail to graduate:

	PERCENT WHO LEAVE AFTER BASIC TRAINING	PERCENT OF ENTERING CLASS WHO GRADUATE
Military Academy	5–7%	85%
Naval Academy	3–4%	85%
Air Force Academy	7%	75–80%
Coast Guard Academy	6–11%	65–75%
Merchant Marines	4%	70–75%

There are several common reasons cadets do not make it to graduation day. During the plebe summer (the period of military training just before classes begin), students typically withdraw because the institution or activities are not what they expected or, as noted above, they are not there for the right reasons (e.g., doing it for parents). Later on in the experience, the most common reasons for withdrawing are academic (e.g., curriculum too rigorous) or disciplinary problems.

**ADMISSIONS DIRECTORS DISCUSS WHO SHOULD NOT
APPLY TO SERVICE ACADEMIES**

Don't apply to the Air Force Academy if you plan to major in art, music, or drama. People who truly want a liberal arts education should consider their desire to come here carefully.　*Rollie Stoneman, U.S. Air Force Academy*

Students not serious about engaging in a disciplined lifestyle and personal challenge ought not apply to the Coast Guard Academy.　*Capt. Susan D. Bibeau, U.S. Coast Guard Academy*

Do not apply to a service academy if you are not interested in being the best possible officer you can be. This is not a place for people who are only looking for a great education. The job that you have to do once you graduate is too important for you not to want it, and not to want to excel at it.　*Maj. William Smith, U.S. Military Academy (West Point)*

If your goal is to major in the humanities, this is not at all the place for you. *Capt. Robert Johnson, U.S. Merchant Marine Academy*

You should not apply to Navy if you are doing it for Mom and Dad. If you apply to a service academy, the motivation for it should be your own, coming from your own heart.　*Capt. Karen Frye, U.S. Naval Academy*

UNDERSTANDING THE SERVICE ACADEMIES

Life at service academies is nothing if not structured. For most of the day, cadets' lives are tied to a strict schedule that leaves no room for actively pursuing leisure activities, holding down a part-time job, or deciding to skip class or blow off studying. This is not to say that there is no room in the day for fun. Service academies are famous for their musical exploits (bands, choirs, and so on); sports teams are vigorous (participation is even required at several service academies); and numerous clubs and activities abound. Still, service academies are not the place for students who prefer a large dose of unstructured and unsupervised time in their day-to-day life.

TYPICAL DAY AT A SERVICE ACADEMY
(DURING THE ACADEMIC YEAR)

5:30–6:00	Physical Training
6:00–6:20	Dress in uniform
6:20–6:40	Breakfast Formation/March to Breakfast
6:40–7:00	Breakfast
7:15–11:40	Morning classes
11:40–12:00	Lunch Formation/March to Lunch
12:00–12:20	Lunch
12:30–13:30	Administrative hour
13:30–15:30	Afternoon classes
15:30–17:40	Athletics, Extracurricular, Parading
17:40–18:00	Dinner Formation/March to Dinner
18:00–18:20	Dinner
18:20–19:30	Free time (clubs, etc.)
19:30–24:00	Study, Barracks

THE CURRICULUM

ACADEMIC PROGRAM

The academic program at military institutions is very different from that at a typical civilian school. Unlike many civilian colleges and universities, service academies do not take a student-centric approach to course selection. Although service academies allow students to choose their own focus and follow their interest to a degree, they also take very seriously the responsibility of ensuring that their students graduate with a requisite education in specific areas crucial to their future military roles.

At West Point, for example, cadets take fourteen elective courses within their chosen major and graduate with a Bachelor of Science (even if they majored in French). Whatever their ultimate major, cadets must complete the core curriculum, which includes an engineering sequence that is the rough equivalent of a minor. Other service academies look even less like liberal arts colleges. At the Coast Guard Academy, for instance, students may choose from only eight majors, four of which are types of engineering.

ADMISSIONS DIRECTORS DISCUSS
SERVICE ACADEMY CURRICULUM AND CULTURE

Although our core curriculum is weighted toward math and engineering, the two most popular majors are management and behavioral science. So, regardless of your area of interest, you should have a solid background in math and the sciences.   *Rollie Stoneman, U.S. Air Force Academy*

All cadets are required to go through an engineering "sequence" similar to a minor. This explains why we are looking for candidates with solid math and science preparation in high school. That said, recently there were more cadets majoring in humanities fields than in math and science fields.   *Maj. William Smith, U.S. Military Academy (West Point)*

Our core curriculum is designed to develop students morally, mentally, and physically.   *Capt. Karen Frye, U.S. Naval Academy*

The curriculum here is fairly scripted. There's not a lot of flexibility. However, with such strong grounding in math and science, cadets are well prepared to pursue graduate studies in nearly any field.   *Capt. Susan D. Bibeau, U.S. Coast Guard Academy*

It's true that the Coast Guard Academy is not part of the Department of Defense. But candidates who expect this to translate to it being less "military" or less rigorous will be disappointed. To do well here, you need to be willing to push yourself every minute of the day.   *Capt. Susan D. Bibeau, U.S. Coast Guard Academy*

The acculturation process at the Coast Guard is different from the other service academies. Where others may have "Warrior" cultures, the Coast Guard has a distinctly humanitarian bent. We are about protecting, rescuing, and helping.   *Capt. Susan D. Bibeau, U.S. Coast Guard Academy*

The Merchant Marine Academy takes a very hands-on approach to education. At sea, you have the opportunity to put into practice everything you have learned in the classroom—to merge the theoretical with the practical.   *Capt. Robert Johnson, U.S. Merchant Marine Academy*

The core curriculum and structure of the majors offered are aimed at one goal: to provide graduates with the requisite knowledge in their field to do their jobs. Although there is some emphasis on creating well-rounded individuals with a grasp of the basics in a variety of fields, the service academies have a distinct bent toward math and applied science. They are not interested in building, for example, their students' fine art skills or knowledge of history.

MILITARY TRAINING

Those at a service academy might be perplexed if you asked what military training takes place there—"It's all military training!" To the extent that the civilian world sees a difference between learning physics in the classroom and driving a tank, however, the military training portion deserves separate mention.

Military training at service academies is not what many might think. During the academic year, cadets are not awakened in their bunks at 4:00 a.m. for a forced march through a muddy marsh. Quite the contrary, during the academic year, the military training component—at least in the physical sense—takes a relative back seat to academics.

There are three main components to military training at service academies: summer training, academic year military roles, and classroom military training.

SUMMER TRAINING

The majority of military training at service academies occurs during the summer. At most service academies, for instance, cadets undergo approximately six weeks of military instruction before first-year classes start. It is not until the summer after the plebe year (first year) that cadets go through a second round of military training, in most cases a type of field training where cadets have the opportunity to put what they have learned in the classroom to work. The summer after the third year is more varied at most service academies. Some cadets might take on leadership roles in the training of a first-year student, while others might run summer field programs. Others might take on quasi-military positions "shadowing" officers in the field. Although cadets are not sent to deployed units (i.e., units engaged in active warfare), there are plenty of domestic and international units they can join for the required summer stint.

ACADEMIC YEAR MILITARY ROLES

During the school year, academics consume the majority of cadets' attention. Still, service academies are organized with a military structure—the more senior you are, the higher your "rank" within the system. Your rank at any particular stage in your service academy career will determine your responsibilities with regard to your fellow cadets. For example, seniors are cadet officers, juniors are sergeants, etc. The purpose behind this military structure is to give the cadets leadership experience in a military setting.

CLASSROOM MILITARY TRAINING

The final piece of military training offered by service academies comes in the form of classroom learning, where cadets are briefed on the basic military knowledge required of officers within their branch. Army cadets, for example, will learn about reading maps, weapon system capabilities, and so forth. Classroom learning is put to direct test during the more hands-on military training during the summer.

THE MERCHANT MARINE TRIMESTER SYSTEM

The Merchant Marine Academy operates on a trimester system that is substantially different from that of the other service academies. All students spend their first year on campus. During their sophomore year, however, cadets spend a trimester at sea applying what they have learned in the classroom. When they start their junior year, cadets take classes one trimester and then are back at sea for two trimesters. This system means that students at the Merchant Marine Academy must take a four-year courseload in three years since they spend three trimesters at sea. Besides gaining meaningful shipboard experience, Merchant Marine Academy graduates are fully licensed as officers by the Coast Guard.

OTHER DIFFERENCES WITH CIVILIAN SCHOOLS

Beyond the curriculum, the service academies are different than civilian schools in a host of other ways, too. Many of these differences are beyond the scope of this book, but a brief list (based on the most military of the academies) includes:

- Students are taught to obey commands immediately, without question.

- Students are given too much to do in too little time. The very demanding environment is meant to foster self-discipline, time-management skills, teamwork (you can accomplish more as part of a team), and the ability to work well when exhausted.

- Individual interests are subordinated to group interests. Thus, your roommate's failure to be dressed properly (shoes shined, etc.) will result in your being punished, too.

- Everyone is equal, regardless of ethnicity, race, family wealth (or lack of wealth), and so on. Everyone has to do the same chores and wear the same clothes.

- Older students (in their third and fourth years) learn how to lead by taking charge of younger students.

■   Students give up virtually all freedom. This extends from how they spend their time to whom they may date: older students are not permitted to date first-year students.

FINANCIAL AID

Part of the reason service academies are so competitive is that tuition, books, board, and medical and dental care are all fully funded all four years. In addition, students receive a monthly stipend. Though stipends may not cover much more than basic expenses during the plebe year (purchasing uniforms, etc.), a gradual increase in stipend plus a corresponding decrease in school-related expenses translates to more money in your pocket the more senior you become.

MILITARY SERVICE OBLIGATIONS

Graduates of service academies receive a Bachelor of Science degree and a guaranteed job as a junior officer in the military (Army, Marine Corps, Navy, Air Force, or Coast Guard, depending on the school attended). This job is, in fact, a minimum service obligation following graduation.

For the Coast Guard Academy, the Naval Academy, the Air Force Academy, and the Military Academy, graduates must serve for five years on active duty and for three years on reserve duty within their assigned branch of the military. Graduates of the Merchant Marine Academy have quite a different service obligation following graduation. They must serve on reserve duty for eight years, but within this constraint they have many options. They may become ships officers at sea (civilian or military), serve ashore in the maritime or intermodal transportation field, or act as active duty officers in one of the Armed Forces. This means, in theory at least, that a graduate of the Merchant Marine Academy can earn a free education *and* take up a well-paid civilian post afterwards in the maritime transportation industry. Approximately 65 percent of Merchant Marine Academy graduates take positions within the civilian maritime transportation industry, and approximately 25 percent assume military posts, while the remaining 10 percent undertake scholarship work, graduate education, and so on.

Note, however, that whenever the military has difficulty filling its roster of soldiers, it may simply forbid officers and enlisted personnel from leaving, whatever their supposed term of service. This is most likely to occur during an unpopular shooting war, when it is difficult to entice new recruits into the military. Thus, during the lengthy, dangerous, and unpopular second Gulf War, the military has invoked these "stop-loss" provisions for many officers, who effectively serve at the military's pleasure. Rather than being able to leave at the end of their five-year tours, for instance, they have had to stay on for as long as the military has wanted them.

POSTGRADUATE SERVICE OBLIGATIONS

SERVICE OBLIGATIONS

SCHOOL	NO. OF YEARS*		TYPE OF SERVICE
	ACTIVE	RESERVE	
U.S. Naval Academy	5**	3	Active duty as ensign in the Navy or a second lieutenant in the Marine Corps
U.S. Air Force Academy	5**	3	Active duty as second lieutenant in the Air Force
U.S. Merchant Marines		6	Maintain a license as a merchant marine officer (issued by the U.S. Coast Guard); must be renewed at year 5, which requires a certain period of time (e.g., 365 days) at sea
		5	Serve as commissioned officer in the U.S. Naval Reserve (including the Merchant Marine Reserve, U.S. Naval Reserve, U.S. Coast Guard Reserve, or any other Reserve unit of an armed force of the United States)
		3	Serve the foreign and domestic commerce and national defense of the United States
U.S. Coast Guard Academy	5	3	Active duty as officer in the U.S. Coast Guard
U.S. Military Academy	5	3	Active duty as officer in the U.S. Army

*This is the minimum number of years required. As the text notes, the "stop-loss" provisions of the agreement officers (and enlisted personnel) sign allows the military to keep them in uniform beyond the five-year mark if it needs them.

**Aviation service commitment depends on type of aircraft and whether you are a pilot or naval flight officer. Most aviators are required to serve seven years on active duty after they complete their initial flight training

ADMISSIONS DIRECTORS ON LIFE AFTER A SERVICE ACADEMY

One of the benefits of the Merchant Marine Academy is that the average nineteen-year-old may not know which branch of the military to join. Merchant Marine Academy graduates can enter any branch of the military upon graduation, giving them a bit more time to choose. *Capt. Robert Johnson, U.S. Merchant Marine Academy*

Attending a service academy allows graduates to take on leadership roles immediately after graduation. You don't have to stand in line at job interviews. You're hired, and you're leading from Day 1.   *Rollie Stoneman, U.S. Air Force Academy*

The job the Coast Guard Academy graduates go on to is extremely satisfying. As a result, Coast Guard graduates stay in service two to three times longer than graduates of other service academies.   *Capt. Susan D. Bibeau, U.S. Coast Guard Academy*

HOW TO GET INTO A SERVICE ACADEMY

WHAT SERVICE ACADEMIES LOOK FOR IN APPLICANTS

ACADEMIC QUALIFICATIONS

Service academies are looking for applicants who have taken a challenging courseload in high school. Some service academies, such as the Merchant Marines, require applicants to have a certain minimum number of credits of certain high school courses. Others merely recommend that candidates complete a desired list of courses. The chart below lays out the basics of what each academy looks for, but you should refer to academy websites and/or admissions materials for details.

REQUIRED/RECOMMENDED HIGH SCHOOL PREREQUISITES (IN UNITS*)

	MATH		SCIENCE		ENGLISH		FOREIGN LANGUAGE		OTHER
	REQ.	REC.	REQ.	REC.	REQ.	REC.	REQ.	REC.	
Army	4	—	2**	—	4	—	2	—	2 units history required; economics, basic computing recommended
Navy	4	—	1	1**	4	—	—	2	Chemistry required; history, physics recommended; familiarity with Windows, word processing,

	MATH		SCIENCE		ENGLISH		FOREIGN LANGUAGE		
	REQ.	REC.	REQ.	REC.	REQ.	REC.	REQ.	REC.	OTHER
Navy (con't)									spreadsheets, and Internet recommended
Air Force	—	4	—	4	—	4	—	2	3 years social science, computer science recommended
Coast Guard	4	—	—	3	4	—	—	2	
Merchant Marines	3	4	3**	4	4	—	—	2	4 units social studies recommended

*One unit is generally equal to a full academic year's worth of study
**Lab science required

Would-be applicants are also advised to be well prepared for their standardized tests. They should also be aware that service academies do not accept nonstandard or untimed administration of the SAT. The minimum acceptable scores for standardized tests are laid out in the chart below.

Standardized Test Scores. The generally acceptable standardized test minimums for admission to service academies appear in the chart below, although admissions officers are quick to point out that these are minimum scores—the class averages are much higher:

		SAT*	ACT
Air Force	Reading	600	26
	Math	600	27
Navy	Reading	600	25
	Math	600	27
Military	Reading	630	26
	Math	630	30
Coast Guard	Reading	600	26
	Math	600	27
Merchant Marines	Reading	510	21
	Math	560	24

*The required scores on the writing section have not yet been established.

LEADERSHIP AND MORAL CHARACTER

Service academies follow general guidelines for measuring *leadership* ability in their applicants. They are looking for candidates who demonstrate extra-curricular interests and who show a drive to lead. Service academies are not looking for candidates who are necessarily well-rounded in terms of their extracurricular participation. Better than actively participating in many teams or clubs is having a leadership role in only one or two.

**WHY SERVICE ACADEMIES VALUE
EXTRACURRICULAR INVOLVEMENT**

The academies value extracurricular involvement for many reasons, all related to their view of what it takes to be an officer. What they learn about candidates differs according to the nature of the extracurricular involvement:

All extracurricular activities:

- Require you to learn to prioritize tasks and to manage your time
- Help you learn to get along with many different sorts of people

Volunteer and service activities:

- Demonstrate a service orientation, which is considered crucial by academies that view themselves as preparing you for a lifetime of service to the country

Varsity athletics:

- All sports signal a competitive instinct and develop resolution as well as physical skill
- Team sports require the subordination of individual to group interests
- Particularly valued are contact sports, such as football, wrestling, and hockey (and to a somewhat lesser extent, lacrosse and soccer), insofar as they develop courage under the most stressful conditions

Leadership of extracurricular activities:

- Require you to be dependable and determined
- Show you have earned the respect of your peers and/or adult supervisors

Lengthy involvement in an activity:

- Shows you are determined, that you don't expect immediate payoffs
- Becoming an Eagle Scout is the prime example (since it takes years to reach this status)

Most helpful to your application may be participation in team sports (as opposed to solitary sports). Being involved in a team sport is very similar to being in the military. If you succeed as a leader of a sports team, service academies take this as a good predictor of your potential to be an effective officer. In spite of their appreciation for team sports, however, service academies do not define leadership too narrowly—it can be demonstrated in nontraditional ways, such as taking over for an absent parent at home.

Each service academy defines *moral character* slightly differently, but all focus on the same set of qualities. The U.S. Air Force Academy, for example, defines character as "qualities of moral excellence which compel a person to do the right things despite pressure or temptations to the contrary." Its stated objective is to graduate officers who:

- Have forthright integrity, voluntarily deciding the right thing to do and doing it
- Are selfless in service to the country, the Air Force, and their subordinates
- Are committed to excellence in the performance of their personal and professional responsibilities
- Respect the dignity of all human beings
- Are decisive, even when faced with high-risk situations
- Take full responsibility for their decisions
- Have the self-discipline, stamina, and courage to do their duty well under even the extreme and prolonged conditions of national defense
- Appreciate the significance of spiritual values and beliefs to their own character development and that of the community

Moral character can be difficult to demonstrate for admissions purposes, but the list above provides a useful guideline for doing so. At the very minimum, candidates must have a clean criminal record, as well as a record free of drug and alcohol abuse. Once offers are extended, the service academies perform a very detailed background and security check. Offers can be withdrawn if harmful information is discovered. Failure to disclose relevant information, even if the underlying issue is a minor one, can also result in withdrawal of an offer.

PUTTING IT TOGETHER: ACADEMICS AND LEADERSHIP

Top civilian colleges are looking for candidates who excel in one or more pursuits, whatever the nature of the pursuits. They are thrilled to find a student who has directed a broadcast documentary, published poetry, or hiked the whole length of the Appalachian trail. Service academies, on the other hand, are looking for well-rounded students who push themselves to be the best leaders they can be, especially in team sports. This means that, at the margins, civilian colleges and service academies will favor different kinds of candidates. Both would love to get a candidate with great academics and great leadership experience, just as both would reject someone with so-so academics and so-so leadership. The differences are to be seen when one or the other dimension has to be sacrificed. As the chart on the next page shows, civilian schools are more likely to take someone with strong academics and acceptable leadership, whereas service academies will prefer the reverse: strong leadership and acceptable academics.

STUDENT ADMISSIBILITY AT CIVILIAN COLLEGES AND SERVICE ACADEMIES		
	ACCEPTABLE ACADEMICS	SUPERIOR ACADEMICS
Acceptable Leadership	Difficult to gain acceptance at either service academies or selective civilian colleges	Selective civilian colleges more likely to admit than service academies
Superior Leadership	Service academies more likely to admit than than selective civilian colleges	Candidate is competitive at both service academies and selective civilian colleges

AN ADMISSIONS DIRECTOR DISCUSSES ADMISSIONS CRITERIA

We walk away from a lot of high scorers in favor of students who have really challenged themselves. *Capt. Susan D. Bibeau, U.S. Coast Guard Academy*

ADMISSIONS DIRECTORS DISCUSS THE
BENEFITS OF EARLY PREPARATION

Do as well as you can in high school—take the right classes that will provide you tools to succeed. Prepare for your standardized tests and do well. And find some way to lead. *Major William Smith, U.S. Military Academy (West Point)*

Academics are the most important component of the application. We cram four years of classroom education into three since cadets spend so much time at sea. Courses will come at you fast and furious and you must have the academic wherewithal to be up for the challenge. *Capt. Robert Johnson, U.S. Merchant Marine Academy*

We are looking for leaders—people who earn the respect of their peers and subordinates. In our experience, it's easier to take someone with leadership ability and teach them math and science by sending them through preparatory school than it is to take someone with great math and science skills and teach them to lead. Leadership ability is more innate. *Maj. William Smith, U.S. Military Academy (West Point)*

We encourage students interested in the Air Force Academy to step out of your comfort zone. Challenge yourself to learn and lead. Not every applicant is going to be class president or team captain of a varsity sport. Knowing this, we are looking for what you have done with the opportunities presented. *Rollie Stoneman, U.S. Air Force Academy*

Service academy attendance is something that needs to be thought through carefully. It's not something you just happen into. *Capt. Susan D. Bibeau, U.S. Coast Guard Academy*

It's not important that you do a lot of activities. Focus on being a leader in one or two things that matter to you. *Maj. William Smith, U.S. Military Academy (West Point)*

Candidates who want to attend the Naval Academy should start thinking about it and preparing for it as early as seventh and eighth grades. This is the time to get on the right math track, to start mapping out a high school curriculum that includes the tough courses, and to start civic or other extracurricular involvement that will allow you to gain leadership. *Capt. Karen Frye, U.S. Naval Academy*

We do see a difference between team sports and individual sports in terms of evaluating applications. Team sport participation is very analogous to interaction on the military level. Seeing leadership qualities in a team sport gives us a little more insight into the person if they are able to succeed in that environment. *Maj. William Smith, U.S. Military Academy (West Point)*

If you have an affinity for leadership, develop those skills by leading a club or sports team, or be a leader at home—there are lots of ways to demonstrate leadership skills. *Capt. Susan D. Bibeau, U.S. Coast Guard Academy*

PHYSICAL AND MEDICAL FITNESS

Being on a high school varsity team will not in itself qualify you physically to attend a service academy. Although such achievement is appreciated by service academy admissions committees, each academy requires applicants to meet defined physical standards that don't necessarily relate to how well you kick a soccer ball. Different service academies have different minimum requirements for the physical aptitude that applicants must be able to demonstrate.

Each candidate is required to take a physical exam to determine his or her readiness to undertake the rigorous physical component of service academy training. The various services have been trying to settle on a common exam for all candidates, but different services currently accept or require different exams. The most common is the Candidate Fitness Assessment (CFA), accepted by the Naval Academy, the Military Academy, and the Air Force Academy. The CFA events are a basketball throw, pull-ups, a shuttle run, crunches, push-ups, and a one-mile run. Candidates are allowed an eight-minute rest between each event. Candidates receive a higher score the better they perform on the CFA. Although there is a minimum that candidates must score to qualify, some schools award candidates more points for more repetitions, faster times, and so on. At each service academy, the physical exam results play a substantial role in the admissions decision.

CANDIDATE FITNESS ASSESSMENT

	B-BALL THROW	PULL-UPS	SHUTTLE RUN	CRUNCHES	PUSH-UPS	1-MILE
Men	102 ft	18 (in 2 min)	7.8 sec, 10 yards four times	95 (in 2 min)	75 (in 2 min)	5:20
Women	66	7	8.6	95	50	6:00

More information on the test requirements and scoring of the three tests currently in use are available at:
CFA: http://admissions.usma.edu/prospectus/CFA_Instructions05.pdf
PFE: http://admissions.uscga.edu/i2e/academy_admission/fitness_exam.asp
PAE: www.academyadmissions.com/admissions/eligibility/pae/instructions.htm

The tests require that you prepare adequately:

Physical preparation. No matter which type of test you take, the best way to prepare is to be in the best physical condition possible. You should have completed the test in simulated conditions (i.e., timed and in order) multiple times before taking it for real.

Proper pacing. Each examination tests your abilities in a series of timed tests one after the other. Use your practice efforts to determine how hard you can push on the first events without exhausting yourself for the following events.

Mental preparation. Applicants should not focus solely on physical training. For some, the physical strain of the test is less than the mental toll. Applicants who score well on practice tests have been known to fail during the actual test due to nervousness. Consider how best to calm your nerves so that you can perform up to your potential.

Each academy requires an extensive examination to determine medical fitness for attendance at the academy and military service beyond. The medical examination is necessary to ensure that cadets will not harm themselves during training because of a medical condition. Although medical evaluation standards differ among the various service academies, only one medical examination is needed to meet the application requirements of all of them. The Department of Defense Medical Examination Review Board (DODMERB) is responsible for scheduling and evaluating the medical examination. Only scholastically qualified applicants will undergo the medical examination portion once the nomination process is complete.

With the medical examination in hand, the different schools will apply their own criteria to determine physical fitness for their program. Some service academies, because of the nature of the activities in that particular branch of the military, have very strict standards in particular areas. For example, if you hope to fly with the Air Force, your vision can be no less than 20/50. If you aim to navigate boats on the open seas for the Coast Guard, the Merchant Marines, or the Navy, you will be disqualified if you are color blind (the ability to distinguish between red and green signals on the high seas is critical).

The Waiver Process. If the DODMERB determines that you have a disqualifying condition, all is not lost. A waiver process is available. If you are an otherwise desirable candidate, and if the disqualifying condition is not too serious, the service academy may pursue a waiver. The most difficult conditions to obtain waivers for are those where recent medical intervention has been necessary. For example, a candidate is more likely to receive a waiver for an ADHD condition if she was medicated for it only as a child, not as a young adult. Those seeking waivers should be forewarned: however much a service academy wants you, it will not risk health problems hampering your ability to perform amid the rigors of the academy and beyond.

THE APPLICATION PROCESS: WHAT IT ENTAILS AND STRATEGIES FOR SUCCESS

The first part of developing an application strategy for service academies is to understand how the application process differs from that at civilian schools.

APPLICATION SCHEDULE

There are more moving pieces in a service academy application than that of civilian schools. Each service academy has its own application process, although they all share the same basic components:

1. Nomination (except Coast Guard Academy)
2. Essays
3. Interviews
4. Recommendations
5. Physical examination
6. Medical examination

The timing of the various components differs from academy to academy, and even changes year to year. Contact the service academy directly for up-to-date information prior to starting the application process.

The Merchant Marine Academy and the U.S. Coast Guard Academy are the only service academies that offer Early Application. The Coast Guard Academy offers a nonbinding Early Action option, while the Merchant Marine Academy offers a binding Early Decision option. All service academies feature a Rolling Admissions model that gives Early applicants an edge over those who wait to apply. The complexity of the process rewards those who start their application efforts early—certainly not later than the winter of their junior year.

TYPICAL APPLICATION SCHEDULE*:
AIR FORCE, ARMY, MERCHANT MARINE, NAVY

TIME FRAME	APPLICATION ACTIVITY
February/March, Junior Year	Submit preliminary application to service academy (e.g., an online application that supplies basic information)
June, Junior Year–September, Senior Year	Submit application to nominating source(s)
October–November, Senior Year	Submit formal application to service academy (including transcripts, scores, recommendations, essays, etc.)
September–March, Senior Year	Submit to medical examination
NOTE: These pieces are scheduled by the Service Academy; timing will depend on when preliminary application/formal application is complete	Submit to physical examination Interview
March–May, Senior Year	Majority of offers of admission extended
May 1, Senior Year	Deadline for accepting offer of admission

*Note that different service academies have their own schedules and order the various elements differently. This breakdown is intended to give only an approximation of the timeline.

TYPICAL APPLICATION SCHEDULE: COAST GUARD

TIME FRAME	APPLICATION ACTIVITY
August 1–March 1, Senior Year	Submit application including essays, recommendation and transcript, PFE, etc.
September–March, Senior Year	Submit to medical examination
November 1, Senior Year	Early Action deadline
December 15, Senior Year	Early Action responses mailed (about half of CGA appointments are given under Early Action)
Mid-April, Senior Year	Majority of offers of admission extended
May 1, Senior Year	Deadline for accepting offer of admission

NOMINATIONS

To win acceptance at a service academy (except the Coast Guard Academy), you must be nominated by an authorized source. Some applicants may qualify for a "military-affiliated nomination." Military-affiliated nominations (also referred to as "service" nominations) are available to candidates who are sons and daughters of career military personnel, sons and daughters of deceased and disabled veterans, sons and daughters of persons awarded the Medal of Honor, persons serving in the military, and those enrolled in ROTC.

Those who do not qualify for a military-affiliated nomination must acquire a nomination from another authorized nominating source—either a member of Congress or the vice president. Congresspersons may submit nominations of candidates residing in their district only, whereas senators may nominate candidates on a statewide basis and the vice president on a nationwide basis.

The Air Force Academy, Naval Academy, and Military Academy share the same nomination process; the Merchant Marine Academy process is slightly different. Each representative is allotted five spaces at each service academy to fill with candidates from his or her state/district. This means that a congressperson only has as many slots to fill as there are vacancies among the five allotted slots. If Congressman Jones has five nominees at the Naval Academy in a given year where two slots are filled by second-year cadets, a third is in her third year, and one will graduate while another withdraws, that means Congressman Jones will have two slots to fill during the next application season. A representative may nominate ten candidates to fill each vacancy. Some years, a representative might need to nominate candidates for all five slots (i.e., fifty nominees); some years, no slots may be open.

The same person may receive nominations from more than one nominating source—for instance, both a congressperson and a senator—and may be nominated for more than one service academy. Those interested in applying to a service academy are encouraged to apply for a nomination from as many sources as possible. For example, apply for a nomination from your congressperson *and* senator. As can be expected, competition at the Senate level is more difficult than it is at the House level. Vice-presidential nominations are the toughest, given the nationwide competition.

EXAMPLE: NUMBER OF SLOTS ALLOTTED TO FILL AT WEST POINT

CONGRESSIONAL

1. Vice President: 5
2. Senate: 500 (100×5)

3. House of Representatives: 2,175 (435×5)
4. Virgin Islands: 2
5. Guam: 2
6. Puerto Rico: 6
7. Samoa: 1

SERVICE CONNECTED

1. President: 400
2. Regular Army/Army Reserve: 340/340
3. ROTC: 80
4. Medal of Honor: Unlimited

OTHER QUALIFIED CANDIDATES

The U.S. Military Academy is authorized to admit applicants (from the list of nominated candidates) beyond the above slots to round out its number to the authorized strength of 4,000.

A certain number of slots is given to the superintendent at West Point to use at his discretion, usually for varsity athletes and for demographic purposes.

NOMINATION PROCESS

Each "nomination source" (such as a congressperson) will have his or her own process for evaluating candidates for nomination. Even nominating sources within the same state may have different procedures and criteria. Therefore the best advice is to contact each to find out the particular process involved, and the criteria used, to evaluate applicants.

Each nominating source will have his or her own deadline. Typically, candidates may submit their nomination applications sometime between June and September leading up to their senior year. Congressional offices must submit their final nominations no later than January 31.

You will need to submit, at a minimum, a high school transcript, standardized test scores, recommendations, a résumé, and an essay explaining why you are interested in attending a service academy. If you pass certain minimum criteria—such as having acceptable test scores and grades—you can also expect to be interviewed. On occasion, the congressperson will conduct the interview. But most likely the interview will be conducted by a congressional staffer or by a review board made up of community members (usually community leaders, persons with backgrounds in education or in the military, and so on).

NOMINATION INTERVIEWS

Applicants who make it to the interview should not expect a hand-holding session like civilian colleges employ. Stressful interviews that probe each aspect of a candidate's academic and leadership record, motivation, and knowledge of what is in store at the academy are by no means uncommon. Don't be surprised if an interviewer acts skeptical about claims you make. In this type of interview, part of what is being assessed is whether you remain calm in the face of difficulty.

Typical questions include:

Why do you want to attend the academy? Instead of just answering, "I've always known I wanted to," you need to reveal your underlying motivations. What do you see yourself doing upon graduation? Why do you want to be in the service? (If you intend to use the academy as a stepping-stone to something other than being an officer, you will in all likelihood fail the interview.) Which of your interests and values will be satisfied? How did you develop your desire to attend the academy? What events developed or crystallized your desire? In addition to understanding your own motivations, you should research the service academy well. Show the interviewer that you are aware of what you will encounter, and that you have given serious thought to what the career entails. Be familiar with the curricular choices and be able to voice your preferences about academic majors. The more knowledge you demonstrate about the institution and the career it enables, the more serious a candidate you will appear.

Why do you want to be an officer? See the discussion above, regarding your desire to attend the academy. Keep in mind that a service academy is considering making a big investment in you. It is paying for your education and training, for which you are expected to pay it back. The more you can demonstrate that you will make good on your commitment to serve, the better. Be prepared to articulate why you want to serve, and where the source of your commitment to serve comes from.

What are your backup plans (if you don't get into the academy)? If you truly intend to become an officer, presumably you will try either to go to another service academy or to find another way (ROTC, perhaps) into the military.

What do your parents think of you attending the academy? It's taken as positive if your parents are supportive of your desire to attend but not if you may be applying largely because of their desire that you do so. The major reason people drop out of a service academy is because they were there more at the behest of relatives than because they themselves wanted to attend.

What does your boyfriend/girlfriend think about you attending the academy? It's perfectly fine that you have a boyfriend (if you're female) or girlfriend (if you're male), but it would be good if he or she were supportive of your intention to attend the academy. If not, the risk of you dropping out due to homesickness or lack of support increases.

What are you doing to prepare for the physical rigors of the academy? Show that you know the importance of being very fit in getting through the academy—especially the first year, when out-of-shape students face extra scrutiny from older students and officers. By all means note your varsity athletic participation and whatever training it involves, but more importantly, discuss the specific workout schedule you have established for yourself.

Who is your hero? You certainly need not name a military figure or an athletic star or someone famous. The hallmarks of this person's heroism might be physical or moral courage. On the other hand, he or she may be your hero because of the contribution made to society (or you), presumably in spite of challenges that had to be overcome in order to contribute.

Have you ever spotted a friend cheating at school? What did you do? The honor code at the academies would require you to turn in someone spotted cheating. Failure to do so would put you at risk of dismissal. Even if you answer that you've never spotted someone cheating, expect a follow-up question as to what you would do if you did spot someone cheating.

How stressful do you think the academy will be? What sort of stress do you expect? What makes you think that you will be able to handle it? Each academy is physically and emotionally stressful, as this chapter points out. (In fact, your own investigation of an academy should reveal that this chapter does not do justice to the level of stress felt by most academy students.) You should be realistic in describing how difficult the experience is for most students and equally realistic in describing both what stresses you have faced to date and what coping mechanisms you have developed.

How will you react to being in what remains largely a man's world? (Asked of women) *How will you react to being ordered about by a woman?* (Asked of men) These questions try to determine whether you are comfortable with the idea of a coed academy and service.

What do you make of [fill in one of the lead stories from the day's newspapers]? To ascertain whether you keep up on what is happening in the world, expect to be quizzed about something currently in the headlines.

Why should we nominate you? Be ready to state your case succinctly. Military officers are expected to be able to communicate effectively, particularly when it comes to questions (such as this one) they should be expecting. Prepare a one- to two-minute response that marshals argument and evidence showing your motivation as well as your physical, mental, and emotional attributes.

General interview advice:

■ Given that military officers are expected to be highly presentable, you should be, too. You certainly do not need to dress expensively. You do need to wear something conservative, pressed, and clean.

■ Shake hands firmly. Look the interviewers in the eye. Stand and sit up straight. Don't fidget.

■ Address your interviewers by title (Mr. Jones, for instance) or by "sir" or "ma'am."

■ Being an officer in the U.S. military requires excellent oral communication skills. Do your best in the interview to articulate clearly, concisely, and confidently.

■ If you are asked a question to which you do not know the answer, you need to respond as an officer would. It is perfectly acceptable to say that you do not know the answer. It is not acceptable to be terribly flustered by the question. You need to appear in control of yourself, particularly when stressed.

■ The interview serves as a key opportunity to evaluate an applicant's character. Think hard ahead of time about ways you can work information about your morals and values into the conversation. Be prepared to discuss your devotion to a team or organization and the reasons why you are or were committed to it; show your willingness to sacrifice for others; demonstrate your notion of doing right; tell a story where you faced pressures (both internal and external) to do something that went against your values and explain how your innate moral character helped you make the right decision; discuss your moral mentors.

■ Given the importance of this interview and the fact that it is likely to be very different than any other interviews you have had, doing a practice interview is particularly valuable. Find a retired or serving officer who will perform the honors.

■ Be yourself. As in any interview situation, it is a poor idea to pretend to be something you are not. You will come across as disingenuous.

TIPS FOR SECURING A NOMINATION

Students applying to service academies face a unique challenge—they must conquer two admissions processes simultaneously: through their nominating source and within the service academy. The more you understand about these processes and how they interact, the better your chances of succeeding.

■ *Know your state.* In some states, nominations are more competitive than they are in others (due to different population size and relative popularity of the military). Among the most competitive states in which to secure a nomination are New York, California, and Texas, along with the home state of the particular service academy to which you are seeking a nomination. Where competition for nomination slots is fierce, a nominating source may require that candidates select only one service academy for which they seek a nomination—that way, the state can nominate the greatest number of candidates. For states where competition is not as tough, a candidate may be nominated for multiple academies. Regardless of the level of competition in your district, you must secure a nomination from within the state where you are a legal resident.

- *Apply Early.* Applying Early not only demonstrates your enthusiasm but also shows that you are organized and able to get things done—traits highly valued by the military. Since many nominating sources fill their slots on a first-come, first-nominated basis, you can be doubly advantaged by applying Early.

- *Get the service academy on your side.* Open your application file at the service academy before applying for a nomination. If the service academy wants you, the admissions director will generally contact your nominating source to indicate interest. Sometimes the service academy will issue a Letter of Assurance, which lets the nominating source know that, based on your preliminary application, you would be accepted if nominated. This may help distinguish you from the pack at the congressional office and pave your way toward being nominated. At the Naval Academy, in fact, you can be accepted for admission *before* you receive a nomination. Though there is no assurance you will receive a nomination just because you've been admitted, sending in an acceptance letter with your nomination materials is very likely to give you a leg up.

- *Cast your net widely.* Although it may seem that you should demonstrate commitment to only one service academy, to maximize the chance of securing a nomination, candidates should list more than one preference (even all four) when they apply to a nominating source.

- *Use all available resources.* In days gone by, securing a nomination was often a political process. A nominating source might have valued your being a member of an important constituency (i.e., important to his or her electoral desires), espousing ideas that he or she valued (or belonging to groups that did), and so on. Now this is the exception rather than the rule. It is unlikely that you will need such advantages to secure a nomination, assuming you are otherwise qualified.

NUMBER OF APPLICANTS IN A REPRESENTATIVE YEAR

	NUMBER OF APPLICANTS	NUMBER OF NOMINATIONS	NUMBER FULLY QUALIFIED	NUMBER ADMITTED
Air Force	9,500	4,300	2,200	1,300
Merchant Marines	2,500	1,500	700	285
Military	12,000	4,000	2,500	1,180
Navy	11,250	4,300	1,800	1,220

As the numbers make clear, securing a nomination is a vital step in the admissions process, one that a majority of applicants fail to manage.

SERVICE ACADEMY APPLICATIONS

Although the nomination process is unique to service academies, other parts of the application process resemble those of civilian schools. Service academies require applicants to submit essays and recommendations and require or recommend interviews. You will find helpful tips elsewhere in this book on these topics. The discussion below highlights strategies in these areas specific to service academy applications.

ESSAYS

Applicants to service academies must write essays on topics relating to their ambition to serve and to their leadership skills. As an example, the U.S. Military Academy asks the following questions:

1. Write an essay explaining why you want to attend the USMA (1 page)

2. Cadets who graduate from West Point serve for a minimum of five years on active duty. Question: Why do you want to serve as an Army officer after earning your degree and commission? (1/2 page)

3. What do you think are the most important qualities in becoming a successful cadet and a successful Army officer? (1/2 page)

At most service academies, the essays must be handwritten (although this is changing as the application process moves online). The most common mistake on handwritten essays tends to be illegibility, but poor grammar and spelling, incoherent organization, and a general inability to communicate effectively are also prevalent. Applicants should remember that they are seeking to become officers—to be a leader requires effective communication skills, and that includes *written* communication skill. This is why English is stressed so heavily both in academic prerequisites and once you are there.

Consult the relevant chapters about writing essays but keep in mind that service academy essays are necessarily limited in their focus. If you can clearly demonstrate your desire to serve and to lead, along with your moral character, a failure to show that you are extraordinarily interesting will probably not be disqualifying.

LOOKING FOR LEADERSHIP

Being a leader is arguably at least as much in your control as getting good grades or passing a physical. Looking to take on leadership roles (not necessarily by title but by impact) is a win-win proposition because in the effort to be seen as a leader by the admissions officers, you will become what you are trying to look like. By trying to make a substantial difference in organizations and learning to make the maximum impact on those around you, you will be doing more than padding your résumé—you will be building the exact set of skills service academies seek.

RECOMMENDATIONS

Most service academies have specific requirements for who must supply recommendation letters. The Air Force Academy, for example, requires one recommendation from an English teacher, one from a math teacher, plus one other. Like in the civilian school application process, students should approach recommenders who know them well. Twenty recommendations from sources who know you only vaguely will do nothing to enhance your application. Service academies do not recommend supplying extra recommendations beyond those required but will accept them.

Successful recommendation letters will show admissions officers that the applicant is of high moral character and possesses the commitment and drive to succeed at the service academy. Your grades and scores will help admissions officers see that you can handle the academic work, but your recommendations should show who you are as a person. As the chapter on recommendations discusses, providing specific examples rather than making broad statements ("showing" rather than "telling") will be most helpful. Finally, it is particularly helpful if the recommender is familiar with service academies' structure and goals. This knowledge will enhance the relevance of the recommendation. A recommender who knows both the applicant and the service academy well is best.

INTERVIEWS

Service academies interview candidates, although the timing and nature varies. Most service academies offer an optional interview at some point during the admissions process. Interviews can occur on campus, during school visits, or in the candidate's hometown or home state. Like civilian schools, service academies typically have a corps of volunteers across the country who interview interested candidates. They supply information about the academy to applicants and gauge candidates' levels of interest and commitment to service. These interviews are similar to the nominating source interviews. (Consult the discussion on page 494 regarding "Nomination Interviews.")

ADMISSIONS DIRECTORS DISCUSS ESSAYS, RECOMMENDATIONS, AND INTERVIEWS

Too often essays fail to answer the question about their motivations for applying, or students don't write essays with sufficient depth to allow us to assess commitment to the Naval Academy and to serving. *Capt. Karen Frye, U.S. Naval Academy*

Students would be wise to request recommendations from individuals who are familiar with service academies. These recommendations are commonly the strongest because they speak to strengths we care about. *Capt. Susan D. Bibeau, U.S. Coast Guard Academy*

We get applicants who give us twenty recommendations from people who barely know them. We far prefer to hear from a select few who know you quite well and can speak from personal knowledge to your character and commitment. *Capt. Karen Frye, U.S. Naval Academy*

We rely heavily on recommendations to determine the moral component of the application. *Capt. Susan D. Bibeau, U.S. Coast Guard Academy*

If you interview at a service academy, think beforehand about why you want to go and be able to articulate this forcefully in the interview. *Capt. Robert Johnson, U.S. Merchant Marine Academy*

The candidate who has an understanding of what he or she would do with a degree from the Naval Academy has an edge in the interview process. Candidates should know the mission and purpose of the academy and the Navy, and how his or her goals fit with those missions and purposes. Do your research before you talk to us. *Capt. Karen Frye, U.S. Naval Academy*

IF YOUR APPLICATION IS NOT QUITE UP TO SNUFF

At top civilian schools, an "almost but not quite" admissions committee decision means rejection. At the service academies, if you show true promise as a leader and pass the physical and medical requirements but your academic skills are not quite up to snuff, you might still be in luck. One solid option is to matriculate at a nonmilitary school and take a demanding courseload, especially in English, math, and sciences. Demonstrate that you can do the work and then reapply. At the U.S. Naval Academy, 7 to 8 percent of the first-year class has typically taken this route (but note that it requires undertaking the first year of college twice).

Another option is to attend a service academy's designated preparatory school. Promising candidates who are not offered appointments at federal service academies may find themselves channeled to a preparatory program designed to hone their skills in advance of matriculating (see the box below).

SERVICE ACADEMY PREPARATORY SCHOOLS

Each of the service academies has a designated preparatory school, where candidates who did not gain entry can go to learn the necessary skills. Most of these preparatory schools do not accept applications directly. Rather, the directors of admissions at the various service academies select applicants who show promise, but for one reason or another (usually academic) did not make the cut for appointment to a service academy. Preparatory programs generally last ten to eleven months, and consist of intensive instruction in English, math, and basic science courses. Many of the students selected for preparatory programs are prior enlisted servicemen and women (i.e., those formerly or currently serving in the Armed Forces) whose college preparatory classes in high school were inadequate. At the Air Force Preparatory School, for example, approximately 20 percent of students are prior enlisted personnel.

Approximately 75 to 80 percent of students entering service academy preparatory schools will secure appointments at the end of their preparatory term.

Some service academies, such as the Air Force, have a preparatory school on or near campus. On the other hand, the Naval Academy Preparatory School (in Maine) serves as a preparatory school for the U.S. Naval Academy, the U.S. Merchant Marine Academy, and the U.S. Coast Guard Academy. Other preparatory schools, not directly affiliated with the service academies, also feed cadets to service academies. Examples include the Service Academy Preparatory Program at the Valley Forge Military Academy and College (in Wayne, PA) and the New Mexico Military Institute.

CONCLUDING THOUGHTS

If you have made it to the end of this chapter, chances are you should take the option of attending a service academy seriously. For those with appropriate ambition and drive, attending a service academy and becoming an officer in the military thereafter can be tremendously fulfilling. But as anyone familiar with life at a service academy and beyond will tell you, a solid understanding of what is involved and thoughtful self-reflection are critical precursors to taking this route.

ATTENDING A FOREIGN UNIVERSITY

— KEY POINTS —

Some students should consider attending a foreign university

Four countries in particular offer attractive options:
—England
—Canada
—Australia
—Scotland

The attractions vary from country to country
—So do the admission requirements

One attraction is constant: Education abroad is nearly always less expensive

INTRODUCTION

Going to college in the United States is certainly the easy and obvious option for American high school graduates. Given that America has what is generally considered the finest university system in the world, it may not be immediately obvious why anyone should even consider doing a degree abroad. In fact, there are a number of potential advantages to attending college abroad:

- Lower overall cost
- Development of language skills
- Cultural understanding
- Development of initiative and independence (due to being far from home)
- Superior education
- Superior reputation

These potential advantages are just that: *potential* advantages. In other words, many of them are decidedly not available at all foreign universities. For example, it is unlikely that one of Italy's enormous state universities or Turkey's Anadolu University, with well over 500,000 students, offers a superior education in many subjects than can be found at leading American schools.

The best bets abroad are to be found in countries that both invest substantially in university education and have a clear hierarchy of schools. France, for instance, has a clearly denoted set of Grandes Ecoles atop its university system. Five of them are of particular interest to those looking for an elite education:

- Ecole Nationale d'Administration (commonly known as ENA), specializing in administration
- Ecole Normale Superieure (Normale Sup), humanities
- Haute Ecole de Commerce (HEC), business
- Ecole Polytechnique (X), engineering
- Institut d'Etudes Politiques de Paris (Sciences Po), social sciences

Germany, on the other hand, does not offer the same possibilities. It has until recently resolutely resisted creating an elite set of universities. As a result, no German university enjoys the same prestige locally that the five French schools listed above have in the Francophone world.

Although it is beyond the scope of this book to explore educational options throughout the world, four countries are worth a look. Australia, Canada, England, and Scotland offer marvelous opportunities for those willing to look outside the United States for a quality education. All of these countries are (generally) English-speaking, meaning that few Americans will be precluded from applying to their universities as a result of language. Just as important, their leading universities enjoy fine reputations worldwide. (After all, those candidates who opt to forgo a degree at a leading American school are likely to value highly an education abroad that resonates with American employers and graduate schools.) We start with England, and focus extra attention on it, because both its universities and their admissions procedures are substantially different from those in the United States. Our detailed analysis of the English university (and secondary education) system and admissions procedures provides a useful example from which readers can benefit even if they choose to apply to schools in other countries. By the same token, the leading English universities enjoy a prestige in America that makes an analysis of who should consider applying, what it takes to get in, and so on too enticing to pass up.

We then examine what is available in Canada; its proximity and the similarity of its education system make it a natural choice for Americans to consider. Next we look at Australia and Scotland; even though Scotland is indeed part of the United Kingdom, as is England, their educational systems differ in important ways. We therefore take a brief look at the key differences.

THE ENGLISH EXAMPLE

The English university system is radically different from our system of higher education. The criteria necessary for successful admission to a university, the expectations of first-year university students, the methods of teaching, and the means of academic evaluation in England are all dramatically different from our own. An average American student would have difficulty trying to transition from high school in the United States to one of England's institutions of higher learning, but the very best and most independent American students preparing to go to the top colleges may be well-suited to the English alternative. Therefore, the option of going to university in England is one very much worth exploring, but only if you feel—after closely examining the English university model—that it is suited to you and your needs.

THE BENEFITS OF ATTENDING AN ENGLISH UNIVERSITY

■ An undergraduate B.A. takes only three years to complete, allowing a student to enter the workforce or graduate school one year earlier than in the United States.

- The three-year plan saves a family (at the very least) a full year of tuition and expenses (generally around $50,000 to $60,000 at the top schools in the United States). In addition, attending university in England can save a family $15,000 to $25,000 a year on annual tuition, for a possible savings of some $100,000 to $130,000.

- Oxford and Cambridge confer honorary master's degrees on their first-degree candidates three years after graduation. A student essentially receives two degrees for three years of actual study in the Oxbridge system.

- There is enormous prestige and credibility attached to the names of universities such as Oxford, Cambridge, and LSE, giving a graduate of one of these schools a secure foundation upon which to build a future.

- The focused programs, one-on-one tutorials (at Oxford and Cambridge), and general intensity of the academics provide a student with excellent preparation for graduate study.

- Many subjects are well pursued in England. LSE, for instance, has some of the best undergraduate departments in the world in fields such as history, international relations, law, politics, and economics.

- Law, medicine, and other professional fields can be studied as first degrees in England, allowing for entry into a professional career at a much younger age than is usual in the United States.

- A student at an English university learns to become more independent and mature than his or her counterparts who remain on American soil throughout college.

- Attending university in another culture enhances a student's worldliness.

- Proximity to continental Europe allows for remarkable travel opportunities and cultural stimulation.

There are hundreds of degree-granting institutions in Britain. But if you plan to return to the United States in later life, you will want to attend a university that not only provides a quality education but also carries strong name recognition and clout beyond the borders of the United Kingdom. Therefore, for the purposes of this chapter, we focus on the University of Oxford, the University of Cambridge, and the London School of Economics and Political Science (LSE), which is one of several colleges within the University of London. (The former two, when referred to together, are often called "Oxbridge" in this book, as they are in their home country.) There are, of course, other famous and reputable colleges in England, including other colleges within the University of London system, such as Imperial College, King's College, and the School of Oriental and African Studies (SOAS). Still, Oxbridge and LSE may be the English options most worth exploring because they offer both a high-quality education and a very strong reputation overseas.

OVERVIEW OF THE ENGLISH EDUCATIONAL SYSTEM

It is important that anyone thinking about applying to university in England understand how the educational system there works and what is expected of students at the upper levels of study.

SECONDARY SCHOOL EDUCATION

At the age of sixteen, English students who plan to pursue a higher-level academic (as opposed to vocational or arts-related) education take GCSE (General Certificate of Secondary Education) examinations in five to ten subjects. After taking their GCSEs, students must decide what subjects to study for the next two years, depending on the field of study they intend to pursue at university. (Note that what we call "colleges" in the United States are called "universities" in the United Kingdom. "College" has a different meaning altogether in Britain—it refers either to what we would call a preparatory high school or to a smaller residential and academic institution within the umbrella of a large university.) In other words, *English students are asked to narrow their focus very early—at the age of sixteen—about four years before American students are usually required to choose a major in college*. Furthermore, in England, no coursework is done in outside fields after beginning university. At an American college, by contrast, usually one- to two-thirds of a student's coursework is done outside of the major.

A-LEVELS

For those who will attend university, the last two years of high school are spent preparing for A-levels (General Certificate of Education, Advanced Level). The level of schooling at which students prepare for A-levels is referred to as the "sixth form." A-levels are subject exams required for admission into university and are graded on a scale, with A being the highest grade and E being the lowest. Students are generally required to have first passed GCSEs in the subjects in which they will take A-levels.

Students can continue to study for their A-levels at the same school they previously attended (whether state-funded or independent) if it offers the sixth form, or they can attend a sixth form "college," the equivalent of a preparatory school in the United States. *The standard pre-university education in England, including the final two years studying for A-levels, requires thirteen years of school rather than our twelve.*

Each A-level is a subject-specific test, like our SAT subject tests. Candidates for admission to an English university must apply to study a certain major or field and are admitted only into that area of study, on the basis of their success on A-levels. Success on A-levels requires an extremely high level of knowledge, so students generally study for two, three, or four exams, rather than pursuing a broad range of subjects in the sixth form.

A-levels are sometimes supplemented by STEP papers, subject-specific examination papers used to assess an applicant's aptitude for study at university. The response written by a student for a STEP paper (unlike the material completed in an A-level exam) is available for view by universities, so it can help admissions committees evaluate students' true strengths and weaknesses. Cambridge in particular is known for requiring students in certain subjects to complete STEP papers for admission.

APPLYING FOR UNIVERSITY-LEVEL EDUCATION

Students apply to all English universities through the Universities and Colleges Admissions Service (UCAS). The UCAS application is due by January 15 of the year in which a student plans to enter university. If a student is applying to Oxford or Cambridge, the form must be received by UCAS three months early, by October 15. A student (whether resident or overseas) can apply to only six universities in a given year. Furthermore, a student can apply to *either* Oxford *or* Cambridge, but not both. Although UCAS facilitates the admissions process for all British universities, the individual schools make their own admissions decisions.

When a student is given an acceptance, it will almost always be a "conditional" offer. Most applicants have not yet taken their A-levels when applying to university. Admission committees therefore make conditional acceptances to their candidates, requiring that they perform to a certain standard on A-levels. If a university notifies a candidate that it grants her a conditional AAB offer, for example, it means she must get at least two As and one B on her A-levels. Each university makes its own offer, so one student may receive different prescriptions from different universities.

When a student is notified of all universities' decisions, she can accept two offers. One is referred to as a "Firm Offer," which she makes to the university she prefers most. The Firm Offer guarantees a university that she will attend if she meets the conditions of her offer. The other acceptance is referred to as an "Insurance Offer," which she makes to a school whose conditional offer she is nearly certain to meet, in case she does not meet the standards of the more selective school.

UCAS operates "the Clearing System" during the summer to place unsuccessful candidates—including those who did not meet the conditions of their offers—in open spots at universities for the fall semester.

UNIVERSITY DEGREES

A bachelor's degree in England is called a "first degree" and generally requires three years of study to complete. Unlike in the United States, where only those in the top part of a graduating class are awarded honors (cum laude, for instance), English first degrees are usually awarded with honors, classified as:

- First class
- Second class—upper division (also designated as "upper second" or 2.1)
- Second class—lower division (also designated as "lower second" or 2.2)
- Third class
- Pass

DEPTH VERSUS BREADTH IN ACADEMICS

Applications to English universities are made for study in a particular subject matter. This presents a mismatch between American students and England's university system. American students often do not know when applying to college what field they want to study. We give our students two or even three years during college to try out different subjects before forcing them to choose a concentration. Many American eighteen-year-olds would be hard-pressed to apply to an English university because they simply have not yet decided what field they want to study. Making a haphazard decision is not advisable, because it is difficult at English institutions to change your field of study once you are enrolled.

American students are usually one year behind their English peers in preparation for college because of our twelve-grade (as opposed to thirteen-year) system. In addition, English sixth formers, as mentioned earlier, study only three or four subjects during their last two years of school. This means that when they arrive at university, they have already built a wealth of knowledge in their chosen fields. Even the brightest and best-schooled Americans might feel they are behind when first arriving at universities in the United Kingdom.

TEACHING AND EXAMINATION SYSTEMS

The teaching and examination systems are different in England as well. There is more small-group interaction in England and less emphasis on large classes and lecture-style learning. The Oxbridge system is based on a one-on-one method of teaching. These sessions, called "tutorials" at Oxford and "supervisions" at Cambridge, are weekly meetings between a student and a supervisor where most teaching takes place. Tutorial sessions involve one teacher and two or three students. In some subjects at Oxbridge, there are essentially no classroom attendance requirements other than tutorials or supervisions. Other English universities also use private tutorial sessions, but not as extensively as do Oxford and Cambridge (and Durham).

The tutorial system requires that students at Oxbridge not be afraid to engage seriously in the learning process. Students cannot sit back and watch while others do the thinking; they are required to be active participants in their own education at all times. Students must be confident and able to conduct prolonged discussions with faculty members. In addition, the small-group emphasis in classrooms requires that students in the Oxbridge system facilitate their own social interactions. This is not particularly difficult, given the active social character of most Oxbridge colleges.

University students in England are generally tested infrequently. In some subjects, students are examined only at the end of each year—and sometimes only at the end of the first and third years. These tests are the only evaluations on which a student's final diploma award is based. Students need a healthy degree of self-motivation to excel in this environment.

CHARACTERISTICS NECESSARY FOR ATTENDING A TOP ENGLISH UNIVERSITY

If you are considering applying to schools like Oxbridge or LSE, you should possess most or all of the attributes listed here—they are important for both gaining admission to an English university and becoming a success once you are there:

- *A superior academic record.* Stellar academic credentials are essential. Your main selling points should be your academic abilities rather than extracurricular or personal accomplishments and roles.

- *Evidence of intellectual vitality.* Show that you have gone beyond the requirements of American high school education in pursuing your academic interests. Study in the English system requires self-motivation and the ability to follow curiosities on your own, with limited direction from faculty members.

- *A firm understanding of what field you want to pursue and why.* When applying to a British university, you must apply to study a certain field or major. You are admitted to university on the basis of your demonstrated interest in and potential for success in that field of study.

- *Independence.* Demonstrate that you can think and work on your own rather than being guided step-by-step through your studies. You must also show that you are ready to live on your own in a foreign country, far away from your family and friends.

- *Maturity.* Be prepared to immerse yourself in an altogether new culture and academic setting.

- *Confidence.* Demonstrate that you are confident in your own academic and presentation abilities. You must be able to both work through material alone and function in the tutorial mode, often one-on-one with faculty members, which can be daunting to those who are timid or unsure of their abilities.

- *Superior organizational and motivational skills.* Show that you can manage your time wisely and structure your own study habits rather than waiting for someone else to tell you what to do next.

- *The ability to reach out socially.* You must be able to form friendships easily and know how to get involved in group activities with your peers. Lack of constant classroom interaction means that friendships and peer groups do not form in the same way they do on American campuses.

- *Secure finances.* Although English universities are less expensive than U.S. colleges, they have very limited funds for overseas undergraduate students. Overseas students can sometimes obtain small bits of financial aid from the British Council, the universities themselves, and other sources to cover small gaps in funding—but an American undergraduate cannot expect to obtain a great deal of merit- or need-based aid in order to attend an English university.

If you possess most or all of these traits, you will likely be able to handle attending a top English university. Those who fit the categories listed here will profit in additional ways from an English university education:

- *Want to study particular subjects.* Leading English universities have strong departments and instruction in a wide range of subjects, in some cases outdoing their American counterparts.

- *Plan to enter graduate school and a career in academia.* Those interested in pursuing graduate study at the master's or doctoral level after a B.A.— whether in the United States or overseas—can benefit from going to a leading school in England. The rigor of the instruction, the independent learning, the one-on-one interaction with professors, and the frequent writing assignments better prepare students for graduate school and careers in academia than do many elite American schools.

- *Want to enter a professional career as early as possible.* In the English system, students pursue the professional fields (medicine, veterinary medicine, dentistry, law, etc.) as first degree or bachelor's degree subjects. Going to university in England means that a student may be able to enter a professional career much sooner than his or her American counterparts, who must undergo four years of college and many more years of graduate school before beginning the same career. Generally speaking, only students studying architecture and engineering can earn first degrees in their fields in the United States.

- *Lack strong extracurricular records.* English universities generally admit students on the basis of academic credentials alone. An American student with top academic performance but little in the way of extracurriculars has only a modest chance of being accepted at the most selective U.S. colleges, but does have a good chance (if he or she possesses the right academic record and capabilities) of getting into Oxford, Cambridge, or LSE.

- *Want to save money.* Although the English schools generally do not offer financial aid to foreign students, they do offer a bargain for those who can pay on their own. Each year of education costs significantly less than a year at a top college in the United States, with the total cost of attendance ranging between about $30,000 and $35,000 (based on the £1 = $1.50 exchange rate in effect as this book went to print) within the Oxbridge and LSE programs, as compared to about $55,000 at the top U.S. colleges. Most Americans attending English universities can thus expect (assuming they would be paying "sticker price" at an American college) to save between $15,000 and $25,000 per year. Furthermore, an undergraduate degree in England takes only three years to complete, saving Americans an additional full year's tuition and expenses at an American school ($50,000 or more), for a total savings of between $100,000 and $130,000 on the entire college education, or a cost reduction of about 45 to 60 percent. Furthermore, if you consider that you receive an honorary master's degree from Oxford and Cambridge after several years, you are arguably getting two degrees for the price of one (or less than one).

AMERICAN COLLEGE VS. ENGLISH UNIVERSITY

	AMERICAN COLLEGE	ENGLISH UNIVERSITY
Apply to . . .	School at large (in most cases)	Particular college and field of study
Accepted on Basis of . . .	Academic and other criteria	Academic criteria
Acceptance Is . . .	Unconditional	Usually conditional (on future test results)

	AMERICAN COLLEGE	ENGLISH UNIVERSITY
Academic Focus	Study many subjects	Study one subject
	Choose major after 1–3 years	Enter major field immediately upon arrival
Can Switch Majors or Departments . . .	Readily	Almost never
Most Classes Are . . .	Interactive group classes	One-on-one tutorials (Cambridge, Oxford) OR largish lecture sessions
Testing	Frequent testing	Infrequent testing
Degree Earned	After four years	After three years

Note that it is difficult to talk of either Oxford or Cambridge as one institution, because student life at both universities is governed by the individual colleges rather than the larger umbrella university. Colleges are independent and self-governing entities responsible for accommodating and feeding students as well as providing sports, entertainment, and activity facilities; giving them a social focus; and overseeing their academic and personal well-being. The characters and personalities of the various colleges differ depending on location, history, academic or nonacademic strengths and weaknesses—and thus the kinds of students they attract—just as individual universities and colleges in the United States do.

ADMISSIONS OF OVERSEAS STUDENTS AT OXBRIDGE AND LSE

Overseas applicants to the leading English universities face one large advantage and one (surmountable) disadvantage. The universities are allowed to charge foreign (non-British and non-European Union) students a hefty premium (although tuition is still lower than at leading U.S. schools), making Americans more desirable than they might otherwise be. Foreign applicants, however, may come from school systems that are difficult for English admissions officers to understand. This is to some extent the case for American applicants.

All candidates to Oxford, Cambridge, or LSE apply for admission to a particular subject. When applying to Oxford or Cambridge, you also apply to a specific college (the situation is a bit different for LSE insofar as it *is* a single college within the University of London). Applying to Oxford or Cambridge requires a separate application form (in addition to the usual UCAS application), which is sent directly to the school rather than to UCAS. LSE, however, requires no extra material beyond the UCAS application from its candidates.

At each Oxford or Cambridge college, as well as at LSE, academic faculty evaluate and admit candidates in their own fields. These faculty members read the admissions files individually as well as meet with others in their departments to discuss their decisions. There are no official ranking systems, although individual faculty members might have their own personal ways of evaluating and ranking candidates. Most candidates are evaluated by at least two people. Because of the faculty role in decision making at English universities, applications can and should be as sophisticated as possible in terms of their academic and intellectual content.

At the Oxford and Cambridge colleges, the admissions officers pass on any attractive candidates for whom their colleges have no space to other colleges within the university for consideration. Cambridge's St. John's College, for example, gets a large number of applicants; about a third of all applicants denied from St. John's are sent on for consideration at other Cambridge colleges.

SPECIAL ADMISSIONS CONSIDERATIONS

Oxford and Cambridge do not accept transfer students. An overseas student possessing an undergraduate degree can apply to Oxford or Cambridge to acquire a second bachelor's degree in only two years, though, in effect becoming transfer students who enter the second-year classes. At LSE, foreign students without degrees can be considered for transfer entry into the second year of study.

AVOID THE OPEN APPLICATION

If you do not want to indicate a college preference at Oxford or Cambridge, you can submit an Open Application, whereby the university will place you in a college if you are accepted into your field of study. This is not necessarily an advisable means of applying to either university, though. The more popular houses do not usually have room for Open applicants, so it is more difficult to be admitted to them through the Open system. Since you could end up anywhere when applying this way, unless you have really investigated each and every college and like all of them (which is highly unlikely, since they are all very different in terms of personality, atmosphere, architecture, size, and numerous other factors), it is not a wise move. Completing an Open Application also forces you to relinquish some control of your positioning efforts. Overseas applicants especially need to prove to the admissions tutors that they know what they are looking for and have what it takes to do well at Oxford and Cambridge academically and socially. Being able to target a particular college as ideal for one's needs, as well as meet and interview with the tutors at the college, can thus be crucial.

DEGREE OF DIFFICULTY IN ADMISSIONS VARIES BY COLLEGE AND FIELD

The degree of difficulty of being admitted to Oxford, Cambridge, or LSE differs by college at the first two universities and by field of study at all three universities. Applying to a less popular college, or a less popular field of study within a particular college, can be much easier than running up against many other candidates for a coveted place elsewhere. In other words, there are ways of getting around the competition to some extent. In a recent year at King's College, Cambridge, for example, acceptance rates ranged from a low of 10 percent (for law) to a high of 50 percent (for three subjects: archaeology and anthropology, classics, and geography).

Oxford, Cambridge, and the University of London (the umbrella university to which LSE belongs) annually publish numbers of applicants and accepted students for each college. Doing your own research will tell you which colleges and subjects of interest are easier to get into than others. This does not mean you should apply to Oxford's St. Hilda's (an all-women's college, which does not receive nearly as many applications as the coed colleges) if you do not want to live and study with only women. You might be easily admitted to a place like St. Hilda's, but would not be satisfied with your experience once there.

Choosing a field of study requires utmost caution because it is difficult to switch subjects once at an English university. Although it is nearly impossible to switch fields after arriving at Oxford or LSE, Cambridge offers a bit more flexibility, allowing many students to change (or combine subjects) after the first year. For example, some students do English for two years and history for one year in a sequential mode of study. With this in mind, some students might consider applying for a field that has higher admissions rates, with the plan to add or switch into another field at a later time. If you plan to take this route, you should investigate the possibilities thoroughly and be aware that it may be risky. It might be difficult in the first place to feign enthusiasm for a subject you do not want to study, and switching subjects later on might become more difficult than you had anticipated.

EVALUATION CRITERIA FOR OVERSEAS STUDENTS: ACADEMICS AND STANDARDIZED TESTS

The problem that the English universities have in admitting American students is that none of our testing options are comparable to A-level performance. Furthermore, American high schoolers have not focused aggressively on one or two fields as English students applying to university have. The colleges like to see candidates' SAT and SAT subject scores (APs are even better for their purposes), but even the best SAT and AP scores do not guarantee you a place at one of the top English universities.

American students thus have several options in submitting academic criteria for admission to English universities:

1. The preferred option is for American students to have followed an IB curriculum in high school. Students who have completed an International Baccalaureate are at an advantage because these courses are recognized by the English system as indicative of the ability to do university work.

2. The next best option is for American students to prove their academic preparedness for an English university not only by submitting high SAT and SAT subject scores (applicants need to score at least 680 on each section to be competitive), but also by showing strong performance on AP exams. Applicants generally need to report three or four tests with scores of 4 or 5 to be competitive. The subjects of the AP tests should correspond with the field to which an applicant is applying.

3. Another option is to take a one-year cram course in England to prepare for A-levels. The candidate would then apply to English universities based on his A-level performance, like English home candidates.

There are two additional options for students wishing to apply to LSE:

1. American applicants can complete one year of study at a U.S. college with a strong GPA and then apply to transfer in to LSE. The GPA itself is of more interest to LSE than the caliber of the school.

2. A final option for American students wanting to attend LSE is to take what is called a bridge or foundation course in England, a thirteenth year of study. At its completion, a student would take LSE's entrance exam (the single exam given to applicants in all subjects who have taken neither A-levels nor AP exams, nor received an IB).

The last two options for those considering LSE are least preferable because they do not allow an American student some of the main benefits of attending an English university, namely the ability to save a great deal of money and time. The last method of gaining entry is also risky because an applicant could potentially waste an entire year. There is no guarantee of admission to candidates planning to succeed this way.

All overseas applicants to Oxbridge or LSE should contact the proper admissions office for advice on how to prepare for the application. This is especially important for those who plan to go to England to take a Bridge or Foundation course before applying. Such programs are not all alike, and many of them are considered inadequate preparation for entry into a top university.

THE NONACADEMIC PROFILE LACKS IMPORTANCE

The nonacademic profile is not as important to admissions at English universities as it is at American universities. It is for this reason that academically competitive American students with little extracurricular strength might well consider applying to English schools. The admissions officers agree that extracurricular activities may make a student interesting, but it is the academic profile that really counts. That said, the one aspect of your personal background that could become important in admission to overseas programs is evidence of study, service, or other experiences abroad. Be sure to highlight any programs abroad as a way of demonstrating that you are prepared for another such situation.

SUPPLEMENTAL ADMISSIONS MATERIALS

Most courses of study at Oxford and Cambridge require supplemental application materials. For example, in modern languages at Oxford, candidates must submit two pieces of recent work for each of the languages they are currently studying. At least one piece should be written in the candidate's target language of study. No matter what field of study an applicant plans to pursue, supplemental materials should generally be pieces marked with teachers' corrections and comments. The colleges generally note that they want to see applicants' own work, not something that has been rewritten and perfected with obvious help from teachers and tutors.

Applications to many subjects at Oxford and Cambridge also require tests or exams to be taken when candidates come to interview. Modern language applicants to Oxford, for example, are required to sit for 30-minute tests in each language.

INTERVIEWS

Admissions tutors at Oxford and Cambridge strongly recommend that overseas applicants do all they can to increase their visibility and improve their chances of getting in by coming for an interview, even though it is not officially required. Interviews are held during a specified admissions period called "Open Days" each year—usually in May or June—although overseas students can often arrange to come at a different time.

Interviews at Oxford and Cambridge colleges are intense and quite different from the more relaxed situations encountered by college applicants in the United

States. Each applicant generally sits through two or three interview sessions, all conducted by experienced members of the faculty rather than by administrators or school alumni. They focus on knowledge of a subject area rather than on general information or a getting-to-know-you type of discussion. They require a student to be able to think on his or her feet, feel confident in the face of challenges, appear well-read and prepared in a field of study, and make impressive oral deliveries of information. Interviewers will evaluate how applicants think, develop ideas, and present them to others.

Oxbridge applicants should definitely seek assistance in this regard before the interview. They should meet with teachers or get in touch with nearby college professors to seek help in preparing for an intense academic interviewing experience. Reviewing test materials in their field of study as well as conducting extra reading is also essential to enter an interview well prepared to share knowledge and demonstrate intellectual interest in a subject beyond basic classroom learning.

Many admissions officers note that the interview helps them identify those with superior intellectual passion and gifts as well as those who will be successful under the tutorial teaching method. The one-on-one interview with a faculty member is itself, after all, somewhat like a tutorial. Thus, the admissions interview at Oxbridge, unlike at U.S. colleges, frequently makes or breaks a candidacy. (There are no interviews for admission at LSE except in the case of older students who are applying after some time out of school.)

RECOMMENDATIONS

A reference from a teacher (often called a "referee" for admissions purposes in England) is required at all three institutions. Admissions officers at Oxford, Cambridge, and LSE primarily want hard academic information, including predictions of final grades if the course is still in session, rather than stories about a candidate's personality or interaction with others in the classroom. Recommendations from supervisors other than academic teachers are discouraged. It is most helpful if the writer of a recommendation is familiar with the English university and its system of education so that he or she can address the student's potential for success in this unique environment. Recommenders writing letters for LSE should also make a realistic assessment of the student's ability to cope with London, a huge international city.

Generally in England the "head teacher" writes the recommendation, pulling together material from all other teachers, as our guidance counselors do in the United States. Thus, for the purposes of applying to English universities, it is advisable for American students to do one of two things:

1. Include a supplemental recommendation from your guidance or college counselor along with a teacher recommendation.

or

2. Ask an academic teacher to write a reference that includes the information gathered from other faculty members that your counselor compiled. Your counselor should understand your concern and agree to hand over her notes or letter for the teacher's use.

Either way, despite the lack of explicit instructions requesting a general guidance recommendation, English universities expect to receive this type of letter on candidates' behalf, so you should prepare to submit one.

ENGLISH UNIVERSITY ADMISSIONS DIRECTORS TALK ABOUT OVERSEAS ADMISSION

WHAT IS THE MOST IMPORTANT ADVICE YOU HAVE FOR OVERSEAS APPLICANTS?

Look at the coursework before applying. People think studying here will be just like being at Harvard—it's not true. You need to look at what you'll be expected to do in your first year. Also, students should know that there are very few subjects you can start at Cambridge—you have to be well into the knowledge of a field to enter university here. *Simon Goldhill, King's College, University of Cambridge*

Prospective overseas applicants may wish to email or call us in advance for advice regarding their plans. Every overseas applicant is different, so our advice is tailored to each individual's needs. *Louise Burton, London School of Economics and Political Science, University of London*

We operate differently than American schools, and applicants should realize this. American students like to know what's expected of them right away, and to get results right away—which is not how things work here. *Ray Jobling, St. John's College, University of Cambridge*

IS THE OPEN APPLICATION A GOOD IDEA?

The Open Application is not a smart idea. We at St. John's end up taking those who didn't mark us as their first choice in only a small number of cases, because there are just too many strong John's applicants. Talk to people and find out which college you want. You should always apply to a particular college in my view. *Ray Jobling, St. John's College, University of Cambridge*

How Is Extracurricular Involvement Evaluated?

We're interested in this sort of thing, but quite frankly, we're much more keen on academics. *Michael Allingham, Magdalen College, University of Oxford*

No personality or extracurricular features will get you in here. *Simon Goldhill, King's College, University of Cambridge*

Should Overseas Candidates Interview?

Americans are told they are not required to come for an interview. But quite honestly, an American student would have a very hard time being admitted if he or she couldn't make him- or herself available for an interview. *Anne Daniel, Christ Church College, University of Oxford*

What Are You Looking for in the Interview?

The interviewers want to see that you can think; how you develop ideas on your own; that you can form an opinion, defend it, revise it, and so on. *Anne Daniel, Christ Church College, University of Oxford*

You must be able to talk about your subject and related materials, and talk about them intelligently. Your experience and intelligence must go beyond the curriculum you've been assigned at school. *Simon Goldhill, King's College, University of Cambridge*

What Are You Looking for in Recommendations?

It's very important that the teacher knows the student very well. The reference also needs to be very distinctive. Teachers need to recognize we're looking for academic *potential*, not just a past show of success. *Ray Jobling, St. John's College, University of Cambridge*

We want hard academic information here, not touchy-feely stuff. *Anne Daniel, Christ Church College, University of Oxford*

It is important that the writer is familiar with Cambridge and what it takes to make it here. Please, no references from tennis coaches! That doesn't cut it here—we want academic information only. *Simon Goldhill, King's College, University of Cambridge*

Are Extra Recommendations Ever Helpful?

It is rare that a reference from someone other than a teacher could really shed light on academic potential, on a candidate's qualifications to study at Oxford. *Anne Daniel, Christ Church College, University of Oxford*

If you're working for someone in your field, in a potentially preprofessional job, then occasionally a reference from this person could help your standing. *Ray Jobling, St. John's College, University of Cambridge*

WHAT DIFFICULTIES DO AMERICAN STUDENTS USUALLY HAVE WHEN ARRIVING AT AN ENGLISH UNIVERSITY?

Our experience is that American students may have trouble when they first get here because they simply aren't used to focusing. They're used to breadth rather than depth. *Anne Daniel, Christ Church College, University of Oxford*

The cultural differences are often hard for American students to digest—just because we both speak English doesn't mean we're the same. Learn to enjoy that fact. *Ray Jobling, St. John's College, University of Cambridge*

WHAT KINDS OF STUDENTS SHOULD APPLY TO AN ENGLISH UNIVERSITY?

You have to be independent-minded, able to organize your life carefully, and mature. We cannot necessarily discern these qualities when admitting a student, so the student needs to decide for himself whether or not British university is right for him. *Michael Allingham, Magdalen College, University of Oxford*

Our degrees are much more specialized than those in the United States. so only those who really know what they want to study should apply. If you're going into maths you'll be entering alongside hundreds of freshers [freshmen] who have specialized in maths over the last several years. So you must be ready to work really hard and make some serious adjustments very quickly, which can be quite difficult. *Ray Jobling, St. John's College, University of Cambridge*

We're looking for students who can cope with a different method of studying plus cope with living in the middle of London for the first time. We especially need kids who've shown initiative—we want to be confident that they'll get up and do something when they get here instead of holing up in their rooms out of fear. *Louise Burton, London School of Economics and Political Science, University of London*

A COMPARISON OF THE APPLICATION PROCESSES AT OXFORD, CAMBRIDGE, AND LSE

	OXFORD	**CAMBRIDGE**	**LSE**
How to Apply	Through UCAS	Through UCAS	Through UCAS
Application Deadline	October 15	October 15	January 15

	OXFORD	CAMBRIDGE	LSE
Apply to . . .	College and Subject	College and Subject	Subject (LSE= one college)
Supplemental Materials	Yes	Yes	No
Interviews	Yes (Recommended)	Yes (Recommended)	No
Recommendations	One required	One required	One required
Ability to Transfer In	No	No	Yes
Overseas Funding*	Essentially none	Essentially none	Essentially none

*American applicants are still eligible for U.S. federally subsidized loans

CANADIAN UNIVERSITIES

REASONS TO ATTEND

The Canadian higher education system is very similar to the American system. Students are permitted to take a broad range of courses (except in highly demanding fields like engineering, which, as in the United States, specify most of a student's curriculum). Most Canadian schools have a semester system, with the summer semester offering optional courses (as in the United States). In addition to being comparable in nature to American schools, the leading Canadian schools are all close to the American border and are readily accessible.

Canadian universities enjoy a very good reputation worldwide. By the same token, the larger ones have a more international feel than do most American universities. In cosmopolitan centers such as Toronto, Montreal, and Vancouver, this is particularly true. Quebec's universities offer a marvelous chance to gain true fluency in French. Even a school like McGill University, which teaches in English, is situated in Francophone Montreal.

Another option is offered by the liberal arts colleges, small institutions similar to America's liberal arts colleges in many respects, but often offering business and other professional courses in addition to traditional liberal arts courses. Many of them are affiliated with the major universities, offering students a chance to take courses at the university as well. Some are akin to residential colleges within a university system, meaning that students live at the college but take most of their courses through the university rather than their college.

LEADING SCHOOLS

The country's leading universities are clustered together in the Group of Thirteen, including the universities of:

- Alberta
- British Columbia
- Calgary
- Dalhousie
- Laval
- McGill
- McMaster
- Montréal
- Ottawa
- Queen's
- Toronto
- Waterloo
- Western Ontario

Most of these schools have more than 20,000 students, with the vast majority being undergraduates. Numerous of them are ranked in the top 200 in the international rankings discussed in Chapter 4, with McGill, the University of Toronto, and the University of British Columbia all frequently ranked in the top fifty worldwide. (These three, plus Queen's University, are commonly termed "Canadian Ivies.") Most of them teach in English, even McGill, despite its location in Montreal. (Montreal could once be described as a bilingual city, but it has become somewhat more Francophone than Anglophone in recent years.) The exceptions are the Université Laval and the Université de Montréal, both of which teach in French.

LIBERAL ARTS COLLEGES

Leading stand-alone liberal arts colleges include Mount Allison University (New Brunswick) and Acadia University (Nova Scotia). But note that many of the leading large universities mentioned above are affiliated with local liberal arts colleges, providing the liberal arts students a small, residential college experience along with the opportunity to take classes at the university. See, for instance, the University of Toronto, which has three affiliated colleges: St. Michael's College, Trinity College, and Victoria University.

APPLICATIONS

Admission requirements at Canadian schools are generally similar to those at American schools. The leading schools, for instance, will generally require SAT I and/or SAT II scores. The primary differences between the two are that Canadian schools:

- Place less emphasis on extracurricular activities and more on academic performance

- Have later application deadlines (often in April or May)

- In Ontario, have applications routed through the provincial clearinghouse, Ontario Universities' Application Center, www.ouac.on.ac; in British Columbia, through the Postsecondary Application Service of British Columbia, www.pas.bc.ca.

KEY ISSUES

In some provinces the standard time to degree is three years rather than four. In some universities offering a three-year degree, those who wish to get an honors degree (demonstrating greater specialization) will require a fourth year of study.

Many Canadian schools, especially the well-known, large universities, have limited dormitory space available. Some guarantee that American students will be housed in university dormitories for their freshman year, but at many housing is allotted on a first-come, first-served basis. If living in the dorms is a priority, be sure to investigate the housing situation at your chosen schools. (Those schools that lack dormitory space do provide help finding suitable local accommodation, so there is no need to panic at the thought of living off-campus.)

FINANCES

Assuming parity between the Canadian and American dollars (the exchange rate in effect at the time of this book's writing), tuition at Canadian schools tends to be less than half that of America's leading private universities. As of this writing, McGill's tuition (CAN$13,965—equal to US$10,742 at the 1.30 exchange rate in effect as this book went to print) is but a fraction of Northwestern University's ($36,756). The cost of living in Canada, by the way, is generally comparable to that in the United States.

Although financial aid for foreign students is limited at Canadian universities, most of them are accredited by the U.S. Department of Education, making American students at them eligible for Federal Student Aid. Some U.S. states have financial aid programs for studying out-of-state. Contact your state's higher education authority for information.

AUSTRALIAN UNIVERSITIES

REASONS TO ATTEND

Australian universities are noted for their informal atmosphere and the welcome given to international students. They are also very inexpensive relative to peer institutions in other countries.

The Australian lifestyle offers many of the advantages of the California lifestyle, making it a magnet for people around the world. The major cities, and major universities, are home to a stunning diaspora, especially of Asians. This offers foreign students a marvelous chance to learn not just about Australian society, but Asian societies as well.

LEADING SCHOOLS

Australia's leading universities are known as the Group of Eight, which comprises the universities of:

- Adelaide
- Australian National
- Melbourne
- Monash
- New South Wales
- Queensland
- Sydney
- Western Australia

Six of these schools—Australian National, Melbourne, Monash, New South Wales, Queensland, and Sydney—are frequently ranked in the top fifty worldwide. Adelaide and Western are often ranked in the top 100 worldwide.

APPLICATIONS

Admission requirements at Australian schools are generally similar to those at American schools. The primary differences between the two are that Australian schools:

- Place less emphasis on extracurricular activities and more on academic performance
- Have later application deadlines (sometimes as late as April or May)

■ May require that applications be made directly to them, or be made through the Universities Admissions Centre (www.uac.edu.au)

KEY ISSUES

Australian universities have traditionally been well regarded internationally. Lately, however, there has been some concern that the beach-and-barbie (barbecue) image the country as a whole has tried to project has encouraged applications by foreign students less intent on studying than on having a good time.

Australia's strength is in its major universities; do not expect to find top-notch, small, liberal arts colleges.

Some programs attract a very large number of foreign students. Be leery of any program that has a majority of non-Australians.

FINANCES

Australian universities offer very good value for money, although they tend to be slightly pricier than Canada's remarkably inexpensive schools. The University of Melbourne's tuition is AUS$19,900 (equal to approximately US$12,839 as of this writing), a substantial savings when compared with Northwestern's ($36,756). Note, however, that not all programs are priced the same at Australian schools. Some, which are generally more expensive to provide (and generally offer better paying job opportunities after graduation), such as engineering, tend to be priced somewhat higher. The cost of living in Australia is generally comparable to that in the United States.

SCOTTISH UNIVERSITIES

REASONS TO ATTEND

The Scottish universities offer many of the advantages of their English counterparts, discussed at length elsewhere in this chapter. By the same token, they offer several more potential advantages of significance. First, Scottish primary and secondary education lasts for twelve years (as in the United States), so Scottish universities have roughly the same expectations for their incoming students as do American universities. English universities, on the other hand, expect students to have completed an extra year of secondary education. Second, Scottish universities generally do not require applicants to commit to the specific subject they will study upon matriculation. (Subjects requiring particularly lengthy and intensive study, such as engineering, are exceptions.) Thus, students can take multiple subjects in their first two years before settling on the one or two in which they will concentrate in their last two years. Third, in many subjects students can readily finish a master's degree, rather than just a bachelor's degree, in four years.

For some students, of course, these potential advantages will be anything but. For instance, some will prefer the English universities' requirement that a student focus on one specific subject throughout university.

LEADING SCHOOLS

The four ancient and traditional universities of Scotland—and the most famous—are Aberdeen, Edinburgh, Glasgow, and St. Andrews. Perhaps because of its connections to the world of golf, the University of St. Andrews is best known in the United States. The University of Edinburgh, however, tends to fare much better in the international rankings. Whereas all four generally rank in the top 200 worldwide, Edinburgh often ranks in the top fifty and Glasgow in the top 100, with St. Andrews and Aberdeen lagging behind somewhat.

APPLICATIONS, KEY ISSUES, FINANCES

See the discussion of the English universities, above.

APPLYING TO LEADING UNIVERSITIES IN CANADA, AUSTRALIA, AND SCOTLAND

	McGILL	UNIVERSITY OF MELBOURNE	St. ANDREWS
How to Apply	Direct	Direct	UCAS (see English universities write-up)
Application Deadline	January 15	December 20	March 1
Apply to	College and subject	College and subject	College and subject
Supplemental materials	Yes (depending on subject)	Yes (depending on subject)	Yes
Interviews	No	No	No
Recommendations	No	No	Yes
Ability to transfer in	Yes	No	Yes
Overseas funding	Yes	No	Yes
Time to Degree	4	3–4 years	4 years
Tuition (2008–9)	USD$10,742	USD$12,839*	USD$17,025

*Depends on which kinds of credits you take (e.g., arts subjects are not as expensive per credit as science subjects)

Part V

FINANCING COLLEGE

FINANCING COLLEGE

— KEY POINTS —

∎

Understand the basics of financial aid

∎

Note how greatly schools' aid policies differ
—Learn to determine a given school's policies

∎

Take financial considerations into account regarding:
—Where to apply
—When to apply

∎

Consider multiple strategies to reduce the cost of college

INTRODUCTION

College financial aid may be second only to the federal tax code for its importance, complexity, and opaqueness. Given the endless increases in college tuition, even at public universities, more and more families need to factor the financial dimension into their college application decisions. This does not mean, of course, that finances alone should determine which college you choose. The primary goal of the college search should be to find one (or more) that will provide an excellent academic and social environment for the student's development. By the same token, however, failing to choose schools with an eye on what is affordable (or will be with suitable financial aid) is likely to lead to trouble.

This subject is too complex to be covered in detail in one chapter. (In fact, we have completely omitted discussion of investment strategies as beyond the scope of the book.) Our purpose, therefore, is to sketch the outline of the subject in a comprehensible fashion, discuss the most important strategies available to you—including how they interact with your application decisions (such as your choice of colleges and the timing of your applications), and point you toward helpful resources for more in-depth research.

FINANCIAL AID BASICS

FEW FAMILIES PAY THE STICKER PRICE

The stated tuitions (or "sticker price") at many colleges—especially the leading private schools—can be daunting. Note, however, that these prices are paid by relatively few families. Many of the priciest colleges have the most generous aid policies and may therefore cost you less than those with lower stated tuitions.

NEED-BASED AND MERIT-BASED AID

Schools can use either or both of two policies for awarding financial aid to families. Those following a need-based approach try to determine how much a family can afford to pay for college. They then subtract this from their stated tuition (plus room and board and other expenses) and look to provide the family with the amount of "need" this formula produces. Those schools following a merit-based approach offer aid on the basis of how attractive an applicant is to them—i.e., his "merit" in their eyes.

CALCULATING FINANCIAL NEED

Unsurprisingly, schools that award aid on the basis of financial need want families to submit substantial information about their finances. Essentially all schools require the filing of the FAFSA (Free Application for Federal Student Aid) form. Many selective colleges require an additional form be filed. Known as the CSS Financial Aid PROFILE (or simply "the PROFILE"), it is designed to capture information (such as home equity) that FAFSA misses. Other schools require families to file a college-specific form.

*Financial aid **base year**.* Those schools that calculate financial need use formulae based on the income and assets of the applicant and his or her family. The crucial starting point is the year before the applicant starts college, known as the "base year."

TYPES OF AID

Grants. Grants (which are also often called scholarships) are forms of financial support that need not be repaid (unlike loans).

Loans. Most loans are federal. Perkins loans are the most desirable of them because interest does not accumulate until after graduation, there are no loan fees, and the interest rate is the lowest available. Stafford loans are next in the loan-desirability hierarchy.

Work-study. The federal work-study program involves a student working ten to fifteen hours per week at a campus job that is likely to pay minimum wage or a bit more.

Note that what colleges call *self-help* usually consists of a combination of loans and work-study, not grants.

COLLEGE FINANCIAL AID POLICIES VARY GREATLY

Need-conscious versus need-blind admissions. Schools that ignore the financial wherewithal of applicants in making admissions decisions are termed "need-blind" schools. Many of the top private schools, including all of the Ivies and "little Ivies" (e.g., Amherst, Wesleyan, and Williams), are currently need-blind. (Whether they will continue to be so during difficult economic times remains to be seen.)

Many schools, however, are "need-conscious" insofar as they take an applicant family's ability to pay into consideration when deciding whether to admit her. At leading schools, this need awareness applies only to some portion of the bottom tier of admitted students. Top candidates are admitted no matter what their financial need; the less-qualified candidates (e.g., perhaps the bottom 5 to 10 percent) are scrutinized carefully to ensure that aid dollars are conserved.

Meeting full need. Some schools meet the full need—as calculated by whatever formula they use—of every student admitted. This is true of most of the ultra-selective private colleges; state schools, on the other hand, generally meet the full need of their residents but not of out-of-state candidates.

Rather than meet the full financial need of candidates, some schools will "gap" them or give them an "admit/deny" decision. These terms refer to the practice of admitting a student, then providing less financial aid than the family needs. This "gap" effectively means that although admitted, the decision is tantamount to denying the candidate—who almost surely will choose to go elsewhere.

Merit aid. Many schools give out financial aid on the basis of how much they want a candidate—without regard to the candidate's financial need (or lack thereof). At many colleges merit aid far outweighs need-based aid. Note, however, that many colleges hide their merit-based aid orientation. Thus, Stanford claims it does not believe in merit-based aid, but it gives out oodles of athletic scholarships. Other schools award merit aid to National Merit Scholars, promising violinists, and so on. Not all schools, however, are shy about their merit aid. Duke and Vanderbilt, for example, have substantial merit scholarship programs that they feature prominently in their marketing materials.

Packaging. How schools combine the different components of a financial aid award is known as "packaging." Most schools package students with loans and work-study first. In other words, the first tier of need in students' packages at most schools is filled with "self-help" (loans and work-study). At some schools, you will receive $7,500 or more of self-help before you see a dime of gift aid. At other schools, the threshold is set much lower. (And at some of the richest schools, such as Harvard and Princeton, self-help has all but disappeared for those of modest means.)

Some schools, especially the most selective, use "equity packaging," meaning that they treat all aid-worthy applicants in the same way. Many schools, however, used "differential packaging," in which highly desirable applicants are given special treatment. Thus, a heavily recruited hockey goalie might be given a package consisting largely of grant aid and relatively little self-help.

Changing packages year to year. Many schools require greater amounts of self-help, in the form of loans or work-study or both, as students progress. Expected contributions from both term-time and summer employment may increase fairly dramatically from freshman to senior year.

Some schools require students to submit financial applications each year the students attend—reevaluating financial need each year. Other schools continue their financial aid package for all four years unless a student notifies them of a substantial change in his or her personal or family financial situation.

**FINANCIAL AID ISSUES FOR STUDENTS
WITH SPECIAL CIRCUMSTANCES**

WAITLISTED STUDENTS

Schools' policies for granting financial aid to students who are accepted off the waitlist vary. Such decisions are often made long after other financial aid decisions have been administered. Some schools treat waitlisted students the same as everyone else, which may mean admitting students off the waitlist on a need-blind basis and giving them full-need packages. Other colleges apply different policies for waitlisted students than they do for regular admits. In such cases, they generally offer less aid to waitlisted students.

TRANSFER STUDENTS

Some colleges treat transfer students the same way they treat incoming freshmen. Other schools consider transfer students as a separate admissions category and do not guarantee them full aid packages.

INTERNATIONAL STUDENTS

Some schools treat international applicants exactly the same as domestic applicants for purposes of determining aid. Other schools meet the full need of all foreign students admitted, but use need-sensitive admissions when deciding which international applicants to accept (without doing so for their domestic applicants). Other colleges provide some international aid packages but cap the awards for overseas applicants. Other schools give no aid to international applicants. The flagship public institutions, for instance, generally have no aid for overseas students.

Most schools do not consider Canadians or legal residents as "international" for purposes of determining financial aid packages.

DETERMINING A SCHOOL'S FINANCIAL AID POLICIES

Your application strategy is likely to depend on a host of factors discussed elsewhere in this book—your individual needs as to learning environment, course offerings, location, and so on. If your financial need is likely to be substantial, however, you will also want to take this into account in your choice of schools and the timing of applications.

To do so, however, you need to know the financial aid policies of schools that interest you. To determine a college's financial aid policies, consult your college counselor (and financial counselor, if you have one). Examine personal finance magazines such as *Kiplinger's, Money,* and so on, which carry annual articles on colleges' financial aid policies. Look, too, for how colleges describe their own policies—but apply a judicious measure of salt if their self-descriptions vary from how others see them.

By all means question the financial aid officers at colleges of interest. The box below provides a set of questions to get you started, but be sure to add those specific to your own situation.

QUESTIONS FOR FINANCIAL AID OFFICERS

- Do you meet the full need of every student? If so, do you meet it for all four years of college?

- What percentage of last year's incoming class received full need?

- What percentage of last year's incoming class received grant funding (i.e., gift funding rather than self-help) from the college?

- What is the minimum student contribution?

- Is there a maximum grant that your institution offers?

- How does your school treat outside scholarships or grants? Does it replace self-help (loan or work-study) or the school's own grant money?

- If I earn significant wages instead of maintaining a work-study job during college, how will that change my aid package?

- What if something unfortunate happens to change my family's financial situation, thus increasing my need later on? Can packages be adjusted midyear, for instance, to account for emergency situations?

FINANCIAL AID AND ADMISSIONS DIRECTORS DISCUSS THE NEW WORLD OF FINANCIAL AID

You need to research the financial aid policies of each school of interest to you because policies differ so much from school to school. Little can be said that is true of schools' financial aid policies in general. Instead, you need to understand that they are absolutely school-dependent. *Janet Lavin Rapelye, Princeton*

Many schools are moving to the "enrollment management" model and using financial aid as a recruiting tool—rather than using it to fill in what needy families cannot afford to pay. *Patricia Coye, Pomona*

FINANCIAL CONSIDERATIONS IN DECIDING WHERE TO APPLY

Apply to a portfolio of schools. To maximize your chances of aid, apply to schools across a range of selectivity and with an appropriate mix of aid policies. For instance, if you need a great deal of aid, consider having several schools on your list that are of the traditional "meet full need" variety. Similarly, apply to schools that are generous with merit aid. If you have a chance for a specific type of scholarship (performing arts, for instance), include schools that offer such merit scholarships. Include slightly less-selective colleges on your list, too, since top applicants are likeliest to get merit scholarships or advantageous need-based packages.

Apply to competing colleges. Being accepted to a set of schools—especially private schools—that compete with one another for students may give you substantial leverage to get more aid or a better need-based aid package. To find out which colleges are most likely to compete with your chosen schools, consult the standard guides to college (many of which list this information), talk with your counselor, and note during your college visits the other schools of interest to those visiting the school.

Apply to schools targeting your chosen field for development. If you have demonstrated potential in a field a college is trying to promote, you may be able to take advantage of its efforts to build strength in that area. Schools trying to support particular departments or areas of study not only give out their own money to promising incoming students in the field but also receive endowments and gift money from corporations and outside sponsors to fund students.

Apply to multiple schools. Your chances of aid are increased by applying to more rather than fewer schools.

FINANCIAL CONSIDERATIONS IN DECIDING WHEN TO APPLY

Early admissions. Consider your financial circumstances when thinking about when to apply to a particular college. As discussed in Chapter 5, your financial circumstances should affect your decision to apply Early under a school's binding Early Decision program. If you have substantial financial need, you should not apply Early Decision to schools that give merit-based aid, design preferential packaging policies based on merit, or do not meet the full financial need of all students. As egregious as the practice may be, many colleges are tempted to offer less desirable packages to students who apply Early Decision because they know these applicants are bound to attend their institutions. Do not apply Early Decision if you intend to decide where to attend based on the aid you receive.

Regular admissions. Apply for admission and financial aid as early as possible. For one thing, many financial aid deadlines are before the final admissions deadline. Failure to submit an application in a timely manner can forfeit aid for which you would otherwise qualify. For another, colleges have a limited financial aid budget each year. As the admissions process continues into the winter and spring, the school's funds may dwindle, putting later applicants at risk of being gapped (i.e., their demonstrated need will not be met by the financial aid package offered).

STRATEGIES TO REDUCE THE COST OF COLLEGE

In addition to trying to get a college to cut its prices (i.e., give you a scholarship or other financial aid), keep in mind the many other ways of reducing the financial burden of college.

SECURE "OUTSIDE" SCHOLARSHIPS

Outside scholarships, meaning grant money that comes from sources outside of the college to which you are applying, come in many forms and are offered for a variety of reasons: academic merit, ethnicity, leadership, musical talent, athletic ability, gender, pursuit of a particular field, geographic location, membership in a particular club, employment at a particular company, and so on.

There are, in total, many grants available, but several cautions are in order:

- Many colleges will deduct some or all of the outside aid from their own grants or loans (so inquire at your chosen college about its policies).
- Most services that charge fees for helping you find outside scholarships are not worth the expense or are outright frauds.
- Don't get your hopes up. The scholarships offered by most other organizations are relatively small—hundreds rather than tens of thousands of dollars—and thus not the basis for funding the entirety of college. Those scholarships that offer anything approaching full tuition and expenses are generally exceptionally difficult to get.

There are, however, other reasons besides money to pursue outside scholarships. A $300 award for being a talented international policy debater, for example, won't help much with college expenses. But if you aspire to keep using these skills, the award can boost your profile as a public speaker interested in international affairs. There is a long-term benefit to earning the award and being able to put in on your résumé.

To find out about the many outside scholarships, start by consulting a scholarship book or website (see the suggestions below). Since the best chance of winning scholarships is generally at the local level, make sure you check your local chamber of commerce and other civic organizations for leads. Your school's counselors should also be able to provide you with a list of the local scholarships awarded in recent years.

WHERE TO LOCATE SCHOLARSHIP INFORMATION

ON THE WEB

Finaid: www.finaid.org/scholarships

College Board Scholarship Search: http://apps.collegeboard.com/cbsearch_ss/welcome.jsp

Fast Web: www.fastweb.com

SRN Express: www.srnexpress.com/index.cfm

HARD COPY

College Aid Resources for Education, published by the National College Scholarship Foundation

Need a Lift, published annually by the American Legion

The Scholarship Book, by the National Scholarship Research Service and Daniel J. Cassidy

---

CHOOSE A COLLEGE WITH A LOWER STICKER PRICE

Even for those who don't qualify for grant aid, there are numerous ways to get a top-notch education without breaking the bank.

Attend a "public Ivy" or flagship public university. State schools are generally much less expensive than private schools. Even out-of-state tuition at a state school tends to be less than tuition at a comparable private school.

States vary in their requirements for becoming residents. Some states, like California, will allow students to become residents within only a year of arrival, as long as they follow a rigorous application program. Other states, like Michigan, make it nearly impossible for students to become residents.

Attend a public or community college and then transfer to a stronger school. This strategy, used either to boost your academic record or to save on a few years of tuition, has become quite common. Beware, though, that some of the selective schools accept few transfer students.

Consider a service academy. As Chapter 18 discusses, the service academies are free.

Go to college overseas. Going to college overseas (as a regular, degree-seeking student rather than as an exchange student) can also be a smart financial move—assuming, of course, that studying overseas meets your life and career goals. As discussed at length in Chapter 19, attending a college in Australia, Canada, England, or Scotland (or elsewhere) can save a family tens of thousands of dollars.

CUT THE COSTS OF TUITION

There are several ways to cut down on the cost of tuition (not including receiving more grant aid from the college you attend).

Accelerate the time it takes to complete your degree. Taking college or AP courses while in high school can cut down on the number of credits needed to graduate. Some 1,200 colleges give credit for passing scores (3, 4, or 5, depending on the college) on AP exams. Taking summer courses at a less expensive school is also a way to finish college sooner.

Another tactic is to take extra classes periodically during college. This can be a risky move because of the potential impact on your GPA if you are overloaded, and should therefore not be undertaken during a busy sports season or during your term as editor-in-chief of the school newspaper, for instance. Although tuition may be based on number of credits taken (so that a three-year program's tuition will be effectively the same as a four-year's), you can still save by eliminating an extra year of living costs—and by getting out into the workforce to start making money a year earlier.

Taking an accelerated load by one of the means above does have its downsides. It may cause students to miss out on the "real college experience," including valuable down-time activities and outlets for developing a student's creativity, talent, and leadership.

Participate in less-expensive study abroad or exchange programs. Especially when offered by a public institution, study abroad programs can be less expensive than a regular semester at college, even after travel expenses are figured in. Some schools require students to pay home-school tuition rates no matter where they study abroad, so check with your financial aid office to see whether it is possible to save money using this tactic. It is also important to check with your school to find out whether any grant aid you receive will apply toward study abroad tuition.

CUT THE COSTS OF ROOM AND BOARD

Choose the least expensive options for housing and meal plans. Living expenses can vary greatly from institution to institution depending on whether a student lives on or off campus, what meal plan is chosen, and so on. Many freshmen, for instance, pay for a complete (20 or 21 meals per week) meal plan, only to skip breakfast throughout the year. Some schools have a set room-and-board cost for students who elect to live on campus; other schools vary the cost depending on the quality of the housing and/or meal plan. At some schools, living off campus can be substantially less expensive, especially with roommates sharing the cost. At other schools, living on campus is a much better financial bet.

Invest in the local real estate market. Another option for parents is to purchase property in the student's college town, investing in the building while also giving the child a place to live. The additional income from renting to other students can help defray mortgage and other costs. After graduation, parents can either sell the property or keep it as an investment. Note, however, that if the local housing market is overvalued, this can easily end up costing rather than saving money. Those best positioned to take advantage of this option are those who expect to use the property for more than four years, either because younger siblings are likely to attend the same school or because the parents look to retire to this area.

CUT THE COST OF HEALTH INSURANCE

Compare the college's health insurance with other policies to make sure you get the most for your money. Most colleges have affordable health care policies, but they also permit students to stay on a parent's plan or obtain other outside health insurance that may be less costly.

CUT THE COST OF BOOKS AND SUPPLIES

You can reduce the cost of books significantly by buying used texts and selling back your books at the end of the semester. Most colleges have on-campus centers that buy and sell course books, and many similar organizations have popped up online. It is also worth your time to check whether copies of texts are available. Professors often make copies available on reserve at the library.

EARN A SUBSTANTIAL INCOME DURING COLLEGE

You can help keep college debt down by opting for higher-paid employment than the common campus jobs in the library, at Starbucks, and so on. Unless those jobs build skills or contacts you plan to use in the future, there is no reason you can't apply yourself to finding work that is more lucrative and may help you figure out what you will do after college.

Too few students take advantage of natural skills, learned talents, and easy-to-access student consumers to set themselves up in constructive jobs that also bring in substantial cash. The ways in which a college student can make a good living while in school depend, naturally, on his or her interests and talents, but also on the campus itself: its location, the makeup of its greater community, the kinds of students it attracts, and its regulations regarding employment. A student at Columbia might not be able to take advantage of her outdoor skills, but she would do well becoming a city dog-walker, charging $10 to $15 per dog, per walk. We are hardly suggesting that students undertake thirty to forty hours per week of money-making activities while in school. Rather, the point is to think broadly about how best to make use of your skills and interests to earn good money in far fewer hours.

In a similar vein, a student could join the Reserve Officer Training Corps (ROTC). Each branch of the military operates a ROTC program. In return for service obligations after college (and training obligations during college), ROTC gives out one-, two-, and four-year scholarships at three levels of tuition payment, ranging from a few thousand dollars to $12,500 per year.

RESOURCES

GENERAL FINANCIAL AID

Each of the websites listed below provides help on multiple financial aid topics as well as links to other resources:

FinAid (www.finaid.org). The premier financial aid site. Covers every aspect of financial aid in-depth—in readable prose, no less. Highly recommended.

The College Board (www.collegeboard.org). In addition to providing registration information for standardized tests, this site offers both a scholarship search component and readily usable calculators for financial aspects of the application: savings, loan repayment, expected family contribution, and so on.

The first two books are good general sources of information, with the Peterson's book being particularly thorough.

College Money Handbook, by Peterson's. Very thorough; covers a wide range of topics in detail.

Getting Financial Aid, by the College Board. Good discussion of most of the key financial aid topics.

101 Tips for Maximizing College Financial Aid, by Alice Orzechowski. Focuses on how to fill out the FAFSA form to your advantage.

WHY COLLEGE COSTS SO MUCH

To understand why college is so expensive, consult Ronald Ehrenberg's *Tuition Rising: Why College Costs So Much*. Although written in the late 1990s, this clear-eyed guide remains the best overview of the subject.

Appendix VI

STRATEGIES TO INCREASE NEED-BASED FINANCIAL AID

The strategies that follow are likely to reduce the amount colleges expect you to pay. That said, however, there are three potential issues to consider before undertaking them:

1. The specifics of your situation may cause one or another of these maneuvers to land you with unforeseen tax consequences. By all means consult your financial or tax adviser before undertaking them.

2. Too much maneuvering—at least of a type visible to college financial aid officers—is likely to work against you. Given the discretionary nature of much financial aid, engaging in very complicated maneuvers risks alienating the financial aid director. In fact, having a lifestyle that seems far beyond the income and assets you report may well cause him or her to investigate your situation and possibly look to limit your aid.

3. Details count. For instance, the specific timing of your efforts, and the particular policies of the college you have targeted, may render a particular strategy ineffective. To get a handle on such issues consult the resources listed elsewhere in this chapter.

Using assets to pay off debt. Your financial aid is based on assets held during the base year (i.e., the year before applying). Debts are not subtracted from assets in this equation. Thus, if you have $60,000 in a savings account but owe $25,000 in credit card or car payment debt, the $60,000 is counted against you in aid formulas, but the $25,000 does nothing to help you qualify for more aid. You would be better off paying down the debt.

Moving assets from student accounts to parental accounts. Money held by parents and students is not considered equally in determining how much a family can afford to pay for college. Parents are generally expected to pay 5.6 percent of their assets, whereas students are expected to spend a whopping 35 percent of their savings on college. Thus, $50,000 in a student savings account results in $17,500 paid to the college, whereas the same amount in a parental account results in only a $2,800 contribution to college costs. If your child holds a trust fund, bonds, or other financial assets in his or her name, move them to your own name (or another relative's) to keep him or her from losing 35 percent of it.

Getting rid of assets through gift donations. You are allowed to give away up to $11,000 per year in untaxed gift money to each recipient. Giving "gifts" to relatives or godchildren in the years before college is a good way to shed extra assets before financial aid calculations get under way.

Making necessary large purchases. If you know the family needs a new car or the house needs a new roof, take care of it before the base year. That way you will gain the object or service you needed anyway while at the same time reducing your reportable assets.

Reducing base pay. If your income fluctuates considerably because of bonuses or commissions, see what you can do to time it so that these extras are earned either before or after the base year.

Taking leave of career (and salary). If one of two wage-earning parents leaves a job to prepare for a future career change, you can maintain a portion of the family income while increasing your eligibility for aid. This is an especially good idea if a large portion of the second wage earner's salary is spent on day care or other expenses not taken into account by many colleges' financial aid calculations. Furthermore, if returning to school is something one parent has wanted to do, the base year would be a good time to begin.

Avoiding capital gains from selling stocks or securities. If you plan to sell appreciated stocks or securities, do so either before the base year begins or after your child has entered college. Capital gains and year-end dividends count as income and are therefore assessed heavily by college financial aid calculators.

Starting a home business. If you have been planning to start a home business, the base year would be a good time to do so. You can cut your current pay and reduce your personal assets by making capital investments in a self-owned business.

Paying off a mortgage. Home equity is not taken into account by the FAFSA form (although it is by the PROFILE). For schools using only the FAFSA form, therefore, you can qualify for much more aid if you get rid of your savings to pay off or pay down your home mortgage.

Appendix VII

Appealing Financial Aid Decisions

Colleges have become accustomed to parents of accepted students appealing for more financial aid. Although a few schools all but encourage this, even offering to match financial aid offers from comparable colleges, most financial aid directors entertain appeals with reluctance. They know that their aid budget is limited, so they cannot readily accede to many, let alone all, requests for increased aid. In addition, financial aid directors are often in the position of earning much less than the parents pleading poverty, making them doubly reluctant to increase the aid offer.

There are some circumstances, however, in which an appeal can succeed—provided it is undertaken in the right manner. The rationales most likely to be deemed legitimate are:

- A special financial circumstance—especially one that other colleges have considered worthy of more aid. For instance, the prospective need to care for a family member diagnosed with Parkinson's is noteworthy. If other colleges have taken this into account but your chosen school has not, pointing this out is certainly warranted.

- A new circumstance has arisen since the aid forms were filed—reduction in pay or loss of a job, for instance.

- A better offer from a competitor school.

- Special (nonfinancial) circumstances that do not fit within the forms' parameters. If the student is going to be running on the cross-country and track teams, which will demand long hours, she may not be able to maintain a part-time job at the same time. Asking that the work-study component of an offer be rescinded in favor of a combination of more grant and loan aid could sound quite reasonable in this case.

The manner in which you make your appeal is likely to matter as much as the rationale for your appeal. Rather than saying that you think you deserve more, or that there must be a mistake, ask the financial aid director to please take another look at your circumstances. Note the items that you think he may have overlooked or not given due weight. If other colleges have been more generous, especially if they are competitor schools, by all means note this (very politely). Because the aid process involves a great deal of judgment—even after all the relevant data is gathered—a financial aid officer does not necessarily believe that his initial opinion was bound to be precisely correct. A reasoned appeal, from pleasant people (who do not come across as stinking with privilege), can be persuasive. This is all the more true when comparable colleges have arrived at different figures. Given the degree of judgment involved, knowing that his peers have seen the matter differently can influence a director to reconsider. If the other colleges are competitor schools, an additional factor comes into play. Colleges naturally dislike losing students they have admitted, particularly to schools they view as rivals.

If the student is capable of doing so, a direct appeal from her can be very effective. If she does not come across as a spoiled kid, she can be very persuasive by pitching for more aid in order to do her part to lessen the burden on her parents. In other words, what would sound like special pleading from the parents can sound like filial devotion from the applicant herself.

The bottom line:

- Bring relevant information to the table
- Make an appeal, rather than negotiating or pushing

Part VI

APPLICATION ESSAY EXAMPLES

This section of the book contains thirty-one successful essays written by eighteen recent applicants to top colleges. We chose our applicants and essays with a number of different criteria in mind. We wanted to include students who represented a wide variety of:

- locations in the United States and the world,
- races, ethnicities, and cultural backgrounds,
- high school types,
- academic and nonacademic interests, and
- writing styles and approaches.

These essays address many different topics from many different perspectives and have been selected in order to give you a wide range of materials from which to profit. Following each applicant's essays are brief comments that will help you understand what went right in the essays. The examples printed here are largely successful, although we have noted what an applicant might have done differently to improve a piece, where appropriate. Of course, you should never copy what these applicants have done. These examples will, however, give you an idea of the kinds of approaches top applicants have taken and what generally works.

Note that actual names have been used, as desired by all of the featured writers. All essays have been reprinted exactly as they appeared to admissions officers; no spelling, grammatical, or other changes of any kind have been made to them here.

APPLICATION ESSAY EXAMPLES

ANNIE PALONE

Notes on her candidacy: An avid photographer and coxswain, Annie's greatest intellectual passion was for the study of the classics. She chose to attend Stanford University.

1. Attach a small photograph of something important to you and explain its significance.

[The attached photograph is of a young woman, presumably the applicant herself.]

I am Annie, a child of the future and one of the past, small-bodied, but strong and determined. In Hebrew, I am the "graceful one." "Maverick," my father calls me, or "Diamond Head," diamonds being stronger than even rock. I am five-three, one fifteen, soft-voiced and a strong believer in equality and experience. I am the older child; I can my strong, slender, almost sixteen-year-old brother, "Little Mickey;" we laugh as he towers over me. I have been a coxswain for three years, the first two filled with laughter and losing, the third with confident joking and a New England Championship we dared not expect. I am a Pisces; I am a fish, a sea nymph and a lover of oceans, lakes, streams, and rivers, even brightly chlorinated swimming pools. I am a photographer and and experienced subject. For two years, I appeared in dozens of my roommate's prints, now I create my own images. I am strong-spirited and open-minded. I have lived in ten houses and known six cities. I am as much American as Canadian. Born in the northern Rocky Mountains and raised in Dallas, San Francisco, and Boston, I spent weeks of each summer on the, "blue lakes and rocky shore," of Ontario's northland. There, the blue sky stretches wider than anywhere and the loons cry eerily in the dark.

In my grandparents coursed the blood of Scotland, Italy, Ireland. I have heard the whispers of my past in the dark rock passages of Edinburgh Castle, seen glimmers of the places my ancestors loved, in the lush greens of Scottish hills and in the brilliant blues of sky and sea. I have read the *Aeneid,* about the brave Trojans who founded the Roman race, and wondered if the genes and spirit of some Trojan hero might not live in me. I cherish the idea that so many people, so many experiences, cultures, and languages come together in me. I am filled with fascination and pride by the diversity of my history.

I have kissed the cheeks of seven-year-old boys, sticky with the juice of mangoes, not yet ripe. I winced as they pulled and braided my hair, wondering at its lightness,

"¡Mira, pelo amarillo!" I knew then, at Atenea, a Venezuelan home for poor, orphaned street children, as I know now, the sadness of their future, the hopelessness of their place in the social strata of their homeland. I feel privileged to be here, to be making a difference. I see the world through the eyes of an artist, notice beautiful light, the sudden permanence of a moment that is captured on film. I revel in the beauty of each instant.

I believe in myself, believe in the words of the lined, turbaned Indian physician-astrologer who examined my palm through his eyepiece when I was five years old. "This little girl will be very rich." I am already rich, blessed by travel, friendships, happy memories of a childhood and growing up, rich because I believe that I will live a life replete with friendships, experiences, travel, and knowledge, rich because the things I value most are not tangible, because it is memories and experiences that I treasure.

2. **Of the activities, interests, and experiences listed above (on the extracurricular and personal activities list), which is the most meaningful to you and why?**

Last fall, I discovered another world behind the lens of a camera. Photography quickly became my passion. I love the process: I love the product. I love the portraits of my friends and family, the people I cherish. Shooting is mysterious; until a roll has been processed, it is impossible to know what treasures will appear. I enjoy poring over contact sheets, choosing the images that I think best represent the subject and the art form. Finally, printing, choosing an exposure time, exposing paper, and waiting over the cool chemicals until the images appears and darkens is wonderful. I spend hours in the darkroom, never running out of things to do. It is enthralling to preserve a moment of laughter or loneliness, of a smile or tear that only film can capture. The sudden permanence that a photograph lends to an instant has made the darkroom my favorite place.

3. **Sharing intellectual interests is an important aspect of university life. Describe an experience, book, class, project, or idea that you find intellectually exciting and explain why.**

A story my Latin teacher told two years ago, about the remarkable trust and persistence of a German banker, who did the impossible by finding the ancient city of Troy, struck a chord with me. Heinrich Schliemann was a businessman who read Homer's *Odyssey* and fell in love. Schliemann believed, contrary to the assertion that it was a fairy tale, that *The Odyssey* was a true story, albeit one filled with romantic exaggeration. He believed that the high citadels of Troy once stood and he used Homer's rich description to find their ancient location on the coast of Turkey. There, he established a dig and found the ruins of the "imagined" city. Schliemann's discovery stimulated a great deal of intellectual discussion. Many scholars who previously believed that the mysterious Homer had imagined every detail of the epic adventure were now uncertain; it led many to believe that at least some of *The Odyssey* was true. The reality of Troy and the fact that archaeological evidence suggested that the city had been sacked and burned contributed further to the wave of questions about the Trojan War. Was *The Odyssey* in fact a history, exaggerated, which was based on fact?

Schliemann was not an expert in the classics. He read *The Odyssey* and intuitively felt that the Trojan War was more than a myth. It is amazing to me that one man, believing in a "fairy tale," encouraged so many analytical questions, and opened a previously unknown door on the ancient world.

Comments

The three essays were submitted as a set.

- Essay 1 is a wonderful piece that expresses exactly what Stanford is looking for in its applicants: intellectual vitality. The essay is cerebral, shows her passionate side, and works on many different levels at once (describing both the tangible and the intangible facets of Annie's existence). It also helps introduce Annie's values, such as her appreciation of her fortunate position in life and her strong friendships.

- Essay 2 builds on the first by again showing Annie's passion for her endeavors, the value she places on personal relationships, and the way in which she is able to cherish a single moment.

■ In essay 3, Annie has wisely taken advantage of her background and interest in the classics (a rarity among applicants these days). She also benefits from developing a unique topic from which a reader is likely to learn something new. The essay would not have been as compelling if she had focused on *The Odyssey* itself, an example used by far too many college applicants when discussing favorite or most influential readings.

ERIC CITRON

Notes on his candidacy: Eric was editor-in-chief of his high school newspaper and intent on a career in law. He selected Harvard University.

1. Evaluate a significant experience or achievement that has special meaning to you.

I blew out a tire today. I was driving home from a football team dinner, perhaps a bit too fast, and a small black cat with shining yellow eyes darted out in front of the car. I swerved. I hit the curb. I heard a pop. I knew I was in trouble. I turned carefully onto the first side street, an unlit, unmarked roadway deep in a town I had never previously visited, and went to size up the damage after seeing those brilliant yellow eyes run safely off the other side of the road. Three gaping holes large enough to fit my fist through were visible—though only as jagged edged shapes even darker than the black wall of the tire—in the dim light cast by the bulb of the open car door. I was walking quite briskly towards the gas station I had passed, now about a hundred feet away, when I stopped myself to collect my thoughts.

As I saw it, the easy answer was only a few feet away. I could simply have walked to the gas station, bestowed my mother's credit card and my problem upon someone else, and have gotten my tired changed. I imagined doing this, however, and found the picture in my mind to be quite distasteful. I saw myself as the quintessential child of privilege, talented and independent in the classroom, perhaps, but helpless as far as completing one of those random and menial challenges that life finds it necessary to confer upon us. So I stopped and stood for a moment, feeling strangely empty in the bare light of a street lamp on Main Street in Dover, before deciding that I would change the tire myself.

Though there is no differential calculus involved in changing a tire, I still found the task to be quite difficult and quite humbling; it requires persistence, along with elbow grease of the most literal sense. After I managed to find the spare tire buried in the Volvo's trunk, I started the dirty task of finding the oil-slicked, sooty place in the undercarriage where the jack attaches to the car. Eventually, I managed to jack the car up, and I removed the busted tire with relative ease. I hit my first "roadblock" when I tried to install the spare. There was a small metal piece on the wheel base which apparently must be lined up with a pea-sized hole in the tire hub, but it took me almost ten minutes to see this metal guide and take appropriate action. So I tried, without success, to simply put the tire on the axle; I was trying to put it on backwards numerous times, dropping it on my own feet often, and becoming more and more frustrated all the while. Suddenly the irony of the situation hit me. Here I am, with grease on my hands and slacks, still wearing my prep-school uniform of shirt and tie, trying to do something which all the classroom time in the world could never possibly teach me.

I have long known that education is not confined to the classroom. So as I sat waiting for a replacement tire at National Tire and Battery—pondering my situation and watching Jeopardy—I realized that part of what makes me a good student is that I do not only learn in class. My private school education may have directly helped me to know that the correct response to the 600 dollar answer in category "B" was "What is Bora-Bora?", but less than a little of what I truly know has come from academic lectures. I read voraciously on a wide range of topics, I do crossword puzzles everyday, and I am often late for upcoming classes because I spend ten minutes after the previous one engaging the teacher in a more in-depth conversation. Even beyond academic pursuits, though, I have learned physical and mental toughness from football and wrestling, I have learned about leadership and journalism from my position on the newspaper, and I have learned much about expression and emotion from music and guitar. I even dropped Homer Simpson in favor of District Attorney Jack McCoy once I figured out how much I could learn from watching "Law and Order" on NBC. In fact, every dimension of my character and each even of my life is an invisible classroom, and so whether I am changing a tire or organizing Holocaust readings at school, I am learning and growing. Accepting the challenges of school and difficult courses is still extremely important to me, but accepting the challenges that life presents can be just as educational and equally important.

Comments

■ This essay is a marvelous "slice-of-life" essay that shows readers who the applicant is and what he stands for. The story is very well written, even funny at times. Notice how effective the details are—the details about watching *Jeopardy* and the play-by-play on jacking up the car and trying to replace the flat tire make the writing sparkle. The essay, most importantly, shows through a very realistic story that the author values his privileged existence but does not wish to rely on his fortunes to get through life the easy way.

ANNE LEE

Notes on her candidacy: Anne was an avid member of the Bethel Korean Presbyterian Church Youth Group and the varsity field hockey team. She chose the University of Pennsylvania.

1. What characteristics of Penn, and yourself, make the University a particularly good match for you? Briefly describe how you envision your first year in college. How will your presence be known on campus?

"... and folks, it's gonna be another beautiful day here in the City of Brotherly Love—mostly sunny with a high of 74 deg—"

Fumbling for the "snooze" button, my hand reaches blindly towards the clock radio, pushing it closer and closer to the desk's edge until the its falls and crashes to the hard floor with a resounding thud. Stupid gravity. Yawning, I pull my pillow over my head, against my ears.

The sound of approaching footsteps . . . a muffled voice calls out . . . "Anne? Anne? What you are you doing still in bed?!?"

"Lemme alone, Zoe," I slur, lazily at the roommate from beneath the pillow. "You know I was up late finishing my paper."

"But Anne, it's almost ten—you're going to be late for your physics class—"

"TEN?!?!?!" OH MY GOSH!!! ZOE, WHY DIDN'T YOU WAKE ME?!?"

"YES!!!! WOOOHOOO—GO QUAKERS!"

Cheers erupt from the stands as the ball slams into the corner of the cage just as the clock runs down to zero. On the field, players raise their hockey sticks jubilantly, and hugs and high-fives abound in celebration over the hard-earned victory. Carrying my notebook and a small tape recorder, I make my way through the crowd, dodging fans and players, until I finally reach the scorer.

"Hi! I'm Anne Lee and I'm here from the Daily Pennsylvanian to cover the game. Congrats on the goal—that was some shot! Do you have any thoughts on today's win?"

"Thanks. I think the team played really well today. Our passing was—hey, are you the Anne Lee who wrote that article about Shakespeare in Highball? That thing was hilarious—I could not stop laughing. The line about Prospero was classic . . ."

"Anne! Over here! I'm open!"

Pivoting to the right, I quickly release the Frisbee and cringe as my pass is intercepted by an opposing player who flings it into the endzone for a goal

"Billy, I thought you said you were open," I ask my teammate.

Billy shrugs, "Sorry, I didn't see that guy coming."

"Yeah, well, you never 'see that guy coming.' . . . hey, find me a substitute—I've got to get to the museum before it closes."

"The Rodin?"

"No, the Philadelphia Museum of Art. There's this new exhibit on Surrealism that I want to see."

"Have fun then. Will you be back in time for the Bible study tonight?"

"Hey, what happened to your clock radio? Is it supposed to have all these cracks in it?"

"Um, it's a long story, Noah, happened months ago . . . I'm starving—let's eat." I open the paper bag and a smell unlike any other pervades the air: the delicious scent of hot, greasy, genuine Philly cheesesteaks. A collective "ooh" escapes from the hungry lips of my friends as the sandwiches are passed around. We sit scattered about the room, a diverse group of different individuals brought together by a love for unhealthy midnight snacks.

"Stop dripping stuff all over the floor!"

"I wish we had cheesesteaks like these back home in China."

"I think I've gained twenty pounds so far."

"You all are so weird . . . where did the admissions people find you guys?"

"Hola, me llamo Ana. Estoy estudiante de primer ano . . ."

I sit at the computer, typing away in virtual conversation at PennMoo. *Professor Hernandez was right; this is a cool way to practice Spanish.*

I glance at my watch. *Fifteen minutes until my freshman seminar starts—I'd better check my e-mail now.* Logging on to my account, I come across a message from my little brother:

"Hey, this is Matt . . . just wanted to say 'hi' . . . school's fine, got an A on my math test . . . thanks for sending me that Upenn sweatshirt . . . Mom and Dad want to know how you're doing . . . write back."

Quickly, I type up a reply: "Hi Matt, I got your e-mail . . . nice job on the test . . . so glad you like the shirt. I'll send you some shorts, too . . . tell everyone I'm doing great and that I miss them . . . and tell Mom and Dad not to worry too much about me—I LOVE IT HERE . . ."

Comments

■ Anne's Penn essay was a favorite among the admissions staff for obvious reasons. She showed not only that she had done her research on the school, but also that she is a real "do-er" who will contribute actively to campus life. The essay is imaginative and demonstrates that Anne has spent time thinking about the realities of college life and picturing what her future will bring. She clearly put a lot of time and effort into this essay (which cannot be used for any other school) and evidenced a high level of enthusiasm for Penn as well.

RYAN CARROLL

Notes on his candidacy: Active in student government, community service, his school's campus ministry program, and cross-country, Ryan selected Boston University.

1. Please describe your greatest academic passion.

I will admit to wrapping a sheet around myself and passing it off as a toga. Most of the conventions I've attended require us to wear it at one point or another.

The most enjoyable classes over my four years in high school have been in Latin. I had taken Spanish for two years in grammar school, so Latin was a big change for me. Although Latin is a "dead" language, I was compelled to take it because it seemed more mystifying and distinctive. This was a subject that I became passionate about. Not to say it wasn't challenging—AP Latin, for example, is one of my most difficult courses this semester, but because I established a fondness for it early, I feel motivated to succeed in it. I ended up winning Latin awards my first three years and I also became a member of the Junior Classical League and was elected by my instructor to the Latin Honor Society. I've attended numerous classical conventions within these organizations where my classmates and I participated in such events as basketball tournaments and Certamen, a Latin quiz game.

I have formed a strong bond with my teacher, who always seems to be there when I need help. She has taught me five classes in my four years of high school. I watched her change from Ms. Fruechtenicht to Mrs. Pollak. Even when the Latin got rather difficult, I could rely on her to guide me in the right direction. In Latin there are such things as deponent verbs, which I had a tough time grasping. These are verbs that look passive, but are actually active in voice! Who would've thought? As most things that are tough at first, though, this one also got easier with help and practice. My instructor would constantly encourage us by writing on the board "Sit vis nobiscum" before our tests, which means, "May the force be with you."

During our classes, we not only learn the Latin language, but also the history behind it and the stories of one of the greatest empires ever. I was a bit disappointed when I discovered that such movies as *Gladiator* and *Troy* weren't entirely factual. Apparently there was no Maximus (Russell Crowe) and also the emperor was supposed to signal thumbs down to the warriors in the Colosseum if their lives were to be spared, which contradicts the movie.

The one thing I'm looking forward to most before college is my school trip to Italy over spring break. I will have the opportunity to finally see for myself the basis of all that I've studied. I take pride in what I've accomplished thus far and I intend to expand on my classical studies in college and also search for other subjects I may become passionate about. The Ancient Roman author Vergil once wrote, "Sic itur ad astra." Literally, this is translated as "Thus one goes to the stars." As a college student I will seek unlimited knowledge and pursue that happiness, or in other words reach for the stars.

Comments

This is a wonderful essay on an academic passion. The introduction is compelling and really helps draw the reader in. The essay helps set Ryan apart by declaring his interest in classical studies, a rarity among many high school students. Admissions officers were no doubt charmed by the fondness and respect Ryan shows for his long-time Latin teacher. And he uses a lot of detail to help illustrate his love for the subject matter as well as the interesting knowledge he has gained over time.

NICOLE PETERSON

Notes on her candidacy: Raised in Elkhorn, Nebraska, Nicole was especially involved in dance activities and instruction, the National Honor Society, her student leadership team at church, and the Japanese Club; in addition, she worked about twenty-five hours a week. Nicole selected Stanford University.

1. **Attach a small photograph of something important to you and explain its significance.**

   (The attached photograph is a silhouette of a woman's profile, presumably the applicant's own.)

   Rhinoplasty. The word alone conjures up images of large prehistoric beasts and horned pachyderms, and for most people who know it by its common name—nose job—it produces pictures of spoiled prima-donnas and aging debutantes. Well, I'm proof enough that the images created by mere words have nothing to do with the real experience.

   Since I was eight years old, I have harbored an intense hatred of as well as an enormous shame for my appearance for one reason: I had an imperfect nose. It was a bit too large and a lot too dramatic for my otherwise acceptable face. I didn't see it as slightly imperfect, however; I saw it as a reason I wasn't worthy to be just like everybody else. I begged my parents to fix it; every time Santa asked what I wanted for Christmas I answered with "rhinoplasty please." Santa never followed through, but my parents promised that one day they would.

   My behavior was greatly affected by my distorted image of my face. When standing in a room, I could always be found in a corner, at the only place where I could see everyone, and no one could get a straight profile view of my nose. When walking past a window or room where people could catch a glimpse of my nose, I'd fake a cough or sneeze as an excuse to cover my hideous birthmark; or else I would turn my face the other way altogether, to spare onlookers from the monster I believed I was.

   I was terrified to meet new people or enter a new situation because I always felt inferior to them and the way they looked. I was a bossy and self-centered child because I felt the need to demand any respect I could from my classmates, since my face couldn't win their instant admiration. I didn't understand then that my few friends didn't even notice my nose except when I pointed it out to them. It wasn't until early adolescence that people began noticing it on their own.

In middle school I found a set of pictures a classmate had drawn during study hall. One was of a tall, thin girl with a horrendously mal-proportioned nose. My name was scrawled across the top. I showed it to him and laughed to appear indifferent to his criticism, but then I went to the bathroom and cried out my pain to my friends. In the ninth grade a teacher told me my friends should call me Jimmy Durante. I just smiled because I didn't get it. When I went home and looked him up in the encyclopedia, I understood. The picture next to the small bio was that of a man with a big, ugly nose.

On June 8, 1994, at the age of fifteen, my greatest wish to date was finally granted. My large, hideous nose was replaced with a magnificent, flawless, new model.

I fully understand that the nose should have no effect on my personality, but it does. It gives me the confidence and self-acceptance I need to enjoy life. Society places so much emphasis on appearance and perfection that it is virtually impossible to grow up, even a little bit, without feeling a need to be flawless. My nose experience taught me compassion and sympathy for people with many problems, physical or otherwise.

In a dance class I teach, one little girl has a defect in her shoulder that makes a bone stick out and form a bump on the front of her upper arm. Because of this bump she will never remove her T-shirt during class. When forced to, she points out the flaw to everyone, so they won't first notice it themselves. She appears indifferent to their "eewws" and "yucks," but I understand how much it truly hurts her. I identify with her because I can still feel the pain of rejection for not being pretty.

I hear people talk about plastic surgery with superior scorn, saying they'd never resort to such superficial nonsense, but, ironically, these people are usually very attractive. I didn't do this so I could be prom queen or win a Miss American title. I did it so I could walk into a room and stand anywhere I want to, and people would notice me, not my nose.

Comments

- Nicole went out on a limb and took a huge risk—one that most applicants could not have managed. The essay is well-written, laugh-out-loud funny, and a bit cynical as well. The author shows that she knows as well as the next person that she should not be praised for having undergone plastic surgery and that she realizes all too well what this stigma suggests about her. Nicole's discussion of superficiality and her inability to cope with a lack of beauty is intelligent and honest—she takes some responsibility for her unhappiness rather than blaming it all on society, which is refreshing. She knows herself so well and delves into the topic with such insight that it is soon clear that she does not fit the "nose job" stereotype and that she in fact has gained life lessons from both her original state and the effects of her surgery. The details she provides about how she used to maneuver her body to avoid the gaze of others as well as the descriptions of others' taunts add depth and believability to her saga. This is a truly remarkable essay.

ATUL JOSHI

Notes on his candidacy: Atul played the trombone in the marching and jazz bands, was a cocaptain of the debate team, and played varsity tennis. He selected the University of Pennsylvania, largely for its Huntsman Program for the study of international relations and business.

1. **Please write an essay about an activity or interest that has been particularly meaningful for you.**

Not many people can see beyond my stern face as I gaze forward into the stands of my high school football field. I plan my next move on an image of the field that is etched in my brain. It is half time, but I am not in the locker room reviewing a football play. Rather, I remain on the field fulfilling one of my most important high school commitments: marching band. To many, the marching band is but an odd assemblage of out-of-shape "band geeks." However, in eighth grade, weighing this stereotype against my interest in the trombone, I signed up for marching band with some reservations. In retrospect, joining the band is one of the best decisions I have ever made.

Often, individuality is seen as the only way to express yourself. The marching band serves as a counterexample. Although we wear the same uniforms and must exercise utmost precision in each formation, our uniformity is essential to our function: entertaining the crowd. Likewise, the strict uniformity of marching band has taught me to recognize that I have a responsibility to a larger entity than myself. For instance, as Section Leader this year, I would gather my entire section in a circle before each rehearsal or performance in order to emphasize key areas of concern, including proper musical tone and balance. No matter how insignificant these team-building and review sessions may sound, in practice, they have tremendously boosted the quality of our performances.

One unique aspect of our marching band is that our director chooses not to compete at band events. Rather, we perform in the "exhibition" category. At first, I felt it was ridiculous to perform but not compete, especially because our band commands a great deal of respect in the region. By removing competition from our agenda, however, our director is able to create riskier and more appealing shows. Thus, my involvement in marching band challenges me to work for nobler causes than medals and prizes: in this case, it is for the sheer pleasure of knowing that the audience has enjoyed our performance and appreciated our effort.

In addition, marching band enriches my appreciation for music through the added dimension of precision choreography. With each position mapped out on an intricate grid of a football field, it seems unlikely that a fifty-page book of positions we must memorize can ever evolve into a beautiful art form. Yet, as we integrate the music with our movement, we express the emotions felt by those whose works we are performing. Our shows have complex structure that follow a story line. The challenge is to communicate this story to our audience with our music and movements. Thus, we are the vehicle that carries a set of instructions and calculated movements into a dynamic display for the spectators to enjoy.

The impact marching band has had on me is not confined to the playing field. Since most aspects of my high school career are somehow related to competition, it is refreshing to know that non-competitive activities are just as enjoyable and rewarding. Marching band has also taught me to respect those I work with, to recognize that leadership does not imply superiority, and to constantly strive for excellence. Finally, I have forged many strong friendships with members of the marching band. These friendships are based on not only a common interest but also a common experience—an experience that has contradicted all of the stereotypes that had originally daunted me.

2. **Discuss your interest in international studies and business. How might this degree program in liberal arts, language, and business help you to meet your goals?**

Friends sometimes ask me, "Atul, how can you possibly be so sure of doing this program? What if you don't like business or Spanish?" In other words, why limit oneself to such a focused program when the purpose of college is to obtain a broad education? However, my friends' opinions reflect a common misperception: I do not view the Huntsman Program as an obstruction to my pursuit of a balanced education; rather, this seemingly rigid structure actually provides the "best of both worlds." Not only will I have the opportunity to enroll in an undergraduate business program whose caliber is second to none, but I will also have, through Penn's manifold liberal arts offerings, the freedom to pursue other interests.

Granted, in spite of the options that are sure to exist, I cannot possibly enroll in the IS&B program without being committed to a career in business. As a boy of nine, I would reach for the Business section of the *New York Times* while my older brother reached for the Comics section of the *Sunday Record*. Since then, this initial interest has grown into a passion for me: I have been fascinated by the dynamics of the global economy and the intricacies of business. Consequently, I plan to seek formal education in this vast field.

While I read the *Economist* and other periodicals at leisure because of my interest in geopolitics and business, my most significant formal education in this topic came this past summer, perhaps my most defining summer to date. At New Jersey's Governor's School for Public Issues, I enrolled in a course entitled, "Global Village or Global Pillage? Globalization, Economic Development, and Democracy in the Changing World." With fundamental principles of economics in mind, we examined the effects of globalization on various areas of the world, studied economic development theories and growth models, and attempted to prescribe remedies for each situation. In doing so, I came to understand the complex difficulties of setting economic policy for different countries and realized the ramifications of poor economic planning.

What I found most interesting through the study of various development models is that, in the end, each one had to be tailored to the culture of the particular area. In realizing this, I understood why policy-makers must keep this in mind when they seek to improve a given economy. At Penn, as I continue my studies of the Spanish language, I will be securing what I consider to be the essential complement to my studies of economics. There are, indeed, many rewarding aspects of the program's interdisciplinary approach. The Huntsman Program's foreign language, study-abroad, and internship components will give me the tools to run a successful business abroad or plan viable economic policy for Spanish-speaking countries.

Nowhere else can I develop my interests in international studies and business so fully and completely as I can through the Huntsman Program. The joint-degree program will not only challenge me to continue to set high goals for myself and help me pursue my current interests, but also develop new interests along the way and make the most our of my college years.

3. **What characteristics of Penn, and yourself, make the University a particularly good match for you? Briefly describe how you envision your first year in college. How will your presence be known on campus?**

Living in a rather small town, I sometimes feel I am missing out on many valuable opportunities, and I long to get "closer to the action." Penn, with its broad range of opportunities and its urban setting, appeals to my interests. I expect myself to contribute to and gain tremendously from the fabric of Penn and its communities. As a student, I consider it imperative to gain experience in various disciplines, and the ability to enroll in courses at Penn's different schools, even outside my intended field, supports my philosophy. Yet, my efforts at Penn will certainly not be confined to academics. The abundance of resources at Penn will be of utmost benefit to me, as I am a person of many interests.

Though I have never seen Penn's musical ensembles perform, friends currently attending Penn have attested to their formidable quality. After downloading soundclips from Penn's website, I became particularly interested in the marching band. Aside from its obvious musical dimensions, high school marching band has instilled in me certain values and leadership qualities that I apply to other activities. By playing trombone in Penn's marching band, I will be pursuing not only my love of music, but also the leadership experiences that I know will help me face challenges and tackle problems.

Another rewarding aspect of Penn is its great diversity. I will be in a setting in which people of different origins have the chance to come together, learn from each other, and commit themselves to the rewards of multiculturalism. At the same time, I feel that in my high school years, I have not been able to develop stronger bonds between myself and others of Indian heritage. Through groups such as Rangoli (IAP) and the South Asia Society, I will be a part of a community that strives to learn and teach others about Indian cultures and works to keep them alive in the United States, an often daunting yet extremely worthwhile task.

Despite the vibrant atmosphere of Penn, I would be remiss if I did not mention a major concern of mine: the contrast between Penn's campus and Philadelphia's struggling underclass. Having recently worked with underprivileged children in the economically depressed Red Bank, New Jersey, I have a new-found devotion to working with and teaching the young. In addition, my experiences with the elderly at Sunrise Assisted Living heightened my awareness of the growing need to address the problems of this often neglected part of our population. The satisfaction of knowing I have touched and influenced the life of someone speaks more to me than medals and awards. Community involvement, in my high school years, has been a major source of my happiness and pride, and I look forward to continuing serving those in need through Penn's volunteer programs.

In my search for a broad range of experiences, I have learned that there is no substitute for dedication, focus, and teamwork. I will bring this understanding to Penn and get involved in areas which currently interest me, such as Penn's musical groups, cultural organizations, and community service programs. My goals, however, must not be limited in scope: I will not keep myself from finding new passions which are bound to arise in the coming years. My various encounters at Penn will continue to fuel my aspirations, shape my future, and define myself as an individual.

4. You have just completed your 300-page autobiography. Please submit page 217.

The cushion hissed as I sat on the bench in my living room. I placed my dry hands on the smooth, plastic keys of my piano, my fingers pressing down to produce a random sequence of notes. In these notes I heard the dissonance in my life. I touched my cold hands to my face and thought of the sorrow-filled wake I had just attended for my piano teacher, Mrs. Formoe. Why was I in the living room? Shouldn't I have simply gone to bed and hoped things would be better the following morning? Despite these thoughts, I instinctively opened a book to the last piece Mrs. Formoe had taught me: Frederic Chopin's "Prelude," Opus 28, Number 4.

Mrs. Formoe, my teacher for seven years, died October 13, 1994 of malignant melanoma. When I had first begun taking weekly piano lessons, I would practice right before she arrived, merely seeing piano lessons as a burden. Only after her passing would I thoroughly grasp the importance of the lessons, during which Mrs. Formoe was letting me discover my own self through music. I would continue to practice and refine my technique, but it took her death to make me understand why I loved playing piano so deeply.

Memories of Mrs. Formoe flooded my mind as I eyed the music for Chopin's "Prelude." I proceeded to take my standard posture, arching my fingers and keeping my elbows above the keyboard. As my right hand formed a perfect octave and played the first two solitary notes of the piece, I remembered Mrs. Formoe's story about how Chopin had composed his famous preludes in a state of depression; I could now understand the depression that went into the creation of this piece. The pulsating, rubato chords began the song and developed in to variations. With each driving beat the pain I felt increased until it reached its apex as the music rose to a powerful climax, the fury of the notes becoming one with the fury inside me. The pain then subsided as the song slowed to the softest, most tender ending I had ever played. For the first time in my life, I experienced the catharsis music can give.

After the night I played that piece, the night I realized the emotional releases music can bring, my passion for music has continued to grow. It has brought great rewards, rewards that go beyond trophies and good grades, rewards such as the magical smiles on the residents' faces as I played them Duke Ellington's "Mood Indigo" at a home for the elderly, or the memories a custodian at the Governor's School recalled as he heard me play Gershwin's "Rhapsody in Blue" on an out-of-tune piano in the grand hall of Woodrow Wilson's "Summer White House." Such is the true splendor of music—how it helps me communication with both myself and others.

Although I enjoy my school subjects, I have never fathomed the complexities of any subject so profoundly as I have with music. The very notion that a precise science of pitch, rhythm, and meter can mesh so beautifully with emotion and soul moves me each time I sit down to play. Through the piano, I find solace in deepening my joys and enduring my frustrations, knowing I can always find a piece that will help me express my emotions. There is no greater pleasure than to leaf through my collection of music and find a piece that "grabs" me because it reflects my mood. Though I sometimes regret that it took her death and the night of her wake for what Mrs. Formoe tried to instill in me to manifest itself, there exists this hope inside me, the hope that a day will come when she will hear me play and realize the impact she made on my life. I will always be grateful to her for showing me how to love and appreciate the piano and the language of music. Beyond the lasting beauty of music, she revealed to me the lasting beauty of reaching out to others and understanding myself.

Comments

Atul submitted essay 1 to several schools; essays 2, 3, and 4 were written exclusively for Penn.

■ Essay 1 is very successful. Not only does Atul show the valuable way in which he utilizes his talents and spends his time, but he also expresses intellectual and personal values. Atul provides a unique discussion of how the marching band encourages a certain positive brand of conformity rather than individuality and shows his sense of responsibility to a group or a team. He also demonstrates immense school spirit, always desirable to admissions committees.

▪ In essays 2 and 3, Atul demonstrates that he knows a lot about the programs to which he is applying and shows that he is a good fit. He does so through discussing both academic and nonacademic pursuits. He shows that he has clear goals, which is especially important for anyone applying for admission to a specific dual-degree and/or non-liberal arts program as an undergraduate, and expresses that his interests in international policy and business have been developed over a long period of time.

LAUREN FOLEY

Notes on her candidacy: A twin, Lauren was an accomplished trumpet player and was involved in many community service projects. She chose Dartmouth College.

1. **If you yourself were in the position to ask a thought-provoking and revealing question of college applicants, what would that question be? Now that you have asked your ideal question, answer it.**

   If you had to choose three bumper stickers that express important aspects of who you are and what you believe in, which would you choose and why?

   As the Foley family's 1989 Oldsmobile, I have experienced much in my day. Recently, when I became the twins' car, I have come to know Lauren a lot better. I have watched her mature physically, intellectually and emotionally. I have great pride in displaying the creative one-liners which she chooses to exhibit on my bumper. She seems to know these messages serve to formulate a first impression of her. Though some have changed, the following three have endured and currently adorn the rusted chrome above my muffler.

HATE IS NOT A FAMILY VALUE

This is certainly true of Lauren and her family. Often, one can see in a young adult evidence of her upbringing. Lauren respects the diversity of people and their different lifestyles. She passionately opposes those who evaluate situations with closed minds and pass judgments stemming from their own ignorance. Lauren knows how to disagree, how to reject, and how to oppose people and issues with fervor. She can dislike people but does not know how to hate them. Her parents simply left hate out when rearing her. An accidental oversight? Probably not. They preach tolerance, acceptance, respect, compassion, understanding, and freedom of expression. Not hate.

EXPECT MIRACLES

This may sound naive and arrogant to some, but to Lauren it expresses a simple truth. Her definition of a miracle is not found in some media hyped "act of God," but instead in the aspects of her life that are often taken for granted. To "expect," then, is to recognize their existence and not to overlook them. Lauren has been radically impacted by her life-long closeness with the person who once shared her egg. The need not to be perceived as a mirror image has caused her individuality to flourish and contributes to her proclivity for deep friendship and closeness. The gift of twinship has been Lauren's greatest miracle.

Another miracle to her is reflected in the "cosmic intelligence" of a flower growing from a seed that is scattered casually on the ground. She observes a child who becomes a teenager and wonders about the natural instinct that allows one to grow into the other. This is a "miracle." The ability to be sensitive in friendship is not taught by rules, but born from intuition and caring. This gift is a "miracle." If a person emerges from a sea of shallow materialism and expresses his or her opposition to drowning in that sea, then that is a "miracle."

Miracles, then, are the perceptions that anything can and does happen. To expect these phenomena is to respect, to acknowledge and to believe in "miracles."

The last sticker is a curiosity to me, yet it is the most important to her. It has been cemented down with glue as strong as the rivets which hold my own bumper. Its true purpose eludes me, but from my experience with Lauren I think I can penetrate its mystery and hypothesize about its true meaning.

The sticker is all white with a simple blue ribbon floating in the middle. Although the blue is bold, the message is subtle. I see motorists pondering this statement at red lights. They seem to be asking themselves, "How can I be for or against this person on this issue if I don't even know what she is saying?" I have concluded that this is Lauren's whole point. Since there are people who create and maintain their impressions of another based on his bumper stickers, the uncertainty about this final sticker keeps them engaged. Lauren has forced them to keep at least a partially open mind. They now have to meet her to solve this riddle and to establish a valid impression of her.

That is just like Lauren. She'll express herself in a brief introduction while deliberately preventing you from establishing a complete image until you know her. She exhibits a bumper sticker that stands for, "Not all I have to say and not all of what I am can be summarized on the rusted exterior of my '89 Olds."

2. What was the highlight of your summer?

I had always told myself that my goal in life was to help others; this was the chance to test my conviction. In February of my Junior year, I was accepted to join a mission trip to Reynosa, Mexico. Our goal: to build houses by hand for people in need.

Each day we worked side-by-side with Mexican families, building their cinder block houses. The immediate gratification I felt from watching the houses rise compelled me to the building site each day, forgetting the heat, forgetting the exhaustion. Everything I experienced, from the strength of our team work to my own enthusiasm, surprised me. Germans, Mexicans, and Anglos, we couldn't speak each other's words, but we shared a common goal as we worked, house by house, seeking better living conditions for these people. I was so heartened by what I was doing that I volunteered to stay late and continue working, even though the majority of the team had left for the day. Upon reflection I noticed that I was often the only woman volunteer.

I'd seen "Save the Children" commercials on TV, but I'd never been exposed to the poverty I saw in Reynosa. The teenagers with whom I mixed cement and laid cinder block will never be offered the opportunities I have. Many of them will remain illiterate and can, at best, anticipate earning a wage of four dollars a day at the local Magnavox or Zenith factories. I realized that my confident teenage self had been muted, my naiveté dissolved, my appreciation for all I have deepened. These were my sobering gifts of the trip.

Immediately after I returned home, I signed up for Habitat for Humanity to continue the experience I gained in Reynosa. As the summer activities fell into place, I relaxed with friends, worked a pleasurable job, and met new people as I volunteered locally. My physical appearance was the same, but inwardly the memories of what I saw and experienced in Mexico have changed me forever.

Comments

Lauren submitted both essays as a set.

■ Essay 1 takes advantage of the open-ended "make up your own question" question to show off a real sense of creativity. The question she poses is unique and Lauren does even more with it by narrating her piece from the point of view of her Oldsmobile. This gives her an opportunity to speak more thoroughly about herself without having to say, "I am x, I am y." The three bumper sticker slogans she chooses demonstrate important aspects of her persona, and she uses tangible details to make her case. She tells us that she is strong and opinionated but not cruel; that she appreciates the little things in life; and that she is interested in engaging others—whether they share her views of the world or not—in a dialogue. Her ending is clever: She is essentially stating that she is a complex, multifaceted character who cannot easily be understood on the basis of her bumper stickers, or, in effect, this one essay.

■ Essay 2 addresses an ordinary topic—a summer community service project—but is effective in its expression of Lauren's personal skills and values. Lauren further demonstrates her humanity and sensitivity to others here.

AMBROSE FATUROTI

Notes on his candidacy: Ambrose, an African American student, played varsity football and basketball, won a nonfiction writing award, and was a counselor and leader at his camp. He selected the University of Virginia.

1. **What work of art, music, science, mathematics, or literature has influenced your thinking, and in what way?**

   Last fall, I took an African American literature course which led to explore areas of myself which were previously uncharted. I read The Souls of Black Folk by W.E.B. DuBois. In his book, DuBois states a theory he calls "double-consciousness." He proposes that blacks in American are indeed dually-conscious of themselves. He muses on how blacks in America are aware that they are both African and equally American as is implied by the politically correct nametag. Not only does this label imply that blacks are aware of themselves in this way, but it also begins to explain a feeling of confusion. This theory tells of an inner struggle African Americans go through between being grounded in their roots in Africa while still being a part of the mainstream United States. More so, while this classification of African Americans as both African and American exists, an "out of place" feeling will continue to exist among African Americans. The sentiment will be that we are still Africans in American which, though more true for me as I am the first generation born in America from my family, is something African Americans have been trying to move away from. This theory, however complex, has opened doors of understanding in my own life that have decisively shaped my outlook on society today and in years past.

2. **Most people belong to many different communities—groups defined by (among other things) shared geography, religion, ethnicity, income, cuisine, interest, race, ideology, or intellectual heritage. Choose one of the communities to which you belong, and describe that community and your place within it.**

   A special community I have been a part of for a significant amount of my life is a seven week overnight camp called Camp Pasquaney. The residents of this community strive, over the course of the summer, to create an atmosphere of trust and to sustain long-lasting friendships among campers and counselors alike. The camp setup is such that each boy lives in a dorm with other boys of his own age. This practice allows campers to grow with each other and foster strong bonds together through living and competing against one another. This competition is focused on pushing campers to be their best as opposed to emphasizing simply on winning. At camp, everyone is relieved of all the over-aggressiveness usually associated with sports and can have fun that is not marred by anyone yelling crudely in the stands.

The youngest are 11 and the last year of camp eligibility is 16. The boy is then required to spend one year away from camp to consider how they have changed in their time there. Afterward, if he wishes to return as a counselor and is wished back, he may do so. This exercise creates continuity at camp and really develops a uniquely warm living environment. Being a part of this community for five summers out of my life instead of being home and working was probably one of the hardest decisions I have been faced with in my life. The part of camp that made this decision a bit easier, however, were the powerful bonds forged in five years with the people there. It was truly hard to confront that last summer might have been the last I would spend on that hill overlooking that lake. Though it was difficult to put aside my own personal interests for so many summers, when I look back on that investment of my time, I am thankful I made the decision I did. When I look at where I had come from and the position I am in now, it is clear to me the Pasquaney seeks to enable an environment where boys can go to become upstanding men in society. Because of all that Pasquaney has given me, it is difficult to say that I will not be back to visit some time next summer. Perhaps even being a counselor may be in my future.

Comments

Ambrose submitted both essays as a set.

- Essay 1 provides a convenient way for the applicant to explore his minority status without resorting to any discussions that suggest he is attempting to gain sympathy for his own experiences of oppression or discrimination. This essay is an intelligent discussion of a classic piece of literature.

- Ambrose wisely utilized the second essay to demonstrate his passion for and devotion to one of his activities. By discussing the way in which his five-year commitment has shaped him, he is also able to bring up values such as cooperation (as opposed to competition).

AINSLEY SEAGO

Notes on her candidacy: Ainsley, the owner of a ferret and two black widow spiders, participated in a Junior Naturalists class for ten years, took college courses in Russian history, and was an active member of her school's pep band. She chose to attend Cornell's College of Agriculture and Life Sciences.

1. **Tell us about a person who has had an important influence on you. What qualities in that person do you most admire, and how have you grown from knowing that person?**

As a small child, I was enthralled by insects, snails, and other wild things. I took to collecting bumblebees, spiders, snakes, and earthworms and went thorough a succession of domestic animals as well, adopting mice, rats, hamsters, and a tarantula.

When these failed to satisfy my interest, I was enrolled at the age of eight in "Junior Naturalists," a class at the nearby Snake Lake Nature Center, an urban nature preserve. For two Saturday mornings each month, I explored the natural world under the tutelage of a man who has become my most beloved and effective teacher. John Slipp, retired biology professor and award-winning aquarist, proved to be the ideal font of knowledge for the inquiring youngster, answering my questions for years to come.

In those years, I found that there was much more to nature than bug collections and caged rodents. John showed me how to identify bird calls and answer back. We analyzed the acidity of pond water and collected salamander eggs. We studied plankton from the lake, mounted insects, and became amateur taxidermists. After one full year of Junior Naturalists, a graduation ceremony was held; we were presented with diplomas and green "naturalist jackets." Most of the graduates, older than I, departed satisfied with their year of education and were ever seen again. I stayed, determined to keep coming back until I decided I had learned enough. I came back for another four years of nature study. Graduation was again suggested, with another recognition ceremony and certificates "for outstanding dedication . . ." I ignored the hint, continuing to learn to track foxes and spot woodpecker nests. The small group of die-hard young naturalists I belonged to was now in middle school, and John began to drop Latin names.

"Hear that? Can you see the bird? Describe it."

"It's a brown bird, robin-sized, red eyes, orange chest . . ."

"That's our native Rufus-Sided Towhee, *Pipillo maculatus*. Related to . . ."

"I know this! Uh . . . Robin! *Turdus migratoris!*"

We brought in recently collected specimens for show and tell, much to the relief of our mothers, whose freezers had contained dead birds for too many days. Numerous highly scientific experiments were conducted, including the great *How Many Other Fish Can We Put in With the Largemouth Bass Before It Stops Eating All of Them* project and the highly amusing *Aerodynamics of the Frozen Crow* test flights (it's all in the wrist). We ignited swamp gas. We dissected a yellow-bellied sapsucker. We hatched salmon eggs and released the fry into local streams. We counted birds around Snake Lake for the Audobon Society's Annual Bird Count. We cared for ill or orphaned animals brought to the Nature Center by worried homeowners, from a shivering baby opossum delivered in an ice chest to an injured weasel and a two-headed garter snake.

We learned to accept death as both an integral counterpart to life and a gift to the studious naturalist, welcoming every chance to inspect and handle a bird that would have been hopelessly elusive when alive. We treasured windshield-casualty butterflies that we never would have had the heart to euthanize, and many a raccoon that would have gnawed our fingers to bits had it not been frozen quite solid. As he pointed out the fantastic design of a specimen, John was frequently heard to quote Blake's famous poem: "What immortal hand or eye . . ." We'd chime in, ". . . could frame thy fearful symmetry."

Now into my tenth year of Junior Naturalism, I still wake up early on Saturdays, looking forward to another episode of nature education with John. I sometimes find myself the only student in attendance. I have begun to take notes, realizing that this class may not continue much longer as my college years approach and John climbs into his eighties. I've learned more from this class than from any other biology course; John has been both a great teacher and a sort of grandfather, combining the wisdom of age with the knowledge of a retired professor. As we've discussed anatomy, whale behavior patterns, bird calls, sea cows, and glaciation, John has not only taught me about natural history but has made a naturalist out of me as well. When I leave for college next fall, I will finally have graduated.

In learning the value of wild things and their habitats, I have become an advocate for conservation of wilderness. I firmly support the Endangered Species Act. I care about manatees and spotted owls. One may call me a tree-hugging, whale-saving nature nerd, but I prefer to answer to the title of Junior Naturalist.

2. Tell us what you would like to study at Cornell. What field(s) of study interest you, and why? How did your interest(s) evolve?

After ten years of examining specimens and spotting wildlife, I've seen most every species of bird and mammal indigenous to the area in which I live. The one taxon that consistently amazes and amuses me is the class Insecta.

I've lived in this city all my life, but it wasn't until last summer that I encountered my first Ten-lined Junebug. I was standing on my front porch looking for moths when I noticed on the doormat, by my foot, the largest beetle I'd ever seen. It was light brown, with white stripes down its back, and as I bent down for a better look, it hissed at me. Hissed! I was taken aback. I'd heard of hissing cockroaches, but this was certainly no cockroach; it had a chubby, fuzzy face, beady eyes, and weird shoehorn-shaped antennae. It hissed again, and I hurried into the house to find a jar.

That Saturday at my nature class, I pulled the jar out of my backpack and presented it to John, the teacher. He squinted at the trapped beetle and pronounced it a *Polyphillus decumlineatus*. Fetching a volume on entomology from the bookshelf, I looked it up and became better acquainted with this monster, the Ten-lined Junebug. According to this book, its hissing was produced by separating and rapidly vibrating the leaf-like layers of its strange, flat antennae. Simply put, this was much cooler than the Big Stupid Garden Beetles (*Caribus hortensis*) that I usually see around my house.

Since then, I've encountered the Pine Sawyer, which is larger by far but hasn't half the charisma of that junebug. I know how to spot ant lion lairs; I've kept water-boatman beetles in aquariums. I've learned a bit about the behavior and identifying characteristics of a number of local insect species, but I still have a great deal to learn about the finer workings of insects. It is for this reason that I would like to study entomology at Cornell's CALS [College of Agriculture and Life Sciences]. After a visit to Cornell and careful study of the Entomology Department's webpages, I am confident that Cornell has a superior entomology program: from Spider Biology to Advanced Coleopterology, CALS offers a better education in entomology than any other school I've looked at. The campus is also patched with and surrounded by green belts and wild places, wherein may be found many a species of insect unseen in the Pacific Northwest. Many of the courses that interest me promise field trips into the local wilderness areas and to collecting sites on and off campus; such opportunities would not exist on an urban campus. In order to eventually build a career in entomology, I see myself learning how insect pests might be deterred from destroying crops without the use of poisons, or which stretch of a forest must be preserved to ensure the continuation of a threatened species of beetle or moth.

Comments

Ainsley submitted these essays as a set.

■ These essays are both well-written and descriptive, and work well together to reinforce themes while also concentrating on different aspects of Ainsley's candidacy. While the first focuses on her interactions with a teacher—the human face of her development—the second focuses on her passion for insects and what she plans to do with that interest in the future.

■ Essay 1 is a beautiful tribute to a teacher who has obviously had a tremendous influence on Ainsley's intellectual and personal growth, even though she never says this in so many words. The essay is comical—especially in its descriptions of the experiments Ainsley has performed over the years—and establishes the roots of her long-term commitment to the study of nature. It shows great intellectual enthusiasm outside of the classroom. It illustrates how Ainsley has allowed herself to be shaped by someone else's knowledge, not only on the subject of biology, but also on the subject of life itself.

■ Essay 2 further establishes Ainsley's fervent intellectual endeavors outside of the classroom. The opening of the essay in fact demonstrates that the author sees the entire world as her classroom or lab. Ainsley also shows that she is serious about Cornell and knows exactly what she is looking for in a college.

WILL SCHER

Notes on his candidacy: An avid writer and lacrosse player, Will Scher chose to attend Emory University.

1. Evaluate a significant experience or achievement that has special meaning for you.

"My Hair-raising Experience"

Though hearing only the first three seconds, I already know the music video—it is one of my favorites. The low, eerie, guitar distortion suddenly explodes into sharp power chords, crashing drums, and earthshaking bass. The televised picture jumps into flashing radiance, illuminating the featured musicians, their heads rising and falling in unison, violently shaking their long, black, dread-locked hair. Leaping from my chair I try to imitate them but something's wrong; something's missing. I then remember that I no longer have the requisite hair-length for such actions and I glumly sink back to listen.

Insignificant as it may seem, growing long hair was a very important experience in my life. While sprouting in ninth grade, the roots of this quest lay firmly planted in the mud of middle school, a time of almost complete social invisibility, where, despite my best efforts, I felt like an imperial storm trooper: nameless, faceless and white. I resolved to forge a new identity in high school, to end my ghost-like status, and most importantly to capture the attention of the fairer sex. After several hours of intense deliberation, I reasoned that long hair could achieve my aims, and so I immediately set to work at not getting a hair cut.

Initially, widespread attention was an endgame I expected to come eventually, if at all. Thus I was unprepared when my barbershop truancy was noticed after only a few weeks. Soon everyone had something to say, and overwhelmingly it was something negative. From my mother dropping subtle hints about a haircut, to my schoolyard chums, whose opposition to my long hair was unanimous as evidenced by their challenges to my manhood. Even my hair itself seemed to protest its new freedom, curling, knotting itself, and hanging in my eyes. Far from the effect intended, however, these deterrents only bolstered my resolve. My juvenile stunt became a determined crusade.

Though myriad in number, the attacks of my opponents remained epidermal in nature, and thus lacked the substance to be truly discouraging. As much fun as was made of my hairstyle, few in my class could deny my strength as student and athlete. Fewer still could equal my capabilities in the weight room or boast a brown belt in Tae Kwan Do. (This is the reason why a secret conspiracy among my classmates to forcibly shave my head never came to fruition.) In time, hallow derision yielded to genuine respect. Paralleling this moral victory was the physical success of my unrelenting campaign to pacify my rebellious locks. Experience, longer hair, and a blow-dryer turned the tide of this war, and ensured a silky flowing mane, as well as the interest (and at times envy) of a great many young ladies. Grown out of insecurity, my hair now filled me with confidence; even the intended derogatory nickname "Sunshine" became a source of pride.

As I run my fingers through my (now) short hair, I again question my judgment in having it cut. While less frequently as time goes on, I still sometimes feel the longer version the way a recent amputee might feel the phantom of a lost appendage. I chose to cut it for many of the same reasons that I chose to grow it out, but the scissors were an even larger gamble for me. Would I lose the identity I had built?

Would I sink back into the murky sea of obscurity? Or, would nothing change, save my shampoo and conditioner consumption, proving that I am more than just skin (or hair) deep? While even more shocking to my friends and peers than my original decision to let my hair grow unchecked, the haircut made no impact on who I was to them. Not even my nickname changed.

Ultimately I realized that my hair had simply been a tool to communicate myself to the world. It was my defiance in growing it, not having it, that had made visible my many previously hidden merits, declared my strength and independence, and yes, attracted a great deal of female attention. The end product originally envisioned was superfluous; my hair had already served its purpose, and that is why I cut it. That, and split ends.

2. Please describe your greatest academic passion.

I was first introduced to poetry in my freshman English class, and what I mean by poetry is real poetry. Until then, I had known only the verses of Hallmark and Poe, and thus maintained that poetry was either pink and lavender, or black and darker black. My teacher, however, was determined to quash the stigma that poetry had for me, and soon broke my resistance to it by suggesting that I write a poem about something I felt strongly about.

With caution and uncertainty, I began to experiment with writing poetry. I like to think that with the completion of my first piece, I conquered poetry. I took it away from the swooning romantics and the cackling Goths; I claimed it in the name of regular people. What really happened, however, was that poetry conquered me, and my prejudices and pre-conceptions.

My first poem was not about love or death. It was an iambic pentameter about surfing, and it showed me that poetry could be whatever I wanted it to be. Once I had discarded my poetic inhibitions it came very easily, naturally, and abundantly. I even began to write outside of class.

I found poetry to be an excellent way to express my thoughts in a concise but very complete and descriptive way. As my experience and proficiency with poetry expanded, the quality of my writing, prose included, benefited stylistically as well as functionally. The challenge of encoding complex and often intangible concepts and ideas into poetry also enabled me to better decode the abstract and symbolic language of others, which proved very useful in all of my classes from algebra to U.S. History. During the classical literature unit in my Spanish class, for example, my incomplete understanding of the language itself was offset by my grounding in the styles in which many of the pieces were written. Poetry for me became a way to write, think, and analyze with greater strength, and at a deeper level.

Comments

■ Both of these essays help to set Will apart from his peers because he shows himself to be willing to go out on a limb, take risks, and be a bit different from the average male high school student—most young men are not willing to endure teasing from their peers over their looks or to admit an interest in writing poetry! This was a clever way of making himself stand out in a competitive pool of applicants. Both essays are well-written and show a creative and fluid use of language.

■ Essay 1 is useful because it discusses something very personal—something admissions officers would certainly not know about Will from other parts of the application—and really uses the subject of growing (and then cutting) his hair to demonstrate important facets of his personality and development during high school.

JAIME SINGLEY

Notes on her candidacy: A dancer, soprano in the Chamber Singers, and writer on the school newspaper, Jaime also worked sixteen hours a week during the school year. She selected Dartmouth College.

1. **If you yourself were in the position to ask a thought-provoking and revealing question of college applicants, what would that question be? Now that you have asked your ideal question, answer it.**

Are you still daddy's little girl?

A monotone buzzing echoed in the distance and my eyes scoured the restaurant to locate the culprit. The word "REMOVE" blinked rapidly above the vat of boiling fries. I began a mad dash towards the fry station, racing to extract the greasy mass and assemble the order on my drive-thru screen before the next car reached my window. As I gingerly placed a Big Mac in a brown paper bag, I narrowly escaped being crushed by two crew members furiously compiling their orders for the multitudes of customers forming lines in the lobby.

Another ringing, this time from the contraption that decorated my head. The clumsy headphones generated the sound of a rumbling car engine. I heard a gruff voice resonate in the drive-thru speaker. "I want two filet-o-fish, a small fry, and a medium coke; that's it." I rattled off the price and directed my latest customer to the second window. By my third year at McDonald's I had memorized the prices of a variety of items and meals, but this combination was new to me. I directed my focus to the bin, spotting the last two filet being eyed by a customer at the front counter. Knowing that it was only seconds before the sandwiches would disappear, I plowed through the masses of workers in front of me. "Out of filet," I shouted back to the grill team, emerging victorious from my quest.

The aroma of fried fish and tartar sauce penetrated my nostrils as I dodged the mop bucket, standing as an obstacle in my return path to the glass windows of the drive-thru station. A familiar face stared at me through the smudged glass shield. Despite a few wrinkles and the absence of hair on his head, I immediately recognized the man whose voice I had not placed. He looked on with an endless gaze that hollowed me from within and I felt slightly relieved when my father did not recognize me. I remembered when my dad used to take me to McDonald's as a young child. Although his order stayed the same, I reminded myself that this was not the same man I had once shared my fries with. Alcohol had transformed him.

My father had been absent for the majority of my life. He had not been there three years earlier when I first entered the shimmering glass doors of McDonald's clutching a job application in my hand in an effort to help my single mother support two children. He had not been there when I became the youngest manager on the staff at seventeen years old. He had not been there when I chose survival over accepting failure, when I learned from his mistakes, nor when I refused to submit to his example. My father had not been a witness to all those small successes that proved any dream attainable and prepared me for my current academic endeavors at Deerfield Academy and those beyond.

I opened the electronic window with a swift gesture of my hand. Trading the precisely creased brown bag for five crumpled dollar bills, I heard the words tumble from my lips, "Thank you and have a nice day." I closed my eyes for a moment until the rumbling of the car engine was nothing more than a dull whisper. A last glance through the foggy glass windows confirmed by suspicion that only a void remained on the other side. I took a step backward, into my world of congested paths and the constant buzzing of timers. With years of experience behind me, I navigated my way around the mop bucket that had previously hindered my course and directed my attention to the daunting lines of ravenous customers in the lobby.

Comments

■ The question that Jaime poses (clearly written after she had composed the essay, and meant only for herself—not a question she would ask every applicant, boys included) immediately makes readers wonder what the essay will be about. The suspense builds as we read the story and see no sign of a discussion of family or father figures. Jaime makes her point—that her father has not been part of her life because of his alcohol problem—by stating it plainly and painting around the critical issue rather than dramatizing it or asking for our sympathy. While describing scenes of family violence or parental alcoholic stupors can be an effective way of telling this kind of story, Jaime's approach is equally if not more effective. The details about being a McDonald's shiftworker help us to feel what her position there is like and how hard she has worked at a job some would call "pointless" in order to help support her family. She deftly includes relevant details—becoming the youngest shift manager, breaking her back to hold down a job and attend Deerfield at the same time—that clarify her fortitude and goal-oriented nature. The ending of the essay is a nice metaphor and forces readers to think a bit more about what the candidate's father stands for in her life.

KASSIDEE KIPP

Notes on her candidacy: After graduating from her public high school in El Paso, Texas, Kassidee attended Dartmouth College.

1. Which of your activities is the most meaningful to you and why?

I ate my bowl of oatmeal at the round, wooden table that now sits in my kitchen in El Paso. It was roundup at the Bar T Ranch, and I scraped every last grain from the bowl, knowing that I would not eat again until sundown. Roundup was my father's holy work, each Spring and Fall; to me it meant riding Go Sierra all day long with my father. I grew up on the backs of those ranch horses, the Quarter horses that the cowboys (including my father) trained and trusted. I rode them day in and day out, during roundup and in gymkhanas in town. They played my games, listened to my stories, knew my secrets. I rode through the desert in Southern New Mexico, completely oblivious to the impact riding would later have on my life. I just loved horses.

My family was forced to leave the ranch when I was still young. I had never lived anywhere where there were more people than Herefords. I will never forget Ms. Hansen, the tough and rugged woman who proved to me that you can live in a city and still ride. I took riding lessons from her, where the objective wasn't just to stay on, but to look good while you did. It fulfilled my instinctual need to be on top of a horse. I learned to ride English and to jump. I learned how to clean my saddle and how to make sure the other horses didn't chew my horse's tail, two principles my father to this day scoffs. I rode in local horse shows and in national horse shows, in Texas and in California. Western always remained my favorite. It reminded me of my roots, of Go Sierra, of roundup at the Bar T.

After I had been riding with Ms. Hansen for a few years, she invited me to be a counselor at a summer camp in the Gila Wilderness. Being only thirteen years old and by far the youngest counselor there, I had quite a time making the campers listen to me. While teaching them to saddle a horse, I seemed more like a comedian than an instructor. I realized that I needed an edge. My ranch skills saved me. I taught them everything that ranch life had taught me, from how to clean out a horse's hoof with a screwdriver to how to lasso a calf. I remember how proud I felt driving home a few weeks later. It allowed me to pass on knowledge others had helped me acquire.

Riding has allowed me to bridge the gap between ranch and city life. My father smiles when he watches me ride the same way he did when came in from roundup, covered from head to toe in dust. By riding, I serve my father's memories just as his sketches of windmills and the country songs he scribbles on his yellow pads of paper at the round wooden table in the kitchen do, and I am able to keep alive the medium by which my family existed for five generations.

2. Tell us about how you spent last summer.

Circle N Number Two is nestled between Juanita Gustavo's beauty shop and Chez Carlos, a thrift store in Downtown El Paso that has been around for at least twenty years. Prior to this summer, it had always been a place where I could take my friends to get a free Slurpee or some Mexican candy. This summer, however, that all changed. Circle N Number Two became my place of employment.

Three middle-aged women usually man the store. Rosa, Esther, and Maria Elena, all first-generation immigrants from Mexico, tell me their stories: some about love, some about hardship, some about each other. Rosa's daughter, Rosio, is getting married next May. She is my age (my age!), and Rosa is thrilled. "I just want to have some *nietos*", she tells me in her thick accent. Esther picks up as many extra hours as she can, and every Saturday she rides the bus over the border to take her weekly earnings to her eleven children in Juarez. Maria Elena spends her spare time at the store touching up her eyeliner and rouge, since she never knows when her boyfriend might stop by. Circle N Number Two isn't a summer job for these women; it is the means by which they survive.

It doesn't take long to get to know all of the "regulars." Many of them live on the streets. Some of them I loved, some of them I pitied, some of them I dreaded. They are war heroes, heroin addicts, truth seekers, drag queens, and drunks. Some silently count out the hundred and nineteen pennies for a Quart of Busch; others show me pictures of their children as I hold my breath, praying that their Lone Star cards have enough money left on them to pay for their "Beans N Weiners." Some are educated; some are mentally ill. They all have one common element: they are good people who have been defeated. I often wonder, was it death, rejection, war, realization, hardship? What changed these people? What caused them to live the lives they do? Being exposed to the people who gave up, who have been defeated by trying times, raised my awareness of the absolute necessity to (as my father says) "keep on truckin'." Life has its highs and lows, and as long as you don't succumb to the lows, a high is bound to follow.

I began working at the store this summer to help my mom out with Circle N Number Two. I ended up helping myself.

3. Please let us know something about you that we might not learn from the rest of your application.

As I walked up to the podium to address the board members of El Paso City Council, my knees trembled just as they had during my first debate round. My research was meticulous, my presentation polished. I was fighting the city's curfew ordinance for minors under the age of seventeen. I felt that I was a mature young adult and that the curfew ordinance, the law that makes it illegal for me to be out past eleven o'clock, violated my civil liberties. I argued my views with passion and confidence. After I finish my three-minute presentation, the final product of my hours on end spent in the library, Mayor Ramirez chuckled and said, "You'll make a fine lawyer one day", and motioned to adjourn. I shuffled out the meeting room with the others, dejected and frustrated. The following evening, as I watched the council deliberate the issue on television, I was thrilled as I watched one of the members vote against the ordinance. This was my first victory, but the war was far from over.

I founded a club at school as a result of my desire to overturn the ordinance, and for the first few months our membership consisted of my closest friends (who were obligated to attend), their younger siblings (who were forced to attend), and me. I planned for us to continue the curfew battle, to readdress city council, but no was willing to do the work. I put up signs, made announcements, and passed out flyers, and at last, our numbers began growing. My peers began showing interest in fighting the curfew ordinance, and they were there to work.

Winter break rolled around, and I decided that we needed to expand our goals, to focus on issues more compelling than the city curfew, and we did just that. We gathered nonperishable goods from local grocery stores and distributed them to the poverty stricken community just over the border in Juarez, Mexico.

Now, the Young Activists Club (as we came to call ourselves) works on multiple projects. We have established a relationship with local elementary schools, and we perform skits for the elementary students, focusing on taking care of the environment and being active in one's community. We have hosted debates in Downtown El Paso in the Plaza Park regarding both local and national issues. We have collected toiletries from hotels and donated them to the Battered Women's Shelter. Curfew still remains my personal focus, however, and I have spoken with lawyers from the American Civil Liberties Union about my viewpoints and continued to perform research on the issue. With the help of several other club members who disagree with the curfew ordinance, I will meet with City Council again in January.

The Young Activists Club began as a result of my frustration with the local curfew ordinance. It has developed into a multipurpose organization with over sixty members, and I am confident it will survive long after my departure from El Paso. I feel our membership has been successful largely because the club serves as a medium for students to realize their ideas and to take an active stance toward issues. Most clubs and other on-campus organizations fail to stretch their focuses beyond the Coronado High School campus. The Young Activists Club, like Japanese class and debate, has allowed me to expand my thought patterns and to see beyond the Friday night lights at a football game.

Comments

■ This is a fantastic set of essays. Each is superbly written and conveys a different theme about Kassidee—you'll notice, however, that the essays work well together because they build a picture of the candidate as a tough, resilient, self-reflective go-getter who will add something unique to her college class. Each portrait of Kassidee helps to demonstrate that her background and experiences are highly unusual, and that she can offer a college what no other candidate can offer. Kassidee was wise to set herself apart from other candidates by emphasizing her family's ranching background, her initiative in founding the Young Activists Club, and her work experience. She shows throughout her set of essays that despite suffering from some hardships and setbacks, she has remained proud as well as determined to stretch herself and reach her goals.

KYLE SEREDA

Notes on his candidacy: A member of the first graduating class of Stuart Hall High School, an independent school for boys in San Francisco, Kyle chose to attend the University of California, Berkeley.

1. Evaluate a significant experience or achievement that has special meaning for you.

Certain conceptions enter my mind when I pass a certain hospital near my school: suffering, fortitude, anguish, and transformation. I was diagnosed with Crohn's disease during my sophomore year, in a bed at this hospital. The week that I spent there represented the beginning of a long recovery period, but I remember it more because the ordeal, and the irrevocability of the change that had occurred in my body, led me to what is now my passion and my calling.

The self-examination prompted by my newly altered life was more profound than any I had ever experienced. So it was natural that when my history teacher assigned a paper on a Renaissance figure, and I chose Machiavelli, I actually found myself buying *The Prince* and reading it. This was a threshold that I crossed because of the reflectivity that a month of pain had put into my head. I wanted to search the wisdom of the past for something, anything, that might satiate my desire for answers. But I was insatiable. *The Prince* was my initiation into the world of philosophy.

I didn't turn back. I only looked forward: forward to Plato, Aristotle, Marcus Aurelius, Rousseau, Kierkegaard, Kant, Mill, Spinoza, and my favorite, Nietzsche. I discovered that I loved philosophy intensely, and consumed the books of these masters, who each had volumes of valuable insights to teach me. Plato and Aristotle introduced me to a world of logic and rationality; Aurelius taught me of my insignificance; Kierkegaard advised me to have faith. But none burrowed into me more deeply than Friedrich Nietzsche. When I read *Twilight of the Idols*, I reexamined every moral, metaphysical, and methodological judgment that I had been taught until then. *Thus Spoke Zarathustra* gave me a character with whom I identified, as a person who often craves solitude. I'm presently reading my eighth Nietzsche work, *The Gay Science*. Nietzsche's work often brings me nearly to tears. When I finished *Ecce Homo*, I marveled at the enduring genius of a man who was about to lose his mental faculties. Nietzsche was sick for a good part of his life and he often wrote about how his suffering inspired flights of reflection on all profound matters; I know what he meant. He wrote about the inseparability of joy from pain, about the augmented beauty of all things perceived by one who has suffered. This I know too. Reading Nietzsche in particular has made my travails worth something.

At the end of the summer that preceded my junior year, I volunteered as a counselor-in-training at a camp for children with my disease. I gave an impromptu speech during an assembly one night in which I described points about suffering from Plato, Machiavelli, and Marcus Aurelius (I had not yet discovered Nietzsche). I intended, as a relative newcomer to the world of Crohn's, to communicate to the kids and adults what I had learned from the philosophers about fate and fortitude. I had only been reading philosophy for about six months, and was in the middle of Plato's *Republic*. Now, it's been nineteen months since I read *The Prince*, and my love for philosophy has been cemented. I love knowledge for its own sake. My idea of a "fun" Saturday or Sunday consists of taking a long, reflective walk and reading philosophy in a park or on a bench somewhere. I've read nine Platonic dialogues, seven works of Nietzsche, two of Aristotle (major works, the *Nichomachean Ethics* and *Politics*), and five other major philosophical works. During my junior year, I taught a session of theology class about Plato's theory of Forms and perception. I plan one day to earn a PhD in philosophy and become a professor. I eagerly anticipate trying to instill a passion for this field into groups of students. Clearly, the changes that occurred in my life nearly two years ago heralded something more significant: I discovered what I was meant to do.

Comments

- The essay shows that Kyle is a mature, thoughtful, intellectual young man with a passion for philosophy and a good idea of what he wants to accomplish both in college and once he graduates. The essay is well-written and full of compelling detail, and also helps admissions officers learn more about Kyle's personal struggles with his health, something that is likely not covered elsewhere in the application.

MARGOT BROOKS

Notes on her candidacy: A nationally ranked competitive swimmer from Ohio, Margot selected Stanford University.

1. Which of your activities is the most meaningful to you and why?

There are few people who devote six hours each day to the pursuit of any single activity other than sleeping. I count myself as one of these people, spending my time traveling back and forth as fast as possible in a large pool of overly chlorinated water. Competitive swimming is the most meaningful activity in my life. I was excited to make the time cuts for my first USA Sectional meet one spring, and then to quality for the bonus final in the 400m freestyle at the next Sectionals that summer. Sectionals is essentially any swimmer's first big meet; the first time a local star will encounter much bigger competition, not win or even place in her races, and realize she is anonymous in the larger scheme of things. For some people, the discovery of being an inexperienced swimmer among the elite is disheartening; for me, it presented new possibilities for my imagination to entertain and provided greater motivation. While I never failed to develop a stomach-wrenching nervousness before big races, the prospect of making new time cuts and the allure of the awards stand always outweighed any anxieties. Keeping my goals in mind, I was able to dedicate more of my physical and mental energy to improving. From the Sectional level I progressed to making National cuts, being a member of the USA National Junior Team, and competing at the Olympic trials. Each time I broke into a new level, I was amazed by the other even better swimmers and wanted to have their speed. Swimming at my level means practices at 5 am, so staying out late with friends is out of the question. I frequently miss school to attend meets, and I have learned how to get my work done efficiently so I don't fall behind. These skills in managing my time and staying dedicated to a goal help me in many areas besides swimming, and will stay with me long after I leave the sport. Swimming has taught me how to take myself seriously and be dedicated to a task.

Comments

■ This is a well-done essay on an athletic topic, often hard to pull off because the material is limiting. Margot does a great job showing why swimming is important to her, providing ample evidence of her success and explaining why her list of extracurricular activities might not be as extensive as the next applicant's, all while writing in a clear and creative fashion.

DANIEL SWISLOW

Notes on his candidacy: Daniel was on one of the country's top-ranked debate teams in high school, a strong positioning point for him in his applications to college. He chose New York University.

1. Evaluate a significant experience or achievement that has special meaning for you.

I eagerly work my way through the crowd, trying to catch a glimpse of the my current fate posted on a small sheet of paper on the cafeteria wall. My dart forward ends as I reach my target and begin scanning the schematic for my team's name: "Maine East HS Novice Policy Debate Opener 2000—Round 1" it reads. Further down the page I find directions to my impending battle: "Room 124—New Trier KM (Aff) vs. Glenbrook North SX (Neg)." This will become a weekend routine for me throughout my high school years.

The judge readily lays his finger on the timer's 'start' button signaling the coming onset of the round and thus my career in debate. My opponent speaks the first word of an unbroken, rapid-talking, eight-minute speech, in what seems to be a foreign language, as I wrote down as much information about racial profiling and the 4th amendment as I can translate.

Unbeknownst to me at the time, this alien language would quickly become my native tongue as I planted the roots of my high school years in an activity that would come to shape my worldview and capture my interest. By the end of my first debate round I knew that I had discovered my first real passion. Enthralled by the political process, critical philosophy and the art of communication, I became eager to uncover everything I could about everything I could. Debate has allowed me to tackle topics that I could have never imagined even skimming over before it, like the effects of community mental health care or the importance of the Coast Guard.

My dedication to debate has evolved into what at some times is my driving force. I remember this past summer pulling an all-nighter, preparing for the final round at the Stanford National Forensic Institute. When 9 a.m. rolled around I should have been falling asleep standing up. I walked into the round, the room packed with hundreds of my peers, and I was more wide awake than at any time I can remember from the past. I realized then that debate, at all times, is that rush of energy, that burst of adrenaline that invigorates my body and conquers my soul.

Debate has pushed me not just to countless hours logged onto LexisNexis in the early morning reading articles about the impacts to Russian nuclear weapon disarmament, but also literally around the country. An incredible amount of traveling has been a great side effect to partaking in debate, but perhaps the best byproduct is meeting throngs of remarkable people along the way. My overflowing AOL Buddy List stands as evidence of the armies of people that I have engaged from coast to coast. In debate, I have found myself through others and continue to do so.

Although other students that I have met have influenced me to a great extent, without question the strongest influence I have encountered was one of my teachers. Since we met the summer after my sophomore year, I have logged innumerable hours of conversation with Jon—even though he lives in Los Angeles we correspond almost daily. Yes, he has taught me invaluable debate lessons, but he has also helped me to discover treasured insights about life. My interest in psychology and the minds of others was realized through experiences with Jon as he has pushed me to relish the uniqueness (forget norms and stereotypes) of everyone that I meet. I have debate to thank for opening up a world to me where friendship between a high school senior and a college grade student not only exist, but can prosper.

The debate community has allowed me to vent my intellectual curiosities and has enabled me to understand myself and the world around me. Ever since that first debate tournament back in October of 2000, my life has been radically transformed—my entrance into the activity brought forth countless experiences that have come to define my life.

Comments

■ This is a wonderful essay on a fairly common subject, high school debate. A strong writer, Daniel does a fantastic job giving personality to the experience and showing how the various people he has encountered through debate have influenced his life.

PING YIU LAI

Notes on his candidacy: Originally from Hong Kong, Ping immigrated to California in middle school and now attends Kenyon College.

1. Write an essay on a topic of your choice.

My name is Ping Yiu Lai.

Many others know me as "Billy". Since July of 1995 I've lived in the United States. My family emigrated from Hong Kong to join my uncles. After I arrived, I embraced a new name, "Billy." In order to fit into the local scene, my parents gave me an Americanized name. Now that I am a little older, I know that the name "Billy" is as American as one can get.

This past February I attended a weeklong leadership conference called Presidential Classroom in Washington D.C. I met many new people from all over the place. Everyone present wore a nametag because of the number of people who attended, and my nametag identified me as Ping. I felt embarrassed about my name—it was unusual and different from all the Joe Schmoe and John Doe names. I was so embarrassed about the name that when I introduced myself I did not identify myself with it. I told everyone present that my name was Billy Lai. When one person from the crowed asked me why my nametag said differently I told them Ping was my old name from Hong Kong. When I finished with my introduction and sat down, I felt ashamed about my name for being different.

Later that night some guy approached me and asked if I was Ping. He introduced himself as "Chris" from New York and told me he would be my roommate. I told him, "Yes I am Ping, however, Billy would be the correct way to address me." He then asked me about the name, "Billy," because he had missed the earlier introduction. So, once again I told him about "Ping" being old and "Billy" being correct. When I thought he had finished asking about it, he raised another question, "Why did you change your name and not keep the original?" After listening to my answer about "Ping" not sounding American he told me that "Ping" actually sounded unique and original. He suggested that I should keep the name "Ping" because there is no reason I should be ashamed about it. At first I rejected the idea of even thinking about it, but I honestly never thought about it that way before. Then I had a revelation. I realized that there is nothing wrong with the name "Ping" or being Chinese. In fact, I should be proud that I am Chinese because of our 5,000 years of history. Although I have moved away from Hong Kong, the long-lived history is still there, and I am still Chinese.

The following day I decided to try out the name "Ping." I did not have much faith in it but the rest of my group loved my name. They liked it so much to a point where they made a song out of it, and the song became our group's theme song for the week. So, for the rest of the week, I felt relieved. I felt like this really is who I am. I acted differently when I returned home. This experience gave me confidence about myself because it helped me discover more of who I am. About a week after I returned, I gave a presentation at our weekly chapel gathering at school to let the rest of the school know that my name is "Ping Yiu Lai" form Hong Kong, China. The student body gladly and supportively gave recognition to my transition, and I am very appreciative for that. Before, it was like I was hiding from "Ping" to be "Billy", but now I am grateful that I am Ping Yiu Lai.

Comments

■ Ping shows maturity and self-reflection here as he examines the way in which he decided to embrace his Chinese heritage at a late age. Note that colleges do not expect applicants for whom English is a second language to have as strong a command of writing and expression as do native speakers.

TYLER THORNTON

Notes on her candidacy: Tyler was a leader in various community service projects and an editor of a literary magazine. She chose Amherst College.

1. Attach a small photograph of something important to you and explain its significance.

[The attached photograph is of a ring.]

I am not a big jewelry person. My friends walk around with fingers and wrists loaded with intricately designed rings and bracelets, but my small fingers and hands have always made such things look gaudy and overdone. I have a box at home where I keep the necklaces, earrings, and pins that I have been given by my mother and grandmother—the small diamond on a chain that my dad bought for my mom, the pearl pin that my grandfather gave my grandmother for their first anniversary, the gold earrings that I was given when I turned sixteen—and I treasure all of them for their sentimental and family value. Yet I wear them only on the rare occasions when I break out the heels and the short black dress. The rest of the time, I wear only two pieces of jewelry without fail: my watch and my Laurel School ring.

The day during my junior year that I received my Laurel School ring was one of the most memorable days of my high school career. I had spent hours the month before pondering what I wanted my ring to look like. Unlike at most schools, where a person has an unlimited supply of stones, metals, and insignias to choose from, I had a say only in what type of gold I got and whether or not my ring was antiqued. In the end, I chose the exact ring that my mother received when she was a junior at Laurel. That, I realized, was the beauty of the ring—knowing that I was being given a simple and elegant connection to my mother, to my grandmother, and great-grandmother, and to every other girl who had a Laurel ring. To me, the actual ring was worth nothing without the tradition and community that it represented.

My great-grandmother's Laurel ring is silver with a big, square green stone in the center. When she went there, the school was housed in a building in the middle of downtown Cleveland instead of in the suburbs, as it is now. My grandmother's Laurel ring is gold with a blue stone. She loves to tell me stories about how she used to live in my sixth grade homeroom when the school had boarders, how she actually showered in the bathroom that my middle school mind was convinced was haunted, and how she used to sneak out of school to go on a date with my grandfather. My mom, who is now a teacher at Laurel, had a few of the same teachers that I have now. There are pictures of her dancing with my dad in old yearbooks, and I love to hear her tell stories about the school pranks that she pulled as a teenager. When my sister is a junior, her ring will look like my mother's and mine—gold with a Laurel leaf insignia and the letters L and S on either side. She and I constitute the fourth generation of our family to attend Laurel, and she will be the sixth Thornton woman to graduate from the school. That is why Laurel is more than a school to me and why I care about Laurel traditions more than most other students. While at school, I feel a connection to my family and am more acutely aware of how traditions like choral concerts, class song contests, and uniforms link current students with those of the past and present. My ring is a symbol of those connections and of our shared values and goals. It is a constant reminder of those who came before me and their love of learning, empathy, tolerance, and discipline.

While Laurel has changed physically since my great-grandmother graduated, the philosophy behind it has remained the same. The school has taught generations of Thornton women to be independent, free-thinking, caring, honest, and responsible people. My teachers, family members, and friends have instilled in me a strong sense of who I am an what I can accomplish, and my ring is a constant reminder of what my classmates and I have learned during our first eighteen years. I have cherished the time that I have spent living at home and going to high school, but I am excited about the new possibilities and adventures that are before me. Luckily, I have been prepared to face new challenges and have been given the tools necessary to control what I do and who I am after I leave home. No matter what happens, I will continue to wear my watch so that I know what time it is. And I will continue to wear my Laurel School ring as both a tangible and intangible connection to the experiences and people who have helped to make me who I am.

2. Evaluate a significant experience or achievement that has special meaning for you.

Having spent my entire life at an independent girls' school, I have grown up surrounded by strong women role models. Feminism has always been a popular topic at school, and history teachers never miss an opportunity to explore the role of women throughout the centuries. In English, we have read the works of great women writers such as Jane Austen and the Bronte sisters. My junior AP English class was famous for its ability to find women's issues to discuss in every book that we read. This feminist training has prepared me well for the leadership roles that I have had the opportunity to assume through sports and extracurricular activities. In short, I have been raised to be an independent and free-thinking individual who was used to seeing no reason why every woman should not be the exact same way. As a result, I joined the many Americans who see their situation in life as superior to that of other cultures and who rush to impose their modern and Americanized views into situations where they simply do not fit.

This realization struck me this past summer while I was in the Dominican Republic helping to construct a church for the impoverished Haitian sugarcane workers who live in tenement slums called batays. This mission trip to the Dominican Republic with Fairmount Presbyterian Church was my third in as many years, yet I had previously worked in a city and had only visited a batay on a bus. One day, we helped the men of the batay to lay the foundation for the new building. One of the men taught me how to lay bricks, and I was lying on my stomach with a bucket of mortar when the women came to bring lunch for the men. I felt a tap on my shoulder and looked up to see one of the men pointing to a young woman and asking me to convince her to join the work. I couldn't understand all of his words, but the few I caught, in conjunction with his motions, conveyed the idea that he was trying to tease the woman into working. And his main argument was that the young woman from America was laying brick and enjoying herself. The young Dominican woman shook her head and shrank away. Without giving it much thought, I joined the man's attempt at persuasion because I could not come up with any reason why the woman would not want to help build the church.

Only later did it strike me how the women in the batay probably felt pressured by our presence. Maybe they even resented us. For not only were we bringing help to these people, we were also bringing our foreign culture and ideas. As a comparatively rich American volunteer who was only visiting the impoverished Dominican Republic, I was able to jump gender boundaries and to pretend to be a carpenter without threatening the identity of either the men or the women in the village. For the young Dominican woman, however, the situation had nothing to do with pretending. If she had joined in the work, her actions would have threatened the established roles of both the men and the women in her society, something that she could not psychologically or economically have afforded to do. The sugarcane workers are oppressed as a group, and the women have to worry about survival before they can worry about being female in a male dominated society. Our presence, therefore, made them uncomfortable, and not because it made them realize their inferior station in life, but because it tested a status quo that they could not risk messing with.

I'm not positive that the young woman in the batay resented my presence, or that she and the other women truly have no problem with their station in life. The experience, however, made me realize how different our culture is from theirs and how dangerous it can be for Americans to assume that our way of thinking should automatically prevail. The brief encounter with the young woman showed me the importance of exploring thoughts, not dictating them, and of realizing that our way is not the only way. Whether or not the women of the batays felt oppressed was not the issue at the time. What was the issue was that my initial reaction was to click into feminist mode and to pressure the young woman while I should have been attempting to understand what factors led her to act as she did. It was a simple lesson in empathy that will forever make me cautious about making patronizing and uninformed assumptions about other cultures.

3. Who is the secondary school teacher who has had the greatest positive impact on your development? Please describe the ways in which this teacher has influenced you.

It was the first day of BC Calculus class, and I was feeling a little anxious. Not only is calculus a notoriously nightmarish class, but I was about to face it as the only junior in a class of three students. In short, there was going to be nowhere to hide. No junior before me had ever taken on the challenge of the BC class, and the reasons why became apparent as Dr. Ellen Stenson entered the room and immediately handed us immense textbooks filled with incredibly tiny print. My anxiety quickly changed to fear as she announced that our lives were going to become calculus and that no one in her right mind took the class. She looked directly at me and expanded that statement—taking the class as a junior was a death sentence. I left that first class with three hours of homework and the feeling that I was never going to survive.

Dr. Stenson may have been the toughest and most intimidating teacher that I have ever encountered, and probably ever will, but she was also the most rewarding. She made it clear from the beginning that she would expect more from us than we would ever dream of expecting from ourselves, and that she would require us to work very hard to meet those expectations. Our lives did become calculus, but she submerged herself right along with us. She was willing to explain every aspect of a concept or problem until I understood exactly what I was dealing with and why, and she and I spent countless hours in her office integrating, differentiating, and finding the volume of the solid created by rotating a line segment around the x-axis. She took the time to go over every step of every problem that we did for homework and to correct our mistakes or congratulate us when we solved a problem differently than she had or finally figured out what we were supposed to be doing. It was apparent that she truly loved calculus and that she wanted nothing more than to share that love with us.

I have never worked harder in my life than I did to succeed in BC Calculus, but all of the work was worth it. Dr. Stenson pushed us hard, and I had to get accustomed to setting anywhere from two to four hours a night aside to find related rates and centroids, but I have never felt as proud as I did when I solved a difficult problem on my own or did well on an exam. I was often frustrated, and there were times when I wanted to give up, but Dr. Stenson was always there to support my efforts and to sit around occasionally and discuss life problems that had absolutely nothing to do with the math world. In my mind, she is a mathematical genius and an excellent teacher who taught me not only to do calculus, but also to stretch my imagination, to think in new ways, and to tackle problems head-on. She prepared me for the AP Calculus BC exam, but she also gave me the self-confidence and the work habits to excel in any math class that I take in the future. I owe a lot to Dr. Stenson, least of which is the five I earned on that AP.

Comments

Tyler submitted each of these essays to different schools.

- In the first essay, Tyler successfully supports with solid evidence her assertion that the ring at the center of the essay is valuable to her because of the traditions and sense of community it symbolizes. She relies on convincing anecdotes to show exactly why Laurel School means so much to her. She demonstrates a deep attachment to and appreciation for her family, recalling three previous generations of relatives who attended her school and connecting the Laurel School bond downward to her younger sister as well. No reader can resist feeling drawn toward an applicant who so believably shows she is pleasantly tickled rather than downright embarrassed to see pictures of her own parents dancing at the prom in old yearbooks! Tyler astutely conveys in the last portion of the essay that she understands that an education comprises more than just classroom learning, something that the top colleges want their students to acknowledge.

- Essay 2 positions Tyler as a unique candidate because of the foundation she has gained by attending an all-girls school her entire life. The piece is also valuable because it hammers home the applicant's commitment to community service (a crucial component of her candidacy), as shown through this description of a third annual mission visit to the Dominican Republic. Most important, though, is Tyler's main message here. The applicant demonstrates maturity and a willingness to take a risk in showing herself to have been at fault in assuming the superiority of her own cultural values. The lesson Tyler ultimately learned shows an open-mindedness that is particularly valuable to her, since she shows in other essays that she is confident, grounded, and shaped by a particularly fortunate and stable family background.

■ In essay 3, the applicant takes advantage of an opportunity to highlight that she was the first person in her school to take BC Calculus as a junior. Unlike most candidates who attempt to answer this question, though, Tyler gets past the emphasis on herself to produce a successful piece about her interaction with a teacher and how that teacher affected her development. The bulk of the essay indeed focuses on Dr. Stenson and why her instructional methods were particularly impressive, as is appropriate for this essay. The calculus-oriented phrases and details personalize the essay and bring it to life.

NICHOLAS HORBACZEWSKI

Notes on his candidacy: Nicholas was involved in the theater and writing for a literary magazine at his high school. He was interested in pursuing a career in film production after completing his undergraduate degree at Harvard.

1. **Please use the space on this page to let us know something about you that we might not learn from the rest of your application.**

I carry a little shard of metal in the coin holder of my wallet. It's maybe two inches long and, as far as I can tell, was once torn from the edge of a some circular metal plate. It falls out every time I dump out my change and people invariably ask me what it is. I tell them part of the story. "It popped my tire on a bike trip from Seattle to San Francisco I took the summer after ninth grade. I only got one flat in twelve hundred miles, and this thing caused it, so I carry it around as a talisman against future accidents." I smile. The subject changes. It really did pop my tire, but the real reason I carry it with me is too intimate to explain in a casual conversation, so I don't go into it.

I have gone to considerable lengths for that shard. I once left my wallet on an airplane and then forced my way back to the gate through the airport security—not for the cash or for my ID's, but because the shard was in it. Once, I reached into a spider infested hole (my personal hell) because I had dropped the shard into it. I don't know why I started to carry it around with me—I just did. I was cycling down the Pacific Coast Highway, it popped my tire and I put it in my wallet. I did not know when I pried it from the rubber somewhere in northern California that it would be my only tangible connection to an experience that changed my life. I had no real reason for keeping it. Only as the trip drew to a close did I begin to see how important it was to me, because it evoked so many memories and emotions. Then I started to hang on to it for dear life.

My rusty sliver of metal seems a humble monument to the experience that was an epiphany in my life. Reveling in my first flush of independence, enjoying the company of unforgettable people and accomplishing a demanding bike ride through the most glorious scenery I had ever seen would have been enough to alter my perspective on life, but the trip means even more than that. Only weeks before I stepped on the airplane for Seattle, I had been an invalid, both biceps ruptured, their blood vessels ripped in two from a catastrophic rowing injury. I had been away from school, my friends, in incredible pain and struggling with the knowledge that I would never regain total use of or strength in my arms. I had returned to school at the very end of the year only to feel isolated from my friends, whom I had been too ashamed to call when I could not even feed myself or straighten my arms. Going back only depressed me more, as I saw that I had lost my place in the highly structured world of high school society.

It seems like a simple story. Boy gets hurt, boy goes on trip, boy feels better. But the trip lifted me out of my daily existence and gave me a broader view of the world and a more positive way to approach life. The adventure, the companionship and the sense of personal accomplishment as we pedaled the final miles across the Golden Gate Bridge would probably have been enough to give me a more positive outlook anyway. It is merely a lucky coincidence that the experience also helped me recover physically and psychologically from my injury. It wasn't so much that the trip gave me back what the injury had taken away, but rather it gave me the perspective to see how much I had not lost: friendships, the joy of the moment, the ability to set physically and emotionally challenging goals and to achieve them. It was this change in attitude about my injury that allowed me to recover. Returning to school after that trip, I tried out, the for the first time, for a part in a play. I began to lift weights so strengthen my body, including my arms in order to minimize the effect of the injury. I found that sports had been pushed aside by these other aspects of my life that mattered more. Perspective is so essential that it can change your whole life. I think, you need to know what's important, like a little metal shard.

Comments

- This essay demonstrates the effect a candidate can have when he orients an ordinary or unoriginal theme around something tangible. The way that Nicholas has pitched his story around the metal shard makes it much more compelling than if he had simply stated, "This summer I learned a lot about myself and learned to appreciate life more" and then told a little bit about the trip. The metal shard draws readers into the story immediately, making them wonder what it stands for as well as feeling fully confident that the summer trip did indeed make a lasting impression on the applicant. Furthermore, the essay is successful because, as the author himself admits, he is revealing something intimate, something that he is not willing to discuss with many people.

INDEX

Page numbers in **bold** indicate tables; those in *italic* indicate figures; those followed by "n" indicate notes.